Ideals and Ideologies

Ideals and Ideologies

A Reader

TERENCE BALL
University of Minnesota

RICHARD DAGGER
Arizona State University

HarperCollins*Publishers*

Sponsoring Editor: Lauren Silverman
Project Editor: Diane Rowell
Art Direction/Cover Coordinator: Heather A. Ziegler
Cover Design: CIRCA 86, Inc.
Cover Photo: Eric Bouvet/Gamma-Liason
Cover Photo Research: Nina Page
Production: Willie Lane/Sunaina Sehwani
Compositor: David E. Seham Associates
Printer and Binder: R. R. Donnelley & Sons Company
Cover Printer: Phoenix Color Corp.

Ideals and Ideologies: A Reader

Library of Congress Cataloging-in-Publication Data

Ideals and ideologies : a reader / [compiled by] Terence Ball, Richard Dagger.
p. cm.
ISBN 0–06–040472–8
1. Political science. 2. Democracy. 3. Ideology. 4. Right and left (Political science) I. Ball, Terence. II. Dagger, Richard.
JA36.I32 1991
320.5—dc20 90-20233
CIP

91 92 93 94 9 8 7 6 5 4 3 2 1

CONTENTS

Preface ix
Introduction xi

PART ONE The Concept of Ideology 1

1. *Ideology: The Career of a Concept,* TERRELL CARVER 4

PART TWO The Democratic Ideal 13

2. *Democracy and Despotism,* EURIPIDES 16
3. *Funeral Oration,* PERICLES 18
4. *Democratic Judgment and the "Middling" Constitution,* ARISTOTLE 23
5. *What's Wrong with Princely Rule?* NICCOLÒ MACHIAVELLI 28
6. *What Is a Republic?* JOHN ADAMS 32
7. *Bill of Rights of the United States* 38
8. *Democracy and Equality,* ALEXIS DE TOCQUEVILLE 40
9. *Democratic Participation and Political Education,* JOHN STUART MILL 48
10. *Town Meetings and Workers' Control,* MICHAEL WALZER 55

PART THREE Liberalism 65

11. *The State of Nature and the Basis of Obligation,* THOMAS HOBBES 68
12. *Toleration and Government,* JOHN LOCKE 75
13. *Government, Rights, and the Bonds between Generations,* THOMAS PAINE 91
14. *Declaration of Independence of the United States* 95
15. *Declaration of the Rights of Man and of Citizens* 99
16. *Private Profit, Public Good,* ADAM SMITH 102
17. *Freedom and Enlightenment,* IMMANUEL KANT 106
18. *Liberty and Individuality,* JOHN STUART MILL 109
19. *According to the Fitness of Things,* WILLIAM GRAHAM SUMNER 116
20. *Liberalism and Positive Freedom,* T. H. GREEN 121
21. *Paternalism vs. Democracy: A Libertarian View,* DONALD ALLEN 125
22. *Libertarian Anarchism,* MURRAY ROTHBARD 129

PART FOUR Conservatism 133

23. *Society, Reverence, and the "True Natural Aristocracy,"* EDMUND BURKE 135
24. *Conservatism as Reaction,* JOSEPH DE MAISTRE 142
25. *The Poet as Conservative,* WILLIAM WORDSWORTH 147
26. *Revolt of the Masses,* JOSÉ ORTEGA Y GASSET 150
27. *On Being Conservative,* MICHAEL OAKESHOTT 154
28. *What Is Neoconservatism?* IRVING KRISTOL 163

PART FIVE Socialism and Communism: More to Marx 167

29. *Utopia,* THOMAS MORE 169
30. *Social Organization,* CHARLES FOURIER 176
31. *The Communist Manifesto,* KARL MARX AND FRIEDRICH ENGELS 180
32. *Socialism: Utopian and Scientific,* FRIEDRICH ENGELS 193

PART SIX Socialism and Communism after Marx 207

33. *Evolutionary Socialism,* EDUARD BERNSTEIN 210
34. *Revisionism, Imperialism, and Revolution,* V. I. LENIN 216
35. *On the People's Democratic Dictatorship,* MAO ZEDONG 233
36. *On Marx and Marxism,* MIKHAIL BAKUNIN 243
37. *Anarchist Communism,* PETER KROPOTKIN 249
38. *Looking Backward,* EDWARD BELLAMY 259
39. *Why We Need Socialism in America,* MICHAEL HARRINGTON 269

PART SEVEN Fascism 279

40. *Civilization and Race,* JOSEPH-ARTHUR DE GOBINEAU 281
41. *The Doctrine of Fascism,* BENITO MUSSOLINI 288
42. *Nation and Race,* ADOLF HITLER 298

PART EIGHT Liberation Ideologies 315

43. *Letter from Birmingham Jail,* MARTIN LUTHER KING, JR. 318
44. *Black Power,* STOKELEY CARMICHAEL AND CHARLES HAMILTON 329
45. *A Vindication of the Rights of Woman,* MARY WOLLSTONECRAFT 336
46. *Oppression,* MARILYN FRYE 344

47. *Gay Liberation,* RICHARD MOHR 353
48. *Liberation Theology,* GUSTAVO GUTIERREZ 358
49. *All Animals Are Equal,* PETER SINGER 368

PART NINE "Green" Politics: Ecology as Ideology 379

50. *The Land Ethic,* ALDO LEOPOLD 381
51. *Earth First!* DAVE FOREMAN 402
52. *What Is Social Ecology?* MURRAY BOOKCHIN 410
53. *What Has Posterity Ever Done for Me?* ROBERT HEILBRONER 420

PART TEN The Future of Ideology 425

54. *The End of Ideology—Revisited,* DANIEL BELL 427
55. *The End of History?* FRANCIS FUKUYAMA 432
56. *Word and Flesh,* WENDELL BERRY 442

PREFACE

"I don't use a textbook. My students read the original sources." This is a common sentiment, and an admirable one. It is surely better for students to read the writings of Mill or Marx or Burke than merely to read about them in a textbook. Most textbooks in "modern political thought" and "contemporary ideologies" offer little more than predigested summaries, while the few available anthologies too often supply only a series of brief snippets from original sources. Understandably dissatisfied, many instructors—and here we speak from long personal experience—have devised their own jerry-rigged packet of photocopied materials, which in the end satisfies neither them nor their students.

Having long felt the dissatisfaction and heard the complaints, we decided to edit an anthology that we hoped would meet many instructors' standards while, at the same time, satisfying students' demands for a readable and reasonably accessible "reader"—an old-fashioned term whose time has come once again. Certainly no textbook summary can convey the power of Burke's prose or capture Marx's outrage over the injustice of capitalism or Mill's misgivings about majority rule or Hitler's hatred of Jews and other supposedly "inferior" peoples. There is simply no substitute for these authors—and many others—speaking in their own voices. But students sometimes find it difficult to read the writings of authors long dead—authors whose prose strike the student as stilted, formal, "flowery," or unnecessarily complex. We know of no entirely satisfactory way of resolving this dilemma. The best we can do is to suggest something like the following.

The ideal anthology or reader for this subject—which probably exists only in Plato's heaven—would combine four features. First, it would represent a wide range of alternative ideological visions, right, left, middle, and unorthodox. Second, it would include a generous sampling of key thinkers in the different ideological traditions, old and new alike. Third, an ideal anthology would, where necessary, modernize the prose of thinkers long dead. Fourth, and finally, it would supply the student with some sense of the intellectual and political context within which these thinkers thought and wrote.

The anthology that follows is, alas, far from ideal. But we have at least tried to satisfy the four aforementioned criteria. First, we have attempted to cover the broad canvas of contemporary political ideologies, from the standard categories of liberalism-conservatism-socialism to a broader range of newly emerging ideological alternatives, including the various "liberation" ideologies and the even more recent ecological or "green" ideology. Second, we have tried to supply a fairly generous and reasonably representative sample of alternative ideological views, including those not represented in any other anthology. Third, we have, where possible, simplified the prose of older thinkers—in some instances providing our own translations of works not written in English. And finally, we have provided brief introductions to place these selections and their authors in their appropriate political and historical context.

In these ways we have tried to supply the student with an accessible and readable book of original sources. Even so, the end result does not necessarily make for easy reading. But then, as we remind our students, the motto, "no pain, no gain," applies to the building not only of muscles, but of minds as well. We have merely attempted to remove some of the unnecessary strain from what is a sometimes painful but always profitable exercise.

This "reader" can be used in several ways. It can be used on its own as a "source book" of original readings from which instructors can assign the selections they think most important. Or it can be used in combination with an accompanying textbook, *Political Ideologies and the Democratic Ideal,* by Terence Ball and Richard Dagger, which contains references keyed to this reader. Either the textbook or reader, or both, may in turn be supplemented with a ten-part video series, "Contemporary Political Ideologies," written and narrated by Terence Ball. Instructors interested in using this series may write to The Director, Media Assisted Instruction, Department of Independent Study, 45 Westbrook Hall, University of Minnesota, Minneapolis, MN 55455.

We would like to thank the following reviewers for their insightful comments throughout the development of this project: Robert Calvert, DePauw University; Phillip Chapman, University of Arizona; Peter Diamond, University of Utah; Larry Elowitz, Georgia College; Andrew Raposa, Westfield State College; Joel Schwartz, College of William and Mary; and Raymond Wrabley, University of Pittsburgh–Johnstown.

We should also note, finally, that many of the readings included here could easily fall under more than one heading. We place Michael Walzer's essay on town meetings and workers' control in Part Two, "The Democratic Ideal," for instance, where others might prefer to use it in the discussion of socialism. Or the selection from Mill's *Representative Government* could appear in Part Three, "Liberalism," and Mao's "On People's Democratic Dictatorship" could fit in Part Two, "The Democratic Ideal." There are many combinations, in short, and many ways to use this book. But whatever the preferred combination, the aim is always the same: to convey to the student-citizen a vivid sense of the centrality and ongoing importance of ideals, ideas, and ideologies in modern politics.

Terence Ball
Richard Dagger

INTRODUCTION

Ideas, it is often said, have consequences. This is especially true of those clusters or systems of ideas called "ideologies." We live in a world that has been, and continues to be, shaped by political ideologies. As we prepare to enter the twenty-first century, some ideologies, such as the Marxist-Leninist version of socialism, seem to be in eclipse, while others—such as a newly emerging ecological or "green" ideology—appear to be gaining in influence and importance. Yet, despite their differences, these ideologies are alike in at least one respect: All have their histories. That is, all have emerged out of particular historical contexts and have changed in response to changing conditions and circumstances. And all have been formed from the ideas of writers old and new. Writing in the 1920s, in the aftermath of the Russian Revolution and just as Hitler and Mussolini were beginning to be heard in Germany and Italy, the economist John Maynard Keynes observed that "Madmen in authority, who hear voices in the air, are distilling their frenzy from some academic scribbler of a few years back."

This is a book about, and by, those "academic scribblers"—and a number of those "madmen in authority" as well. Their ideas have, for better or worse, formed the ideologies and fueled the conflicts that have shaped and reshaped the political landscape of our century. We live in the shadow, and under the influence, of thinkers long dead. To be ignorant of their influence is not to escape it. By tracing modern ideologies back to their original sources, we can see more clearly how our own outlooks—and those of our enemies—have been shaped by earlier thinkers. When a character in one of Peter DeVries' novels exclaims, "We must get Aristotle out of our system!" another objects that Aristotle is not in *his* system because he has never even read Aristotle. "Oh, he's there, all right," says the first character, "whether you know it or not." The same can be said of other thinkers long dead—Plato, Machiavelli, Hobbes, Locke, Mandeville, Smith, Marx, Mill, and many others. To return to, and read, these authors is to gain some insight into the shaping of the modern political mind—or rather minds, plural, since ideological disagreement continues unabated.

Some modern commentators claim—wrongly, we believe—that ideological disagreements are at last coming to an end. "The age of ideology," they say, is over. As evidence they cite the ending of the Cold War, the emancipation of Eastern Europe from Soviet domination, and the democratizing of former dictatorships. Important as they are, however, these events do not presage "the end of ideology." Rather, they suggest that ours is an age of important ideological realignments. Marxism-Leninism may be dead or dying in Eastern Europe and even in the Soviet Union, but other versions of it continue to dominate the politics of China, Vietnam, Cuba, and other countries. And, of course, conservatives continue to disagree with liberals, socialists disagree among themselves, animal liberationists fight for animal rights, and "Greens" organize and act to protect the environment. Other movements, motivated by other ideologies, are no less active.

So ours is now, and is likely to remain, an age of ideological diversity and disagreement. The selections that follow include some, though scarcely all, of the sources that have helped to form the ideologically varied political terrain on which we dwell together, if not always amicably or harmoniously.

T. B.
R. D.

Ideals and Ideologies

PART ONE
THE CONCEPT OF IDEOLOGY

The persistence of ideologies and ideological conflict throughout modern history should come as no surprise, for ideologies are born of crisis and conflict. People need help to comprehend and cope with turbulent times and confusing circumstances, and ideologies provide this help. An ideology does this by performing four important and perhaps indispensable functions for those who subscribe to it. First, it helps to *explain* political phenomena that would otherwise remain mysterious or puzzling. Why are there wars and rumors of war? Why are there conflicts between nations, between classes, and between races? What causes depressions? The answer that one gives to these, and to many other questions, depends to some degree on the ideology to which one subscribes. A Marxian socialist will answer one way, a fascist another, and a feminist yet another.

Second, an ideology provides its adherents with criteria and standards of *evaluation*—of deciding what is right and wrong, good and bad. Are class differences and vast disparities of wealth a good or a bad thing? Is interracial harmony possible, and, if so, is it desirable? Is censorship permissible, and, if so, under what conditions? Again, the answer one gives will depend on which ideology one accepts.

Third, an ideology *orients* its adherents, giving them a sense of who they are and where they belong—a social and cultural compass with which to define and affirm their individual and collective identity. A fascist, for example, will typically think of himself as a member of a superior nation or race. A Communist will conceive of herself as a defender of the working class against capitalist oppression and exploitation. An animal liberationist will identify herself as a defender of animals that are unable to defend themselves from human abuse and exploitation.

Fourth and finally, an ideology supplies its adherents with a rudimentary political *program*. This program provides an answer to the question posed by Lenin, among many others: What is to be done? And, no less important: Who is to do it? A Marxist-Leninist, for instance, will answer these questions as follows: The working class must be emancipated from capitalist exploitation by means of a revolution led by a vanguard party. Fascists, feminists, "greens," liberals, conservatives, and others will, of course, opt for other programs of political action.

To summarize, a political ideology is a more or less systematic set of ideas that performs four functions for those who hold it: the explanatory, the evaluative, the orientative, and the programmatic functions. An ideology, in short, serves as a guide and compass through the thicket of political life.

There are, as we shall see, many different political ideologies in the modern world. But what of democracy? Is it an ideology? In our view democracy is not an ideology, but an *ideal* that different ideologies interpret in different ways. For the ancient Greeks—and for modern Marxists—democracy (or "people's democracy") means rule by, and in the interest of, the working class. For liberals, "democracy" means "liberal democracy"—that is, majority rule, but with ample provision for the protection of minority rights. For modern "greens," democracy means decentralized "participatory" or "grass-roots" democracy. Other ideologies interpret the democratic ideal in other ways. Democracy is, then, an *essentially contested concept* whose meaning is disputed and defined in different ways by different ideologies.

As with democracy, so too with freedom. Different ideologies conceive of freedom in different ways. "Freedom" means something quite different for liberals from what it means for fascists, for example. We can see this more clearly by thinking of freedom (or liberty) as a triadic or three-sided relation among an *agent*, a *goal*, and any *obstacle* standing between the agent and the goal that he, she, or they seek to achieve. We represent this relationship in the following diagram.

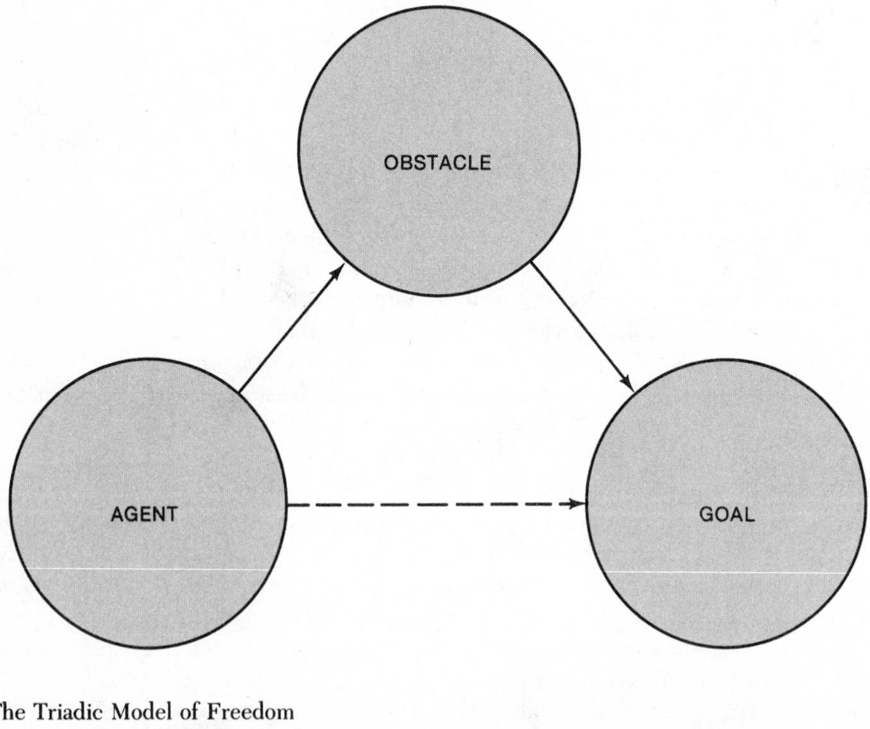

The Triadic Model of Freedom

Every ideology identifies the three elements of the triad in its own way. A liberal, for instance, will typically identify the agent as an individual, the goal as the satisfaction of an individual's own desires, and the obstacle as any unreasonable restraint or restriction on such "want-satisfaction." A Marxist, by contrast, will characteristically identify the agent as an entire class—the working class or "proletariat"—that struggles to overcome capitalist exploitation in order to achieve a classless communist society. A fascist will conceive of the agent as a whole nation or race attempting to overcome "inferior" nations or races in a collective search for racial or national supremacy and purity. And other ideologies, of course, conceive of freedom in still other ways.

So we can see that two of the watchwords of modern politics—"democracy" and "freedom"—have no fixed or final meaning apart from that given them by various ideologies. Americans and Europeans are apt to think of freedom and democracy in broadly liberal terms, while Chinese Communists decry these as "bourgeois" distortions of "true" freedom and democracy. Such disagreements are deep-seated because they derive from ideological differences. These and many other disagreements are not likely to end soon, if ever, for political and economic crises are endemic to the modern age. So long as there are crises, people will require the means to comprehend and cope with troubled times. There is, then, plenty of reason to expect political ideologies and ideological conflict to persist well into the new century.

1

IDEOLOGY: THE CAREER OF A CONCEPT

TERRELL CARVER

The concept of ideology has undergone dramatic changes in meaning since the term *ideologie* was first coined in eighteenth-century France. In an essay written expressly for this volume the Anglo-American political theorist Terrell Carver (1946–   ) traces these changes, concluding with a critical consideration of the ways in which the term "ideology" is used today.

As a coined word, the term "ideology" has a precise origin in the era of the French Revolution. The decisive shifts in its meaning, moreover, have been associated with some of the most colorful and influential figures in modern history—Napoleon Bonaparte (1769–1821), Karl Marx (1818–1883), Friedrich Engels (1820–1895), and V. I. Lenin (1870–1924). From its very inception, in fact, ideology has been associated with highly abstract philosophy and forceful, even brutal, political repression.

Behind the term "ideology" are the familiar features of politics—ideas and power. Philosophers have not been conspicuous for their participation in politics, but through the actions of others they have been influential at times. Improving the connection between philosopher and politician to extend this influence was one of the main concerns of Antoine Louis Claude Destutt, Comte de Tracy (1754–1836), one of the Enlightenment *philosophes*. De Tracy coined the term "ideology" during the wild revolutionary decade in France when ideas inspired many thousands to test their powers in politics and to put their immediate material interests, even lives, at risk. Although the substance of de Tracy's thought drew on the specific philosophies of Étienne Bonnot de Condillac (1715–1780) and John Locke (1632–1704), amongst others, his work was explicitly directed toward political action. He assumed that criteria for the truth and falsity of ideas could be established and definitively employed, and that there was a point to doing so. That point was overtly political.

De Tracy and his colleagues aimed to promote progress in all areas of human endeavor, theoretical and practical, by reforming elite and middle-class opinion. Their Institut de France was established by the Convention in 1795 to disseminate higher learning as the *savants* of the revolution defined it. Their work began with three assumptions: that progress in social life is desirable; that progress comes only from correct ideas; and that incorrect ideas must be resisted, especially in the schools. In opposition to the traditions of the Catholic Church and to the personal authority of anointed monarchs, de Tracy and his colleagues in the Institut favored the ideals of the new science associated with Francis Bacon (1561–1626), Galileo Galilei (1564–1642), Réné Descartes (1596–1650), and other thinkers who espoused rational inquiry into the natural and social world. The rationalism of the Institut was especially hostile to religious thought if conceived mystically.

In 1796 a British commentator reported that de Tracy had read a paper at the Institut in which he proposed to call the philosophy of mind "ideology." Five years later, in his *Elements of Ideology* (1801; translated into English by Thomas Jefferson for an edition of 1817), de Tracy summarized the results of his logic within a "plan of the elements of ideology . . . to give a complete knowledge of our intellectual faculties, and to deduce from that knowledge the first principles of all other branches of our knowledge." Without these first principles "our knowledge" could "never be founded on any other solid base."[1] With correct ideas would come a correct psychology or theory of human behavior, and with that the justification for such political prescriptions as intellectuals might devise and enlightened politicians might enforce.

De Tracy's system, while sweeping, was disarmingly simplistic, dismissive of scepticism, and surprisingly concise. Even at the time it must have raised some strong doubts amongst philosophers. Indeed, the association of ideology with intellectual shortcuts, oversimplification, and distortion seems inherent in de Tracy's original conception. That de Tracy also associated his ideology with a political program and authoritarian politics provides further clues to the way the concept has functioned since his day.

There are three important features of de Tracy's conception of ideology: (1) the explicit linkage between logic, psychology, and politics, set down in a "table" of simple propositions and backed up with more extensive observations; (2) the assumption that intellectuals discover the truth and that well-advised political authorities implement policies to match; and (3) the claim that logic, psychology, and politics, as linked, are coincident with science and history, properly understood.

In 1797 Napoleon Bonaparte, the leading general of the revolutionary army, became an honorary member of the Institut, and his fellow "ideologues" supported the coup d'etat by which he seized power in 1799. With their boundless faith in reason, the "ideologues," de Tracy amongst them, expected to achieve the same success in psychology, morality, social and economic relations, and politics that the new "natural philosophers" had achieved in studying planetary and terrestrial motion, optics, and mathematics. Such was their certainty that they committed themselves to an administrative structure to promote their ideas and to discourage what they termed prejudices—and with that they necessarily engaged in politics. As their concept of truth presupposed the authority of the intellectual (validated by the "correct" assumptions and methods), so their politics created no great obstacles to authoritarian rule—provided, of course, that the authority had proper intellectual guidance. There was little in the doctrines of the "ideologues" to favor the unenlightened intellect or to afford it any great role in decisionmaking. Because politics was supposed to be subject to the new science, democracy with its popular decisionmaking would have little to recommend itself to the Enlightenment intellectual unless it were properly guided. Tutoring rulers was obviously the easier and more immediately efficacious task. With Napoleon a member of the Institut, furthermore, the "ideologues" could expect enlightenment and progress to spread all the more quickly throughout France and beyond its borders. The forces of reaction were to be swept away by the enlightened use of political power as the resources of the state were made available to the intellectual élite.

The crucial event in the development of the concept of ideology came when Napoleon turned against the "ideologues" and decisively reversed their interpretation of the proper relationship between intellectuals and rulers, philosophers and politicians. Around 1812 he dismissed de Tracy's work and the work of the Institut de France as "ideology, that sinister metaphysics." This hostility to the "ideologues" apparently reflected a shift in Napoleon's political tactics—from alliance with the rationalists of the Institut against religion and the Church, to the reverse. Eradicating what the "ideologues" saw as prejudice was politically costly, and Napoleon sought to increase his personal power by making peace with the Church and allying himself with other conservative forces.[2]

About thirty years later the German Communist Karl Marx seized on "ideology" as a term of abuse. He criticized German intellectuals whose philosophy and politics displeased him by dismissing them as "ideologists," proponents of "the German ideology." He and Friedrich Engels co-authored a manuscript of that name which remained unpublished as a whole until 1932, though sections of the large work appeared in excerpts from 1903 onwards.[3] In other published works that circulated during his lifetime and in his private correspondence, Marx used the term "ideology" in ways that drew on the more extensive airing he had given the concept in *The German Ideology*.

Ideologies and ideologists arise in class-divided societies, according to Marx. In particular, "the class which has the means of material production at its disposal consequently also controls the means of mental production." Thinkers are "producers of ideas," in other words, while ruling classes regulate "the production and distribution of the ideas of their age." Thus "the ideas of the ruling class are in every epoch the ruling ideas: i.e., the class which is the ruling *material* force of society is at the same time its ruling *intellectual* force." Within the ruling class the division of labor divides mental from material tasks, so that:

> Inside this class one part appears as the thinkers of the class (its active, conceptualizing ideologists, who make the formation of the illusions of the class about itself their chief source of livelihood), while the other's attitude to these ideas

> and illusions is more passive and receptive, because they are in reality the active members of this class and have less time to make up illusions and ideas about themselves.[4]

The German ideology was to be explained, Marx argued, "from its connection with the illusion of ideologists in general, e.g., the illusions of the jurists, politicians (including practical statesmen), from the dogmatic dreamings and distortions of these fellows." All those illusions and distortions were "explained perfectly easily from their practical position in life, their job, and the division of labour."[5] In this realm of jobs and economic activity, Marx introduced a notion of material interest which made illusions demonstrably functional for some individuals and classes in societies as they pursued economic advantages for themselves at others' expense. Some of these useful illusions were dressed up as claims about nature or God—for example, "some people are slaves by nature," "God made woman to serve man"—and some were more elaborately cloaked in a universalism that Marx dismissed as spurious. He argued, for example, that the "rights of man and the citizen" proclaimed in the French Revolution ultimately worked for the benefit of owners of private property at the expense of workers, who had no property to sell but their own labor. Thus in Marx's analysis an ideology came to mean not just a body of ideas that conformed to certain formal characteristics, such as those of de Tracy's system, but any ideas, however unsophisticated, that gave apparent validity and assumed authority to the claims that members of different classes might make when they pursued their various interests. Those who characteristically made such claims were deemed "ideologists"; others merely repeated in their speech or reflected in their behavior an "ideology."

In Marx's view ideologies could be reactionary, conservative, reformist, or revolutionary, depending on the way that material interests (typically the use and control of resources, goods, and services) were pursued by individuals and then protected socially and politically. In keeping with his depiction of history as the history of class struggles—now hidden, now open—Marx defined ideologies as the "legal, political, religious, aesthetic or philosophic—in short, ideological—forms" in which people become conscious of class conflict "and fight it out."[6] In that way, "the existence of revolutionary ideas in a particular period," he wrote, "presupposes the existence of a revolutionary class."[7]

Marx thus extended de Tracy's term "ideology" to cover ideas that reflected, and were somehow useful in pursuing, the material interests of classes. But his own work was supposed to identify, explain, and promote working-class interests in current political struggles. It might seem, therefore, to be ideological itself. Marx did not refer to his work in those terms, however, nor to the pursuit of working-class politics as requiring an ideology. He identified the working class as a revolutionary class, but one distinguished from previous revolutionary classes in that it was becoming a majority and already expressed "the dissolution of all classes, nationalities etc., within present society."[8] A revolutionary class was to overthrow a ruling class, as had already happened many times, but with the *proletarian* revolution would come the abolition of class-society altogether. This could happen, Marx said, because the interest of the proletariat coincides with the interests of all individuals "as individuals."[9]

Marx's arguments for the proletariat's abolition of class-divided society are sketchy and unconvincing, but they are quite distinct from the views he described as ideological. His communism, and the theory behind it, were not ideologies on his definition, because the formal properties and political reference were profoundly different. Instead, Marx considered his work to be scientific, taking due regard for the historical character of the social phenomena under investigation. It was also supposed to have political significance in the struggle for socialism. But it was not formally identical to the pattern for an "ideology" established by de Tracy because there was no Marxian logic and psychology from which his politics were deduced. Rather he worked from a less comprehensive conception, that of economic activity ("so-called material interests"), towards prescriptions that could be useful, so he argued, in proletarian politics.[10] The role of the theoretically informed individual or group was said, in the *Communist Manifesto* and elsewhere, to be advisory, not authoritative. Marx contemptuously dismissed sects and other ways in which ideals were supposed to be imposed on people so that reality could be created, in a sense, by ideas. Communism, he claimed, was a "real movement" already in existence, to which his science was intended to contribute.[11]

Friedrich Engels was the architect of a Marxism that fitted the formal requirements of an ideology, though he himself dismissed ideology all too simplistically as mere "false consciousness," a phrase not used by Marx.[12] While he did not term Marx's work an ideology, but a science—namely, "scientific socialism"—Engels elaborated a view that Marx's science had specified fundamental laws of dialectics in the realm of "thought" (presumably a proto-psychology), in the development of human behavior in history, and in the matter-in-motion of the universe itself. Engels's widely circulated *Anti-Dühring* (1878) advertised those pretensions, producing extended discussions of historical and contemporary economic development that were supposed to substantiate his claims for a materialistic dialectic in logic. These were repeated in his later *Ludwig Feuerbach and the End of Classical German Philosophy* (1888) and the posthumously published *Dialectics of Nature* (1925), edited from notebooks largely contemporary with *Anti-Dühring*.

Whether Marx shared Engels's views is a matter of controversy.[13] There is no explicit endorsement of them in his works. Indeed, as I am arguing here, the way that Marx identified such logico-deductive constructions as "ideological" suggests that he could not have agreed with Engels's views without major inconsistency.

Thus Marx's followers did their best to make his ideas fit the formal and political definitions of ideology that Marx himself had applied to other systems of ideas. In doing so his followers seemed to undermine the pejorative connotations of the term. This introduced an obvious contradiction between Marx's own consistently pejorative usage with respect to German ideologists and other apologists for the ruling classes, on the one hand, and his followers' use of the term in an approving sense, on the other, to identify his work as a comprehensive system that promoted the interests of one particular class in society—the working class. This working-class or proletarian "ideology" was a science, Marx's followers said, precisely because it was a body of thought reflecting proletarian interests. As a result we have Marxism identified by Soviet philosophers and many others as a "scientific ideology"—a contradiction in terms from Marx's own point of view.

The Russian revolutionary Lenin (pseudonym for Vladimir Ilich Ulyanov) followed Engels in identifying Marxism as a comprehensive science derived from an abstract logic, thus accepting it formally as an ideology. While this identification was merely tacit in Engels's case, Lenin made it specific and went one stage further in his highly influential *What Is to Be Done?* (1902). Citing Engels on the necessity for political, economic, and theoretical struggle in pursuing working-class interests, Lenin concluded very generally and with particular reference to Russia that "without revolutionary theory there can be no revolutionary practice." "Modern socialist consciousness," he wrote, "can only arise on the basis of profound scientific knowledge."[14]

Lenin identified this science as "socialist ideology" and claimed that the only political choice available in his time was between the bourgeois ideology and the socialist one. He thus defined ideologies as doctrines reflecting class interests that were in some sense products of theoretical thinking, not the commonplace consciousness of class-members themselves. For the working class this was crucial in Lenin's eyes, because he viewed them as likely victims of bourgeois ideology (or unwitting servants of it via "trade union consciousness"), unless socialist intellectuals and party workers, using the "socialist ideology," awakened the workers to the "irreconcilable antagonism of their interests to the whole of the modern political and social system."[15] On this view it was a matter of fact that science served proletarian interests because it revealed the true character of class antagonism in capitalist society, the very truth that bourgeois ideology had veiled in illusions, such as "self-help," "parliamentary democracy," "market forces," etc.

Presumably Lenin's use of "ideology" to include science, as well as the interest-serving mystifications Marx had loosely identified as ideologies, was a kind of shorthand. Lenin conceived of a "scientific ideology" opposed to unscientific ones, all serving different class interests. In that political sense—ideology as ideas serving class interests—Lenin made Marxism ideological. By the early twentieth century, then, ideology had wandered in meaning from a science of ideas, to a sinister metaphysics, to class-serving illusions, to false consciousness as opposed to scientific socialism, to scientific socialism as one ideology competing with others.

The "science" within the socialism of Engels and Lenin was very vulnerable to criticism, as the first principles of their dialectical materialism were incomplete and unconvincing. But the insight, derived ultimately from Marx, that ideas serve the interests of individuals, groups, and classes, and that individuals, groups, and classes often generate and defend the ideas that do this, has made a systematic sociology of consciousness possible. This project was set out by the German sociologist Karl Mannheim (1893–1947), who explained that the principal thesis of his "sociology of knowledge" is that there are modes of thought which cannot be adequately understood as long as their social origins are obscured. In his view the study of these "ideologies" involves unmasking the more or less conscious deceptions and disguises of interest groups, particularly those of political parties.[16] For Mannheim "ideology" was a name for two related conceptions which he distinguished as "particular" and "total":

> The particular conception of ideology is implied when the term denotes that we are sceptical of the ideas and representations advanced by our opponent. They are regarded as more or less conscious disguises of the real nature of a situation, the true recognition of which would not be in accord with his interests. . . .

"This conception of ideology," wrote Mannheim, "has only gradually become differentiated from the commonsense notion of the lie." It was "particular" by comparison with the more inclusive "total" conception of ideology: "Here we refer to the ideology of an age or of a concrete historico-social group, e.g., of a class, when we are concerned with the characteristics and composition of the total structure of the mind of this epoch or of this group."[17]

Mannheim argued that this total conception of ideology raised the problem of "false consciousness" as "the totally distorted mind which falsified everything." The possibility that our whole conception of reality might be systematically distorted and continuously distorting had "a special significance and relevance for the understanding of our social life." From the awareness of this possibility arose a "profound disquietude" which Mannheim felt very deeply.[18]

De Tracy confidently described his ideology, a general grammar and logic, as a science, about whose methods, truth and timelessness he had no doubts. Since the time of the *philosophes* confidence has given way to scepticism, and the term ideology has reflected this exactly. When there was certainty about truth and science, a new word, "ideology," was coined. This fell victim to a vengeful politics when Napoleon dismissed it as "sinister metaphysics," and the term came to stand for illusion as opposed to science. Because of Marx's attacks on the élitism of the philosopher-politicians and his pithy theorizing on the origins of ideas in class-divided societies, the concept has almost become synonymous with ax-grinding. Engels's "scientific socialism" and Lenin's "proletarian ideology" reincarnate de Tracy's confidence, but to less than universal satisfaction, as modern scepticism about truth admits no conclusive grounds for the judgments that those doctrines claim to justify. Ideology has thus been moved from denoting the elements of a comprehensive, programmatic politics to functioning as an element in a supremely doubtful academic taxonomy. It is confused to the point of babel, as it variously signifies unambiguous truth, myth or illusion, false consciousness, scientific socialism, and ideas that distort and conceal a dynamically changing social reality.

This has not stopped contemporary writers from trying to extract order from chaos. Recently Malcolm B. Hamilton has formulated no less than 27 "definitional elements" of the concept from no less than 85 sources. His own selective synthesis is as follows: "An ideology is a system of collectively held normative and reputedly factual ideas and beliefs and attitudes advocating a particular pattern of social relationships and arrangements, and/or aimed at justifying a particular pattern of conduct, which its proponents seek to promote, realize, pursue or maintain."[19]

Hamilton recommends this definition for purposes of "empirical application and research," and so excludes some of the "definitional elements" that have historically been important to participants in and theorists of political action. Hence the association of ideology with class interest that has been so important to Marxist politics is rejected, as is the whole question of relationship between ideology and science. Indeed, a number of other issues that have been famously explored in discussions about what ideology is and what are examples of it are rather flippantly discarded, as if specialists in epistemology or philosophy of science were the only ones competent to "settle" such questions. These include the way that ideas are determined in society, the distinction between descriptive and explanatory claims, the relationship between political advocacy and social science, and the way in which ideas are or are not "functional." In justifying his exclusions Hamilton appeals to a realm of "reason, logic or . . . evidence" that he believes is independent of the interests of the human beings who use such concepts.[20] One can argue, however, that this claim is not only impossible to sustain, but that it lays the author open to the very kind of scrutiny in which the term ideology has figured. What exactly are the interests of social scientists? Are these not reflected in their concept of an "empirical fact"? Can they escape their own social and political context so easily by modeling themselves on what they take to be the natural sciences? Can they appeal so conveniently to what philosophers term reason and logic?

Ideology, in sum, is not a concept that denotes some particular phenomenon in the world. It is not a template against which something is or is not an ideology; nor is it a recipe stating how to make an ideology correctly. Rather it is an agenda of things to discuss, questions to ask, hypotheses to make. We should be able to use it when considering the interaction between ideas and politics, especially systems of ideas that make claims, whether justificatory or hortatory. Cutting the concept off from its history, even if historically it has been used in contradictory ways, is no service. Political theory is not an exercise in grave-digging, so that inconvenient problems can be "disappeared." Instead, it provides a wealth of critical perspective, if only we are prepared to use it.

NOTES

1. Count Destutt de Tracy, *A Treatise on Political Economy; to Which Is Prefixed a Supplement to a Preceding Work on the Understanding, or Elements of Ideology; with an Analytical Table, and an Introduction on the Faculty of the Will*, translated by Thomas Jefferson, in John M. Dorsey, *Psychology of Political Science* (Detroit: Center for Health Education, 1973), "Advertisement" ix.

2. George Lichtheim, *The Concept of Ideology and Other Essays* (New York: Random House, 1967), pp. 4–5.
3. Karl Marx and Friedrich Engels, *Collected Works,* vol. 5 (London: Lawrence & Wishart, 1976), pp. 586–587.
4. Ibid., pp. 59–60.
5. Ibid., p. 62.
6. Karl Marx and Friedrich Engels, *Selected Works in One Volume* (London: Lawrence & Wishart, 1984), p. 183.
7. Marx and Engels, *Collected Works,* vol. 5, p. 60.
8. Ibid., p. 52.
9. Ibid., p. 80.
10. Marx and Engels, *Selected Works in One Volume,* p. 181.
11. Marx and Engels, *Collected Works,* vol. 5, p. 49.
12. Terrell Carver, *Marx's Social Theory* (Oxford: Oxford University Press, 1982), p. 44.
13. See Terrell Carver, *Marx and Engels: The Intellectual Relationship* (Brighton: Wheatsheaf Books, 1983), *passim.*
14. V. I. Lenin, *Collected Works,* vol. 5, translated by Joe Fineberg and George Hanna, ed. Victor Jerome (Moscow: Progress Publishers, 1973), pp. 369, 370, 383–384.
15. Ibid., pp. 375, 383–384.
16. Karl Mannheim, *Ideology and Utopia,* translated by Louis Wirth and Edward Shils (London: Routledge & Kegan Paul, 1948), pp. 2, 238.
17. Ibid., pp. 49–50.
18. Ibid., p. 62.
19. Malcolm B. Hamilton, "The Elements of the Concept of Ideology," *Political Studies* 35 (1987), p. 38.
20. Ibid., p. 32.

PART TWO
THE DEMOCRATIC IDEAL

Some politicians, scholars, and journalists speak of democracy as if it were an ideology, distinct from and in opposition to other ideologies—especially communism and fascism. But surely this is mistaken. Democracy is not itself an ideology, but an *ideal* that different ideologies define and pursue in different ways. Everyone agrees that "democracy" means "rule by the people," of course, but what *is* rule by the people? Who are *the people*, and *how* are they to rule? On these points there is little agreement, as each ideology answers these questions in its own way. With the exception of fascism and Nazism, however, all the ideologies now agree that democracy is certainly the most desirable form of government—an ideal toward which all societies should strive.

The popularity of democracy at the end of the twentieth century is extraordinary not only because so many people of such different views claim to be democrats, but also because democracy was long regarded as a bad or corrupt form of government. The word "democracy" itself first came into use in ancient Greece, where a conflict developed between those who favored democracy—rule by the *demos*, or people—and those who preferred aristocracy—literally, "rule by the best." In Athens in the fifth century B.C. the *demos*, or people, found a leader in Pericles, whose "Funeral Oration" was one of the first defenses of democracy as a way of life. The Athenian democracy was short-lived, however, and philosophers such as Plato (c. 428–348 B.C.) and Aristotle (384–322 B.C.) concluded that democracy is inherently unstable. The common people, Plato argued, are simply too shortsighted and too unruly to govern wisely. Democracy will soon descend into anarchy, a lawless condition that will lead the people to call for some strong leader to restore law and order. But that strong leader will be a despot who subjects everyone else to slavery. From democracy, according to Plato, it is but a short step to despotism, the worst of all forms of government.

Like Plato, Aristotle regarded democracy as a selfish or corrupt form of government. Democracy is "rule by the many" in the selfish interest of the common people as a distinct class, he said, not rule in the interest of the community as a whole. But Aristotle did note that democracy has some desirable features—enough to make it the least bad of the corrupt forms—and he went further to argue that rule by the many in the interests of the whole community is not only possible, but probably the best of all forms of government.

Aristotle called this best form of government a polity, but it became better known later by the Roman name of "republic," from the Latin *res publica* (meaning "public thing" or "public business"). The republican idea was that the forms of government must be mixed in such a way that some power is in the hands of the common people, some in the hands of the aristocratic few, and some in the hands of a single person. Because each element of society would have some power, but not enough to rule without the cooperation of the other two elements, a system of checks and balances would lead to a government that ruled in the common interest. It would then be a popular government because the people *(populus)* would have a significant voice, but it would not be a democracy. In a republic the power of the people would be tempered and guided by the wisdom of the few.

For centuries the republic, and not democracy, was considered the ideal form of popular government. Its supporters included Niccolò Machiavelli (1469–1527), the Italian author of the notorious *The Prince*, and John Adams (1735–1826), the second President of the United States. But in the late eighteenth and early nineteenth centuries sentiment began to shift in favor of democracy. Exactly why this happened is not clear. But with the growth of cities and industry came increasing literacy and improved means of communication, and the nineteenth century soon came to be known as the age of "the common man." In the United States this change was associated with Jacksonian Democracy, as the period of Andrew Jackson's presidency (1829–1837) was called. Democracy was taken to be a means of expression, or self-government, for the common man, as well as a device by which he could protect his rights and interests. But "rule by the people" did not then include women and those other groups, such as slaves in the United States, who were not yet counted among "the people."

To some observers the rise of democracy was a mixed blessing. Alexis de Tocqueville (1805–1859), a French aristocrat who traveled throughout the United States in the 1830s, welcomed the increased opportunities that democracy brought to common people. In his *Democracy in America*, de Tocqueville particularly praised the opportunities for participation in local government that democracy made possible. But he also worried that democracy placed so much emphasis on equality that a new form of tyranny would emerge—the "tyranny of the majority." The emphasis on equality will lead to the pressure to conform, de Tocqueville feared, so that people will be afraid to think and act for themselves. In England John Stuart Mill (1806–1873) reached much the same conclusion. The old days of tyrannical rule by kings and emperors were vanishing, he wrote in *On Liberty*, but now the individual's ability to think and live freely was subject to "the moral coercion of public opinion" (see the selection from *On Liberty* in Part Three). Like de Tocqueville, Mill welcomed the increased opportunities for political participation that democracy opened, for he saw participation as a way of educating and improving men and women. But he also suggested that it might be prudent, at least temporarily, to give the wiser, better informed, and more responsible members of societies more votes than the common person.

Despite these concerns, democracy became more widespread throughout the nineteenth century. Voting rights were extended to almost all adult males in the industrialized countries of Europe and America by the end of the century, then to women in the early years of this century. Fascism reacted against this democratic trend in the years following World War I, but the defeat of Germany, Italy, and Japan in World War II seems to have crushed fascism as a significant antidemocratic force. Throughout the world, democracy is hailed as the best of all forms of government.

But "democracy" means different things to different people. In particular, three conceptions of democracy have competed with one another in the twentieth century. The most familiar in the English-speaking world is *liberal democracy*. For liberals like Mill democracy is indeed government by the people, but the people must be willing to respect the rights and liberties of the individuals who compose society. In liberal democracy, then, the chief concern is to prevent majority rule from becoming the tyranny of the majority. The advocates of *social democracy* accept the need to protect individual rights, but they argue that some of these rights—especially the right to own and dispose of property—may be used to frustrate true democracy. Like Michael Walzer, whose essay "Town Meetings and Workers' Control" is reprinted below, social democrats take the socialist point of view that property ought to be controlled directly for the public good, not the private benefit of individuals. Property and wealth are forms of power, they say, and no society can be truly democratic when some people have far more power than others. Social democrats thus stress the importance of equality for democracy, where equality is understood as a roughly equal chance to influence the decisions that govern one's society.

The third conception of democracy competing for acceptance in this century is *people's democracy*. This view is linked most closely with communism, or Marxism-Leninism. In this view democracy is rule by, or *in the interests of*, the common people, which means that it is possible for a single group, such as the Communist party, to wield power democratically so long as it acts to promote the interests of the working class, or proletariat. Democracy and dictatorship are compatible with one another, in other words, as the Chinese leader Mao Zedong (1893–1976) insisted in his essay "On the People's Democratic Dictatorship" (in Part Six).

In the last decade of the twentieth century the idea of the "people's democracy" seems to have few adherents outside the ranks of the leaders of the Chinese Communist party. But democracy in general is more popular than ever, and the question we now face is whether liberals and socialists will continue to quarrel over the proper definition of "democracy," or whether they will find enough common ground to satisfy—and perhaps unite—the two groups.

2

DEMOCRACY AND DESPOTISM

EURIPIDES

Greeks of fifth and fourth centuries B.C. Athens took pride in a form of government that they had invented—democracy (from *demos*, meaning "people" or "common people," and *kratein*, meaning "rule"). While other peoples chafed under the rule of despots, the Athenians ruled themselves. In his play *The Suppliants*, first performed in 422 B.C., Euripides (c. 485–407 B.C.) contrasts democratic and despotic government, celebrating the former while condemning the latter. The occasion is the arrival of an envoy from Thebes, which was then ruled by the tyrant Creon. The envoy cannot quite believe that the people are capable of ruling themselves.

Source: Euripides, The Suppliants, 11. *394–465; translated by Terence Ball.*

THEBAN MESSENGER: Who is the tyrant who rules this land? To whom must I deliver my message from Creon, ruler of Thebes?

THESEUS: Noble visitor, your speech proceeds from a false premise. No tyrant rules here, for this city is free. Here the people rule, each taking his turn without respect of wealth or poverty.

THEBAN MESSENGER: Surely you are playing games with me. The city from which I come is ruled not by the gullible multitude but by one man only. No one there uses high-sounding words to pander to the crowd, manipulating them for his own advantage while cloaking his crimes and failures in fair-sounding phrases. So I ask you: Since the people are such poor judges of everything, how can they possibly govern the city? They have neither the time nor the talent to understand the intricacies of politics. Even if he had been educated, a poor working stiff would have no time or energy left over from his labors to learn about political affairs. Besides, wiser and better people would recoil from a system in which such a man might, through his own way with words, fool the people and rise from being a nobody to occupy a position of political prominence.

THESEUS: You yourself have a way with words and would, if you could, fool us with your kit of clever verbal tricks. But since you have chosen to play this game of words, permit me to take my turn while you listen. Nothing is worse for a city than a tyrant. Wherever he rules, the law does not. In his hands there is no law that rules over all alike. But where the laws rule, all—rich and poor, powerful and weak—are equal before them. There the poor are able to speak the same language as the strong—the language of law and justice. If his cause be just, the poor man can prevail against a wealthy adversary. The hallmark of freedom is this: Anyone having good advice to give to the city should be heard, and anyone with nothing to say may choose to remain silent. What greater equality can exist in a city? Where all the citizens rule, they take pride in their young people. But where a tyrant rules, he fears them, and, seeing the most talented among them as a threat to his own power, he puts them to the sword. How can the city survive and prosper, where its ruler stifles all initiative and uses his sword like a scythe, cutting down its youths like the flowers of spring? Why work and save for the sake of your children, only to have the tyrant take it all away? Why raise your daughters to be virtuous, when they can be ravished at whim by a lustful tyrant while their tearful parents are powerless to prevent it? I would rather die than have my children be subjected to such arbitrary power!

This thunderbolt I hurl in answer to your words. . . . If you weren't a messenger and therefore under the protection of the law, you would pay dearly for your outrageous remarks. It is the messenger's duty to deliver one message and to return with another. So take this reply back to Creon: Next time, send to our city a messenger who talks less foolishly than this one.

3

FUNERAL ORATION

PERICLES

After defeating the numerically larger forces of the despotic Persian Empire in 480 B.C., democratic Athens assumed a preeminent position among the city-states of Greece. Wary of Athens' growing power and arrogance, several other city-states, led by Sparta, waged war—the Peloponnesian War—against Athens. In his famous "Funeral Oration" (430 B.C.) the statesman Pericles (c. 495–429 B.C.) commemorates the sacrifice of the Athenians who fell in the first years of the war and celebrates the ideals of Athenian democracy.

Source: Thucydides, *2nd ed., revised, vol. I, translated by Benjamin Jowett (Oxford: Clarendon Press, 1900), pp. 126–135. The editors have altered the translation slightly.*

Most of those who have spoken here before me have commended the lawgiver who added this oration to our other funeral customs; it seemed to them a worthy thing that such an honour should be given at their burial to the dead who have fallen on the field of battle. But I should have preferred that, when men's deeds have been brave, they should be honoured in deed only, and with such an honour as this public funeral, which you are now witnessing. Then the reputation of many would not have been imperilled on the eloquence or want of eloquence of one, and their virtues believed or not as he spoke well or ill. For it is difficult to say neither too little nor too much; and even moderation is apt not to give the impression of truthfulness. The friend of the dead who knows the facts is likely to think that the words of the speaker fall short of his knowledge and of his wishes; another who is not so well informed, when he hears of anything which surpasses his own powers, will be envious and will suspect exaggeration. Mankind are tolerant of the praises of others so long as each hearer thinks that he can do as well or nearly as well himself, but, when the speaker rises above him, jealousy is aroused and he begins to be incredulous. However, since our ancestors have set the seal of their approval upon the practice, I must obey, and to the utmost of my power shall endeavour to satisfy the wishes and beliefs of all who hear me.

I will speak first of our ancestors, for it is right and seemly that now, when we are lamenting the dead, a tribute should be paid to their memory. There has never been a time when they did not inhabit this land, which by their valour they have handed down from generation to generation, and we have received from them a free state. But if they were worthy of praise, still more were our fathers, who added to their inheritance, and after many a struggle transmitted to us their sons this great empire. And we ourselves assembled here today, who are still most of us in the vigour of life, have carried the work of improvement further, and have richly endowed our city with all things, so that she is sufficient for herself both in peace and war. Of the military exploits by which our various possessions were acquired, or of the energy with which we or our fathers drove back the tide of war, Hellenic or Barbarian, I will not speak; for the tale would be long and is familiar to you. But before I praise the dead, I should like to point out by what principles of action we rose to power, and under what institutions and through what manner of life our empire became great. For I conceive that such thoughts are not unsuited to the occasion, and that this numerous assembly of citizens and strangers may profitably listen to them.

Our form of government does not enter into rivalry with the institutions of others. We do not copy our neighbours, but are an example to them. It is true that we are called a democracy, for the administration is in the hands of the many and not of the few. But while the law secures equal justice to all alike in their private disputes, the claim of excellence is also recognised; and when a citizen is in any way distinguished, he is preferred to the public service, not as a matter of privilege, but as the reward of merit. Neither is poverty a bar, but a man may benefit his country whatever be the obscurity of his condition. There is no exclusiveness in our public life, and in our private intercourse we are not suspicious of one another, nor angry with our neighbour if he does what he likes; we do not put on sour looks at him which, though harmless, are not pleasant. While we are thus unconstrained in our private intercourse, a spirit of reverence pervades our public acts; we are prevented from doing wrong by respect for the authorities and for the laws, having an especial regard to those which are ordained for the protection of the injured as well as to those unwritten laws which bring upon the transgressor of them the reprobation of the general sentiment.

And we have not forgotten to provide for our weary spirits many relaxations from toil; we have regular games and sacrifices throughout the year; our homes are beautiful and elegant; and the delight which we daily feel in all these things helps to banish melancholy. Because of the greatness of our city the fruits of the whole earth flow in upon us; so that we enjoy the goods of other countries as freely as of our own.

Then, again, our military training is in many respects superior to that of our adversaries. Our city is thrown open to the world, and we never expel a foreigner or prevent him from seeing or learning anything of which the secret if revealed to an enemy might profit him. We rely not upon management or trickery, but upon our own hearts and hands. And in the matter of education, whereas they from early youth are always undergoing laborious exercises which are to make them brave, we live at ease, and yet are equally ready to face the perils which they face. And here is the proof. The Lacedaemonians come into Attica not by themselves, but with their whole confederacy following; we go alone into a neighbour's country; and although our opponents are fighting for their homes and we on a foreign soil, we have seldom any difficulty in overcoming them. Our enemies have never yet felt our united strength; the care of a navy divides our attention, and on land we are obliged to send our own citizens everywhere. But they, if they meet and defeat a part of our army, are as proud as if they had routed us all, and when defeated they pretend to have been vanquished by us all.

If then we prefer to meet danger with a light heart but without laborious training, and with a courage which is gained by habit and not enforced by law, are we not greatly the gainers? Since we do not anticipate the pain, although, when the hour comes, we can be as brave as those who never allow themselves to rest; and thus too our city is equally admirable in peace and in war. For we are lovers of the beautiful, yet simple in our tastes, and we cultivate the mind without loss of manliness. Wealth we employ, not for talk and ostentation, but when there is a real use for it. To avow poverty with us is no disgrace; the true disgrace is in doing nothing to avoid it. An Athenian citizen does not neglect the state because he takes care of his own household; and even those of us who are engaged in business have a very fair idea of politics. We alone regard a man who takes no interest in public affairs, not as a harmless, but as a useless character; and if few of us are originators, we are all sound judges of a policy. The great impediment to action is, in our opinion, not discussion, but the want of that knowledge which is gained by discussion preparatory to action. For we have a peculiar power of thinking before we act and of acting too, whereas other men are courageous from ignorance but hesitate upon reflection. And they are surely to be esteemed the bravest spirits who, having the clearest sense both of the pains and pleasures of life, do not on that account shrink from danger. In doing good, again, we are unlike others; we make our friends by conferring, not by receiving favours. Now he who confers a favor is the firmer friend, because he would fain by kindness keep alive the memory of an obligation; but the recipient is colder in his feelings, because he knows that in requiting another's generosity he will not be winning gratitude but only paying a debt. We alone do good to our neighbours not upon a calculation of interest, but in the confidence of freedom and in a frank and fearless spirit. To sum up: I say that Athens is the school of Hellas, and that the individual Athenian in his own person seems to have the power of adapting himself to the most varied forms of action with the utmost versatility and grace. This is no passing and idle word, but truth and fact; and the assertion is verified by the position to which these qualities have raised the state. For in the hour of trial Athens alone among her contemporaries is superior to the report of her. No enemy who comes against her is indignant at the reverses which he sustains at the hands of such a city; no subject complains that his masters are unworthy of him. And we shall assuredly not be without witnesses; there are mighty monuments of our power which will make us the wonder of this and of succeeding ages; we shall not need the praises of Homer or of any other panegyrist whose poetry may please for the moment, although his representation of the facts will not bear the light of day. For we have compelled every land and every sea to open a path for our valour, and have everywhere planted eternal memorials of our friendship and of our enmity. Such is the city for whose sake these men nobly fought and died; they could not bear the thought that she might be taken from them; and every one of us who survive should gladly toil on her behalf.

I have dwelt upon the greatness of Athens because I want to show you that we are contending for a higher prize than those who enjoy none of these privileges, and to establish by manifest proof the merit of these men whom I am now commemorating. Their loftiest praise has been already spoken. For in magnifying the city I have magnified them, and men like them whose virtues made her glorious. And of how few Hellenes can it be said as of them, that their deeds when weighed in the balance have been found equal to their fame! I believe that a death such as theirs has been gives the true measure of a man's worth; it may be the first revelation of his virtues, but is at any rate their final seal. For even those who come short in other ways may justly plead the valour with which they have fought for their country; they have blotted out the evil with the good, and have benefited the state more by their public services than they have injured her by their private actions. None of these men were weakened by wealth or hesitated to forgo the pleasures of life; none of them put off the evil day in the hope, natural to poverty, that a man, though poor, may one day become rich. But, deeming that the punishment of their enemies was sweeter than any of these things, and that they could fall in no nobler cause, they determined at the hazard of their lives to be honourably avenged, and to leave the rest. They resigned to hope their unknown chance of happiness; but in the face of death they resolved to rely upon themselves alone. And when the moment came they were minded to resist and suffer, rather than to flee and save their lives; they ran away from the word of dishonour, but on the battle-field their feet stood fast, and in an instant, at the height of their fortune, they passed away from the scene, not of their fear, but of their glory.

Such was the end of these men; they were worthy of Athens, and the living need not desire to have a more heroic spirit, although they may pray for a less fatal result. The value of such a spirit is not to be expressed in words. Any one can talk to you for ever about the advantages of a brave defence, which you know already. But instead of listening to him I would have you day by day fix your eyes upon the greatness of Athens, until you become filled with the love of her; and when you are impressed by the spectacle of her glory, reflect that this empire has been acquired by men who knew their duty and had the courage to do it, who in the hour of conflict had the fear of dishonour always present to them, and who, if ever they failed in an enterprise, would not allow their virtues to be lost to their country, but freely gave their lives to her as the fairest offering which they could present at her feast. The sacrifice which they collectively made was individually repaid to them; for they received again each one for himself a praise which grows not old, and the noblest of all sepulchres—I speak not of that in which their remains are laid, but of that in which their glory survives, and is proclaimed always and on every fitting occasion both in word and deed. For the whole earth is the sepulchre of famous men; not only are they commemorated by columns and inscriptions in their own country, but in foreign lands there dwells also an unwritten memorial of them, graven not on stone but in the hearts of men. Make them your examples, and, esteeming courage to be freedom and freedom to be happiness, do not weigh too nicely the perils of war. The unfortunate who has no hope of a change for the better has less reason to throw away his life than the prosperous who, if he survive, is always liable to a change for the worse, and to whom any accidental fall makes the most serious difference. To a man of spirit, cowardice and disaster coming together are far more bitter than death striking him unperceived at a time when he is full of courage and animated by the general hope.

Wherefore I do not now commiserate the parents of the dead who stand here; I would rather comfort them. You know that your life has been passed amid many great changes; and that they may be deemed fortunate who have gained most honour, whether an honourable death like theirs, or an honourable sorrow like yours, and whose days have been so ordered that the term of their happiness is likewise the term of their life. I know how hard it is to make you feel this, when the good fortune of others will too often remind you of the gladness which once lightened your hearts. And sorrow is felt at the want of those blessings, not which a man never knew, but which were a part of his life before they were taken from him. Some of you are of an age at which they may hope to have other children, and they ought to bear their sorrow better; not only will the children who may hereafter be born make them forget their own lost ones, but the city will be doubly a gainer. She will not be left desolate, and she will be safer. For a man's counsel cannot have equal weight or worth, when he alone has no children to risk in the general danger. To those of you who have passed their prime, I say: "Congratulate yourselves that you have been happy during the greater part of your days; remember that your life of sorrow will not last long, and be comforted by the glory of those who are gone. For the love of honour alone is ever young, and not riches, as some say, but honour is the delight of men when they are old and useless."

To you who are the sons and brothers of the departed, I see that the struggle to emulate them will be an arduous one. For all men praise the dead, and, however preeminent your virtue may be, hardly will you be thought, I do not say to equal, but even to approach them. The living have their rivals and detractors, but when a man is out of the way, the honour and good-will which he receives is unalloyed. And, if I am to speak of womanly virtues to those of you who will henceforth be widows, let me sum them up in one short admonition: To a woman not to show more weakness than is natural to her sex is a great glory, and not to be talked about for good or for evil among men.

I have paid the required tribute, in obedience to the law, making use of such fitting words as I had. The tribute of deeds has been paid in part; for the dead have been honourably buried, and it remains only that their children should be maintained at the public charge until they are grown up: this is the solid prize with which, as with a wreath, Athens crowns her sons living and dead, after a struggle like theirs. For where the rewards of virtue are greatest, there the noblest citizens are enlisted in the service of the state. And now, when you have duly lamented, every one his own dead, you may depart.

4

DEMOCRATIC JUDGMENT AND THE "MIDDLING" CONSTITUTION

ARISTOTLE

Although critical of democracy as a form of government, the Greek philosopher Aristotle (384–322 B.C.) nevertheless recognized the democratic principle that "many heads are better than one." Just as a feast to which many people contribute is richer, more varied, and more nourishing than that prepared by one or a few, so a government that makes use of many talents and perspectives is wiser than one that does not. But the best form of government, he goes on to say, is not democracy but "polity," that is, rule by the many in the interest of all. Aristotle thus anticipates the kind of popular self-rule that came to be called "republican." On the republican form of government, see selections 5 and 7.

Source: Aristotle, The Politics, *translated by Benjamin Jowett (New York: Modern Library, 1943), pp. 145–149, 189–193. The editors have altered the translation slightly.*

BOOK III

. . .

CHAPTER 11

. . . The principle that the multitude ought to be supreme rather than the few best is one that is maintained, and, though not free from difficulty, yet seems to contain an element of truth. For the many, of whom each individual is but an ordinary person, when they meet together may very likely be better than the few good, if regarded not individually but collectively, just as a feast to which many contribute is better than a dinner provided out of a single purse. For each individual among the many has a share of virtue and prudence, and when they meet together, they become in a manner one man, who has many feet, and hands, and senses; that is a figure of their mind and disposition. Hence the many are better judges than a single man of music and poetry; for some understand one part, and some another, and among them they understand the whole. There is a similar combination of qualities in good men, who differ from any individual of the many, as the beautiful are said to differ from those who are not beautiful, and works of art from realities, because in them the scattered elements are combined, although, if taken separately, the eye of one person or some other feature in another person would be fairer than in the picture. Whether this principle can apply to every democracy, and to all bodies of men, is not clear. Or rather, by heaven, in some cases it is impossible of application; for the argument would equally hold about animals; and wherein, it will be asked, do some men differ from animals? But there may be bodies of men about whom our statement is nevertheless true. And if so, the difficulty which has been already raised, and also another which is akin to it—viz. what power should be assigned to the mass of freemen and citizens, who are not rich and have no personal merit—are both solved. There is still a danger in allowing them to share the great offices of state, for their folly will lead them into error, and their dishonesty into crime. But there is a danger also in not letting them share, for a state in which many poor men are excluded from office will necessarily be full of enemies. The only way of escape is to assign to them some deliberative and judicial functions. For this reason Solon and certain other legislators give them the power of electing to offices, and of calling the magistrates to account, but they do not allow them to hold office singly. When they meet together their perceptions are quite good enough, and combined with the better class they are useful to the state (just as impure food when mixed with what is pure sometimes makes the entire mass more wholesome than a small quantity of the pure would be), but each individual, left to himself, forms an imperfect judgement. On the other hand, the popular form of government involves certain difficulties. In the first place, it might be objected that he who can judge of the healing of a sick man would be one who could himself heal his disease, and make him whole—that is, in other words, the physician; and so in all professions and arts. As, then, the physician ought to be called to account by physicians, so ought men in general to be called to account by their peers. But physicians are of three kinds: there is the ordinary practitioner, and there is the physician of the higher class, and thirdly the intelligent man who has studied the art: in all arts there is such a class; and we attribute the power of judging to them quite as much as to professors of the art. Secondly, does not the same principle apply to elections? For a right election can only be made by those who have knowledge; those who know geometry, for example, will choose a geometrician rightly, and those who know how to steer, a pilot; and, even if there be some occupations and arts in which private persons share in the ability to choose, they certainly cannot choose better than those who know. So that, according to this argument, neither the election of magistrates, nor the calling of them to account, should be entrusted to the many. Yet possibly these objections are to a great extent met by our old answer, that if the people are not utterly degraded, although individually they may be worse judges than those who have special knowledge: as a body they are as good or better. Moreover, there are some arts whose products are not judged of solely, or best, by the artists themselves, namely those arts whose products are recognized even by those who do not possess the art; for example, the knowledge of the house is not limited to the builder only; the user, or, in other words, the master, of the house will be even a better judge than the builder, just as the pilot will judge better of a rudder than the carpenter, and the guest will judge better of a feast than the cook.

This difficulty seems now to be sufficiently answered, but there is another akin to it. That inferior persons should have authority in greater matters than the good would appear to be a strange thing, yet the election and calling to account of the magistrates is the greatest of all. And these, as I was saying, are functions which in some states are assigned to the people, for the assembly is supreme in all such matters. Yet persons of any age, and having but a small property qualification, sit in the assembly and deliberate and judge, although for the great officers of state, such as treasurers and generals, a high qualification is required. This difficulty may be solved in the same manner as the preceding, and the present practice of democracies may be really defensible. For the power does not reside in the juror, or senator, or assemblyman, but in the court, and the senate, and the assembly, of which individual senators, or assemblyman or jurors, are only parts or members. And for this reason the many may claim to have a higher authority than the few; for the people, and the senate, and the courts consist of many persons, and their property collectively is greater than the property of one or of a few individuals holding great offices. But enough of this.

The discussion of the first question shows nothing so clearly as that laws, when good, should be supreme; and that the magistrate or magistrates should regulate those matters only on which the laws are unable to speak with precision owing to the difficulty of any general principle embracing all particulars. But what are good laws has not yet been clearly explained; the old difficulty remains. The goodness or badness, justice or injustice, of laws varies of necessity with the constitutions of states. This, however, is clear, that the laws must be adapted to the constitutions. But if so, true forms of government will of necessity have just laws, and perverted forms of government will have unjust laws.

CHAPTER 12

In all sciences and arts the end is a good, and the greatest good and in the highest degree a good in the most authoritative of all—this is the political science of which the good is justice, in other words, the common interest. All men think justice to be a sort of equality; and to a certain extent they agree in the philosophical distinctions which have been laid down by us about Ethics. For they admit that justice is a thing and has a relation to persons, and that equals ought to have equality.

BOOK IV

. . .

CHAPTER 11

We have now to inquire what is the best constitution for most states, and the best life for most men, neither assuming a standard of virtue which is above ordinary persons, nor an education which is exceptionally favoured by nature and circumstances, nor yet an ideal state which is an aspiration only, but having regard to the life in which the majority are able to share, and to the form of government which states in general can attain. As to those aristocracies, as they are called, of which we were just now speaking, they either lie beyond the possibilities of the greater number of states, or they approximate to the so-called constitutional government, and therefore need no separate discussion. And in fact the conclusion at which we arrive respecting all these forms rests upon the same grounds. For if what was said in the *Ethics* is true, that the happy life is the life according to virtue lived without impediment, and that virtue is a mean, then the life which is in a mean, and in a mean attainable by every one, must be the best. And the same principles of virtue and vice are characteristic of cities and of constitutions; for the constitution is in a figure the life of the city.

Now in all states there are three elements: one class is very rich, another very poor, and a third in a mean. It is admitted that moderation and the mean are best, and therefore it will clearly be best to possess the gifts of fortune in moderation; for in that condition of life men are most ready to follow rational principle. But he who greatly excels in beauty, strength, birth, or wealth, or on the other hand who is very poor, or very weak, or very much disgraced, finds it difficult to follow rational principle. Of these two the one sort grow into violent and great criminals, the others into rogues and petty rascals. And two sorts of offences correspond to them, the one committed from violence, the other from roguery. Again, the middle class is least likely to shrink from rule, or to be overambitious for it; both of which are injuries to the state. Again, those who have too much of the goods of fortune, strength, wealth, friends, and the like, are neither willing nor able to submit to authority. The evil begins at home; for when they are boys, by reason of the luxury in which they are brought up, they never learn, even at school, the habit of obedience. On the other hand, the very poor, who are in the opposite extreme, are too degraded. So that the one class cannot obey, and can only rule despotically; the other knows not how to command and must be ruled like slaves. Thus arises a city, not of freemen, but of masters and slaves, the one despising, the other envying; and nothing can be more fatal to friendship and good fellowship in states than this: for good fellowship springs from friendship; when men are at enmity with one another, they would rather not even share the same path. But a city ought to be composed, as far as possible, of equals and similars; and these are generally the middle classes. Wherefore the city which is composed of middle-class citizens is necessarily best constituted in respect of the elements of which we say the fabric of the state naturally consists. And this is the class of citizens which is most secure in a state, for they do not, like the poor, covet their neighbours' goods; nor do others covet theirs, as the poor covet the goods of the rich; and as they neither plot against others, nor are themselves plotted against, they pass through life safely. Wisely then did Phocylides pray—"Many things are best in the mean; I desire to be of a middle condition in my city."

Thus it is manifest that the best political community is formed by citizens of the middle class, and that those states are likely to be well-administered, in which the middle class is large, and stronger if possible than both the other classes, or at any rate than either singly; for the addition of the middle class turns the scale, and prevents either of the extremes from being dominant. Great then is the good fortune of a state in which the citizens have a moderate and sufficient property; for where some possess much, and the others nothing, there may arise an extreme democracy, or a pure oligarchy; or a tyranny may grow out of either extreme—either out of the most rampant democracy, or out of an oligarchy; but it is not so likely to arise out of the middle constitutions and those akin to them. I will explain the reason of this hereafter, when I speak of the revolutions of states. The mean condition of states is clearly best, for no other is free from faction; and where the middle class is large, there are least likely to be factions and dissensions. For a similar reason large states are less liable to faction than small ones, because in them the middle class is large; whereas in small states it is easy to divide all the citizens into two classes who are either rich or poor, and to leave nothing in the middle. And democracies are safer and more permanent than oligarchies, because they have a middle class which is more numerous and has a greater share in the government; for when there is no middle class, and the poor greatly exceed in number, troubles arise, and the state soon comes to an end. A proof of the superiority of the middle class is that the best legislators have been of a middle condition; for example, Solon, as his own verses testify; and Lycurgus, for he was not a king; and Charondas, and almost all legislators.

These considerations will help us to understand why most governments are either democratical or oligarchical. The reason is that the middle class is seldom numerous in them, and whichever party, whether the rich or the common people, transgresses the mean and predominates, draws the constitution its own way, and thus arises either oligarchy or democracy. There is another reason—the poor and the rich quarrel with one another, and whichever side gets the better, instead of establishing a just or popular government, regards political supremacy as the prize of victory, and the one party sets up a democracy and the other an oligarchy. Further, both the parties which had the supremacy in Hellas looked only to the interest of their own form of government, and established in states, the one, democracies, and the other, oligarchies; they thought of their own advantage, of the public not at all. For these reasons the middle form of government has rarely, if ever, existed, and among a very few only. One man alone of all who ever ruled in Hellas was induced to give this middle constitution to states. But it has now become a habit among the citizens of states, not even to care about equality; all men are seeking for dominion, or, if conquered, are willing to submit.

What then is the best form of government, and what makes it the best, is evident; and of other constitutions, since we say that there are many kinds of democracy and many of oligarchy, it is not difficult to see which has the first and which the second or any other place in the order of excellence, now that we have determined which is the best. For that which is nearest to the best must of necessity be better, and that which is furthest from it worse, if we are judging absolutely and not relatively to given conditions: I say "relatively to given conditions," since a particular government may be preferable, but another form may be better for some people.

5

WHAT'S WRONG WITH PRINCELY RULE?

NICCOLÒ MACHIAVELLI

The Italian Renaissance of the fifteenth and sixteenth centuries saw the rebirth of many of the ideals of classical Greece and Rome, including the ideal of self-government. Among those who celebrated the rebirth of "republican" government was Niccolò Machiavelli (1469–1527). Here he criticizes the claim that the people, acting collectively, are less wise than a single king or prince.

Source: N. Machiavelli, The Discourses, *translated by Christian Detmold (Boston: James R. Osgood & Co., 1882), Chapter 58,* pp. 214–219.

THE PEOPLE ARE WISER AND MORE CONSTANT THAN PRINCES

TITUS LIVIUS as well as all other historians affirm that nothing is more uncertain and inconstant than the multitude; for it appears from what he relates of the actions of men, that in many instances the multitude, after having condemned a man to death, bitterly lamented it, and most earnestly wished him back. This was the case with the Roman people and Manlius Capitolinus, whom they had condemned to death and afterwards most earnestly desired him back, as our author says in the following words: "No sooner had they found out that they had nothing to fear from him, than they began to regret and to wish him back." And elsewhere, when he relates the events that occurred in Syracuse after the death of Hieronymus, nephew of Hiero, he says: "It is the nature of the multitude either humbly to serve or insolently to dominate." I know not whether, in undertaking to defend a cause against the accusations of all writers, I do not assume a task so hard and so beset with difficulties as to oblige me to abandon it with shame, or to go on with it at the risk of being weighed down by it. Be that as it may, however, I think, and ever shall think, that it cannot be wrong to defend one's opinions with arguments founded upon reason, without employing force or authority.

I say, then, that individual men, and especially princes, may be charged with the same defects of which writers accuse the people; for whoever is not controlled by laws will commit the same errors as an unbridled multitude. This may easily be verified, for there have been and still are plenty of princes, and a few good and wise ones, such, I mean, as needed not the curb that controlled them. Amongst these, however, are not to be counted either the kings that lived in Egypt at that ancient period when that country was governed by laws, or those that arose in Sparta; neither such as are born in our day in France, for that country is more thoroughly regulated by laws than any other of which we have any knowledge in modern times. And those kings that arise under such constitutions are not to be classed amongst the number of those whose individual nature we have to consider, and see whether it resembles that of the people; but they should be compared with a people equally controlled by law as those kings were, and then we shall find in that multitude the same good qualities as in those kings, and we shall see that such a people neither obey with servility nor command with insolence. Such were the people of Rome, who, so long as that republic remained uncorrupted, neither obeyed basely nor ruled insolently, but rather held its rank honorably, supporting the laws and their magistrates. And when the unrighteous ambition of some noble made it necessary for them to rise up in self-defence, they did so, as in the case of Manlius, the Decemvirs, and others who attempted to oppress them; and so when the public good required them to obey the Dictators and Consuls, they promptly yielded obedience. And if the Roman people regretted Manlius Capitolinus after his death, it is not to be wondered at; for they regretted his virtues, which had been such that the remembrance of them filled every one with pity, and would have had the power to produce the same effect upon any prince; for all writers agree that virtue is to be admired and praised, even in one's enemies. And if intense desire could have restored Manlius to life, the Roman people would nevertheless have pronounced the same judgment against him as they did the first time, when they took him from prison and condemned him to death. And so we have seen princes that were esteemed wise, who have caused persons to be put to death and afterwards regretted it deeply; such as Alexander the Great with regard to Clitus and other friends, and Herod with his wife Mariamne. But what our historian says of the character of the multitude does not apply to a people regulated by laws, as the Romans were, but to an unbridled multitude, such as the Syracusans; who committed all the excesses to which infuriated and unbridled men abandon themselves, as did Alexander the Great and Herod in the above-mentioned cases.

Therefore, the character of the people is not to be blamed any more than that of princes, for both alike are liable to err when they are without any control. Besides the examples already given, I could adduce numerous others from amongst the Roman Emperors and other tyrants and princes, who have displayed as much inconstancy and recklessness as any populace ever did. Contrary to the general opinion, then, which maintains that the people, when they govern, are inconsistent, unstable, and ungrateful, I conclude and affirm that these defects are not more natural to the people than they are to princes. To charge the people and princes equally with them may be the truth, but to except princes from them would be a great mistake. For a people that governs and is well regulated by laws will be stable, prudent, and grateful, as much so, and even more, according to my opinion, than a prince, although he be esteemed wise; and, on the other hand, a prince, freed from the restraints of the law, will be more ungrateful, inconstant, and imprudent than a people similarly situated. The difference in their conduct is not due to any difference in their nature (for that is the same, and if there be any difference for good, it is on the side of the people); but to the greater or less respect they have for the laws under which they respectively live. And whoever studies the Roman people will see that for four hundred years they have been haters of royalty, and lovers of the glory and common good of their country; and he will find any number of examples that will prove both the one and the other. And should any one allege the ingratitude which the Roman people displayed towards Scipio, I shall reply the same as I have said in another place on this subject, where I have demonstrated that the people are less ungrateful than princes. But as regards prudence and stability, I say that the people are more prudent and stable, and have better judgment than a prince; and it is not without good reason that it is said, "The voice of the people is the voice of God"; for we see popular opinion prognosticate events in such a wonderful manner that it would almost seem as if the people had some occult virtue, which enables them to foresee the good and the evil. As to the people's capacity of judging of things, it is exceedingly rare that, when they hear two orators of equal talents advocate different measures, they do not decide in favor of the best of the two; which proves their ability to discern the truth of what they hear. And if occasionally they are misled in matters involving questions of courage or seeming utility (as has been said above), so is a prince also many times misled by his own passions, which are much greater than those of the people. We also see that in the election of their magistrates they make far better choices than princes; and no people will ever be persuaded to elect a man of infamous character and corrupt habits to any post of dignity, to which a prince is easily influenced in a thousand different ways. When we see a people take an aversion to anything, they persist in it for many centuries, which we never find to be the case with princes. Upon both these points the Roman people shall serve me as a proof, who in the many elections of Consuls and Tribunes had to regret only four times the choice they had made. The Roman people held the name of king in such detestation, as we have said, that no extent of services rendered by any of its citizens who attempted to usurp that title could save him from his merited punishment. We furthermore see the cities where the people are masters make the greatest progress in the least possible time, and much greater than such as have always been governed by princes; as was the case with Rome after the expulsion of the kings, and with Athens after they rid themselves of Pisistratus; and this can be attributed to no other cause than that the governments of the people are better than those of princes.

It would be useless to object to my opinion

by referring to what our historian has said in the passages quoted above, and elsewhere; for if we compare the faults of a people with those of princes, as well as their respective good qualities, we shall find the people vastly superior in all that is good and glorious. And if princes show themselves superior in the making of laws, and in the forming of civil institutions and new statutes and ordinances, the people are superior in maintaining those institutions, laws, and ordinances, which certainly places them on a par with those who established them.

And finally to sum up this matter, I say that both governments of princes and of the people have lasted a long time, but both required to be regulated by laws. For a prince who knows no other control but his own will is like a madman, and a people that can do as it pleases will hardly be wise. If now we compare a prince who is controlled by laws, and a people that is untrammelled by them, we shall find more virtue in the people than in the prince; and if we compare them when both are freed from such control, we shall see that the people are guilty of fewer excesses than the prince, and that the errors of the people are of less importance, and therefore more easily remedied. For a licentious and mutinous people may easily be brought back to good conduct by the influence and persuasion of a good man, but an evil-minded prince is not amenable to such influences, and therefore there is no other remedy against him but cold steel. We may judge then from this of the relative defects of the one and the other; if words suffice to correct those of the people, whilst those of the prince can only be remedied by violence, no one can fail to see that where the greater remedy is required, there also the defects must be greater. The follies which a people commits at the moment of its greatest license are not what is most to be feared; it is not the immediate evil that may result from them that inspires apprehension, but the fact that such general confusion might afford the opportunity for a tyrant to seize the government. But with evil-disposed princes the contrary is the case; it is the immediate present that causes fear, and there is hope only in the future; for men will persuade themselves that the termination of his wicked life may give them a chance of liberty. Thus we see the difference between the one and the other to be, that the one touches the present and the other the future. The excesses of the people are directed against those whom they suspect of interfering with the public good; whilst those of princes are against apprehended interference with their individual interests. The general prejudice against the people results from the fact that everybody can freely and fearlessly speak ill of them in mass, even whilst they are at the height of their power; but a prince can only be spoken of with the greatest circumspection and apprehension.

6

WHAT IS A REPUBLIC?

JOHN ADAMS

The ideal of republican self-rule was revived in eighteenth-century America. Thomas Paine and Thomas Jefferson used republican arguments during the American Revolution to justify independence from Great Britain, and the founding fathers drafted a republican constitution in 1787. In 1776 John Adams (1735–1826) wrote the following selection, *Thoughts on Government,* in which he expounds and defends the principles of republican government.

Source: The Works of John Adams, *ed. C. F. Adams (Boston: Little, Brown, 1851), pp. 193–200.*

THOUGHTS ON GOVERNMENT

My Dear Sir,—If I was equal to the task of forming a plan for the government of a colony, I should be flattered with your request, and very happy to comply with it; because, as the divine science of politics is the science of social happiness, and the blessings of society depend entirely on the constitutions of government, which are generally institutions that last for many generations, there can be no employment more agreeable to a benevolent mind than a research after the best.

Pope flattered tyrants too much when he said,

For forms of government let fools contest,
That which is best administered is best.

Nothing can be more fallacious than this. But poets read history to collect flowers, not fruits; they attend to fanciful images, not the effects of social institutions. Nothing is more certain, from the history of nations and nature of man, than that some forms of government are better fitted for being well administered than others.

We ought to consider what is the end of government, before we determine which is the best form. Upon this point all speculative politicians will agree, that the happiness of society is the end of government, as all divines and moral philosophers will agree that the happiness of the individual is the end of man. From this principle it will follow, that the form of government which communicates ease, comfort, security, or, in one word, happiness, to the greatest number of persons, and in the greatest degree, is the best.

All sober inquirers after truth, ancient and modern, pagan and Christian, have declared that the happiness of man, as well as his dignity, consists in virtue. Confucius, Zoroaster, Socrates, Mahomet, not to mention authorities really sacred, have agreed in this.

If there is a form of government, then, whose principle and foundation is virtue, will not every sober man acknowledge it better calculated to promote the general happiness than any other form?

Fear is the foundation of most governments; but it is so sordid and brutal a passion, and renders men in whose breasts it predominates so stupid and miserable, that Americans will not be likely to approve of any political institution which is founded on it.

Honor is truly sacred, but holds a lower rank in the scale of moral excellence than virtue. Indeed, the former is but a part of the latter, and consequently has not equal pretensions to support a frame of government productive of human happiness.

The foundation of every government is some principle or passion in the minds of the people. The noblest principles and most generous affections in our nature, then, have the fairest chance to support the noblest and most generous models of government.

A man must be indifferent to the sneers of modern Englishmen, to mention in their company the names of Sidney, Harrington, Locke, Milton, Nedham, Neville, Burnet, and Hoadly. No small fortitude is necessary to confess that one has read them. The wretched condition of this country, however, for ten or fifteen years past, has frequently reminded me of their principles and reasonings. They will convince any candid mind, that there is no good government but what is republican. That the only valuable part of the British constitution is so; because the very definition of a republic is "an empire of laws, and not of men." That, as a republic is the best of governments, so that particular arrangement of the powers of society, or, in other words, that form of government which is best contrived to secure an impartial and exact execution of the laws, is the best of republics.

Of republics there is an inexhaustible variety, because the possible combinations of the powers of society are capable of innumerable variations.

As good government is an empire of laws, how shall your laws be made? In a large society, inhabiting an extensive country, it is impossible that the whole should assemble to make laws. The first necessary step, then, is to depute power from the many to a few of the most wise and good. But by what rules shall you choose your representatives? Agree upon the number and qualifications of persons who shall have the benefit of choosing, or annex this privilege to the inhabitants of a certain extent of ground.

The principal difficulty lies, and the greatest care should be employed, in constituting this representative assembly. It should be in miniature an exact portrait of the people at large. It should think, feel, reason, and act like them. That it may be the interest of this assembly to do strict justice at all times, it should be an equal representation, or, in other words, equal interests among the people should have equal interests in it. Great care should be taken to effect this, and to prevent unfair, partial, and corrupt elections. Such regulations, however, may be better made in times of greater tranquillity than the present; and they will spring up themselves naturally, when all the powers of government come to be in the hands of the people's friends. At present, it will be safest to proceed in all established modes, to which the people have been familiarized by habit.

A representation of the people in one assembly being obtained, a question arises, whether all the powers of government, legislative, executive, and judicial, shall be left in this body? I think a people cannot be long free, nor ever happy, whose government is in one assembly. My reasons for this opinion are as follow:—

1. A single assembly is liable to all the vices, follies, and frailties of an individual; subject to fits of humor, starts of passion, flights of enthusiasm, partialities, or prejudice, and consequently productive of hasty results and absurd judgments. And all these errors ought to be corrected and defects supplied by some controlling power.

2. A single assembly is apt to be avaricious, and in time will not scruple to exempt itself from burdens, which it will lay, without compunction, on its constituents.

3. A single assembly is apt to grow ambitious, and after a time will not hesitate to vote itself perpetual. This was one fault of the Long Parliament; but more remarkably of Holland, whose assembly first voted themselves from annual to septennial, then for life, and after a course of years, that all vacancies happening by death or otherwise, should be filled by themselves, without any application to constituents at all.

4. A representative assembly, although extremely well qualified, and absolutely necessary, as a branch of the legislative, is unfit to exercise the executive power, for want of two essential properties, secrecy and despatch.

5. A representative assembly is still less qualified for the judicial power, because it is too numerous, too slow, and too little skilled in the laws.

6. Because a single assembly, possessed of all the powers of government, would make arbitrary laws for their own interest, execute all laws arbitrarily for their own interest, and adjudge all controversies in their own favor.

But shall the whole power of legislation rest in one assembly? Most of the foregoing reasons apply equally to prove that the legislative power ought to be more complex; to which we may add, that if the legislative power is wholly in one assembly, and the executive in another, or in a single person, these two powers will oppose and encroach upon each other, until the contest shall end in war, and the whole power, legislative and executive, be usurped by the strongest.

The judicial power, in such case, could not mediate, or hold the balance between the two contending powers, because the legislative would undermine it. And this shows the necessity, too, of giving the executive power a negative upon the legislative, otherwise this will be continually encroaching upon that.

To avoid these dangers, let a distinct assembly be constituted, as a mediator between the two extreme branches of the legislature, that which represents the people, and that which is vested with the executive power.

Let the representative assembly then elect by ballot, from among themselves or their constituents, or both, a distinct assembly, which, for the sake of perspicuity, we will call a council. It may consist of any number you please, say twenty or thirty, and should have a free and independent exercise of its judgment, and consequently a negative voice in the legislature.

These two bodies, thus constituted, and made integral parts of the legislature, let them unite, and by joint ballot choose a governor, who, after being stripped of most of those badges of domination, called prerogatives, should have a free and independent exercise of his judgment, and be made also an integral part of the legislature. This, I know, is liable to objections; and, if you please, you may make him only president of the council, as in Connecticut. But as the governor is to be invested with the executive power, with consent of council, I think he ought to have a negative upon the legislative. If he is annually elective, as he ought to be, he will always have so much reverence and affection for the people, their representatives and counsellors, that, although you give him an independent exercise of his judgment, he will seldom use it in opposition to the two houses, except in cases the public utility of which would be conspicuous; and some such cases would happen.

In the present exigency of American affairs, when, by an act of Parliament, we are put out of the royal protection, and consequently discharged from our allegiance, and it has become necessary to assume government for our immediate security, the governor, lieutenant-governor, secretary, treasurer, commissary, attorney-general, should be chosen by joint ballot of both houses. And these and all other elections, especially of representatives and counsellors, should be annual, there not being in the whole circle of the sciences a maxim more infallible than this, "where annual elections end, there slavery begins."

These great men, in this respect, should be, once a year,

Like bubbles on the sea of matter borne,
They rise, they break, and to that sea
return.

This will teach them the great political virtues of humility, patience, and moderation, without which every man in power becomes a ravenous beast of prey.

This mode of constituting the great offices of state will answer very well for the present; but if by experiment it should be found inconvenient, the legislature may, at its leisure, devise other methods of creating them, by elections of the people at large, as in Connecticut, or it may enlarge the term for which they shall be chosen to seven years, or three years, or for life, or make any other alterations which the society shall find productive of its ease, its safety, its freedom, or, in one word, its happiness.

A rotation of all offices, as well as of representatives and counsellors, has many advocates, and is contended for with many plausible arguments. It would be attended, no doubt, with many advantages; and if the society has a sufficient number of suitable characters to supply the great number of vacancies which would be made by such a rotation, I can see no objection to it. These persons may be allowed to serve for three years, and then be excluded three years, or for any longer or shorter term.

Any seven or nine of the legislative council may be made a quorum, for doing business as a privy council, to advise the governor in the exercise of the executive branch of power, and in all acts of state.

The governor should have the command of the militia and of all your armies. The power of pardons should be with the governor and council.

Judges, justices, and all other officers, civil and military, should be nominated and appointed by the governor, with the advice and consent of council, unless you choose to have a government more popular; if you do, all officers, civil and military, may be chosen by joint ballot of both houses; or, in order to preserve the independence and importance of each house, by ballot of one house, concurred in by the other. Sheriffs should be chosen by the freeholders of counties; so should registers of deeds and clerks of counties.

All officers should have commissions, under the hand of the governor and seal of the colony.

The dignity and stability of government in all its branches, the morals of the people, and every blessing of society depend so much upon an upright and skilful administration of justice, that the judicial power ought to be distinct from both the legislative and executive, and independent upon both, that so it may be a check upon both, as both should be checks upon that. The judges therefore, should be always men of learning and experience in the laws, of exemplary morals, great patience, calmness, coolness and attention. Their minds should not be distracted with jarring interests; they should not be dependent upon any man, or body of men. To these ends, they should hold estate for life in their offices; or, in other words, their commission should be during good behavior, and their salaries ascertained and established by law. For misbehavior, the grand inquest of the colony, the house of representatives, should impeach them before the governor and council, where they should have time and opportunity to make their defence; but, if convicted, shall be removed from their offices, and subjected to such other punishment as shall be thought proper.

A militia law, requiring all men, or with very few exceptions besides cases of conscience, to be provided with arms and ammunition, to be trained at certain seasons; and requiring counties, towns, or other small districts, to be provided with public stocks of ammunition and intrenching utensils, and with some settled plans for transporting provisions after the militia, when marched to defend their country against sudden invasions; and requiring certain districts to be provided with field-pieces, companies of matrosses, and perhaps some regiments of light-horse, is always a wise institution, and, in the present circumstances of our country, indispensable.

Laws for the liberal education of youth, especially of the lower class of people, are so extremely wise and useful, that, to a humane and generous mind, no expense for this purpose would be thought extravagant.

The very mention of sumptuary laws will excite a smile. Whether our countrymen have wisdom and virtue enough to submit to them, I know not; but the happiness of the people might be greatly promoted by them, and a revenue saved sufficient to carry on this war forever. Frugality is a great revenue, besides curing us of vanities, levities, and fopperies, which are real antidotes to all great, manly, and warlike virtues.

But must not all commissions run in the name of a king? No. Why may they not as well run thus, "The colony of ____ to A. B. greeting," and be tested by the governor?

Why may not writs, instead of running in the name of the king, run thus, "The colony of ____ to the sheriff," etc., and be tested by the chief justice?

Why may not indictments conclude, "against the peace of the colony of ____ and the dignity of the same?"

A constitution founded on these principles introduces knowledge among the people, and inspires them with a conscious dignity becoming freemen; a general emulation takes place, which causes good humor, sociability, good manners, and good morals to be general. That elevation of sentiment inspired by such a government, makes the common people brave and enterprising. That ambition which is inspired by it makes them sober, industrious, and frugal. You will find among them some elegance, perhaps, but more solidity; a little pleasure, but a great deal of business; some politeness, but more civility. If you compare such a country with the regions of domination, whether monarchical or aristocratical, you will fancy yourself in Arcadia or Elysium.

If the colonies should assume governments separately, they should be left entirely to their own choice of the forms; and if a continental constitution should be formed, it should be a congress, containing a fair and adequate representation of the colonies, and its authority should sacredly be confined to these cases, namely, war, trade, disputes between colony and colony, the post-office, and the unappropriated lands of the crown, as they used to be called.

These colonies, under such forms of government, and in such a union, would be unconquerable by all the monarchies of Europe.

You and I, my dear friend, have been sent into life at a time when the greatest lawgivers of antiquity would have wished to live. How few of the human race have ever enjoyed an opportunity of making an election of government, more than of air, soil, or climate, for themselves or their children! When, before the present epoch, had three millions of people full power and a fair opportunity to form and establish the wisest and happiest government that human wisdom can contrive? I hope you will avail yourself and your country of that extensive learning and indefatigable industry which you possess, to assist her in the formation of the happiest governments and the best character of a great people. For myself, I must beg you to keep my name out of sight; for this feeble attempt, if it should be known to be mine, would oblige me to apply to myself those lines of the immortal John Milton, in one of his sonnets:—

I did but prompt the age to quit their clogs
By the known rules of ancient liberty,
When straight a barbarous noise environs me
Of owls and cuckoos, asses, apes, and dogs.

7

BILL OF RIGHTS OF THE UNITED STATES

One of the central tensions within the democratic tradition concerns the conflict between majority rule and minority rights. How can the one be reconciled with the other? The men who drafted the U.S. Constitution thought that the separation of governmental powers and the system of checks and balances incorporated into the Constitution would protect the rights and interests of individuals from the power of the majority, but many others believed that a list of specific limits on government authority was needed to guarantee individual rights. When the first Congress met, it moved to add the following ten amendments to the Constitution. These amendments, known as the Bill of Rights, took effect November 3, 1791.

Articles in addition to, and Amendment of the Constitution of the United States of America, proposed by Congress, and ratified by the Legislatures of the several States, pursuant to the fifth Article of the original Constitution.

ART. I

Congress shall make no law respecting an establishment of religion, or prohibiting the free exercise thereof; or abridging the freedom of speech, or of the press; or the right of the people peaceably to assemble, and to petition the government for a redress of grievances.

ART. II

A well regulated Militia, being necessary to the security of a free State, the right of the people to keep and bear Arms, shall not be infringed.

ART. III

No Soldier shall, in time of peace be quartered in any house, without the consent of the Owner, nor in time of war, but in a manner to be prescribed by law.

ART. IV

The right of the people to be secure in their persons, houses, papers, and effects, against unreasonable searches and seizures, shall not be violated, and no Warrants shall issue, but upon probable cause, supported by Oath or affirmation, and particularly describing the place to be searched, and the persons or things to be seized.

ART. V

No person shall be held to answer for a capital, or otherwise infamous crime, unless on a presentment or indictment of a Grand Jury, except in cases arising in the land or naval forces, or in the Militia, when in actual service in time of War or public danger; nor shall any person be subject for the same offence to be twice put in jeopardy of life or limb; nor shall be compelled in any criminal case to be a witness against himself, nor be deprived of life, liberty, or property, without due process of law; nor shall private property be taken for public use, without just compensation.

ART. VI

In all criminal prosecutions, the accused shall enjoy the right to a speedy and public trial, by an impartial jury of the State and district wherein the crime shall have been committed, which district shall have been previously ascertained by law, and to be informed of the nature and cause of the accusation; to be confronted with the witnesses against him; to have compulsory process for obtaining witnesses in his favor, and to have the Assistance of Counsel for his defence.

ART. VII

In Suits at common law, where the value in controversy shall exceed twenty dollars, the right of trial by jury shall be preserved, and no fact tried by a jury, shall be otherwise re-examined in any Court of the United States, than according to the rules of the common law.

ART. VIII

Excessive bail shall not be required, nor excessive fines imposed, nor cruel and unusual punishments inflicted.

ART. IX

The enumeration in the Constitution, of certain rights, shall not be construed to deny or disparage others retained by the people.

ART. X

The powers not delegated to the United States by the Constitution, nor prohibited by it to the States, are reserved to the States respectively, or to the people.

8

DEMOCRACY AND EQUALITY

ALEXIS DE TOCQUEVILLE

One of the key features of democracy is its emphasis on equality. Among the first to trace the implications of this theme was the French writer and statesman Alexis de Tocqueville (1805–1859). After visiting the United States in 1831–1832, de Tocqueville wrote *Democracy in America,* one of the first—and, some say, still the greatest—explorations of the American democratic experience. When de Tocqueville analyzed American democracy, moreover, he did so with an eye to the implications of democracy for Europe as well.

Source: Alexis de Tocqueville, Democracy in America, *vol. I, translated by Henry Reeve (New York: Henry G. Langley, 1845), pp. 1–13.*

INTRODUCTION

Among the novel objects that attracted my attention during my stay in the United States, nothing struck me more forcibly than the general equality of conditions. I readily discovered the prodigious influence which this primary fact exercises on the whole course of society, by giving a certain direction to public opinion, and a certain tenor to the laws; by imparting new maxims to the governing powers, and peculiar habits to the governed.

I speedily perceived that the influence of this fact extends far beyond the political character and the laws of the country, and that it has no less empire over civil society than over the government; it creates opinions, engenders sentiments, suggests the ordinary practices of life, and modifies whatever it does not produce.

The more I advanced in the study of American society, the more I perceived that the equality of conditions is the fundamental fact from which all others seem to be derived, and the central point at which all my observations constantly terminated.

I then turned my thoughts to our own hemisphere, where I imagined that I discerned something analogous to the spectacle which the New World presented to me. I observed that the equality of conditions is daily advancing toward those extreme limits which it seems to have reached in the United States; and that the democracy which governs the American communities, appears to be rapidly rising into power in Europe.

I hence conceived the idea of the book which is now before the reader.

It is evident to all alike that a great democratic revolution is going on among us; but there are two opinions as to its nature and consequences. To some it appears to be a novel accident, which as such may still be checked; to others it seems irresistible, because it is the most uniform, the most ancient, and the most permanent tendency which is to be found in history.

Let us recollect the situation of France seven hundred years ago, when the territory was divided among a small number of families, who were the owners of the soil and the rulers of the inhabitants; the right of governing descended with the family inheritance from generation to generation; force was the only means by which man could act on man; and landed property was the sole source of power.

Soon, however, the political power of the clergy was founded, and began to exert itself; the clergy opened its ranks to all classes, to the poor and the rich, the villain and the lord; equality penetrated into the government through the church, and the being who, as a serf, must have vegetated in perpetual bondage, took his place as a priest in the midst of nobles, and not unfrequently above the heads of kings.

The different relations of men became more complicated and more numerous, as society gradually became more stable and more civilized. Thence the want of civil laws was felt; and the order of legal functionaries soon rose from the obscurity of the tribunals and their dusty chambers, to appear at the court of the monarch, by the side of the feudal barons in their ermine and their mail.

While the kings were ruining themselves by their great enterprises, and the nobles exhausting their resources by private wars, the lower orders were enriching themselves by commerce. The influence of money began to be perceptible in state affairs. The transactions of business opened a new road to power, and the financier rose to a station of political influence in which he was at once flattered and despised.

Gradually the spread of mental acquirements, and the increasing taste for literature and art, opened chances of success to talent; science became the means of government, intelligence led to social power, and the man of letters took a part in the affairs of the state.

The value attached to the privileges of birth, decreased in the exact proportion in which new paths were struck out to advancement. In the eleventh century nobility was beyond all price; in the thirteenth it might be purchased; it was conferred for the first time in 1270; and equality was thus introduced into the government by the aristocracy itself.

In the course of these seven hundred years, it sometimes happened that, in order to resist the authority of the crown or to diminish the power of their rivals, the nobles granted a certain share of political rights to the people. Or, more frequently, the king permitted the lower orders to enjoy a degree of power, with the intention of repressing the aristocracy.

In France the kings have always been the most active and the most constant of levellers. When they were strong and ambitious, they spared no pains to raise the people to the level of the nobles; when they were temperate or weak, they allowed the people to rise above themselves. Some assisted the democracy by their talents, others by their vices. Louis XI and Louis XIV reduced every rank beneath the throne to the same subjection; Louis XV descended, himself and all his court, into the dust.

As soon as land was held on any other than a feudal tenure, and personal property began in its turn to confer influence and power, every improvement which was introduced in commerce or manufacture, was a fresh element of the equality of conditions. Henceforward every new discovery, every new want which it engendered, and every new desire which craved satisfaction, was a step toward the universal level. The taste for luxury, the love of war, the sway of fashion, the most superficial, as well as the deepest passions of the human heart, co-operated to enrich the poor and to empoverish the rich.

From the time when the exercise of the intellect became the source of strength and of wealth, it is impossible not to consider every addition to science, every fresh truth, and every new idea, as a germ of power placed within the reach of the people. Poetry, eloquence, and memory, the grace of wit, the glow of imagination, the depth of thought, and all the gifts which are bestowed by Providence with an equal hand, turned to the advantage of the democracy; and even when they were in the possession of its adversaries, they still served its cause by throwing into relief the natural greatness of man; its conquests spread, therefore, with those of civilization and knowledge; and literature became an arsenal, where the poorest and weakest could always find weapons to their hand.

In perusing the pages of our history, we shall scarcely meet with a single great event, in the lapse of seven hundred years, which has not turned to the advantage of equality.

The crusades and the wars of the English decimated the nobles, and divided their possessions; the erection of communes introduced an element of democratic liberty into the bosom of feudal monarchy; the invention of firearms equalized the villain and the noble on the field of battle; printing opened the same resources to the minds of all classes; the post was organized so as to bring the same information to the door of the poor man's cottage and to the gate of the palace; and protestantism proclaimed that all men are alike able to find the road to heaven. The discovery of America offered a thousand new paths to fortune, and placed riches and power within the reach of the adventurous and the obscure.

If we examine what has happened in France at intervals of fifty years, beginning with the eleventh century, we shall invariably perceive that a twofold revolution has taken place in the state of society. The noble has gone down on the social ladder, and the *roturier* has gone up; the one descends as the other rises. Every half-century brings them nearer to each other, and they will very shortly meet.

Nor is this phenomenon at all peculiar to France. Whithersoever we turn our eyes, we shall discover the same continual revolution throughout the whole of Christendom.

The various occurrences of national existence have everywhere turned to the advantage of democracy; all men have aided it by their exertions: those who have intentionally laboured in its cause, and those who have served it unwittingly—those who have fought for it, and those who have declared themselves its opponents—

have all been driven along in the same track, have all laboured to one end, some ignorantly, and some unwillingly; all have been blind instruments in the hands of God.

The gradual development of the equality of conditions is, therefore, a providential fact, and it possesses all the characteristics of a divine decree: it is universal, it is durable, it constantly eludes all human interference, and all events as well as all men contribute to its progress.

Would it, then, be wise to imagine that a social impulse which dates from so far back, can be checked by the efforts of a generation? Is it credible that the democracy which has annihilated the feudal system, and vanquished kings, will respect the citizen and the capitalist? Will it stop now that it has grown so strong and its adversaries so weak?

None can say which way we are going, for all terms of comparison are wanting: the equality of conditions is more complete in the Christian countries of the present day, than it has been at any time, or in any part of the world; so that the extent of what already exists prevents us from foreseeing what may be yet to come.

The whole book which is here offered to the public, has been written under the impression of a kind of religious dread, produced in the author's mind by the contemplation of so irresistible a revolution, which has advanced for centuries in spite of such amazing obstacles, and which is still proceeding in the midst of the ruins it has made.

It is not necessary that God himself should speak in order to disclose to us the unquestionable signs of his will; we can discern them in the habitual course of nature, and in the invariable tendency of events; I know, without a special revelation, that the planets move in the orbits traced by the Creator's finger.

If the men of our time were led by attentive observation and by sincere reflection, to acknowledge that the gradual and progressive development of social equality is at once the past and future of their history, this solitary truth would confer the sacred character of a divine decree upon the change. To attempt to check democracy would be in that case to resist the will of God; and the nations would then be constrained to make the best of the social lot awarded to them by Providence.

The Christian nations of our age seem to me to present a most alarming spectacle; the impulse which is bearing them along is so strong that it cannot be stopped, but it is not yet so rapid that it cannot be guided: their fate is in their hands; yet a little while and it may be so no longer.

The first duty which is at this time imposed upon those who direct our affairs is to educate the democracy; to warm its faith, if that be possible; to purify its morals; to direct its energies; to substitute a knowledge of business for its inexperience, and an acquaintance with its true interests for its blind propensities; to adapt its government to time and place, and to modify it in compliance with the occurrences and the actors of the age.

A new science of politics is indispensable to a new world.

This, however, is what we think of least; launched in the middle of a rapid stream, we obstinately fix our eyes on the ruins which may still be descried upon the shore we have left, while the current sweeps us along, and drives us backward toward the gulf.

In no country in Europe has the great social revolution which I have been describing, made such rapid progress as in France; but it has always been borne on by chance. The heads of the state have never had any forethought for its exigences, and its victories have been obtained without their consent or without their knowledge. The most powerful, the most intelligent, and the most moral classes of the nation have never attempted to connect themselves with it in order to guide it. The people have consequently been abandoned to its wild propensities, and it has grown up like those outcasts who receive their education in the public streets, and who are unacquainted with aught but the vices and wretchedness of society. The existence of a democracy was seemingly unknown, when, on a sudden, it took possession of the supreme power. Everything was then submitted to its caprices; it was worshipped as the idol of strength; until, when it was enfeebled by its own excesses, the legislator conceived the rash project of annihilating its power, instead of instructing it and correcting its vices; no attempt was made to fit it to govern, but all were bent on excluding it from the government.

The consequence of this has been that the democratic revolution has been effected only in the material parts of society, without that concomitant change in laws, ideas, customs, and manners, which was necessary to render such a revolution beneficial. We have gotten a democracy, but without the conditions which lessen its vices, and render its natural advantages more prominent; and although we already perceive the evils it brings, we are ignorant of the benefits it may confer.

While the power of the crown, supported by the aristocracy, peaceably governed the nations of Europe, society possessed, in the midst of its wretchedness, several different advantages which can now scarcely be appreciated or conceived.

The power of a parts of his subjects was an insurmountable barrier to the tyranny of the prince; and the monarch who felt the almost divine character which he enjoyed in the eyes of the multitude, derived a motive for the just use of his power from the respect which he inspired.

High as they were placed above the people, the nobles could not but take that calm and benevolent interest in its fate which the shepherd feels toward his flock; and without acknowledging the poor as their equals, they watched over the destiny of those whose welfare Providence had intrusted to their care.

The people, never having conceived the idea of a social condition different from its own, and entertaining no expectation of ever ranking with its chiefs, received benefits from them without discussing their rights. It grew attached to them when they were clement and just, but it submitted without resistance or servility to their exactions, as to the inevitable visitations of the arm of God. Custom, and the manners of the time, had moreover created a species of law in the midst of violence, and established certain limits to oppression.

As the noble never suspected that any one would attempt to deprive him of the privileges which he believed to be legitimate, and as the serf looked upon his own inferiority as a consequence of the immutable order of nature, it is easy to imagine that a mutual exchange of goodwill took place between two classes so differently gifted by fate. Inequality and wretchedness were then to be found in society; but the souls of neither rank of men were degraded.

Men are not corrupted by the exercise of power or debased by the habit of obedience; but by the exercise of power which they believe to be illegal, and by obedience to a rule which they consider to be usurped and oppressive.

On one side were wealth, strength, and leisure, accompanied by the refinement of luxury, the elegance of taste, the pleasures of wit, and the religion of art. On the other were labor, and a rude ignorance; but in the midst of this coarse and ignorant multitude, it was not uncommon to meet with energetic passions, generous sentiments, profound religious convictions, and independent virtues.

The body of a state thus organized, might boast of its stability, its power, and above all, of its glory.

But the scene is now changed, and gradually the two ranks mingle; the divisions which once severed mankind, are lowered; property is divided, power is held in common, the light of intelligence spreads, and the capacities of all classes are equally cultivated; the state becomes democratic, and the empire of democracy is slowly and peaceably introduced into the institutions and manners of the nation.

I can conceive a society in which all men would profess an equal attachment and respect for the laws of which they are the common authors; in which the authority of the state would be respected as necessary, though not as divine; and the loyalty of the subject to the chief magistrate would not be a passion, but a quiet and rational persuasion. Every individual being in the possession of rights which he is sure to retain, a kind of manly reliance and reciprocal courtesy would arise between all classes, alike removed from pride and meanness.

The people, well acquainted with its true interests, would allow, that in order to profit by the advantages of society, it is necessary to satisfy its demands. In this state of things, the voluntary association of the citizens might supply the individual exertions of the nobles, and the community would be alike protected from anarchy and from oppression.

I admit that in a democratic state thus constituted, society will not be stationary; but the impulses of the social body may be regulated and directed forward; if there be less splendour than in the halls of an aristocracy, the contrast of misery will be less frequent also; the pleasures of enjoyment may be less excessive, but those of comfort will be more general; the sciences may be less perfectly cultivated, but ignorance will be less common; the impetuosity of the feelings will be repressed, and the habits of the nation softened; there will be more vices and fewer crimes.

In the absence of enthusiasm and of an ardent faith, great sacrifices may be obtained from the members of a commonwealth by an appeal to their understandings and their experience: each individual will feel the same necessity for uniting with his fellow-citizens to protect his own weakness; and as he knows that if they are to assist he must co-operate, he will readily perceive that his personal interest is identified with the interest of the community.

The nation, taken as a whole, will be less brilliant, less glorious, and perhaps less strong; but the majority of the citizens will enjoy a greater degree of prosperity, and the people will remain quiet, not because it despairs of melioration, but because it is conscious of the advantages of its condition.

If all the consequences of this state of things were not good or useful, society would at least have appropriated all such as were useful and good; and having once and for ever renounced the social advantages of aristocracy, mankind would enter into possession of all the benefits which democracy can afford.

But here it may be asked what we have adopted in the place of those institutions, those ideas, and those customs of our forefathers which we have abandoned.

The spell of royalty is broken, but it has not been succeeded by the majesty of the laws; the people have learned to despise all authority. But fear now extorts a larger tribute of obedience than that which was formerly paid by reverence and by love.

I perceive that we have destroyed those independent beings which were able to cope with tyranny single-handed; but it is the government that has inherited the privileges of which families, corporations, and individuals, have been deprived; the weakness of the whole community has, therefore, succeeded to that influence of a small body of citizens, which, if it was sometimes oppressive, was often conservative.

The division of property has lessened the distance which separated the rich from the poor; but it would seem that the nearer they draw to each other, the greater is their mutual hatred, and the more vehement the envy and the dread with which they resist each other's claims to power; the notion of right is alike insensible to both classes, and force affords to both the only argument for the present, and the only guarantee for the future.

The poor man retains the prejudices of his forefathers without their faith, and their ignorance without their virtues; he has adopted the doctrine of self-interest as the rule of his actions, without understanding the science which controls it, and his egotism is no less blind than his devotedness was formerly.

If society is tranquil, it is not because it relies upon its strength and its well-being, but because it knows its weakness and its infirmities: a single effort may cost it its life; everybody feels the evil, but no one has courage or energy enough to seek the cure; the desires, the regret, the sorrows, and the joys of the time, produce nothing that is visible or permanent, like the passions of old men which terminate in impotence.

We have, then, abandoned whatever advantages the old state of things afforded, without receiving any compensation from our present condition; having destroyed an aristocracy, we seem inclined to survey its ruins with complacency, and to fix our abode in the midst of them.

The phenomena which the intellectual world presents are not less deplorable. The democracy of France, checked in its course or abandoned to its lawless passions, has overthrown whatever crossed its path, and has shaken all that it has not destroyed. Its control over society has not been gradually introduced, or peaceably established, but it has constantly advanced in the midst of disorder, and the agitation of a conflict. In the heat of the struggle each partisan is hurried beyond the limits of his opinions by the opinions and the excesses of his opponents, until he loses sight of the end of his exertions, and holds a language which disguises his real sentiments or secret instincts. Hence arises the strange confusion which we are beholding.

I cannot recall to my mind a passage in history more worthy of sorrow and of pity than the scenes which are happening under our eyes; it is as if the natural bond which unites the opinions of man to his tastes, and his actions to his principles, was now broken; the sympathy which has always been acknowledged between the feelings and the ideas of mankind, appears to be dissolved, and all the laws of moral analogy to be abolished.

Zealous Christians may be found among us, whose minds are nurtured in the love and knowledge of a future life, and who readily espouse the cause of human liberty, as the source of all moral greatness. Christianity, which has declared that all men are equal in the sight of God, will not refuse to acknowledge that all citizens are equal in the eye of the law. But, by a singular concourse of events, religion is entangled in those institutions which democracy assails, and it is not unfrequently brought to reject the equality it loves, and to curse that cause of liberty as a foe, which it might hallow by its alliance.

By the side of these religious men I discern others whose looks are turned to the earth more than to heaven; they are the partisans of liberty, not only as the source of the noblest virtues, but more especially as the root of all solid advantages; and they sincerely desire to extend its sway, and to impart its blessings to mankind. It is natural that they should hasten to invoke the assistance of religion, for they must know that liberty cannot be established without morality, nor morality without faith; but they have seen religion in the ranks of their adversaries, and they inquire no farther; some of them attack it openly, and the remainder are afraid to defend it.

In former ages slavery has been advocated by the venal and slavish-minded, while the independent and the warm-hearted were struggling without hope to save the liberties of mankind. But men of high and generous characters are now to be met with, whose opinions are at variance with their inclinations, and who praise that servility which they have themselves never known. Others, on the contrary, speak in the name of liberty as if they were able to feel its sanctity and its majesty, and loudly claim for humanity those rights which they have always disowned.

There are virtuous and peaceful individuals whose pure morality, quiet habits, affluence, and talents, fit them to be the leaders of the surrounding population; their love of their country is sincere, and they are prepared to make the greatest sacrifices to its welfare, but they confound the abuses of civilization with its benefits, and the idea of evil is inseparable in their minds from that of novelty.

Not far from this class is another party, whose object is to materalise mankind, to hit upon what is expedient without heeding what is just; to acquire knowledge without faith, and prosperity apart from virtue; assuming the title of the champions of modern civilization, and placing themselves in a station which they usurp with insolence, and from which they are driven by their own unworthiness.

Where are we then?

The religionists are the enemies of liberty, and the friends of liberty attack religion; the high-minded and the noble advocate subjection, and the meanest and most servile minds preach independence; honest and enlightened citizens are opposed to all progress, while men without patriotism and without principles, are the apostles of civilization and of intelligence.

Has such been the fate of the centuries which have preceded our own? and has man always inhabited a world, like the present, where nothing is linked together, where virtue is without genius, and genius without honour; where the love of order is confounded with a taste for oppression, and the holy rites of freedom with a contempt of law; where the light thrown by conscience on human actions is dim, and where nothing seems to be any longer forbidden or allowed, honorable or shameful, false or true?

I cannot, however, believe that the Creator made man to leave him in an endless struggle with the intellectual miseries which surround us: God destines a calmer and a more certain future to the communities of Europe; I am unacquainted with his designs, but I shall not cease to believe in them because I cannot fathom them, and I had rather mistrust my own capacity than his justice.

There is a country in the world where the great revolution which I am speaking of seems nearly to have reached its natural limits; it has been effected with ease and simplicity, say rather that this country has attained the consequences of the democratic revolution which we are undergoing, without having experienced the revolution itself.

The emigrants who fixed themselves on the shores of America in the beginning of the seventeenth century, severed the democratic principle from all the principles which repressed it in the old communities of Europe, and transplanted it unalloyed to the New World. It has there been allowed to spread in perfect freedom, and to put forth its consequences in the laws by influencing the manners of the country.

It appears to me beyond a doubt, that sooner or later we shall arrive, like the Americans, at an almost complete equality of conditions. But I do not conclude from this, that we shall ever be necessarily led to draw the same political consequences which the Americans have derived from a similar social organization. I am far from supposing that they have chosen the only form of government which a democracy may adopt; but the identity of the efficient cause of laws and manners in the two countries is sufficient to account for the immense interest we have in becoming acquainted with its effects in each of them.

It is not, then, merely to satisfy a legitimate curiosity that I have examined America; my wish has been to find instruction by which we may ourselves profit. Whoever should imagine that I have intended to write a panegyric would be strangely mistaken, and on reading this book, he will perceive that such was not my design: nor has it been my object to advocate any form of government in particular, for I am of opinion that absolute excellence is rarely to be found in any legislation; I have not even affected to discuss whether the social revolution, which I believe to be irresistible, is advantageous or prejudicial to mankind; I have acknowledged this revolution as a fact already accomplished or on the eve of its accomplishment; and I have selected the nation, from among those which have undergone it, in which its development has been the most peaceful and the most complete, in order to discern its natural consequences, and, if it be possible, to distinguish the means by which it may be rendered profitable. I confess that in America I saw more than America; I sought the image of democracy itself, with its inclinations, its character, its prejudices, and its passions, in order to learn what we have to fear or to hope from its progress.

9

DEMOCRATIC PARTICIPATION AND POLITICAL EDUCATION

JOHN STUART MILL

There are, as the English philosopher John Stuart Mill (1806–1873) noted, several reasons for preferring democracy to other forms of government. One is that it enables individuals to speak up for—and thus protect—their own interests. But, in addition to this "protectionist" argument, there is a second and perhaps more important argument to be made in favor of democracy: That it educates and improves citizens by providing them with "hands on" experience of self-rule.

Source: John Stuart Mill, Considerations on Representative Government, in Liberty, Utilitarianism, and Representative Government, *ed. A. D. Lindsay (New York: E. P. Dutton & Co., 1910), chapter 3, pp. 202–205, 207–208, 211–218.*

THAT THE IDEALLY BEST FORM OF GOVERNMENT IS REPRESENTATIVE GOVERNMENT

It has long (perhaps throughout the entire duration of British freedom) been a common saying, that if a good despot could be ensured, despotic monarchy would be the best form of government. I look upon this as a radical and most pernicious misconception of what good government is; which, until it can be got rid of, will fatally vitiate all our speculations on government.

The supposition is, that absolute power, in the hands of an eminent individual, would ensure a virtuous and intelligent performance of all the duties of government. Good laws would be established and enforced, bad laws would be reformed; the best men would be placed in all situations of trust; justice would be as well administered, the public burthens would be as light and as judiciously imposed, every branch of administration would be as purely and as intelligently conducted, as the circumstances of the country and its degree of intellectual and moral cultivation would admit. I am willing, for the sake of the argument, to concede all this: but I must point out how great the concession is; how much more is needed to produce even an approximation to these results, than is conveyed in the simple expression, a good despot. Their realization would in fact imply, not merely a good monarch, but an all-seeing one. He must be at all times informed correctly, in considerable detail, of the conduct and working of every branch of administration, in every district of the country, and must be able, in the twenty-four hours per day which are all that is granted to a king as to the humblest labourer, to give an effective share of attention and superintendence to all parts of this vast field; or he must at least be capable of discerning and choosing out, from among the mass of his subjects, not only a large abundance of honest and able men, fit to conduct every branch of public administration under supervision and control, but also the small number of men of eminent virtues and talents who can be trusted not only to do without that supervision, but to exercise it themselves over others. So extraordinary are the faculties and energies required for performing this task in any supportable manner, that the good despot whom we are supposing can hardly be imagined as consenting to undertake it, unless as a refuge from intolerable evils, and a transitional preparation for something beyond. But the argument can do without even this immense item in the account. Suppose the difficulty vanquished. What should we then have? One man of superhuman mental activity managing the entire affairs of a mentally passive people. Their passivity is implied in the very idea of absolute power. The nation as a whole, and every individual composing it, are without any potential voice in their own destiny. They exercise no will in respect to their collective interests. All is decided for them by a will not their own, which it is legally a crime for them to disobey. What sort of human beings can be formed under such a regimen? What development can either their thinking or their active faculties attain under it? On matters of pure theory they might perhaps be allowed to speculate, so long as their speculations either did not approach politics, or had not the remotest connexion with its practice. On practical affairs they could at most be only suffered to suggest; and even under the most moderate of despots, none but persons of already admitted or reputed superiority could hope that their suggestions would be known to, much less regarded by, those who had the management of affairs. A person must have a very unusual taste for intellectual exercise in and for itself, who will put himself to the trouble of thought when it is to have no outward effect, or qualify himself for functions which he has no chance of being allowed to exercise. The only sufficient incitement to mental exertion, in any but a few minds in a generation, is the prospect of some practical use to be made of its results. It does not follow that the nation will be wholly destitute of intellectual power. The common business of life, which must necessarily be performed by each individual or family for themselves, will call forth some amount of intelligence and practical ability, within a certain narrow range of ideas. There may be a select class of *savants*, who cultivate science with a view to its physical uses, or for the pleasure of the pursuit. There will be a bureaucracy, and persons in training for the bureaucracy, who will be taught at least some empirical maxims of government and public administration. There may be, and often has been, a systematic organization of the best mental power in the country in some special direction (commonly military) to promote the grandeur of the despot. But the public at large remain without information and without interest on all the greater matters of practice; or, if they have any knowledge of them, it is but a *dilettante* knowledge, like that which people have of the mechanical arts who have never handled a tool. Nor is it only in their intelligence that they suffer. Their moral capacities are equally stunted. Wherever the sphere of action of human beings is artificially circumscribed, their sentiments are narrowed and dwarfed in the same proportion. The food of feeling is action: even domestic affection lives upon voluntary good offices. Let a person have nothing to do for his country, and he will not care for it. It has been said of old, that in a despotism there is at most but one patriot, the despot himself; and the saying rests on a just appreciation of the effects of absolute subjection, even to a good and wise master. Religion remains: and here at least, it may be thought, is an agency that may be relied on for lifting men's eyes and minds above the dust at their feet. But religion, even supposing it to escape perversion for the purposes of despotism, ceases in these circumstances to be a social concern, and narrows into a personal affair between an individual and his Maker, in which the issue at stake is but his private salvation. Religion in this shape is quite consistent with the most selfish and contracted egoism, and identifies the votary as little in feeling with the rest of his kind as sensuality itself.

A good despotism means a government in which, so far as depends on the despot, there is no positive oppression by officers of state, but in which all the collective interests of the people are managed for them, all the thinking that has relation to collective interests done for them, and in which their minds are formed by, and consenting to, this abdication of their own energies. Leaving things to the Government, like leaving them to Providence, is synonymous with caring nothing about them, and accepting their results, when disagreeable, as visitations of Nature. With the exception, therefore, of a few studious men who take an intellectual interest in speculation for its own sake, the intelligence and sentiments of the whole people are given up to the material interests, and when these are provided for, to the amusement and ornamentation, of private life. But to say this is to say, if the whole testimony of history is worth anything, that the era of national decline has arrived: that is, if the nation had ever attained anything to decline from. If it has never risen above the condition of an Oriental people, in that condition it continues to stagnate. But if, like Greece or Rome, it had realized anything higher, through the energy, patriotism, and enlargement of mind, which as national qualities are the fruits solely of freedom, it relapses in a few generations into the Oriental state. And that state does not mean stupid tranquillity, with security against change for the worse; it often means being overrun, conquered, and reduced to domestic slavery, either by a stronger despot, or by the nearest barbarous people who retain along with their savage rudeness the energies of freedom. . . .

There is no difficulty in showing that the ideally best form of government is that in which the sovereignty, or supreme controlling power in the last resort, is vested in the entire aggregate of the community; every citizen not only having a voice in the exercise of that ultimate sovereignty, but being, at least occasionally, called on to take an actual part in the government, by the personal discharge of some public function, local or general.

To test this proposition, it has to be examined in reference to the two branches into which, as pointed out in the last chapter, the inquiry into the goodness of a government conveniently divides itself, namely, how far it promotes the good management of the affairs of society by means of the existing faculties, moral, intellectual, and active, of its various members, and what is its effect in improving or deteriorating those faculties.

The ideally best form of government, it is scarcely necessary to say, does not mean one which is practicable or eligible in all states of civilization, but the one which, in the circumstances in which it is practicable and eligible, is attended with the greatest amount of beneficial consequences, immediate and prospective. A completely popular government is the only polity which can make out any claim to this character. It is pre-eminent in both the departments between which the excellence of a political constitution is divided. It is both more favourable to present good government, and promotes a better and higher form of national character, than any other polity whatsoever.

Its superiority in reference to present well-being rests upon two principles, of as universal truth and applicability as any general propositions which can be laid down respecting human affairs. The first is, that the rights and interests of every or any person are only secure from being disregarded, when the person interested is himself able, and habitually disposed, to stand up for them. The second is, that the general prosperity attains a greater height, and is more widely diffused, in proportion to the amount and variety of the personal energies enlisted in promoting it.

Putting these two propositions into a shape more special to their present application; human beings are only secure from evil at the hands of others, in proportion as they have the power of being, and are, self-*protecting;* and they only achieve a high degree of success in their struggle with Nature, in proportion as they are self-*dependent*, relying on what they themselves can do, either separately or in concert, rather than on what others do for them. . . .

If we now pass to the influence of the form of government upon character, we shall find the superiority of popular government over every other to be, if possible, still more decided and indisputable.

This question really depends upon a still more fundamental one—viz., which of two common types of character, for the general good of humanity, it is most desirable should predominate—the active, or the passive type; that which struggles against evils, or that which endures them; that which bends to circumstances, or that which endeavours to make circumstances bend to itself.

The commonplaces of moralists, and the general sympathies of mankind, are in favour of the passive type. Energetic characters may be admired, but the acquiescent and submissive are those which most men personally prefer. The passiveness of our neighbours increases our sense of security, and plays into the hands of our wilfulness. Passive characters, if we do not happen to need their activity, seem an obstruction the less in our own path. A contented character is not a dangerous rival. Yet nothing is more certain, than that improvement in human affairs is wholly the work of the uncontented characters; and, moreover, that it is much easier for an active mind to acquire the virtues of patience, than for a passive one to assume those of energy.

Of the three varieties of mental excellence, intellectual, practical, and moral, there never could be any doubt in regard to the first two, which side had the advantage. All intellectual superiority is the fruit of active effort. Enterprise, the desire to keep moving, to be trying and accomplishing new things for our own benefit or that of others, is the parent even of speculative, and much more of practical, talent. The intellectual culture compatible with the other type is of that feeble and vague description, which belongs to a mind that stops at amusement, or at simple contemplation. The test of real and vigorous thinking, the thinking which ascertains truths instead of dreaming dreams, is successful application to practice. Where that purpose does not exist, to give definiteness, precision, and an intelligible meaning to thought, it generates nothing better than the mystical metaphysics of the Pythagoreans or the Vedas. With respect to practical improvement, the case is still more evident. The character which improves human life is that which struggles with natural powers and tendencies, not that which gives way to them. The self-benefiting qualities are all on the side of the active and energetic character: and the habits and conduct which promote the advantage of each individual member of the community, must be at least a part of those which conduce most in the end to the advancement of the community as a whole.

But on the point of moral preferability, there seems at first sight to be room for doubt. I am not referring to the religious feeling which has so generally existed in favour of the inactive character, as being more in harmony with the submission due to the divine will. Christianity as well as other religions has fostered this sentiment; but it is the prerogative of Christianity, as regards this and many other perversions, that it is able to throw them off. Abstractedly from religious considerations, a passive character, which yields to obstacles instead of striving to overcome them, may not indeed be very useful to others, no more than to itself, but it might be expected to be at least inoffensive. Contentment is always counted among the moral virtues. But it is a complete error to suppose that contentment is necessarily or naturally attendant on passivity of character; and unless it is, the moral consequences are mischievous. Where there exists a desire for advantages not possessed, the mind which does not potentially possess them by means of its own energies, is apt to look with hatred and malice on those who do. The person bestirring himself with hopeful prospects to improve his circumstances, is the one who feels goodwill towards others engaged in, or who have succeeded in, the same pursuit. And where the majority are so engaged, those who do not attain the object have had the tone given to their feelings by the general habit of the country, and ascribe their failure to want of effort or opportunity, or to their personal ill luck. But those who, while desiring what others possess, put no energy into striving for it, are either incessantly grumbling that fortune does not do for them what they do not attempt to do for themselves, or overflowing with envy and ill-will towards those who possess what they would like to have. . . .

There are, no doubt, in all countries, really contented characters, who not merely do not seek, but do not desire, what they do not already possess, and these naturally bear no ill-will towards such as have apparently a more favoured lot. But the great mass of seeming contentment is real discontent, combined with indolence or self-indulgence, which, while taking no legitimate means of raising itself, delights in bringing others down to its own level. And if we look narrowly even at the cases of innocent contentment, we perceive that they only win our admiration, when the indifference is solely to improvement in outward circumstances, and there is a striving for perpetual advancement in spiritual worth, or at least a disinterested zeal to benefit others. The contented man, or the contented family, who have no ambition to make any one else happier, to promote the good of their country or their neighbourhood, or to improve themselves in moral excellence, excite in us neither admiration nor approval. We rightly ascribe this sort of contentment to mere unmanliness and want of spirit. The content which we approve, is an ability to do cheerfully without what cannot be had, a just appreciation of the comparative value of different objects of desire, and a willing renunciation of the less when incompatible with the greater. These, however, are excellences more natural to the character, in proportion as it is actively engaged in the attempt to improve its own or some other lot. He who is continually measuring his energy against difficulties, learns what are the difficulties insuperable to him, and what are those which though he might overcome, the success is not worth the cost. He whose thoughts and activities are all needed for, and habitually employed in, practicable and useful enterprises, is the person of all others least likely to let his mind dwell with brooding discontent upon things either not worth attaining, or which are not so to him. Thus the active, self-helping character is not only intrinsically the best, but is the likeliest to acquire all that is really excellent or desirable in the opposite type. . . .

Now there can be no kind of doubt that the passive type of character is favoured by the government of one or a few, and the active self-helping type by that of the Many. Irresponsible rulers need the quiescence of the ruled, more than they need any activity but that which they can compel. Submissiveness to the prescriptions of men as necessities of nature, is the lesson inculcated by all governments upon those who are wholly without participation in them. The will of superiors, and the law as the will of superiors, must be passively yielded to. But no men are mere instruments or materials in the hands of their rulers, who have will or spirit or a spring of internal activity in the rest of their proceedings: and any manifestation of these qualities, instead of receiving encouragement from despots, has to get itself forgiven by them. Even when irresponsible rulers are not sufficiently conscious of danger from the mental activity of their subjects to be desirous of repressing it, the position itself is a repression. Endeavour is even more effectually restrained by the certainty of its impotence, than by any positive discouragement. Between subjection to the will of others, and the virtues of self-help and self-government, there is a natural incompatibility. This is more or less complete, according as the bondage is strained or relaxed. Rulers differ very much in the length to which they carry the control of the free agency of their subjects, or the supersession of it by managing their business for them. But the difference is in degree, not in principle; and the best despots often go the greatest lengths in chaining up the free agency of their subjects. A bad despot, when his own personal indulgences have been provided for, may sometimes be willing to let the people alone; but a good despot insists on doing them good, by making them do their own business in a better way than they themselves know of. The regulations which restricted to fixed processes all the leading branches of French manufacturers, were the work of the great Colbert.

Very different is the state of the human faculties where a human being feels himself under no other external restraint than the necessities of nature, or mandates of society which he has his share in imposing, and which it is open to him, if he thinks them wrong, publicly to dissent from, and exert himself actively to get altered. No doubt, under a government partially popular, this freedom may be exercised even by those who are not partakers in the full privileges of citizenship. But it is a great additional stimulus to any one's self-help and self-reliance when he starts from even ground, and has not to feel that his success depends on the impression he can make upon the sentiments and dispositions of a body of whom he is not one. It is a great discouragement to an individual, and a still greater one to a class, to be left out of the constitution; to be reduced to plead from outside the door to the arbiters of their destiny, not taken into consultation within. The maximum of the invigorating effect of freedom upon the character is only obtained, when the person acted on either is, or is looking forward to becoming, a citizen as fully privileged as any other. What is still more important than even this matter of feeling, is the practical discipline which the character obtains, from the occasional demand made upon the citizens to exercise, for a time and in their turn, some social function. It is not sufficiently considered how little there is in most men's ordinary life to give any largeness either to their conceptions or to their sentiments. Their work is a routine; not a labour of love, but of self-interest in the most elementary form, the satisfaction of daily wants; neither the thing done, nor the process of doing it, introduces the mind to thoughts or feelings extending beyond individuals; if instructive books are within their reach, there is no stimulus to read them; and in most cases the individual has no access to any person of cultivation much superior to his own. Giving him something to do for the public, supplies, in a measure, all these deficiencies. If circumstances allow the amount of public duty assigned him to be considerable, it makes him an educated man. Notwithstanding the defects of the social system and moral ideas of antiquity, the practice of the dicastery and the ecclesia raised the intellectual standard of an average Athenian citizen far beyond anything of which there is yet an example in any other mass of men, ancient or modern. The proofs of this are apparent in every page of our great historian of Greece; but we need scarcely look further than to the high quality of the addresses which their great orators deemed best calculated to act with effect on their understanding and will. A benefit of the same kind, though far less in degree, is produced on Englishmen of the lower middle class by their liability to be placed on juries and to serve parish offices; which, though it does not occur to so many, nor is so continuous, nor introduces them to so great a variety of elevated considerations, as to admit of comparison with the public education which every citizen of Athens obtained from her democratic institutions, must make them nevertheless very different beings, in range of ideas and development of faculties, from those who have done nothing in their lives but drive a quill, or sell goods over a counter. Still more salutary is the moral part of the instruction afforded by the participation of the private citizen, if even rarely, in public functions. He is called upon, while so engaged, to weigh interests not his own; to be guided, in case of conflicting claims, by another rule than his private partialities; to apply, at every turn, principles and maxims which have for their reason of existence the common good: and he usually finds associated with him in the same work minds more familiarized than his own with these ideas and operations, whose study it will be to supply reasons to his understanding, and stimulation to his feeling for the general interest. He is made to feel himself one of the public, and whatever is for their benefit to be for his benefit. Where this school of public spirit does not exist, scarcely any sense is entertained that private persons, in no eminent social situation, owe any duties to society, except to obey the laws and submit to the government. There is no unselfish sentiment of identification with the public. Every thought or feeling, either of interest or of duty, is absorbed in the individual and in the family. The man never thinks of any collective interest, of any objects to be pursued jointly with others, but only in competition with them, and in some measure at their expense. A neighbour, not being an ally or an associate, since he is never engaged in any common undertaking for joint benefit, is therefore only a rival. Thus even private morality suffers, while public is actually extinct. Were this the universal and only possible state of things, the utmost aspirations of the lawgiver or the moralist could only stretch to making the bulk of the community a flock of sheep innocently nibbling the grass side by side.

From these accumulated considerations it is evident, that the only government which can fully satisfy all the exigencies of the social state, is one in which the whole people participate; that any participation, even in the smallest public function, is useful; that the participation should everywhere be as great as the general degree of improvement of the community will allow; and that nothing less can be ultimately desirable, than the admission of all to a share in the sovereign power of the state. But since all cannot, in a community exceeding a single small town, participate personally in any but some very minor portions of the public business, it follows that the ideal type of a perfect government must be representative.

10

TOWN MEETINGS AND WORKERS' CONTROL

MICHAEL WALZER

To have a say in determining the direction of one's country or community is part of the idea of democracy. But how far should this principle extend? A self-styled "radical democrat," Michael Walzer (1935–) maintains that "What touches all should be decided by all." As he suggests in his fable of "J-town," this principle requires that much of what is considered "private" life in liberal societies ought to be subject to public control. Only socialism is consistent with democracy—or at least with *social democracy*.

Source: Michael Walzer, "Town Meetings and Workers' Control," Dissent *(Summer 1978), pp. 325–333. Reprinted by permission of Michael Walzer and* Dissent.

TOWN MEETINGS AND WORKERS' CONTROL: A STORY FOR SOCIALISTS

INTRODUCTION TO THE STORY

There are thirteen arguments for socialism; they have to do with distributive justice, equality, the need for planning, self-respect, fraternity, and so on. But the one that seems to me the easiest and best is a political argument, an extension of the defense of democracy. It has been put forward often over the last one hundred years, but it has never, in this country at least, commanded general acceptance. I suppose no doctrine commands general acceptance that is, as Hobbes wrote, "contrary to any man's right of dominion or to the interest of men that have dominion."[1] And yet there is some sense in which we are all democrats, so I shall start from there, assuming that we have good reasons, and see how far I can go.

The central commitment of socialist politics has often been put in a phrase that must be intuitively appealing to democrats: *the abolition of the power of man over man*. Neither democrats nor socialists begin with an assertion of popular sovereignty. Since they everywhere encounter established sovereigns, authorities, hierarchies, conventional claims to rule, they begin with denials and rejections. They are abolitionists. They aim at abolishing two kinds of authority relations, those in which men and women are directly, and those in which they are indirectly, subject to the arbitrary will of another. I will consider these two separately. Direct subjection suggests the immediacy of bondage; it describes the slave, the serf, the servant, all those who bow before some powerful person, defer to him, obey his every command. Direct subjection is pervasive in the old regime, and it is not missing in the new. One recognizes it in those forms of speech, those bodily postures and motions that connote weakness, inferiority, humility, a certain zeal for service, which we are disinclined to accept as spontaneous or voluntary.

Indirect subjection is not so easy to recognize, for it has to do not with relationships but with systems of relationships, and the systems are invisible. What is at issue here is the right of a single person, acting on his own, for reasons of his own, to make decisions seriously affecting the welfare of his fellowmen, without the agreement of those whom his decisions affect. Now we all make decisions all the time that seriously affect others: when I decide to accept a job, for example, my decision has an immediate impact on the life of the next candidate, who would have received an offer had I declined. But it would be odd to think of him as my subject, and I am certainly not required to seek his agreement before making up my own mind. In every society, however, there are positions of recognized power, offices within some organizational structure, from which decisions of a different sort are made. The best way to characterize these is to say that they are authoritative decisions, for that invites us to inquire as to the source of the authority. And what is crucial in systems of indirect subjection is that the subjects are not the source. Men and women ruled by an absolute monarch are directly subject in that they must obey his commands and indirectly subject in that they must live with the consequences of his political, economic, and military decisions. Clearly, democratic argument must challenge and does challenge both these forms of subjection.

The principle of the second challenge is nicely expressed in an old maxim, a rule of law, I believe, in medieval times, honored regularly in the breach: *what touches all should be decided by all.* It's not every decision affecting others that must be democratically made, but only those affecting everyone. That does not mean everyone in the world; I think we should take it to mean everyone associated in some common enterprise the existence or success of which requires that decisions be made. Thus the medieval maxim was invoked in disputes about authority relations in guilds, churches, towns, and states. No doubt, there are problems with this (and every other) restriction on the reach of the maxim, for decisions made within some particular association are certain to affect not only members, but nonmembers as well—and may affect them seriously indeed, as the example of state decisions and international politics suggests. But since this is a general difficulty for democratic theory, and not a special difficulty for socialists, I am going to put it aside (I'll come back to it briefly later on). My own argument requires only this much: that for any authoritative decision seriously affecting others, there is some subset of those affected who ought to authorize the decision or to make it or approve it themselves. The subset includes, but is not necessarily limited to, those people whose association makes the decision possible or necessary—as the association of Frenchmen, for example, makes possible the French king's decision to go to war or requires him to oppose an armed invasion.

The argument also assumes that the king cannot decide to break up the association (or to cooperate with the invaders) rather than allow its members to join him in decision making. It is not the case that the authorities can seek support for their decisions just anywhere. Thus Bertolt Brecht's satiric poem, written in Berlin, 1953:[2]

After the rising of the 17th of June
The Secretary of the Writers' Union
Had leaflets distributed in the Stalinallee
In which you could read that the People
Had lost the Government's confidence
Which it could only regain
By redoubled efforts. Would it in that
case
Not be simpler if the Government
Dissolved the People
And elected another?

The satire depends on the commonly accepted principle that the dissolution of the government is a popular right. But it should also be said that the dissolution of the *people* is a popular right. The cohesion that makes it possible to speak of "touching all" and being "decided by all" can only be dissolved by all. And this is true however the association was made and whatever the role of the king or the authorities in making it. The argument is not dependent upon an original contract; it works whatever stories about the origin and foundation of the common enterprise are accepted by the participants, including stories about great men, godlike acts. vanguard revolutions, and so on.

Now, it is the socialist claim that neither direct nor indirect subjection, neither the arbitrary power of persons nor that of positions has been abolished through the establishment of a democratic state. For the state is not our only common enterprise; nor do the laws of the state constitute the only disciplinary system to which we are subject. The capitalist economy proliferates what are plausibly called private governments. Within capitalist organizations a process of decision making can be marked out, dominated by officials, which has the crucial characteristics of a political regime. The process has outcomes that seriously affect thousands and hundreds of thousands of people, including men and women whose cooperative activity underlies the organization and who are in some sense its members. These outcomes take the form of decisions and rules that can be opposed or ignored by the members only at the risk of penalties. Here are participants who are subjects, officials who act with authority. What is the source of that authority? It clearly does not derive from the participants, else it would not be called private. It derives instead, or it is said to derive, from the ownership of the organization by particular persons. Their claim to govern, to make decisions affecting others, rests on the legal and, what is more important, the moral implications of private property. Socialists argue that this is not a tenable claim, and it is at this point that many democrats part company with them, insisting that economic enterprises are unlike political associations precisely because the former are subject to ownership and the latter are not.

It should be said, however, that in their time democrats also challenged the implications of ownership—as these were understood within the feudal economy. Feudalism, like capitalism, rested on a certain view of property rights, specifically on the view that the ownership of land entitled the owner to exercise direct disciplinary (judicial and police) powers over the men and women who lived on the land and also to make decisions (to go to war with some neighboring landowner, for example) seriously affecting their lives. In the course of many years of political conflict and revolutionary activity, the formal structure of feudal rights was abolished and the disciplinary powers of the feudal lords were socialized. Taxation, law enforcement, conscription: all these ceased to be property rights. In Marxist terms, the state was emancipated from civil society, that is, from the property system. The implications of ownership were redefined so as to exclude certain sorts of decision making that, it was thought, could only be authorized by the political community as a whole. This redefinition establishes the central division along which social life is organized today. On the one side are activities called political; on the other, activities called economic. On both sides, men and women make authoritative decisions affecting others, but the maxim *what touches all should be decided by all* applies only in the realm of politics. Hence socialism has commonly been described as the extension of democratic decision making from the political to the economic realm.

But this description may be misleading, for the two realms do not seem to me at all distinct. They are subject, of course, to conventional definition, but there is no need for us to accept the conventions of 1789. Indeed, the political argument for socialism is strongest insofar as it suggests the radical similarity of decision making in the two realms. What justifies the contemporary version of property rights, we are commonly told, is the entrepreneurial zeal, the risk taking, the inventiveness, the capital investment, through which economic enterprises are founded, sustained, and expanded. Whereas feudal property was founded on armed force and sustained and expanded through the power of the sword (even though it was also traded and inherited), capitalist property rests upon forms of activity that are intrinsically noncoercive. The factory is distinguished from the manor, the disciplinary system of the first is upheld and that of the second condemned, because men and women come willingly to work in the factory, drawn by the wages, working conditions, prospects for the future that the owner offers, which are made possible by his energy and enterprise, while the workers on the manor are serfs, prisoners of their noble lords. All this may well be true; in any case, I will not question it now; it helps us understand why feudalism was not an ideal political or economic arrangement. But it does not draw the line between democratic politics and the capitalist economy, nor does it justify the present authority of owners. For political communities are also created by entrepreneurial energy and enterprise, and it's not implausible to say of cities and towns, if not always of states, that they recruit and hold their citizens by offering them an attractive place to live. Yet ownership is not an acceptable source of governmental authority in cities and towns. If we consider deeply why this is so, we will have to conclude, I think, that it should not be acceptable in companies or factories either. What is necessary is to imagine a man who claims to own a town, to tell a story—it must be a success story—about the life of a political entrepreneur.

THE STORY

Long ago, when the frontier was still somewhere east of the Great Plains, a young man named J.J. set out to make his fortune. He was bold, adventurous, energetic, and very smart, and he left Boston and New York, even Pittsburgh and Cincinnati behind him. After hardships and excitements not worth mentioning, he staked out a claim to a large and rich piece of land at the bend of a river, one of the smaller western tributaries of the Mississippi. But J.J.

was not a farmer. He hated domestic animals, and while he could plow as straight a furrow as anyone in the West, the accomplishment gave him no joy. Soon, he acquired land on the other side of the river and built a ferry, which he ran himself. It was a well-built and well-run ferry. J.J. was a gregarious man, and he entertained his passengers as he took them across; he was warm and funny and full of stories. The enterprise was a success, and after a year or so a few men settled nearby, a storekeeper, a blacksmith, even a preacher, renting the land from J.J. He provided a small lot for a small church and happily watched the settlement grow. When word came of a threatened Indian attack, he organized its defense, bringing in (and paying for) vital supplies from the East. There was an attack of sorts, though only by a small raiding party, and J.J. was in the forefront of the defenders—twelve or fifteen people now, mostly heads of families, who recognized and accepted him as their leader. He would have been the newest of new men in Boston or New York, but in this little settlement, he was the oldest, the richest, the most well-established of the inhabitants.

About this time, J.J. went East to borrow some money. He now had visions of a city, for the river bend was a good location, the ferry was busy, there were new farms on both sides of the river, and the farmers needed supplies, schools, sermons, and company. He got the money from a young banker who was bold, adventurous, energetic, and very smart. Back home, he bought more land, laid out a square, set aside lots for a school and a town hall. Though no one had yet died in the settlement, he provided a cemetery too, sure that people would die and not unhappy about that. Dead bodies lend dignity to the place where they lie; a town with a cemetery has staying power. He incorporated the town in accordance with territorial law and gave it the name he had always had in mind: J-town. The law did not specify any particular form of government, but J.J. again had something in mind. When the town hall was built (at his own expense), he moved in. The settlers were not surprised; nor was there any opposition. J.J. was still a gregarious man; he knew them all, talked to them all, always consulted with them about matters of common interest. As at the time of the Indian raid, his leadership was recognized and accepted. Anyway, they all paid him rent, and it did not seem strange to pay him taxes too—a per-capita levy for the salary of the schoolteacher, the maintenance of public buildings, and other minor expenses. J.J. himself took no salary. His ferry was doing well, and he had begun to transport goods up and down the river. His enterprises expanded as the town grew and, to a considerable extent, the town grew because his enterprises expanded.

Years went by. J.J. prospered, paid off the loan, delighting himself and the Eastern banker. J-town prospered; new settlers arrived every year; there was money in the treasury. The town lines were redrawn. Now there were tax-payers who did not pay rent to J.J., though he still owned most of the town and continued to serve as mayor. When it became necessary to appoint other town officers, he talked to his friends and neighbors and always picked the right person. He had a knack for making decisions, not only decisions that paid off, but ones that pleased people. And if anyone wasn't pleased, he could always move on; J.J. would pat him on the back and talk about the wide Western spaces. He treated criminals the same way. He didn't like locking people up, and he thought it enough of a punishment to have to leave J-town.

J.J. was a natural leader, a man of substance, a man of power. He proved himself again when the flood came, risking his boats on the rapidly rising river in order to evacuate the settlers and their movable possessions, contributing freely to the relief fund. Later on, he went East for a second time to raise money, signing the papers in his own name and bringing home the capital that made it possible to rebuild J-town. The townspeople could hardly imagine another mayor. Nor could J.J.

Life was placid in J-town; time passed quickly. Revivalist preachers came and went; a labor organizer arrived one day and departed the next; the Republican party sent someone to talk to J.J., and the visitor did not find it necessary to talk to anyone else. The dissidence of dissent was absent. Or so it was until J.J., aging now, appointed his son chief of police. Perhaps there had been murmurings before that, but they were scarcely audible. Many of the new settlers did not remember J.J.'s earlier days, did not really believe the stories of his heroic exploits, or—what was worse—did not think the stories mattered. But the town was well run, and they were content not to worry about it; they didn't think of politics as something that was missing from their lives; to all appearances they didn't think about it at all.

Still, the appointment of his son was a political mistake—J.J.'s first. His son wasn't particularly bold, adventurous, energetic, or smart, and everyone in town knew it. A few of the newer inhabitants called a meeting at the Odd Fellow's Lodge (the town hall had no assembly room). Only a small number of people came, but they shouted a lot, worked one another up, formed a citizen's committee, and called another meeting. This time more people came; the speeches were exciting, and the participants went home feeling differently about J-town than they had ever felt before. There was a third meeting, and on the following afternoon a delegation of citizens called on J.J.

No one took notes that afternoon, but what was said was repeated all over town. The citizens told the mayor that he could appoint his son to any position he liked in J's River Haulage, Inc., but the town, they said, was not one of his businesses. Town government was the *public* business, and henceforth the public would have to be brought into it in some regularized manner. What touches all should be decided by all, they said. They demanded that elections be held, and they intimated that they had a candidate for mayor in mind whom they preferred to J.J.

J.J.'s reply was a passionate defense of entrepreneurial rights. What do you mean? he said. *This is my town.* I found this place; I built my ferry here, and other people came because of the ferry. I risked my life against the Indians. I risked my capital to buy this land and raise on it the buildings people needed. Your children are studying, right now, in schools I made possible; your dead are buried on land I gave. When the flood came, I did it all again, giving money, raising money, organizing reconstruction. This town wouldn't exist without me and, what's more, I still own most of it. All of you came here with your eyes open; you knew how this town was run; you knew who made the decisions around here. Don't talk to me about elections. . . .

J.J. had never lacked for words. And everything he said was true. He did not have to make things up, for he was indeed a great man and had done great things. If it were possible to own a town, he certainly deserved to own this one. The citizens insisted, however, that it wasn't possible. J.J. was the founder, not the owner of J-town, they said, and they would happily put up a statue of him in Central Park. (On land I gave you, muttered J.J.) He was entitled to honor and glory, but not to obedience. He was entitled to rent, but they would tax themselves. They did not mean to sound ungrateful, they said; they weren't ungrateful, but political foundation and public service did not give a man the right to tyrannize over others.

How can I be a tyrant, shouted J.J., when it's my own town?

The next weeks were exciting, but the events are not worth mentioning here. The citizens' insurrection was successful. J.J. fell. His son never became chief of police. J.J. withdrew from public life, did not vote in the first town elections, never attended town meetings, turned away from his friends and neighbors. When he died, not long after, the town council commissioned a statue, as the insurgent citizens had promised. The new mayor made a fine speech when the statue was unveiled. J.J., he said, was a heroic figure, a man of the pioneering past, a founding father. The town owed him a profound debt, a spiritual debt, of which the statue could only be a lasting reminder. It was true, the mayor said, that J.J. had occasionally confused business and politics, but, after all, that was a confusion not uncommon in American life.

J.J.'s son had occasion to reflect upon that last remark when the town council, only a few years later, tried to take over the river haulage company. They would have paid him handsomely, had the state supreme court allowed the take-over, but money, they insisted, was all he was entitled to in return for his father's investment. Decisions about whether or not to expand the ferry service, buy new boats, and so on—those could not be made by one man, they said, considering only his private profit. The whole town was a transportation center; all its citizens depended on the haulage company; most of them worked for it. And what touches all, they said, should be decided by all. . . .

INTERPRETATION OF THE STORY

I had originally planned to write about a company town, drawing upon actual historical accounts. The story would then have described how the owners of an economic enterprise created a political community, so to speak, on the side, as a place for their employees to live. Upon reflection, it seemed better to imagine a case where the major entrepreneurial activity was focused on the town itself, so that J.J. would stand in the great tradition of the political founder. He represents the liberal form of that tradition, which is to say, he has no deep convictions about the shape of the town or the moral character of its citizens. He merely wants them to live peaceably and to prosper. But he is clearly comparable, despite that, to the figures celebrated by Machiavelli and Rousseau—Lycurgus, Solon, Romulus—who made or remade the political community. Now, in that tradition, founding or reforming the state generates no right of ownership and none of the subsidiary rights that ownership brings with it in feudal manors or in capitalist factories or companies. Most important, it does not give rise to any sort of disciplinary authority over those who join the new community. That authority belongs to the members, even if they were passive or entirely absent during the period of foundation.

Why are economic associations any different? *Not because of the entrepreneurial vision, energy, inventiveness, and so on, that go into the making of the company:* the making of J-town required exactly the same qualities. There are certainly objects in the world that a man can acquire through enterprise and invention. Making them or mixing his labor with them, as John Locke argued, produces at least a presumption of ownership.[3] But it's not the case that *anything* can be acquired that way, and if towns cannot be, there is no reason to think that companies can. These two are much nearer to one another than either is to the land I cultivate, the wood I cut, the chair I build, the book I write—the examples that Locke had in mind. What brings them close together is that both of them involve other people, shared interests, cooperative activity.

Not because of the investment of capital: J.J. invested his own money in J-town without becoming an owner. Nor do men and women who buy municipal bonds come to own the municipality. They acquire no political rights at all. Unless they are already citizens, they cannot even participate in deciding how to spend their own money. They are entitled to a specified rate of interest, and that is their only entitlement. The members of the political community are conceived to have rights of a different sort, simply by virtue of their membership, whether they have invested money in the community or not. There seems no reason not to make the same distinction in economic associations, marking off investors from participants, a just return from authoritative decision making.

Not because men and women join a company voluntarily, with full knowledge of the established structure of authority: the settlers in J-town arrived freely, and the same knowledge was available to them, as J.J. told the citizens' delegation. If I settle in a state founded and ruled by a powerful despot, my knowledge of his despotism does not make the act of settlement into an act of consent. Nor is my prompt departure the only way I can express my opposition to despotic government. That may be the case with a man who joins a monastic order requiring strict and unquestioning obedience. Here the new member seems to be choosing a way of life, and his choice entails a particular disciplinary rule. We would not be paying him proper respect if we denied the efficacy of his choice; its purpose and its moral effect are precisely to authorize his superior; he can't withdraw that authority without himself withdrawing from the common life it makes possible.

But that is not true of a man who joins a company or who comes to work in a factory. In these associations, the common life does not require unquestioning obedience, and we respect the new member only if we assume that he does not seek subjection. Of course, he encounters supervisors, foremen, company police, as he knew he would, and it may be that the success of the economic enterprise requires his obedience, just as the success of the political association requires that citizens obey public officials. But in neither case do we want to say (what we might say to the novice monk): if you don't like these officials and the orders they give, you can always leave. It is important that there be options short of leaving, connected with the appointment of the officials and the making of the rules they enforce. We see this clearly in the case of towns and also, curiously, in the case of labor unions. In the United States today, the democratic rights of union members are legally protected. But the rights of company employees are only indirectly protected insofar as they are unionized (and insofar as their union has won some share in company decision making).[4]

Entrepreneurial vision, capital investment, the freedom to join or not to join: none of these satisfactorily distinguishes economic from political associations. None of them accounts for, let alone justifies, the privacy of a private government.

But there are two differences between towns and companies that I have not yet considered. First of all, a town is an association of residents; a company is an association of workers, who live somewhere else. Perhaps the maxim, *what touches all should be decided by all,* only applies to residential communities. Monasteries and unions are immediate counterexamples, monasteries because they are residential communities to which the maxim does not apply, unions because they are nonresidential communities to which it does apply. Nevertheless, it is true that ordinary democrats have generally tried to organize people where they live, socialists where they work (though not only there), and some distinction might be drawn along these lines. The self-government of residents, it might be said, is more obvious and important than that of workers. Men and women must collectively control the place where they live in order to be safe in their own homes.

There is certainly no other place where it is so important to be safe. Hence another ancient maxim: *a man's home is his castle.* I will assume that this maxim expresses a genuine moral imperative. What does it require? Not self-government, but rather the protection of a private sphere, a piece of nonpolitical space for withdrawal, rest, secrecy, and solitude. As a feudal baron retired to his castle to brood over public slights, so I retire to my home. But the political community is not a collection of brooding places, or not only that. It is a common enterprise, a public place where we are seen and heard by others, where we quarrel over the public interest, where we sometimes work together. That is why the meetings in J-town were so exciting. They represented the discovery or creation of a local republic, a public thing, which by its very nature had to be shared once it was known to exist. And in this sense, an economic enterprise seems to be very like a town, even though, or in part because, it is so unlike a home. It is not a place of withdrawal, but of cooperative activity. It is not a place that anyone needs to own in order to safeguard his independence and solitude. No one ever thought of saying, a man's factory is his castle. The moral independence of the men and women who work in a factory requires shared decision making and not the protection of a private sphere. Surely we grant that point whenever we require union democracy, and having done that, there seems no principled reason to stop short of company democracy.

But let's think about stopping short, exactly as we currently do. Imagine that the inhabitants of J-town, instead of calling for elections, had organized a citizens' union and bargained collectively with J.J. and his heirs. It is interesting to speculate on the ranges of issues they might have bargained about. Which matters would lie beyond their reach, once they had conceded the issue of ownership? Presumably, they would not have had much to say if J.J. had decided to relocate the town (since it was "his" town). But they could have bargained in detail about living conditions within it, about zoning laws, traffic control, sewage disposal, and so on. They could not have vetoed his choice for chief of police, but it is possible to imagine grievance machinery that would function somewhat like a civilian board of review. The picture is not entirely unattractive, but it is not what we mean by democracy or, at least, it is not all that we mean. Particular groups of city employees do form unions and negotiate with the mayor, but their members also vote for the mayor with whom they negotiate. Members of pressure groups participate in the same dual way, though the arrangements are less formal. They bargain and they vote, acting simultaneously as men and women with particular interests and as men and women with general interests. That seems the right arrangement for economic enterprises also, whose participants are concerned both with their immediate returns and with the well-being of the enterprise as a whole.

The second difference between towns and companies follows from the separation of residence and work. The citizens of a town are also the consumers of the goods and services the town provides—and they are, except for occasional visitors, the only consumers of those goods and services. But the "citizens" of a company are producers of goods and services; they are only sometimes consumers, and they are never the only consumers. Hence there are large numbers of other people, outside the company, who have a direct and material interest in what goes on inside. What should their role be in company decision making? The question is often raised in the literature on workers' control, and it is variously answered. Here I don't want to answer it again, only to insist that the sorts of arrangements required in a fully developed industrial democracy are not all that different from those required in a political democracy. For we don't, after all, grant absolute authority to town governments, even over the goods and services they produce for internal consumption. We enmesh our towns in a federal structure, and we regulate what they can and cannot do in areas like education, criminal justice, environmental use, and so on. No doubt, companies would be similarly enmeshed. In a developed economy, as in a developed polity, different decisions are made by different groups of people at different levels. The division of power in both these cases is only partly a matter of principle; it is also a matter of circumstance and expediency.

The case is similar with the particular constitutional arrangements necessary within companies and factories. There will, of course, be many difficulties in working these out; there will be false starts and failed experiments, as there have been in the previous history of political democracy. Nor should we expect a single resolution of all problems. Proportional representation, single member constituencies, mandated and independent representatives, bicameral and unicameral legislatures, city managers, regulatory commissions, public corporations—the common business is done and should continue to be done in many ways. What is important is that it be known to be common and that our participation in it be recognized as a matter of right.

Today, there are many men and women who preside over enterprises in which hundreds and thousands of their fellow citizens are involved, who make decisions that shape the lives of their fellows, and who defend and justify themselves exactly as J.J. did. I own this place, they say, I built this factory, I founded this company, I risked my capital, I make the decisions around here. It has been my purpose to argue that people who speak this way are wrong. They misunderstand the prerogatives of foundation and investment. They claim an authority to which they have no right. It has not been my purpose, however, to deny the significance of entrepreneurial activity. In both towns and companies one looks for energetic people, willing to innovate and take risks. It would be foolish to create a system that did not bring them forward. They are of no use to us if they just brood in their castles.

On the other hand, nothing they do or can do gives them a right to rule over others—unless they win the agreement of the others. This means that at a certain point in the development of an enterprise, it must pass out of entrepreneurial control. Its founders have created, or they have led other men and women in creating, a public thing, which must now be run in some public way. It is often said that economic entrepreneurs will not come forward if they cannot hope to own the companies they make. The best response is to point to the other side of that all-important but entirely conventional dividing line: we do not lack for political entrepreneurs, though they cannot hope to own the state. Possession is not the goal of public life, but that does not mean that there are not attractive and even compelling goals. For one thing, we can go on building statues of worthy men and women—the founders but not the owners of our common wealth.

NOTES

1. *Leviathan,* Part I, chap. 11.
2. Quoted in Martin Esslin, *Brecht: The Man and His Work* (Garden City, N.Y., 1961), p. 183.
3. *The Second Treatise of Government,* chap. 5, para. 27.
4. There are other sorts of organizations that raise more difficult problems. What about bureaucracies, for example, or schools? Or consider an example that Marx used (in *Capital,* vol. 3) to illustrate the nature of authority in a Communist factory: cooperative labor requires, he wrote, "one commanding will," and he compared this will to that of an orchestra conductor. A strange comparison, for conductors have historically been tyrannical figures. Should their will be commanding? Perhaps it should, but I doubt that Marx's comparison is a good one, for orchestras must express a single interpretation of the music they play, while patterns of work in a factory are more readily negotiated. The political rights of individuals are relative to the character of the activities in which they voluntarily engage. But this general principle needs to be worked out in detail.

PART THREE
LIBERALISM

Like "liberty," the word "liberal" derives from the Latin *liber*, meaning free. Liberals usually see themselves as champions of individual liberty who work to create or preserve an open and tolerant society—a society whose members are free to pursue their own ideas and interests with as little interference as possible. An ideology with a long history, liberalism began as a reaction against two features of medieval society in Europe: religious conformity and ascribed status.

Religious conformity was taken for granted in a society in which the Church and the state were supposed to be partners in the defense of "Christendom." Indeed, there was no clear distinction between Church and state in the Middle Ages. The Christian Church saw its mission as saving souls for the kingdom of God—something that could best be done by teaching and upholding orthodoxy, or "correct belief." Those who took an unorthodox view of Christianity or rejected it altogether thus threatened the Church's attempts to do what it saw as the will of God. To counter this threat, the Church called on the kings, princes, and other rulers of Christendom to use their power to enforce conformity to the Church's doctrines. This the secular authorities were usually willing to do.

The other feature of medieval society against which liberalism reacted was ascribed status, wherein a person's social standing was based not on achievement, but on the status of his or her parents. One was simply born a nobleman, a free commoner, or a serf—and that, with few exceptions, was all there was to it. People may have been equal in the eyes of God, as the Church taught, but men and women of different social ranks were not equals on God's earth or in man's state.

Against this society rooted in ascribed status and religious conformity, liberalism emerged as the first distinctive political ideology. Yet this liberal reaction did not take form until a series of social, economic, and cultural crises shook the medieval order to its foundations. Many of these changes were directly related to the outburst of creativity in the fourteenth and fifteenth centuries known as the Renaissance. But the most important change leading to the rise of liberalism was probably the Protestant Reformation of the sixteenth century. When Martin Luther (1483–1546) and other "reformers" taught that salvation comes through faith alone, they encouraged people to value the individual conscience more than the preservation of unity and orthodoxy. Without intending to do so, then, they prepared the way for liberalism. The step from individual conscience to individual liberty was still radical for the time, but it was a step that liberals began to take in the seventeenth and eighteenth centuries.

The first book of philosophical significance to bear the distinctive stamp of liberalism was Thomas Hobbes's *Leviathan* (1651). All individuals are equals, Hobbes argued. Everyone has a natural right to be free, and no one has the right to rule another without that person's consent. From these liberal premises, however, Hobbes reached the distinctly illiberal conclusion that the people, for the sake of their security, must voluntarily grant absolute power over themselves to a sovereign ruler.

Other writers, such as John Locke (1632–1704), used similar arguments to reach very different conclusions. Locke argued for a measure of religious liberty in his *Letter Concerning Toleration* (1689), for instance, and defended in his *Second Treatise of Government* the right of the people to overthrow any government that does not protect their natural right to life, liberty, and property. The arguments he mustered—the natural equality of men, natural rights, government founded on the consent of the governed—were invoked throughout the eighteenth century. They proved particularly attractive to revolutionaries in North America and France, where they found lasting expression in the Declaration of Independence of the United States (1776) and the French Declaration of the Rights of Man (1789).

In their efforts to remove obstacles to individual liberty, many liberals began to argue that economic exchanges are a private matter between persons who ought to be free from government regulation. In France a group of thinkers called the physiocrats captured this view in the phrase, *"Laissez faire, laissez passer"*—let it be, leave it alone. This is the core of capitalism, which found its most influential defense in Adam Smith's *Wealth of Nations* (1776). Smith argued that an economic policy that would allow individuals to compete freely in the marketplace would be not only the most efficient, but the fairest policy, since it gives everyone an equal opportunity to compete.

Throughout the eighteenth century, then, liberalism was a revolutionary doctrine that reshaped the religious, political, social, and economic relations of people in Europe and North America. Although it continued to play this part in the nineteenth century, liberalism began to take new directions. Perhaps the best way to describe these new directions is to say that the liberal attitude toward democracy and government shifted in the course of the 1800s. Whereas earlier liberals had spoken the language of equality, liberals in the nineteenth century went further to call for expansions of voting rights; and whereas earlier liberals regarded government as, in Thomas Paine's words, a "necessary evil," some in the nineteenth century came to see it as a necessary ally in the struggle to promote individual liberty. In both cases, John Stuart Mill (1806–1873) played a vital part.

An early supporter of women's rights, Mill argued that all sane adults should have the right to vote. Yet he believed that it would be foolish to entrust the ignorant and uninformed with an equal voice in public decisions. Almost every person should have a vote, he concluded, but those with higher levels of education should have two, three, or more. This ambivalence toward democracy follows from Mill's fear of the "tyranny of the majority." Now that government is responsible to the people, he said in *On Liberty* (1859), the majority of voters could conceivably use the government to deny liberty to those who do not agree with them. More directly, the "moral coercion of public opinion" can and does stifle freedom of thought and action by making a social outcast of anyone who does not conform to social customs and beliefs. Mill's argument against this new tyranny rests on the claim that not only individuals, but society as a whole will benefit if people are encouraged to act and think freely, for progress is possible only where there is open competition among different ideas, opinions, and beliefs—a marketplace of ideas.

With its distinction between private and public matters and its suggestion that individual liberty must be protected from interference by government and society, Mill's defense of liberty took a form familiar to earlier liberals. There was another dimension to Mill's view, however, that marked a shift in many liberals' attitude toward government. Freedom, as Mill conceived it, is largely a matter of being free to develop one's potential. In some of Mill's later work, and especially in the writings of T. H. Green (1836–1882), this conception of freedom suggested that government could and should be something more than a nightwatchman protecting the life, liberty, and property of its citizens. Instead, government should promote the welfare of its people—and should do so in the name of individual liberty. Only in this way could people overcome some of the obstacles—for example, poverty, illness, ignorance, and prejudice—that prevented them from being truly free.

This led to a split between those who clung to the older views—the neoclassical liberals—and those who followed Green along the path of "welfare" or "reform" liberalism. In the late 1800s the most prominent version of neoclassical liberalism was the Social Darwinism of such writers as Herbert Spencer (1820–1903) and William Graham Sumner (1840–1910). As the franchise expanded to include the working class and the welfare state began to emerge, however, neoclassical liberalism began to fade. Welfare liberalism came gradually to be known simply as liberalism.

This is not to say that neoclassical liberalism ever entirely disappeared, for some economists (e.g., Friedrich Hayek [b. 1899] and Milton Friedman [b. 1912]) and at least one novelist (Ayn Rand [1905–1982]) continued to press the case against active government and the welfare state in their writings. Some, such as Murray Rothbard [b. 1926], have even argued for anarchism on the grounds that government is an entirely *un*necessary evil. So the debate within liberalism that began over one hundred years ago continues today. Both groups agree on the end they want to achieve—an open and tolerant society in which every person has an equal opportunity to live as freely as possible. But what are the best means to achieve this end? Is government the chief obstacle to individual liberty, as the neoclassical liberals claim, or an aid and ally useful in removing other barriers to freedom, as the welfare liberals insist? On this point, welfare and neoclassical liberals continue to disagree, with no resolution or agreement in sight.

11

THE STATE OF NATURE AND THE BASIS OF OBLIGATION

THOMAS HOBBES

Thomas Hobbes (1588–1679) might best be described as a pre-liberal, or perhaps a proto-liberal, thinker. The main features of liberalism are to be found in his *Leviathan* (1651), particularly in the imaginary "state of nature," but his conclusions are seldom considered liberal. Writing in the aftermath of the English civil war, Hobbes invited his readers to imagine a world without laws, police, courts, and prisons—a world of "perfect" liberty and equality—and then went on to show "scientifically" that such a world would be nothing less than a "war of every man against every man." Thus, he concluded, rational, self-interested people would have every reason to enter into a "social contract" to put themselves under the unlimited authority of a sovereign ruler.

Source: The English Works of Thomas Hobbes of Malmesbury, *vol. III, ed. Sir William Molesworth (London: John Bohm, 1839), chapters 13 and 14, pp. 110–130. The editors have modernized the spelling of some words.*

OF THE NATURAL CONDITION OF MANKIND AS CONCERNING THEIR FELICITY AND MISERY

Nature has made men so equal, in the faculties of the body, and mind; as that though there be found one man sometimes manifestly stronger in body, or of quicker mind than another; yet when all is reckoned together, the difference between man, and man, is not so considerable, as that one man can thereupon claim to himself any benefit, to which another may not pretend, as well as he. For as to the strength of body, the weakest has strength enough to kill the strongest, either by secret machination, or by confederacy with others, that are in the same danger with himself.

And as to the faculties of the mind, setting aside the arts grounded upon words, and especially that skill of proceeding upon general, and infallible rules, called science; which very few have, and but in few things; as being not a native faculty, born with us; nor attained, as prudence, while we look after somewhat else, I find yet a greater equality amongst men, than that of strength. For prudence, is but experience; which equal time, equally bestows on all men, in those things they equally apply themselves unto. That which may perhaps make such equality incredible, is but a vain conceit of one's own wisdom, which almost all men think they have in a greater degree, than the vulgar; that is, than all men but themselves, and a few others, whom by fame, or for concurring with themselves, they approve. For such is the nature of men, that howsoever they may acknowledge many others to be more witty, or more eloquent, or more learned; yet they will hardly believe there be many so wise as themselves; for they see their own wit at hand, and other men's at a distance. But this proves rather that men are in that point equal, than unequal. For there is not ordinarily a greater sign of the equal distribution of any thing, than that every man is contented with his share.

From this equality of ability, arises equality of hope in the attaining of our ends. And therefore if any two men desire the same thing, which nevertheless they cannot both enjoy, they become enemies; and in the way to their end, which is principally their own conservation, and sometimes their delectation only, endeavour to destroy, or subdue one another. And from hence it comes to pass, that where an invader has no more to fear, than another man's single power; if one plant, sow, build, or possess a convenient seat, others may probably be expected to come prepared with forces united, to dispossess, and deprive him, not only of the fruit of his labour, but also of his life, or liberty. And the invader again is in the like danger of another.

And from this diffidence of one another, there is no way for any man to secure himself, so reasonable, as anticipation; that is, by force, or wiles, to master the persons of all men he can, so long, till he see no other power great enough to endanger him: and this is no more than his own conservation requires, and is generally allowed. Also because there be some, that taking pleasure in contemplating their own power in the acts of conquest, which they pursue farther than their security requires; if others, that otherwise would be glad to be at ease within modest bounds, should not by invasion increase their power, they would not be able, long time, by standing only on their defence, to subsist. And by consequence, such augmentation of dominion over men being necessary to a man's conservation, it ought to be allowed him.

Again, men have no pleasure, but on the contrary a great deal of grief, in keeping company, where there is no power able to over-awe them all. For every man looks that his companion should value him, at the same rate he sets upon himself: and upon all signs of contempt, or undervaluing, naturally endeavours, as far as he dares, (which amongst them that have no common power to keep them in quiet, is far enough to make them destroy each other), to extort a greater value from his contemners, by damage; and from others, by the example.

So that in the nature of man, we find three principal causes of quarrel. First, competition; secondly, diffidence; thirdly, glory.

The first, makes men invade for gain; the second, for safety; and the third, for reputation. The first use violence, to make themselves masters of other men's persons, wives, children, and cattle; the second, to defend them; the third, for trifles, as a word, a smile, a different opinion, and any other sign of undervalue, either direct in their persons, or by reflection in their kindred, their friends, their nation, their profession, or their name.

Hereby it is manifest, that during the time men live without a common power to keep them all in awe, they are in that condition which is called war; and such a war, as is of every man, against every man. For WAR, consists not in battle only, or the act of fighting; but in a tract of time, wherein the will to contend by battle is sufficiently known: and therefore the notion of *time*, is to be considered in the nature of war; as it is in the nature of weather. For as the nature of foul weather, lies not in a shower or two of rain; but in an inclination thereto of many days together: so the nature of war, consists not in actual fighting; but in the known disposition thereto, during all the time there is no assurance to the contrary. All other time is PEACE.

Whatsoever therefore is consequent to a time of war, where every man is enemy to every man; the same is consequent to the time, wherein men live without other security, than what their own strength, and their own invention shall furnish them withal. In such condition, there is no place for industry; because the fruit thereof is uncertain: and consequently no culture of the earth; no navigation, nor use of the commodities that may be imported by sea; no commodious building; no instruments of moving, and removing, such things as require much force; no knowledge of the face of the earth; no account of time; no arts; no letters; no society; and which is worst of all, continual fear, and danger of violent death; and the life of man, solitary, poor, nasty, brutish, and short.

It may seem strange to some man, that has not well weighed these things; that nature should thus dissociate, and render men apt to invade, and destroy one another: and he may therefore, not trusting to this inference, made from the passions, desire perhaps to have the same confirmed by experience. Let him therefore consider with himself, when taking a journey, he arms himself, and seeks to go well accompanied; when going to sleep, he locks his doors; when even in his house he locks his chests; and this when he knows there be laws, and public officers, armed, to revenge all injuries shall be done him; what opinion he has of his fellow-subjects, when he rides armed; of his fellow citizens, when he locks his doors; and of his children, and servants, when he locks his chests. Does he not there as much accuse mankind by his actions, as I do by my words? But neither of us accuse man's nature in it. The desires, and other passions of man, are in themselves no sin. No more are the actions, that proceed from those passions, till they know a law that forbids them: which till laws be made they cannot know: nor can any law be made, till they have agreed upon the person that shall make it.

It may peradventure be thought, there was never such a time, nor condition of war as this; and I believe it was never generally so, over all the world: but there are many places, where they live so now. For the savage people in many places of America, except the government of small families, the concord whereof depends on natural lust, have no government at all; and live at this day in that brutish manner, as I said before. Howsoever, it may be perceived what manner of life there would be, where there were no common power to fear, by the manner of life, which men that have formerly lived under a peaceful government, use to degenerate into, in a civil war.

But though there had never been any time, wherein particular men were in a condition of war one against another; yet in all times, kings, and persons of sovereign authority, because of their independency, are in continual jealousies, and in the state and posture of gladiators; having their weapons pointing, and their eyes fixed on one another; that is, their forts, garrisons, and guns upon the frontiers of their kingdoms; and continual spies upon their neighbours; which is a posture of war. But because they uphold thereby, the industry of their subjects; there does not follow from it, that misery, which accompanies the liberty of particular men.

To this war of every man, against every man, this also is consequent; that nothing can be unjust. The notions of right and wrong, justice and injustice have there no place. Where there is no common power, there is no law: where no law, no injustice. Force, and fraud, are in war the two cardinal virtues. Justice, and injustice are none of the faculties neither of the body, nor mind. If they were, they might be in a man that were alone in the world, as well as his senses, and passions. They are qualities, that relate to men in society, not in solitude. It is consequent also to the same condition, that there be no propriety, no dominion, no *mine* and *thine* distinct; but only that to be every man's, that he can get: and for so long, as he can keep it. And thus much for the ill condition, which man by mere nature is actually placed in; though with a possibility to come out of it, consisting partly in the passions, partly in his reason.

The passions that incline men to peace, are fear of death; desire of such things as are necessary to commodious living; and a hope by their industry to obtain them. And reason suggests convenient articles of peace, upon which men may be drawn to agreement. These articles, are they, which otherwise are called the Laws of Nature: whereof I shall speak more particularly, in . . . following chapters.

OF THE FIRST AND SECOND NATURAL LAWS, AND OF CONTRACTS

THE RIGHT OF NATURE, which writers commonly call *jus naturale*, is the liberty each man has, to use his own power, as he will himself, for the preservation of his own nature; that is to say, of his own life; and consequently, of doing any thing, which in his own judgment, and reason, he shall conceive to be the aptest means thereunto.

BY LIBERTY, is understood, according to the proper signification of the word, the absence of external impediments: which impediments, may oft take away part of a man's power to do what he would; but cannot hinder him from using the power left him, according as his judgment, and reason shall dictate to him.

A LAW OF NATURE, *lex naturalis*, is a precept or general rule, found out by reason, by which a man is forbidden to do that, which is destructive of his life, or takes away the means of preserving the same; and to omit that, by which he thinks it may be best preserved. For though they that speak of this subject, use to confound *jus*, and *lex*, *right* and *law:* yet they ought to be distinguished; because RIGHT, consists in liberty to do, or to forbear: whereas LAW, determines, and binds to one of them: so that law, and right, differ as much, as obligation, and liberty; which in one and the same matter are inconsistent.

And because the condition of man, as has been declared in the precedent chapter, is a condition of war of every one against every one; in which case every one is governed by his own reason; and there is nothing he can make use of, that may not be a help unto him, in preserving his life against his enemies; it follows, that in such a condition, every man has a right to every thing; even to one another's body. And therefore, as long as this natural right of every man to every thing endures, there can be no security to any man, how strong or wise soever he be, of living out the time, which nature ordinarily allows men to live. And consequently it is a precept, or general rule of reason, *that every man, ought to endeavour peace, as far as he has hope of obtaining it; and when he cannot obtain it, that he may seek, and use, all helps, and advantages of war*. The first branch of which rule, contains the first, and fundamental law of nature; which is, *to seek peace, and follow it*. The second, the sum of the right of nature; which is, *by all means we can, to defend ourselves*.

From this fundamental law of nature, by which men are commanded to endeavour peace, is derived this second law; *that a man be willing, when others are so too, as far-forth, as for peace, and defence of himself he shall think it necessary, to lay down this right to all things; and be contented with so much liberty against other men, as he would allow other men against himself*. For as long as every man holds this right, of doing any thing he likes; so long are all men in the condition of war. But if other men will not lay down their right, as well as he; then there is no reason for any one, to divest himself of his: for that were to expose himself to prey, which no man is bound to, rather than to dispose himself to peace. This is that law of the Gospel; *whatsoever you require that others should do to you, that do ye to them*. And that law of all men, *quod tibi fieri non vis, alteri ne feceris [what you don't want done to you, don't do to others]*.

To *lay down* a man's *right* to any thing, is to *divest* himself of the *liberty*, of hindering another of the benefit of his own right to the same. For he that renounces, or passes away his right, gives not to any other man a right which he had not before; because there is nothing to which every man had not right by nature: but only stands out of his way, that he may enjoy his own original right, without hindrance from him; not without hindrance from another. So that the effect which redounds to one man, by another man's defect of right, is but so much diminution of impediments to the use of his own right original.

Right is laid aside, either by simply renouncing it; or by transferring it to another. By *simply* RENOUNCING; when he cares not to whom the benefit thereof redounds. By TRANSFERRING; when he intends the benefit thereof to some certain person, or persons. And when a man has in either manner abandoned, or granted away his right; then he is said to be OBLIGED, or BOUND, not to hinder those, to whom such right is granted, or abandoned, from the benefit of it: and that he *ought*, and it is his DUTY, not to make void that voluntary act of his own: and that such hindrance is INJUSTICE, and INJURY, as being *sine jure;* the right being before renounced, or transferred. So that *injury*, or *injustice*, in the controversies of the world, is somewhat like to that, which in the disputations of scholars is called *absurdity*. For as it is there called an absurdity, to contradict what one maintained in the beginning: so in the world, it is called injustice, and injury, voluntarily to undo that, which from the beginning he had voluntarily done. The way by which a man either simply renounces, or transfers his right, is a declaration, or signification, by some voluntary and sufficient sign, or signs, that he does so renounce, or transfer; or has so renounced, or transferred the same, to him that accepts it. And these signs are either words only, or actions only; or, as it happens most often, both words, and actions. And the same are the BONDS, by which men are bound, and obliged: bonds, that have their strength, not from their own nature, for nothing is more easily broken than a man's word, but from fear of some evil consequence upon the rupture.

Whensoever a man transfers his right, or renounces it; it is either in consideration of some right reciprocally transferred to himself; or for some other good he hopes for thereby. For it is a voluntary act: and of the voluntary acts of every man, the object is some *good to himself*. And therefore there be some rights, which no man can be understood by any words, or other signs, to have abandoned, or transferred. As first a man cannot lay down the right of resisting them, that assault him by force, to take away his life; because he cannot be understood to aim thereby, at any good to himself. The same may be said of wounds, and chains, and imprisonment; both because there is no benefit consequent to such patience; as there is to the patience of suffering another to be wounded, or imprisoned: as also because a man cannot tell, when he sees men proceed against him by violence, whether they intend his death or not. And lastly the motive, and end for which this renouncing, and transferring of right is introduced, is nothing else but the security of a man's person, in his life, and in the means of so preserving life, as not to be weary of it. And therefore if a man by words, or other signs, seem to despoil himself of the end, for which those signs were intended; he is not to be understood as if he meant it, or that it was his will; but that he was ignorant of how such words and actions were to be interpreted.

The mutual transferring of right, is that which men call CONTRACT.

There is a difference between transferring of right to the thing; and transferring, or tradition, that is delivery of the thing itself. For the thing may be delivered together with the translation of the right; as in buying and selling with ready-money; or exchange of goods, or lands: and it may be delivered some time after.

Again, one of the contractors, may deliver the thing contracted for on his part, and leave the other to perform his part at some determinate time after, and in the mean time be trusted; and then the contract on his part, is called PACT, or COVENANT: or both parts may contract now, to perform hereafter: in which cases, he that is to perform in time to come, being trusted, his performance is called *keeping of promise*, or faith; and the failing of performance, if it be voluntary, *violation of faith*.

When the transferring of right, is not mutual: but one of the parties transfers, in hope to gain thereby friendship, or service from another, or from his friends; or in hope to gain the reputation of charity, or magnanimity; or to deliver his mind from the pain of compassion; or in hope of reward in heaven; this is not contract, but GIFT, FREE-GIFT, GRACE: which words signify one and the same thing.

Signs of contract, are either *express*, or *by inference*. Express, are words spoken with understanding of what they signify: and such words are either of the time *present*, or *past;* as, *I give, I grant, I have given, I have granted, I will that this be yours:* or of the future; as, *I will give, I will grant:* which words of the future are called PROMISE.

Signs by inference, are sometimes the consequence of words; sometimes the consequence of silence; sometimes the consequence of actions; sometimes the consequence of forbearing an action: and generally a sign of inference, of any contract, is whatsoever sufficiently argues the will of the contractor.

Words alone, if they be of the time to come, and contain a bare promise, are an insufficient sign of a free-gift, and therefore not obligatory. For if they be of the time to come, as *tomorrow I will give,* they are a sign I have not given yet, and consequently that my right is not transferred, but remains till I transfer it by some other act. But if the words be of the time present, or past, as, *I have given*, or, *do give to be delivered to-morrow,* then is my to-morrow's right given away to-day; and that by the virtue of the words, though there were no other argument of my will. And there is a great difference in the signification of these words, *volo hoc tuum esse cras*, and *cras dabo;* that is, between *I will that this be thine to-morrow,* and, *I will give it thee to-morrow:* for the word *I will,* in the former manner of speech, signifies an act of the will present; but in the latter, it signifies a promise of an act of the will to come: and therefore the former words, being of the present, transfer a future right; the latter, that be of the future, transfer nothing. But if there be other signs of the will to transfer a right, besides words; then, though the gift be free, yet may the right be understood to pass by words of the future: as if a man propound a prize to him that comes first to the end of a race, the gift is free; and though the words be of the future, yet the right passes: for if he would not have his words so be understood, he should not have let them run.

In contracts, the right passes, not only where the words are of the time present, or past, but also where they are of the future: because all contract is mutual translation, or change of right; and therefore he that promises only, because he has already received the benefit for which he promises, is to be understood as if he intended the right should pass: for unless he had been content to have his words so understood, the other would not have performed his part first. And for that cause, in buying, and selling, and other acts of contract, a promise is equivalent to a covenant; and therefore obligatory. . . .

If a covenant be made, wherein neither of the parties perform presently, but trust one another; in the condition of mere nature, which is a condition of war of every man against every man, upon any reasonable suspicion, it is void: but if there be a common power set over them both, with right and force sufficient to compel performance, it is not void. For he that performs first, has no assurance the other will perform after; because the bonds of words are too weak to bridle men's ambition, avarice, anger, and other passions, without the fear of some coercive power; which in the condition of mere nature, where all men are equal, and judges of the justness of their own fears, cannot possibly be supposed. And therefore he which performeth first, does but betray himself to his enemy; contrary to the right, he can never abandon, of defending his life, and means of living.

But in a civil estate, where there is a power set up to constrain those that would otherwise violate their faith, that fear is no more reasonable; and for that cause, he which by the covenant is to perform first, is obliged so to do. . . .

Covenants entered into by fear, in the condition of mere nature, are obligatory. For example, if I covenant to pay a ransom, or service for my life, to an enemy; I am bound by it: for it is a contract, wherein one receives the benefit of life; the other is to receive money, or service for it; and consequently, where no other law, as in the condition of mere nature, forbids the performance, the covenant is valid. Therefore prisoners of war, if trusted with the payment of their ransom, are obliged to pay it: and if a weaker prince, make a disadvantageous peace with a stronger, for fear; he is bound to keep it; unless, as hath been said before, there arises some new, and just cause of fear, to renew the war. And even in commonwealths, if I be forced to redeem myself from a thief by promising him money, I am bound to pay it, till the civil law discharge me. For whatsoever I may lawfully do without obligation, the same I may lawfully covenant to do through fear: and what I lawfully covenant, I cannot lawfully break.

A former covenant, makes void a later. For a man that has passed away his right to one man to-day, has it not to pass to-morrow to another: and therefore the later promise passes no right, but is null.

A covenant not to defend myself from force, by force, is always void. For, as I have showed before, no man can transfer, or lay down his right to save himself from death, wounds, and imprisonment, the avoiding whereof is the only end of laying down any right; and therefore the promise of not resisting force, in no covenant transfers any right; nor is obliging. For though a man may covenant thus, *unless I do so, or so, kill me;* he cannot covenant thus, *unless I do so, or so, I will not resist you, when you come to kill me.* For man by nature chooses the lesser evil, which is danger of death in resisting; rather than the greater, which is certain and present death in not resisting. And this is granted to be true by all men, in that they lead criminals to execution, and prison, with armed men, notwithstanding that such criminals have consented to the law, by which they are condemned.

A covenant to accuse oneself, without assurance of pardon, is likewise invalid. For in the condition of nature, where every man is judge, there is no place for accusation: and in the civil state, the accusation is followed with punishment; which being force, a man is not obliged not to resist. . . .

12

TOLERATION AND GOVERNMENT

JOHN LOCKE

Although the word "liberal" was not used to describe a political position until the early 1800s, John Locke (1632–1704) is usually considered the first philosopher to adopt a clearly liberal stance. The power of a political society or "commonwealth," Locke claimed, is limited to the protection of its members' "civil interests." These include life, liberty, and property, but not the private sphere of religious belief—as he argued in *A Letter Concerning Toleration* (1689). In his *Second Treatise of Government*—published in 1690 after the Glorious Revolution of 1688, but written earlier—Locke began from premises quite similar to those of Thomas Hobbes, but arrived at conclusions more recognizably liberal. Everyone has a natural right to life, liberty, and property, Locke said, and no one has authority over us without our consent. Any government that violates our rights releases us from any obligation to obey it and may, indeed, entitle us to overthrow it and establish a new government.

Sources: The Works of John Locke, *10 vols. (London: Thomas Tegg; W. Sharpe and Son; G. Offor; G. and J. Robinson; J. Evans and Co., 1823), pp. 9–21 (vol. VI) and 339–347, 352–367, 469–472 (vol. V).*

A LETTER CONCERNING TOLERATION

. . .

The commonwealth seems to me to be a society of men constituted only for the procuring, preserving, and advancing their own civil interests.

Civil interest I call life, liberty, health, and indolency of body; and the possession of outward things, such as money, lands, houses, furniture, and the like.

It is the duty of the civil magistrate, by the impartial execution of equal laws, to secure unto all the people in general, and to every one of his subjects in particular, the just possession of these things belonging to this life. If any one presume to violate the laws of public justice and equity, established for the preservation of these things, his presumption is to be checked by the fear of punishment, consisting in the deprivation or diminution of those civil interests, or goods, which otherwise he might and ought to enjoy. But seeing no man does willingly suffer himself to be punished by the deprivation of any part of his goods, and much less of his liberty or life, therefore is the magistrate armed with the force and strength of all his subjects, in order to the punishment of those that violate any other man's rights.

Now that the whole jurisdiction of the magistrate reaches only to these civil concernments; and that all civil power, right, and dominion, is bounded and confined to the only care of promoting these things; and that it neither can nor ought in any manner to be extended to the salvation of souls, these following considerations seem unto me abundantly to demonstrate.

First, Because the care of souls is not committed to the civil magistrate, any more than to other men. It is not committed unto him, I say, by God; because it appears not that God has ever given any such authority to one man over another, as to compel any one to his religion. Nor can any such power be vested in the magistrate by the consent of the people; because no man can so far abandon the care of his own salvation as blindly to leave it to the choice of any other, whether prince or subject, to prescribe to him what faith or worship he shall embrace. For no man can, if he would, conform his faith to the dictates of another. All the life and power of true religion consists in the inward and full persuasion of the mind; and faith is not faith without believing. Whatever profession we make, to whatever outward worship we conform, if we are not fully satisfied in our own mind that the one is true, and the other well-pleasing unto God, such profession and such practice, far from being any furtherance, are indeed great obstacles to our salvation. For in this manner, instead of expiating other sins by the exercise of religion, I say in offering thus unto God Almighty such a worship as we esteem to be displeasing unto him, we add unto the number of our other sins, those also of hypocrisy, and contempt of his Divine Majesty.

In the second place, The care of souls cannot belong to the civil magistrate, because his power consists only in outward force: but true and saving religion consists in the inward persuasion of the mind, without which nothing can be acceptable to God. And such is the nature of the understanding, that it cannot be compelled to the belief of any thing by outward force. Confiscation of estate, imprisonment, torments, nothing of that nature can have any such efficacy as to make men change the inward judgment that they have framed of things.

It may indeed be alleged that the magistrate may make use of arguments, and thereby draw the heterodox into the way of truth, and procure their salvation. I grant it; but this is common to him with other men. In teaching, instructing, and redressing the erroneous by reason, he may certainly do what becomes any good man to do. Magistracy does not oblige him to put off either humanity or Christianity. But it is one thing to persuade, another to command; one thing to press with arguments, another with penalties. This the civil power alone has a right to do; to the other, good-will is authority enough. Every man has commission to admonish, exhort, convince another of error, and by reasoning to draw him into truth: but to give laws, receive obedience, and compel with the sword, belongs to none but the magistrate. And upon this ground I affirm, that the magistrate's power extends not to the establishing of any articles of faith, or forms of worship, by the force of his laws. For laws are of no force at all without penalties, and penalties in this case are absolutely impertinent; because they are not proper to convince the mind. Neither the profession of any articles of faith, nor the conformity to any outward form of worship, as has been already said, can be available to the salvation of souls, unless the truth of the one, and the acceptableness of the other unto God, be thoroughly believed by those that so profess and practise. But penalties are no ways capable to produce such belief. It is only light and evidence that can work a change in men's opinions; and that light can in no manner proceed from corporal sufferings, or any other outward penalties.

In the third place, The care of the salvation of men's souls cannot belong to the magistrate; because, though the rigour of laws and the force of penalties were capable to convince and change men's minds, yet would not that help at all to the salvation of their souls. For, there being but one truth, one way to heaven; what hopes is there that more men would be led into it, if they had no other rule to follow but the religion of the court, and were put under a necessity to quit the light of their own reason, to oppose the dictates of their own consciences, and blindly to resign up themselves to the will of their governors, and to the religion, which either ignorance, ambition, or superstition had chanced to establish in the countries where they were born? In the variety and contradiction of opinions in religion, wherein the princes of the world are as much divided as in their secular interests, the narrow way would be much straitened; one country alone would be in the right, and all the rest of the world put under an obligation of following their princes in the ways that lead to destruction: and that which heightens the absurdity, and very ill suits the notion of a Deity, men would owe their eternal happiness or misery to the places of their nativity.

These considerations, to omit many others that might have been urged to the same purpose, seem unto me sufficient to conclude, that all the power of civil government relates only to men's civil interests, is confined to the care of the things of this world, and hath nothing to do with the world to come.

Let us now consider what a church is. A church then I take to be a voluntary society of men, joining themselves together of their own accord, in order to the public worshipping of God, in such a manner as they judge acceptable to him, and effectual to the salvation of their souls.

I say, it is a free and voluntary society. Nobody is born a member of any church; otherwise the religion of parents would descend unto children, by the same right of inheritance as their temporal estates, and every one would hold his faith by the same tenure he does his lands; than which nothing can be imagined more absurd. Thus therefore that matter stands. No man by nature is bound unto any particular church or sect, but every one joins himself voluntarily to that society in which he believes he has found that profession and worship which is truly acceptable to God. The hopes of salvation, as it was the only cause of his entrance into that communion, so it can be the only reason of his stay there. For if afterwards he discover any thing either erroneous in the doctrine, or incongruous in the worship of that society to which he has joined himself, why should it not be as free for him to go out as it was to enter? No member of a religious society can be tied with any other bonds but what proceed from the certain expectation of eternal life. A church then is a society of members voluntarily uniting to this end.

It follows now that we consider what is the power of this church, and unto what laws it is subject.

Forasmuch as no society, how free soever, or upon whatsoever slight occasion instituted, (whether of philosophers for learning, of merchants for commerce, or of men of leisure for mutual conversation and discourse) no church or company, I say, can in the least subsist and hold together, but will presently dissolve and break to pieces, unless it be regulated by some laws, and the members all consent to observe some order. Place and time of meeting must be agreed on; rules for admitting and excluding members must be established; distinction of officers, and putting things into a regular course, and such like, cannot be omitted. But since the joining together of several members into this church-society, as has already been demonstrated, is absolutely free and spontaneous, it necessarily follows, that the right of making its laws can belong to none but the society itself, or at least, which is the same thing, to those whom the society by common consent has authorized thereunto.

Some perhaps may object, that no such society can be said to be a true church, unless it have in it a bishop, or presbyter, with ruling authority derived from the very apostles, and continued down unto the present time by an uninterrupted succession.

To these I answer: In the first place, Let them show me the edict by which Christ has imposed that law upon his church. And let not any man think me impertinent, if, in a thing of this consequence, I require that the terms of that edict be very express and positive. For the promise he has made us, that "wheresoever two or three are gathered together in his name, he will be in the midst of them," Matth, xviii, 20, seems to imply the contrary. Whether such an assembly want any thing necessary to a true church, pray do you consider. Certain I am, that nothing can be there wanting unto the salvation of souls, which is sufficient for our purpose.

Next, pray observe how great have always been the divisions amongst even those who lay so much stress upon the divine institution, and continued succession of a certain order of rulers in the church. Now their very dissension unavoidably puts us upon a necessity of deliberating, and consequently allows a liberty of choosing that, which upon consideration, we prefer.

And, in the last place, I consent that these men have a ruler of their church, established by such a long series of succession as they judge necessary, provided I may have liberty at the same time to join myself to that society, in which I am persuaded those things are to be found which are necessary to the salvation of my soul. In this manner ecclesiastical liberty will be preserved on all sides, and no man will have a legislator imposed upon him, but whom himself has chosen.

But since men are so solicitous about the true church, I would only ask them here by the way, if it be not more agreeable to the church of Christ to make the conditions of her communion consist in such things, and such things only, as the Holy Spirit has in the holy Scriptures declared, in express words, to be necessary to salvation? I ask, I say, whether this be not more agreeable to the church of Christ, than for men to impose their own inventions and interpretations upon others, as if they were of divine authority; and to establish by ecclesiastical laws, as absolutely necessary to the profession of Christianity such things as the holy Scriptures do either not mention, or at least not expressly command? Whosoever requires those things in order to ecclesiastical communion, which Christ does not require in order to life eternal, he may perhaps indeed constitute a society accommodated to his own opinion, and his own advantage; but how that can be called the church of Christ, which is established upon laws that are not his, and which excludes such persons from its communion as he will one day receive into the kingdom of heaven, I understand not. But this being not a proper place to enquire into the marks of the true church, I will only mind those that contend so earnestly for the decrees of their own society, and that cry out continually the Church, the Church, with as much noise, and perhaps upon the same principle, as the Ephesian silversmiths did for their Diana; this, I say, I desire to mind them of, that the Gospel frequently declares, that the true disciples of Christ must suffer persecution; but that the church of Christ should persecute others, and force others by fire and sword to embrace her faith and doctrine, I could never yet find in any of the books of the New Testament.

The end of a religious society, as has already been said, is the public worship of God, and by means thereof the acquisition of eternal life. All discipline ought therefore to tend to that end, and all ecclesiastical laws to be thereunto confined. Nothing ought, nor can be transacted in this society, relating to the possession of civil and worldly goods. No force is here to be made use of, upon any occasion whatsoever: for force belongs wholly to the civil magistrate, and the possession of all outward goods is subject to his jurisdiction.

But it may be asked, by what means then shall ecclesiastical laws be established, if they must be thus destitute of all compulsive power? I answer they must be established by means suitable to the nature of such things, whereof the external profession and observation, if not proceeding from a thorough conviction and approbation of the mind, is altogether useless and unprofitable. The arms by which the members of this society are to be kept within their duty, are exhortations, admonitions, and advice. If by these means the offenders will not be reclaimed, and the erroneous convinced, there remains nothing farther to be done, but that such stubborn and obstinate persons, who give no ground to hope for their reformation, should be cast out and separated from the society. This is the last and utmost force of ecclesiastical authority: no other punishment can thereby be inflicted, than that the relation ceasing between the body and the member which is cut off, the person so condemned ceases to be a part of that church.

These things being thus determined, let us inquire, in the next place, how far the duty of toleration extends, and what is required from every one by it.

And first, I hold, that no church is bound by the duty of toleration to retain any such person in her bosom, as after admonition, continues obstinately to offend against the laws of the society. For these being the condition of communion, and the bond of society, if the breach of them were permitted without any animadversion, the society would immediately be thereby dissolved. But nevertheless, in all such cases care is to be taken that the sentence of excommunication, and the execution thereof, carry with it no rough usage, of word or action, whereby the ejected person may any ways be damnified in body or estate. For all force, as has often been said, belongs only to the magistrate, nor ought any private persons, at any time, to use force; unless it be in self-defence against unjust violence. Excommunication neither does nor can deprive the excommunicated person of any of those civil goods that he formerly possessed. All those things belong to the civil government, and are under the magistrate's protection. The whole force of excommunication consists only in this, that the resolution of the society in that respect being declared, the union that was between the body and some member, comes thereby to be dissolved; and that relation ceasing, the participation of some certain things, which the society communicated to its members, and unto which no man has any civil right, comes also to cease. For there is no civil injury done unto the excommunicated person, by the church-minister's refusing him that bread and wine, in the celebration of the Lord's supper, which was not bought with his, but other men's money.

Secondly, No private person has any right in any manner to prejudice another person in his civil enjoyments, because he is of another church or religion. All the rights and franchises that belong to him as a man, or as a denizen, are inviolably to be preserved to him. These are not the business of religion. No violence nor injury is to be offered him, whether he be Christian or pagan. Nay, we must not content ourselves with the narrow measures of bare justice: charity, bounty, and liberality must be added to it. This the Gospel enjoins, this reason directs, and this that natural fellowship we are born into requires of us. If any man err from the right way, it is his own misfortune, no injury to thee: nor therefore art thou to punish him in the things of this life, because thou supposest he will be miserable in that which is to come.

What I say concerning the mutual toleration of private persons differing from one another in religion, I understand also of particular churches; which stand as it were in the same relation to each other as private persons among themselves; nor has any one of them any manner of jurisdiction over any other, no, not even when the civil magistrate, as it sometimes happens, comes to be of this or the other communion. For the civil government can give no new right to the church, nor the church to the civil government. So that whether the magistrate join himself to any church, or separate from it, the church remains always as it was before, a free and voluntary society. It neither acquires the power of the sword by the magistrate's coming to it, nor does it lose the right of instruction and excommunication by his going from it. This is the fundamental and immutable right of a spontaneous society, that it has to remove any of its members who transgress the rules of its institution: but it cannot, by the accession of any new members, acquire any right of jurisdiction over those that are not joined with it. And therefore peace, equity, and friendship, are always mutually to be observed by particular churches, in the same manner as by private persons, without any pretence of superiority or jurisdiction over one another. . . .

Nobody therefore, in fine, neither single persons, nor churches, nay, nor even commonwealths, have any just title to invade the civil rights and worldly goods of each other, upon pretence of religion. Those that are of another opinion, would do well to consider with themselves how pernicious a seed of discord and war, how powerful a provocation to endless hatreds, rapines, and slaughters, they thereby furnish unto mankind. No peace and security, no, not so much as common friendship, can ever be established or preserved amongst men, so long as this opinion prevails, "that dominion is founded in grace, and that religion is to be propagated by force of arms."

In the third place, Let us see what the duty of toleration requires from those who are distinguished from the rest of mankind, from the laity, as they please to call us, by some ecclesiastical character and office; whether they be bishops, priests, presbyters, ministers, or however else dignified or distinguished. It is not my business to inquire here into the origins of the power or dignity of the clergy. This only I say, that whencesoever their authority be sprung, since it is ecclesiastical, it ought to be confined within the bounds of the church, nor can it in any manner be extended to civil affairs; because the church itself is a thing absolutely separate and distinct from the commonwealth. The boundaries on both sides are fixed and immoveable. He jumbles heaven and earth together, the things most remote and opposite, who mixes these societies, which are, in their origins, end, business, and in every thing, perfectly distinct, and infinitely different from each other. No man therefore, with whatsoever ecclesiastical office he be dignified, can deprive another man, that is not of his church and faith, either of liberty, or of any part of his worldly goods, upon the account of that difference which is between them in religion. For whatsoever is not lawful to the whole church cannot, by any ecclesiastical right, become lawful to any of its members.

SECOND TREATISE OF GOVERNMENT

. . .

OF THE STATE OF NATURE

4. To understand political power right, and derive it from its origins, we must consider what state all men are naturally in, and that is, a state of perfect freedom to order their actions and dispose of their possessions and persons, as they think fit, within the bounds of the law of nature;

without asking leave, or depending upon the will of any other man.

A state also of equality, wherein all the power and jurisdiction is reciprocal, no one having more than another; there being nothing more evident than that creatures of the same species and rank, promiscuously born to all the same advantages of nature, and the use of the same faculties, should also be equal one amongst another without subordination or subjection; unless the Lord and Master of them all should, by any manifest declaration of his will, set one above another, and confer on him, by an evident and clear appointment, an undoubted right to dominion and sovereignty. . . .

6. But though this be a state of liberty, yet it is not a state of licence: though man in that state have an uncontrollable liberty to dispose of his person or possessions, yet he has not liberty to destroy himself, or so much as any creature in his possession, but where some nobler use than its bare preservation calls for it. The state of nature has a law of nature to govern it, which obliges every one: and reason, which is that law, teaches all mankind, who will but consult it, that being all equal and independent, no one ought to harm another in his life, health, liberty, or possessions: for men being all the workmanship of one omnipotent and infinitely wise Maker; all the servants of one sovereign Master, sent into the world by his order, and about his business; they are his property, whose workmanship they are, made to last during his, not another's pleasure: and being furnished with like faculties, sharing all in one community of nature, there cannot be supposed any such subordination among us that may authorize us to destroy another, as if we were made for one another's uses, as the inferior ranks of creatures are for ours. Every one, as he is bound to preserve himself, and not to quit his station wilfully, so by the like reason, when his own preservation comes not in competition, ought he, as much as he can, to preserve the rest of mankind, and may not, unless it be to do justice to an offender, take away or impair the life, or what tends to the preservation of life, the liberty, health, limb, or goods of another.

7. And that all men may be restrained from invading others' rights, and from doing hurt to one another, and the law of nature be observed, which willeth the peace and preservation of all mankind, the execution of the law of nature is, in that state, put into every man's hands, whereby every one has a right to punish the transgressors of that law to such a degree as may hinder its violation: for the law of nature would, as all other laws that concern men in this world, be in vain, if there were nobody that in the state of nature had a power to execute that law, and thereby preserve the innocent, and restrain offenders. And if any one in the state of nature may punish another for any evil he has done, every one may do so: for in that state of perfect equality, where naturally there is no superiority or jurisdiction of one over another, what any may do in prosecution of that law every one must needs have a right to do.

8. And thus, in the state of nature, one man comes by a power over another, but yet no absolute or arbitrary power to use a criminal, when he has got him in his hands, according to the passionate heats or boundless extravagancy of his own will; but only to retribute to him, so far as calm reason and conscience dictate, what is proportionate to his transgression; which is so much as may serve for reparation and restraint: for these two are the only reasons why one man may lawfully do harm to another, which is that we call punishment. In transgressing the law of nature, the offender declares himself to live by another rule than that of reason and common equity, which is that measure God has set to the actions of men for their mutual security; and so he becomes dangerous to mankind, the tie, which is to secure them from injury and violence, being slighted and broken by him: which being a trespass against the whole species, and the peace and safety of it, provided for by the law of nature; every man upon this score, by the right he hath to preserve mankind in general, may restrain, or, where it is necessary, destroy things noxious to them, and so may bring such evil on any one, who hath transgressed that law, as may make him repent the doing of it, and thereby deter him, and by his example others,

from doing the like mischief. And in this case, and upon this ground, every man hath a right to punish the offender, and be executioner of the law of nature.

9. I doubt not but this will seem a very strange doctrine to some men: but, before they condemn it, I desire them to resolve me by what right any prince or state can put to death or punish an alien for any crime he commits in their country? It is certain their laws, by virtue of any sanction they receive from the promulgated will of the legislative, reach not a stranger: they speak not to him, nor, if they did, is he bound to hearken to them. The legislative authority, by which they are in force over the subjects of that commonwealth, hath no power over him. Those who have the supreme power of making laws in England, France, or Holland, are to an Indian but like the rest of the world, men without authority: and therefore, if by the law of nature every man hath not a power to punish offences against it, as he soberly judges the case to require, I see not how the magistrates of any community can punish an alien of another country; since, in reference to him, they can have no more power than what every man naturally may have over another.

10. Besides the crime which consists in violating the law, and varying from the right rule of reason, whereby a man so far becomes degenerate, and declares himself to quit the principles of human nature, and to be a noxious creature, there is commonly injury done to some person or other, and some other man receives damage by his transgression: in which case he who hath received any damage, has, besides the right of punishment common to him with other men, a particular right to seek reparation from him that has done it: and any other person, who finds it just, may also join with him that is injured, and assist him in recovering from the offender so much as may make satisfaction for the harm he has suffered.

11. From these two distinct rights, the one of punishing the crime for restraint, and preventing the like offence, which right of punishing is in every body; the other of taking reparation, which belongs only to the injured party; comes it to pass that the magistrate, who by being magistrate hath the common right of punishing put into his hands, can often, where the public good demands not the execution of the law, remit the punishment of criminal offences by his own authority, but yet cannot remit the satisfaction due to any private man for the damage he has received. That he who has suffered the damage has a right to demand in his own name, and he alone can remit: the damnified person has this power of appropriating to himself the goods or service of the offender, by right of self-preservation, as every man has a power to punish the crime, to prevent its being committed again, by the right he has of preserving all mankind, and doing all reasonable things he can in order to that end: and thus it is that every man, in the state of nature, has a power to kill a murderer, both to deter others from doing the like injury, which no reparation can compensate, by the example of the punishment that attends it from every body; and also to secure men from the attempts of a criminal, who having renounced reason, the common rule and measure God hath given to mankind, hath, by the unjust violence and slaughter he hath committed upon one, declared war against all mankind; and therefore may be destroyed as a lion or a tiger, one of those wild savage beasts with whom men can have no society nor security: and upon this is grounded that great law of nature, "Whoso sheddeth man's blood, by man shall his blood be shed." And Cain was so fully convinced that every one had a right to destroy such a criminal, that, after the murder of his brother, he cries out, "Every one that findeth me shall slay me," so plain was it writ in the hearts of all mankind.

12. By the same reason may a man in the state of nature punish the lesser breaches of that law. It will perhaps be demanded, with death? I answer, each transgression may be punished to that degree, and with so much severity, as will suffice to make it an ill bargain to the offender, give him cause to repent, and terrify others from doing the like. Every offence that

can be committed in the state of nature, may in the state of nature be also punished equally, and as far forth, as it may in a commonwealth: for though it would be beside my present purpose to enter here into the particulars of the law of nature, or its measures of punishment, yet it is certain there is such a law, and that too as intelligible and plain to a rational creature, and a studier of that law, as the positive laws of commonwealths; nay, possibly plainer, as much as reason is easier to be understood than the fancies and intricate contrivances of men, following contrary and hidden interests put into words; for so truly are a great part of the municipal laws of countries, which are only so far right, as they are founded on the law of nature, by which they are to be regulated and interpreted.

13. To this strange doctrine, viz. That in the state of nature every one has the executive power of the law of nature, I doubt not but it will be objected, that it is unreasonable for men to be judges in their own cases, that self-love will make men partial to themselves and their friends: and, on the other side, that ill-nature, passion, and revenge will carry them too far in punishing others; and hence nothing but confusion and disorder will follow: and that therefore God hath certainly appointed government to restrain the partiality and violence of men. I easily grant, that civil government is the proper remedy for the inconveniencies of the state of nature, which must certainly be great, where men may be judges in their own case; since it is easy to be imagined, that he who was so unjust as to do his brother an injury, will scarce be so just as to condemn himself for it: but I shall desire those who make this objection to remember, that absolute monarchs are but men; and if government is to be the remedy of those evils, which necessarily follow from men's being judges in their own cases, and the state of nature is therefore not to be endured; I desire to know what kind of government that is, and how much better it is than the state of nature, where one man, commanding a multitude, has the liberty to be judge in his own case, and may do to all his subjects whatever he pleases, without the least liberty to any one to question or control those who execute his pleasure? and in whatsoever he doth, whether led by reason, mistake, or passion, must be submitted to? Much better it is in the state of nature, wherein men are not bound to submit to the unjust will of another: and if he that judges, judges amiss in his own, or any other case, he is answerable for it to the rest of mankind.

14. It is often asked, as a mighty objection, "where are or ever were there any men in such a state of nature?" To which it may suffice as an answer at present, that since all princes and rulers of independent governments, all through the world, are in a state of nature, it is plain the world never was, nor never will be, without numbers of men in that state. I have named all governors of independent communities, whether they are, or are not, in league with others: for it is not every compact that puts an end to the state of nature between men, but only this one of agreeing together mutually to enter into one community, and make one body politic; other promises and compacts men may make one with another, and yet still be in the state of nature. The promises and bargains for truck, etc., between the two men in the desert island, mentioned by Garcilasso de la Vega, in his history of Peru; or between a Swiss and an Indian, in the woods of America; are binding to them, though they are perfectly in a state of nature, in reference to one another: for truth and keeping of faith belongs to men as men, and not as members of society.

15. To those that say, there were never any men in the state of nature, I . . . affirm, that all men are naturally in that state, and remain so, till by their own consents they make themselves members of some politic society; and I doubt not in the sequel of this discourse to make it very clear. . . .

OF PROPERTY

. . .

26. God, who hath given the world to men in common, hath also given them reason to make use of it to the best advantage of life and conve-

nience. The earth, and all that is therein, is given to men for the support and comfort of their being. And though all the fruits it naturally produces, and beasts it feeds, belong to mankind in common, as they are produced by the spontaneous hand of nature; and nobody has originally a private dominion, exclusive of the rest of mankind, in any of them, as they are thus in their natural state: yet being given for the use of men, there must of necessity be a means to appropriate them some way or other before they can be of any use, or at all beneficial to any particular man. The fruit, or venison, which nourishes the wild Indian, who knows no enclosure, and is still a tenant in common, must be his, and so his, *i.e.*, a part of him, that another can no longer have any right to it, before it can do him any good for the support of his life.

27. Though the earth, and all inferior creatures, be common to all men, yet every man has a property in his own person: this nobody has any right to but himself. The labour of his body, and the work of his hands, we may say, are properly his. Whatsoever then, he removes out of the state that nature hath provided, and left it in, he hath mixed his labour with, and joined to it something that is his own, and thereby makes it his property. It being by him removed from the common state nature hath placed it in, it hath by this labour something annexed to it that excludes the common right of other men. For this labour being the unquestionable property of the labourer, no man but he can have a right to what that is once joined to, at least where there is enough, and as good, left in common for others.

28. He that is nourished by the acorns he picked up under an oak, or the apples he gathered from the trees in the wood, has certainly appropriated them to himself. Nobody can deny but the nourishment is his. I ask then, when did they begin to be his? when he digested? or when he ate? or when he boiled? or when he brought them home? or when he picked them up? and it is plain, if the first gathering made them not his, nothing else could. That labour put a distinction between them and common: that added something to them more than nature, the common mother of all, had done; and so they became his private right. And will any one say, he had no right to those acorns or apples he thus appropriated, because he had not the consent of all mankind to make them his? Was it a robbery thus to assume to himself what belonged to all in common? If such a consent as that was necessary, man had starved, notwithstanding the plenty God had given him. We see in commons, which remain so by compact, that it is the taking any part of what is common, and removing it out of the state nature leaves it in, which begins the property; without which the common is of no use. And the taking of this or that part does not depend on the express consent of all the commoners. Thus the grass my horse has bit; the turfs my servant has cut; and the ore I have digged in any place, where I have a right to them in common with others; become my property, without the assignation or consent of any body. The labour that was mine, removing them out of that common state they were in, hath fixed my property in them.

29. By making an explicit consent of every commoner necessary to any one's appropriating to himself any part of what is given in common, children or servants could not cut the meat, which their father or master had provided for them in common, without assigning to every one his peculiar part. Though the water running in the fountain be every one's, yet who can doubt but that in the pitcher is his only who drew it out? His labour hath taken it out of the hands of nature, where it was common, and belonged equally to all her children, and hath thereby appropriated it to himself.

30. Thus this law of reason makes the deer that Indian's who hath killed it; it is allowed to be his goods who hath bestowed his labour upon it, though before it was the common right of every one. And amongst those who are counted the civilized part of mankind, who have made and multiplied positive laws to determine property, this original law of nature, for the beginning of property, in what was before common,

still takes place; and by virtue thereof, what fish any one catches in the ocean, that great and still remaining common of mankind; or what ambergris any one takes up here, is by the labour that removes it out of that common state nature left it in made his property who takes that pains about it. And even amongst us, the hare that any one is hunting is thought his who pursues her during the chase: for being a beast that is still looked upon as common, and no man's private possession; whoever has employed so much labour about any of that kind, as to find and pursue her, has thereby removed her from the state of nature, wherein she was common, and hath begun a property.

31. It will perhaps be objected to this, that "if gathering the acorns, or other fruits of the earth, etc., makes a right to them, then any one may engross as much as he will." To which I answer, Not so. The same law of nature, that does by this means give us property, does also bound that property too. "God has given us all things richly," 1 Tim. vi 17, is the voice of reason confirmed by inspiration. But how far has he given it us? To enjoy. As much as any one can make use of to any advantage of life before it spoils, so much he may by his labour fix a property in: whatever is beyond this, is more than his share, and belongs to others. Nothing was made by God for man to spoil or destroy. And thus, considering the plenty of natural provisions there was a long time in the world, and the few spenders; and to how small a part of that provision the industry of one man could extend itself, and engross it to the prejudice of others; especially keeping within the bounds, set by reason, of what might serve for his use; there could be then little room for quarrels or contentions about property so established.

32. But the chief matter of property being now not the fruits of the earth, and the beasts that subsist on it, but the earth itself; as that which takes in, and carries with it all the rest; I think it is plain, that property in that too is acquired as the former. As much land as a man tills, plants, improves, cultivates, and can use the product of, so much is his property. He by his labour does, as it were, enclose it from the common. Nor will it invalidate his right, to say every body else has an equal title to it, and therefore he cannot appropriate, he cannot enclose, without the consent of all his fellow-commoners, all mankind. God, when he gave the world in common to all mankind, commanded man also to labour, and the penury of his condition required it of him. God and his reason commanded him to subdue the earth, *i.e.*, improve it for the benefit of life, and therein lay out something upon it that was his own, his labour. He that, in obedience to this command of God, subdued, tilled, and sowed any part of it, thereby annexed to it something that was his property, which another had no title to, nor could without injury take from him.

33. Nor was this appropriation of any parcel of land, by improving it, any prejudice to any other man, since there was still enough, and as good left; and more than the yet unprovided could use. So that, in effect, there was never the less left for others because of his enclosure for himself: for he that leaves as much as another can make use of, does as good as take nothing at all. Nobody could think himself injured by the drinking of another man, though he took a good draught, who had a whole river of the same water left him to quench his thirst; and the case of land and water, where there is enough of both, is perfectly the same.

34. God gave the world to men in common; but since he gave it them for their benefit, and the greatest conveniencies of life they were capable to draw from it, it cannot be supposed he meant it should always remain common and uncultivated. He gave it to the use of the industrious and rational (and labour was to be his title to it), not to the fancy or covetousness of the quarrelsome and contentious. He that had as good left for his improvement as was already taken up, needed not complain, ought not to meddle with what was already improved by another's labour: if he did, it is plain he desired the benefit of another's pains, which he had no right to, and not the ground which God had given him in common with others to labour on,

and whereof there was as good left as that already possessed, and more than he knew what to do with, or his industry could reach to.

35. It is true, in land that is common in England, or any other country, where there are plenty of people under government, who have money and commerce, no one can enclose or appropriate any part without the consent of all his fellow-commoners; because this is left common by compact, *i.e.*, by the law of the land, which is not to be violated. And though it be common, in respect of some men, it is not so to all mankind, but is the joint property of this county, or this parish. Besides, the remainder, after such enclosure, would not be as good to the rest of the commoners as the whole was when they could all make use of the whole; whereas in the beginning and first peopling of the great common of the world it was quite otherwise. The law man was under was rather for appropriating. God commanded, and his wants forced him to labour. That was his property which could not be taken from him wherever he had fixed it. And hence subduing or cultivating the earth, and having dominion, we see are joined together. The one gave title to the other. So that God, by commanding to subdue, gave authority so far to appropriate: and the condition of human life, which requires labour and materials to work on, necessarily introduces private possessions.

36. The measure of property nature has well set by the extent of men's labour and the conveniencies of life: no man's labour could subdue, or appropriate all; nor could his enjoyment consume more than a small part; so that it was impossible for any man, this way, to entrench upon the right of another, or acquire to himself a property, to the prejudice of his neighbour, who would still have room for as good and as large a possession (after the other had taken out his) as before it was appropriated. This measure did confine every man's possession to a very moderate proportion, and such as he might appropriate to himself, without injury to any body, in the first ages of the world, when men were more in danger to be lost, by wandering from their company, in the then vast wilderness of the earth, than to be straitened for want of room to plant in. . . .

40. . . . It is labour indeed that put the difference of value on every thing; and let any one consider what the difference is between an acre of land planted with tobacco or sugar, sown with wheat or barley, and an acre of the same land lying in common, without any husbandry upon it, and he will find, that the improvement of labour makes the far greater part of the value. I think it will be but a very modest computation to say, that of the products of the earth useful to the life of man, nine-tenths are the effects of labour: nay, if we will rightly estimate things as they come to our use, and cast up the several expenses about them, what in them is purely owing to nature, and what to labour, we shall find, that in most of them ninety-nine hundredths are wholly to be put on the account of labour.

41. There cannot be a clearer demonstration of any thing, than several nations of the Americans are of this, who are rich in land, and poor in all the comforts of life; whom nature having furnished as liberally as any other people with the materials of plenty, *i.e.*, a fruitful soil, apt to produce in abundance; yet, for want of improving it by labour, have not one-hundredth part of the conveniencies we enjoy: and a king of a large and fruitful territory there feeds, lodges, and is clad worse than a day-labourer in England.

42. To make this a little clearer, let us but trace some of the ordinary provisions of life, through their several progresses, before they come to our use, and see how much of their value they receive from human industry. Bread, wine, and cloth, are things of daily use, and great plenty; yet notwithstanding, acorns, water, and leaves, or skins, must be our bread, drink, and clothing, did not labour furnish us with these more useful commodities: for whatever bread is more worth than acorns, wine than water, and cloth or silk than leaves, skins, or moss, that is wholly owing to labour and industry; the one of these being the food and rai-

ment which unassisted nature furnishes us with; the other, provisions which our industry and pains prepare for us; which, how much they exceed the other in value, when any one hath computed, he will then see how much labour makes the far greatest part of the value of things we enjoy in this world: and the ground which produces the materials is scarce to be reckoned in as any, or, at most, but a very small part of it; so little, that even amongst us, land that is left wholly to nature, that hath no improvement of pasturage, tillage, or planting, is called, as indeed it is, waste; and we shall find the benefit of it amount to little more than nothing.

This shows how much numbers of men are to be preferred to largeness of dominions; and that the increase of lands, and the right of employing of them, is the great art of government: and that prince, who shall be so wise and godlike, as by established laws of liberty to secure protection and encouragement to the honest industry of mankind, against the oppression of power and narrowness of party, will quickly be too hard for his neighbours: but this by the by. To return to the argument in hand.

43. An acre of land, that bears here twenty bushels of wheat, and another in America, which, with the same husbandry, would do the like, are, without doubt, of the same natural intrinsic value: but yet the benefit mankind receives from the one in a year is worth 5£. and from the other possibly not worth a penny, if all the profit an Indian received from it were to be valued, and sold here; at least, I may truly say, not one thousandth. It is labour, then, which puts the greatest part of value upon land, without which it would scarcely be worth any thing: it is to that we owe the greatest part of all its useful products; for all that the straw, bran, bread, of that acre of wheat, is more worth than the product of an acre of as good land, which lies waste, is all the effect of labour: for it is not barely the ploughman's pains, the reaper's and thresher's toil, and the baker's sweat, is to be counted into the bread we eat; the labour of those who broke the oxen, who digged and wrought the iron and stones, who felled and framed the timber employed about the plough, mill, oven, or any other utensils, which are a vast number, requisite to this corn, from its being seed to be sown to its being made bread, must all be charged on the account of labour, and received as an effect of that: nature and the earth furnished only the almost worthless materials, as in themselves. It would be a strange catalogue of things, that industry provided and made use of, about every loaf of bread, before it came to our use, if we could trace them; iron, wood, leather, bark, timber, stone, bricks, coals, lime, cloth, dyeing, drugs, pitch, tar, masts, ropes, and all the materials made use of in the ship, that brought any of the commodities used by any of the workmen, to any part of the work, all which it would be almost impossible, at least too long, to reckon up.

44. From all which it is evident, that though the things of nature are given in common, yet man, by being master of himself, and proprietor of his own person, and the actions or labour of it, had still in himself the great foundation of property; and that which made up the greater part of what he applied to the support or comfort of his being, when invention and arts had improved the conveniencies of life, was perfectly his own, and did not belong in common to others.

45. Thus labour, in the beginning, gave a right of property, wherever any one was pleased to employ it, upon what was common, which remained a long while the far greater part, and is yet more than mankind makes use of. Men, at first, for the most part, contented themselves with what unassisted nature offered to their necessities: and though afterwards, in some parts of the world, (where the increase of people and stock, with the use of money, had made land scarce, and so of some value) the several communities settled the bounds of their distinct territories, and by laws within themselves regulated the properties of the private men of their society, and so, by compact and agreement, settled the property which labour and industry began: and the leagues that have been made between several states and kingdoms, either

expressly or tacitly disowning all claim and right to the land in the others' possession, have, by common consent, given up their pretences to their natural common right, which originally they had to those countries, and so have, by positive agreement, settled a property amongst themselves, in distinct parts and parcels of the earth; yet there are still great tracts of ground to be found, which (the inhabitants thereof not having joined with the rest of mankind in the consent of the use of their common money) lie waste, and are more than the people who dwell on it do or can make use of, and so still lie in common; though this can scarce happen amongst that part of mankind that have consented to the use of money.

46. The greatest part of things really useful to the life of man, and such as the necessity of subsisting made the first commoners of the world look after, as it doth the Americans now, are generally things of short duration; such as, if they are not consumed by use, will decay and perish of themselves: gold, silver, and diamonds, are things that fancy or agreement hath put the value on, more than real use, and the necessary support of life. Now of those good things which nature hath provided in common, every one had a right (as hath been said) to as much as he could use, and had property in all that he could effect with his labour; all that his industry could extend to, to alter from the state nature had put it in, was his. He that gathered a hundred bushels of acorns or apples, had thereby a property in them; they were his goods as soon as gathered. He was only to look that he used them before they spoiled, else he took more than his share, and robbed others. And indeed it was a foolish thing, as well as dishonest, to hoard up more than he could make use of. If he gave away a part to any body else, so that it perished not uselessly in his possession, these he also made use of. And if he also bartered away plums, that would have rotted in a week, for nuts that would last good for his eating a whole year, he did no injury; he wasted not the common stock; destroyed no part of the portion of goods that belonged to others, so long as nothing perished uselessly in his hands. Again, if he would give his nuts for a piece of metal, pleased with its colour; or exchange his sheep for shells, or wool for a sparkling pebble or a diamond, and keep those by him all his life, he invaded not the right of others; he might heap as much of these durable things as he pleased; the exceeding of the bounds of his just property not lying in the largeness of his possession, but the perishing of any thing uselessly in it.

47. And thus came in the use of money, some lasting thing that men might keep without spoiling, and that by mutual consent men would take in exchange for the truly useful, but perishable supports of life.

48. And as different degrees of industry were apt to give men possessions in different proportions, so this invention of money gave them the opportunity to continue and enlarge them. . . .

51. And thus, I think, it is very easy to conceive, how labour could at first begin a title of property in the common things of nature, and how the spending it upon our uses bounded it. . . . This left no room for controversy about the title, nor for encroachment on the right of others; what portion a man carved to himself was easily seen: and it was useless, as well as dishonest, to carve himself too much, or take more than he needed. . . .

OF THE DISSOLUTION OF GOVERNMENT

222. The reason why men enter into society is the preservation of their property; and the end why they choose and authorize a legislative is, that there may be laws made, and rules set, as guards and fences to the properties of all the members of the society: to limit the power, and moderate the dominion, of every part and member of the society: for since it can never be supposed to be the will of the society that the legislative should have a power to destroy that which every one designs to secure by entering into society, and for which the people submitted them-

selves to legislators of their own making; whenever the legislators endeavour to take away and destroy the property of the people, or to reduce them to slavery under arbitrary power, they put themselves into a state of war with the people, who are thereupon absolved from any farther obedience, and are left to the common refuge, which God hath provided for all men, against force and violence. Whensoever therefore the legislative shall transgress this fundamental rule of society; and either by ambition, fear, folly, or corruption, endeavour to grasp themselves, or put into the hands of any other, an absolute power over the lives, liberties, and estates of the people; by this breach of trust they forfeit the power the people had put into their hands for quite contrary ends, and it devolves to the people, who have a right to resume their original liberty, and, by the establishment of a new legislative, (such as they shall think fit), provide for their own safety and security, which is the end for which they are in society. What I have said here, concerning the legislative in general, holds true also concerning the supreme executor, who having a double trust put in him, both to have a part in the legislative, and the supreme execution of the law, acts against both, when he goes about to set up his own arbitrary will as the law of the society. He acts also contrary to his trust, when he either employs the force, treasure, and offices of the society to corrupt the representatives, and gain them to his purposes; or openly pre-engages the electors, and prescribes to their choice, such, whom he has, by solicitations, threats, promises, or otherwise, won to his designs; and employs them to bring in such, who have promised beforehand what to vote, and what to enact. Thus to regulate candidates and electors, and new-model the ways of election, what is it but to cut up the government by the roots, and poison the very fountain of public security? for the people having reserved to themselves the choice of their representatives, as the fence to their properties, could do it for no other end, but that they might always be freely chosen, and so chosen, freely act, and advise, as the necessity of the commonwealth and the public good should, upon examination and mature debate, be judged to require. This, those who give their votes before they hear the debate, and have weighed the reasons on all sides, are not capable of doing. To prepare such an assembly as this, and endeavour to set up the declared abettors of his own will, for the true representatives of the people, and the law-makers of the society, is certainly as great a breach of trust, and as perfect a declaration of a design to subvert the government, as is possible to be met with. To which if one shall add rewards and punishments visibly employed to the same end, and all the arts of perverted law made use of, to take off and destroy all that stand in the way of such a design, and will not comply and consent to betray the liberties of their country, it will be past doubt what is doing. What power they ought to have in the society, who thus employ it contrary to the trust that went along with it in its first institution, is easy to determine; and one cannot but see, that he, who has once attempted any such thing as this, cannot any longer be trusted. . . .

224. . . . The people generally ill-treated, and contrary to right, will be ready upon any occasion to ease themselves of a burden that sits heavy upon them. They will wish, and seek for the opportunity, which in the change, weakness, and accidents of human affairs, seldom delays long to offer itself. He must have lived but a little while in the world, who has not seen examples of this in his time; and he must have read very little, who cannot produce examples of it in all sorts of governments in the world.

225. Such revolutions happen . . . not upon every little mismanagement in public affairs. Great mistakes in the ruling part, many wrong and inconvenient laws, and all the slips of human frailty, will be borne by the people without mutiny or murmur. But if a long train of abuses, prevarications, and artifices, all tending the same way, make the design visible to the people, and they cannot but feel what they lie under, and see whither they are going; it is not to be wondered, that they should then rouse themselves, and endeavour to put the rule into

such hands which may secure to them the ends for which government was at first erected, and without which, ancient names, and specious forms, are so far from being better, that they are much worse, than the state of nature, or pure anarchy; the inconveniencies, being all as great and as hear, but the remedy farther off and more difficult.

13

GOVERNMENT, RIGHTS, AND THE BONDS BETWEEN GENERATIONS

THOMAS PAINE

Although he spent his first 38 years in Great Britain, Thomas Paine (1737–1809) is most often associated with the American and French revolutions. Paine moved to Pennsylvania in 1775, and in February of the following year he published a pamphlet, *Common Sense*, that urged the colonists to declare themselves independent of Britain. He later moved to France, where he actively supported the French Revolution. The second selection is from *The Rights of Man* (1791, 1792), which Paine wrote to defend the revolution against Edmund Burke's *Reflections on the Revolution in France* (see Part IV, selection 23).

Sources: Common Sense, *from* The Life and Writings of Thomas Paine, *vol.2, ed. Daniel Edwin Wheeler (New York: Vincent Parke and Co., 1915), pp. 1–7; and* The Rights of Man: Being an Answer to Mr. Burke's Attack on the French Revolution *(Dublin: G. Burnet, R. Cross, P. Wogan et al., 1791), pp. 8–9.*

COMMON SENSE

Some writers have so confounded society with government, as to leave little or no distinction between them; whereas they are not only different, but have different origins. Society is produced by our wants, and government by our wickedness; the former promotes our happiness *positively* by uniting our affections, the latter *negatively* by restraining our vices. The one encourages intercourse, the other creates distinctions. The first is a patron, the last a punisher.

Society in every state is a blessing, but government even in its best state is but a necessary evil; in its worst state an intolerable one; for when we suffer, or are exposed to the same miseries *by a government*, which we might expect in a country *without government*, our calamities are heightened by reflecting that we furnish the means by which we suffer. Government, like dress, is the badge of lost innocence; the palaces of kings are built on the ruins of the bowers of paradise. For were the impulses of conscience clear, uniform, and irresistibly obeyed, man would need no other lawgiver; but that not being the case, he finds it necessary to surrender up a part of his property to furnish means for the protection of the rest; and this he is induced to do by the same prudence which in every other case advises him out of two evils to choose the least. *Wherefore*, security being the true design and end of government, it unanswerably follows that whatever *form* thereof appears most likely to ensure it to us, with the least expense and greatest benefit, is preferable to all others.

In order to gain a clear and just idea of the design and end of government, let us suppose a small number of persons settled in some sequestered part of the earth, unconnected with the rest, they will then represent the first peopling of any country, or of the world. In this state of natural liberty, society will be their first thought. A thousand motives will excite them thereto, the strength of one man is so unequal to his wants, and his mind so unfitted for perpetual solitude, that he is soon obliged to seek assistance and relief of another, who in his turn requires the same. Four or five united would be able to raise a tolerable dwelling in the midst of a wilderness, but *one* man might labour out the common period of life without accomplishing any thing; when he had felled his timber he could not remove it, nor erect it after it was removed; hunger in the mean time would urge him from his work, and every different want call him a different way. Disease, nay even misfortune, would be death, for though neither might be mortal, yet either would disable him from living, and reduce him to a state in which he might rather be said to perish than to die.

Thus necessity, like a gravitating power, would soon form our newly arrived emigrants into society, the reciprocal blessings of which would supersede and render the obligations of law and government unnecessary while they remained perfectly just to each other; but as nothing but heaven is impregnable to vice, it will unavoidably happen, that in proportion as they surmount the first difficulties of emigration, which bound them together in a common cause, they will begin to relax in their duty and attachment to each other; and this remissness, will point out the necessity, of establishing some form of government to supply the defect of moral virtue.

Some convenient tree will afford them a State-House, under the branches of which, the whole colony may assemble to deliberate on public matters. It is more than probable that their first laws will have the title only of REGULATIONS, and be enforced by no other penalty than public disesteem. In this first parliament every man, by natural right will have a seat.

But as the colony increases, the public concerns will increase likewise, and the distance at which the members may be separated, will render it too inconvenient for all of them to meet on every occasion as at first, when their number was small, their habitations near, and the public concerns few and trifling. This will point out the convenience of their consenting to leave the legislative part to be managed by a select number chosen from the whole body, who are supposed to have the same concerns at stake which those have who appointed them, and who will act in the same manner as the whole body would act were they present. If the colony continue increasing, it will become necessary to augment the number of the representatives, and that the interest of every part of the colony may be attended to, it will be found best to divide the whole into convenient parts, each part sending its proper number; and that the *elected* might never form to themselves an interest separate from the *electors*, prudence will point out the propriety of having elections often; because as the *elected* might by that means return and mix again with the general body of the *electors* in a few months, their fidelity to the public will be secured by the prudent reflection of not making a rod for themselves. And as this frequent interchange will establish a common interest with every part of the community, they will mutually and naturally support each other, and on this (not on the unmeaning name of king) depends the *strength of government, and the happiness of the governed.*

Here then is the origin and rise of government; namely, a mode rendered necessary by the inability of moral virtue to govern the world; here too is the design and end of government, viz. freedom and security. And however our eyes may be dazzled with snow, or our ears deceived by sound; however prejudice may warp our wills, or interest darken our understanding, the simple voice of nature and of reason will say, it is right.

I draw my idea of the form of government from a principle in nature, which no art can overturn, viz. that the more simple any thing is, the less liable it is to be disordered, and the easier repaired when disordered; and with this maxim in view, I offer a few remarks on the so much boasted constitution of England. That it was noble for the dark and slavish times in which it was erected is granted. When the world was overrun with tyranny the least remove therefrom was a glorious rescue. But that it is imperfect, subject to convulsions, and incapable of producing what it seems to promise, is easily demonstrated.

Absolute governments (tho' the disgrace of human nature) have this advantage with them, that they are simple; if the people suffer, they know the head from which their suffering springs, know likewise the remedy, and are not bewildered by a variety of causes and cures. . . .

There is something exceedingly ridiculous in the composition of monarchy; it first excludes a man from the means of information, yet empowers him to act in cases where the highest judgement is required. The state of a king shuts him from the world, yet the business of a king requires him to know it thoroughly; wherefore the different parts, unnaturally opposing and destroying each other, prove the whole character to be absurd and useless.

THE RIGHTS OF MAN

. . .

Every age and generation must be as free to act for itself, *in all cases*, as the ages and generation which preceded it. The vanity and presumption of governing beyond the grave, is the most ridiculous and insolent of all tyrannies.

Man has no property in man; neither has any generation a property in the generations which are to follow. The Parliament or the people of 1688, or of any other period, had no more right to dispose of the people of the present day, or to bind or to control them *in any shape whatever*, than the Parliament or the people of the present day have to dispose of, bind, or control those who are to live a hundred or a thousand years hence.

Every generation is, and must be, competent

to all the purposes which its occasions require. It is the living, and not the dead, that are to be accommodated. When man ceases to be, his power and his wants cease with him; and having no longer any participation in the concerns of this world, he has no longer any authority in directing who shall be its governors, or how its government shall be organized, or how administered.

I am not contending for nor against any form of government, nor for nor against any party here or elsewhere. That which a whole nation chooses to do, it has a right to do. Mr. Burke says, No. Where then *does* the right exist? I am contending for the rights of the *living*, and against their being willed away, and controlled and contracted for, by the manuscript assumed authority of the dead; and Mr. Burke is contending for the authority of the dead over the rights and freedom of the living.

There was a time when kings disposed of their crowns by will upon their death-beds, and consigned the people, like beasts of the field, to whatever successor they appointed. This is now so exploded as scarcely to be remembered, and so monstrous as hardly to be believed. But the parliamentary clauses upon which Mr. Burke builds his political church, are of the same nature.

The laws of every country must be analogous to some common principle. In England, no parent or master, nor all the authority of Parliament, omnipotent as it has called itself, can bind or control the personal freedom even of an individual beyond the age of twenty-one years. On what ground of right, then, could the Parliament of 1688, or any other parliament, bind all posterity for ever?

Those who have quitted the world, and those who are not yet arrived in it, are as remote from each other, as the utmost stretch of moral imagination can conceive. What possible obligation, then, can exist between them; what rule or principle can be laid down, that two nonentities, the one out of existence, and the other not in, and who never can meet in this world, that the one should control the other to the end of time?

14

DECLARATION OF INDEPENDENCE OF THE UNITED STATES

On June 7, 1776 Richard Henry Lee, a representative to the Continental Congress from Virginia, introduced a resolution proclaiming that "these United Colonies are, and of right ought to be, free and independent States. . . ." Three days later Congress appointed a committee to prepare a declaration of independence. One member of the committee, Thomas Jefferson (1743–1826), wrote the initial draft, which the other members of the committee and then the Congress as a whole modified. Jefferson later characterized the Declaration in this way: "Neither aiming at originality of principle or sentiment, nor yet copied from any particular and previous writing, it was intended to be an expression of the American mind. . . ."

THE UNANIMOUS DECLARATION OF THE THIRTEEN UNITED STATES OF AMERICA

When in the Course of human events, it becomes necessary for one people to dissolve the political bands which have connected them with another, and to assume among the Powers of the earth, the separate and equal station to which the Laws of Nature and of Nature's God entitle them, a decent respect to the opinions of mankind requires that they should declare the causes which impel them to the separation.

We hold these truths to be self-evident, that all men are created equal, that they are endowed by their Creator with certain unalienable Rights, that among these are Life, Liberty and the pursuit of Happiness. That to secure these rights, Governments are instituted among Men, deriving their just powers from the consent of the governed. That whenever any Form of Government becomes destructive of these ends, it is the Right of the People to alter or to abolish it, and to institute new Government, laying its foundation on such principles and organizing its powers in such form, as to them shall seem most likely to effect their Safety and Happiness. Prudence, indeed, will dictate that Governments long established should not be changed for light and transient causes; and accordingly all experience hath shown, that mankind are more disposed to suffer, while evils are sufferable, than to right themselves by abolishing the forms to which they are accustomed. But when a long train of abuses and usurpations, pursuing invariably the same Object evinces a design to reduce them under absolute Despotism, it is their right, it is their duty, to throw off such Government, and to provide new Guards for their future security—Such has been the patient sufferance of these Colonies; and such is now the necessity which constrains them to alter their former Systems of Government. The history of the present King of Great Britain is a history of repeated injuries and usurpations, all having in direct object the establishment of an absolute Tyranny over these States. To prove this, let Facts be submitted to a candid world.

He has refused his Assent to Laws, the most wholesome and necessary for the public good.

He has forbidden his Governors to pass Laws of immediate and pressing importance, unless suspended in their operation till his Assent should be obtained; and when so suspended, he has utterly neglected to attend to them.

He has refused to pass other Laws for the accommodation of large districts of people, unless those people would relinquish the right of Representation in the Legislature, a right inestimable to them and formidable to tyrants only.

He has called together legislative bodies at places unusual, uncomfortable, and distant from the depository of their Public Records, for the sole purpose of fatiguing them into compliance with his measures.

He has dissolved Representative Houses repeatedly, for opposing with manly firmness his invasions on the rights of the people.

He has refused for a long time, after such dissolutions, to cause others to be elected; whereby the Legislative Powers, incapable of Annihilation, have returned to the People at large for their exercise; the State remaining in the mean time exposed to all the dangers of invasion from without, and convulsions within.

He has endeavoured to prevent the population of these States; for that purpose obstructing the Laws of Naturalization of Foreigners; refusing to pass others to encourage their migration hither, and raising the conditions of new Appropriations of Lands.

He has obstructed the Administration of Justice, by refusing his Assent to Laws for establishing Judiciary Powers.

He has made Judges dependent on his Will alone, for the tenure of their offices, and the amount and payment of their salaries.

He has erected a multitude of New Offices,

and sent hither swarms of Officers to harass our People, and eat out their substance.

He has kept among us, in times of peace, Standing Armies without the Consent of our legislature.

He has affected to render the Military independent of and superior to the Civil Power.

He has combined with others to subject us to a jurisdiction foreign to our constitution, and unacknowledged by our laws; giving his Assent to their acts of pretended legislation:

For quartering large bodies of armed troops among us:

For protecting them, by a mock Trial, from Punishment for any Murders which they should commit on the Inhabitants of these States:

For cutting off our Trade with all parts of the world:

For imposing taxes on us without our Consent:

For depriving us in many cases, of the benefits of Trial by Jury:

For transporting us beyond Seas to be tried for pretended offences:

For abolishing the free System of English Laws in a neighbouring Province, establishing therein an Arbitrary government, and enlarging its Boundaries so as to render it at once an example and fit instrument for introducing the same absolute rule into these Colonies:

For taking away our Charters, abolishing our most valuable Laws, and altering fundamentally the Forms of our Governments:

For suspending our own Legislature, and declaring themselves invested with Power to legislate for us in all cases whatsoever.

He has abdicated Government here, by declaring us out of his Protection and waging War against us.

He has plundered our seas, ravaged our Coasts, burnt our towns, and destroyed the lives of our people.

He is at this time transporting large armies of foreign mercenaries to compleat the works of death, desolation and tyranny, already begun with circumstances of Cruelty & perfidy scarcely paralleled in the most barbarous ages, and totally unworthy the Head of a civilized nation.

He has constrained our fellow Citizens taken Captive on the high Seas to bear Arms against their Country, to become the executioners of their friends and Brethren, or to fall themselves by their Hands.

He has excited domestic insurrections amongst us, and has endeavoured to bring on the inhabitants of our frontiers, the merciless Indian Savages, whose known rule of warfare, is an undistinguished destruction of all ages, sexes and conditions.

In every stage of these Oppressions We have Petitioned for Redress in the most humble terms: Our repeated Petitions have been answered only by repeated injury. A Prince, whose character is thus marked by every act which may define a Tyrant, is unfit to be the ruler of a free People.

Nor have We been wanting in attention to our British brethren. We have warned them from time to time of attempts by their legislature to extend an unwarrantable jurisdiction over us. We have reminded them of the circumstances of our emigration and settlement here. We have appealed to their native justice and magnanimity, and we have conjured them by the ties of our common kindred to disavow these usurpations, which, would inevitably interrupt our connections and correspondence. They too have been deaf to the voice of justice and of consanguinity. We must, therefore, acquiesce in the necessity, which denounces our Separation, and hold them, as we hold the rest of mankind, Enemies in War, in Peace Friends.

We, therefore, the Representatives of the united States of America, in General Congress, Assembled, appealing to the Supreme Judge of the world for the rectitude of our intentions, do, in the Name, and by Authority of the good People of these Colonies, solemnly publish and declare, That these United Colonies are, and of Right ought to be Free and Independent States; that they are Absolved from all Allegiance to the

British Crown, and that all political connection between them and the State of Great Britain, is and ought to be totally dissolved; and that as Free and Independent States, they have full Power to levy War, conclude Peace, contract Alliances, establish Commerce, and to do all other Acts and Things which Independent States may of right do. And for the support of this Declaration, with a firm reliance on the Protection of Divine Providence, we mutually pledge to each other our Lives, our Fortunes and our sacred Honor.

15

DECLARATION OF THE RIGHTS OF MAN AND OF CITIZENS

In 1788, faced with a financial crisis, King Louis XVI of France called the Estates-General into session for the first time in over 170 years. The traditional representative body of France, the Estates-General consisted of representatives of the Church, the nobility, and the people. When the Estates-General convened in 1789, the representatives of the Third Estate (the people) defied the king and declared themselves the National Assembly of France. As one of its first acts, the Assembly approved a declaration of rights that was to serve as the basis of a constitution. The Declaration appears here in Thomas Paine's translation, included in his book, *The Rights of Man* (see selection 13).

DECLARATION OF THE RIGHTS OF MAN AND OF CITIZENS

BY THE NATIONAL ASSEMBLY OF FRANCE

The representatives of the people of FRANCE, *formed into a* NATIONAL ASSEMBLY, considering that ignorance, neglect, or contempt of human rights, are the sole causes of public misfortunes and corruptions of government, have resolved to set forth in a solemn declaration, these natural, imprescriptible, and unalienable rights: that this declaration, being constantly present to the minds of the members of the body social, they may be ever kept attentive to their rights and their duties: that the acts of the legislative and executive powers of government, being capable of being every moment compared with the end of political institutions, may be more respected: and also, that the future claims of the citis, being directed by simple and incontestible principles, may always tend to the maintenance of the Constitution, and the general happiness.

For these reasons the NATIONAL ASSEMBLY doth recognize and declare, in the presence of the Supreme Being, and with the hope of His blessing and favor, the following *sacred* rights of men and of citizens:

I. *Men are born, and always continue, free, and equal in respect of their rights. Civil distinctions, therefore, can be founded only on public utility.*

II. *The end of all political associations, is, the preservation of the natural and imprescriptible rights of man; and these rights are liberty, property, security, and resistance of oppression.*

III. *The nation is essentially the source of all sovereignty; nor can any* INDIVIDUAL, *or* ANY BODY OF MEN, *be entitled to any authority which is not expressly derived from it.*

IV. Political liberty consists in the power of doing whatever does not injure another. The exercise of the natural rights of every man has no other limits than those which are necessary to secure to every *other* man the free exercise of the same rights; and these limits are determinable only by the law.

V. The law ought to prohibit only actions hurtful to society. What is not prohibited by the law, should not be hindered; nor should any one be compelled to that which the law does not require.

VI. The law is an expression of the will of the community. All citizens have a right to concur, either personally, or by their representatives, in its formation. It should be the same to all, whether it protects or punishes; and *all being equal in its sight, are equally eligible to all honors, places, and employments, according to their different abilities, without any other distinction than that created by their virtues and talents.*

VII. No man should be accused, arrested, or held in confinement, except in cases determined by the law, and according to the forms which it has prescribed. All who promote, solicit, execute, or cause to be executed, arbitrary orders, ought to be punished; and every citizen called upon or apprehended by virtue of the law, ought immediately to obey, and renders himself culpable by resistance.

VIII. The law ought to impose no other penalties but such as are absolutely and evidently necessary: and no one ought to be punished, but in virtue of a law promulgated before the offense, and legally applied.

IX. Every man being presumed innocent till he has been convicted, whenever his detention becomes indispensable, all rigor to him, more than is necessary to secure his person, ought to be provided against by the law.

X. No man ought to be molested on account of his opinions, not even on account of his *religious* opinions, provided his avowal of them does not disturb the public order established by the law.

XI. The unrestrained communication of thoughts and opinions being one of the most precious rights of man, every citizen may speak, write, and publish freely, provided he is responsible for the abuse of this liberty in cases determined by the law.

XII. A public force being necessary to give security to the rights of men and of citizens, that force is instituted for the benefit of the community, and not for the particular benefit of the persons with whom it is intrusted.

XIII. A common contribution being necessary for the support of the public force, and for defraying the other expenses of government, it ought to be divided equally among the members of the community, according to their abilities.

XIV. Every citizen has a right, either by himself or his representative, to a free voice in determining the necessity of public contributions, the appropriation of them, and their amount, mode of assessment, and duration.

XV. Every community has a right to demand of all its agents, an account of their conduct.

XVI. Every community in which a separation of powers and a security of rights is not provided for, wants a constitution.

XVII. The rights to property being inviolable and sacred, no one ought to be deprived of it, except in cases of evident public necessity, legally ascertained, and on condition of a previous just indemnity.

16

PRIVATE PROFIT, PUBLIC GOOD

ADAM SMITH

Although he was one of the major philosophers of the Scottish Enlightenment, Adam Smith (1723–1790) is best known for his work in political economy, notably his *An Inquiry into the Nature and Causes of the Wealth of Nations* (1776). Other writers had developed the laissez faire theory that government should leave people alone in the economic marketplace, but Smith provided the most thorough and influential defense of this doctrine.

Source: Adam Smith, An Inquiry into the Nature and Causes of the Wealth of Nations, *vol. 1 (London: T. Cadell and W. Davies, 1805), Book I, chapter 2, pp. 20–27.*

OF THE PRINCIPLE WHICH GIVES OCCASION TO THE DIVISION OF LABOR

THIS division of labor, from which so many advantages are derived, is not originally the effect of any human wisdom which foresees and intends that general opulence to which it gives occasion. It is the necessary, though very slow and gradual, consequence of a certain propensity in human nature which has in view no such extensive utility: the propensity to truck, barter, and exchange one thing for another.

Whether this propensity be one of those original principles in human nature, of which no further account can be given; or whether, as seems more probable, it be the necessary consequence of the faculties of reason and speech, it belongs not to our present subject to enquire. It is common to all men, and to be found in no other race of animals, which seem to know neither this nor any other species of contracts. Two greyhounds, in running down the same hare, have sometimes the appearance of acting in some sort of concert. Each turns her toward his companion, or endeavors to intercept her when his companion turns her toward himself. This, however, is not the effect of any contract, but of the accidental concurrence of their passions in the same object at that particular time. Nobody ever saw a dog make a fair and deliberate exchange of one bone for another with another dog. Nobody ever saw one animal by its gestures and natural cries signify to another, this is mine, that yours; I am willing to give this for that. When an animal wants to obtain something either of a man or of another animal, it has no other means of persuasion but to gain the favor of those whose service it requires. A puppy fawns upon its dam, and a spaniel endeavors by a thousand attractions to engage the attention of its master who is at dinner, when it wants to be fed by him. Man sometimes uses the same arts with his brethren, and when he has no other means of engaging them to act according to his inclinations, endeavors by every servile and fawning attention to obtain their good will. He has not time, however, to do this upon every occasion. In civilized society he stands at all times in need of the co-operation and assistance of great multitudes, while his whole life is scarce sufficient to gain the friendship of a few persons. In almost every other race of animals each individual, when it is grown up to maturity, is entirely independent, and in its natural state has occasion for the assistance of no other living creature. But man has almost constant occasion for the help of his brethren, and it is in vain for him to expect it from their benevolence only. He will be more likely to prevail if he can interest their self-love in his favor, and show them that it is for their own advantage to do for him what he requires of them. Whoever offers to another a bargain of any kind, proposes to do this. Give me that which I want, and you shall have this which you want, is the meaning of every such offer; and it is in this manner that we obtain from one another the far greater part of those good offices which we stand in need of. It is not from the benevolence of the butcher, the brewer, or the baker, that we expect our dinner, but from their regard to their own interest. We address ourselves, not to their humanity but to their self-love, and never talk to them of our own necessities but of their advantages. Nobody but a beggar chooses to depend chiefly upon the benevolence of his fellow-citizens. Even a beggar does not depend upon it entirely. The charity of well-disposed people, indeed, supplies him with the whole fund of his subsistence. But though this principle ultimately provides him with all the necessaries of life which he has occasion for, it neither does nor can provide him with them as he has occasion for them. The greater part of his occasional wants are supplied in the same manner as those of other people, by treaty, by barter, and by purchase. With the money which one man gives him he purchases food. The old clothes which another bestows upon him he exchanges for other old clothes which suit him better, or for lodging, or for food, or for money, with which he can buy either food, clothes, or lodging, as he has occasion.

As it is by treaty, by barter, and by purchase that we obtain from one another the greater part of those mutual good offices which we stand in need of, so it is this same trucking disposition which originally gives occasion to the division of labor. In a tribe of hunters or shepherds a particular person makes bows and arrows, for example, with more readiness and dexterity than any other. He frequently exchanges them for cattle or for venison with his companions; and he finds at last that he can in this manner get more cattle and venison than if he himself went to the field to catch them. From a regard to his own interest, therefore, the making of bows and arrows grows to be his chief business, and he becomes a sort of armorer. Another excels in making the frames and covers of their little huts or movable houses. He is accustomed to be of use in this way to his neighbors, who reward him in the same manner with cattle and with venison till at last he finds it his interest to dedicate himself entirely to this employment, and to become a sort of house carpenter. In the same manner a third becomes a smith or a brazier; a fourth a tanner or dresser of hides or skins, the principal part of the clothing of savages. And thus the certainty of being able to exchange all that surplus part of the produce of his own labor, which is over and above his own consumption, for such parts of the produce of other men's labor as he may have occasion for, encourages every man to apply himself to a particular occupation, and to cultivate and bring to perfection whatever talent or genius he may possess for that particular species of business.

The difference of natural talents in different men is, in reality, much less than we are aware of; and the very different genius which appears to distinguish men of different professions, when grown up to maturity, is not upon many occasions so much the cause as the effect of the division of labor. The difference between the most dissimilar characters, between a philosopher and a common street porter, for example, seems to arise not so much from nature as from habit, custom, and education. When they came into the world, and for the first six or eight years of their existence, they were, perhaps, very much alike, and neither their parents nor playfellows could perceive any remarkable difference. About that age, or soon after, they come to be employed in very different occupations. The difference of talents comes then to be taken notice of, and widens by degrees, till at last the vanity of the philosopher is willing to acknowledge scarce any resemblance. But without the disposition to truck, barter, and exchange, every man must have procured to himself every necessary and conveniency of life which he wanted. All must have had the same duties to perform, and the same work to do, and there could have been no such difference of employment as could alone give occasion to any great difference of talents.

As it is this disposition which forms that difference of talents so remarkable among men of different professions, so it is this same disposition which renders that difference useful. Many tribes of animals acknowledged to be all of the same species derive from nature a much more remarkable distinction of genius than what, antecedent to custom and education, appears to take place among men. By nature a philosopher is not in genius and disposition half so different from a street porter as a mastiff is from a greyhound, or a greyhound from a spaniel, or this last from a shepherd's dog. Those different tribes of animals, however, though all of the same species, are of scarce any use to one another. The strength of the mastiff is not in the least supported either by the swiftness of the greyhound, or by the sagacity of the spaniel, or by the docility of the shepherd's dog. The effects of those different geniuses and talents, for want of the power or disposition to barter and exchange, cannot be brought into a common stock, and do not in the least contribute to the better accommodation and conveniency of the species. Each animal is still obliged to support and defend itself separately and independently, and derives no sort of advantage from that variety of talents with which nature has distinguished its fellows. Among men, on the contrary, the most dissimilar geniuses are of use to one another; the different produces of their respective talents, by the general disposition to truck, barter, and exchange, being brought, as it were, into a common stock, where every man may purchase whatever part of the produce of other men's talents he has occasion for.

17

FREEDOM AND ENLIGHTENMENT

IMMANUEL KANT

Immanuel Kant (1724–1804), the eminent German philosopher, wrote several influential books, including *The Critique of Pure Reason* (1781) and the *Groundwork of the Metaphysics of Morals* (1785). Kant held that autonomy, or self-rule, is the mark of a fully mature and moral person, and he believed that the eighteenth-century intellectual movement known as the Enlightenment embodied that ideal. He wrote the following essay, "What Is Enlightenment?," as a newspaper article in 1784 to describe and defend the ideals of the Enlightenment against some of its critics.

Source: "Was Ist Aufklarung?" in Kants Sämmtliche Werke *(1838), vol. 7; translated and abridged by Terence Ball.*

WHAT IS ENLIGHTENMENT?

Enlightenment is mankind's leaving behind its self-imposed immaturity. Immaturity is the inability to employ one's own intelligence without being directed by someone else. This immaturity is self-imposed if it results not from lack of intellect but from a lack of willingness and courage to use it without another's guidance. *Sapere Aude!*—"Have the courage to use your own mind!"—that is the motto of the enlightenment.

Because of laziness and cowardice, many supposedly grown men remain happily immature throughout their lives, readily allowing others to serve as their guardians. After all, it is so easy to remain immature! If I have a book which does my thinking for me, a priest or pastor who serves as my conscience, and a doctor who tells me what to eat, then I need not take the trouble to think for myself. If I have the money to pay them, others will perform that troublesome task for me. The guardians who have so kindly agreed to supervise me will warn me and others like me—including the entire "fair sex"—that any move toward adult maturity is not merely difficult but downright dangerous. Having already made their domestic animals dumb by seeing that these placid creatures remain on a short leash, our guardians likewise warn us of the danger of attempting to stand and walk on our own two feet. In fact, however, the danger is not all that great, since after falling a few times, one finally learns to walk by oneself. Even so, most people are so frightened by the warning that they dare not venture out on their own.

It is no easy task for a lone individual to outgrow the immaturity which has become second nature for him. He has grown fond of his infantile dependency, and is for the moment unable to employ his reason, since no one has previously permitted him to try. Rules and regulations—those mechanical tools of the use, or rather misuse, of his natural talents—are the chains which keep him bound to an endless childhood. Whoever broke these chains would have great difficulty in jumping over the smallest ditch, because he would be unused to moving freely. Thus only a handful of human beings have heretofore succeeded in freeing themselves from their childish dependency on others by cultivating their own minds at their own steady pace.

But it is even more possible that the public can enlighten itself. In fact, such enlightenment is virtually assured under conditions of freedom. . . . The only thing needed for such enlightenment is freedom, and particularly . . . the freedom to make public use of one's reason in every case. And yet I hear people shout from all sides: "Don't argue!" The officer says: "Don't argue, drill!" The tax collector: "Don't argue, pay!" The priest or pastor: "Don't argue, believe!" . . . Everywhere there are restrictions on freedom.

Which of these restrictions hinders enlightenment, and which does not? I answer: The public use of one's reason must always be free, and this by itself can bring about enlightenment among human beings. By contrast, the private use of one's reason may be rather tightly restricted without necessarily impeding the progress of enlightenment. By the public use of one's reason I mean, for example, the way in which a scholar uses reason before the reading public. The private use of reason is the use which one may make of reason in a civil position or office with which he is entrusted. In the latter case, the public interest is served by the office-holder's neutrality and obedience—not by his argument and disagreement, which would be divisive and disruptive. Civil servants should not argue but obey. . . . A soldier, for example, should not argue with a superior officer who gives him a command. . . . Nor should a citizen refuse to pay his taxes. . . . Nor may a priest publicly disagree with the teachings of his church, offering instead his own personal interpretation of the gospel. But in their capacity as scholars, those same people would have the freedom and indeed the duty to criticize the military, the system of taxation, and the teachings of the church. . . . The scholar, speaking to the world through his writings, has an unrestricted freedom to use his own reason and to speak in his own voice. To insist that the people's spiritual guardians should themselves remain immature children would only perpetuate present-day ignorance.

But should an organization of clergymen be permitted to pledge itself to teach a particular unchanging doctrine, now and forevermore, in order to perpetuate its dominion over its members and their congregations? I say no. Any such agreement which aims to prevent the enlightenment of mankind is null and void. One generation cannot enter into a contract to stifle the intellectual and moral development of a later generation by making it impossible for the latter to expand its knowledge, to expose and eliminate error, and thereby to become ever more enlightened. To do so would be to commit a crime against human nature, whose destiny is to grow and progress. Later generations are utterly justified in ignoring or overturning such an agreement as unjust and illegal. . . . An individual may for a time hesitate to enlighten himself. But to opt out of such enlightenment entirely, either for oneself or one's descendants, is to ride roughshod over the sacred rights of mankind. . . .

We can now pose the question: Is ours an enlightened age? I answer no: Ours is not an enlightened age, but it *is* an age of enlightenment. Many things continue to prevent people from using their own minds in matters of religion. But there is every indication that even this area is being opened up to critical scrutiny, thereby permitting people to escape from self-imposed immaturity. . . .

I have stressed the primary point of enlightenment—i.e., of man's release from his self-imposed immaturity—mainly in matters of religion . . . because immaturity in this area is the most unfortunate and reprehensible kind. The ruler of a free state recognizes that there is no danger in legislation allowing his people to make public use of their own reason in publicly discussing and criticizing existing or proposed legislation. . . . A very large degree of civic freedom appears to be beneficial for the freedom of the spirit of a people. . . . Thus nature has nurtured, inside its tough shell, the embryo of the interest in and need for free thought. This free thought acts slowly but surely upon the mind of the people, permitting them to become ever more able to act freely. Eventually even the government will be influenced by this free thought, and will begin to treat men not as automata but as autonomous and responsible human beings.

18

LIBERTY AND INDIVIDUALITY

JOHN STUART MILL

Like Alexis de Tocqueville (see selection 9), whose work he admired, John Stuart Mill (1806–1873) feared that the advent of democracy was bringing with it a stifling pressure to conform to the conventional or popular opinion. In Mill's view no one could live a fully human life unless he—or she, as he made clear in *The Subjection of Women* (1869)—was free to think and act for him- or herself. In the following excerpt from *On Liberty* (1859), Mill proposes "one very simple principle" for deciding just when society or government may rightfully regulate the individual's conduct and when the individual should be free to do as he or she sees fit.

Source: John Stuart Mill, Utilitarianism, Liberty, and Representative Government, *ed. A.D. Lindsay (New York: E.P. Dutton, 1910), pp. 72–77, 79, 111–112, 123–128.*

INTRODUCTORY

The object of this Essay is to assert one very simple principle, as entitled to govern absolutely the dealings of society with the individual in the way of compulsion and control, whether the means used be physical force in the form of legal penalties, or the moral coercion of public opinion. That principle is, that the sole end for which mankind are warranted, individually or collectively, in interfering with the liberty of action of any of their number, is self-protection. That the only purpose for which power can be rightfully exercised over any member of a civilized community, against his will, is to prevent harm to others. His own good, either physical or moral, is not a sufficient warrant. He cannot rightfully be compelled to do or forbear because it will be better for him to do so, because it will make him happier, because, in the opinions of others, to do so would be wise, or even right. These are good reasons for remonstrating with him, or reasoning with him, or persuading him, or entreating him, but not for compelling him, or visiting him with any evil in case he do otherwise. To justify that, the conduct from which it is desired to deter him, must be calculated to produce evil to some one else. The only part of the conduct of any one, for which he is amenable to society, is that which concerns others. In the part which merely concerns himself, his independence is, of right, absolute. Over himself, over his own body and mind, the individual is sovereign.

It is, perhaps, hardly necessary to say that this doctrine is meant to apply only to human beings in the maturity of their faculties. We are not speaking of children, or of young persons below the age which the law may fix as that of manhood or womanhood. Those who are still in a state to require being taken care of by others, must be protected against their own actions as well as against external injury. For the same reason, we may leave out of consideration those backward states of society in which the race itself may be considered as in its nonage. The early difficulties in the way of spontaneous progress are so great, that there is seldom any choice of means for overcoming them; and a ruler full of the spirit of improvement is warranted in the use of any expedients that will attain an end, perhaps otherwise unattainable. Despotism is a legitimate mode of government in dealing with barbarians, provided the end be their improvement, and the means justified by actually effecting that end. Liberty, as a principle, has no application to any state of things anterior to the time when mankind have become capable of being improved by free and equal discussion. Until then, there is nothing for them but implicit obedience to an Akbar or a Charlemagne, if they are so fortunate as to find one. But as soon as mankind have attained the capacity of being guided to their own improvement by conviction or persuasion (a period long since reached in all nations with whom we need here concern ourselves), compulsion, either in the direct form or in that of pains and penalties for non-compliance, is no longer admissible as a means to their own good, and justifiable only for the security of others.

It is proper to state that I forgo any advantage which could be derived to my argument from the idea of abstract right, as a thing independent of utility. I regard utility as the ultimate appeal on all ethical questions; but it must be utility in the largest sense, grounded on the permanent interests of man as a progressive being. Those interests, I contend, authorize the subjection of individual spontaneity to external control, only in respect to those actions of each, which concern the interest of other people. If any one does an act hurtful to others, there is a prima facie case for punishing him, by law, or, where legal penalties are not safely applicable, by general disapprobation. There are also many positive acts for the benefit of others, which he may rightfully be compelled to perform; such as, to give evidence in a court of justice; to bear his fair share in the common defence, or in any other joint work necessary to the interest of the society of which he enjoys the protection; and to perform certain acts of individual beneficence, such as saving a fellow creature's life, or interposing to protect the defenceless against ill-usage, things which whenever it is obviously a man's duty to do, he may rightfully be made responsible to society for not doing. A person may cause evil to others not only by his actions but by his inaction, and in either case he is justly accountable to them for the injury. The latter case, it is true, requires a much more cautious exercise of compulsion than the former. To make any one answerable for doing evil to others, is the rule; to make him answerable for not preventing evil, is, comparatively speaking, the exception. Yet there are many cases clear enough and grave enough to justify that exception. In all things which regard the external relations of the individual, he is *de jure* amenable to those whose interests are concerned, and if need be, to society as their protector. There are often good reasons for not holding him to the responsibility; but these reasons must arise from the special expediencies of the case: either because it is a kind of case in which he is on the whole likely to act better, when left to his own discretion, than when controlled in any way in which society have it in their power to control him; or because the attempt to exercise control would produce other evils, greater than those which it would prevent. When such reasons as these preclude the enforcement of responsibility, the conscience of the agent himself should step into the vacant judgement-seat, and protect those interests of others which have no external protection; judging himself all the more rigidly, because the case does not admit of his being made accountable to the judgement of his fellow creatures.

But there is a sphere of action in which society, as distinguished from the individual, has, if any, only an indirect interest; comprehending all that portion of a person's life and conduct which affects only himself, or if it also affects others, only with their free, voluntary, and undeceived consent and participation. When I say only himself, I mean directly, and in the first instance: for whatever affects himself, may affect others through himself; and the objection which may be grounded on this contingency will receive consideration in the sequel. This, then, is the appropriate region of human liberty. It comprises, first, the inward domain of consciousness; demanding liberty of conscience, in the most comprehensive sense; liberty of thought and feeling; absolute freedom of opinion and sentiment on all subjects, practical or speculative, scientific, moral, or theological. The liberty of expressing and publishing opinions may seem to fall under a different principle, since it belongs to that part of the conduct of an individual which concerns other people; but, being almost of as much importance as the liberty of thought itself, and resting in great part on the same reasons, is practically inseparable from it. Secondly, the principle requires liberty of tastes and pursuits; of framing the plan of our life to suit our own character; of doing as we like, subject to such consequences as may follow: without impediment from our fellow creatures, so long as what we do does not harm them, even though they should think our conduct foolish, perverse, or wrong. Thirdly, from this liberty of each individual, follows the liberty, within the same limits, of combination among individuals; freedom to unite, for any purpose not involving harm to others: the persons combining being supposed to be of full age, and not forced or deceived.

No society in which these liberties are not, on the whole, respected, is free, whatever may be its form of government; and none is completely free in which they do not exist absolute and unqualified. The only freedom which deserves the name, is that of pursuing our own good in our own way, so long as we do not attempt to deprive others of theirs, or impede their efforts to obtain it. Each is the proper guardian of his own health, whether bodily, or mental and spiritual. Mankind are greater gainers by suffering each other to live as seems good to themselves, than by compelling each to live as seems good to the rest. . . .

Apart from the peculiar tenets of individual thinkers, there is also in the world at large an increasing inclination to stretch unduly the powers of society over the individual, both by the force of opinion and even by that of legislation: and as the tendency of all the changes taking place in the world is to strengthen society, and diminish the power of the individual, this encroachment is not one of the evils which tend spontaneously to disappear, but, on the contrary, to grow more and more formidable. The disposition of mankind, whether as rulers or as fellow citizens, to impose their own opinions and inclinations as a rule of conduct on others, is so energetically supported by some of the best and by some of the worst feelings incident to human nature, that it is hardly ever kept under restraint by anything but want of power; and as the power is not declining, but growing, unless a strong barrier of moral conviction can be raised against the mischief, we must expect, in the present circumstances of the world, to see it increase.

OF THE LIBERTY OF THOUGHT AND DISCUSSION

. . .

If all mankind minus one, were of one opinion, and only one person were of the contrary opinion, mankind would be no more justified in silencing that one person, than he, if he had the power, would be justified in silencing mankind. Were an opinion a personal possession of no value except to the owner; if to be obstructed in the enjoyment of it were simply a private injury, it would make some difference whether the injury was inflicted only on a few persons or on many. But the peculiar evil of silencing the expression of an opinion is, that it is robbing the human race; posterity as well as the existing generation; those who dissent from the opinion, still more than those who hold it. If the opinion is right, they are deprived of the opportunity of exchanging error for truth: if wrong, they lose, what is almost as great a benefit, the clearer perception and livelier impression of truth, produced by its collision with error.

It is necessary to consider separately these two hypotheses, each of which has a distinct branch of the argument corresponding to it. We can never be sure that the opinion we are endeavouring to stifle is a false opinion; and if we were sure, stifling it would be an evil still. . . .

We have now recognized the necessity to the mental well-being of mankind (on which all their other well-being depends) of freedom of opinion, and freedom of the expression of opinion, on four distinct grounds; which we will now briefly recapitulate.

First, if any opinion is compelled to silence, that opinion may, for aught we can certainly know, be true. To deny this is to assume our own infallibility.

Secondly, though the silenced opinion be an error, it may, and very commonly does, contain a portion of truth; and since the general or prevailing opinion on any subject is rarely or never the whole truth, it is only by the collision of adverse opinions that the remainder of the truth has any chance of being supplied.

Thirdly, even if the received opinion be not only true, but the whole truth; unless it is suffered to be, and actually is, vigorously and earnestly contested, it will, by most of those who receive it, be held in the manner of a prejudice, with little comprehension or feeling of its rational grounds. And not only this, but, fourthly, the meaning of the doctrine itself will be in danger of being lost, or enfeebled, and deprived of its vital effect on the character and conduct: the dogma becoming a mere formal profession, inefficacious for good, but cumbering the ground, and preventing the growth of any real and heartfelt conviction, from reason or personal experience. . . .

Persons of genius, it is true, are, and are always likely to be, a small minority; but in order to have them, it is necessary to preserve the soil in which they grow. Genius can only breathe freely in an *atmosphere* of freedom. Persons of genius are, *ex vi termini, more* individual than any other people—less capable, consequently, of fitting themselves, without hurtful compression, into any of the small number of moulds which society provides in order to save its members the trouble of forming their own character. If from timidity they consent to be forced into one of these moulds, and to let all that part of themselves which cannot expand under the pressure remain unexpanded, society will be little the better for their genius. If they are of a strong character, and break their fetters, they become a mark for the society which has not succeeded in reducing them to commonplace, to point at with solemn warning as "wild," "erratic," and the like; much as if one should complain of the Niagara river for not flowing smoothly between its banks like a Dutch canal.

I insist thus emphatically on the importance of genius, and the necessity of allowing it to unfold itself freely both in thought and in practice, being well aware that no one will deny the position in theory, but knowing also that almost every one, in reality, is totally indifferent to it. People think genius a fine thing if it enables a man to write an exciting poem, or paint a picture. But in its true sense, that of originality in thought and action, though no one says that it is not a thing to be admired, nearly all, at heart, think that they can do very well without it. Unhappily this is too natural to be wondered at. Originality is the one thing which unoriginal minds cannot feel the use of. They cannot see what it is to do for them: how should they? If they could see what it would do for them, it would not be originality. The first service which originality has to render them, is that of opening their eyes: which being once fully done, they would have a chance of being themselves original. Meanwhile, recollecting that nothing was ever yet done which some one was not the first to do, and that all good things which exist are the fruits of originality, let them be modest enough to believe that there is something still left for it to accomplish, and assure themselves that they are more in need of originality, the less they are conscious of the want.

In sober truth, whatever homage may be professed, or even paid, to real or supposed mental superiority, the general tendency of things throughout the world is to render mediocrity the ascendant power among mankind. In ancient history, in the middle ages, and in a diminishing degree through the long transition from feudality to the present time, the individual was a power in himself; and if he had either great talents or a high social position, he was a considerable power. At present individuals are lost in the crowd. In politics it is almost a triviality to say that public opinion now rules the world. The only power deserving the name is that of masses, and of governments while they make themselves the organ of the tendencies and instincts of masses. This is as true in the moral and social relations of private life as in public transactions. Those whose opinions go by the name of public opinion, are not always the same sort of public: in America they are the whole white population; in England, chiefly the middle class. But they are always a mass, that is to say, collective mediocrity. And what is a still greater novelty, the mass do not now take their opinions from dignitaries in Church or State, from ostensible leaders, or from books. Their thinking is done for them by men much like themselves, addressing them or speaking in their name, on the spur of the moment, through the newspapers. I am not complaining of all this. I do not assert that anything better is compatible, as a general rule, with the present low state of the human mind. But that does not hinder the government of mediocrity from being mediocre government. No government by a democracy or a numerous aristocracy, either in its political acts or in the opinions, qualities, and tone of mind which it fosters, ever did or could rise above mediocrity, except in so far as the sovereign Many have let themselves be guided (which in their best times they always have done) by the counsels and influence of a more highly gifted and instructed One or Few. The initiation of all wise or noble things, comes and must come from individuals; generally at first from some one individual. The honour and glory of the average man is that he is capable of following that initiative; that he can respond internally to wise and noble things, and be led to them with his eyes open. I am not countenancing the sort of "hero-worship" which applauds the strong man of genius for forcibly seizing on the government of the world and making it do his bidding in spite of itself. All he can claim is, freedom to point out the way. The power of compelling others into it, is not only inconsistent with the freedom and development of all the rest, but corrupting to the strong man himself. It does seem, however, that when the opinions of masses of merely average men are everywhere become or becoming the dominant power, the counterpoise and corrective to that tendency would be, the more and more pronounced individuality of those who stand on the higher eminences of thought. It is in these circumstances most especially, that exceptional individuals, instead of being deterred, should be encouraged in acting differently from the mass. In other times there was no advantage in their doing so, unless they acted not only differently, but better. In this age, the mere example of nonconformity, the mere refusal to bend the knee to custom, is itself a service. Precisely because the tyranny of opinion is such as to make eccentricity a reproach, it is desirable, in order to break through that tyranny, that people should be eccentric. Eccentricity has always abounded when and where strength of character has abounded; and the amount of eccentricity in a society has generally been proportional to the amount of genius, mental vigour, and moral courage which it contained. That so few now dare to be eccentric, marks the chief danger of the time. . . .

. . . [N]or is it only persons of decided mental superiority who have a just claim to carry on their lives in their own way. There is no reason that all human existence should be constructed on some one or some small number of patterns. If a person possesses any tolerable amount of common sense and experience, his own mode of laying out his existence is the best, not because it is the best in itself, but because it is his own mode. Human beings are not like sheep; and even sheep are not undistinguishably alike. A man cannot get a coat or a pair of boots to fit him, unless they are either made to his measure, or he has a whole warehouseful to choose from: and is it easier to fit him with a life than with a coat, or are human beings more like one another in their whole physical and spiritual conformation than in the shape of their feet? If it were only that people have diversities of taste, that is reason enough for not attempting to shape them all after one model. But different persons also require different conditions for their spiritual development; and can no more exist healthily in the same moral, than all the variety of plants can in the same physical, atmosphere and climate. The same things which are helps to one person towards the cultivation of his higher nature, are hindrances to another. The same mode of life is a healthy excitement to one, keeping all his faculties of action and enjoyment in their best order, while to another it is a distracting burden, which suspends or crushes all internal life. Such are the differences among human beings in their sources of pleasure, their susceptibilities of pain, and the operation on them of different physical and moral agencies, that unless there is a corresponding diversity in their modes of life, they neither obtain their fair share of happiness, nor grow up to the mental, moral, and aesthetic stature of which their nature is capable. . . .

There is one characteristic of the present direction of public opinion, peculiarly calculated to make it intolerant of any marked demonstration of individuality. The general average of mankind are not only moderate in intellect, but also moderate in inclinations: they have no tastes or wishes strong enough to incline them to do anything unusual, and they consequently do not understand those who have, and class all such with the wild and intemperate whom they are accustomed to look down upon. Now, in addition to this fact which is general, we have only to suppose that a strong movement has set in towards the improvement of morals, and it is evident what we have to expect. In these days such a movement has set in; much has actually been effected in the way of increased regularity of conduct, and discouragement of excesses; and there is a philanthropic spirit abroad, for the exercise of which there is no more inviting field than the moral and prudential improvement of our fellow creatures. These tendencies of the times cause the public to be more disposed than at most former periods to prescribe general rules of conduct, and endeavour to make every one conform to the approved standard. And that standard, express or tacit, is to desire nothing strongly. Its ideal of character is to be without any marked character; to maim by compression, like a Chinese lady's foot, every part of human nature which stands out prominently, and tends to make the person markedly dissimilar in outline to commonplace humanity. . . .

The despotism of custom is everywhere the standing hindrance to human advancement, being in unceasing antagonism to that disposition to aim at something better than customary, which is called, . . . the spirit of liberty. . . .

The combination of all these causes forms so great a mass of influences hostile to Individuality, that it is not easy to see how it can stand its ground. It will do so with increasing difficulty, unless the intelligent part of the public can be made to feel its value—to see that it is good there should be differences, even though not for the better, even though, as it may appear to them, some should be for the worse. If the claims of Individuality are ever to be asserted, the time is now, while much is still wanting to complete the enforced assimilation. It is only in the earlier stages that any stand can be successfully made against the encroachment. The demand that all other people shall resemble ourselves, grows by what it feeds on. If resistance waits till life is reduced *nearly* to one uniform type, all deviations from that type will come to be considered impious, immoral, even monstrous and contrary to nature. Mankind speedily become unable to conceive diversity, when they have been for some time unaccustomed to see it.

19

ACCORDING TO THE FITNESS OF THINGS

WILLIAM GRAHAM SUMNER

Like his English contemporary, Herbert Spencer, the American sociologist William Graham Sumner (1840–1910) vigorously developed and defended the theory of Social Darwinism. According to this theory, individual humans are locked in a competition for survival—a competition that the strong will win if nature is allowed to take its course. Spencer's and Sumner's adaptations of Darwin's theory of evolution to human society thus provided one of the first important statements of neoclassical liberalism.

Source: William Graham Sumner, What Social Classes Owe to Each Other *(New York: Harper & Brothers, 1883), chapters 7–9, pp. 112–133.*

ON THE VALUE, AS A SOCIOLOGICAL PRINCIPLE, OF THE RULE TO MIND ONE'S OWN BUSINESS.

The passion for dealing with social questions is one of the marks of our time. Every man gets some experience of, and makes some observations on social affairs. Except matters of health, probably none have such general interest as matters of society. Except matters of health, none are so much afflicted by dogmatism and crude speculation as those which appertain to society. The amateurs in social science always ask: What shall we do? What shall we do with Neighbor A? What shall we do for Neighbor B? What shall we make Neighbor A do for Neighbor B? It is a fine thing to be planning and discussing broad and general theories of wide application. The amateurs always plan to use the individual for some constructive and inferential social purpose, or to use the society for some constructive and inferential individual purpose. For A to sit down and think, What shall I do? is commonplace; but to think what B ought to do is interesting, romantic, moral, self-flattering, and public-spirited all at once. It satisfies a great number of human weaknesses at once. To go on and plan what a whole class of people ought to do is to feel one's self a power on earth, to win a public position, to clothe one's self in dignity. Hence we have an unlimited supply of reformers, philanthropists, humanitarians, and would-be managers-in-general of society.

Every man and woman in society has one big duty. That is, to take care of his or her own self. This is a social duty. For, fortunately, the matter stands so that the duty of making the best of one's self individually is not a separate thing from the duty of filling one's place in society, but the two are one, and the latter is accomplished when the former is done. The common notion, however, seems to be that one has a duty to society, as a special and separate thing, and that this duty consists in considering and deciding what other people ought to do. Now, the man who can do anything for or about anybody else than himself is fit to be head of a family; and when he becomes head of a family he has duties to his wife and his children, in addition to the former big duty. Then again, any man who can take care of himself and his family is in a very exceptional position, if he does not find in his immediate surroundings people who need his care and have some sort of a personal claim upon him. If, now, he is able to fulfill all this, and to take care of anybody outside his family and his dependents, he must have a surplus of energy, wisdom, and moral virtue beyond what he needs for his own business. No man has this; for a family is a charge which is capable of infinite development, and no man could suffice to the full measure of duty for which a family may draw upon him. Neither can a man give to society so advantageous an employment of his services, whatever they are, in any other way as by spending them on his family. Upon this, however, I will not insist. I recur to the observation that a man who proposes to take care of other people must have himself and his family taken care of, after some sort of a fashion, and must have an as yet unexhausted store of energy.

The danger of minding other people's business is twofold. First, there is the danger that a man may leave his own business unattended to; and, second, there is the danger of an impertinent interference with another's affairs. The "friends of humanity" almost always run into both dangers. I am one of humanity, and I do not want any volunteer friends. I regard friendship as mutual, and I want to have my say about it. I suppose that other components of humanity feel in the same way about it. If so, they must regard any one who assumes the *rôle* of a friend of humanity as impertinent. The reference to the friend of humanity back to his own business is obviously the next step.

Yet we are constantly annoyed, and the legislatures are kept constantly busy, by the people who have made up their minds that it is wise and conducive to happiness to live in a certain way, and who want to compel everybody else to live in their way. Some people have decided to spend Sunday in a certain way, and they want laws passed to make other people spend Sunday in the same way. Some people have resolved to be teetotalers, and they want a law passed to make everybody else a teetotaler. Some people have resolved to eschew luxury, and they want taxes laid to make others eschew luxury. The taxing power is especially something after which the reformer's finger always itches. Sometimes there is an element of self-interest in the proposed reformation, as when a publisher wanted a duty imposed on books, to keep Americans from reading books which would unsettle their Americanisms; and when artists wanted a tax laid on pictures, to save Americans from buying bad paintings. . . .

The amateur social doctors are like the amateur physicians—they always begin with the question of *remedies*, and they go at this without any diagnosis or any knowledge of the anatomy or physiology of society. They never have any doubt of the efficacy of their remedies. They never take account of any ulterior effects which may be apprehended from the remedy itself. It generally troubles them not a whit that their remedy implies a complete reconstruction of society, or even a reconstitution of human nature. Against all such social quackery the obvious injunction to the quacks is, to mind their own business. . . .

ON THE CASE OF A CERTAIN MAN WHO IS NEVER THOUGHT OF

The type and formula of most schemes of philanthropy or humanitarianism is this: A and B put their heads together to decide what C shall be made to do for D. The radical vice of all these schemes, from a sociological point of view, is that C is not allowed a voice in the matter, and his position, character, and interests, as well as the ultimate effects on society through C's interests, are entirely overlooked. I call C the Forgotten Man. For once let us look him up and consider his case, for the characteristic of all social doctors is, that they fix their minds on some man or group of men whose case appeals to the sympathies and the imagination, and they plan remedies addressed to the particular trouble; they do not understand that all the parts of society hold together, and that forces which are set in action act and react throughout the whole organism, until an equilibrium is produced by a readjustment of all interests and rights. They therefore ignore entirely the source from which they must draw all the energy which they employ in their remedies, and they ignore all the effects on other members of society than the ones they have in view. They are always under the dominion of the superstition of government, and, forgetting that a government produces nothing at all, they leave out of sight the first fact to be remembered in all social discussion—that the State cannot get a cent for any man without taking it from some other man, and this latter must be a man who has produced and saved it. This latter is the Forgotten Man.

The friends of humanity start out with certain benevolent feelings toward "the poor," "the weak," "the laborers," and others of whom they make pets. They generalize these classes, and render them impersonal, and so constitute the classes into social pets. They turn to other classes and appeal to sympathy and generosity, and to all the other noble sentiments of the human heart. Action in the line proposed consists in a transfer of capital from the better off to the worse off. Capital, however, as we have seen, is the force by which civilization is maintained and carried on. The same piece of capital cannot be used in two ways. Every bit of capital, therefore, which is given to a shiftless and inefficient member of society, who makes no return for it, is diverted from a reproductive use; but if it was put to reproductive use, it would have to be granted in wages to an efficient and productive laborer. Hence the real sufferer by that kind of benevolence which consists in an expenditure of capital to protect the good-for-nothing is the industrious laborer. The latter, however, is never thought of in this connection. It is assumed that he is provided for and out of the account. Such a notion only shows how little true notions of political economy have as yet become popularized. There is an almost invincible prejudice that a man who gives a dollar to a beggar is generous and kind-hearted, but that a man who refuses the beggar and puts the dollar in a savings-bank is stingy and mean. The former is putting capital where it is very sure to be wasted, and where it will be a kind of seed for a long succession of future dollars, which must be wasted to ward off a greater strain on the sympathies than would have been occasioned by a refusal in the first place. Inasmuch as the dollar might have been turned into capital and given to a laborer who, while earning it, would have reproduced it, it must be regarded as taken from the latter. When a millionaire gives a dollar to a beggar the gain of utility to the beggar is enormous, and the loss of utility to the millionaire is insignificant. Generally the discussion is allowed to rest there. But if the millionaire makes capital of the dollar, it must go upon the labor market, as a demand for productive services. Hence there is another party in interest—the person who supplies productive services. There always are two parties. The second one is always the Forgotten Man, and any one who wants to truly understand the matter in question must go and search for the Forgotten Man. He will be found to be worthy, industrious, independent, and self-supporting. He is not, technically, "poor" or "weak"; he minds his own business, and makes no complaint. Consequently the philanthropists never think of him, and trample on him. . . .

Society . . . maintains police, sheriffs, and various institutions, the object of which is to protect people against themselves—that is, against their own vices. Almost all legislative effort to prevent vice is really protective of vice, because all such legislation saves the vicious man from the penalty of his vice. Nature's remedies against vice are terrible. She removes the victims without pity. A drunkard in the gutter is just where he ought to be, according to the fitness and tendency of things. Nature has set up on him the process of decline and dissolution by which she removes things which have survived their usefulness. Gambling and other less mentionable vices carry their own penalties with them.

Now, we never can annihilate a penalty. We can only divert it from the head of the man who has incurred it to the heads of others who have not incurred it. A vast amount of "social reform" consists in just this operation. The consequence is that those who have gone astray, being relieved from Nature's fierce discipline, go on to worse, and that there is a constantly heavier burden for the others to bear. Who are the others? When we see a drunkard in the gutter we pity him. If a policeman picks him up, we say that society has interfered to save him from perishing. "Society" is a fine word, and it saves us the trouble of thinking. The industrious and sober workman, who is mulcted of a percentage of his day's wages to pay the policeman, is the one who bears the penalty. But he is the Forgotten Man. He passes by and is never noticed, because he has behaved himself, fulfilled his contracts, and asked for nothing.

The fallacy of all prohibitory, sumptuary, and moral legislation is the same. A and B determine to be teetotalers, which is often a wise determination, and sometimes a necessary one. If A and B are moved by considerations which seem to them good, that is enough. But A and B put their heads together to get a law passed which shall force C to be a teetotaler for the sake of D, who is in danger of drinking too much. There is no pressure on A and B. They are having their own way, and they like it. There is rarely any pressure on D. He does not like it, and evades it. The pressure all comes on C. The question then arises, Who is C? He is the man who wants alcoholic liquors for any honest purpose whatsoever, who would use his liberty without abusing it, who would occasion no public question, and trouble nobody at all. He is the Forgotten Man again, and as soon as he is drawn from his obscurity we see that he is just what each one of us ought to be.

20

LIBERALISM AND POSITIVE FREEDOM

T. H. GREEN

Contrary to the Social Darwinists and other neoclassical liberals, the English philosopher Thomas Hill Green (1836–1882) insisted that liberalism requires an active government to ensure and promote individual liberty. In this excerpt from his speech, "Liberal Legislation and Freedom of Contract" (1880), Green draws a distinction between two kinds of freedom, negative and positive. He then uses this distinction as the basis for his claim that government has a duty to promote the welfare of the people so that they can become free. In this and his other essays and books, Green thus helped to create welfare liberalism.

Source: The Works of Thomas Hill Green, *ed. R. L. Nettleship, vol. 3 (London: Longmans, Green and Co., 1888), pp. 370–376.*

We shall probably all agree that freedom, rightly understood, is the greatest of blessings; that its attainment is the true end of all our efforts as citizens. But when we thus speak of freedom, we should consider carefully what we mean by it. We do not mean merely freedom from restraint or compulsion. We do not mean merely freedom to do as we like irrespectively of what it is that we like. We do not mean a freedom that can be enjoyed by one man or one set of men at the cost of a loss of freedom to others. When we speak of freedom as something to be so highly prized, we mean a positive power or capacity of doing or enjoying something worth doing or enjoying, and that, too, something that we do or enjoy in common with others. We mean by it a power which each man exercises through the help or security given him by his fellow-men, and which he in turn helps to secure for them. When we measure the progress of a society by its growth in freedom, we measure it by the increasing development and exercise on the whole of those powers of contributing to social good with which we believe the members of the society to be endowed; in short, by the greater power on the part of the citizens as a body to make the most and best of themselves. Thus, though of course there can be no freedom among men who act not willingly but under compulsion, yet on the other hand the mere removal of compulsion, the mere enabling a man to do as he likes, is in itself no contribution to true freedom. In one sense no man is so well able to do as he likes as the wandering savage. He has no master. There is no one to say him nay. Yet we do not count him really free, because the freedom of savagery is not strength, but weakness. The actual powers of the noblest savage do not admit of comparison with those of the humblest citizen of a law-abiding state. He is not the slave of man, but he is the slave of nature. Of compulsion by natural necessity he has plenty of experience, though of restraint by society none at all. Nor can he deliver himself from that compulsion except by submitting to this restraint. So to submit is the first step in true freedom, because the first step towards the full exercise of the faculties with which man is endowed. But we rightly refuse to recognize the highest development on the part of an exceptional individual or exceptional class, as an advance towards the true freedom of man, if it is founded on a refusal of the same opportunity to other men. The powers of the human mind have probably never attained such force and keenness, the proof of what society can do for the individual has never been so strikingly exhibited, as among the small groups of men who possessed civil privileges in the small republics of antiquity. The whole framework of our political ideas, to say nothing of our philosophy, is derived from them. But in them this extraordinary efflorescence of the privileged class was accompanied by the slavery of the multitude. That slavery was the condition on which it depended, and for that reason it was doomed to decay. There is no clearer ordinance of that supreme reason, often dark to us, which governs the course of men's affairs, than that no body of men should in the long run be able to strengthen itself at the cost of others' weakness. The civilization and freedom of the ancient world were short-lived because they were partial and exceptional. If the ideal of true freedom is the maximum of power for all members of human society alike to make the best of themselves, we are right in refusing to ascribe the glory of freedom to a state in which the apparent elevation of the few is founded on the degradation of the many, and in ranking modern society, founded as it is on free industry, with all its confusion and ignorant licence and waste of effort, above the most splendid of ancient republics.

If I have given a true account of that freedom which forms the goal of social effort, we shall see that freedom of contract, freedom of all the forms of doing what one will with one's own, is valuable only as a means to an end. That end is what I call freedom in the positive sense: in other words, like liberation of the powers of all men equally for contributions to a common good. No one has a right to do what he will with his own in such a way as to contravene this end. It is only through the guarantee which society gives him that he has property at all, or, strictly speaking, any right to his possessions. This guarantee is founded on a sense of common interest. Every one has an interest in securing to every one else the free use and enjoyment and disposal of his possessions, so long as that freedom on the part of one does not interfere with a like freedom on the part of others, because such freedom contributes to that equal development of the faculties of all which is the highest good for all. This is the true and the only justification of rights of property. Rights of property, however, have been and are claimed which cannot thus be justified. We are all now agreed that men cannot rightly be the property of men. The institution of property being only justifiable as a means to the free exercise of the social capabilities of all, there can be no true right to property of a kind which debars one class of men from such free exercise altogether. We condemn slavery no less when it arises out of a voluntary agreement on the part of the enslaved person. A contract by which anyone agreed for a certain consideration to become the slave of another we should reckon a void contract. Here, then, is a limitation upon freedom of contract which we all recognize as rightful. No contract is valid in which human persons, willingly or unwillingly, are dealt with as commodities, because such contracts of necessity defeat the end for which alone society enforces contracts at all.

Are there no other contracts which, less obviously perhaps but really, are open to the same objection? In the first place, let us consider contracts affecting labor. Labor, the economist tells us, is a commodity exchangeable like other commodities. This is in a certain sense true, but it is a commodity which attaches in a peculiar manner to the person of man. Hence restrictions may need to be placed on the sale of this commodity which would be unnecessary in other cases, in order to prevent labor from being sold under conditions which make it impossible for the person selling it ever to become a free contributor to social good in any form. This is most plainly the case when a man bargains to work under conditions fatal to health, in an unventilated factory. Every injury to the health of the individual is, so far as it goes, a public injury. It is an impediment to the general freedom; so much deduction from our power, as members of society, to make the best of ourselves. Society is, therefore, plainly within its right when it limits freedom of contract for the sale of labor, so far as is done by our laws for the sanitary regulations of factories, workshops, and mines. It is equally within its right in prohibiting the labor of women and young persons beyond certain hours. If they work beyond those hours, the result is demonstrably physical deterioration; which, as demonstrably, carries with it a lowering of the moral forces of society. For the sake of that general freedom of its members to make the best of themselves, which it is the object of civil society to secure, a prohibition should be put by law, which is the deliberate voice of society, on all such contracts of service as in a general way yield such a result. The purchase or hire of unwholesome dwellings is properly forbidden on the same principle. Its application to compulsory education may not be quite so obvious, but it will appear on a little reflection. Without a command of certain elementary arts and knowledge, the individual in modern society is as effectually crippled as by the loss of a limb or a broken constitution. He is not free to develop his faculties. With a view to securing such freedom among its members it is as certainly within the province of the state to prevent children from growing up in that kind of ignorance which practically excludes them from a free career in life, as it is within its province to require the sort of building and drainage necessary for public health.

Our modern legislation then with reference to labor, and education, and health, involving as it does manifold interference with freedom of contract, is justified on the ground that it is the business of the state, not indeed directly to promote moral goodness, for that, from the very nature of moral goodness, it cannot do, but to maintain the conditions without which a free exercise of the human faculties is impossible. . . .

Now, we shall probably all agree that a society in which the public health was duly protected, and necessary education duly provided for, by the spontaneous action of individuals, was in a higher condition than one in which the compulsion of law was needed to secure those ends. But we must take men as we find them. Until such a condition of society is reached, it is the business of the state to make the best security it can for the young citizens' growing up in such health and with so much knowledge as is necessary for their real freedom. In so doing it need not at all interfere with the independence and self-reliance of those whom it requires to do what they would otherwise do for themselves. The man who, of his own right feeling, saves his wife from overwork and sends his children to school, suffers no moral degradation from a law which, if he did not do this for himself, would seek to make him do it. Such a man does not feel the law as constraint at all. To him it is simply a powerful friend. It gives him security for that being done efficiently which, with the best wishes, he might have much trouble in getting done efficiently if left to himself. No doubt it relieves him from some of the responsibility which would otherwise fall to him as head of a family, but, if he is what we are supposing him to be, in proportion as he is relieved of responsibilities in one direction he will assume them in another. The security which the state gives him for the safe housing and sufficient schooling of his family will only make him the more careful for their well-being in other respects, which he is left to look after for himself. We need have no fear, then, of such legislation having an ill-effect on those who, without the law, would have seen to that being done, though probably less efficiently, which the law requires to be done. But it was not their case that the laws we are considering were especially meant to meet. It was the overworked women, the ill-housed and untaught families, for whose benefit they were intended. And the question is whether without these laws the suffering classes could have been delivered quickly or slowly from the condition they were in. Could the enlightened self-interest or benevolence of individuals, working under a system of unlimited freedom of contract, have ever brought them into a state compatible with the free development of the human faculties? No one considering the facts can have any doubt as to the answer to this question. Left to itself, or to the operation of casual benevolence, a degraded population perpetuates and increases itself. Read any of the authorized accounts, given before royal or parliamentary commissions, of the state of the laborers, especially of the women and children, as they were in our great industries before the law was first brought to bear on them, and before freedom of contract was first interfered with in them. Ask yourself what chance there was of a generation, born and bred under such conditions, ever contracting itself out of them. Given a certain standard of moral and material well-being, people may be trusted not to sell their labor, or the labor of their children, on terms which would not allow that standard to be maintained. But with large masses of our population, until the laws we have been considering took effect, there was no such standard. There was nothing on their part, in the way either of self-respect or established demand for comforts, to prevent them from working and living, or from putting their children to work and live, in a way in which no one who is to be a healthy and free citizen can work and live. No doubt there were many high-minded employers who did their best for their work-people before the days of state-interference, but they could not prevent less scrupulous hirers of labor from hiring it on the cheapest terms.

21

PATERNALISM VS. DEMOCRACY: A LIBERTARIAN VIEW

DONALD ALLEN

In the last twenty years or so neoclassical liberalism has enjoyed a revival in the form of the libertarian movement. In the United States the Libertarian party regularly nominates and supports candidates for public office, including president, and libertarian scholars are also quite active in academe. In an essay written for this volume the libertarian writer Donald Allen (1944–   ) argues that democracy can survive only when individuals are free from government interference to control their own lives.

Paternalism—the doctrine that the state knows better than its citizens what is good for them—is especially insidious in a democracy. The most morally and intellectually demanding form of government, democracy requires the free flow of information about alternatives and choices. Inasmuch as they propose to dam and channel that flow as they see fit, paternalists are inherently antidemocratic.

Censorship has always been the paternalist's weapon of choice. And it is easy to see why. The paternalist wishes not only to deliver us from evil but to prevent us from even being led into temptation in the first place. By blocking information about attractive but "unacceptable" alternatives, censorship precludes the possibility that some citizens will make the "wrong" choices about what to read, see, say, or smoke.

Now it might be objected that paternalists are good people who have the best of intentions and the interests of others at heart. And so they may be. But in matters moral and political, consequences count for more than intentions. And the consequences of paternalism, whether intended or not, are dangerous to the health of a democratic body politic and the individual citizens who comprise it. If you doubt it, consider the case of Prohibition.

Led by well-intentioned zealots like Carry A. Nation—who, incidentally, believed that God had given her her name so that she might "carry a nation"—the Prohibitionists singled out for special censure not the consumers who abused alcohol but those who distilled and sold it. The Prohibitionists sincerely believed that their aim was noble and their cause a righteous one, and many Americans apparently agreed. After all, there were drunkards who were killing themselves with Demon Drink. To save such people from themselves the Congress in 1919 passed the Volstead Act outlawing the production, sale, and distribution of intoxicating liquors. (These rather primitive paternalists had not yet hit upon the idea of adding advertising to their list of unlawful activities.) Like many a well-intentioned scheme, this one went badly awry. The free market in alcohol became a black market in bootleg whiskey and bathtub gin. The supply of alcohol kept pace with the undiminished demand, even as the quality of the alcohol decreased and the price consumers paid for it (in dollars and in damaged livers) increased. And—not least—politicians and policemen were corrupted and organized crime gained a foothold in America that it has never lost. The harm caused by America's paternalistic experiment with Prohibition is with us even today.

One might think that Americans would have learned by now that paternalism will not and cannot work in a society supposedly blessed with free institutions and free markets. Apparently not, alas. Despite our many virtues, we Americans have, as Alexis de Tocqueville noted nearly a century and a half ago, two particularly nasty vices. The first is that we know next to nothing about history. And knowing so little about the past, we are in no position to learn from it, although we are all too apt to repeat its mistakes. We are therefore unable to follow Bismarck's dictum that "The truly wise man does not learn from his mistakes; he learns from other people's mistakes." Ignorant even of our own recent history, we muddle on, naively trusting a new generation of elected or self-appointed Prohibitionists to tell us which products, ideas, and information we may or may not be exposed to.

Our second vice is one to which democracies may be peculiarly prone. Tocqueville, along with James Madison and John Stuart Mill, observed that in democracies without strong constitutional safeguards, a tyrannical majority can very easily ride roughshod over the rights of unpopular minorities. That is why a Bill of Rights was added to the U.S. Constitution and why the First Amendment comes first in that list of liberties. And that is why the whole of Mill's magnificent *On Liberty* (1859) is devoted to defending the right of free expression for all citizens, however obnoxious or distasteful others may think their views to be. Mill's essay is also a defense of diversity and a thoroughgoing critique of paternalism. "The only purpose for which power can be rightfully exercised over any member of a civilized community, against his will," wrote Mill, "is to prevent harm to others. His own good, either physical or moral, is not a sufficient warrant. He cannot rightfully be compelled to do or forbear because it will be better for him to do so, because it will make him happier, because, in the opinions of others, to do so would be wise or even right. . . . Over himself, over his own body and mind, the individual is sovereign." It is just this individual sovereignty that the New Prohibitionists find so intolerable.

The New Prohibitionists have in recent years turned their attention not to alcohol but toward drugs, tobacco, and pornography, in particular. To stop the flow of drugs into the United States they propose more laws, stiffer penalties, more police—in short, more state power devoted to preventing people from doing what they like with, and to, their own bodies. It has not worked, and will not work. Exactly the same things that happened during Prohibition are happening all over again. People who want to drink—or take drugs or view pornography or to have sex with another consenting adult—will do so. And if there is no free market in any product or service that is in demand, whether it be drugs or pornography or prostitution, there will inevitably be a black market in that product or service. Because black market goods and services are much more expensive than those sold on the free market, some consumers will pay for them by turning to other illegal, but profitable activities, including prostitution, theft, and the selling of drugs. This of course is exactly what has happened. The result is that our jails and prisons are overflowing, our police officers overworked or corrupted, and our taxes raised in a Canute-like effort to turn back the tide. Once again, well-meaning paternalists, in attempting to solve one "problem," have not only failed to solve it but have created many additional problems as well.

Not content to restrict or outlaw certain kinds of purely private conduct by or between consenting adults, the New Prohibitionists have recently turned their attention to public speech. Their most recent efforts include proposing legislation to restrict or outlaw the production, sale, and distribution of pornography and a ban on tobacco advertising. The first comes from paternalists on the religious Right, the second from the liberal Left. No matter what their motives, however, their message is essentially the same. Their claim is that certain words and pictures ought to be prohibited by law, lest people be tempted to think, and perchance to act, in ways that the state deems socially unacceptable. And the aim in both cases is to de-diversify a pluralistic society whose strength has traditionally resided in its citizens' diverse and often opposing outlooks, opinions, and tastes. This is, of course, a tall order. It requires nothing less than an assault on our fundamental freedoms, as articulated in the Bill of Rights, and the First Amendment in particular.

Since a full frontal assault on these freedoms would never be tolerated, the New Prohibitionists have turned to other tactics. Scare tactics, for example: some kinds of speech or expression are said to pose too great a danger to our morals or our health to be tolerated or otherwise countenanced. They must therefore be silenced. But, we are assured, this silencing isn't "really" censorship because "free speech" isn't involved. In the case of sexually explicit materials, they say, it isn't words—that is, speech—but morally objectionable pictures that the state should outlaw. The outlawing of tobacco ads is also said not to be censorship, but something else. Casting about for some less loaded euphemism, our Washington wordsmiths have coined the phrase, "ban on advertising." This ban, or whatever it is, is supposed to be highly selective. It is to be aimed only at a small minority whose activities are said to be injurious to the health or morals of the vast majority.

Who in good conscience could object to these or any other measure claiming to promote health or moral decency or any similarly admirable goal?

Answer: I can. And I think that any liberty-loving democrat can, too.

Let me be blunt: I have no particular affection for drug dealers (or users), or for pornographers and their customers, or for tobacco companies or smokers. Nor do I use any of their products. But the fact that they make such tempting targets for the New Prohibitionists should give us pause. It is precisely because there is so little love lost on drug dealers, pornographers, and tobacco producers that those who love democracy had better have a care. As Mill warned—and as the history of our century shows with alarming clarity—scapegoating is always selective at first. Although the members of a particular unpopular minority are always the first to lose their liberty, they are never the last to lose it.

The modern movement toward the all-powerful paternal state has proceeded in a piecemeal way. It is a revolution wrought not by the single great bite but by a long series of small, highly selective nibbles around the unguarded edges of our liberties. For this reason the movement's most fitting symbol would not be the biblical whale Leviathan, as Thomas Hobbes suggested in the seventeenth century, but the humble piranha. The bite of a single piranha, I am told—though I have no wish to test this myself—is neither fatal nor even particularly painful. But the cumulative effect of a series of nibbles by a school of these tiny creatures is dreadful to behold.

So it is with censorship. A tiny bite here, a little nibble there, and we are very soon stripped of our liberties and the life and health of our greater public body—the body politic—is gravely imperiled. However small, however "selective" its target, however carefully it is aimed, the paternalist's favorite weapon must eventually destroy the liberties, and perchance even the lives, of those whose interests it initially purported to protect.

Like it or not, any government restriction on any form of speech—including advertising—amounts to an abridgement of the free speech and expression protected by the First Amendment. If it is to survive and flourish, democracy requires an intelligent and informed citizenry, just as the free market requires intelligent and informed consumers. Because the free society and the free market are alike in requiring the free flow of information in all its forms, a ban on the advertising of any product makes a mockery of both. Censorship—for that is what such restrictions amount to—is nothing less than the constricting of choice through the withholding of ideas and information about alternative ways of thinking and acting and living one's life as one sees fit.

The New Prohibitionists are right in at least one respect. They are correct in casting their crusade against free choice and free speech as a public health issue. The kind of legislation they wish to enact does raise profound questions about health, all right—the health of our democratic body politic. The real issue, in the final analysis, is not whether alcohol, drugs, tobacco, or any other product is bad for one's health but whether a democratic polity can survive the ministrations of well-meaning paternalists bent on protecting us from ourselves.

Every well-intentioned proposal to outlaw or restrict any sort of self-regarding or private action and speech in all its forms should be required to carry a label reading "Warning: Paternalism Is Dangerous to the Health of the Body Politic."

Paternalism promises illusory cures for imaginary ailments. In a free society paternalism can never be the remedy for anything. Paternalism is, instead, the disease for which the libertarian philosophy is the cure.

22

LIBERTARIAN ANARCHISM

MURRAY ROTHBARD

One of the best-known contemporary libertarian or neoclassical liberal writers, Murray Rothbard (1926–) is an economist by profession. Rothbard believes not that government should be kept small, but that it should be abolished altogether. Rothbard is a libertarian anarchist, who contends that government is an entirely *un*necessary evil.

Source: Murray Rothbard, For a New Liberty *(New York: Macmillan, 1973), pp. 8–12, 18–19, 34–35, 40. Reprinted by permission of Murray Rothbard and the Libertarian Review Foundation.*

Throughout the numerous factions and splinters of the movement, . . . there is agreement on the central core of the libertarian creed. The crucial axiom of that creed is: no man or group of men have the right to aggress against the person or property of anyone else. This might be called the "nonaggression" axiom. "Aggression" is defined as the initiation of the use or threat of physical violence against the person or property of someone else. Aggression is therefore synonymous with "invasion." How this axiom may be arrived at will be discussed below, and the paths toward attaining the axiom vary among different groups of libertarians. But all libertarians agree on nonagression as the central axiom of their doctrine.

If no man may aggress against—invade—the person or property of another, this means that every man is free to do whatever he wishes, except commit such aggression. The great nineteenth-century libertarian theorist Herbert Spencer formulated a similar axiom: "Law of Equal Liberty." "Freedom" or "liberty" is therefore rigorously defined in such a credo as: the absence of invasion. A man is free when he is not being aggressed against; and all men, or "society," is free when no aggression or invasion is being committed.

If no man may aggress against another; if, in short, everyone has the absolute right to be "free" from aggression, then this at once implies that the libertarian stands foursquare for what are generally known as "civil liberties": the freedom to speak, publish, assemble, and to engage in such "victimless crimes" as pornography, sexual deviation, and prostitution (which the libertarian does not regard as "crimes" at all, since he defines a "crime" as violent invasion of someone else's person or property). Furthermore, he regards conscription as slavery on a massive scale. And since war, especially modern war, entails the mass slaughter of civilians, the libertarian regards such conflicts as mass murder and therefore totally illegitimate.

All of these positions are now considered "leftist" on the contemporary ideological scale. On the other hand, since the libertarian also opposes invasion of the rights of private property, this also means that he just as emphatically opposes government interference with property rights or with the free market economy through controls, regulations, subsidies, or prohibitions. For if every individual has the right to his own property without having to suffer aggressive depredation, then he also has the right to give away his property (bequest and inheritance) and to exchange it for the property of others (free contract and the free market economy) without interference. The libertarian favors the right to unrestricted private property and free-exchange; hence, a system of "laissez-faire capitalism."

In current terminology again, the libertarian position on property and economics would be called "extreme right wing." But the libertarian sees no inconsistency in being "leftist" on some issues and "rightist" on others. On the contrary, he sees his own position as virtually the *only* consistent one, consistent on behalf of the liberty of every individual. For how can the leftist be opposed to the violence of war and conscription while at the same time supporting the violence of taxation and government control? And how can the rightist trumpet his devotion to private property and free enterprise while at the same time favoring war, conscription, and the outlawing of noninvasive activities and practices that he deems immoral? And how can the rightist favor a free market while seeing nothing amiss in the vast subsidies, distortions, and unproductive inefficiencies involved in the military-industrial complex?

While opposing any and all private or group aggression against the rights of person and property, the libertarian sees that throughout history and into the present day, there has been one central, dominant, and overriding aggressor upon all of these rights: the State. In contrast to all other thinkers, left, right, or in-between, the libertarian refuses to give the State the moral sanction to commit actions that almost everyone agrees would be immoral, illegal, and criminal if committed by any person or group in society. The libertarian, in short, insists on applying the general moral law to everyone, and makes no special exemptions for any person or group. But if we look at the State naked, as it were, we see that it is universally allowed, and even encouraged, to commit all the acts which even nonlibertarians concede are reprehensible crimes. The State habitually commits mass murder, which it calls "war," or sometimes "suppression of subversion"; the State engages in enslavement into its military forces, which it calls "conscription"; and it lives and has its being in the practice of forcible theft, which it calls "taxation." The libertarian insists that whether or not such practices are supported by the majority of the population is not germane to their nature: that, regardless of popular sanction, War is Mass Murder, Conscription is Slavery, and Taxation is Robbery. The libertarian, in short, is almost completely the child in the fable, pointing out insistently that the emperor has no clothes.

Throughout the ages, the emperor has had a series of pseudo-clothes provided for him by the nation's intellectual caste. In past centuries, the intellectuals informed the public that the State or its rulers were divine, or at least clothed in divine authority, and therefore what might *look* to the naïve and untutored eye as despotism, mass murder, and theft on a grand scale was only the divine working its benign and mysterious ways in the body politic. In recent decades, as the divine sanction has worn a bit threadbare, the emperor's "court intellectuals" have spun ever more sophisticated apologia: informing the public that what the government does is for the "common good" and the "public welfare," that the process of taxation-and-spending works through the mysterious process of the "multiplier" to keep the economy on an even keel, and that, in any case, a wide variety of governmental "services" could not possibly be performed by citizens acting voluntarily on the market or in society. All of this the libertarian denies: he sees the various apologia as fraudulent means of obtaining public support for the State's rule, and he insists that whatever services the government actually performs could be supplied far more efficiently and far more morally by private and cooperative enterprise.

The libertarian therefore considers one of his prime educational tasks is to spread the demystification and desanctification of the State among its hapless subjects. His task is to demonstrate repeatedly and in depth that not only the emperor but even the "democratic" state has no clothes; that all governments subsist by exploitive rule over the public; and that such rule is the reverse of objective necessity. He strives to show that the very existence of taxation and the State necessarily sets up a class division between the exploiting rulers and the exploited ruled. He seeks to show that the task of the court intellectuals who have always supported the State has ever been to weave mystification in order to induce the public to accept State rule, and that these intellectuals obtain, in return, a share in the power and pelf extracted by the rulers from their deluded subjects.

Take, for example, the institution of taxation, which statists have claimed is in some sense really "voluntary." Anyone who truly believes in the "voluntary" nature of taxation is invited to refuse to pay taxes and to see what then happens to him. If we analyze taxation, we find that, among all the persons and institutions in society, only the government acquires its revenues through coercive violence. Everyone else in society acquires income *either* through voluntary gift (lodge, charitable society, chess club) *or* through the sale of goods or services voluntarily purchased by consumers. If anyone *but* the government proceeded to "tax," this would clearly be considered coercion and thinly disguised banditry. Yet the mystical trappings of "sovereignty" have so veiled the process that only libertarians are prepared to call taxation what it is: legalized and organized theft on a grand scale. . . .

Further, if taxation is robbery, then it becomes clear that a tax or monopoly-coercing government is a robber band, and deserves not reverence but abolition—or, if abolition cannot be achieved, at the least there should be a relentless whittling down of governmental power and activity. Civil disobedience to unjust laws and decrees—including not only the draft but taxation itself—becomes morally legitimate if not always strategically or tactically prudent.

Superpatriotism is at the least very difficult for any anarchist, so the great bulk of anarcho-capitalists have abandoned their former rightist devotion to the Cold War and to American foreign policy. Generally, they have adopted an "ultra-isolationist" foreign policy as the external corollary to their opposition to domestic statism. . . .

If . . . land is nature- or God-given then so are the people's talents, health, and beauty. And just as all these attributes are given to specific individuals and not to "society," so then are land and natural resources. All of these resources are given to individuals and not to "society," which is an abstraction that does not actually exist. There is no existing entity called "society": there are only interacting individuals. To say that "society" should own land or any other property in common, then, must mean that a group of oligarchs—in practice, government bureaucrats—should own the property, and at the expense of expropriating the creator or the homesteader who had originally brought this product into existence.

Moreover, no one can produce *anything* without the cooperation of original land, if only as standing room. No man can produce or create anything by his labor alone; he must have the cooperation of land and other natural raw materials.

Man comes into the world with just himself and the world around him—the land and natural resources given him by nature. He takes these resources and transforms them by his labor and mind and energy into goods more useful to man.

Therefore, if an individual cannot own original land, neither can he in the full sense own any of the fruits of his labor. The farmer cannot own his wheat crop if he cannot own the land on which the wheat grows. Now that his labor has been inextricably mixed with the land, he cannot be deprived of one without being deprived of the other.

Moreover, if a producer is *not* entitled to the fruits of his labor, who is? . . . Land in its original state is unused and unowned. Georgists[1] and other land communalists may claim that the whole world population *really* "owns" it, but if no one has yet used it, it is in the real sense owned and controlled by no one. The pioneer, the homesteader, the first user and transformer of this land, is the man who first brings this simple valueless thing into production and social use. It is difficult to see the morality of depriving him of ownership in favor of people who have never gotten within a thousand miles of the land, and who may not even know of the existence of the property over which they are supposed to have a claim.

The moral, natural rights issue involved here is even clearer if we consider the case of animals. Animals are "economic land," since they are original nature-given resources. Yet will anyone deny full title to a horse to the man who finds and domesticates it—is this any different from the acorns and berries that are generally conceded to the gatherer? Yet in land, too, some homesteader takes the previously "wild," undomesticated land, and "tames" it by putting it to productive use.

The central core of the libertarian creed, then, is to establish the absolute right to private property of every man; first, in his own body, and second, in the previously unused natural resources which he first transforms by his labor. These two axioms, the right of self-ownership and the right to "homestead," establish the complete set of principles of the libertarian system. The entire libertarian doctrine then becomes the spinning out and the application of all the implications of this central doctrine.

EDITORS' NOTE

1. Followers of Henry George (1839–1897), an American economist.

PART FOUR

CONSERVATISM

Conservatism is both easy and difficult to define. It is easy because conservatives share a desire to conserve something—usually the traditions or customary way of life of their societies. Thus conservatives, as a rule, generally resist change, preferring to cling to the "tried and true" ways. But different conservatives will have different ideas about what is valuable and worth preserving. Besides that, traditions and customs vary widely from one society to another so that a conservative in one society may want to preserve traditions that are at odds with the traditions of another society. Conservatives may all want to conserve something, in other words, but they do not all want to conserve the same things—and that is what makes their ideology difficult to define.

In the case of Edmund Burke (1729–1797), widely regarded as the father of conservatism, the desire to conserve a traditional way of life is quite clear. The most famous writings of Burke—an Irishman who served for many years as a member of the British Parliament—were directed against the French Revolution, which he saw as a misguided attempt to create an entirely new kind of society based on abstract reason. The revolutionaries, he charged in *Reflections on the Revolution in France* (1790), are attacking all the institutions—the king, the aristocracy, the Church—that give order and stability to their country. If they succeed, Burke said, they will find themselves and their society adrift in a storm-tossed sea, all sail and no anchor.

Burke, like conservatives since his time, recognized that change is an inevitable part of life. But he believed that change can occur in either a healthy or a dangerous way. If it is the result of gradual or piecemeal reform, it will promote the health of society. But rapid change and radical innovation are likely to prove disastrous. Revolutionaries who want to transform whole societies overnight are like people who tear down their old house, only to find themselves freezing to death before they can build a new one.

Burke wrote his *Reflections* less out of concern for the future of France than out of fear that the revolution would inspire a similar upheaval in England. He did not argue, in any case, that France could and should go back to the way things were before the revolution. But a more extreme group of conservatives reacted in just this way. These "reactionaries," such as Joseph de Maistre (1753–1821), hoped to turn back the clock, returning to a prerevolutionary France guided by "throne and altar," or king and church. Since then, "reactionary" refers to anyone who wants to restore or return to an earlier way of life.

During the first half of the nineteenth century conservatives generally opposed liberalism and democracy, two impulses that they blamed for upsetting the established social order. Liberalism, with its emphasis on the rights and interests of the individual, threatened to tear the delicate fabric of society. A person is not merely an individual, the conservatives maintained, but a part of a larger whole who has a duty to other members of the society. When all people are joined together, like the criss-crossing threads of a fabric, the society is strong and beautiful. When each goes his or her own way, however, the social fabric frays and begins to unravel. Life then becomes dull and drab, especially as capitalism turns the individual's attention to commerce—to "getting and spending" that "lay waste our powers," as the English poet William Wordsworth (1770–1850) put it. Nature, literature, and religion are all reduced to the lowest common denominator in the age of commerce—money.

Many conservatives also regarded democracy as a threat to social order. Like Burke, they believed that human beings are ruled more by their passions than by their reason. If the people govern, who will govern the people? Who, or what, will keep the common people from destroying their society? At the worst, according to conservatives, democracy will lead to chaos and anarchy because the common people will be too shortsighted to take measures that will restrain their passions and desires. At best, democracy will "level" society by reducing everyone to the same condition. Either way, conservatives warned of the dangers of "mass society"—a warning still sounded in the twentieth century by José Ortega y Gasset (1883–1955) and other writers.

But something curious happened in the late nineteenth century. In England, and especially in the United States, "conservative" came to be applied to those who held to the views of the early liberals. As more liberals adopted the "welfare liberal" position that government should be used to promote individual liberty, anyone who resisted this change began to seem old-fashioned. Those who continued to accept the classical or neoclassical liberal view that government is a necessary evil now seemed to be resisting change, and therefore taking a "conservative" position.

Throughout the twentieth century there has been an uneasy alliance between "Burkean" or "classical" conservatives, such as Michael Oakeshott (1901–), and modern conservatives, such as Margaret Thatcher and Ronald Reagan, who declare that government should not "interfere" with individuals competing in the marketplace. The alliance has held together in large part because conservatives of both sorts share a respect for private property, a (sometimes grudging) acceptance of democracy, and a fear of communism. Now that the communist threat seems to be receding, this conservative alliance may come under increasing strain.

Conservatism comes in many varieties these days, including the conservatism of the evangelical Protestants who compose the New Right (or the New Christian Right) in the United States and the conservatism of the disenchanted welfare liberals called neoconservatives. As we noted earlier, all wish to conserve something. But what they wish to conserve, and how they propose to do it, remain matters of difference and dispute.

23

SOCIETY, REVERENCE, AND THE "TRUE NATURAL ARISTOCRACY"

EDMUND BURKE

When the French Revolution began in 1789, many in England greeted it with enthusiasm. But Edmund Burke (1729–1797), an Irishman who moved to England and served for many years in Parliament, saw the revolution as a threat to order and liberty. In his *Reflections on the Revolution in France* (1790), Burke not only criticized the revolutionaries, but virtually predicted that the revolution would end in chaos. This and his other speeches and writings—such as the *Appeal from the New to the Old Whigs* (1791), from which the second selection is drawn—have won Burke the title of father of conservatism.

Source: The Works of Edmund Burke *(London: George Bell and Sons, 1901), vols. II, pp. 332–335, 359, 364–369, and III, pp. 85–87.*

REFLECTIONS ON THE REVOLUTION IN FRANCE

. . .

Government is not made in virtue of natural rights, which may and do exist in total independence of it; and exist in much greater clearness, and in a much greater degree of abstract perfection: but their abstract perfection is their practical defect. By having a right to every thing they want every thing. Government is a contrivance of human wisdom to provide for human *wants*. Men have a right that these wants should be provided for by this wisdom. Among these wants is to be reckoned the want, out of civil society, of a sufficient restraint upon their passions. Society requires not only that the passions of individuals should be subjected, but that even in the mass and body as well as in the individuals, the inclinations of men should frequently be thwarted, their will controlled, and their passions brought into subjection. This can only be done *by a power out of themselves;* and not, in the exercise of its function, subject to that will and to those passions which it is its office to bridle and subdue. In this sense the restraints on men, as well as their liberties, are to be reckoned among their rights. But as the liberties and the restrictions vary with times and circumstances, and admit of infinite modifications, they cannot be settled upon any abstract rule; and nothing is so foolish as to discuss them upon that principle.

The moment you abate any thing from the full rights of men, each to govern himself, and suffer any artificial positive limitation upon those rights, from that moment the whole organization of government becomes a consideration of convenience. This it is which makes the constitution of a state, and the due distribution of its powers, a matter of the most delicate and complicated skill. It requires a deep knowledge of human nature and human necessities, and of the things which facilitate or obstruct the various ends which are to be pursued by the mechanism of civil institutions. The state is to have recruits to its strength, and remedies to its distempers. What is the use of discussing a man's abstract right to food or to medicine? The question is upon the method of procuring and administering them. In that deliberation I shall always advise to call in the aid of the farmer and the physician, rather than the professor of metaphysics.

The science of constructing a commonwealth, or renovating it, or reforming it, is, like every other experimental science, not to be taught *a priori*. Nor is it a short experience that can instruct us in that practical science; because the real effects of moral causes are not always immediate; but that which in the first instance is prejudicial may be excellent in its remoter operation; and its excellence may arise even . . . from the ill effects it produces in the beginning. The reverse also happens; and very plausible schemes, with very pleasing commencements, have often shameful and lamentable conclusions. In states there are often some obscure and almost latent causes, things which appear at first view of little moment, on which a very great part of its prosperity or adversity may most essentially depend. The science of government being therefore so practical in itself, and intended for such practical purposes, a matter which requires experience, and even more experience than any person can gain in his whole life, however sagacious and observing he may be, it is with infinite caution that any man ought to venture upon pulling down an edifice which has answered in any tolerable degree for ages the common purposes of society, or on building it up again, without having models and patterns of approved utility before his eyes.

These metaphysic rights entering into common life, like rays of light which pierce into a dense medium, are, by the laws of nature, refracted from their straight line. Indeed in the gross and complicated mass of human passions and concerns, the primitive rights of men undergo such a variety of refractions and reflections, that it becomes absurd to talk of them as if they continued in the simplicity of their original direction. The nature of man is intricate; the objects of society are of the greatest possible complexity; and therefore no simple disposition or direction of power can be suitable either to man's nature, or to the quality of his affairs. When I hear the simplicity of contrivance aimed at and boasted of in any new political constitutions, I am at no loss to decide that the artificers are grossly ignorant of their trade, or totally negligent of their duty. The simple governments are fundamentally defective, to say no worse of them. If you were to contemplate society in but one point of view, all these simple modes of polity are infinitely captivating. In effect each would answer its single end much more perfectly than the more complex is able to attain all its complex purposes. But it is better that the whole should be imperfectly and anomalously answered, than that, while some parts are provided for with great exactness, others might be totally neglected, or perhaps materially injured, by the over-care of a favourite member.

The pretended rights of these theorists are all extremes; and in proportion as they are metaphysically true, they are morally and politically false. The rights of men are in a sort of *middle*, incapable of definition, but not impossible to be discerned. The rights of men in governments are their advantages; and these are often in balances between differences of good; in compromises sometimes between good and evil, and sometimes, between evil and evil. Political reason is a computing principle; adding, subtracting, multiplying, and dividing, morally and not metaphysically or mathematically, true moral denominations.

By these theorists the right of the people is almost always sophistically confounded with their power. The body of the community, whenever it can come to act, can meet with no effectual resistance; but till power and right are the same, the whole body of them has no right inconsistent with virtue, and the first of all virtues, prudence. Men have no right to what is not reasonable, and to what is not for their benefit. . . .

We preserve the whole of our feelings still native and entire, unsophisticated by pedantry and infidelity. We have real hearts of flesh and blood beating in our bosoms. We fear God; we look up with awe to kings; with affection to parliaments; with duty to magistrates; with reverence to priests; and with respect to nobility. Why? Because when such ideas are brought before our minds, it is *natural* to be so affected; because all other feelings are false and spurious, and tend to corrupt our minds, to vitiate our primary morals, to render us unfit for rational liberty; and by teaching us a servile, licentious, and abandoned insolence, to be our low sport for a few holidays to make us perfectly fit for, and justly deserving of slavery, through the whole course of our lives.

You see, Sir, that in this enlightened age I am bold enough to confess, that we are generally men of untaught feelings; that instead of casting away all our old prejudices, we cherish them to a very considerable degree, and, to take more shame to ourselves, we cherish them because they are prejudices; and the longer they have lasted, and the more generally they have prevailed, the more we cherish them. We are afraid to put men to live and trade each on his own private stock of reason; because we suspect that this stock in each man is small, and that the individuals would do better to avail themselves of the general bank and capital of nations, and of ages. Many of our men of speculation, instead of exploding general prejudices, employ their sagacity to discover the latent wisdom which prevails in them. If they find what they seek, and they seldom fail, they think it more wise to continue the prejudice, with the reason involved, than to cast away the coat of prejudice, and to leave nothing but the naked reason; because prejudice, with its reason, has a motive to give action to that reason, and an affection which will give it permanence. Prejudice is of ready application in the emergency; it previously engages the mind in a steady course of wisdom and virtue, and does not leave the man hesitating in the moment of decision, sceptical, puzzled, and unresolved. Prejudice renders a man's virtue his habit; and not a series of unconnected acts. Through just prejudice, his duty becomes a part of his nature. . . .

The consecration of the state, by a state religious establishment, is necessary also to operate with an wholesome awe upon free citizens; because, in order to secure their freedom, they must enjoy some determinate portion of power. To them therefore a religion connected with the state, and with their duty towards it, becomes even more necessary than in such societies, where the people by the terms of their subjection are confined to private sentiments, and the management of their own family concerns. All persons possessing any portion of power ought to be strongly and awefully impressed with an idea that they act in trust; and that they are to account for their conduct in that trust to the one great master, author and founder of society.

This principle ought even to be more strongly impressed upon the minds of those who compose the collective sovereignty than upon those of single princes. Without instruments, these princes can do nothing. Whoever uses instruments, in finding helps, finds also impediments. Their power is therefore by no means compleat; nor are they safe in extreme abuse. Such persons, however elated by flattery, arrogance, and self-opinion, must be sensible that, whether covered or not by positive law, in some way or other they are accountable even here for the abuse of their trust. If they are not cut off by a rebellion of their people, they may be strangled by the very Janissaries kept for their security against all other rebellion. Thus we have seen the king of France sold by his soldiers for an encrease of pay. But where popular authority is absolute and unrestrained, the people have an infinitely greater, because a far better founded confidence in their own power. They are themselves, in a great measure, their own instruments. They are nearer to their objects. Besides, they are less under responsibility to one of the greatest controlling powers on earth, the sense of fame and estimation. The share of infamy that is likely to fall to the lot of each individual in public acts, is small indeed; the operation of opinion being in the inverse ratio to the number of those who abuse power. Their own approbation of their own acts has to them the appearance of a public judgment in their favour. A perfect democracy is therefore the most shameless thing in the world. As it is the most shameless, it is also the most fearless. No man apprehends in his person he can be made subject to punishment. Certainly the people at large never ought: for as all punishments are for example towards the conservation of the people at large, the people at large can never become the subject of punishment by any human hand. It is therefore of infinite importance that they should not be suffered to imagine that their will, any more than that of kings, is the standard of right and wrong. They ought to be persuaded that they are full as little entitled, and far less qualified, with safety to themselves, to use any arbitrary power whatsoever; that therefore they are not, under a false shew of liberty, but, in truth, to exercise an unnatural inverted domination, tyrannically to exact, from those who officiate in the state, not an entire devotion to their interest, which is their right, but an abject submission to their occasional will; extinguishing thereby, in all those who serve them, all moral principle, all sense of dignity, all use of judgment, and all consistency of character, whilst by the very same process they give themselves up a proper, a suitable, but a more contemptible prey to the servile ambition of popular sycophants or courtly flatterers.

When the people have emptied themselves of all the lust of selfish will, which without religion it is utterly impossible they ever should, when they are conscious that they exercise, and exercise perhaps in an higher link of the order of delegation, the power, which to be legitimate must be according to that eternal immutable law, in which will and reason are the same, they will be more careful how they place power in base and incapable hands. In their nomination to office, they will not appoint to the exercise of authority, as to a pitiful job, but as to an holy function; not according to their sordid selfish interest, nor to their wanton caprice, nor to their arbitrary will; but they will confer that power (which any man may well tremble to give or to receive) on those only, in whom they may discern that predominant proportion of active virtue and wisdom, taken together and fitted to the charge, such, as in the great and inevitable mixed mass of human imperfections and infirmities, is to be found.

When they are habitually convinced that no evil can be acceptable, either in the act or the permission, to him whose essence is good, they will be better able to extirpate out of the minds of all magistrates, civil, ecclesiastical, or military, any thing that bears the least resemblance to a proud and lawless domination.

But one of the first and most leading principles on which the commonwealth and the laws are consecrated, is lest the temporary possessors and life-renters in it, unmindful of what they have received from their ancestors, or of what is due to their posterity, should act as if they were the entire masters; that they should not think it amongst their rights to cut off the entail, or commit waste on the inheritance, by destroying at their pleasure the whole original fabric of their society; hazarding to leave to those who come after them, a ruin instead of an habitation—and teaching these successors as little to respect their contrivances, as they had themselves respected the institutions of their forefathers. By this unprincipled facility of changing the state as often, and as much, and in as many ways as there are floating fancies or fashions, the whole chain and continuity of the commonwealth would be broken. No one generation could link with the other. Men would become little better than the flies of a summer.

And first of all the science of jurisprudence, the pride of the human intellect, which, with all its defects, redundancies, and errors, is the collected reason of ages, combining the principles of original justice with the infinite variety of human concerns, as a heap of old exploded errors, would be no longer studied. Personal self-sufficiency and arrogance (the certain attendants upon all those who have never experienced a wisdom greater than their own) would usurp the tribunal. Of course, no certain laws, establishing invariable grounds of hope and fear, would keep the actions of men in a certain course, or direct them to a certain end. Nothing stable in the modes of holding property, or exercising function, could form a solid ground on which any parent could speculate in the education of his offspring, or in a choice for their future establishment in the world. No principles would be early worked into the habits. As soon as the most able instructor had completed his laborious course of instruction, instead of sending forth his pupil, accomplished in a virtuous discipline, fitted to procure him attention and respect, in his place in society, he would find every thing altered; and that he had turned out a poor creature to the contempt and derision of the world, ignorant of the true grounds of estimation. Who would insure a tender and delicate sense of honour to beat almost with the first pulses of the heart, when no man could know what would be the test of honour in a nation, continually varying the standard of its coin? No part of life would retain its acquisitions. Barbarism with regard to science and literature, unskilfulness with regard to arts and manufactures, would infallibly succeed to the want of a steady education and settled principle; and thus the commonwealth itself would, in a few generations, crumble away, be disconnected into the dust and powder of individuality, and at length dispersed to all the winds of heaven.

To avoid therefore the evils of inconstancy and versatility, ten thousand times worse than those of obstinacy and the blindest prejudice, we have consecrated the state, that no man should approach to look into its defects or corruptions but with due caution; that he should never dream of beginning its reformation by its subversion; that he should approach to the faults of the state as to the wounds of a father, with pious awe and trembling sollicitude. By this wise prejudice we are taught to look with horror on those children of their country who are prompt rashly to hack that aged parent in pieces, and put him into the kettle of magicians, in hopes that by their poisonous weeds, and wild incantations, they may regenerate the paternal constitution, and renovate their father's life.

Society is indeed a contract. Subordinate

contracts for objects of mere occasional interest may be dissolved at pleasure—but the state ought not to be considered as nothing better than a partnership agreement in a trade of pepper and coffee, callico or tobacco, or some other such low concern, to be taken up for a little temporary interest, and to be dissolved by the fancy of the parties. It is to be looked on with other reverence; because it is not a partnership in things subservient only to the gross animal existence of a temporary and perishable nature. It is a partnership in all science; a partnership in all art; a partnership in every virtue, and in all perfection. As the ends of such a partnership cannot be obtained in many generations, it becomes a partnership not only between those who are living, but between those who are living, those who are dead, and those who are to be born. Each contract of each particular state is but a clause in the great primaeval contract of eternal society, linking the lower with the higher natures, connecting the visible and invisible world, according to a fixed compact sanctioned by the inviolable oath which holds all physical and all moral natures, each in their appointed place.

APPEAL FROM THE NEW TO THE OLD WHIGS

. . .

. . . To enable men to act with the weight and character of a people, and to answer the ends for which they are incorporated into that capacity, we must suppose them (by means immediate or consequential) to be in that state of habitual social discipline in which the wiser, the more expert, and the more opulent conduct, and by conducting enlighten and protect, the weaker, the less knowing, and the less provided with the goods of fortune. When the multitude are not under this discipline, they can scarcely be said to be in civil society. . . .

A true natural aristocracy is not a separate interest in the state, or separable from it. It is an essential integrant part of any large body rightly constituted. It is formed out of a class of legitimate presumptions, which, taken as generalities, must be admitted for actual truths. To be bred in a place of estimation; to see nothing low and sordid from one's infancy; to be taught to respect one's self; to be habituated to the censorial inspection of the public eye; to look early to public opinion; to stand upon such elevated ground as to be enabled to take a large view of the wide-spread and infinitely diversified combinations of men and affairs in a large society; to have leisure to read, to reflect, to converse; to be enabled to draw the court and attention of the wise and learned, wherever they are to be found; to be habituated in armies to command and to obey; to be taught to despise danger in the pursuit of honor and duty; to be formed to the greatest degree of vigilance, foresight, and circumspection, in a state of things in which no fault is committed with impunity and the slightest mistakes draw on the most ruinous consequences; to be led to a guarded and regulated conduct, from a sense that you are considered as an instructor of your fellow-citizens in their highest concerns, and that you act as a reconciler between God and man; to be employed as an administrator of law and justice, and to be thereby amongst the first benefactors to mankind; to be a professor of high science, or of liberal and ingenuous art; to be amongst rich traders, who from their success are presumed to have sharp and vigorous understandings, and to possess the virtues of diligence, order, constancy, and regularity, and to have cultivated an habitual regard to commutative justice: these are the circumstances of men that form what I should call a *natural* aristocracy, without which there is no nation.

The state of civil society which necessarily generates this aristocracy is a state of Nature,—and much more truly so than a savage and incoherent mode of life. For man is by nature reasonable; and he is never perfectly in his natural state, but when he is placed where reason may be best cultivated and most predominates. Art is man's nature. We are as much, at least, in a state of Nature in formed manhood as in immature and helpless infancy. Men, qualified in the manner I have just described, form in Nature, as she operates in the common modification of society, the leading, guiding, and governing part. It is the soul to the body, without which the man does not exist. To give, therefore, no more importance, in the social order, to such descriptions of men than that of so many units is a horrible usurpation.

When great multitudes act together, under that discipline of Nature, I recognize the PEOPLE. I acknowledge something that perhaps equals, and ought always to guide, the sovereignty of convention. In all things the voice of this grand chorus of national harmony ought to have a mighty and decisive influence. But when you disturb this harmony,—when you break up this beautiful order, this array of truth and Nature, as well as of habit and prejudice,—when you separate the common sort of men from their proper chieftains, so as to form them into an adverse army,—I no longer know that venerable object called the people in such a disbanded race of deserters and vagabonds. For a while they may be terrible, indeed,—but in such a manner as wild beasts are terrible. The mind owes to them no sort of submission. They are, as they have always been reputed, rebels.

24

CONSERVATISM AS REACTION

JOSEPH DE MAISTRE

On the European continent some of the aristocratic opponents of the French Revolution saw it as the logical, if terrible, outcome of the eighteenth century, with its glorification of reason. Because they reacted against the revolution, these writers came to be known as the "reactionaries." Perhaps the most important writer who sought to restore the old order of European society—with the Church, monarchy, and aristocracy firmly in control—was Joseph de Maistre (1753–1821). The following selections are from de Maistre's *Considerations on France* (1796) and *Study on Sovereignty* (first published in 1884).

Source: The Works of Joseph de Maistre *(New York: Macmillan, 1965), pp. 77–80, 102–105, 108–110, 113–114, 118. Reprinted with permission of Macmillan Publishing Company from* The Works of Joseph de Maistre, *edited and translated by Jack Lively.*

CONSIDERATIONS ON FRANCE

. . .

The 1795 [French] constitution, like its predecessors, was made for *man*. But there is no such thing as *man* in the world. During my life, I have seen, Frenchmen, Italians, Russians, and so on; thanks to Montesquieu, I even know that one can be *Persian;* but I must say, as for *man*, I have never come across him anywhere; if he exists, he is completely unknown to me.

Is there a single country in the world in which there is a council of five hundred, a council of elders, and five leaders? Such a constitution may be offered to every human association from China to Geneva. But a constitution that is made for all nations is made for none: it is a pure abstraction, an academic exercise of the mind, according to some hypothetical ideal, that should be addressed to *man*, in whatever imaginary realm he inhabits.

Is not a constitution a solution to the following problem: *Given the population, customs, religion, geographical situation, political relations, wealth, good and bad qualities of a particular nation, to find the laws which suit it?*

Yet this problem is not even approached in the 1795 constitution, which was aimed solely at *man*.

Thus every imaginable reason combines to show that this enterprise has not the divine blessing. It is no more than a schoolboy's exercise.

STUDY ON SOVEREIGNTY

THE FOUNDERS

The government of a nation is no more its own work than its language. Just as in nature the seeds of an infinite number of plants are destined to perish unless the wind or the hand of man puts them where they can germinate, so also there are in nations certain qualities and powers which are ineffective until they get a stimulus from circumstances either alone or used by a skillful hand.

The founder of a nation is precisely this skillful hand. Gifted with an extraordinary penetration or, what is more probable, with an infallible instinct (for often personal genius does not realize what it is achieving, which is what distinguishes it above all from intelligence), he divines those hidden powers and qualities which shape a nation's character, the means of bringing them to life, putting them into action, and making the greatest possible use of them. He is never to be seen writing or debating; his mode of acting derives from inspiration; and if sometimes he takes up a pen, it is not to argue but to command.

One of the greatest errors of this age is to believe that the political constitution of nations is the work of man alone and that a constitution can be made as a watchmaker makes a watch. This is quite false; but still more false is the belief that this great work can be executed by an assembly of men. The author of all things has only two ways of giving a government to a people. Most often he reserves to himself its formation more directly by making it grow, as it were, imperceptibly like a plant, through the conjunction of a multitude of those circumstances we call fortuitous. But when he wants to lay quickly the foundations of a political structure and to show the world a creation of this kind, he confides his power to rare men, the true Elect. Scattered thinly over the centuries, they rise like obelisks on time's path, and, as humanity grows older, they appear the less. To fit them for these unusual tasks, God invests them with unusual power, often unknown to their contemporaries and perhaps to themselves. . . .

No important and truly constitutional reform ever establishes anything new; it simply declares and defends previously existing rights. This is why the constitution of a country can never be known from its written constitutional laws, because these laws are made at different periods only to lay down forgotten or contested rights, and because there are always a host of things which are not written. . . .

The different forms and degrees of sovereignty have given rise to the belief that it is the work of nations which have modified it at will. Nothing could be further from the truth. Every nation has the government suited to it, and none has chosen it. The remarkable thing is that, nearly every time a nation tries to give itself a government, or more accurately every time too great a section of the people set out with such an aim, the attempt works to its misfortune; for in this fatal confusion, it is too easy for a nation to mistake its real interests, to chase desperately after what cannot be suitable for it, and at the same time reject what is best for it: and we all know how harmful errors in this field are. . . .

. . . Men never respect what they have made. This is why an elective king never possesses the moral force of a hereditary sovereign because he is not sufficiently *noble,* that is to say, he does not possess that kind of grandeur independent of men which is the work of time. . . .

The mass of men play no part in political events. They even respect government only because it is not their work. This feeling is written indelibly on their hearts. They submit to sovereignty because they feel that it is something sacred that they can neither create nor destroy. If, through corruption and treacherous suggestions, they reach the point of effacing in themselves this preserving sentiment, if they have the misfortune to think that they are called as a body to reform the state, everything is lost. This is why, even in free states, it is extremely important for rulers to be separated from the mass of the people by that personal respect which stems from birth and wealth; for if opinion does not put a barrier between itself and authority, if power is not outside its scope, if the governed many can think themselves the equals of the governing few, government will collapse. Thus the aristocracy is a sovereign or ruling class by nature, and the principle of the French Revolution runs directly contrary to the eternal laws of nature. . . .

THE NATIONAL SOUL

All known nations have been happy and powerful to the degree that they have faithfully obeyed this national mind, which is nothing other than the destruction of individual dogmas and the absolute and general rule of national dogmas, that is to say, useful prejudices. Once let everyone rely on his individual reason in religion, and you will see immediately the rise of anarchy of belief or the annihilation of religious sovereignty. Likewise, if each man makes himself the judge of the principles of government you will see immediately the rise of civil anarchy or the annihilation of political sovereignty. Government is a true religion; it has its dogmas, its mysteries, its priests; to submit it to individual discussion is to destroy it; it has life only through the national mind, that is to say, political faith, which is a *creed.* Man's primary need is that his nascent reason should be curbed under a double yoke; it should be frustrated, and it should lose itself in the national mind, so that it changes its individual existence for another communal existence, just as a river which flows into the ocean still exists in the mass of water, but without name and distinct reality.

What is patriotism? It is this national mind of which I am speaking; it is individual *abnegation.* Faith and patriotism are the two great thaumaturges of the world. Both are divine. All their actions are miracles. Do not talk to them of scrutiny, choice, discussion, for they will say that you blaspheme. They know only two words, *submission* and *belief;* with these two levers, they raise the world. Their very errors are sublime. These two infants of Heaven prove their origin to all by creating and conserving; and if they unite, join their forces and together take possession of a nation, they exalt it, make it divine and increase its power a hundredfold. . . .

But can you, insignificant man, light this sacred fire that inflames nations? Can you give a common soul to several million men? Unite them under your laws? Range them closely around a common center? Shape the mind of men yet unborn? Make future generations obey you and create those age-old customs, those conserving *prejudices*, which are the father of the laws and stronger than them? What nonsense! . . .

APPLICATION OF THE PRECEDING PRINCIPLES

There is no doubt that, in a certain sense, reason is good for nothing. We have the scientific knowledge necessary for the maintenance of society; we have made conquests in mathematics and what is called natural science; but, once we leave the circle of our needs, our knowledge becomes either useless or doubtful. The human mind, ever restless, proliferates constantly succeeding theories. They are born, flourish, wither, and fall like leaves from the trees; the only difference is that their year is longer.

And in the whole of the moral and political world, what do we know, and what are we able to do? We *know* the morality handed down to us by our fathers, as a collection of dogmas or useful prejudices adopted by the national mind. But on this point we owe nothing to any man's individual reason. On the contrary, every time this reason has interfered, it has perverted morality.

In politics, we *know* that it is necessary to respect those powers established we know not how or by whom. When time leads to abuses capable of altering the root principle of a government, we *know* that it is necessary to remove these abuses, but without touching the principle itself, an act of delicate surgery; and we *are able* to carry through these salutary reforms until the time when the principle of life is totally vitiated and the death of the body politic is inevitable. . . .

MONARCHY

It can be said in general that all men are born for monarchy. This form of government is the most ancient and the most universal. . . . Monarchical government is so natural that, without realizing it, men identify it with sovereignty. They seem tacitly to agree that, wherever there is no king, there is no real *sovereign*. . . .

This is particularly striking in everything that has been said on both sides of the question that formed the subject of the first book of this work. The adversaries of divine origin always hold a grudge against *kings* and talk only of *kings*. They do not want to accept that the authority of kings comes from God: but it is not a question of *royalty* in particular but of *sovereignty* in general. Yes, all sovereignty derives from God; whatever form it takes, it is not the work of man. It is one, absolute and inviolable of its nature. Why, then, lay the blame on royalty, as though the inconveniences which are relied on to attack this system are not the same in any form of government? Once again, it is because royalty is *the natural government* and because in common discourse men confuse it with sovereignty by disregarding other governments, just as they neglect the exception when enunciating the general rule. . . .

Man must always be brought back to history, which is the first and indeed the only teacher in politics. Whoever says that man is born for liberty is speaking nonsense. If a being of a superior order undertook the *natural history* of man, surely he would seek his directions in the history of facts. When he knew what man is and has always been, what he does and has always done, he would write; and doubtless he would reject as foolish the notion that man is not what he should be and that his condition is contrary to the laws of creation. The very expression of this proposition is sufficient to refute it.

History is experimental politics; and just as, in the physical sciences, a hundred books of speculative theories disappear before a single experiment, in the same way in political science no theory can be allowed if it is not the more or less probable corollary of well-attested facts. If the question is asked, "What is the most natural government to man," history will reply, *It is monarchy*. . . .

How many faults power has committed! And

how steadfastly it ignores the means of conserving itself! Man is insatiable for power, he is infinite in his desires and, always discontented with what he has, loves only what he has not. People complain of the despotism of princes; they ought to complain of the despotism of *man*. We are all born despots, from the most absolute monarch of Asia to the infant who smothers a bird with its hand for the pleasure of seeing that there exists in the world a being weaker than itself. There is not a man who does not abuse power, and experience shows that the most abominable despots, if they manage to seize the scepter, are precisely those who rant against despotism. But the Author of nature has set bounds to the abuse of power: He has willed that it destroys itself once it goes beyond its natural limits. Everywhere He has written this law; in the physical as in the moral world, it surrounds us and makes itself constantly heard. Look at this gun: up to a certain point, the longer you make it, the more effective it will be; but once you go at all beyond this limit, its effectiveness will be reduced. Look at this telescope; up to a certain point, the bigger you make it, the more powerful it will be; but go beyond that, and invincible nature will turn all your efforts to perfect the instrument against you. This is a crude image of power. To conserve itself, it must restrain itself, and it must always keep away from that point at which its most extreme effort leads to its own death.

Certainly I do not like *popular* assemblies any more than the next man; but French folly ought not to turn us aside from the truth and wisdom of the happy mean. If there is any indisputable maxim, it is that, in all mutinies, insurrections, and revolutions *the people always start by being right and always end by being wrong.*

25

THE POET AS CONSERVATIVE

WILLIAM WORDSWORTH

One of the greatest poets in English literature, William Wordsworth (1770–1850) welcomed the French Revolution as a young man—as he acknowledged wistfully in the first selection. But Wordsworth later turned against the revolution and other sweeping attempts to remake society. Like Edmund Burke, he became a defender of "ordered liberty," an idea at the center of his "Sonnets Dedicated to Liberty and Order" (1838).

Source: The Complete Poetical Works of William Wordsworth, *edited by Andrew J. George (Boston and New York: Houghton, Mifflin and Co., 1904), pp. 340, 761, and 758, respectively.*

FRENCH REVOLUTION AS IT APPEARED TO ENTHUSIASTS AT ITS COMMENCEMENT*

Oh! pleasant exercise of hope and joy!
For mighty were the auxiliars which then stood
Upon our side, we who were strong in love!
Bliss was it in that dawn to be alive,
But to be young was very heaven!—Oh! times,
In which the meagre, stale, forbidding ways
Of custom, law, and statute, took at once
The attraction of a country in romance!
When Reason seemed the most to assert her rights,
When most intent on making of herself
A prime Enchantress—to assist the work
Which then was going forward in her name!
Not favoured spots alone, but the whole earth,
The beauty wore of promise, that which sets
(As at some moment might not be unfelt
Among the bowers of paradise itself)
The budding rose above the rose full blown.
What temper at the prospect did not wake
To happiness unthought of? The inert
Were roused, and lively natures rapt away!
They who had fed their childhood upon dreams,
The playfellows of fancy, who had made
All powers of swiftness, subtilty, and strength
Their ministers,—who in lordly wise had stirred
Among the grandest objects of the sense,
And dealt with whatsoever they found there
As if they had within some lurking right
To wield it;—they, too, who, of gentle mood,
Had watched all gentle motions, and to these
Had fitted their own thoughts, schemers more mild,
And in the region of their peaceful selves;—
Now was it that both found, the meek and lofty
Did both find, helpers to their hearts desire,
And stuff at hand, plastic as they could wish;
Were called upon to exercise their skill,
Not in Utopia, subterranean fields,
Or some secreted island, Heaven knows where!
But in the very world, which is the world
Of all of us,—the place where in the end
We find our happiness, or not at all!

SONNETS DEDICATED TO LIBERTY AND ORDER‡

IV

Blest Statesman He, whose Mind's unselfish will
Leaves him at ease among grand thoughts: whose eye
Sees that, apart from magnanimity,
Wisdom exists not; nor the humbler skill
Of Prudence, disentangling good and ill
With patient care, What tho' assaults run high,
They daunt not him who holds his ministry,
Resolute, at all hazards, to fulfil
Its duties;—prompt to move, but firm to wait,—
Knowing, things rashly sought are rarely found;
That, for the functions of an ancient State—
Strong by her charters, free because imbound,
Servant of Providence, not slave of Fate—
Perilous is sweeping change, all chance unsound.

**Composed 1804, published October 26, 1809 in* The Friend.
‡*Composed and published 1838.*

AT BOLOGNA, IN REMEMBRANCE OF THE LATE INSURRECTIONS, 1837*

As leaves are to the tree whereon they grow
And wither, every human generation
Is to the Being of a mighty nation,
Locked in our world's embrace through weal and woe;
Thought that should teach the zealot to forego
Rash schemes, to abjure all selfish agitation,
And seek through noiseless pains and moderation
The unblemished good they only can bestow.
Alas! with most, who weigh futurity
Against time present, passion holds the scales:
Hence equal ignorance of both prevails,
And nations sink; or, struggling to be free,
Are doomed to flounder on, like wounded whales
Tossed on the bosom of a stormy sea.

**Composed probably 1837, published 1842. Third of three sonnets.*

26

REVOLT OF THE MASSES

JOSÉ ORTEGA Y GASSET

De Tocqueville and Mill, with their warnings of the "tyranny of the majority," sounded a theme that became a favorite of conservative writers in the nineteenth and twentieth centuries. One of the most forceful criticisms of "mass society" came from the Spanish philosopher, José Ortega y Gasset (1883–1955). Although Ortega, like de Tocqueville, does not fit neatly into either the liberal or conservative category, his *Revolt of the Masses* (1930) issues a protest and a warning against many of the "progressive" and "levelling" features of a democratic age.

Source: The Revolt of the Masses *(New York: W. W. Norton, 1932), pp. 127–135. Reprinted from* The Revolt of the Masses *by José Ortega y Gasset, by permission of W. W. Norton & Company Inc. Copyright renewed 1960 by Teresa Carey.*

THE GREATEST DANGER, THE STATE

In a right ordering of public affairs, the mass is that part which does not act of itself. Such is its mission. It has come into the world in order to be directed, influenced, represented, organised—even in order to cease being mass, or at least to aspire to this. But it has not come into the world to do all this by itself. It needs to submit its life to a higher court, formed of the superior minorities. The question as to who are these superior individuals may be discussed *ad libitum,* but that without them, whoever they be, humanity would cease to preserve its essentials is something about which there can be no possible doubt, though Europe spend a century with its head under its wing, ostrich-fashion, trying if she can to avoid seeing such a plain truth. For we are not dealing with an opinion based on facts more or less frequent and probable, but on a law of social "physics," much more immovable than the laws of Newton's physics. The day when a genuine philosophy[1] once more holds sway in Europe—it is the one thing that can save her—that day she will once again realise that man, whether he like it or no, is a being forced by his nature to seek some higher authority. If he succeeds in finding it of himself, he is a superior man; if not, he is a mass-man and must receive it from his superiors.

For the mass to claim the right to act of itself is then a rebellion against its own destiny, and because that is what it is doing at present, I speak of the rebellion of the masses. For, after all, the one thing that can substantially and truthfully be called rebellion is that which consists in not accepting one's own destiny, in rebelling against one's self. The rebellion of the archangel Lucifer would not have been less if, instead of striving to be God—which was not his destiny—he had striven to be the lowest of the angels—equally not his destiny. (If Lucifer had been a Russian, like Tolstoi, he would perhaps have preferred this latter form of rebellion, none the less against God than the other more famous one.)

When the mass acts on its own, it does so only in one way, for it has no other: it lynches. It is not altogether by chance that lynch law comes from America, for America is, in a fashion, the paradise of the masses. And it will cause less surprise, nowadays, when the masses triumph, that violence should triumph and be made the one *ratio,* the one doctrine. It is now some time since I called attention to this advance of violence as a normal condition.[2] To-day it has reached its full development, and this is a good symptom, because it means that automatically the descent is about to begin. To-day violence is the rhetoric of the period, the empty rhetorician has made it his own. When a reality of human existence has completed its historic course, has been shipwrecked and lies dead, the waves throw it up on the shores of rhetoric, where the corpse remains for a long time. Rhetoric is the cemetery of human realities, or at any rate a Home for the Aged. The reality itself is survived by its name, which, though only a word, is after all at least a word and preserves something of its magic power.

But though it is not impossible that the prestige of violence as a cynically established rule has entered on its decline, we shall still continue under that rule, though in another form. I refer to the gravest danger now threatening European civilisation. Like all other dangers that threaten it, this one is born of civilisation itself. More than that, it constitutes one of its glories: it is the State as we know it to-day. We are confronted with a replica of what we said in the previous chapter about science: the fertility of its principles brings about a fabulous progress, but this inevitably imposes specialisation, and specialisation threatens to strangle science.

The same thing is happening with the State. Call to mind what the State was at the end of the XVIIIth Century in all European nations. Quite a small affair! . . .

In our days the State has come to be a formidable machine which works in marvellous fashion; of wonderful efficiency by reason of the quantity and precision of its means. Once it is set up in the midst of society, it is enough to touch a button for its enormous levers to start working and exercise their overwhelming power on any portion whatever of the social framework.

The contemporary State is the easiest seen and best-known product of civilisation. And it is an interesting revelation when one takes note of the attitude that mass-man adopts before it. He sees it, admires it, knows that *there it is*, safeguarding his existence; but he is not conscious of the fact that it is a human creation invented by certain men and upheld by certain virtues and fundamental qualities which the men of yesterday had and which may vanish into air to-morrow. Furthermore, the mass-man sees in the State an anonymous power, and feeling himself, like it, anonymous, he believes that the State is something of his own. Suppose that in the public life of a country some difficulty, conflict, or problem presents itself, the mass-man will tend to demand that the State intervene immediately and undertake a solution directly with its immense and unassailable resources.

This is the gravest danger that to-day threatens civilisation: State intervention; the absorption of all spontaneous social effort by the State, that is to say, of spontaneous historical action, which in the long run sustains, nourishes, and impels human destinies. When the mass suffers any ill-fortune or simply feels some strong appetite, its great temptation is that permanent, sure possibility of obtaining everything—without effort, struggle, doubt, or risk—merely by touching a button and setting the mighty machine in motion. The mass says to itself, *"L'État, c'est moi,"* which is a complete mistake. The State is the mass only in the sense in which it can be said of two men that they are identical because neither of them is named John. The contemporary State and the mass coincide only in being anonymous. But the mass-man does in fact believe that he is the State, and he will tend more and more to set its machinery working on whatsoever pretext, to crush beneath it any creative minority which disturbs it—disturbs it in any order of things: in politics, in ideas, in industry.

The result of this tendency will be fatal. Spontaneous social action will be broken up over and over again by State intervention; no new seed will be able to fructify. Society will have to live *for* the State, man *for* the governmental machine. And as, after all, it is only a machine whose existence and maintenance depend on the vital supports around it, the State, after sucking out the very marrow of society, will be left bloodless, a skeleton, dead with that rusty death of machinery, more gruesome than the death of a living organism. . . .

Is the paradoxical, tragic process of Statism now realised? Society, that it may live better, creates the State as an instrument. Then the State gets the upper hand and society has to begin to live for the State. . . . This is what State intervention leads to: the people are converted into fuel to feed the mere machine which is the State. The skeleton eats up the flesh around it. The scaffolding becomes the owner and tenant of the house.

When this is realised, it rather confounds one to hear Mussolini heralding as an astounding discovery just made in Italy, the formula: "All for the State; nothing outside the State; nothing against the State." This alone would suffice to reveal in Fascism a typical movement of mass-men. Mussolini found a State admirably built up—not by him, but precisely by the ideas and the forces he is combating: by liberal democracy. He confines himself to using it ruthlessly, and, without entering now into a detailed examination of his work, it is indisputable that the results obtained up to the present cannot be compared with those obtained in political and administrative working by the liberal State. If he has succeeded in anything, it is so minute, so little visible, so lacking in substance as with difficulty to compensate for the accumulation of the abnormal powers which enable him to make use of that machine to its full extent.

Statism is the higher form taken by violence

and direct action when these are set up as standards. Through and by means of the State, the anonymous machine, the masses act for themselves. The nations of Europe have before them a period of great difficulties in their internal life, supremely arduous problems of law, economics, and public order. Can we help feeling that under the rule of the masses the State will endeavour to crush the independence of the individual and the group, and thus definitely spoil the harvest of the future?

A concrete example of this mechanism is found in one of the most alarming phenomena of the last thirty years: the enormous increase in the police force of all countries. The increase of population has inevitably rendered it necessary. However accustomed we may be to it, the terrible paradox should not escape our minds that the population of a great modern city, in order to move about peaceably and attend to its business, necessarily requires a police force to regulate the circulation. But it is foolishness for the party of "law and order" to imagine that these "forces of public authority" created to preserve order are always going to be content to preserve the order that that party desires. Inevitably they will end by themselves defining and deciding on the order they are going to impose—which, naturally, will be that which suits them best.

NOTES

1. For philosophy to rule, it is not necessary that philosophers be the rulers—as Plato at first wished—nor even for rulers to be philosophers—as was his later, more modest, wish. Both these things are, strictly speaking, most fatal. For philosophy to rule, it is sufficient for it to exist; that is to say, for the philosophers to be philosophers. For nearly a century past, philosophers have been everything but that—politicians, pedagogues, men of letters, and men of science.
2. Vide *España Invertebrada,* 1912.

27

ON BEING CONSERVATIVE

MICHAEL OAKESHOTT

One of the leading representatives of "classical" conservatism in this century, the British philosopher Michael Oakeshott (1901–) insists that politics must be rooted in tradition and experience, not abstract reason or principles. As he says in his essay, "Political Education," "In political activity . . . men sail a boundless and bottomless sea; there is neither harbour for shelter nor floor for anchorage, neither starting-place nor appointed destination. The enterprise is to keep afloat on an even keel; the sea is both friend and enemy; and the seamanship consists in using the resources of a traditional manner of behaviour in order to make a friend of every hostile occasion." The following selection is from Oakeshott's essay, "On Being Conservative."

ON BEING CONSERVATIVE

I

The common belief that it is impossible (or, if not impossible, then so unpromising as to be not worth while attempting) to elicit explanatory general principles from what is recognized to be conservative conduct is not one that I share. It may be true that conservative conduct does not readily provoke articulation in the idiom of general ideas, and that consequently there has been a certain reluctance to undertake this kind of elucidation; but it is not to be presumed that conservative conduct is less eligible than any other for this sort of interpretation, for what it is worth. Nevertheless, this is not the enterprise I propose to engage in here. My theme is not a creed or a doctrine, but a disposition. To be conservative is to be disposed to think and behave in certain manners; it is to prefer certain kinds of conduct and certain conditions of human circumstances to others; it is to be disposed to make certain kinds of choices. And my design here is to construe this disposition as it appears in contemporary character, rather than to transpose it into the idiom of general principles.

The general characteristics of this disposition are not difficult to discern, although they have often been mistaken. They centre upon a propensity to use and to enjoy what is available rather than to wish for or to look for something else; to delight in what is present rather than what was or what may be. Reflection may bring to light an appropriate gratefulness for what is available, and consequently the acknowledgment of a gift or an inheritance from the past; but there is no mere idolizing of what is past and gone. What is esteemed is the present; and it is esteemed not on account of its connections with a remote antiquity, nor because it is recognized to be more admirable than any possible alternative, but on account of its familiarity: not, *Verweile doch, du bist so schön,*[1] but, *Stay with me because I am attached to you.*

If the present is arid, offering little or nothing to be used or enjoyed, then this inclination will be weak or absent; if the present is remarkably unsettled, it will display itself in a search for a firmer foothold and consequently in a recourse to and an exploration of the past; but it asserts itself characteristically when there is much to be enjoyed, and it will be strongest when this is combined with evident risk of loss. In short, it is a disposition appropriate to a man who is acutely aware of having something to lose which he has learned to care for; a man in some degree rich in opportunities for enjoyment, but not so rich that he can afford to be indifferent to loss. It will appear more naturally in the old than in the young, not because the old are more sensitive to loss but because they are apt to be more fully aware of the resources of their world and therefore less likely to find them inadequate. In some people this disposition is weak merely because they are ignorant of what their world has to offer them: the present appears to them only as a residue of inopportunities.

To be conservative, then, is to prefer the familiar to the unknown, to prefer the tried to the untried, fact to mystery, the actual to the possible, the limited to the unbounded, the near to the distant, the sufficient to the superabundant, the convenient to the perfect, present laughter to utopian bliss. Familiar relationships and loyalties will be preferred to the allure of more profitable attachments; to acquire and to enlarge will be less important than to keep, to cultivate and to enjoy; the grief of loss will be more acute than the excitement of novelty or promise. It is to be equal to one's own fortune, to live at the level of one's own means, to be content with the want of greater perfection which belongs alike to oneself and one's circumstances. With some people this is itself a choice; in others it is a disposition which appears, frequently or less frequently, in their preferences and aversions, and is not itself chosen or specifically cultivated.

Now, all this is represented in a certain attitude towards change and innovation; change denoting alterations we have to suffer and innovation those we design and execute.

Changes are circumstances to which we have to accommodate ourselves, and the disposition to be conservative is both the emblem of our difficulty in doing so and our resort in the attempts we make to do so. Changes are without effect only upon those who notice nothing, who are ignorant of what they possess and apathetic to their circumstances; and they can be welcomed indiscriminately only by those who esteem nothing, whose attachments are fleeting and who are strangers to love and affection. The conservative disposition provokes neither of these conditions: the inclination to enjoy what is present and available is the opposite of ignorance and apathy and it breeds attachment and affection. Consequently, it is averse from change, which appears always, in the first place, as deprivation. A storm which sweeps away a copse and transforms a favourite view, the death of friends, the sleep of friendship, the desuetude of customs of behaviour, the retirement of a favourite clown, involuntary exile, reversals of fortune, the loss of abilities enjoyed and their replacement by others—these are changes, none perhaps without its compensations, which the man of conservative temperament unavoidably regrets. But he has difficulty in reconciling himself to them, not because what he has lost in them was intrinsically better than any alternative might have been or was incapable of improvement, nor because what takes its place is inherently incapable of being enjoyed, but because what he has lost was something he actually enjoyed and had learned how to enjoy and what takes its place is something to which he has acquired no attachment. Consequently, he will find small and slow changes more tolerable than large and sudden; and he will value highly every appearance of continuity. Some changes, indeed, will present no difficulty; but, again, this is not because they are manifest improvements but merely because they are easily assimilated: the changes of the seasons are mediated by their recurrence and the growing up of children by its continuousness. And, in general, he will accommodate himself more readily to changes which do not offend expectation than to the destruction of what seems to have no ground of dissolution within itself.

Moreover, to be conservative is not merely to be averse from change (which may be an idiosyncrasy); it is also a manner of accommodating ourselves to changes, an activity imposed upon all men. For, change is a threat to identity, and every change is an emblem of extinction. But a man's identity (or that of a community) is nothing more than an unbroken rehearsal of contingencies, each at the mercy of circumstance and each significant in proportion to its familiarity. It is not a fortress into which we may retire, and the only means we have of defending it (that is, ourselves) against the hostile forces of change is in the open field of our experience; by throwing our weight upon the foot which for the time being is most firmly placed, by cleaving to whatever familiarities are not immediately threatened and thus assimilating what is new without becoming unrecognizable to ourselves. The Masai, when they were moved from their old country to the present Masai reserve in Kenya, took with them the names of their hills and plains and rivers and gave them to the hills and plains and rivers of the new country. And it is by some such subterfuge of conservatism that every man or people compelled to suffer a notable change avoids the shame of extinction.

Changes, then, have to be suffered; and a man of conservative temperament (that is, one strongly disposed to preserve his identity) cannot be indifferent to them. In the main, he judges them by the disturbance they entail and, like everyone else, deploys his resources to meet them. The idea of innovation, on the other hand, is improvement. Nevertheless, a man of this temperament will not himself be an ardent innovator. In the first place, he is not inclined to think that nothing is happening unless great changes are afoot and therefore he is not worried by the absence of innovation: the use and enjoyment of things as they are occupies most of his attention. Further, he is aware that not all innovation is, in fact, improvement; and he will think that to innovate without improving is either designed or inadvertent folly. Moreover, even when an innovation commends itself as a convincing improvement, he will look twice at its claims before accepting them. From his point of view, because every improvement involves change, the disruption entailed has always to be set against the benefit anticipated. But when he has satisfied himself about this, there will be other considerations to be taken into the account. Innovating is always an equivocal enterprise, in which gain and loss (even excluding the loss of familiarity) are so closely interwoven that it is exceedingly difficult to forecast the final up-shot: there is no such thing as an unqualified improvement. For, innovating is an activity which generates not only the "improvement" sought, but a new and complex situation of which this is only one of the components. The total change is always more extensive than the change designed; and the whole of what is entailed can neither be foreseen nor circumscribed. Thus, whenever there is innovation there is the certainty that the change will be greater than was intended, that there will be loss as well as gain and that the loss and the gain will not be equally distributed among the people affected; there is the chance that the benefits derived will be greater than those which were designed; and there is the risk that they will be off-set by changes for the worse.

From all this the man of conservative temperament draws some appropriate conclusions. First, innovation entails certain loss and possible gain, therefore, the onus of proof, to show that the proposed change may be expected to be on the whole beneficial, rests with the would-be innovator. Secondly, he believes that the more closely an innovation resembles growth (that is, the more clearly it is intimated in and not merely imposed upon the situation) the less likely it is to result in a preponderance of loss. Thirdly, he thinks that an innovation which is a response to some specific defect, one designed to redress some specific disequilibrium, is more desirable than one which springs from a notion of a generally improved condition of human circumstances, and is far more desirable than one generated by a vision of perfection. Consequently, he prefers small and limited innovations to large and indefinite. Fourthly, he favours a slow rather than a rapid pace, and pauses to observe current consequences and make appropriate adjustments. And lastly, he believes the occasion to be important; and, other things being equal, he considers the most favourable occasion for innovation to be when the projected change is most likely to be limited to what is intended and least likely to be corrupted by undesired and unmanageable consequences.

The disposition to be conservative is, then, warm and positive in respect of enjoyment, and correspondingly cool and critical in respect of change and innovation: these two inclinations support and elucidate one another. The man of conservative temperament believes that a known good is not lightly to be surrendered for an unknown better. He is not in love with what is dangerous and difficult; he is unadventurous; he has no impulse to sail uncharted seas; for him there is no magic in being lost, bewildered or shipwrecked. If he is forced to navigate the unknown, he sees virtue in heaving the lead every inch of the way. What others plausibly identify as timidity, he recognizes in himself as rational prudence; what others interpret as inactivity, he recognizes as a disposition to enjoy rather than to exploit. He is cautious, and he is disposed to indicate his assent or dissent, not in absolute, but in graduated terms. He eyes the situation in terms of its propensity to disrupt the familiarity of the features of his world.

2

It is commonly believed that this conservative disposition is pretty deeply rooted in what is called "human nature." Change is tiring, innovation calls for effort, and human beings (it is said) are more apt to be lazy than energetic. If they have found a not unsatisfactory way of getting along in the world, they are not disposed to go looking for trouble. They are naturally apprehensive of the unknown and prefer safety to danger. They are reluctant innovators, and they accept change not because they like it but (as Rochefoucauld says they accept death) because it is inescapable. Change generates sadness rather than exhilaration: heaven is the dream of a changeless no less than of a perfect world. Of course, those who read "human nature" in this way agree that this disposition does not stand alone; they merely contend that it is an exceedingly strong, perhaps the strongest, of human propensities. And, so far as it goes, there is something to be said for this belief: human circumstances would certainly be very different from what they are if there were not a large ingredient of conservatism in human preferences. Primitive peoples are said to cling to what is familiar and to be averse from change; ancient myth is full of warnings against innovation; our folklore and proverbial wisdom about the conduct of life abounds in conservative precepts; and how many tears are shed by children in their unwilling accommodation to change. Indeed, wherever a firm identity has been achieved, and wherever identity is felt to be precariously balanced, a conservative disposition is likely to prevail. On the other hand, the disposition of adolescence is often predominantly adventurous and experimental: when we are young, nothing seems more desirable than to take a chance; *pas de risque, pas de plaisir.* And while some peoples, over long stretches of time, appear successfully to have avoided change, the history of others displays periods of intense and intrepid innovation. There is, indeed, not much profit to be had from general speculation about "human nature," which is no steadier than anything else in our acquaintance. What is more to the point is to consider current human nature, to consider ourselves.

With us, I think, the disposition to be conservative is far from being notably strong. Indeed, if he were to judge by our conduct during the last five centuries or so, an unprejudiced stranger might plausibly suppose us to be in love with change, to have an appetite only for innovation and to be either so out of sympathy with ourselves or so careless of our identity as not to be disposed to give it any consideration. In general, the fascination of what is new is felt far more keenly than the comfort of what is familiar. We are disposed to think that nothing important is happening unless great innovations are afoot, and that what is not being improved must be deteriorating. There is a positive prejudice in favour of the yet untried. We readily presume that all change is, somehow, for the better, and we are easily persuaded that all the consequences of our innovating activity are either themselves improvements or at least a reasonable price to pay for getting what we want. While the conservative, if he were forced to gamble, would bet on the field, we are disposed to back our individual fancies with little calculation and no apprehension of loss. We are acquisitive to the point of greed; ready to drop the bone we have for its reflection magnified in the mirror of the future. Nothing is made to outlast probable improvement in a world where everything is undergoing incessant improvement: the expectation of life of everything except human beings themselves continuously declines. Pieties are fleeting, loyalties evanescent, and the pace of change warns us against too deep attachments. We are willing to try anything once, regardless of the consequences. One activity vies with another in being "up-to-date": discarded motor-cars and television sets have their counterparts in discarded moral and religious beliefs: the eye is ever on the new model. To see is to imagine what might be in the place of what is; to touch is to transform. Whatever the shape or quality of the world, it is not for long as we want it. And those in the van of movement infect those behind with their energy and enterprise. *Omnes eodem cogemur:* when we are no longer light-footed we find a place for ourselves in the band.[2]

Of course, our character has other ingredients besides this lust for change (we are not devoid of the impulse to cherish and preserve), but there can be little doubt about its pre-eminence. And, in these circumstances, it seems appropriate that a conservative disposition should appear, not as an intelligible (or even plausible) alternative to our mainly "progressive" habit of mind, but either as an unfortunate hindrance to the movement afoot, or as the custodian of the museum in which quaint examples of superseded achievement are preserved for children to gape at, and as the guardian of what from time to time is considered not yet ripe for destruction, which we call (ironically enough) the amenities of life.

Here our account of the disposition to be conservative and its current fortunes might be expected to end, with the man in whom this disposition is strong last seen swimming against the tide, disregarded not because what he has to say is necessarily false but because it has become irrelevant; outmanoeuvred, not on account of any intrinsic demerit but merely by the flow of circumstance; a faded, timid, nostalgic character, provoking pity as an outcast and contempt as a reactionary. Nevertheless, I think there is something more to be said. Even in these circumstances, when a conservative disposition in respect of things in general is unmistakably at a discount, there are occasions when this disposition remains not only appropriate, but supremely so; and there are connections in which we are unavoidably disposed in a conservative direction.

In the first place, there is a certain kind of activity (not yet extinct) which can be engaged in only in virtue of a disposition to be conservative, namely, activities where what is sought is present enjoyment and not a profit, a reward, a prize or a result in addition to the experience itself. And when these activities are recognized as the emblems of this disposition, to be conservative is disclosed, not as prejudiced hostility to a "progressive" attitude capable of embracing the whole range of human conduct, but as a disposition exclusively appropriate in a large and significant field of human activity. And the man in whom this disposition is pre-eminent appears as one who prefers to engage in activities where to be conservative is uniquely appropriate, and not as a man inclined to impose his conservatism indiscriminately upon all human activity. In short, if we find ourselves (as most of us do) inclined to reject conservatism as a disposition appropriate in respect of human conduct in general, there still remains a certain kind of human conduct for which this disposition is not merely appropriate but a necessary condition. . . .

This is so of friendship. Here, attachment springs from an intimation of familiarity and subsists in a mutual sharing of personalities. To go on changing one's butcher until one gets the meat one likes, to go on educating one's agent until he does what is required of him, is conduct not inappropriate to the relationship concerned; but to discard friends because they do not behave as we expected and refuse to be educated to our requirements is the conduct of a man who has altogether mistaken the character of friendship. Friends are not concerned with what might be made of one another, but only with the enjoyment of one another; and the condition of this enjoyment is a ready acceptance of what is and the absence of any desire to change or to improve. A friend is not somebody one trusts to behave in a certain manner, who supplies certain wants, who has certain useful abilities, who possesses certain merely agreeable qualities, or who holds certain acceptable opinions; he is somebody who engages the imagination, who excites contemplation, who provokes interest, sympathy, delight and loyalty simply on account of the relationship entered into. One friend cannot replace another; there is all the difference in the world between the death of a friend and the retirement of one's tailor from business. The relationship of friend to friend is dramatic, not utilitarian; the tie is one of familiarity, not usefulness; the disposition engaged is conservative, not "progressive." And what is true of friendship is not less true of other experiences—of patriotism, for example, and of conversation—each of which demands a conservative disposition as a condition of its enjoyment.

But further, there are activities, not involving human relationships, that may be engaged in, not for a prize, but for the enjoyment they generate, and for which the only appropriate disposition is the disposition to be conservative. Consider fishing. If your project is merely to catch fish it would be foolish to be unduly conservative. You will seek out the best tackle, you will discard practices which prove unsuccessful, you will not be bound by unprofitable attachments to particular localities, pieties will be fleeting, loyalties evanescent; you may even be wise to try anything once in the hope of improvement. But fishing is an activity that may be engaged in, not for the profit of a catch, but for its own sake; and the fisherman may return home in the evening not less content for being empty-handed. Where this is so, the activity has become a ritual and a conservative disposition is appropriate. Why worry about the best gear if you do not care whether or not you make a catch? What matters is the enjoyment of exercising skill (or, perhaps, merely passing the time), and this is to be had with any tackle, so long as it is familiar and is not grotesquely inappropriate.

All activities, then, where what is sought is enjoyment springing, not from the success of the enterprise but from the familiarity of the engagement, are emblems of the disposition to be conservative. . . .

3

How, then, are we to construe the disposition to be conservative in respect of politics? . . . To state my view briefly before elaborating it, what makes a conservative disposition in politics intelligible is nothing to do with a natural law or a providential order, nothing to do with morals or religion; it is the observation of our current manner of living combined with the belief (which from our point of view need be regarded as no more than an hypothesis) that governing is a specific and limited activity, namely the provision and custody of general rules of conduct, which are understood, not as plans for imposing substantive activities, but as instruments enabling people to pursue the activities of their own choice with the minimum frustration, and therefore something which it is appropriate to be conservative about. . . .

. . . [T]he office of government is not to impose other beliefs and activities upon its subjects, not to tutor or to educate them, not to make them better or happier in another way, not to direct them, to galvanize them into action, to lead them or to coordinate their activities so that no occasion of conflict shall occur; the office of government is merely to rule. This is a specific and limited activity, easily corrupted when it is combined with any other, and, in the circumstances, indispensable. The image of the ruler is the umpire whose business is to administer the rules of the game, or the chairman who governs the debate according to known rules but does not himself participate in it.

Now people of this disposition commonly defend their belief that the proper attitude of government towards the current condition of human circumstance is one of acceptance by appealing to certain general ideas. They contend that there is absolute value in the free play of human choice, that private property (the emblem of choice) is a natural right, that it is only in the enjoyment of diversity of opinion and activity that true belief and good conduct can be expected to disclose themselves. But I do not think that this disposition requires these or any similar beliefs in order to make it intelligible. Something much smaller and less pretentious will do: the observation that this condition of human circumstance is, in fact, current, and that we have learned to enjoy it and how to manage it; that we are not children *in statu pupillari*[3] but adults who do not consider themselves under any obligation to justify their preference for making their own choices; and that it is beyond human experience to suppose that those who rule are endowed with a superior wisdom which discloses to them a better range of beliefs and activities and which gives them authority to impose upon their subjects a quite different manner of life. In short, if the man of this disposition is asked: Why ought governments to accept the current diversity of opinion and activity in preference to imposing upon their subjects a dream of their own? it is enough for him to reply: Why not? Their dreams are no different from those of anyone else; and if it is boring to have to listen to dreams of others being recounted, it is insufferable to be forced to re-enact them. We tolerate monomaniacs, it is our habit to do so; but why should we be *ruled* by them? Is it not (the man of conservative disposition asks) an intelligible task for a government to protect its subjects against the nuisance of those who spend their energy and their wealth in the service of some pet indignation, endeavouring to impose it upon everybody, not by suppressing their activities in favour of others of a similar kind, but by setting a limit to the amount of noise anyone may emit?

Nevertheless, if this acceptance is the spring of the conservative's disposition in respect of government, he does not suppose that the office of government is to do nothing. As he understands it, there is work to be done which can be done only in virtue of a genuine acceptance of current beliefs simply because they are current and current activities simply because they are afoot. And, briefly, the office he attributes to government is to resolve some of the collisions which this variety of beliefs and activities generates; to preserve peace, not by placing an interdict upon choice and upon the diversity that springs from the exercise of preference, not by imposing substantive uniformity, but by enforcing general rules of procedure upon all subjects alike.

Government, then, as the conservative in this matter understands it, does not begin with a vision of another, different and better world, but with the observation of the self-government practised even by men of passion in the conduct of their enterprises; it begins in the informal adjustments of interests to one another which are designed to release those who are apt to collide from the mutual frustration of a collision. Sometimes these adjustments are no more than agreements between two parties to keep out of each other's way; sometimes they are of wider application and more durable character, such as the International Rules for the prevention of collisions at sea. In short, the intimations of government are to be found in ritual, not in religion or philosophy; in the enjoyment of orderly and peaceable behaviour, not in the search for truth or perfection. . . .

. . . Innovation, then, is called for if the rules are to remain appropriate to the activities they govern. But, as the conservative understands it, modification of the rules should always reflect, and never impose, a change in the activities and beliefs of those who are subject to them, and should never on any occasion be so great as to destroy the *ensemble*. Consequently, the conservative will have nothing to do with innovations designed to meet merely hypothetical situations; he will prefer to enforce a rule he has got rather than invent a new one; he will think it appropriate to delay a modification of the rules until it is clear that the change of circumstance it is designed to reflect has come to stay for a while; he will be suspicious of proposals for change in excess of what the situation calls for, of rulers who demand extra-ordinary powers in order to make great changes and whose utterances are tied to generalities like "the public good" or "social justice," and of Saviours of Society who buckle on armour and seek dragons to slay; he will think it proper to consider the occasion of the innovation with care; in short, he will be disposed to regard politics as an activity in which a valuable set of tools is renovated from time to time and kept in trim rather than as an opportunity for perpetual re-equipment. . . .

To some people, "government" appears as a vast reservoir of power which inspires them to dream of what use might be made of it. They have favourite projects, of various dimensions, which they sincerely believe are for the benefit of mankind, and to capture this source of power, if necessary to increase it, and to use it for imposing their favourite projects upon their fellows is what they understand as the adventure of governing men. They are, thus, disposed to recognize government as an instrument of passion; the art of politics is to inflame and direct desire. In short, governing is understood to be just like any other activity—making and selling a brand of soap, exploiting the resources of a locality, or developing a housing estate—only the power here is (for the most part) already mobilized, and the enterprise is remarkable only because it aims at monopoly and because of its promise of success once the source of power has been captured. Of course a private enterprise politician of this sort would get nowhere in these days unless there were people with wants so vague that they can be prompted to ask for what he has to offer, or with wants so servile that they prefer the promise of a provided abundance to the opportunity of choice and activity on their own account. And it is not all as plain sailing as it might appear: often a politician of this sort misjudges the situation; and then, briefly, even in democratic politics, we become aware of what the camel thinks of the camel driver.

Now, the disposition to be conservative in respect of politics reflects a quite different view of the activity of governing. The man of this disposition understands it to be the business of a government not to inflame passion and give it new objects to feed upon, but to inject into the activities of already too passionate men an ingredient of moderation; to restrain, to deflate, to pacify and to reconcile; not to stoke the fires of desire, but to damp them down. And all this, not because passion is vice and moderation virtue, but because moderation is indispensable if passionate men are to escape being locked in an encounter of mutual frustration. . . .

Nobody pretends that it is easy to acquire or to sustain the mood of indifference which this manner of politics calls for. To rein-in one's own beliefs and desires, to acknowledge the current shape of things, to feel the balance of things in one's hand, to tolerate what is abominable, to distinguish between crime and sin, to respect formality even when it appears to be leading to error, these are difficult achievements; and they are achievements not to be looked for in the young.

Everybody's young days are a dream, a delightful insanity, a sweet solipsism. Nothing in them has a fixed shape, nothing a fixed price; everything is a possibility, and we live happily on credit. There are no obligations to be observed; there are no accounts to be kept. Nothing is specified in advance; everything is what can be made of it. The world is a mirror in which we seek the reflection of our own desires. The allure of violent emotions is irresistible. When we are young we are not disposed to make concessions to the world; we never feel the balance of a thing in our hands—unless it be a cricket bat. We are not apt to distinguish between our liking and our esteem; urgency is our criterion of importance; and we do not easily understand that what is humdrum need not be despicable. We are impatient of restraint; and we readily believe, like Shelley, that to have contracted a habit is to have failed. These, in my opinion, are among our virtues when we are young; but how remote they are from the disposition appropriate for participating in the style of government I have been describing. Since life is a dream, we argue (with plausible but erroneous logic) that politics must be an encounter of dreams, in which we hope to impose our own. Some unfortunate people, like Pitt (laughably called "the Younger"), are born old, and are eligible to engage in politics almost in their cradles; others, perhaps more fortunate, belie the saying that one is young only once, they never grow up. But these are exceptions. For most there is what Conrad called the "shadow line" which, when we pass it, discloses a solid world of things, each with its fixed shape, each with its own point of balance, each with its price; a world of fact, not poetic image, in which what we have spent on one thing we cannot spend on another; a world inhabited by others besides ourselves who cannot be reduced to mere reflections of our own emotions. And coming to be at home in this commonplace world qualifies us (as no knowledge of "political science" can ever qualify us), if we are so inclined and have nothing better to think about, to engage in what the man of conservative disposition understands to be political activity.

NOTES

1. Editors' note: "Stay with me, you are so beautiful."
2. "Which of us," asks a contemporary (not without some equivocation), "would not settle, at whatever cost in nervous anxiety, for a febrile and creative rather than a static society?"
3. In the status of pupils.

28

WHAT IS NEOCONSERVATISM?

IRVING KRISTOL

In response to the "counterculture" that emerged in the 1960s, a group of former socialists and welfare liberals in the United States turned in a conservative direction—a turn that earned them the name, neoconservatives. Among the influential intellectuals often included in this group are Senator Daniel Patrick Moynihan, former U.S. Secretary to the United Nations Jeane Kirkpatrick, editors and writers Norman Podhoretz and Daniel Bell (see selection 54 in Part Ten), and Irving Kristol (1920–)—author of the following "Confessions of a True, Self-Confessed—Perhaps the Only—'Neoconservative.' "

Source: Public Opinion *(October/November 1979). Reprinted with the permission of the American Enterprise Institute for Public Policy Research, Washington, D.C.*

CONFESSIONS OF A TRUE, SELF-CONFESSED—PERHAPS THE ONLY—"NEOCONSERVATIVE"

It has long been a cliché of liberal discourse that what this country needs is a truly intelligent and sophisticated conservatism to replace the rather primitive, philistine, and often racist conservatism that our history is only too familiar with. This new and desirable conservatism should have a philosophic and literary dimension which would rectify the occasional excesses of liberal ideology. It should even have a nebulous but definitely genteel political dimension, since it is likely that we shall always, at intervals, need a brief interregnum of conservative government whose function it is to consolidate and ratify liberal reforms. The ideal conservative president, from this liberal point of view, would be a Dwight Eisenhower who read Lionel Trilling instead of paperback Westerns, who listened to chamber music instead of playing golf—but who would be, in all other respects, as inert as the real President Eisenhower in fact was.

What we absolutely do *not* need or want, from this liberal perspective, is a conservatism with strong ideas of its own about economic policy, social policy, or foreign policy—especially if these ideas can pass academic muster and survive intellectual debate. Such a conservatism might actually affect public policy, even become a shaping force in American politics, and this is simply impermissible. The very possibility of such a conservatism is a specter that haunts the liberal imagination and can propel it into frenzies of exorcism.

It is because the liberal intellectual community—and particularly the liberal-Left intellectual community, which is not quite the same thing, if almost the same thing—sees "neoconservatism" as representing such an awful possibility that it is so terribly agitated about it. Note: It is *they*, not us, who are excited. It is even they who gave us our name in the first place (specifically, it was Michael Harrington). *We* don't go around talking about neoconservatism. Indeed, such supposed representatives of this "movement" as Daniel Bell, Daniel Patrick Moynihan, Nathan Glazer, Norman Podhoretz, Aaron Wildavsky, Samuel Huntington, Roger Starr, Seymour Martin Lipset, and James Q. Wilson all shy away from the designation—some of them quite violently. Others, such as Robert Nisbet and Edward Banfield, call themselves "conservatives," without benefit of qualification. I myself have accepted the term, perhaps because, having been named Irving, I am relatively indifferent to baptismal caprice. But I may be the only living and self-confessed neoconservative, at large or in captivity.

It was to be expected, therefore, that the first book on neoconservatism would be written by one of *them*, not by one of *us*. Peter Steinfels is a Left-liberal journalist, a "democratic socialist" apparently, and his book, *The Neoconservatives: The Men Who Are Changing America's Politics* (Simon & Schuster, 1979), is a polemic disguised as a report and "fair" commentary. The pretense is even more annoying than the polemic, which takes the form of interspersing summaries of our presumed views with constant reminders—lest the reader be contaminated—of just how far short these fall from wholesome "progressive" opinion. (There is also the insinuation that neoconservatism is really a profit-making enterprise disguised as intellectual work.) This rhetorical strategy makes for a long but tedious book, the reading of which is a wearying experience. It is as if Mr. Steinfels, morally opposed to capital punishment, had decided to nag neoconservatism to death.

I do not wish to suggest that the book is without merit. There is, for instance, an excellent couple of sentences on page 4:

> Political thought—in the United States today—is moving steadily in two directions. There are those, like democratic socialists, who feel they must reach beyond contemporary liberalism in order to fulfil its promises. And there are those, like the neoconservatives, who feel they must reach beyond contemporary liberalism to preserve its heritage.

That is very well put—though it would be more correct to talk not of the promises *of* liberalism, but of the promises generated *by* and grafted *onto* liberalism in the course of this century. Democratic socialism can be seen as the fulfillment of liberalism only in a Hegelian sense—that is, it absorbs, transcends, and nullifies it, all at the same time. Neoconservatism, on the other hand, is indeed "reformationist" as Mr. Steinfels suggests. It tries to "reach beyond" contemporary liberalism in the way that all reformations, religious or political, do—by a return to the original sources of liberal vision and liberal energy so as to correct the warped version of liberalism that is today's orthodoxy.

Another way of defining these two antithetical tendencies is to say that the one is modern-utopian, the other classical-realist in temper and intellectual inclination. Nothing reveals this more clearly than Mr. Steinfels's accusation against neoconservatism that it is committed to "stability as the prerequisite for justice rather than the other way around." I do not know of a single political philosopher, from Plato to Tocqueville, or any of the founding fathers (always excepting an occasional wayward remark by Jefferson), who would have thought such a commitment anything but obviously sensible. To demand "justice" as a precondition for political or social stability is to make a demand on this world which the world has ever refused to concede. Mr. Steinfels, who is a Catholic intellectual—he is executive editor of *Commonweal*—has, in his passion for "justice now," forgotten everything he may once have learned from reading St. Augustine or St. Thomas.

It should be clear by now that I do think there really is such a thing as neoconservatism—but it is most misleading to think of it as any kind of "movement." It holds no meetings, has no organizational form, has no specific programmatic goals, and when two neoconservatives meet they are more likely to argue with one another than to confer or conspire. But it is there, nevertheless—an impulse that ripples through the intellectual world; a "persuasion," to use a nice old-fashioned term; a mode of thought (but not quite a school of thought).

What are its distinctive features? I shall list them as I see them—but to say that this listing is unofficial would be the understatement of the decade.

1. Neoconservatism is a current of thought emerging out of the academic-intellectual world and provoked by disillusionment with contemporary liberalism. Its relation to the business community—the traditional source of American conservatism—is loose and uneasy, though not necessarily unfriendly.

2. Unlike previous such currents of thought—for example, the Southern Agrarians or the Transcendentalists of the nineteenth century—neoconservatism is antiromantic in substance and temperament. Indeed, it regards political romanticism—and its twin, political utopianism—of any kind as one of the plagues of our age. This is but another way of saying it is a philosophical-political impulse rather than a literary-political impulse. Or, to put it still another way: Its approach to the world is more "rabbinic" than "prophetic."

3. The philosophical roots of neoconservatism are to be found mainly in classical—that is, premodern, preideological—political philosophy. Here the teaching and writing of the late Leo Strauss (never mentioned by Mr. Steinfels) are of importance, though many neoconservatives find him somewhat too wary of modernity. Neoconservatives are admiring of Aristotle, respectful of Locke, distrustful of Rousseau.

4. The attitude of neoconservatives to bourgeois society and the bourgeois ethos is one of detached attachment. In the spirit of Tocqueville, neoconservatives do not think that liberal-democratic capitalism is the best of all imaginable worlds—only the best, under the circumstances, of all possible worlds. This *modest* enthusiasm distinguishes neoconservatism from the Old Right and the New Right—both of which are exceedingly suspicious of it.

5. Neoconservatism is inclined to the belief that a predominantly market economy—just

how "predominant" is a matter for some disagreement—is a necessary if not sufficient precondition for a liberal society (Daniel Bell, as the theoretician for what may be called our "social-democratic wing," would presumably take issue with this judgment.) It also sees a market economy as favorable to economic growth.

6. Neoconservatives believe in the importance of economic growth, not out of any enthusiasm for the material goods of this world, but because they see economic growth as indispensable for social and political stability. It is the prospect of economic growth that has made it possible to think—against the grain of premodern political thought—of democracy as a viable and enduring sociopolitical system.

7. Neoconservatives, though respecting the market as an economic mechanism, are not libertarian in the sense, say, that Milton Friedman and Friedrich A. von Hayek are. A conservative welfare state—what once was called a "social insurance" state—is perfectly consistent with the neoconservative perspective. So is a state that takes a degree of responsibility for helping to shape the preferences that the people exercise in a free market—to "elevate" them, if you will. Neoconservatives, moreover, believe that it is natural for people to *want* their preferences to be elevated. The current version of liberalism, which prescribes massive government intervention in the marketplace but an absolute laissez-faire attitude toward manners and morals, strikes neoconservatives as representing a bizarre inversion of priorities.

8. Neoconservatives look upon family and religion as indispensable pillars of a decent society. Indeed, they have a special fondness for all of those intermediate institutions of a liberal society which reconcile the need for community with the desire for liberty.

Karl Marx once wrote that the human race would eventually face the choice between socialism and barbarism. Well, we have seen enough of socialism in our time to realize that, in actuality as distinct from ideality, it can offer neither stability nor justice, and that in many of its versions it seems perfectly compatible with barbarism. So most neoconservatives believe that the last, best hope of humanity at this time is an intellectually and morally reinvigorated liberal capitalism.

I could go on but I had better not. I suspect that too many of my neoconservative friends will already have taken exception to one or another thing I have said. For this is an intellectual current full of all sorts of little knotty whirlpools, each being agitated by some problem in political, social, or economic theory that needs further exploration, further thought. And that, I think, is what makes neoconservatism so interesting—the fact that it is as concerned with the questions it cannot yet satisfactorily answer as with those it thinks contemporary liberalism has answered incorrectly.

PART FIVE

SOCIALISM AND COMMUNISM: MORE TO MARX

Although socialism and communism are by no means identical, they belong to a common family of ideologies and spring from a common impulse. Both envision a society in which everyone contributes time, labor, and talent to a common pool and receives in return enough goods to satisfy his or her needs. Both condemn the exploitation of one individual or class by another that occurs, for example, when one profits from another's labor. And both believe that property should be so distributed as to benefit not the wealthy few, but the public at large. Both are, therefore, critical of capitalism as an economic system and of liberalism (or liberal individualism) as an ideology.

But socialism and communism are different in other respects. One crucial difference concerns the means for attaining their ends. Socialists are more apt to favor peaceful and piecemeal reforms as a way of bringing about a socialist society, while Communists—at least in the late nineteenth and the twentieth centuries—have often opted for violent revolutionary transformations spearheaded by an elite "vanguard" party. Moreover, the kind of society that each hopes to create differs to some degree. Socialists envision a society in which the major means of production—mines, mills, factories, power plants, and so on—are either publicly owned or at least operated for the public benefit. Modern Communists, by contrast, tend to favor public ownership and bureaucratic control of virtually all enterprises, large and small.

Socialism and communism come in a variety of forms and share a long history. In the fifth century B.C., for example, Plato in his *Republic* envisioned an ideal society in which one class, the Guardians, shared everything, including spouses and children, in common. Many early Christians were communists who shared all their worldly goods with one another—a practice that persists even today in some monasteries. This early conception of communism is perhaps most memorably sketched in St. Thomas More's *Utopia* (1516). There he imagines a society from which the forces of envy and greed have been banished. Private property and money have been abolished. The Utopians work not for profit, but for the common good. Although the

Utopians are pagans, More maintains that they put "Christian" Europe to shame by behaving selflessly and charitably toward each other.

Later idealistic or "utopian" socialists, such as Charles Fourier (1772–1837) and Robert Owen (1771–1858), provided more secular variations on More's theme. Fourier, for example, imagined an ideal society in which all would work for the common good, even if they did exactly as they pleased. The socialist principle of "harmonism" would harmonize diverse interests or "passions" and would make social cooperation not only possible, but pleasant. Owen, a capitalist turned socialist, tried to put his plans for a perfect society into practice. Believing that human labor should be not only productive but morally uplifting, he designed and built factories and adjoining towns to promote these two ideals.

These and other schemes for socialist transformation were derided and condemned by those who thought of themselves as "scientific" socialists. Against the "utopianism" of earlier socialists, Karl Marx (1818–1883) and Friedrich Engels (1820–1895) argued that society is changed not through moral suasion, but by understanding the hidden processes of material production and historical progress. The key, they thought, was the "materialist conception of history." Unlike the "idealist" view of history advanced by G. W. F. Hegel (1770–1831), Marx and Engels' "materialist" view made material production and class struggle the primary determinants of social stability and change. All previously existing societies were divided along class lines. On the one side was the dominant or ruling class, the owners of the means of material production; on the other, a subservient class condemned to do the bidding of the ruling class. Who the rulers and the ruled are depends on the type of society or "social formation" one is talking about. In slave society, masters rule over slaves; in feudal society, lords rule over serfs; in capitalist society, the ruling capitalist class or *bourgeoisie* rules over the working class or *proletariat.* These "social relations of production" do not rest on force alone. If a class-divided society is to be stable and long-lived, its members must view it as legitimate. The social order, with its inequalities of wealth and opportunity, must be seen as "normal," "natural," "necessary," or "inevitable." This is the function of ideology: to put the stamp of legitimacy on existing social arrangements. The "ruling ideas"—that is, the respectable or mainstream ideas—"are in every society the ideas of the ruling class." Only the ideas that serve the interests of the ruling class by helping it to perpetuate its rule will be disseminated from the pulpit, in the classroom, in the mass media, and elsewhere. All others will be regarded with suspicion or contempt.

Marx viewed his own theory as critical, that is, subversive of the orthodox opinions prevalent in capitalist society. The ideological prop and mainstay of such a society, he held, was "political economy"—the nineteenth-century term for the "science" of economics—with its "laws" of supply and demand, and so on. Marx tried to show that political economy was really a smokescreen to obscure the system of exploitative social relations upon which capitalism rested. By exposing the exploitative nature of the system, Marx hoped to enlighten or raise the consciousness of the proletariat, thereby paving the way for a revolution that would free them from the system that oppressed them. Only then, he thought, could the workers begin to bring about a classless communist society operating according to the principle, "From each according to his ability, to each according to his need."

29

UTOPIA

THOMAS MORE

Thomas More (1478–1535) was an important political and literary figure of the "Northern Renaissance" of the early sixteenth century. At one time a close advisor to King Henry VIII, More fell into disfavor when Henry broke with the Roman Catholic Church to establish the Church of England with himself as head. For refusing to approve Henry's action, More was beheaded. Four centuries later the Roman Catholic Church recognized him as a saint. Before his difficulties with Henry VIII began, More wrote *Utopia* (1516), a book in which he imagined a society from which the evils of envy and poverty had been banished. In the following selection More's main character, Raphael Hythloday, traces the evils of European society to the private ownership of property, which he contrasts to the virtues of the island commonwealth of Utopia, where private property and even money have been abolished.

Source: More wrote Utopia *in Latin. The following selections are from the first English translation, by Ralph Robynson in 1551. We have made numerous changes, including some minor abridgments, to put these passages in a style and language more accessible to today's reader.*

UTOPIA

FROM BOOK I

"I have no doubt, Master More," said Hythloday, "that wherever men have private property and money is the measure of everything, there it is hardly possible for the commonwealth to be justly governed or to flourish in prosperity. Unless, that is, you think that justice is done when all things are in the hands of evil men, or that prosperity and happiness are found when everything is divided among a few—and even those few do not really thrive—while all the rest live in misery and wretchedness.

"This is so different from the wise and godly ordinances of the Utopians, among whom a few laws are sufficient to keep everything well and happily ordered. In Utopia virtue is greatly esteemed, and even though all things are owned in common, everyone has everything in abundance. Now compare them with the many nations that are always making new, but unsatisfactory, laws. In these countries every man claims that he has his own property, or private goods; but the new laws they make every day are not enough to enable everyone to enjoy or defend those things that he calls his own. This much is made plain by the never-ending legal suits that constantly arise. When I consider these things, then, I have to agree with Plato, and I do not wonder that he made no laws for those who refused to share their wealth equally. For this wise man clearly foresaw that the only way to promote the well-being of the public as a whole is to establish equality of all goods.[1] Such equality can never be found where every man's goods are his private property. For there every man lays claim to as much as he can get. Then, no matter how great the abundance, a few divide all the riches among themselves, leaving the rest in poverty. And for the most part, the poor are more worthy to be happy and prosperous than the others. The rich are covetous, crafty, and really quite useless; the poor, on the other hand, are lowly, simple, and by their daily labor more beneficial to the common welfare than to themselves.

"Thus I am fully persuaded that no equitable and just distribution of goods can be made, and that there can be no true well-being in human affairs, unless private property is outlawed and banished. But as long as private property is the rule, the heavy and inevitable burden of poverty and wretchedness will weigh down the largest and best part of mankind. I grant that this burden may be eased, but it cannot be wholly removed while private property reigns. There might be a law that prohibits anyone from possessing more than a certain measure of land, perhaps, or more than a certain sum of money. Or there might be laws preventing the king from being too powerful, or the people from being too proud and unruly. Still other laws might proclaim that public offices must not be obtained by bribes and gifts, or that they cannot be bought or sold. Putting offices up for sale simply encourages the officials to regain the money they spent by defrauding and plundering the public; and if the offices go to those who offer bribes and gifts, the government will be in the hands of the rich, not the wise. By laws such as these, in short, the evils of which I have been speaking can be lightened and mitigated, just as people who are desperately ill and beyond cure can be kept alive with constant care. But these nations will never be completely cured and brought to a healthy condition while every man is master of his own property. You may cure one part, but in doing so you aggravate the illness of another. Helping one person harms another, for nothing can be given to anyone unless it is taken from someone else. . . ."

FROM BOOK II (HYTHLODAY'S ACCOUNT OF UTOPIA)

. . .

[W]here money is the standard of everything, many vain and superfluous occupations must be pursued, although they serve only for wanton luxury and false pleasure. If the same multitude that now is occupied in work were divided into the few occupations that the truly necessary work requires, the abundance of goods that would ensue would be so great that the prices would doubtless be too low for the craftsmen to maintain their livelihood. But if all these who are now busy in useless occupations, with the whole flock of those who live idly and slothfully, consuming and wasting every one of them more of those things that come from other men's labor than two of the workers themselves do—if all these, I say, were set to useful occupations, you can easily see how little would be enough, even too much, to supply us with everything we require for the sake of necessity or comfort. Yes, or even for pleasure, as long as the pleasure be true and natural.

This is made plain by the life of Utopia itself. There in each city, including the adjoining countryside, scarcely 500 persons of all those who are neither too old nor to weak to work are excused from labor. Among these are the Syphogrants,[2] who are exempted by law from labor. Yet they do not take advantage of the exemption because they want to set an example by their labor that will encourage others to work. There are also the scholars to whom the people, upon the recommendation of the priests and secret election by the Syphogrants, give an exemption from labor so that they may devote themselves to learning. But if any of the scholars fails to meet the expected standards, he is immediately plucked back to the company of workers. On the other hand, it often happens that a craftsman so earnestly devotes his free time to learning, and so profits by his diligence, that he is taken from his handicraft and promoted to the company of the learned.

From these scholars the ambassadors, priests, and tranibors[3] are chosen, as is the prince himself, whom they in their old tongue called Barzanes, and now call Ademus.[4] The rest of the people are neither idle nor occupied with useless work, so it may easily be judged how much good work they may do in a few hours. They also have the advantage that in most of the necessary trades they need not work as much as other nations do. First of all, the building or repairing of houses takes everywhere else so many men's time because the careless heir allows the house his father built to fall into decay. So while he might have preserved it at little cost, his successor is now constrained to build it anew at great expense. Many times also one man has so refined and delicate a taste that he sets no value on a house that cost another man much money. As the house is neglected and shortly falls into ruin, the man of refined taste builds another one in another place at no less cost. But among the Utopians, where all things are in good order and the commonwealth is well-regulated, it very seldom happens that they choose a new plot to build a house upon. They not only find quick remedies for existing faults, but also prevent those that are likely to occur. In this way their houses last long with little labor and small repairs—so long that their carpenters and builders sometimes have almost nothing to do, in which case they hew timber at home, and square and trim stones, so that if any work needs to be done, it may be finished even more speedily.

Now note how few workers their clothing requires. First of all, while they are at work they are dressed in simple leather or skins that will last seven years. When they go out they put on a cloak which hides the other homely apparel. These cloaks throughout the island are all the same color, and that is the natural color of the wool. They therefore not only need much less wool than people in other countries, but the wool they do need costs them much less. Linen is made with less labor, so it is used more. But in linen only whiteness is valued, and in wool only cleanliness. As for the fineness of the thread, they don't care. Yet this is why in other places four or five cloth gowns of diverse colors, and as many silk coats, are not enough for one man. Yes, and if he is the fashionable sort, even ten are too few. But in Utopia one garment will serve a man very well for two years. Why should he desire more? If he had them, he would be neither better protected from the cold nor in any way appear better dressed.

Because they are all engaged in useful occupations, there is plenty of everything they need;

and because a few workers are enough for each craft, they sometimes bring out great numbers of people to repair the highways, if any need repair. Many times, also, when they have no such work to do, an open proclamation is made that they should devote fewer hours to work. For the authorities do not force the citizens to labor unnecessarily. Why should they? The chief aim of the constitution and government is to spare people as much time as possible from necessary occupations so that they can leave the labor of the body and give time to the freedom and culture of the mind. For this, they suppose, is what makes for a truly happy life. . . .

The Utopians use gold and silver in such a way as to prevent anyone from placing a greater value on these metals than they naturally deserve. Who does not see that these metals are less valuable than iron? Men can live no better without iron than without fire and water. But nature has given gold and silver no use that we could not do without. It is the folly of men that sets a higher value on them because they are rare. Nature, however, as a tender and loving mother, has placed the best and most necessary things in the open all about us, such as air, water, and the earth itself, and has hidden farthest from us vain and useless things. . . .

The Utopians have devised, then, a plan that is as consistent with their laws and customs as it is contrary to ours, where gold is so cherished. The plan may even seem incredible, as a result, to those unfamiliar with it. They eat and drink from earthen and glass vessels, which are well and cleverly made, but which have little value. Of gold and silver, however, they make chamber pots and similar containers that serve for the most vile uses, not only in their common halls, but in everyone's private house.[5] Furthermore, they make great chains and fetters of these metals to bind their slaves.[6] Finally, those who commit crimes must wear gold rings on their ears and fingers, gold chains around their necks, and gold crowns around their heads. In this way the Utopians arrange to have gold and silver serve as marks of reproach and infamy. Other peoples grieve if they must do without these metals, as if gold and silver were their own lives. But if they should be taken all at once from the Utopians, no one there would think he had lost as much as a penny.

They gather pearls from the sea and diamonds and rubies from certain rocks. They do not search for them, but if they find them by chance they cut and polish them, then decorate their infants with them. In their early years the children are fond and proud of such ornaments. When they are a little older and wiser, though, they see that only children wear such trifles, and they put them away as shameful, without any bidding from their parents, just as our children cast away their marbles, rattles, and dolls when they grow older. How these laws and customs, so different from other nations, lead to different ideas and desires was made most clear to me by the arrival of the ambassadors of the Anemolians.[7]

These ambassadors came to Amaurot[8] while I was there. Because they came to negotiate great and weighty matters, three representatives from each Utopian city gathered before them. The ambassadors of other countries who had been there before knew the manners of the Utopians, so they knew that no honor was given to sumptuous and costly apparel—silks were condemned, gold considered disgraceful—and they came to Amaurot in plain and simple clothing. But the Anemolians, who lived far away and had little acquaintance with Utopia, decided upon hearing that Utopians all wore the same simple clothing that they must not have the things they did not wear. Being more proud than wise, the Anemolians determined to dress as gorgeously as the gods themselves, and thus to dazzle the eyes of the poor Utopians with their glistening clothes. So in came the three ambassadors with 100 servants dressed in many colors, most of them in silk. The ambassadors themselves, who were noblemen in their own country, wore clothes of gold, with great gold chains, gold hanging from their ears, gold rings on their fingers, brooches and strings of gold glistening with pearls and jewels upon their caps—trimmed and adorned, in short, with all those things which among the Utopians were either the punishment of slaves, the mark of disgrace upon wrong-doers, or trifles for young children's play. It would have done a man good, therefore, to have seen how proudly they displayed their peacock feathers, how much they made of their painted sheaths, and how loftily they advanced themselves when they compared their brilliant apparel with the poor garments of the Utopians, who swarmed into the streets. On the other hand, it was no less pleasant to see how much they were deceived and how far they missed their purpose. For to the eyes of the Utopians, except for the few who had been in other countries, all that gorgeous apparel seemed shameful. In fact, they saluted the lowest and most abject of the Anemolians, mistaking them for the nobles, while they ignored the ambassadors, whom they judged to be slaves because of their golden chains. You should have seen the children who had thrown away their pearls and jewels dig and push when they saw these items on the ambassadors' capes. "Look Mother," they said, "at that big ninny who still wears pearls and jewels like a little child." But the mother would earnestly say, "Hush, Son, I think he is one of the ambassador's fools." Others found fault with the golden chains because they were so small and weak that a slave could easily break them; or so large that he might slip them off and run away.

But when the ambassadors had been there a day or two and saw so much gold so little esteemed, and more gold in the chains of one fugitive slave than in all their costly ornaments, they put away shamefully all that gorgeous array of which they had been so proud. For their part, the Utopians marveled that anyone who may behold the stars or the sun could be so foolish as to delight in the sparkling of a trifling stone, or that any man is so mad as to count himself a better person for the fine quality of the wool he wears. No matter how fine, they say, the same wool was once worn by a sheep, which was nothing but a sheep the whole time she wore it.

They marvel also that gold, so useless in itself, is now valued so highly among all people that man himself is held in less esteem than gold. A lumpish blockhead, with no more wit than an ass, nevertheless shall have many wise and good men at his command simply because he has a great heap of gold. But if the gold should be taken from him and given to the lowest servant in his household either by fortune or by some subtle trick of the law (which no less than fortune raises up the low and pulls down the high), then he as well as his money shall shortly go into the service of his servant. . . .

I have described to you as truly as I could the form and order of that commonwealth which in my judgment is not only the best, but the only one that can rightly claim the name of a commonwealth or republic. In other places they speak of the common good, but every man procures his private good. Here, where nothing is private, the common affairs are their real concern. In both cases they have good reason to act as they do. For in other countries, no matter how prosperous the country may be, who knows that he will not starve if he makes no special provision for himself? Therefore he is compelled to look out for himself rather than the people—that is, for others. Where all things are owned in common, on the contrary, no one shall lack anything necessary for his private use, so long as the common storehouses and barns are sufficiently stocked. There nothing is distributed in a niggardly way, nor is anyone poor. And though no one owns anything, yet everyone is rich. For what can be richer than to live joyfully, free from worries about making a living? No man is vexed by his wife's importunate complaints, nor dreads poverty for his sons, nor sorrows because he cannot provide a dowry for his daughter. Instead, the Utopians do not worry at all about the livelihood and prosperity of themselves and their kin: their wives, their children, their nephews, their children's children, and all that shall follow in their posterity. Besides this, they provide as much for those who were once laborers, but are now too weak to work, as for those who are still working.

Now I would like to see if anyone is so bold

as to compare this with the so-called justice of other nations—among whom, upon my soul, I can find no sign of equity and justice. Is it justice when a rich goldsmith or moneylender, or anyone who either does nothing at all or nothing necessary to the common good, has a pleasant and prosperous life, while poor laborers, carters, ironsmiths, carpenters, and plowmen by great and continual toil are barely able to stay alive? Their work is so necessary that no commonwealth could last a year without it; yet their lives are so wretched and miserable that the condition of the beasts of burden may seem better. . . . Not only are these wretched workers tormented with hard and unprofitable labor, but they must also suffer the prospect of a penniless old age. For their daily wage is so little that it will not suffice for that day, much less yield any surplus that may be saved for the relief of old age.

Is this not an unjust country?[9] It gives great rewards to so-called gentlemen, goldsmiths, and other idlers and flatterers, or to those who devise useless pleasures, on the one hand; then, on the other, it fails to provide for poor plowmen, coal miners, laborers, carters, ironsmiths, and carpenters, without whom no commonwealth can survive. After it has abused the labors of their lusty and flowering years, it abandons them to a miserable death. Besides this, the rich men every day snatch away from the poor some part of their livelihood, either by private fraud or public law. So to their despicable treatment of the workers whose pains promote the public good, the rich now give the name of justice under law.

Therefore when I consider all these commonwealths which nowadays flourish everywhere, God help me but I perceive nothing but a conspiracy of the rich, who serve their own interests under the name of the common good. They invent all sorts of ways to keep what they have unjustly acquired, as well as ways to employ the labor of the poor for as little money as possible. These devices, the rich declare, must be kept and observed for the sake of the common good—that is, for the welfare also of the poor people—and so they are made laws. But when these most wicked and vicious men have by their insatiable covetousness divided among themselves all those things that would suffice for *all* men, they are still far from enjoying the happiness of the Utopian commonwealth. In Utopia, where the desire for money is banished along with its use, how great a heap of cares is cut away! How great an occasion for wickedness and mischief is pulled up by the roots! Who does not know that fraud, theft, plunder, brawling, quarreling, faction, strife, chiding, contention, murder, treason, and poisoning, which are revenged but not prevented by punishment, die out when money dies? Or that fear, grief, care, toils, and anxiety perish the same moment that money perishes? Yes, poverty itself, which only seemed to be the lack of money, would vanish if money were gone.

That you may perceive this more plainly, consider some barren and unfruitful year in which many thousands of people have starved. I dare to say that at the end of that desperate time enough grain might have been found in the rich men's barns to feed everyone whom famine and pestilence killed. So easily might men make their living if that worthy princess, Lady Money, did not stand in the way. I am sure that the rich understand this. Even they must know that it is better to lack nothing one really needs than to have many unnecessary things—better to be rid of innumerable cares and troubles than to be besieged with great riches. I do not doubt that every man's respect for his private interest, or the authority of our savior Christ (who knew and counselled what is best), would have brought all the world long ago into the ways of the public welfare if it were not for that one beast, the princess and mother of all wrongdoing—pride. Pride measures happiness and prosperity not by her own advantages, but by the miseries and disadvantages of others. She would not be content if there were no wretches to mock and scorn, no one whose misery might bring out her happiness, no one whose poverty she might torment and increase by gorgeously displaying her riches. This hellhound creeps into men's hearts and keeps them from entering the right path of life. Pride is so deeply rooted in men's breasts that she cannot easily be plucked out.

Although I would gladly wish the form of a true commonwealth for all nations, I am glad that it has chanced to fall to the Utopians. They have laid such foundations of their commonwealth as shall endure forever, as far as one can foresee. Because the chief causes of ambition and factions and the other vices have been pulled up by the roots, the Utopians are in no jeopardy of the domestic dissension that has brought to ruin the well fortified and strongly defended wealth and riches of many cities. And as long as perfect concord remains and wholesome laws are enforced at home, the envy of foreign princes will not be able to conquer or shake Utopia, for they have tried many times and always been driven back.

EDITORS' NOTES

1. In the just society Plato envisions in his *Republic,* the rulers, or Guardians, share everything in common, although most of the people are allowed to own private property.
2. Hythloday had earlier explained that Utopian cities are divided into groups of 30 households, with each group electing an official called a Syphogrant.
3. A Tranibor is an official, elected annually, with authority over ten Syphogrants and the 300 families they represent.
4. In classical Greek, Barzanes means "Son of Zeus"; Ademus, "without people."
5. Strictly speaking, houses are not privately owned in Utopia. According to Hythloday's account, moreover, all houses are alike and every ten years they are redistributed by lottery.
6. Most slaves in Utopia are either prisoners of war or people guilty of heinous offenses. There is also a group of what we now would call servants, comprising foreigners who prefer "slavery" in Utopia to life in their native land.
7. Anemolian is Greek for "windy people."
8. Amaurot is the capital city of Utopia.
9. That is, England, and other European countries, and not Utopia.

30

SOCIAL ORGANIZATION

CHARLES FOURIER

Like many socialists, the French writer Charles Fourier (1772–1837) attributed the ills of his society to private property and the profit motive. Yet human history was destined, he believed, to progress beyond the lower stage of self-interest to a higher stage of social harmony and "collective interest." Fourier lacked the resources to put his ideas into practice, but several attempts were made to establish utopian communities based on his ideas. One of these, the Brook Farm community in Massachusetts, was the project of several New England transcendentalist thinkers in the 1840s. Nathaniel Hawthorne spent some time at Brook Farm, then made it the setting for his novel, *The Blithedale Romance.*

Source: Design for Utopia: Selected Writings of Charles Fourier, *translated by Julia Franklin (London: Swan Sonnenschein and Co., 1901), pp. 51–54, 82–89.*

Our destiny is to advance; every social period must progress towards the one above it: it is Nature's wish that barbarism should tend towards civilisation and attain to it by degrees; that civilisation should tend to guaranteeism, that guaranteeism should tend to simple association, and so of the other periods. The same is true of phases: the first must tend towards the second, this to the third, this again to the fourth, this to transition state, and so on in succession. If a society lingers too long in a period or phase, it engenders corruption like stagnant water. (This rule is subject to certain exceptions for the periods inferior to civilisation.)

It is only during the past hundred years that we have been in the third phase of civilisation; but in this short space of time the phase has advanced very rapidly, owing to the colossal progress of industry; so that to-day the third phase exceeds its natural limits. We have too much material for a stage so little advanced; and, this material not finding its natural employment, there is a consequent overloading and discomfort in the social mechanism. This results in a fermentation which taints it; it develops a great number of malevolent characteristics, symptoms of lassitude, effects of the disproportion which exists between our industrial means and the inferior stage to which they are applied. We have too much industry for a civilisation so little advanced, detained in the third phase; it is besieged by the need of raising itself at least to the fourth; thence arise the properties of exuberance and deterioration. . . .

We shall not follow the right path until we establish guaranteeism. It is a stratagem which ought to be employed to oppose liberalism, a stationary spirit which is incapable of advancing, and which is enamoured of a characteristic of the second phase, the *representative system*, a little scheme good in a small republic such as Sparta or Athens, but altogether illusory in a vast and opulent empire like France. . . .

Every society has a greater or less admixture of characteristics taken from superior or inferior periods; the French, for instance, have lately adopted the *unity of industrial and administrative relations;* this method, which is one of the characteristics of the sixth period, was introduced by the uniform metric system and the civil code of Napoleon, two institutions opposed to the civilised Order, one of whose characteristics is the *incoherence of industrial and administrative relations.* We have, then, on this point, *deviated from Civilisation and worked into the sixth period.* We have worked into it on other points also, notably by *religious toleration.* The English, who practise a degree of intolerance worthy of the twelfth century, are in this respect more civilised than we. The Germans likewise are more civilised than we as regards the incoherence of laws, customs, and industrial relations; in Germany one encounters at every turn different measures, sorts of money, laws, and usages, by which means a stranger is robbed and cheated far more easily than if there were but one kind of measure, money, code, etc. This chaos of relations is favourable to the mechanism of civilisation, which seeks, as its aim, to raise knavery to the highest point; and this would be attained by fully developing the sixteen special characteristics of civilisation.

Nevertheless philosophers maintain "that civilisation has been raised by the adoption of religious toleration, industrial and administrative unity." That is expressing one's self very poorly; they should have said that *the social Order has been raised and Civilisation lowered;* in reality, if all the sixteen characteristics of the sixth period were successively adopted it would result in the total annihilation of Civilisation—it would be destroyed under the belief that it was being perfected. The social Order would be better organised, but the fifth would have been replaced by the sixth period. These distinctions of characteristics lead to an amusing conclusion: it is that *the little good to be found in the Civilised Order is due only to features that are contrary to Civilisation.* . . .

The associative[1] Order will fulfil the wish of the nations, by securing to all progressive wealth, the object of everyone's desire: as for Civilisation, from which we are going to emerge, far from its being the industrial destiny of man, it is but a passing scourge with which most of the planets are afflicted during their first ages; it is for the human race a temporary malady, like teething for infants; it has been prolonged two thousand five hundred years too long through the inadvertence or the pride of the sophists who have disdained all investigation of Association and Attraction; in fine, the Savage, Patriarchal, Barbarous, and Civilised forms of society are but the thorny paths, the ladders which are to lead us up to the social state which is the destiny of Man, and outside of which all the efforts of the best rulers are unable in any way to remedy the ills of mankind.

It is in vain, then, Philosophers, that you accumulate libraries to search for happiness, while the root of all the social ills has not been eradicated—*industrial parcelling* or incoherent labour which is the antipodes of God's designs. You complain that Nature refuses you the knowledge of her laws: well! if you have, up to the present, been unable to discover them, why do you hestitate to recognise the insufficiency of your methods and to seek new ones? Either Nature does not desire the happiness of man, or your methods are reproved by her, since they have not been able to wrest from her the secret which you are endeavouring to obtain. Do you see her refractory to the efforts of physicists as she is to yours? No, for they study her laws instead of dictating laws to her; and you only study to stifle the voice of Nature, to stifle the Attraction which is the interpreter of her designs, since it leads on every hand to domestic-agricultural Association.

What a contrast, therefore, between your blunderings and the achievements of the exact sciences! Each day you add new errors to the old ones, while each day sees the physical sciences advancing upon the road of truth and shedding a lustre upon modern times equal to the opprobrium which has been cast upon them by the visions of regeneration of the sophists. . . .

. . . Our sciences, which boast their love of the people, are totally ignorant of the means of protecting them.

It is to chance, therefore, and not to the political and moral sciences that we owe our feeble advances in the spirit of society; but chance makes us purchase each discovery with centuries of stormy trials. The movement of our societies may be compared to that of the sloth, whose every step is counted by a groan; like it, civilisation advances with an inconceivable slowness through political torments; with each generation it tries new systems which only serve, like briars, to stain with blood those who take hold of them. . . .

It is, above all, in industrial policy that our century displays its pride; proud of some material strides, it does not perceive that it is retrograding politically, and that its rapid advance is that of the crab, which moves, but moves backward.

Industrialism is the latest of our scientific chimeras; it is the mania of producing in confusion, without any system of proportional compensation, without any guarantee to the producer or wage-earner that he will participate in the increase of wealth; accordingly, we find the industrial regions sprinkled with beggars to as great, or, perhaps, a greater extent than those countries which are indifferent to this sort of progress. . . .

. . . [M. Sismondi] has recognised that consumption operates in an *inverted manner*, that it is based upon the whims of the idle, and not upon the well-being of the producer; this is at any rate a first step towards analytical sincerity. But this inverted mechanism, is it limited to consumption? is it not evident:

That *exchange is inverted*, carried on by intermediaries called *merchants*, *traders*, who, becoming owners of the product, levy tribute upon the producer and the consumer, and sow disorder in the industrial system by their underhand dealings in monopolies, stock-jobbing, cheating, extortion, bankruptcy, etc.

That competition is inverted, tending to the reduction of wages, and leading the people to indigence through the progress in industry; the more it increases, the more is the labourer obliged to accept very low remuneration for labour too much contended for; and on the other hand, the more the number of merchants increases, the more are they drawn to cheating, through the difficulty of realising any profit.

Here are already three forces directed in an inverted manner, in the industrial mechanism; I could readily name thirty of them; why admit only one, that of inverted consumption?

Industry offers a subversion far more striking; this is the *opposition of the two kinds of interest, collective and individual.* Every person engaged in an industry is at war with the mass, and malevolent toward it from personal interest. A physician wishes his fellow-citizens good, genuine cases of fevers, and an attorney good lawsuits in every family. An architect has need for a good conflagration which should reduce a quarter of the city to ashes, and a glazier desires a good hail-storm which should break all the panes of glass. A tailor, a shoemaker, wishes the public to use only poorly-dyed stuffs and shoes made of bad leather, so that a triple amount may be consumed—for the benefit of trade; that is their refrain. A court of justice regards it opportune that France continues to commit a hundred and twenty thousand crimes and actionable offences, that number being necessary to maintain the criminal courts. It is thus that in civilised industry every individual is in intentional war against the mass; necessary result of anti-associative industry or an inverted world. We shall see this absurdity disappear in the associative *régime,* where each individual will find his advantage only in that of the mass. . . .

This vicious circle of industry has been so clearly recognised, that people on all sides are beginning to suspect it, and feel astonished *that, in civilisation, poverty should be the offspring of abundance.*

After having proved that the lot of the civilised masses must of necessity be unfortunate, let us remark that the progress of industry adds little or nothing to the happiness of the rich. The *bourgeoisie* of Paris, to-day, has more beautiful furniture, prettier gew-gaws, than the great of the seventeenth century; what does that add to happiness? Our ladies with their cashmere shawls, are they happier than the Sévignés, the Ninons? We see at present the petty *bourgeois* of Paris served in vessels of gilded porcelain; are they happier than the ministers of Louis XIV, the Colberts, the Louvois, who had dishes of earthenware?

There is beyond doubt real enjoyment in improvements affecting comfort and health such, for example, as the springs of carriages; but one grows *blasé* after a week regarding the refinements of visual luxury, such as porcelain; they only serve to excite the cupidity of the poor, who imagine that the wealthy classes find great happiness in the possession of these baubles. They will only be useful in the associative order, where they will have the double property of stimulating industrial attraction and of multiplying the harmonies of the passions, which are indeed a real enjoyment, and which will be shared by the poor, as well as the rich, in spite of the extreme inequality of fortunes. Then the poorest of men will have many more pleasures than the most opulent monarch of to-day, because the order termed passionate Series creates social harmonies of pleasures of the soul, which at present are well-nigh unknown to the great, and it raises sensual refinements to a perfection of which the civilised world is incapable of forming any conception.

NOTE

1. The word "associative" seems to be better fitted than any other English word to convey the meaning implied by Fourier's term *"sociétaire,"* and has been used as the equivalent of that term in this translation.—Tr.

31

THE COMMUNIST MANIFESTO

KARL MARX AND FRIEDRICH ENGELS

Originally written at the request of a small group of radicals known as the Communist League, the *Manifesto of the Communist Party* (1848) has become the most famous, and perhaps the most influential, statement of Karl Marx's views. In other writings Marx (1818–1883) delves more deeply into philosophical, economic, and social issues, but none of these is as comprehensive or clear as the *Manifesto*. The clarity may be due largely to Friedrich Engels (1820–1895), Marx's longtime friend and collaborator, but the ideas were chiefly Marx's—as Engels himself acknowledged. Beginning with the statement, "The history of all hitherto existing society is the history of class struggles," the *Manifesto* sets out Marx's materialist conception of history in bold terms, then draws on this analysis of history and economics to offer a program for radical change. If some of Marx's and Engels's proposals no longer seem radical—a "heavy progressive or graduated income tax," for example, or "free education for all children in public schools"—this is a sign of the changes since 1848. But even by today's standards, some of their proposals—for example, "abolition of property in land" and "equal liability of all to labour"—may seem very radical indeed.

Source: The following is an abridged version of the English edition of 1888, translated by Samuel Moore.

MANIFESTO OF THE COMMUNIST PARTY

A spectre is haunting Europe—the spectre of Communism. All the Powers of old Europe have entered into a holy alliance to exorcise this spectre: Pope and Czar, Metternich and Guizot, French Radicals and German police-spies.

Where is the party in opposition that has not been decried as Communistic by its opponents in power? Where the Opposition that has not hurled back the branding reproach of Communism, against the more advanced opposition parties, as well as against its reactionary adversaries?

Two things result from this fact.

I. Communism is already acknowledged by all European Powers to be itself a Power.

II. It is high time that Communists should openly, in the face of the whole world, publish their views, their aims, their tendencies, and meet this nursery tale of the Spectre of Communism with a Manifesto of the party itself.

To this end, Communists of various nationalities have assembled in London, and sketched the following Manifesto, to be published in the English, French, German, Italian, Flemish and Danish languages.

I BOURGEOIS AND PROLETARIANS

The history of all hitherto existing society is the history of class struggles.

Freeman and slave, patrician and plebeian, lord and serf, guild-master and journeyman, in a word, oppressor and oppressed, stood in constant opposition to one another, carried on an uninterrupted, now hidden, now open fight, a fight that each time ended, either in a revolutionary re-constitution of society at large, or in the common ruin of the contending classes.

In the earlier epochs of history, we find almost everywhere a complicated arrangement of society into various orders, a manifold gradation of social rank. In ancient Rome we have patricians, knights, plebeians, slaves; in the Middle Ages, feudal lords, vassals, guild-masters, journeymen, apprentices, serfs; in almost all of these classes, again, subordinate gradations.

The modern bourgeois society that has sprouted from the ruins of feudal society has not done away with class antagonisms. It has but established new classes, new conditions of oppression, new forms of struggle in place of the old ones.

Our epoch, the epoch of the bourgeoisie, possesses, however, this distinctive feature: it has simplified the class antagonisms: Society as a whole is more and more splitting up into two great hostile camps, into two great classes directly facing each other: Bourgeoisie and Proletariat.

From the serfs of the Middle Ages sprang the chartered burghers of the earliest towns. From these burgesses the first elements of the bourgeoisie were developed.

The discovery of America, the rounding of the Cape, opened up fresh ground for the rising bourgeoisie. The East-Indian and Chinese markets, the colonisation of America, trade with the colonies, the increase in the means of exchange and in commodities generally, gave to commerce, to navigation, to industry, an impulse never before known, and thereby, to the revolutionary element in the tottering feudal society, a rapid development.

The feudal system of industry, under which industrial production was monopolised by closed guilds, now no longer sufficed for the growing wants of the new markets. The manufacturing system took its place. The guild-masters were pushed on one side by the manufacturing middle class; division of labour between the different corporate guilds vanished in the face of division of labour in each single workshop.

Meantime the markets kept ever growing, the demand ever rising. Even manufacture no longer sufficed. Thereupon, steam and machinery revolutionised industrial production. The place of manufacture was taken by the giant, Modern Industry, the place of the industrial middle class, by industrial millionaires, the leaders of whole industrial armies, the modern bourgeois.

Modern industry has established the world-market, for which the discovery of America paved the way. This market has given an immense development to commerce, to navigation, to communication by land. This development has, in its turn, reacted on the extension of industry; and in proportion as industry, commerce, navigation, railways extended, in the same proportion the bourgeoisie developed, increased its capital, and pushed into the background every class handed down from the Middle Ages.

We see, therefore, how the modern bourgeoisie is itself the product of a long course of development, of a series of revolutions in the modes of production and of exchange.

Each step in the development of the bourgeoisie was accompanied by a corresponding political advance of that class. An oppressed class under the sway of the feudal nobility, an armed and self-governing association in the mediaeval commune here independent urban republic (as in Italy and Germany), there taxable "third estate" of the monarchy (as in France), afterwards, in the period of manufacture proper, serving either the semi-feudal or the absolute monarchy as a counterpoise against the nobility, and, in fact, corner-stone of the great monarchies in general, the bourgeoisie has at last, since the establishment of Modern Industry and of the world-market, conquered for itself, in the modern representative State, exclusive political sway. The executive of the modern State is but a committee for managing the common affairs of the whole bourgeoisie.

The bourgeoisie, historically, has played a most revolutionary part.

The bourgeoisie, wherever it has got the upper hand, has put an end to all feudal, patriarchal, idyllic relations. It has pitilessly torn asunder the motley feudal ties that bound man to his "natural superiors," and has left remaining no other nexus between man and man than naked self-interest, than callous "cash payment." It has drowned the most heavenly ecstasies of religious fervour, of chivalrous enthusiasm, of philistine sentimentalism, in the icy water of egotistical calculation. It has resolved personal worth into exchange value, and in place of the numberless indefeasible chartered freedoms, has set up that single, unconscionable freedom—Free Trade. In one word, for exploitation, veiled by religious and political illusions, it has substituted naked, shameless, direct, brutal exploitation.

The bourgeoisie has stripped of its halo every occupation hitherto honoured and looked up to with reverent awe. It has converted the physician, the lawyer, the priest, the poet, the man of science, into its paid wage-labourers.

The bourgeoisie has torn away from the family its sentimental veil, and has reduced the family relation to a mere money relation.

The bourgeoisie has disclosed how it came to pass that the brutal display of vigour in the Middle Ages, which Reactionists so much admire, found its fitting complement in the most slothful indolence. It has been the first to show what man's activity can bring about. It has accomplished wonders far surpassing Egyptian pyramids, Roman aqueducts, and Gothic cathedrals; it has conducted expeditions that put in the shade all former Exoduses of nations and crusades.

The bourgeoisie cannot exist without constantly revolutionising the instruments of production, and thereby the relations of production, and with them the whole relations of society. Conservation of the old modes of production in unaltered form was, on the contrary, the first condition of existence for all earlier industrial classes. Constant revolutionising of production, uninterrupted disturbance of all social conditions, everlasting uncertainty and agitation distinguish the bourgeois epoch from all earlier ones. All fixed, fast-frozen relations, with their train of ancient and venerable prejudices and opinions, are swept away, all new-formed ones become antiquated before they can ossify. All that is solid melts into air, all that is holy is profaned, and man is at last compelled to face with sober senses, his real conditions of life, and his relations with his kind.

The need of a constantly expanding market

for its products chases the bourgeoisie over the whole surface of the globe. It must nestle everywhere, settle everywhere, establish connexions everywhere.

The bourgeoisie has through its exploitation of the world-market given a cosmopolitan character to production and consumption in every country. To the great chagrin of Reactionists, it has drawn from under the feet of industry the national ground on which it stood. All old-established national industries have been destroyed or are daily being destroyed. They are dislodged by new industries, whose introduction becomes a life and death question for all civilised nations, by industries that no longer work up indigenous raw material, but raw material drawn from the remotest zones; industries whose products are consumed, not only at home, but in every quarter of the globe. In place of the old wants, satisfied by the productions of the country, we find new wants, requiring for their satisfaction the products of distant lands and climes. In place of the old local and national seclusion and self-sufficiency, we have intercourse in every direction, universal inter-dependence of nations. And as in material, so also in intellectual production. The intellectual creations of individual nations become common property. National one-sidedness and narrow-mindedness become more and more impossible, and from the numerous national and local literatures, there arises a world literature.

The bourgeoisie, by the rapid improvement of all instruments of production, by the immensely facilitated means of communication, draws all, even the most barbarian, nations into civilisation. The cheap prices of its commodities are the heavy artillery with which it batters down all Chinese walls, with which it forces the barbarians' intensely obstinate hatred of foreigners to capitulate. It compels all nations, on pain of extinction, to adopt the bourgeois mode of production; it compels them to introduce what it calls civilisation into their midst, *i.e.*, to become bourgeois themselves. In one word, it creates a world after its own image.

The bourgeoisie has subjected the country to the rule of the towns. It has created enormous cities, has greatly increased the urban population as compared with the rural, and has thus rescued a considerable part of the population from the idiocy of rural life. Just as it has made the country dependent on the towns, so it has made barbarian and semi-barbarian countries dependent on the civilised ones, nations and peasants on nations of bourgeois, the East on the West.

The bourgeoisie keeps more and more doing away with the scattered state of the population, of the means of production, and of property. It has agglomerated population, centralised means of production, and has concentrated property in a few hands. The necessary consequence of this was political centralisation. Independent, or but loosely connected provinces, with separate interests, laws, governments and systems of taxation, became lumped together into one nation, with one government, one code of laws, one national class-interest, one frontier and one customs-tariff.

The bourgeoisie, during its rule of scarce one hundred years, has created more massive and more colossal productive forces than have all preceding generations together. Subjection of Nature's forces to man, machinery, application of chemistry to industry and agriculture, steam-navigation, railways, electric telegraphs, clearing of whole continents for cultivation, canalisation of rivers, whole populations conjured out of the ground—what earlier century had even a presentiment that such productive forces slumbered in the lap of social labour?

We see then: the means of production and of exchange, on whose foundation the bourgeoisie built itself up, were generated in feudal society. At a certain stage in the development of these means of production and of exchange, the conditions under which feudal society produced and exchanged, the feudal organisation of agriculture and manufacturing industry, in one word, the feudal relations of property became no longer compatible with the already developed productive forces; they became so many fetters. They had to be burst asunder; they were burst asunder.

Into their place stepped free competition, accompanied by a social and political constitution adapted to it, and by the economical and political sway of the bourgeois class.

A similar movement is going on before our own eyes. Modern bourgeois society with its relations of production, of exchange and of property, a society that has conjured up such gigantic means of production and of exchange, is like the sorcerer, who is no longer able to control the powers of the nether world whom he has called up by his spells. For many a decade past the history of industry and commerce is but the history of the revolt of modern productive forces against modern conditions of production, against the property relations that are the conditions for the existence of the bourgeoisie and of its rule. It is enough to mention the commercial crises that by their periodical return put on its trial, each time more threateningly, the existence of the entire bourgeois society. In these crises a great part not only of the existing products, but also of the previously created productive forces, are periodically destroyed. In these crises there breaks out an epidemic that, in all earlier epochs, would have seemed an absurdity—the epidemic of over-production. Society suddenly finds itself put back into a state of momentary barbarism; it appears as if a famine, a universal war of devastation had cut off the supply of every means of subsistence; industry and commerce seem to be destroyed; and why? Because there is too much civilisation, too much means of subsistence, too much industry, too much commerce. The productive forces at the disposal of society no longer tend to further the development of the conditions of bourgeois property; on the contrary, they have become too powerful for these conditions, by which they are fettered, and so soon as they overcome these fetters, they bring disorder into the whole of bourgeois society, endanger the existence of bourgeois property. The conditions of bourgeois society are too narrow to comprise the wealth created by them. And how does the bourgeoisie get over these crises? On the one hand by enforced destruction of a mass of productive forces; on the other, by the conquest of new markets, and by the more thorough exploitation of the old ones. That is to say, by paving the way for more extensive and more destructive crises, and by diminishing the means whereby crises are prevented.

The weapons with which the bourgeoisie felled feudalism to the ground are now turned against the bourgeoisie itself.

But not only has the bourgeoisie forged the weapons that bring death to itself; it has also called into existence the men who are to wield those weapons—the modern working class—the proletarians.

In proportion as the bourgeoisie, *i.e.*, capital, is developed, in the same proportion is the proletariat, the modern working class, developed—a class of labourers, who live only so long as they find work, and who find work only so long as their labour increases capital. These labourers, who must sell themselves piece-meal, are a commodity, like every other article of commerce, and are consequently exposed to all the vicissitudes of competition, to all the fluctuations of the market.

Owing to the extensive use of machinery and to division of labour, the work of the proletarians has lost all individual character, and consequently, all charm for the workman. He becomes an appendage of the machine, and it is only the most simple, most monotonous, and most easily acquired knack, that is required of him. Hence, the cost of production of a workman is restricted, almost entirely, to the means of subsistence that he requires for his maintenance, and for the propagation of his race. But the price of a commodity, and therefore also of labour, is equal to its cost of production. In proportion, therefore, as the repulsiveness of the work increases, the wage decreases. Nay more, in proportion as the use of machinery and division of labour increases, in the same proportion the burden of toil also increases, whether by prolongation of the working hours, by increase of the work exacted in a given time or by increased speed of the machinery, etc.

Modern industry has converted the little

workshop of the patriarchal master into the great factory of the industrial capitalist. Masses of labourers, crowded into the factory, are organized like soldiers. As privates of the industrial army they are placed under the command of a perfect hierarchy of officers and sergeants. Not only are they slaves of the bourgeois class, and of the bourgeois State; they are daily and hourly enslaved by the machine, by the over-looker, and, above all, by the individual bourgeois manufacturer himself. The more openly this despotism proclaims gain to be its end and aim, the more petty, the more hateful and the more embittering it is.

The less the skill and exertion of strength implied in manual labour, in other words, the more modern industry becomes developed, the more is the labour of men superseded by that of women. Differences of age and sex have no longer any distinctive social validity for the working class. All are instruments of labour, more or less expensive to use, according to their age and sex.

No sooner is the exploitation of the labourer by the manufacturer, so far, at an end, that he receives his wages in cash, than he is set upon by the other portions of the bourgeoisie, the landlord, the shopkeeper, the pawnbroker, etc.

The lower strata of the middle class—the small tradespeople, shopkeepers, and retired tradesmen generally, the handicraftsmen and peasants—all these sink gradually into the proletariat, partly because their diminutive capital does not suffice for the scale on which Modern Industry is carried on, and is swamped in the competition with the large capitalists, partly because their specialised skill is rendered worthless by new methods of production. Thus the proletariat is recruited from all classes of the population.

The proletariat goes through various stages of development. With its birth begins its struggle with the bourgeoisie. At first the contest is carried on by individual labourers, then by the workpeople of a factory, then by the operatives of one trade, in one locality, against the individual bourgeois who directly exploits them. They direct their attacks not against the bourgeois conditions of production, but against the instruments of production themselves; they destroy imported wares that compete with their labour, they smash to pieces machinery, they set factories ablaze, they seek to restore by force the vanished status of the workman of the Middle Ages.

At this stage the labourers still form an incoherent mass scattered over the whole country, and broken up by their mutual competition. If anywhere they unite to form more compact bodies, this is not yet the consequence of their own active union, but of the union of the bourgeoisie, which class, in order to attain its own political ends, is compelled to set the whole proletariat in motion, and is moreover yet, for a time, able to do so. At this stage, therefore, the proletarians do not fight their enemies, but the enemies of their enemies, the remnants of absolute monarchy, the landowners, the non-industrial bourgeois, the petty bourgeoisie. Thus the whole historical movement is concentrated in the hands of the bourgeoisie; every victory so obtained is a victory for the bourgeoisie.

But with the development of industry the proletariat not only increases in number; it becomes concentrated in greater masses, its strength grows, and it feels that strength more. The various interests and conditions of life within the ranks of the proletariat are more and more equalised, in proportion as machinery obliterates all distinctions of labour, and nearly everywhere reduces wages to the same low level. The growing competition among the bourgeois, and the resulting commercial crises, make the wages of the workers ever more fluctuating. The unceasing improvement of machinery, ever more rapidly developing, makes their livelihood more and more precarious; the collisions between individual workmen and individual bourgeois take more and more the character of collisions between two classes. Thereupon the workers begin to form combinations (Trade Unions) against the bourgeois; they club together in order to keep up the rate of wages; they found permanent associations in order to make provision beforehand for these occasional revolts. Here and there the contest breaks out into riots.

Now and then the workers are victorious, but only for a time. The real fruit of their battles lies, not in the immediate result, but in the ever-expanding union of the workers. This union is helped on by the improved means of communication that are created by modern industry and that place the workers of different localities in contact with one another. It was just this contact that was needed to centralise the numerous local struggles, all of the same character, into one national struggle between classes. But every class struggle is a political struggle. And that union, to attain which the burghers of the Middle Ages, with their miserable highways, required centuries, the modern proletarians, thanks to railways, achieve in a few years.

This organisation of the proletarians into a class, and consequently into a political party, is continually being upset again by the competition between the workers themselves. But it ever rises up again, stronger, firmer, mightier. It compels legislative recognition of particular interests of the workers, by taking advantage of the divisions among the bourgeoisie itself. Thus the ten-hours' bill in England was carried.

Altogether collisions between the classes of the old society further, in many ways, the course of development of the proletariat. The bourgeoisie finds itself involved in a constant battle. At first with the aristocracy; later on, with those portions of the bourgeoisie itself, whose interests have become antagonistic to the progress of industry; at all times, with the bourgeoisie of foreign countries. In all these battles it sees itself compelled to appeal to the proletariat, to ask for its help, and thus, to drag it into the political arena. The bourgeoisie itself, therefore, supplies the proletariat with its own elements of political and general education, in other words, it furnishes the proletariat with weapons for fighting the bourgeoisie.

Further, as we have already seen, entire sections of the ruling classes are, by the advance of industry, precipitated into the proletariat, or are at least threatened in their conditions of existence. These also supply the proletariat with fresh elements of enlightenment and progress.

Finally, in times when the class struggle nears the decisive hour, the process of dissolution going on within the ruling class, in fact within the whole range of society, assumes such a violent, glaring character, that a small section of the ruling class cuts itself adrift, and joins the revolutionary class, the class that holds the future in its hands. Just as, therefore, at an earlier period, a section of the nobility went over to the bourgeoisie, so now a portion of the bourgeoisie goes over to the proletariat, and in particular, a portion of the bourgeois ideologists, who have raised themselves to the level of comprehending theoretically the historical movement as a whole.

Of all the classes that stand face to face with the bourgeoisie today, the proletariat alone is a really revolutionary class. The other classes decay and finally disappear in the face of Modern Industry; the proletariat is its special and essential product.

The lower middle class, the small manufacturer, the shopkeeper, the artisan, the peasant, all these fight against the bourgeoisie, to save from extinction their existence as fractions of the middle class. They are therefore not revolutionary, but conservative. Nay more, they are reactionary, for they try to roll back the wheel of history. If by chance they are revolutionary, they are so only in view of their impending transfer into the proletariat, they thus defend not their present, but their future interests, they desert their own standpoint to place themselves at that of the proletariat.

The "dangerous class," the social scum, that passively rotting mass thrown off by the lowest layers of old society, may, here and there, be swept into the movement by a proletarian revolution; its conditions of life, however, prepare it far more for the part of a bribed tool of reactionary intrigue.

In the conditions of the proletariat, those of old society at large are already virtually swamped. The proletarian is without property; his relation to his wife and children has no longer anything in common with the bourgeois family-relations; modern industrial labour, modern subjection to capital, the same in England as in France, in America as in Germany, has stripped him of every trace of national character. Law, morality, religion, are to him so many bourgeois prejudices, behind which lurk in ambush just as many bourgeois interests.

All the preceding classes that got the upper hand, sought to fortify their already acquired status by subjecting society at large to their conditions of appropriation. The proletarians cannot become masters of the productive forces of society, except by abolishing their own previous mode of appropriation, and thereby also every other previous mode of appropriation. They have nothing of their own to secure and to fortify; their mission is to destroy all previous securities for, and insurances of, individual property.

All previous historical movements were movements of minorities, or in the interests of minorities. The proletarian movement is the self-conscious, independent movement of the immense majority, in the interests of the immense majority. The proletariat, the lowest stratum of our present society, cannot stir, cannot raise itself up, without the whole superincumbent strata of official society being sprung into the air.

Though not in substance, yet in form, the struggle of the proletariat with the bourgeoisie is at first a national struggle. The proletariat of each country must, of course, first of all settle matters with its own bourgeoisie.

In depicting the most general phases of the development of the proletariat, we traced the more or less veiled civil war, raging within existing society, up to the point where that war breaks out into open revolution, and where the violent overthrow of the bourgeoisie lays the foundation for the sway of the proletariat.

Hitherto, every form of society has been based, as we have already seen, on the antagonism of oppressing and oppressed classes. But in order to oppress a class, certain conditions must be assured to it under which it can, at least, continue its slavish existence. The serf, in the period of serfdom, raised himself to membership in the commune, just as the petty bourgeois, under the yoke of feudal absolutism, managed to develop into a bourgeois. The modern labourer, on the contrary, instead of rising with the progress of industry, sinks deeper and deeper below the conditions of existence of his own class. He becomes a pauper, and pauperism develops more rapidly than population and wealth. And here it becomes evident, that the bourgeoisie is unfit any longer to be the ruling class in society, and to impose its conditions of existence upon society as an over-riding law. It is unfit to rule because it is incompetent to assure an existence to its slave within his slavery, because it cannot help letting him sink into such a state, that it has to feed him, instead of being fed by him. Society can no longer live under this bourgeoisie, in other words, its existence is no longer compatible with society.

The essential condition for the existence, and for the sway of the bourgeois class, is the formation and augmentation of capital; the condition for capital is wage-labour. Wage-labour rests exclusively on competition between the labourers. The advance of industry, whose involuntary promoter is the bourgeoisie, replaces the isolation of the labourers, due to competition, by their revolutionary combination, due to association. The development of Modern Industry, therefore, cuts from under its feet the very foundation on which the bourgeoisie produces and appropriates products. What the bourgeoisie, therefore, produces, above all, is its own grave-diggers. Its fall and the victory of the proletariat are equally inevitable.

II PROLETARIANS AND COMMUNISTS

In what relation do the Communists stand to the proletarians as a whole?

The Communists do not form a separate party opposed to other working-class parties.

They have no interests separate and apart from those of the proletariat as a whole.

They do not set up any sectarian principles of their own, by which to shape and mould the proletarian movement.

The Communists are distinguished from the other working-class parties by this only: (1) In the national struggles of the proletarians of the different countries, they point out and bring to the front the common interests of the entire proletariat, independently of all nationality. (2) In the various stages of development which the struggle of the working class against the bourgoisie has to pass through, they always and everywhere represent the interests of the movement as a whole.

The Communists, therefore, are on the one hand, practically, the most advanced and resolute section of the working-class parties of every country, that section which pushes forward all others; on the other hand, theoretically, they have over the great mass of the proletariat the advantage of clearly understanding the line of march, the conditions, and the ultimate general results of the proletarian movement.

The immediate aim of the Communists is the same as that of all the other proletarian parties: formation of the proletariat into a class, overthrow of the bourgeois supremacy, conquest of political power by the proletariat.

The theoretical conclusions of the Communists are in no way based on ideas or principles that have been invented, or discovered, by this or that would-be universal reformer.

They merely express, in general terms, actual relations springing from an existing class struggle, from a historical movement going on under our very eyes. The abolition of existing property relations is not at all a distinctive feature of Communism.

All property relations in the past have continually been subject to historical change consequent upon the change in historical conditions.

The French Revolution, for example, abolished feudal property in favour of bourgeois property.

The distinguishing feature of Communism is not the abolition of property generally, but the abolition of bourgeois property. But modern bourgeois private property is the final and most complete expression of the system of producing and appropriating products, that is based on class antagonisms, on the exploitation of the many by the few.

In this sense, the theory of the Communists may be summed up in the single sentence: Abolition of private property.

We Communists have been reproached with the desire of abolishing the right of personally acquiring property as the fruit of a man's own labour, which property is alleged to be the groundwork of all personal freedom, activity and independence.

Hard-won, self-acquired, self-earned property! Do you mean the property of the petty artisan and of the small peasant, a form of property that preceded the bourgeois form? There is no need to abolish that; the development of industry has to a great extent already destroyed it, and is still destroying it daily.

Or do you mean modern bourgeois private property?

But does wage-labour create any property for the labourer? Not a bit. It creates capital, *i.e.*, that kind of property which exploits wage-labour, and which cannot increase except upon condition of begetting a new supply of wage-labour for fresh exploitation. Property, in its present form, is based on the antagonism of capital and wage-labour. Let us examine both sides of this antagonism.

To be a capitalist, is to have not only a purely personal, but a social *status* in production. Capital is a collective product, and only by the united action of many members, nay, in the last resort, only by the united action of all members of society, can it be set in motion.

Capital is, therefore, not a personal, it is a social power.

When, therefore, capital is converted into common property, into the property of all members of society, personal property is not thereby transformed into social property. It is only the social character of the property that is changed. It loses its class-character. Let us now take wage-labour.

The average price of wage-labour is the minimum wage, *i.e.*, that quantum of the means of subsistence, which is absolutely requisite to keep the labourer in bare existence as a labourer. What, therefore, the wage-labourer appropriates by means of his labour, merely suffices to prolong and reproduce a bare existence. We by no means intend to abolish this personal appropriation of the products of labour, an appropriation that is made for the maintenance and reproduction of human life, and that leaves no surplus wherewith to command the labour of others. All that we want to do away with, is the miserable character of this appropriation, under which the labourer lives merely to increase capital, and is allowed to live only in so far as the interest of the ruling class requires it.

In bourgeois society, living labour is but a means to increase accumulated labour. In Communist society, accumulated labour is but a means to widen, to enrich, to promote the existence of the labourer. In bourgeois society, therefore, the past dominates the present; in Communist society, the present dominates the past. In bourgeois society capital is independent and has individuality, while the living person is dependent and has no individuality.

And the abolition of this state of things is called by the bourgeois, abolition of individuality and freedom! And rightly so. The abolition of bourgeois individuality, bourgeois independence, and bourgeois freedom is undoubtedly aimed at.

By freedom is meant, under the present bourgeois conditions of production, free trade, free selling and buying.

But if selling and buying disappears, free selling and buying disappears also. This talk about free selling and buying, and all the other "brave words" of our bourgeoisie about freedom in general, have a meaning, if any, only in contrast with restricted selling and buying, with the fettered traders of the Middle Ages, but have no meaning when opposed to the Communistic abolition of buying and selling, of the bourgeois conditions of production, and of the bourgeoisie itself.

You are horrified at our intending to do away with private property. But in your existing society, private property is already done away with for nine-tenths of the population; its existence for the few is solely due to its non-existence in the hands of those nine-tenths. You reproach us, therefore, with intending to do away with a form of property, the necessary condition for whose existence is the non-existence of any property for the immense majority of society.

In one word, you reproach us with intending to do away with your property. Precisely so; that is just what we intend.

From the moment when labour can no longer be converted into capital, money, or rent, into a social power capable of being monopolised, *i.e.*, from the moment when individual property can no longer be transformed into bourgeois property, into capital, from that moment, you say, individuality vanishes.

You must, therefore, confess that by "individual" you mean no other person than the bourgeois, than the middle-class owner of property. This person must, indeed, be swept out of the way, and made impossible.

Communism deprives no man of the power to appropriate the products of society; all that it does is to deprive him of the power to subjugate the labour of others by means of such appropriation.

It has been objected that upon the abolition of private property all work will cease, and universal laziness will overtake us.

According to this, bourgeois society ought long ago to have gone to the dogs through sheer idleness; for those of its members who work, acquire nothing, and those who acquire anything, do not work. The whole of this objection is but another expression of the tautology: that there can no longer be any wage-labour when there is no longer any capital.

All objections urged against the Communistic mode of producing and appropriating material products, have, in the same way, been urged against the Communistic modes of producing and appropriating intellectual products. Just as, to the bourgeois, the disappearance of class property is the disappearance of production itself, so the disappearance of class culture is to him identical with the disappearance of all culture.

That culture, the loss of which he laments, is, for the enormous majority, a mere training to act as a machine.

But don't wrangle with us so long as you apply, to our intended abolition of bourgeois property, the standard of our bourgeois notions of freedom, culture, law, &c. Your very ideas are but the outgrowth of the conditions of your bourgeois production and bourgeois property, just as your jurisprudence is but the will of your class made into a law for all, a will, whose essential character and direction are determined by the economical conditions of existence of your class.

The selfish misconception that induces you to transform into eternal laws of nature and of reason, the social forms springing from your present mode of production and form of property—historical relations that rise and disappear in the progress of production—this misconception you share with every ruling class that has preceded you. What you see clearly in the case of ancient property, what you admit in the case of feudal property, you are of course forbidden to admit in the case of your own bourgeois form of property.

Abolition of the family! Even the most radical flare up at this infamous proposal of the Communists.

On what foundation is the present family, the bourgeois family, based? On capital, on private gain. In its completely developed form this family exists only among the bourgeoisie. But this state of things finds its complement in the practical absence of the family among the proletarians, and in public prostitution.

The bourgeois family will vanish as a matter of course when its complement vanishes, and both will vanish with the vanishing of capital.

Do you charge us with wanting to stop the exploitation of children by their parents? To this crime we plead guilty.

But, you will say, we destroy the most hallowed of relations, when we replace home education by social.

And your education! Is not that also social, and determined by the social conditions under which you educate, by the intervention, direct or indirect, of society, by means of schools, &c.? The Communists have not invented the intervention of society in education; they do but seek to alter the character of that intervention, and to rescue education from the influence of the ruling class.

The bourgeois clap-trap about the family and education, about the hallowed co-relation of parent and child, becomes all the more disgusting, the more, by the action of Modern Industry, all family ties among the proletarians are torn asunder, and their children transformed into simple articles of commerce and instruments of labour.

But you Communists would introduce community of women, screams the whole bourgeoisie in chorus.

The bourgeois sees in his wife a mere instrument of production. He hears that the instruments of production are to be exploited in common, and, naturally, can come to no other conclusion than that the lot of being common to all will likewise fall to the women.

He has not even a suspicion that the real point aimed at is to do away with the status of women as mere instruments of production.

For the rest, nothing is more ridiculous than the virtuous indignation of our bourgeois at the community of women which, they pretend, is to be openly and officially established by the Communists. The Communists have no need to introduce community of women; it has existed almost from time immemorial.

Our bourgeois, not content with having the wives and daughters of their proletarians at their disposal, not to speak of common prostitutes, take the greatest pleasure in seducing each other's wives.

Bourgeois marriage is in reality a system of wives in common and thus, at the most, what the Communists might possibly be reproached with, is that they desire to introduce, in substitution for a hypocritically concealed, an openly legalised community of women. For the rest, it is self-evident that the abolition of the present system of production must bring with it the abolition of the community of women springing from that system, *i.e.*, of prostitution both public and private.

The Communists are further reproached with desiring to abolish countries and nationality.

The working men have no country. We cannot take from them what they have not got. Since the proletariat must first of all acquire political supremacy, must rise to be the leading class of the nation, must constitute itself *the* nation, it is, so far, itself national, though not in the bourgeois sense of the word.

National differences and antagonisms between peoples are daily more and more vanishing, owing to the development of the bourgeoisie, to freedom of commerce, to the world-market, to uniformity in the mode of production and in the conditions of life corresponding thereto.

The supremacy of the proletariat will cause them to vanish still faster. United action, of the leading civilised countries at least, is one of the first conditions for the emancipation of the proletariat.

In proportion as the exploitation of one individual by another is put an end to, the exploitation of one nation by another will also be put an end to. In proportion as the antagonism between classes within the nation vanishes, the hostility of one nation to another will come to an end.

The charges against Communism made from a religious, a philosophical, and, generally, from an ideological standpoint, are not deserving of serious examination.

Does it require deep intuition to comprehend that man's ideas, views and conceptions, in one word, man's consciousness, changes with every change in the conditions of his material existence, in his social relations and in his social life?

What else does the history of ideas prove, than that intellectual production changes its character in proportion as material production is changed? The ruling ideas of each age have ever been the ideas of its ruling class.

When people speak of ideas that revolutionise society, they do but express the fact, that within the old society, the elements of a new one have been created, and that the dissolution of the old ideas keeps even pace with the dissolution of the old conditions of existence.

When the ancient world was in its last throes, the ancient religions were overcome by Christianity. When Christian ideas succumbed in the 18th century to rationalist ideas, feudal society fought its death battle with the then revolutionary bourgeoisie. The ideas of religious liberty and freedom of conscience merely gave expression to the sway of free competition within the domain of knowledge.

"Undoubtedly," it will be said, "religious, moral, philosophical and juridical ideas have been modified in the course of historical development. But religion, morality, philosophy, political science, and law, constantly survived this change."

"There are, besides, eternal truths, such as Freedom, Justice, etc., that are common to all states of society. But Communism abolishes eternal truths, it abolishes all religion, and all morality, instead of constituting them on a new basis; it therefore acts in contradiction to all past historical experience."

What does this accusation reduce itself to? The history of all past society has consisted in the development of class antagonisms, antagonisms that assumed different forms at different epochs.

But whatever form they may have taken, one fact is common to all past ages, *viz.*, the exploitation of one part of society by the other. No wonder, then, that the social consciousness of past ages, despite all the multiplicity and variety it displays, moves within certain common forms, or general ideas, which cannot completely vanish except with the total disappearance of class antagonisms.

The Communist revolution is the most radical rupture with traditional property relations; no wonder that its development involves the most radical rupture with traditional ideas.

But let us have done with the bourgeois objections to Communism.

We have seen above, that the first step in the revolution by the working class, is to raise the proletariat to the position of ruling class, to win the battle of democracy.

The proletariat will use its political suprem acy to wrest, by degrees, all capital from the bourgeoisie, to centralise all instruments of production in the hands of the State, *i.e.*, of the proletariat organised as the ruling class; and to increase the total of productive forces as rapidly as possible.

Of course, in the beginning, this cannot be effected except by means of despotic inroads on the rights of property, and on the conditions of bourgeois production; by means of measures, therefore, which appear economically insufficient and untenable, but which, in the course of the movement, outstrip themselves, necessitate further inroads upon the old social order, and are unavoidable as a means of entirely revolutionising the mode of production.

These measures will of course be different in different countries.

Nevertheless in the most advanced countries, the following will be pretty generally applicable.

1. Abolition of property in land and application of all rents of land to public purposes.
2. A heavy progressive or graduated income tax.
3. Abolition of all right of inheritance.
4. Confiscation of the property of all emigrants and rebels.
5. Centralisation of credit in the hands of the State, by means of a national bank with State capital and an exclusive monopoly.
6. Centralisation of the means of communication and transport in the hands of the State.
7. Extension of factories and instruments of production owned by the State; the bringing into cultivation of waste-lands, and the improvement of the soil generally in accordance with a common plan.
8. Equal liability of all to labour. Establishment of industrial armies, especially for agriculture.
9. Combination of agriculture with manufacturing industries; gradual abolition of the distinction between town and country, by a more equable distribution of the population over the country.
10. Free education for all children in public schools. Abolition of children's factory labour in its present form. Combination of education with industrial production, &c., &c.

When, in the course of development, class distinctions have disappeared, and all production has been concentrated in the hands of a vast association of the whole nation, the public power will lose its political character. Political power, properly so called, is merely the organised power of one class for oppressing another. If the proletariat during its contest with the bourgeoisie is compelled, by the force of circumstances, to organise itself as a class, if, by means of a revolution, it makes itself the ruling class, and, as such, sweeps away by force the old conditions of production, then it will, along with these conditions, have swept away the conditions for the existence of class antagonisms and of classes generally, and will thereby have abolished its own supremacy as a class.

In place of the old bourgeois society, with its classes and class antagonisms, we shall have an association, in which the free development of each is the condition for the free development of all. . . .

In short, the Communists everywhere support every revolutionary movement against the existing social and political order of things.

In all these movements they bring to the front, as the leading question in each, the property question, no matter what its degree of development at the time.

Finally, they labour everywhere for the union and agreement of the democratic parties of all countries.

The Communists disdain to conceal their views and aims. They openly declare that their ends can be attained only by the forcible overthrow of all existing social conditions. Let the ruling classes tremble at a Communistic revolution. The proletarians have nothing to lose but their chains. They have a world to win.

WORKING MEN OF ALL COUNTRIES, UNITE!

32

SOCIALISM: UTOPIAN AND SCIENTIFIC

FRIEDRICH ENGELS

Neither of those great enemies of capitalism, Karl Marx or his collaborator, Friedrich Engels (1820–1895), was part of the proletariat, or working class. Indeed, Engels was the son of a prosperous capitalist, and he spent some twenty years in Manchester, England, helping to manage a textile firm in which his family owned an interest. If anything, however, Engels's years as a capitalist increased his sympathy for socialism—but not just any sort of socialism. Marx and Engels took pains to distinguish their brand of socialism from others, especially the "utopian" socialism of thinkers like Saint-Simon, Robert Owen, and Charles Fourier. While others spent their time sketching pretty pictures of how society ought to be, Marx and Engels declared, only they understood that socialism requires a scientific understanding of history and society. The basis of this "scientific socialism" is the materialist conception of history, which Engels undertook to explain in *Socialism: Utopian and Scientific* (first published in 1878 as part of Engels's *Herr Eugen Dühring's Revolution in Science*). Although Engels seemed confident that his views and Marx's were substantially the same, some scholars today argue that Engels's writings not only simplified, but distorted, Marx's ideas.

Source: Friedrich Engels, Socialism, Utopian and Scientific, *translated by Edward Aveling (London: Swan Sonnenschein and Co., 1892).*

III

The materialist conception of history starts from the proposition that the production of the means to support human life and, next to production, the exchange of things produced, is the basis of all social structure; that in every society that has appeared in history, the manner in which wealth is distributed and society divided into classes or orders is dependent upon what is produced, how it is produced, and how the products are exchanged. From this point of view the final causes of all social changes and political revolutions are to be sought, not in men's brains, not in men's better insight into eternal truth and justice, but in changes in the modes of production and exchange. They are to be sought not in the *philosophy*, but in the *economics* of each particular epoch. The growing perception that existing social institutions are unreasonable and unjust, that reason has become unreason and right wrong, is only proof that in the modes of production and exchange changes have silently taken place with which the social order, adapted to earlier economic conditions, is no longer in keeping. From this it also follows that the means of getting rid of the incongruities that have been brought to light must also be present, in a more or less developed condition, within the changed modes of production themselves. These means are not to be invented by deduction from fundamental principles, but are to be discovered in the stubborn facts of the existing system of production.

What is, then, the position of modern socialism in this connection?

The present structure of society—this is now pretty generally conceded—is the creation of the ruling class of today, of the bourgeoisie. The mode of production peculiar to the bourgeoisie, known, since Marx, as the capitalist mode of production, was incompatible with the feudal system, with the privileges it conferred upon individuals, entire social ranks and local corporations, as well as with the hereditary ties of subordination which constituted the framework of its social organisation. The bourgeoisie broke up the feudal system and built upon its ruins the capitalist order of society, the kingdom of free competition, of personal liberty, of the equality, before the law, of all commodity owners, of all the rest of the capitalist blessings. Thenceforward the capitalist mode of production could develop in freedom. Since steam, machinery, and the making of machines by machinery transformed the older manufacture into modern industry, the productive forces evolved under the guidance of the bourgeoisie developed with a rapidity and in a degree unheard of before. But just as the older manufacture, in its time, and handicraft, becoming more developed under its influence, had come into collision with the feudal [limits] of the guilds, so now modern industry, in its more complete development, comes into collision with the bounds within which the capitalistic mode of production holds it confined. The new productive forces have already outgrown the capitalistic mode of using them. And this conflict between productive forces and modes of production is not a conflict engendered in the mind of man, like that between original sin and divine justice. It exists, in fact, objectively, outside us, independently of the will and actions even of the men that have brought it on. Modern socialism is nothing but the reflex, in thought, of this conflict in fact; its ideal reflection in the minds, first, of the class directly suffering under it, the working class.

Now, in what does this conflict consist?

Before capitalistic production, i.e., in the Middle Ages, the system of petty industry obtained generally, based upon the private property of the labourers in their means of production; in the country, the agriculture of the small peasant, freeman or serf; in the towns, the handicrafts organised in guilds. The instruments of labour—land, agricultural implements, the workshop, the tool—were the instruments of labour of single individuals, adapted for the use of one worker, and, therefore, of necessity, small, dwarfish, circumscribed. But, for this very reason they belonged, as a rule, to the producer himself. To concentrate these scattered, limited means of production, to enlarge them, to turn them into the powerful levers of production of the present day—this was precisely the historic role of capitalist production and of its upholder, the bourgeoisie. In the fourth section of *Capital* Marx has explained in detail how since the fifteenth century this has been historically worked out through the three phases of simple co-operation, manufacture and modern industry. But the bourgeoisie, as is also shown there, could not transform these puny means of production into mighty productive forces without transforming them, at the same time, from means of production of the individual into *social* means of production only workable by a collectivity of men. The spinning-wheel, the hand-loom, the blacksmith's hammer, were replaced by the spinning-machine, the power-loom, the steam-hammer; the individual workshop, by the factory implying the co-operation of hundreds and thousands of workmen. In like manner, production itself changed from a series of individual into a series of social acts, and the products from individual to social products. The yarn, the cloth, the metal articles that now came out of the factory, were the joint product of many workers, through whose hands they had successively to pass before they were ready. No one person could say of them; "I made that; this is *my* product."

But where, in a given society, the fundamental form of production is that spontaneous division of labour which creeps in gradually and not upon any preconceived plan, there the products take on the form of *commodities*, whose mutual exchange, buying and selling, enable the individual producers to satisfy their manifold wants. And this was the case in the Middle Ages. The peasant, *e.g.*, sold to the artisan agricultural products and bought from him the products of handicraft. Into this society of individual producers, of commodity producers, the new mode of production thrust itself. In the midst of the old division of labour, grown up spontaneously and upon *no definite plan*, which had governed the whole of society, now arose division of labour upon a *definite* plan, as organised in the factory; side by side with *individual* production appeared *social* production. The products of both were sold in the same market, and, therefore, at prices at least approximately equal. But organisation upon a definite plan was stronger than spontaneous division of labour. The factories working with the combined social forces of a collectivity of individuals produced their commodities far more cheaply than the individual small producers. Individual production succumbed in one department after another. Socialised production revolutionised all the old methods of production. But its revolutionary character was, at the same time, so little recognised that it was, on the contrary, introduced as a means of increasing and developing the production of commodities. When it arose, it found ready-made, and made liberal use of, certain machinery for the production and exchange of commodities: merchants' capital, handicraft, wage-labour. Socialised production thus introducing itself as a new form of the production of commodities, it was a matter of course that under it the old forms of appropriation remained in full swing, and were applied to its products as well.

In the mediaeval stage of evolution of the production of commodities, the question as to the owner of the product of labour could not arise. The individual producer, as a rule, had, from raw material belonging to himself, and generally his own handiwork, produced it with his own tools, by the labour of his own hands or of his family. There was no need for him to appropriate the new product. It belonged wholly to him, as a matter of course. His property in the product was, therefore, based *upon his own labour*. Even where external help was used, this was, as a rule, of little importance, and very generally was compensated by something other than wages. The apprentices and journeymen of the guilds worked less for board and wages than for education, in order that they might become master craftsmen themselves.

Then came the concentration of the means of production and of the producers in large workshops and manufactories, their transformation into actual socialised means of production and socialised producers. But the socialised producers and means of production and their products were still treated, after this change, just as they had been before, i.e., as the means of production and the products of individuals. Hitherto, the owner of the instruments of labour had himself appropriated the product, because, as a rule, it was his own product and the assistance of others was the exception. Now the owner of the instruments of labour always appropriated to himself the product, although it was no longer *his* product but exclusively the product of the *labour of others.* Thus, the products now produced socially were not appropriated by those who had actually set in motion the means of production and actually produced the commodities, but by the *capitalists.* The means of production, and production itself, had become in essence socialised. But they were subjected to a form of appropriation which presupposes the private production of individuals, under which, therefore, everyone owns his own product and brings it to market. The mode of production is subjected to this form of appropriation, although it abolishes the conditions upon which the latter rests.[1]

This contradiction, which gives to the new mode of production its capitalistic character, *contains the germ of the whole of the social antagonisms of today.* The greater the mastery obtained by the new mode of production over all important fields of production and in all manufacturing countries, the more it reduced individual production to an insignificant residuum, *the more clearly was brought out the incompatibility of socialised production with capitalistic appropriation.*

The first capitalists found, as we have said, alongside of other forms of labour, wage-labour ready-made for them on the market. But it was exceptional, complementary, accessory, transitory wage labour. The agricultural labourer, though, upon occasion, he hired himself out by the day, had a few acres of his own land on which he could at all events live at a pinch. The guilds were so organized that the journeyman of today became the master of tomorrow. But all this changed as soon as the means of production became socialised and concentrated in the hands of capitalists. The means of production, as well as the product, of the individual producer became more and more worthless; there was nothing left for him but to turn wage-worker under the capitalist. Wage-labour, aforetime the exception and accessory, now became the rule and basis of all production; aforetime complementary, it now became the sole remaining function of the workers. The wage-worker for a time became a wage-worker for life. The number of these permanent wage-workers was further enormously increased by the breaking-up of the feudal system that occurred at the same time, by the disbanding of the retainers of the feudal lords, the eviction of the peasants from their homesteads, etc. The separation was made complete between the means of production concentrated in the hands of the capitalists, on the one side, and the producers, possessing nothing but their labour-power, on the other. *The contradiction between socialised production and capitalistic appropriation manifested itself as the antagonism of proletariat and bourgeoisie.*

We have seen that the capitalistic mode of production thrust its way into a society of commodity-producers, of individual producers, whose social bond was the exchange of their products. But every society based upon the production of commodities has this peculiarity: that the producers have lost control over their own social interrelations. Each man produces for himself with such means of production as he may happen to have, and for such exchange as he may require to satisfy his remaining wants. No one knows how much of his particular article is coming on the market, nor how much of it will be wanted. No one knows whether his individual product will meet an actual demand, whether he will be able to make good his costs of production or even to sell his commodity at all. Anarchy reigns in socialised production.

But the production of commodities, like every other form of production, has its peculiar, inherent laws inseparable from it; and these laws work, despite anarchy, in and through anarchy. They reveal themselves in the only persistent form of social inter-relations, i.e., in exchange, and here they affect the individual producers as compulsory laws of competition. They are, at first, unknown to these producers themselves, and have to be discovered by them gradually and as the result of experience. They work themselves out, therefore, independently of the producers, and in antagonism to them, as inexorable natural laws of their particular form of production. The product governs the producers.

In mediaeval society, especially in the earlier centuries, production was essentially directed towards satisfying the wants of the individual. It satisfied, in the main, only the wants of the producer and his family. Where relations of personal dependence existed, as in the country, it also helped to satisfy the wants of the feudal lord. In all this there was, therefore, no exchange; the products, consequently, did not assume the character of commodities. The family of the peasant produced almost everything they wanted: clothes and furniture, as well as means of subsistence. Only when it began to produce more than was sufficient to supply its own wants and the payments in kind to the feudal lord, only then did it also produce commodities. This surplus, thrown into socialised exchange and offered for sale, became commodities.

The artisans of the towns, it is true, had from the first to produce for exchange. But they, also, themselves supplied the greatest part of their own individual wants. They had gardens and plots of land. They turned their cattle out into the communal forest, which, also, yielded them timber and firing. The women spun flax, wool, and so forth. Production for the purpose of exchange, production of commodities, was only in its infancy. Hence, exchange was restricted, the market narrow, the methods of production stable; there was local exclusiveness without, local unity within; the Mark in the country; in the town, the guild.

But with the extension of the production of commodities, and especially with the introduction of the capitalist mode of production, the laws of commodity production, hitherto latent, came into action more openly and with greater force. The old bonds were loosened, the old exclusive limits broken through, the producers were more and more turned into independent, isolated producers of commodities. It became apparent that the production of society at large was ruled by absence of plan, by accident, by anarchy; and this anarchy grew to greater and greater height. But the chief means by aid of which the capitalist mode of production intensified this anarchy of socialised production was the exact opposite of anarchy. It was the increasing organisation of production, upon a social basis, in every individual productive establishment. By this, the old, peaceful, stable condition of things was ended. Wherever this organisation of production was introduced into a branch of industry, it brooked no other method of production by its side. The field of labour became a battle-ground. The great geographical discoveries, and the colonisation following upon them, multiplied markets and quickened the transformation of handicraft into manufacture. The war did not simply break out between the individual producers of particular localities. The local struggles begot in their turn national conflicts, the commercial wars of the seventeenth and eighteenth centuries.

Finally, modern industry and the opening of the world market made the struggle universal, and at the same time gave it an unheard-of virulence. Advantages in natural or artificial conditions of production now decide the existence or non-existence of individual capitalists, as well as of whole industries and countries. He that falls is remorselessly cast aside. It is the Darwinian struggle of the individual for existence transferred from Nature to society with intensified violence. The conditions of existence natural to the animal appear as the final term of human development. The contradiction between socialised production and capitalistic appropriation now presents itself as *an antagonism between the organisation of production in the individual workshop and the anarchy of production in society generally.*

The capitalistic mode of production moves in these two forms of the antagonism immanent to it from its very origin. It is never able to get out of that "vicious circle" which Fourier had already discovered. What Fourier could not, indeed, see in his time is that this circle is gradually narrowing; that the movement becomes more and more a spiral, and must come to an end, like the movement of the planets, by collision with the centre. It is the compelling force of anarchy in the production of society at large that more and more completely turns the great majority of men into proletarians; and it is the masses of the proletariat again who will finally put an end to anarchy in production. It is the compelling force of anarchy in social production that turns the limitless perfectibility of machinery under modern industry into a compulsory law by which every individual industrial capitalist must perfect his machinery more and more, under penalty of ruin.

But the perfecting of machinery is making human labour superfluous. If the introduction and increase of machinery means the displacement of millions of manual by a few machine-workers, improvement in machinery means the displacement of more and more of the machine-workers themselves. It means, in the last instance, the production of a number of available wage-workers in excess of the average needs of capital, the formation of a complete industrial reserve army, as I called it in 1845, available at the times when industry is working at high pressure, to be cast out upon the street when the inevitable crash comes, a constant dead weight upon the limbs of the working class in its struggle for existence with capital, a regulator for the keeping of wages down to the low level that suits the interests of capital. Thus it comes about, to quote Marx, that machinery becomes the most powerful weapon in the war of capital against the working class; that the instruments of labour constantly tear the means of subsistence out of the hands of the labourer; that the very product of the worker is turned into an instrument for his subjugation. Thus it comes about that the economising of the instruments of labour becomes at the same time, from the outset, the most reckless waste of labour power, and robbery based upon the normal conditions under which labour functions; that machinery, "the most powerful instrument for shortening labour time, becomes the most unfailing means for placing every moment of the labourer's time and that of his family at the disposal of the capitalist for the purpose of expanding the value of his capital." *(Capital)* Thus it comes about that the overwork of some becomes the preliminary condition for the idleness of others, and that modern industry, which hunts after new consumers over the whole world, forces the consumption of the masses at home down to a starvation minimum, and in doing thus destroys its own home market. "The law that always equilibrates the relative surplus population, or industrial reserve army, to the extent and energy of accumulation, this law rivets the labourer to capital more firmly than the wedges of Vulcan did Prometheus to the rock. It establishes an accumulation of misery, corresponding with accumulation of capital. Accumulation of wealth at one pole is, therefore, at the same time, accumulation of misery, agony of toil, slavery, ignorance, brutality, mental degradation, at the opposite pole, i.e. on the side of the class that produces *its own product in the form of capital.*" *(Capital)* And to expect any other division of the products from the capitalistic mode of production is the same as expecting the electrodes of a battery not to decompose acidulated water, not to liberate oxygen at the positive, hydrogen at the negative pole, so long as they are connected with the battery.

We have seen that the ever-increasing perfectibility of modern machinery is, by the anarchy of social production, turned into a compulsory law that forces the individual industrial capitalist always to improve his machinery, always to increase its productive force. The bare possibility of extending the field of production is transformed for him into a similar compulsory law. The enormous expansive force of modern industry, compared with which that of gases is mere child's play, appears to us now as a *necessity* for expansion, both qualitative and quantitative, that laughs at all resistance. Such resistance is offered by consumption, by sales, by the markets for the products of modern industry. But the capacity for extension, extensive and intensive, of the markets is primarily governed by quite different laws that work much less energetically. The extension of the markets cannot keep pace with the extension of production. The collision becomes inevitable, and as this cannot produce any real solution so long as it does not break in pieces the capitalist mode of production, the collisions become periodic. Capitalist production has begotten another "vicious circle."

As a matter of fact, since 1825, when the first general crisis broke out, the whole industrial and commercial world, production and exchange among all civilised peoples and their more or less barbaric hangers-on, are thrown out of joint about once every ten years. Commerce is at a standstill, the markets are glutted, products accumulate, as multitudinous as they are unsaleable, hard cash disappears, credit vanishes, factories are closed, the mass of the workers are in want of the means of subsistence, because they have produced too much of the means of subsistence; bankruptcy follows upon bankruptcy, execution upon execution. The stagnation lasts for years; productive forces and products are wasted and destroyed wholesale, until the accumulated mass of commodities finally filters off, more or less depreciated in value, until production and exchange gradually begin to move again. Little by little the pace quickens. It becomes a trot. The industrial trot breaks into a canter, the canter in turn grows into the headlong gallop of a perfect steeplechase of industry, commercial credit, and speculation which finally, after breakneck leaps, ends where it began—in the ditch of a crisis. And so over and over again. We have now, since the year 1825, gone through this five times, and at the present moment (1877) we are going through it for the sixth time. And the character of these crises is so clearly defined that Fourier hit all of them off when he described the first as "*crise pléthorique*," a crisis from plethora.

In these crises, the contradiction between socialised production and capitalist appropriation ends in a violent explosion. The circulation of commodities is, for the time being, stopped. Money, the means of circulation, becomes a hindrance to circulation. All the laws of production and circulation of commodities are turned upside down. The economic collision has reached its apogee. *The mode of production is in rebellion against the mode of exchange.*

The fact that the socialised organisation of production within the factory has developed so far that it has become incompatible with the anarchy of production in society, which exists side by side with and dominates it, is brought home to the capitalists themselves by the violent concentration of capital that occurs during crises, through the ruin of many large, and a still greater number of small, capitalists. The whole mechanism of the capitalist mode of production breaks down under the pressure of the productive forces, its own creations. It is no longer able to turn all this mass of means of production into capital. They lie fallow, and for that very reason the industrial reserve army must also lie fallow. Means of production, means of subsistence, available labourers, all the elements of production and of general wealth, are present in abundance. But "abundance becomes the source of distress and want" (Fourier), because it is the very thing that prevents the transformation of the means of production and subsistence into capital. For in capitalistic society the means of production can only function when they have undergone a preliminary transformation into capital, into the means of exploiting human labour power. The necessity of this transformation into capital of the means of production and subsistence stands like a ghost between these and the workers. It alone prevents the coming together of the material and personal levers of production; it alone forbids the means of production to function, the workers to work and live. On the one hand, therefore, the capitalistic mode of production stands convicted of its own incapacity to further direct these productive forces. On the other, these productive forces themselves, with increasing energy, press forward to the removal of the existing contradiction to the abolition of their quality as capital, to the *practical recognition of their character as social productive forces.*

This rebellion of the productive forces, as they grow more and more powerful, against their quality as capital, this stronger and stronger command that their social character shall be recognised, forces the capitalist class itself to treat them more and more as social productive forces, so far as this is possible under capitalist conditions. The period of industrial high pressure, with its unbounded inflation of credit, not less than the crash itself, by the collapse of great capitalist establishments, tends to bring about that form of the socialisation of great masses of means of production which we meet with in the different kinds of joint-stock companies. Many of these means of production and of distribution are, from the outset, so colossal that, like the railways, they exclude all other forms of capitalistic exploitation. At a further stage of evolution this form also becomes insufficient. The producers on a large scale in a particular branch of industry in a particular country unite in a trust, a union for the purpose of regulating production. They determine the total amount to be produced, parcel it out among themselves, and thus enforce the selling price fixed beforehand. But trusts of this kind, as soon as business becomes bad, are generally liable to break up, and on this very account compel a yet greater concentration of association. The whole of the particular industry is turned into one gigantic joint-stock company; internal competition gives place to the internal monopoloy of this one company. This has happened in 1890 with the English alkali production, which is now, after the fusion of 48 large works, in the hands of one company, conducted upon a single plan, and with a capital of £6,000,000.

In the trusts, freedom of competition changes into its very opposite—into monopoly; and the production without any definite plan of capitalistic society capitulates to the production upon a definite plan of the invading socialistic society. Certainly this is so far still to the benefit and advantage of the capitalists. But in this case the exploitation is so palpable that it must break down. No nation will put up with production conducted by trusts, with so barefaced an exploitation of the community by a small band of dividend-mongers.

In any case, with trusts or without, the official representative of capitalist society—the state—will ultimately have to undertake the direction of production.[2] This necessity for conversion into state property is felt first in the great institutions for intercourse and communication—the post office, the telegraphs, the railways.

If the crises demonstrate the incapacity of the bourgeoisie for managing any longer modern productive forces, the transformation of the great establishments for production and distribution into joint-stock companies, trusts and state property shows how unnecessary the bourgeoisie are for that purpose. All the social functions of the capitalist are now performed by salaried employees. The capitalist has no further social function than that of pocketing dividends, tearing off coupons, and gambling on the Stock Exchange, where the different capitalists despoil one another of their capital. At first the capitalistic mode of production forces out the workers. Now it forces out the capitalists, and reduces them, just as it reduced the workers, to the ranks of the surplus population, although not immediately into those of the industrial reserve army.

But the transformation, either into joint-stock companies and trusts, or into state ownership, does not do away with the capitalistic nature of the productive forces. In the joint-stock companies and trusts this is obvious. And the modern state, again, is only the organisation that bourgeois society takes on in order to support the external conditions of the capitalist mode of production against the encroachments as well of the workers as of individual capitalists.

The modern state, no matter what its form, is essentially a capitalist machine, the state of the capitalists, the ideal personification of the total national capital. The more it proceeds to the taking over of productive forces, the more does it actually become the national capitalist, the more citizens does it exploit. The workers remain wage-workers—proletarians. The capitalist relation is not done away with. It is rather brought to a head. But, brought to a head, it topples over. State ownership of the productive forces is not the solution of the conflict, but concealed within it are the technical conditions that form the elements of that solution.

This solution can only consist in the practical recognition of the social nature of the modern forces of production, and therefore in the harmonising of the modes of production, appropriation, and exchange with the socialised character of the means of production. And this can only come about by society openly and directly taking possession of the productive forces which have outgrown all control except that of society as a whole. The social character of the means of production and of the products today reacts against the producers, periodically distrupts all production and exchange, acts only like a law of Nature working blindly, forcibly, destructively. But with the taking over by society of the productive forces, the social character of the means of production and of the products will be utilised by the producers with a perfect understanding of its nature, and instead of being a source of disturbance and periodical collapse, will become the most powerful lever of production itself.

Active social forces work exactly like natural forces: blindly, forcibly, destructively, so long as we do not understand, and reckon with, them. But when once we understand them, when once we grasp their action, their direction, their effects, it depends only upon ourselves to subject them more and more to our own will, and by means of them to reach our own ends. And this holds quite especially of the mighty productive forces of today. As long as we obstinately refuse to understand the nature and the character of these social means of action—and this understanding goes against the grain of the capitalist mode of production and its defenders—so long these forces are at work in spite of us, in opposition to us, so long they master us, as we have shown above in detail.

But when once their nature is understood, they can, in the hands of the producers working together, be transformed from master demons into willing servants. The difference is as that between the destructive force of electricity in the lightning of the storm, and electricity under command in the telegraph and the voltaic arc; the difference between a conflagration, and fire working in the service of man. With this recognition, at last, of the real nature of the productive forces of today, the social anarchy of production gives place to a social regulation of production upon a definite plan, according to the needs of the community and of each individual. Then the capitalist mode of appropriation, in which the product enslaves first the producer and then the appropriator, is replaced by the mode of appropriation of the products that is based upon the nature of the modern means of production; upon the one hand, direct social appropriation, as means to the maintenance and extension of production—on the other, direct individual appropriation, as means of subsistence and of enjoyment.

Whilst the capitalist mode of production more and more completely transforms the great majority of the population into proletarians, it creates the power which, under penalty of its own destruction, is forced to accomplish this revolution. Whilst it forces on more and more the transformation of the vast means of production, already socialised, into state property, it shows itself the way to accomplishing this revolution. *The proletariat seizes political power and turns the means of production into state property.*

But, in doing this, it abolishes itself as proletariat, abolishes all class distinctions and class antagonisms, abolishes also the state as state. Society thus far, based upon class antagonisms, had need of the state. That is, of an organisation of the particular class which was *pro tempore* the exploiting class, an organisation for the purpose of preventing any interference from without with the existing conditions of production, and, therefore, especially, for the purpose of forcibly keeping the exploited classes in the condition of oppression corresponding with the given mode of production (slavery, serfdom, wage-labour). The state was the official representative of society as a whole; the gathering of it together into a visible embodiment. But it was this only in so far as it was the state of that class which itself represented, for the time being, society as a whole: in ancient times, the state of slaveowning citizens; in the Middle Ages, the feudal lords; in our own time, the bourgeoisie. When at last it becomes the real representative of the whole of society, it renders itself unnecessary. As soon as there is no longer any social class to be held in subjection; as soon as class rule, and the individual struggle for existence based upon our present anarchy in production, with the collisions and excesses arising from these, are removed, nothing more remains to be repressed, and a special repressive force, a state, is no longer necessary. The first act by virtue of which the state really constitutes itself the representative of the whole of society—this is, at the same time, its last independent act as a state. State interference in social relations becomes, in one domain after another, superfluous, and then dies out of itself; the government of persons is replaced by the administration of things, and by the conduct of processes of production. The state is not "abolished." *It dies out.* This gives the measure of the value of the phrase "*a free state*," both as to its justifiable use at times by agitators, and as to its ultimate scientific insufficiency; and also of the demands of the so-called anarchists for the abolition of the state out of hand.

Since the historical appearance of the capitalist mode of production, the appropriation by society of all the means of production has often been dreamed of, more or less vaguely, by individuals, as well as by sects, as the ideal of the future. But it could become possible, could become a historical necessity, only when the actual conditions for its realisation were there. Like every other social advance, it becomes practicable, not by men understanding that the existence of classes is in contradiction to justice, equality, etc., not by the mere willingness to abolish these classes, but by virtue of certain new economic conditions. The separation of society into an exploiting and an exploited class, a ruling and an oppressed class, was the necessary consequence of the deficient and restricted development of production in former times. So long as the total social labour only yields a product which but slightly exceeds that barely necessary for the existence of all; so long, therefore, as labour engages all or almost all the time of the great majority of the members of society—so long, of necessity, this society is divided into classes. Side by side with the great majority, exclusively bond slaves to labour, arises a class freed from directly productive labour, which looks after the general affairs of society: the direction of labour, state business, law, science, art, etc. It is, therefore, the law of division of labour that lies at the basis of the division into classes. But this does not prevent this division into classes from being carried out by means of violence and robbery, trickery and fraud. It does not prevent the ruling class, once having the upper hand, from consolidating its power at the expense of the working class, from turning its social leadership into an intensified exploitation of the masses.

But if, upon this showing, division into classes has a certain historical justification, it has this only for a given period, only under given social conditions. It was based upon the insufficiency of production. It will be swept away by the complete development of modern productive forces. And, in fact, the abolition of classes in society presupposes a degree of historical evolution at which the existence, not simply of this or that particular ruling class, but of any ruling class at all, and, therefore, the existence of class distinction itself has become an obsolete anachronism. It presupposes, therefore, the development of production carried out to a degree at which appropriation of the means of production and of the products, and, with this, of political domination, of the monopoly of culture, and of intellectual leadership by a particular class of society, has become not only superfluous but economically, politically, intellectually, a hindrance to development.

This point is now reached. Their political and intellectual bankruptcy is scarcely any longer a secret to the bourgeoisie themselves. Their economic bankruptcy recurs regularly every ten years. In every crisis, society is suffocated beneath the weight of its own productive forces and products, which it cannot use, and stands helpless, face to face with the absurd contradiction that the producers have nothing to consume, because consumers are wanting. The expansive force of the means of production bursts the bonds that the capitalist mode of production had imposed upon them. Their deliverance from these bonds is the one precondition for an unbroken, constantly accelerated development of the productive forces, and therewith for a practically unlimited increase of production itself. Nor is this all. The socialised appropriation of the means of production does away, not only with the present artificial restrictions upon production, but also with the positive waste and devastation of productive forces and products that are at the present time the inevitable concomitants of production, and that reach their height in the crises. Further, it sets free for the community at large a mass of means of production and of products, by doing away with the senseless extravagance of the ruling classes of today and their political representatives. The possibility of securing for every member of society, by means of socialised production, an existence not only fully sufficient materially, and becoming day by day more full, but an existence guaranteeing to all the free development and exercise of their physical and mental faculties—this possibility is now for the first time here, but *it is here.*[3]

With the seizing of the means of production by society, production of commodities is done away with, and, simultaneously, the mastery of the product over the producer. Anarchy in social production is replaced by systematic, definite organisation. The struggle for individual existence disappears. Then for the first time man, in a certain sense, is finally marked off from the rest of the animal kingdom, and emerges from mere animal conditions of existence into really human ones. The whole sphere of the conditions of life which environ man, and which have hitherto ruled man, now comes under the dominion and control of man, who for the first time becomes the real, conscious lord of Nature, because he has now become master of his own social organisation. The laws of his own social action, hitherto standing face to face with man as laws of Nature foreign to, and dominating him, will then be used with full understanding, and so mastered by him. Man's own social organisation, hitherto confronting him as a necessity imposed by Nature and history, now becomes the result of his own free action. The extraneous objective forces that have hitherto governed history pass under the control of man himself. Only from that time will man himself, more and more consciously, make his own history—only from that time will the social causes set in movement by him have, in the main and in a constantly growing measure, the results intended by him. It is the ascent of man from the kingdom of necessity to the kingdom of freedom.

Let us briefly sum up our sketch of historical evolution.

I. *Mediaeval Society.* Individual production on a small scale. Means of production adapted for individual use; hence primitive, ungainly, petty, dwarfed in action. Production for immediate consumption, either of the producer himself or of his feudal lord. Only where an excess of production over this consumption occurs is such excess offered for sale, enters into exchange. Production of commodities, therefore, only in its infancy. But already it contains within itself, in embryo, *anarchy in the production of society at large.*

II. *Capitalist Revolution.* Transformation of industry, at first by means of simple cooperation and manufacture. Concentration of the means of production, hitherto scattered, into great workshops. As a consequence, their transformation from individual to social means of production—a transformation which does not, on the whole, affect the form of exchange. The old forms of appropriation remain in force. The capitalist appears. In his capacity as owner of the means of production, he also appropriates the products and turns them into commodities. Production has become a *social* act. Exchange and appropriation continue to be *individual* acts, the acts of individuals. *The social product is appropriated by the individual capitalist.* Fundamental contradiction, whence arise all the contradictions in which our present-day society moves, and which modern industry brings to light.

A. Severance of the producer from the means of production. Condemnation of the worker to wage-labour for life. *Antagonism between the proletariat and the bourgeoisie.*

B. Growing predominance and increasing effectiveness of the laws governing the production of commodities. Unbridled competition. *Contradiction between socialised organisation in the individual factory and social anarchy in production as a whole.*

C. On the one hand, perfecting of machinery, made by competition compulsory for each individual manufacturer, and complemented by a constantly growing displacement of labourers. *Industrial reserve army.* On the other hand, unlimited extension of production, also compulsory under competition, for every manufacturer. On both sides, unheard-of development of productive forces, excess of supply over demand, over-production, glutting of the markets, crises every ten years, the vicious circle: excess here, of means of production and products—excess there, of labourers, without employment and without means of existence. But these two levers of production and of social well-being are unable to work together, because the capitalist form of production prevents the productive forces from working and the products from circulating, unless they are first turned into capital—which their very superabundance prevents. The contradiction has grown into an absurdity. *The mode of production rises in rebellion against the form of exchange.* The bourgeoisie are convicted of incapacity further to manage their own social productive forces.

D. Partial recognition of the social character of the productive forces forced upon the capitalists themselves. Taking over of the great institutions for production and communication, first by joint-stock companies, later on by trusts, then by the state. The bourgeoisie demonstrated to be a superfluous class. All its social functions are now performed by salaried employees.

III. *Proletarian Revolution.* Solution of the contradictions. The proletariat seizes the public power, and by means of this transforms the socialised means of production, slipping from the hands of the bourgeoisie, into public property. By this act, the proletariat frees the means of production from the character of capital they have thus far borne, and gives their socialised character complete freedom to work itself out. Socialised production upon a predetermined plan becomes henceforth possible. The development of production makes the existence of different classes of society thenceforth an anachronism. In proportion as anarchy in social production vanishes, the political authority of the state dies out. Man, at last the master of his own form of social organisation, becomes at the same time the lord over Nature, his own master—free.

To accomplish this act of universal emancipation is the historical mission of the modern proletariat. To thoroughly comprehend the historical conditions and thus the very nature of this act, to impart to the new oppressed proletarian class a full knowledge of the conditions and of the meaning of the momentous act it is called upon to accomplish, this is the task of the theoretical expression of the proletarian movement, scientific socialism.

NOTES

1. It is hardly necessary in this connection to point out that, even if the *form* of appropriation remains the same, the *character* of the appropriation is just as much revolutionized as production is by the changes described above. It is, of course, a very different matter whether I appropriate to myself my own product or that of another. Note in passing that wage-labour, which contains the whole capitalistic mode of production in embryo, is very ancient; in a sporadic, scattered form it existed for centuries alongside of slave-labour. But the embryo could duly develop into the capitalistic mode of production only when the necessary historical preconditions had been furnished.
2. I say "have to." For only when the means of production and distribution have *actually* outgrown the form of management by joint-stock companies, and when, therefore, the taking them over by the state has become *economically* inevitable, only then—even if it is the state of today that effects this—is there an economic advance, the attainment of another step preliminary to the taking over of all productive forces by society itself. But of late, since Bismarck went in for state ownership of industrial establishments, a kind of spurious socialism has arisen, degenerating, now and again, into something of flunkeyism, that without more ado declares *all* state ownership, even of the Bismarckian sort, to be socialistic. Certainly, if the taking over by the state of the tobacco industry, is socialistic, then Napoleon and Metternich must be numbered among the founders of socialism. If the Belgian state, for quite ordinary political and financial reasons, itself constructed its chief railway lines; if Bismarck, not under any economic compulsion, took over for the state the chief Prussian lines, simply to be the better able to have them in hand in case of war, to bring up the railway employees as voting cattle for the government, and especially to create for himself a new source of income independent of parliamentary votes—this was, in no sense, a socialistic measure, directly or indirectly, consciously or unconsciously. Otherwise, the Royal Maritime Company, the Royal porcelain manufacture, and even the regimental tailor shops of the Army would also be socialistic institutions, or even, as was seriously proposed by a sly dog in Frederick William III's reign, the taking over by the state of the brothels.
3. A few figures may serve to give an approximate idea of the enormous expansive force of the modern means of production, even under capitalist pressure. According to Mr. Giffen, the total wealth of Great Britain and Ireland amounted, in round numbers in

   1814 to £2,200,000,000.
   1865 to £6,100,000,000.
   1875 to £8,500,000,000.

As an instance of the squandering of means of production and of products during a crisis, the total loss in the German iron industry alone, in the crisis 1873–78, was given at the second German Industrial Congress (Berlin, February 21, 1878) as £22,750,000.

PART SIX

SOCIALISM AND COMMUNISM AFTER MARX

Much has happened to the ideologies of socialism and communism in the last century. The most momentous developments include the fact that several revolutions have been made, and regimes ruled, in Marx's name. No less momentous is the fact that those regimes began to unravel and lose their legitimacy in the latter part of the twentieth century. In the Soviet Union, in Eastern Europe, and even in China, the chorus of criticism grew into a crescendo. Communist parties in Hungary and elsewhere changed their names and in some cases their policies. Old hard-line leaders were expelled or jailed or, as in Romania, executed. Clearly, communism—and, as some have said, socialism as well—was experiencing a crisis of unprecedented proportions. Whether communism will survive—and if so, in what form—no one can say for sure. But the best way of guessing where it might be going is to turn to the past, to see where it has been and how it reached its present predicament. Even the briefest backward glance is sufficient to show how radically Marx's ideas have been interpreted and reinterpreted by disciples who called themselves Marxists.

Karl Marx died in 1883. It was not long before various sects of "Marxists" sprang up in Europe and elsewhere. Each claimed to be the only "true" or "real" Marxists. Each was critical of the others, and all were adamantly opposed to non-Marxian Socialists of various stripes. The one thing on which they could all agree was that the end of capitalism was in sight.

One group of Marxists, the so-called "revisionists," held that Marx's theory must, in the best scientific spirit, be subjected to criticism and revision in the light of new factual evidence. This was the argument advanced by Eduard Bernstein (1850–1932) in his book *Evolutionary Socialism* (1899). Contrary to Marx's prediction about the ever-increasing "immiseration of the proletariat," the working class in Europe and North America had become better-off: Real wages had risen, working conditions had improved, and so had the average worker's standard of living. This was not, he hastened to add, because the capitalists had become benign or kindly employers, but because the working class had developed its political muscles. Laborers had organized trade unions and called strikes to raise their wages and improve their working conditions. And they had organized and supported working-class parties to elect representatives pledged to promote their interests. By these means the proletariat had forced concessions from a reluctant ruling class that was beginning to lose its legitimacy and authority. Thus, Bernstein believed, violent revolution was no longer necessary (if indeed it ever had been). Capitalist society was slowly but surely "evolving" into a more egalitarian, just, and humane socialist society. Instead of focusing on a distant utopian end—the creation of a communist society—Marxists should devote their energies to day-to-day trade union activities and parliamentary politics.

Bernstein's "revisionist" message met with harsh criticism from other Marxists. Rosa Luxemburg (1871–1919), Karl Kautsky (1854–1938), and other prominent German Marxists were highly critical of Bernstein's nonrevolutionary version of Marxism. But the harshest criticisms came from the East. Marxists in Russia—including Georgi Plekhanov (1856–1918) and Vladimir Ilich Ulyanov (1870–1924), better known as Lenin—condemned Bernstein as a "bourgeois" traitor to Marxism.

The only Marxism worthy of the name, Lenin argued, was radical in its aims and revolutionary in its strategy. The aim was nothing less than the creation of a classless communist society. And this aim, he argued, could be accomplished only with the assistance of a revolutionary vanguard party whose leadership was composed of radicalized "bourgeois" intellectuals like himself. After all, as Lenin often noted, Marx and Engels were not workers, but members of the intelligentsia. Left to themselves, the workers would behave just as Bernstein had said they would: That is, workers would organize themselves into trade unions and form working-class political parties in hopes of "reforming" the capitalist system from within. To cooperate with the capitalist system, said Lenin, was to be corrupted by it. Better to bury it once and for all. Hence the need for a relatively small, tightly knit, highly organized conspiratorial party to raise class consciousness, educate the workers about where their "real" interests lay, and prepare the way for a revolution made in the name of, but not directly by, the proletariat.

Yet Russia at the beginning of the twentieth century was an odd place for a "proletarian" revolution, if only because the vast majority of Russian workers were neither factory workers nor wage laborers, but peasants who tilled the soil. Set in their ways, suspicious of outsiders, and often superstitious, such people seemed the very embodiment of what Marx had called "the idiocy of rural life." They appeared to be singularly ill-suited to be the agents of radical revolutionary transformation, as Lenin acknowledged. But the peasants were discontented and they were numerous. They could therefore be the clay fit for molding by a vanguard party.

Lenin's reinterpretation of Marxism had two novel aspects, neither of which Marx had anticipated: the idea that revolutionary political consciousness had to be brought to the proletariat and the peasantry from outside and the idea that the source of such consciousness was to be a vanguard party. It is indeed this version of Marxism—"Marxism-Leninism"—that proved to be the single most influential and important variant of Marxism through the twentieth century. In the Soviet Union, China, Cuba, Vietnam, Eastern Europe, and elsewhere, the Marxist-Leninist model, as modified by Joseph Stalin (1879–1953), Mao Zedong (1893–1976), and others, served as an ideology to legitimize an all-powerful party ruling over a highly centralized government and a planned economy managed by government bureaucrats. It is this ideology, and the system it spawned and justified, that in the 1980s and early 1990s came under withering attack from within those countries and even from factions within their respective Communist parties. Whether those reforms will succeed, and what forms they will take, remains an open question. But there can be no question that communism as we have known it is rapidly ceasing to exist.

Ironically, the demise of Communism, or at least its Marxist-Leninist variant, could conceivably be a boon for non-Communist socialism. Other varieties of socialism—Christian socialism, democratic socialism, market socialism, even anarchocommunism—have long been eclipsed by Marxism-Leninism. Now that the latter is collapsing, the former may be revived in some form or other. Reformers in the Soviet Union and in Eastern Europe are now turning to other sorts of socialism that were until recently condemned as "reactionary," "revisionist," or "bourgeois." Bernstein may turn out to have been a better prophet than Marx.

33

EVOLUTIONARY SOCIALISM

EDUARD BERNSTEIN

Eduard Bernstein (1850–1932) believed that Marx's theory of social change was generally correct in outline but false or mistaken in several important details. He therefore favored revising Marx's theory to make it consistent with newly emerging facts—the fact including that the predicted "immiseration of the proletariat" had not occurred. Rather than becoming worse off, Bernstein noted, European and North American workers were increasingly prosperous. This had happened, he claimed, because the capitalist system was "evolving" into socialism as it was transformed by trade unions and working-class or socialist political parties. Bernstein's book *Evolutionary Socialism* (originally published in 1899) provided the classic statement of "revisionist" Marxism.

Source: Eduard Bernstein, Evolutionary Socialism, *translated by Edith C. Harvey (New York: B. W. Huebsch, 1909), pp. 203–213, 216–222, 224.*

. . . No socialist capable of thinking, dreams to-day in England of an imminent victory for socialism by means of a violent revolution—none dreams of a quick conquest of Parliament by a revolutionary proletariat. But they rely more and more on work in the municipalities and other self-governing bodies. The early contempt for the trade union movement has been given up; a closer sympathy has been won for it and, here and there also, for the co-operative movement.

And the ultimate aim? Well, that just remains an ultimate aim. "The working classes have no fixed and perfect Utopias to introduce by means of a vote of the nation. They know that in order to work out their own emancipation—and with it that higher form of life which the present form of society irresistibly makes for by its own economic development—they, the working classes, have to pass through long struggles, a whole series of historical processes, by means of which men and circumstances will be completely transformed. They have no ideals to realise, they have only to set at liberty the elements of the new society which have already been developed in the womb of the collapsing bourgeois society." So writes Marx in *Civil War in France*. I was thinking of this utterance, not in every point, but in its fundamental thought in writing down the sentence about the ultimate aim. For after all what does it say but that the movement, the series of processes, is everything, whilst every aim fixed beforehand in its details is immaterial to it. I have declared already that I willingly abandon the form of the sentence about the ultimate aim as far as it admits the interpretation that every general aim of the working class movement formulated as a principle should be declared valueless. But the preconceived theories about the drift of the movement which go beyond such a generally expressed aim, which try to determine the direction of the movement and its character without an ever-vigilant eye upon facts and experience, must necessarily always pass into Utopianism, and at some time or other stand in the way, and hinder the real theoretical and practical progress of the movement.

Whoever knows even but a little of the history of German social democracy also knows that the party has become important by continued action in contravention of such theories and of infringing resolutions founded on them. What Engels says in the preface to the new edition of *Civil War* with regard to the Blanquists and Proudhonists in the Paris Commune of 1871, namely that they both had been obliged in practice to act against their own theory, has often been repeated in another form. A theory or declaration of principle which does not allow attention being paid at every stage of development to the actual interests of the working classes, will always be set aside just as all foreswearing of reforming detail work and of the support of neighbouring middle class parties has again and again been forgotten; and again and again at the congresses of the party will the complaint be heard that here and there in the electoral contest the ultimate aim of socialism has not been put sufficiently in the foreground.

[Some of my Marxist critics] . . . cart me over to the "opponents of scientific socialism."

Unfortunately for "scientific" socialism, the Marxist propositions on the hopelessness of the position of the worker have been upset in a book [by Marx himself] which bears the title, *Capital: A Criticism of Political Economy*. There we read of the "physical and moral regeneration" of the textile workers in Lancashire through the Factory Law of 1847, which "struck the feeblest eye." A bourgeois republic was not even necessary to bring about a certain improvement in the situation of a large section of workers! In the same book we read that the society of to-day is no firm crystal, but an organism capable of change and constantly engaged in a process of change, that also in the treatment of economic questions on the part of the official representatives of this society an "improvement was unmistakable." Further that the author had devoted so large a space in his book to the results of the English Factory Laws in order to spur the Continent to imitate them and thus to work so that the process of transforming society may be accomplished in ever more humane forms. All of which signifies not hopelessness but capability of improvement in the condition of the worker. And, as since 1866, when this was written, the legislation depicted has not grown weaker but has been improved, made more general, and has been supplemented by laws and organisations working in the same direction, there can be no more doubt to-day than formerly of the hopefulness of the position of the worker. If to state such facts means following the "immortal Bastiat," then among the first ranks of these followers is—Karl Marx.

Now, it can be asserted against me that Marx certainly recognised those improvements, but that the chapter on the historical tendency of capitalist accumulation at the end of the first volume of *Capital* shows how little these details influenced his fundamental mode of viewing things. To which I answer that as far as that is correct it speaks against that chapter and not against me.

One can interpret this chapter in very different kinds of ways. I believe I was the first to point out, and indeed repeatedly, that it was a summary characterisation of the tendency of a development which is found in capitalist accumulation, but which in practice is not carried out completely and which therefore need not be driven to the critical point of the antagonism there depicted. Engels has never expressed himself against this interpretation of mine, never, either verbally or in print, declared it to be wrong. Nor did he say a word against me when I wrote, in 1891: "It is clear that where legislation, this systematic and conscious action of society, interferes in an appropriate way, the working of the tendencies of economic development is thwarted, under some circumstances can even be annihilated. Marx and Engels have not only never denied this, but, on the contrary, have always emphasised it." If one reads the chapter mentioned with this idea, one will also, in a few sentences, silently place the word "tendency" and thus be spared the need of bringing this chapter into accord with reality by distorting arts of interpretation. But then the chapter itself would become of less value the more progress is made in actual evolution. For its theoretic importance does not lie in the argument of the general tendency to capitalistic centralisation and accumulation which had been affirmed long before Marx by bourgeois economists and socialists, but in the presentation, peculiar to Marx, of circumstances and forms under which it would work at a more advanced stage of evolution, and of the results to which it would lead. But in this respect actual evolution is really always bringing forth new arrangements, forces, facts, in face of which that presentation seems insufficient and loses to a corresponding extent the capability of serving as a sketch of the coming evolution. That is how I understand it.

One can, however, understand this chapter differently. One can conceive it in this way, that all the improvements mentioned there, and some possibly ensuing, only create temporary remedies against the oppressive tendencies of capitalism, that they signify unimportant modifications which cannot in the long run effect anything substantially against the critical point of antagonisms laid down by Marx, that this will finally appear—if not literally yet substantially—in the manner depicted, and will lead to catastrophic change by violence. This interpretation can be founded on the categoric wording of the last sentences of the chapter, and receives a certain confirmation because at the end reference is again made to the *Communist Manifesto*, whilst Hegel also appeared shortly before with his negation of the negation—the restoration on a new foundation of individual property negated by the capitalist manner of production.

According to my view, it is impossible simply to declare the one conception right and the other absolutely wrong. To me the chapter illustrates a dualism which runs through the whole monumental work of Marx, and which also finds expression in a less pregnant fashion in other passages—a dualism which consists in this, that the work aims at being a scientific inquiry and also at proving a theory laid down long before its drafting; a formula lies at the basis of it in which the result to which the exposition should lead is fixed beforehand. The return to the *Communist Manifesto* points here to a real residue of Utopianism in the Marxist system. Marx had accepted the solution of the Utopians in essentials, but had recognised their means and proofs as inadequate. He therefore undertook a revision of them, and this with the zeal, the critical acuteness, and love of truth of a scientific genius. He suppressed no important fact, he also forebore belittling artificially the importance of these facts as long as the object of the inquiry had no immediate reference to the final aim of the formula to be proved. To that point his work is free of every tendency necessarily interfering with the scientific method.

For the general sympathy with the strivings for emancipation of the working classes does not in itself stand in the way of the scientific method. But, as Marx approaches a point when that final aim enters seriously into the question, he becomes uncertain and unreliable. Such contradictions then appear as were shown in the book under consideration, for instance, in the section on the movement of incomes in modern society. It thus appears that this great scientific spirit was, in the end, a slave to a doctrine. To express it figuratively, he has raised a mighty building within the framework of a scaffolding he found existing, and in its erection he kept strictly to the laws of scientific architecture as long as they did not collide with the conditions which the construction of the scaffolding prescribed, but he neglected or evaded them when the scaffolding did not allow of their observance. Where the scaffolding put limits in the way of the building, instead of destroying the scaffolding, he changed the building itself at the cost of its right proportions and so made it all the more dependent on the scaffolding. Was it the consciousness of this irrational relation which caused him continually to pass from completing his work to amending special parts of it? However that may be, my conviction is that wherever that dualism shows itself the scaffolding must fall if the building is to grow in its right proportions. In the latter, and not in the former, is found what is worthy to live in Marx.

Nothing confirms me more in this conception than the anxiety with which some persons seek to maintain certain statements in *Capital*, which are falsified by facts. It is just some of the more deeply devoted followers of Marx who have not been able to separate themselves from the dialectical form of the work—that is the scaffolding alluded to—who do this. At least, that is only how I can explain the words of a man, otherwise so amenable to facts as Karl Kautsky, who, when I observed in Stuttgart that the number of wealthy people for many years had increased, not decreased, answered: "If that were true then the date of our victory would not only be very long postponed, but we should never attain our goal. If it be capitalists who increase and not those with no possessions, then we are going ever further from our goal the more evolution progresses, then capitalism grows stronger, not socialism."

That the number of the wealthy increases and does not diminish is not an invention of bourgeois "harmony economists," but a fact established by the boards of assessment for taxes, often to the chagrin of those concerned, a fact which can no longer be disputed. But what is the significance of this fact as regards the victory of socialism? Why should the realisation of socialism depend on its refutation? Well, simply for this reason: because the dialectical scheme seems so to prescribe it; because a post threatens to fall out of the scaffolding if one admits that the social surplus product is appropriated by an increasing instead of a decreasing number of possessors. But it is only the speculative theory that is affected by this matter; it does not at all affect the actual movement. Neither the struggle of the workers for democracy in politics nor their struggle for democracy in industry is touched by it. The prospects of this struggle do not depend on the theory of concentration of capital in the hands of a diminishing number of magnates, nor on the whole dialectical scaffolding of which this is a plank, but on the growth of social wealth and of the social productive forces, in conjunction with general social progress, and, particularly, in conjunction with the intellectual and moral advance of the working classes themselves.

Suppose the victory of socialism depended on the constant shrinkage in the number of capitalist magnates, social democracy, if it wanted to act logically, either would have to support the heaping up of capital in ever fewer hands, or at least to give no support to anything that would stop this shrinkage. As a matter of fact it often enough does neither the one nor the other. These considerations, for instance, do not govern its votes on questions of taxation. From the standpoint of the catastrophic theory a great part of this practical activity of the working classes is an undoing of work that ought to be allowed to be done. It is not social democracy which is wrong in this respect. The fault lies in the doctrine which assumes that progress depends on the deterioration of social conditions. . . .

[In earlier] circumstances a reference to politics could appear only to be a turning aside from more pressing duties. To-day these conditions have been to some extent removed, and therefore no person capable of reflecting will think of criticising political action. . . .

[L]aw, or the path of legislative reform, is the slower way, and revolutionary force the quicker and more radical. But that only is true in a restricted sense. Whether the legislative or the revolutionary method is the more promising depends entirely on the nature of the measures and on their relation to different classes and customs of the people.

In general, one may say here that the revolutionary way (always in the sense of revolution by violence) does quicker work as far as it deals with removal of obstacles which a privileged minority places in the path of social progress: that its strength lies on its negative side.

Constitutional legislation works more slowly in this respect as a rule. Its path is usually that of compromise, not the prohibition, but the buying out of acquired rights. But it is stronger than the revolution scheme where prejudice and the limited horizon of the great mass of the people appear as hindrances to social progress, and it offers greater advantages where it is a question of the creation of permanent economic arrangements capable of lasting; in other words, it is best adapted to positive social-political work.

In legislation, intellect dominates over emotion in quiet times; during a revolution emotion dominates over intellect. But if emotion is often an imperfect leader, the intellect is a slow motive force. Where a revolution sins by over haste, the every-day legislator sins by procrastination. Legislation works as a systematic force, revolution as an elementary force.

As soon as a nation has attained a position where the rights of the propertied minority have ceased to be a serious obstacle to social progress, where the negative tasks of political action are less pressing than the positive, then the appeal to a revolution by force becomes a meaningless phrase. One can overturn a government or a privileged minority, but not a nation. When the working classes do not possess very strong economic organisations of their own, and have not attained, by means of education on self-governing bodies, a high degree of mental independence, the dictatorship of the proletariat means the dictatorship of club orators and writers. I would not wish that those who see in the oppression and tricking of the working men's organisations and in the exclusion of working men from the legislature and government the highest point of the art of political policy should experience their error in practice. Just as little would I desire it for the working class movement itself.

One has not overcome Utopianism if one assumes that there is in the present, or ascribes to the present, what is to be in the future. We have to take working men as they are. And they are neither so universally pauperised as was set out in the *Communist Manifesto,* nor so free from prejudices and weaknesses as their courtiers wish to make us believe. They have the virtues and failings of the economic and social conditions under which they live. And neither these conditions nor their effects can be put on one side from one day to another.

Have we attained the required degree of development of the productive forces for the abolition of classes? In face of the fantastic figures which were formerly set up in proof of this and which rested on generalisations based on the development of particularly favoured industries, socialist writers in modern times have endeavoured to reach by carefully detailed calculations, appropriate estimates of the possibilities of production in a socialist society, and their results are very different from those figures. Of a general reduction of hours of labour to five, four, or even three or two hours, such as was formerly accepted, there can be no hope at any time within sight, unless the general standard of life is much reduced. Even under a collective organisation of work, labour must begin very young and only cease at a rather advanced age, it is to be reduced considerably below an eight-hours' day. Those persons ought to understand this first of all who indulge in the most extreme exaggerations regarding the ratio of the number of the nonpropertied classes to that of the propertied. But he who thinks irrationally on one point does so usually on another. . . .

[H]e who surveys the actual workers' movement will also find that the freedom from those qualities which appeared Philistine to a person born in the bourgeoisie, is very little valued by the workers, that they in no way support the morale of proletarianism, but, on the contrary, tend to make a Philistine out of a proletarian. With the roving proletarian without a family and home, no lasting, firm trade union movement would be possible. It is no bourgeois prejudice, but a conviction gained through decades of labour organisation, which has made so many of the English labour leaders—socialists and non-socialists—into zealous adherents of the temperance movement. The working class socialists know the faults of their class, and the most conscientious among them, far from glorifying these faults, seek to overcome them with all their power.

We cannot demand from a class, the great majority of whose members live under crowded conditions, are badly educated, and have an uncertain and insufficient income, the high intellectual and moral standard which the organisation and existence of a socialist community presupposes. We will, therefore, not ascribe it to them by way of fiction. Let us rejoice at the great stock of intelligence, renunciation, and energy which the modern working class movement has partly revealed, partly produced; but we must not assign, without discrimination to the masses, the millions, what holds good, say, of hundreds of thousands. I will not repeat the declarations which have been made to me on this point by working men [themselves]. . . . [I]t is not every epoch that produces a Marx, and even for a man of equal genius the working class movement of to-day is too great to enable him to occupy the position which Marx fills in its history. To-day it needs, in addition to the fighting spirit, the co-ordinating and constructive thinkers who are intellectually enough advanced to be able to separate the chaff from the wheat, who are great enough in their mode of thinking to recognise also the little plant that has grown on another soil than theirs, and who, perhaps, though not kings, are warm-hearted republicans in the domain of socialist thought.

34

REVISIONISM, IMPERIALISM, AND REVOLUTION

V. I. LENIN

Marxism-Leninism, as the ideology of the Soviet Union was officially called before the dramatic changes of the late 1980s, was largely the creation of one man. Vladimir Ilich Ulyanov (1870–1924)—better known by his revolutionary name, Lenin—was until his death the preeminent Russian revolutionary and Marxian theorist. In "adapting" Marxism to Russian conditions, Lenin made several significant changes. For one, he held that a proletarian revolution could occur in Russia, despite the fact that Russia in the early twentieth century had a relatively small proletariat (the overwhelming majority of Russian workers were peasants who tilled the soil). For another, he claimed that only a small, highly organized, conspiratorial party could supply the political will (or "consciousness") and leadership required to transform radically such an economically and politically backward country. A fiercely combative critic of other interpretations of Marxism, Lenin claimed that his alone was the "true" interpretation; all others—including the "revisionist" view espoused by Bernstein—were deviations from or distortions of Marx's "scientific" outlook. If revolution had not come to the advanced capitalist countries, as Marx had predicted, that was because the workers in those countries were afflicted with "trade-union consciousness," that is, the mistaken view that they could organize themselves into unions and political parties to press for their interests. This strategy was successful, said Lenin, only because the capitalist countries were exploiting the workers of nonindustrial countries. Such exploitation would cease—and revolution would come to capitalist countries themselves—when workers in those underdeveloped countries made their own anti-colonial or anti-imperial revolutions.

Source: "Marxism and Revisionism," from V. I. Lenin, Selected Works *(Moscow: Progress Publishers, 1967), pp. 25–32; "Imperialism, the Highest Stage of Capitalism," ibid., pp. 260–263; and "State and Revolution," ibid., pp. 322–337.*

MARXISM AND REVISIONISM

There is a well-known saying that if geometrical axioms affected human interests attempts would certainly be made to refute them. Theories of natural history which conflicted with the old prejudices of theology provoked, and still provoke, the most rabid opposition. No wonder, therefore, that the Marxian doctrine, which directly serves to enlighten and organise the advanced class in modern society, indicates the tasks facing this class and demonstrates the inevitable replacement (by virtue of economic development) of the present system by a new order—no wonder that this doctrine has had to fight for every step forward in the course of its life.

Needless to say, this applies to bourgeois science and philosophy, officially taught by official professors in order to befuddle the rising generation of the propertied classes and to "coach" it against internal and foreign enemies. This science will not even hear of Marxism, declaring that it has been refuted and annihilated. Marx is attacked with equal zest by young scholars who are making a career by refuting socialism, and by decrepit elders who are preserving the tradition of all kinds of outworn "systems." The progress of Marxism, the fact that its ideas are spreading and taking firm hold among the working class, inevitably increase the frequency and intensity of these bourgeois attacks on Marxism, which becomes stronger, more hardened and more vigorous every time it is "annihilated" by official science.

But even among doctrines connected with the struggle of the working class, and current mainly among the proletariat, Marxism by no means consolidated its position all at once. In the first half-century of its existence (from the 1840s on) Marxism was engaged in combating theories fundamentally hostile to it. In the early forties Marx and Engels settled accounts with the radical Young Hegelians whose viewpoint was that of philosophical idealism. At the end of the forties the struggle began in the field of economic doctrine, against Proudhonism. The fifties saw the completion of this struggle in criticism of the parties and doctrines which manifested themselves in the stormy year of 1848. In the sixties the struggle shifted from the field of general theory to one closer to the direct labour movement: the ejection of Bakuninism from the International. In the early seventies the stage in Germany was occupied for a short while by the Proudhonist Mühlberger, and in the late seventies by the positivist Dühring. But the influence of both on the proletariat was already absolutely insignificant. Marxism was already gaining an unquestionable victory over all other ideologies in the labour movement.

By the nineties this victory was in the main completed. Even in the Latin countries, where the traditions of Proudhonism held their ground longest of all, the workers' parties in effect built their programmes and their tactics on Marxist foundations. The revived international organisation of the labour movement—in the shape of periodical international congresses—from the outset, and almost without a struggle, adopted the Marxist standpoint in all essentials. But after Marxism had ousted all the more or less integral doctrines hostile to it, the tendencies expressed in those doctrines began to seek other channels. The forms and causes of the struggle changed, but the struggle continued. And the second half-century of the existence of Marxism began (in the nineties) with the struggle of a trend hostile to Marxism within Marxism itself.

Bernstein, a one-time orthodox Marxist, gave his name to this trend, by coming forward with the most noise and with the most purposeful expression of amendments to Marx, revision of Marx, revisionism. Even in Russia where—owing to the economic backwardness of the country and the preponderance of a peasant population weighed down by the relics of serfdom—non-Marxist socialism has naturally held its ground longest of all, it is plainly passing into revisionism before our very eyes. Both in the agrarian question (the programme of the municipalisation of all land) and in general questions of programme and tactics, our Social-Narod-niks are more and more substituting "amendments" to Marx for the moribund and obsolescent remnants of their old system, which in its own way was integral and fundamentally hostile to Marxism.

Pre-Marxist socialism has been defeated. It is continuing the struggle, no longer on its own independent ground, but on the general ground of Marxism, as revisionism. Let us, then, examine the ideological content of revisionism.

In the sphere of philosophy revisionism followed in the wake of bourgeois professional "science." The professors went "back to Kant"—and revisionism dragged along after the neo-Kantians. The professors repeated the platitudes that priests have uttered a thousand times against philosophical materialism—and the revisionists, smiling indulgently, mumbled . . . that materialism had been "refuted" long ago. The professors treated Hegal as a "dead dog," and while themselves preaching idealism, only an idealism a thousand times more petty and banal than Hegel's, contemptuously shrugged their shoulders at dialectics—and the revisionists floundered after them into the swamp of philosophical vulgarisation of science, replacing "artful" (and revolutionary) dialectics by "simple" (and tranquil) "evolution." The professors earned their official salaries by adjusting both their idealist and their "critical" systems to the dominant medieval "philosophy" (i.e., to theology)—and the revisionists drew close to them, trying to make religion a "private affair," not in relation to the modern state, but in relation to the party of the advanced class.

What such "amendments" to Marx really meant in class terms need not be stated: it is self-evident. . . .

Passing to political economy, it must be noted first of all that in this sphere the "amendments" of the revisionists were much more comprehensive and circumstantial; attempts were made to influence the public by "new data on economic development." It was said that concentration and the ousting of small-scale production by large-scale production do not occur in agriculture at all, while they proceed very slowly in commerce and industry. It was said that crises had now become rarer and weaker, and that cartels and trusts would probably enable capital to eliminate them altogether. It was said that the "theory of collapse" to which capitalism is heading was unsound, owing to the tendency of class antagonisms to become milder and less acute. It was said, finally, that it would not be amiss to correct Marx's theory of value, too . . .

The fight against the revisionists on these questions resulted in as fruitful a revival of the theoretical thought in international socialism as did Engels's controversy with Dühring twenty years earlier. The arguments of the revisionists were analysed with the help of facts and figures. It was proved that the revisionists were systematically painting a rose-coloured picture of modern small-scale production. The technical and commercial superiority of large-scale *production* over small-scale production not only in industry, but also in agriculture, is proved by irrefutable facts. But commodity production is far less developed in agriculture, and modern statisticians and economists are, as a rule, not very skilful in picking out the special branches (sometimes even the operations) in agriculture which indicate that agriculture is being progressively drawn into the process of *exchange* in world economy. Small-scale production maintains itself on the ruins of natural economy by constant worsening of diet, by chronic starvation, by lengthening of the working day, by deterioration in the quality and the care of cattle, in a word, by the very methods whereby handicraft production maintained itself against capitalist manufacture. Every advance in science and technology inevitably and relentlessly undermines the foundations of small-scale production in capitalist society; and it is the task of socialist political economy to investigate this process in all its forms, often complicated and intricate, and to demonstrate to the small producer the impossibility of his holding his own under capitalism, the hopelessness of peasant farming under capitalism, and the necessity for the peasant to adopt the standpoint of the proletarian. On this question the revisionists sinned, in the scientific sense, by superficial generalisations based on facts selected one-sidedly and without reference to the system of capitalism as a whole. From the political point of view, they sinned by the fact that they inevitably, whether they wanted to or not, invited or urged the peasant to adopt the attitude of a small proprietor (i.e., the attitude of the bourgeoisie) instead of urging him to adopt the point of view of the revolutionary proletarian.

The position of revisionism was even worse as regards the theory of crises and the theory of collapse. Only for a very short time could people, and then only the most short-sighted, think of refashioning the foundations of Marx's theory under the influence of a few years of industrial boom and prosperity. Realities very soon made it clear to the revisionists that crises were not a thing of the past: prosperity was followed by a crisis. The forms, the sequence, the picture of particular crises changed, but crises remained an inevitable component of the capitalist system. While uniting production, the cartels and trusts at the same time, and in a way that was obvious to all, aggravated the anarchy of production, the insecurity of existence of the proletariat and the oppression of capital, thereby intensifying class antagonisms to an unprecedented degree. That capitalism is heading for a breakdown—in the sense both of individual political and economic crises and of the complete collapse of the entire capitalist system—has been made particularly clear, and on a particularly large scale, precisely by the new giant trusts. The recent financial crisis in America and the appalling increase of unemployment all over Europe, to say nothing of the impending industrial crisis to which many symptoms are pointing—all this has resulted in the recent "theories" of the revisionists having been forgotten by everybody, including, apparently, many of the revisionists themselves. But the lessons which this instability of the intellectuals had given the working class must not be forgotten.

As to the theory of value, it need only be said that . . . the revisionists have contributed absolutely nothing, and have therefore left no traces whatever on the development of scientific thought.

In the sphere of politics, revisionism did really try to revise the foundation of Marxism, namely, the doctrine of the class struggle. Political freedom, democracy and universal suffrage remove the ground for the class struggle—we were told—and render untrue the old proposition of the *Communist Manifesto* that the working men have no country. For, they said, since the "will of the majority" prevails in a democracy, one must neither regard the state as an organ of class rule, nor reject alliances with the progressive, social-reform bourgeoisie against the reactionaries.

It cannot be disputed that these arguments of the revisionists amounted to a fairly well-balanced system of views, namely, the old and well-known liberal-bourgeois views. The liberals have always said that bourgeois parliamentarism destroys classes and class divisions, since the right to vote and the right to participate in the government of the country are shared by all citizens without distinction. The whole history of Europe in the second half of the nineteenth century, and the whole history of the Russian revolution in the early twentieth, clearly show how absurd such views are. Economic distinctions are not mitigated but aggravated and intensified under the freedom of "democratic" capitalism. Parliamentarism does not eliminate, but lays bare the innate character even of the most democratic bourgeois republics as organs of class oppression. By helping to enlighten and to organise immeasurably wider masses of the population than those which previously took an active part in political events, parliamentarism does not make for the elimination of crises and political revolutions, but for the maximum intensification of civil war during such revolutions. The events in Paris in the spring of 1871 and the events in Russia in the winter of 1905 showed as clearly as could be how inevitably this intensification comes about. The French bourgeoisie without a moment's hesitation made a deal with the enemy of the whole nation, with the foreign army which had ruined its country, in order to crush the proletarian movement. Whoever does not understand the inevitable inner dialectics of parliamentarism and bourgeois democracy—which leads to an even sharper decision of the argument by mass violence than formerly—will never be able on the basis of this parlimentarism to conduct propaganda and agitation consistent in principle, really preparing the working-class masses for victorious participation in such "arguments." The experience of alliances, agreements and blues with the social-reform liberals in the West and with the liberal reformists (Cadets) in the Russian revolution, has convincingly shown that these agreements only blunt the consciousness of the masses, that they do not enhance but weaken the actual significance of their struggle, by linking fighters with elements who are least capable of fighting and most vacillating and treacherous. Millerandism in France—the biggest experiment in applying revisionist political tactics on a wide, a really national scale—has provided a practical appraisal of revisionism that will never be forgotten by the proletariat all over the world.

A natural complement to the economic and political tendencies of revisionism was its attitude to the ultimate aim of the socialist movement. "The movement is everything, the ultimate aim is nothing"—this catch-phrase of Bernstein's expresses the substance of revisionism better than many long disquisitions. To determine its conduct from case to case, to adapt itself to the events of the day and to the chopping and changing of petty politics, to forget the primary interests of the proletariat and the basic features of the whole capitalist system, of all capitalist evolution, to sacrifice these primary interests for the real or assumed advantages of the moment—such is the policy of revisionism. And it patently follows from the very nature of this policy that it may assume an infinite variety of forms, and that every more or less "new" question, every more or less unexpected and unforeseen turn of events, even though it changes the basic line of development only to an insignificant degree and only for the briefest period, will always inevitably give rise to one variety of revisionism or another.

The inevitably of revisionism is determined by its class roots in modern society. Revisionism is an international phenomenon. No thinking socialist who is in the least informed can have the slightest doubt that the relation between the orthodox and the Bernsteinians in Germany [and elsewhere] is similar. . . .

Wherein lies its inevitability in capitalist society? Why is it more profound than the differences of national peculiarities and of degrees of capitalist development? Because in every capitalist country, side by side with the proletariat, there are always broad strata of the petty bourgeoisie, small proprietors. Capitalism arose and is constantly arising out of small production. A number of new "middle strata" are inevitably brought into existence again and again by capitalism (appendages to the factory, work at home, small workshops scattered all over the country to meet the requirements of big industries, such as the bicycle and automobile industries, etc.). These new small producers are just as inevitably being cast again into the ranks of the proletariat. It is quite natural that the petty-bourgeois world outlook should again and again crop up in the ranks of the broad workers' parties. It is quite natural that this should be so and always will be so, right up to the changes of fortune that will take place in the proletarian revolution. For it would be a profound mistake to think that the "complete" proletarianisation of the majority of the population is essential for bringing about such a revolution. What we now frequently experience only in the domain of ideology, namely, disputes over theoretical amendments to Marx; what now crops up in practice only over individual partial issues of the labour movement, as tactical differences with the revisionists and splits on this basis—is bound to be experienced by the working class on an incomparably larger scale when the proletarian revolution will sharpen all disputed issues, will focus all differences on points which are of the most immediate importance in determining the conduct of the masses, and will make it necessary in the heat of the fight to distinguish enemies from friends, and to cast out bad allies in order to deal decisive blows at the enemy.

The ideological struggle waged by revolutionary Marxism against revisionism at the end of the nineteenth century is but the prelude to the great revolutionary battles of the proletariat, which is marching forward to the complete victory of its cause despite all the waverings and weaknesses of the petty bourgeoisie.

. . .

IMPERIALISM: THE HIGHEST STAGE OF CAPITALISM

. . . [W]hen nine-tenths of Africa had been seized (by 1900), when the whole world had been divided up, there was inevitably ushered in the era of monopoly possession of colonies and, consequently, of particularly intense struggle for the division and the redivision of the world.

The extent to which monopolist capital has intensified all the contradictions of capitalism is generally known. It is sufficient to mention the high cost of living and the tyranny of the cartels. This intensification of contradictions constitutes the most powerful driving force of the transitional period of history, which began from the time of the final victory of world finance capital.

Monopolies, oligarchy, the striving for domination and not for freedom, the exploitation of an increasing number of small or weak nations by a handful of the richest or most powerful nations—all these have given birth to those distinctive characteristics of imperialism which compel us to define it as parasitic or decaying capitalism. More and more prominently there emerges, as one of the tendencies of imperialism, the creation of the "rentier state," the usurer state, in which the bourgeoisie to an ever-increasing degree lives on the proceeds of capital exports and by "clipping coupons." It would be a mistake to believe that this tendency to decay precludes the rapid growth of capitalism. It does not. In the epoch of imperialism, certain branches of industry, certain strata of the bourgeoisie and certain countries betray, to a greater or lesser degree, now one and now another of these tendencies. One the whole, capitalism is growing far more rapidly than before; but this growth is not only becoming more and more uneven in general, its unevenness also manifests itself, in particular, in the decay of the countries which are richest in capital (Britain).

In regard to the rapidity of Germany's economic development, Riesser, the author of the book of the big German banks, states: "The progress of the preceding period (1848–1870), which had not been exactly slow, compares with the rapidity with which the whole of Germany's national economy, and with it German banking, progressed during this period (1870–1905) in about the same way as the speed of the mail coach in the good old days compares with the speed of the present-day automobile . . . which is whizzing past so fast that it endangers not only innocent pedestrians in its path, but also the occupants of the car." In its turn, this finance capital which has grown with such extraordinary rapidity is not unwilling, precisely because it has grown so quickly, to pass on to a more "tranquil" possession of colonies which have to be seized—and not only by peaceful methods—from richer nations. In the United States, economic development in the last decades has been even more rapid than in Germany, *and for this very reason*, the parasitic features of modern American capitalism have stood out with particular prominence. On the other hand, a comparison of, say, the republican American bourgeoisie with the monarchist Japanese or German bourgeoisie shows that the most pronounced political distinction diminishes to an extreme degree in the epoch of imperialism—not because it is unimportant in general, but because in all these cases we are talking about a bourgeoisie which has definite features of parasitism.

The receipt of high monopoly profits by the capitalists in one of the numerous branches of industry, in one of the numerous countries, etc., makes it economically possible for them to bribe certain sections of the workers, and for a time a fairly considerable minority of them, and win them to the side of the bourgeoisie of a given industry or given nation against all the others. The intensification of antagonisms between imperialist nations for the division of the world increases this urge. And so there is created that bond between imperialism and opportunism, which revealed itself first and most clearly in Great Britain, owing to the fact that certain features of imperialist development were observable there much earlier than in other countries. Some writers, L. Martov, for example, are prone to wave aside the connection between imperialism and opportunism in the working-class movement—a particularly glaring fact at the present time—by resorting to "official optimism" (*à la* Kautsky and Huysmans) like the following: the cause of the opponents of capitalism would be hopeless if it were progressive capitalism that led to the increase of opportunism, or, if it were the best-paid workers who were inclined towards opportunism, etc. We must have no illusions about "optimism" of this kind. It is optimism in respect of opportunism; it is optimism which serves to conceal opportunism. As a matter of fact the extraordinary rapidity and the particularly revolting character of the development of opportunism is by no means a guarantee that its victory will be durable: the rapid growth of a painful abcess on a healthy body can only cause it to burst more quickly and thus relieve the body of it. The most dangerous of all in this respect are those who do not wish to understand that the fight against imperialism is a sham and humbug unless it is inseparably bound up with the fight against opportunism.

From all that has been said in this book on the economic essence of imperialism, it follows that we must define it as capitalism in transition, or, more precisely, as moribund capitalism. It is very instructive in this respect to note that bourgeois economists, in describing modern capitalism, frequently employ catchwords and phrases like "interlocking," "absence of isolation," etc.; "in conformity with their functions and course of development," banks are "not purely private business enterprises; they are more and more outgrowing the sphere of purely private business regulation." And this very Riesser, whose words I have just quoted, declares with all seriousness that the "prophecy" of the Marxists concerning "socialisation" has "not come true"!

What then does this catchword "interlocking" express? It merely expresses the most striking feature of the process going on before our eyes. It shows that the observer counts the separate trees, but cannot see the woods. It slavishly copies the superficial, the fortuitous, the chaotic. It reveals the observer as one who is overwhelmed by the mass of raw material and is utterly incapable of appreciating its meaning and importance. Ownership of shares, the relations between owners of private property "interlock in a haphazard way." But underlying this interlocking, its very base, are the changing social relations of production. When a big enterprise assumes gigantic proportions, and, on the basis of an exact computation of mass data, organises according to plan the supply of primary raw materials to the extent of two-thirds, or three-fourths, of all that is necessary for tens of millions of people; when the raw materials are transported in a systematic and organised manner to the most suitable places of production, sometimes situated hundreds or thousands of miles from each other; when a single centre directs all the consecutive stages of processing the material right up to the manufacture of numerous varieties of finished articles; when these products are distributed according to a single plan among tens and hundreds of millions of consumers (the marketing of oil in America and Germany by the American oil trust)—then it becomes evident that we have socialisation of production, and not mere "interlocking"; that private economic and private property relations constitute a shell which no longer fits its contents, a shell which must inevitably decay if its removal is artifically delayed, a shell which may remain in a state of decay for a fairly long period (if, at the worst, the cure of the opportunist abscess is protracted), but which will inevitably be removed. . . .

STATE AND REVOLUTION

In the usual arguments about the state, the mistake is constantly made against which Engels warned and which we have in passing indicated above, namely, it is constantly forgotten that the abolition of the state means also the abolition of democracy: that the withering away of the state means the withering away of democracy.

At first sight this assertion seems exceedingly strange and incomprehensible; indeed, someone may even suspect us of expecting the advent of a system of society in which the principle of subordination of the minority of the majority will not be observed—for democracy means the recognition of this very principle.

No, democracy is *not* identical with the subordination of the minority to the majority. Democracy is a *state* which recognises the subordination of the minority to the majority, i.e., an organisation for the systematic use of *force* by one class against another, by one section of the population against another.

We set ourselves the ultimate aim of abolishing the state, i.e., all organised and systematic violence, all use of violence against people in general. We do not expect the advent of a system of society in which the principle of subordination of the minority is the majority will not be observed. In striving for socialism, however, we are convinced that it will develop into communism and, therefore, that the need for violence against people in general, for the *subordination* of one man to another, and of one section of the population to another, will vanish altogether since people will *become accustomed* to observing the elementary conditions of social life *without violence* and *without subordination*.

In order to emphasise this element of habit, Engels speaks of a new *generation*, "reared in new, free social conditions," which will "be able to discard the entire lumber of the state"—of any state, including the democratic-republican state.

In order to explain this, it is necessary to analyse the economic basis of the withering away of the state.

Marx explains this question most thoroughly in his *Critique of the Gotha Programme*. . . . The polemical part of this remarkable work, which contains a criticism of Lassalleanism, has, so to speak, overshadowed its positive part, namely, the analysis of the connection between the development of communism and the withering away of the state.

1 Presentation of the Question by Marx

From a superficial comparison of Marx's letter to Bracke of May 5, 1875, with Engels's letter of Bebel of March 28, 1875, which we examined above, it might appear that Marx was much more of a "champion of the state" than Engels, and that the difference of opinion between the two writers on the question of the state was very considerable.

Engels suggested to Bebel that all chatter about the state be dropped altogether, that the word "state" be eliminated from the programme altogether and the word "community" substituted for it. Engels even declared that the Commune was no longer a state in the proper sense of the word. Yet Marx even spoke of the "future state in comunist society," i.e., he would seem to recognise the need for the state even under communism.

But such a view would be fundamentally wrong. A closer examination shows that Marx's and Engels's views on the state and its withering away were completely identical, and that Marx's expression quoted above refers to the state in the process of *withering away*.

Clearly there can be no question of specifying the moment of the *future* "withering away," the more so since it will obviously be a lengthy process. The apparent difference between Marx and Engels is due to the fact that they dealt with different subjects and pursued different aims. Engels set out to show Bebel graphically, sharply and in broad outline the utter absurdity of the current prejudices concerning the state (shared to no small degree by Lassalle). Marx only touched upon *this* question is passing, being interested in another subject, namely, the *development* of communist society.

The whole theory of Marx is the application of the theory of development—in its most consistent, complete, considered and pithy form—to modern capitalism. Naturally, Marx was faced with the problem of applying this theory both to the *forthcoming* collapse of capitalism and to the *future* development of *future* communism.

On the basis of what *facts*, then, can the question of the future development of future communism be dealt with?

On the basis of the fact that it *has its origin* in capitalism, that it develops historically from capitalism, that it is the result of the action of a social force to which capitalism *gave birth*. There is no trace of an attempt on Marx's part to make up a utopia, to indulge in idle guesswork about what cannot be known. Marx treated the question of communism in the same way as a naturalist would treat the question of the development of, say, a new biological variety, once he knew that it had originated in such and such a way and was changing in such and such a definite direction.

To begin with, Marx brushed aside the confusion the Gotha Programme brought into the question of the relationship between state and society. He wrote:

> . . . "Present-day society" is capitalist society, which exists in all civilised countries, being more or less free from medieval admixture, more or less modified by the particular historical development of each country, more or less developed. On the other hand, the 'present-day state' changes with a country's frontier. It is different in the Prusso-German Empire from what it is in Switzerland, and different in England from what it is in the United States. '*The* present-day state' is, therefore, a fiction.
>
> Nevertheless, the different states of the different civilised countries, in spite of their motley diversity of form, all have this in common, that they are based on modern bourgeois society, only one more or less capitalistically developed. They have, therefore, also certain essential characteristics in common. In this sense it is possible to speak of the "present-day state," in contrast with the future, in which its present root, bourgeois society, will have died off.
>
> The question then arises: what transformation will the state undergo in communist society? In other words, what social functions will remain in existence there that are analogous to present state functions? This question can only be answered scientifically, and one does not get a flea-hop nearer to the problem by a thousandfold combination of the word people with the word state.

After thus ridiculing all talk about a "people's state," Marx formulated the question and gave warning, as it were, that those seeking a scientific answer to it should use only firmly-established scientific data.

The first fact that has been established most accurately by the whole theory of development, by science as a whole—a fact that was ignored by the utopians, and is ignored by the present-day opportunists, who are afraid of the socialist revolution—is that, historically, there must undoubtedly be a special stage, or a special phase, of *transition* from capitalism to communism.

2 The Transition From Capitalism to Communism

Marx continued:

> . . . Between capitalist and communist society lies the period of the revolutionary transformation of the one into the other. Corresponding to this is also a political transition period in which the state can be nothing but the *revolutionary dictatorship of the proletariat*.

Marx bases this conclusion on an analysis of the role played by the proletariat in modern capitalist society, on the data concerning the development of this society, and on the irreconcilability of the antagonistic interests of the proletariat and the bourgeoisie.

Previously the question was put as follows: to achieve its emancipation, the proletariat must overthrow the bourgeoisie, win political power and establish its revolutionary dictatorship.

Now the question is put somewhat differently: the transition from capitalist society—which is developing towards communism—to communist society is impossible without a "political transition period," and the state in this period can only be the revolutionary dictatorship of the proletariat.

What, then, is the relation of this dictatorship to democracy?

We have seen that the *Communist Manifesto* simply places side by side the two concepts: "to raise the proletariat to the position of the ruling class" and "to win the battle of democracy." On the basis of all that has been said above, it is possible to determine more precisely how democracy changes in the transition from capitalism to communism.

In capitalist society, providing it develops under the most favourable conditions, we have a more or less complete democracy in the democratic republic. But this democracy is always hemmed in by the narrow limits set by capitalist exploitation, and consequently always remains, in effect, a democracy for the minority, only for the propertied classes, only for the rich. Freedom in capitalist society always remains about the same as it was in the ancient Greek republics: freedom for the slave-owners. Owing to the conditions of capitalist exploitation, the modern wage slaves are so crushed by want and poverty that "they cannot be bothered with democracy," "cannot be bothered with politics"; in the ordinary, peaceful course of events, the majority of the population is debarred from participation in public and political life.

The correctness of this statement is perhaps most clearly confirmed by Germany, because constitutional legality steadily endured there for a remarkably long time—nearly half a century (1871–1914)—and during this period the Social-Democrats were able to achieve far more than in other countires in the way of "utilising legality," and organised a larger proportion of the workers into a political party than anywhere else in the world.

What is this largest proportion of politically conscious and active wage slaves that has so far been recorded in capitalist society? One million members of the Social-Democratic Party—out of fifteen million wage-workers! Three million organised in trade unions—out of fifteen million!

Democracy for an insignificant minority, democracy for the rich—that is the democracy of capitalist society. If we look more closely into the machinery of capitalist democracy, we see everywhere, in the "petty"—supposedly petty—details of the suffrage (residential qualification, exclusion of women, etc.), in the technique of the representative institutions, in the actual obstacles to the right of assembly (public buildings are not for "paupers"!), in the purely capitalist organisation of the daily press, etc., etc.—we see restriction after restriction upon democracy. These restrictions, exceptions, exclusions, obstacles for the poor seem slight, especially in the eyes of one who has never known want himself and has never been in close contact with the oppressed classes in their mass life (and nine out of ten, if not ninety-nine out of a hundred, bourgeois publicists and politicians come under this category); but in their sum total these restrictions exclude and squeeze out the poor from politics, from active participation in democracy.

Marx grasped this *essence* of capitalist democracy splendidly when, in analysing the experience of the Commune, he said that the oppressed are allowed once every few years to decide which particular representatives of the oppressing class shall represent and repress them in parliament!

But from this capitalist democracy—that is inevitably narrow and stealthily pushes aside the poor, and is therefore hypocritical and false through and through—forward development does not proceed simply, directly and smoothly, towards "greater and greater democracy," as the liberal professors and petty-bourgeois opportunists would have us believe. No, forward development, i.e., development towards communism, proceeds through the dictatorship of the proletariat, and cannot do otherwise, for the *resistance* of the capitalist exploiters cannot be *broken* by anyone else or in any other way.

And the dictatorship of the proletariat, i.e., the organisation of the vanguard of the oppressed as the ruling class for the purpose of suppressing the oppressors, cannot result merely in an expansion of democracy. *Simultaneously* with an immense expansion of democracy, which *for the first time* becomes democracy for the poor, democracy for the people, and not democracy for the money-bags, the dictatorship of the proletariat imposes a series of restrictions on the freedom of the oppressors, the exploiters, the capitalists. We must suppress them in order to free humanity from wage slavery, their resistance must be crushed by force; it is clear that there is no freedom and no democracy where there is suppression and where there is violence.

Engels expressed this splendidly in his letter to Bebel when he said, as the reader will remember, that "the proletariat needs the state, not in the interests of freedom but in order to hold down its adversaries, and as soon as it becomes possible to speak of freedom the state as such ceases to exist."

Democracy for the vast majority of the people, and suppression by force, i.e., exclusion from democracy, of the exploiters and oppressors of the people—this is the change democracy undergoes during the *transition* from capitalism to communism.

Only in communist society, when the resistance of the capitalists has been completely crushed, when the capitalists have disappeared when there are no classes (i.e., when there is no distinction between the members of society as regards their relation to the social means of production), *only* then "the state . . . ceases to exist," and "*it becomes possible to speak of freedom.*" Only then will a truly complete democracy become possible and be realised, a democracy without any exceptions whatever. And only then will democracy begin to *wither away*, owing to the simple fact that, freed from capitalist slavery, from the untold horrors, savagery, absurdities and infamies of capitalist exploitation, people will gradually *become accustomed* to observing the elementary rules of social intercourse that have been known for centuries and repeated for thousands of years in all copy-book maxims. They will become accustomed to observing them without force, without coercion, without subordination, *without the special apparatus* for coercion called the state.

The expression "the state *withers away*" is very well chosen, for it indicates both the gradual and the spontaneous nature of the process. Only habit can, and undoubtedly will, have such an effect; for we see around us on millions of occasions how readily people become accustomed to observing the necessary rules of social intercourse when there is no exploitation, when there is nothing that arouses indignation, evokes protest and revolt, and creates the need for *suppression*.

And so in capitalist society we have a democracy that is curtailed, wretched, false, a democracy only for the rich, for the minority. The dictatorship of the proletariat, the period of transition to communism, will for the first time create democracy for the people, for the majority, along with the necessary suppression of the exploiters, of the minority. Communism alone is capable of providing really complete democracy, and the more complete it is, the sooner it will become unnecessary and wither away of its own accord.

In other words, under capitalism we have the state in the proper sense of the word, that is, a special machine for the suppression of one class by another, and, what is more, of the majority by the minority. Naturally, to be successful, such an undertaking as the systematic suppression of the exploited majority by the exploiting minority calls for the utmost ferocity and savagery in the matter of suppressing, it calls for seas of blood, through which mankind is actually wading its way in slavery, serfdom and wage labour.

Furthermore, during the *transition* from capitalism to communism suppression is *still* necessary, but it is now the suppression of the exploiting minority by the exploited majority. A special apparatus, a special machine for suppression, the "state," is *still* necessary, but this is now a transitional state. It is no longer a state in the proper sense of the word; for the suppression of the minority of exploiters by the majority of the wage slaves of *yesterday* is comparatively so easy, simple and natural a task that it will entail far less bloodshed than the suppression of the risings of slaves, serfs or wage-labourers, and it will cost mankind far less. And it is compatible with the extension of democracy to such an overwhelming majority of the population that the need for a *special machine* of suppression will begin to disappear. Naturally, the exploiters are unable to suppress the people without a highly complex machine for performing this task, but *the people* can suppress the exploiters even with a very simple "machine," almost without a "machine," without a special apparatus, by the simple *organisation of the armed people* (such as the Soviets of Workers' and Soldiers' Deputies, we would remark, running ahead).

Lastly, only communism makes the state absolutely unnecessary, for there is *nobody* to be suppressed—"nobody" in the sense of a *class*, of a systematic struggle against a definite section of the population. We are not utopians, and do not in the least deny the possibility and inevitability of excesses on the part of *individual persons*, or the need to stop *such* excesses. In the first place, however, no special machine, no special apparatus of suppression, is needed for this; this will be done by the armed people themselves, as simply and as readily as any crowd of civilised people, even in modern society, interferes to put a stop to a scuffle or to prevent a woman from being assaulted. And, secondly, we know that the fundamental social cause of excesses, which consist in the violation of the rules of social intercourse, is the exploitation of the people, their want and their poverty. With the removal of this chief cause, excesses will inevitably begin to "*wither away.*" We do not know how quickly and in what succession, but we do know they will wither away. With their withering away the state will also *wither away*.

Without building utopias, Marx defined more fully what can be defined *now* regarding this future, namely, the difference between the lower and higher phases (levels, stages) of communist society.

3 The First Phase of Communist Society

In the *Critique of the Gotha Programme*, Marx goes into detail to disprove Lassalle's idea that under socialism the worker will receive the "undiminished" or "full product of his labour." Marx shows that from the whole of the social labour of society there must be deducted a reserve fund, a fund for the expansion of production, a fund for the replacement of the "wear and tear" of machinery, and so on. Then, from the means of consumption must be deducted a fund for administrative expenses, for schools, hospitals, old people's homes, and so on.

Instead of Lassalle's hazy, obscure, general phrase ("the full product of his labour to the worker"), Marx makes a sober estimate of exactly how socialist society will have to manage its affairs. Marx proceeds to make a *concrete* analysis of the conditions of life of a society in which there will be no capitalism, and says:

> What we have to deal with here [in analysing the programme of the workers' party] is a communist society, not as it has *developed* on its own foundations, but, on the contrary, just as it *emerges* from capitalist society; which is, therefore, in every respect, economically, morally and intellectually, still stamped with the birthmarks of the old society from whose womb it comes.

It is this communist society, which has just emerged into the light of day out of the womb of capitalism and which is in every respect stamped with the birthmarks of the old society, that Marx terms the "first," or lower, phrase of communist society.

The means of production are no longer the private property of individuals. The means of production belong to the whole of society. Every member of society, performing a certain part of the socially necessary work, receives a certificate from society to the effect that he has done a certain amount of work. And with this certificate he receives from the public store of consumer goods a corresponding quantity of products. After a deduction is made of the amount of labour which goes to the public fund, every worker, therefore, receives from society as much as he has given to it.

"Equality" apparently reigns supreme.

But when Lassalle, having in view such a social order (usually called socialism, but termed by Marx the first phase of communism), says that this is "equitable distribution," that this is "the equal right of all to an equal product of labour," Lassalle is mistaken and Marx exposes the mistake.

"Equal right," says Marx, we certainly do have here; but it is *still* a "bourgeois right," which, like every right, *implies inequality*. Every right is an application of an *equal* measure of *different* people who in fact are not alike, are not equal to one another. That is why "equal right" is a violation of equality and an injustice. In fact, everyone, having performed as much social labour as another, receives an equal share of the social product (after the above-mentioned deductions).

But people are not alike: one is strong, another is weak; one is married, another is not; one has more children, another has less, and so on. And the conclusion Marx draws is:

> . . . With an equal performance of labour, and hence an equal share in the social consumption fund, one will in fact receive more than another, one will be richer than another, and so on. To avoid all these defects, right would have to be unequal rather than equal.

The first phase of communism, therefore, cannot yet provide justice and equality: differences, and unjust differences, in wealth will still persist, but the *exploitation* of man by man will have become impossible because it will be impossible to seize the *means of production*—the factories, machines, land, etc.—and make them private property. In smashing Lassalle's petty-bourgeois, vague phrases about "equality" and "justice" *in general*, Marx shows the *course of development* of communist society, which is *compelled* to abolish at first *only* the "injustice" of the means of production seized by individuals, and which is *unable* at once to eliminate the other injustice, which consists in the distribution of consumer goods "according to the amount of labour performed" (and not according to needs).

The vulgar economists, including the bourgeois professors and "our" Tugan, constantly reproach the socialists with forgetting the inequality of people and with "dreaming" of eliminating this inequality. Such a reproach, as we see, only proves the extreme ignorance of the bourgeois ideologists.

Marx not only most scrupulously takes account of the inevitable inequality of men, but he also takes into account the fact that the mere conversion of the means of production into the common property of the whole of society (commonly called "socialism") *does not remove* the defects of distribution and the inequality of "bourgeois right," which *continues to prevail* so long as products are divided "according to the amount of labour performed." Continuing, Marx says:

> . . . But these defects are inevitable in the first phase of communist society as it is when it has just emerged, after prolonged birth pangs, from capitalist society. Right can never be higher than the economic structure of society and its cultural development conditioned thereby.

And so, in the first phase of communist society (usually called socialism) "bourgeois right" is *not* abolished in its entirety, but only in part, only in proportion to the economic revolution so far attained, i.e., only in respect of the means of production. "Bourgeois right" recognises them as the private property of individuals. Socialism converts them into *common* property. *To that extent*—and to that extent alone—"bourgeois right" disappears.

However, it persists as far as its other part is concerned; it persists in the capacity of regulator (determining factor) in the distribution of products and the allotment of labour among the members of society. The socialist principle, "He who does not work shall not eat," is *already* realised; the other socialist principle, "An equal amount of products for an equal amount of labour," is also *already* realised. But this is not yet communism, and it does not yet abolish "bourgeois right," which gives unequal individuals, in return for unequal (really unequal) amounts of labour, equal amounts of products.

This is a "defect," says Marx, but it is unavoidable in the first phase of communism; for if we are not to indulge in utopianism, we must not think that having overthrown capitalism people will at once learn to work for society *without any standard of right*. Besides, the abolition of capitalism *does not immediately create* the economic prerequisites for *such a* change.

Now, there is no other standard than that of "bourgeois right." To this extent, therefore, there still remains the need for a state, which, while safeguarding the common ownership of the means of production, would safeguard equality in labour and in the distribution of products.

The state withers away insofar as there are no longer any capitalists, any classes, and, consequently, no *class* can be *suppressed*.

But the state has not yet completely withered away, since there still remains the safeguarding of "bourgeois right," which sanctifies actual inequality. For the state to wither away completely, complete communism is necessary.

4 The Higher Phase of Communist Society

Marx continues:

> . . . In a higher phase of communist society, after the enslaving subordination of the individual to the division of labour and with it also the antithesis between mental and physical labour has vanished, after labour has become not only a livelihood but life's prime want, after the productive forces have increased with the all-round development of the individual, and all the springs of co-operative wealth flow more abundantly—only then can the narrow horizon of bourgeois right be crossed in its entirely and society inscribe on its banner: From each according to his ability, to each according to his needs!

Only now can we fully appreciate the correctness of Engels's remarks mercilessly ridiculing the absurdity of combining the words "freedom" and "state." So long as the state exists there is no freedom. When there is freedom, there will be no state.

The economic basis for the complete withering away of the state is such a high stage of development of communism at which the antithesis between mental and physical labour disappears, at which there consequently disappears one of the principal sources of modern *social* inequality—a source, moreover, which cannot on any account be removed immediately by the mere conversion of the means of production into public property, by the mere expropriation of the capitalists.

This expropriation will make it *possible* for the productive forces to develop to a tremendous extent. And when we see how incredibly capitalism is already *retarding* this development, when we see how much progress could be achieved on the basis of the level of technique already attained, we are entitled to say with the fullest confidence that the expropriation of the capitalists will inevitably result in an enormous development of the productive forces of human society. But how rapidly this development will proceed, how soon it will reach the point of breaking away from the division of labour, of doing away with the antithesis between mental and physical labour, of transforming labour into "life's prime want"—we do not and *cannot* know.

That is why we are entitled to speak only of the inevitable withering away of the state, emphasising the protracted nature of this process and its dependence upon the rapidity of development of the *higher phase* of communism, and leaving the question of the time required for, or the concrete forms of, the withering away quite open, because there is *no* material for answering these questions.

The state will be able to wither away completely when society adopts the rule: "From each according to his ability, to each according to his needs", i.e., when people have become so accustomed to observing the fundamental rules of social intercourse and when their labour has become so productive that they will voluntarily work *according to their ability.* "The narrow horizon of bourgeois right," which compels one to calculate with the heartlessness of a Shylock whether one has not worked half an hour more than somebody else, whether one is not getting less pay than somebody else—this narrow horizon will then be crossed. There will then be no need for society, in distributing products, to regulate the quantity to be received by each; each will take freely "according to his needs."

From the bourgeois point of view, it is easy to declare that such a social order is "sheer utopia" and to sneer at the socialists for promising everyone the right to receive from society, without any control over the labour of the individual citizen, any quantity of truffles, cars, pianos, etc. Even to this day, most bourgeois "savants" confine themselves to sneering in this way, thereby betraying both their ignorance and their selfish defence of capitalism.

Ignorance—for it has never entered the head of any socialist to "promise" that the higher phase of the development of communism will arrive; as for the great socialists' *forecast* that it will arrive, it presupposes not the present productivity of labour and *not the present* ordinary run of people, who, like the seminary students in Pomyalovsky's stories, are capable of damaging the stocks of public wealth "just for fun," and of demanding the impossible. Until the "higher" phase of communism arrives, the socialists demand the *strictest* control by society *and by the state* over the measure of labour and the measure of consumption; but this control must *start* with the expropriation of the capitalists, with the establishment of workers' control over the capitalists, and must be exercised not by a state of bureaucrats, but by a state of *armed workers.*

The selfish defence of capitalism by the bourgeois ideologists . . . consists in that they *substitute* arguing and talk about the distant future for the vital and burning question of *present-day* politics, namely, the expropriation of the capitalists, the conversion of *all* citizens into workers and other employees of *one* huge "syndicate"—the whole state—and the complete subordination of the entire work of this syndicate to a genuinely democratic state, the *state of the Soviets of Workers' and Soldiers' Deputies.*

In fact, when a learned professor . . . talks of wild utopias, of the demagogic promises of the Bolsheviks, of the impossibility of "introducing" socialism, it is the higher state, or phase, of communism he has in mind, which no one has ever promised or even thought to "introduce," because, generally speaking, it cannot be "introduced."

And this brings us to the question of the scientific distinction between socialism and communism which Engels touched on in his above-quoted argument about the incorrectness of the name "Social-Democrat." Politically, the distinction between the first, or lower, and the higher phase of communism will in time, probably, be tremendous. But it would be ridiculous to recognise this distinction now, under capitalism, and only individual anarchists, perhaps, could invest it with primary importance (if there still are people among the anarchists who have learned nothing from the "Plekhanov" conversion of the Kropotkins, of Grave, Cornelissen and other stars' of anarchism into social-chauvinists or "anarchotrenchists," as Ghe, one of the few anarchists who have still preserved a sense of honour and a conscience, has put it).

But the scientific distinction between socialism and communism is clear. What is usually called socialism was termed by Marx the "first," or lower, phase of communist society. Insofar as the means of production become *common* property, the word "communism" is also applicable here, providing we do not forget that this is *not* complete communism. The great significance of Marx's explanations is that here, too, he consistenly applies materialist dialectics, the theory of development, and regards communism as something which develops *out of* capitalism. Instead of scholastically invented, "concocted" definitions and fruitless disputes over words (What is socialism? What is communism?), Marx gives an analysis of what might be called the stages of the economic maturity of communism.

In its first phase, or first stage, communism *cannot* as yet be fully mature economically and entirely free from traditions or vestiges of capitalism. Hence the interesting phenomenon that communism in its first phase retains "the narrow horizon of *bourgeois* right." Of course, bourgeois right in regard to the distribution of *consumer* goods inevitably presupposes the existence of the *bourgeois state,* for right is nothing without an apparatus capable of *enforcing* the observance of the standards of right.

It follows that under communism there remains for a time not only bourgeois right, but even the bourgeois state, without the bourgeoisie!

This may sound like a paradox or simply a dialectical conundrum, of which Marxism is often accused by people who have not taken the slightest trouble to study its extraordinary profound content.

But in fact, remnants of the old, surviving in the new, confront us in life at every step, both in nature and in society. And Marx did not arbitrarily insert a scrap of "bourgeois" right into communism, but indicated what is economically and politically inevitable in a society emerging *out of the womb* of capitalism.

Democracy is of enormous importance to the working class in its struggle against the capitalists for its emancipation. But democracy is by no means a boundary not to be overstepped; it is only one of the stages on the road from feudalism to capitalism, and from capitalism to communism.

Democracy means equality. The great significance of the proletariat's struggle for equality and of equality as a slogan will be clear if we correctly interpret it as meaning the abolition of *classes.* But democracy means only *formal* equality. And as soon as equality is achieved for all members of society in *relation* to ownership of the means of production, that is, equality of labour and wages, humanity will inevitably be confronted with the question of advancing farther, from formal equality to actual equality, i.e., to the operation of the rule "from each according to his ability, to each according to his needs." By what stages, by means of what practical measures humanity will proceed to this supreme aim we do not and cannot know. But it is important to realise how infinitely mendacious is the ordinary bourgeois conception of socialism as something lifeless, rigid, fixed once and for all, whereas in reality *only* socialism will be the beginning of a rapid, genuine, truly mass forward movement, embracing first the *majority* and then the whole of the population, in all spheres of public and private life.

Democracy is a form of the state, one of its varieties. Consequently, it, like every state, represents, on the one hand, the organised, systematic use of force against persons; but, on the other hand, it signifies the formal recognition of equality of citizens, the equal right of all to determine the structure of, and to administer, the state. This, in turn, results in the fact that, at a certain stage in the development of democracy, it first welds together the class that wages a revolutionary struggle against capitalism—the proletariat—and enables it to crush, smash to atoms, wipe off the face of the earth the bourgeois, even the republican-bourgeois, state machine, the standing army, the police and the bureaucracy and to substitute for them a *more* democratic state machine, but a state machine nevertheless, in the shape of armed workers who proceed to form a militia involving the entire population.

Here "quantity turns into quality": *such* a degree of democracy implies overstepping the boundaries of bourgeois society and beginning its socialist reorganisation. If really *all* take part in the administration of the state, capitalism cannot retain its hold. The development of capitalism, in turn, creates the *preconditions* that *enable* really "all" to take part in the administration of the state. Some of these preconditions are: universal literacy, which has already been achieved in a number of the most advanced capitalist countries, then the "training and disciplining" of millions of workers by the huge, complex, socialised apparatus of the postal service, railways, big factories, large-scale commerce, banking, etc., etc.

Given these *economic* preconditions, it is quite possible, after the overthrow of the capitalists and the bureaucrats, to proceed immediately, overnight, to replace them in the *control* over production and distribution, in the work of *keeping account* of labour and products, by the armed workers, by the whole of the armed population. (The question of control and accounting should not be confused with the question of the scientifically trained staff of engineers, agronomists and so on. These gentlemen are working today in obedience to the wishes of the capitalists, and will work even better tomorrow in obedience to the wishes of the armed workers.)

Accounting and control—that is *mainly* what is needed for the "smooth working," for the proper functioning, of the *first phase* of communist society. *All* citizens are transformed into hired employees of the state, which consists of the armed workers. *All* citizens become employees and workers of a *single* country-wide state "syndicate." All that is required is that they should work equally, do their proper share of work, and get equal pay. The accounting and control necessary for this have been *simplified* by capitalism to the utmost and reduced to the extraordinarily simple operations—which any literate person can perform—of supervising and recording, knowledge of the four rules of arithmetic, and issuing appropriate receipts.

When the *majority* of the people begin independently and everywhere to keep such accounts and exercise such control over the capitalists (now converted into employees) and over the intellectual gentry who preserve their capitalist habits, this control will really become universal, general and popular; and there will be no getting away from it, there will be "nowhere to go."

The whole of society will have become a single office and a single factory, with equality of labour and pay.

But this "factory" discipline, which the proletariat, after defeating the capitalists, after overthrowing the exploiters, will extend to the whole of society, is by no means our ideal, or our ultimate goal. It is only a necessary *step* for thoroughly cleaning society of all the infamies and abominations of capitalist exploitation, *and for further* progress.

From the moment all members of society, or at least the vast majority, have learned to administer the state *themselves*, have taken this work into their own hands, have organised control over the insignificant capitalist minority, over the gentry who wish to preserve their capitalist habits and over the workers who have been thoroughly corrupted by capitalism—from this moment the need for government of any kind begins to disappear altogether. The more complete the democracy, the nearer the moment when it becomes unnecessary. The more democratic the "state" which consists of the armed workers, and which is "no longer a state in the proper sense of the word," the more rapidly *every form* of state begins to wither away.

For when *all* have learned to administer and actually do independently administer social production, independently keep accounts and exercise control over the parasites, the sons of the wealthy, the swindlers and other "guardians of capitalist traditions," the escape from this popular accounting and control will inevitably become so incredibly difficult, such a rare exception, and will probably be accompanied by such swift and severe punishment (for the armed workers are practical men and not sentimental intellectuals, and they will scarcely allow anyone to trifle with them), that the *necessity* of observing the simple, fundamental rules of the community will very soon become a *habit*.

Then the door will be thrown wide open for the transition from the first phase of communist society to its higher phase, and with it to the complete withering away of the state.

35

ON THE PEOPLE'S DEMOCRATIC DICTATORSHIP

MAO ZEDONG

In the "liberation" of 1949 the Chinese Communist forces, led by Mao Zedong (1893–1976), routed the Nationalist forces of Chiang Kai-chek. Adapting Marxism-Leninism to Chinese conditions, Mao set even greater store by the peasantry than had Lenin. After the revolution the "people"—by which Mao meant the peasantry, under the guidance of the Chinese Communist party—were to rule. The "people's democratic dictatorship" meant rule not so much by as on behalf of the numerically largest class, namely, the peasantry. This interim "dictatorship" was to be a period of civic "education" for the peasantry. Once in power, however, Mao—like Stalin in the Soviet Union—made himself an object of veneration and worship.

Source: Mao Zedong, "On the People's Democratic Dictatorship," Selected Works *(Beijing: Foreign Languages Press, 1971), pp. 411–423.*

ON THE PEOPLE'S DEMOCRATIC DICTATORSHIP

IN COMMEMORATION OF THE TWENTY-EIGHTH ANNIVERSARY OF THE COMMUNIST PARTY OF CHINA

June 30, 1949 The first of July 1949 marks the fact that the Communist Part of China has already lived through twenty-eight years. Like a man, a political party has its childhood, youth, manhood and old age. The Communist Party of China is no longer a child or a lad in his teens but has become an adult. When a man reaches old age, he will die; the same is true of a party. When classes disappear, all instruments of class struggle—parties and the state machinery—will lose their function, cease to be necessary, therefore gradually wither away and end their historical mission; and human society will move to a higher stage. We are the opposite of the political parties of the bourgeoisie. They are afraid to speak of the extinction of classes, state power and parties. We, on the contrary, declare openly that we are striving hard to create the very conditions which will bring about their extinction. The leadership of the Communist Party and the state power of the people's dictatorship are such conditions. Anyone who does not recognize this truth is no communist. Young comrades who have not studied Marxism-Leninism and have only recently joined the Party may not yet understand this truth. They must understand it—only then can they have a correct world outlook. They must understand that the road to the abolition of classes, to the abolition of state power and to the abolition of parties is the road all mankind must take; it is only a question of time and conditions. Communists the world over are wiser than the bourgeoisie, they understand the laws governing the existence and development of things, they understand dialectics and they can see farther. The bourgeoisie does not welcome this truth because it does not want to be overthrown. To be overthrown is painful and is unbearable to contemplate for those overthrown, for example, for the Kuomintang reactionaries whom we are now overthrowing and for Japanese imperialism which we together with other peoples overthrew some time ago. But for the working class, the labouring people and the Communist Party the question is not one of being overthrown, but of working hard to create the conditions in which classes, state power and political parties will die out very naturally and mankind will enter the realm of Great Harmony.[1] We have mentioned in passing the long-range perspective of human progress in order to explain clearly the problems we are about to discuss.

As everyone knows, our Party passed through these twenty-eight years not in peace but amid hardships, for we had to fight enemies, both foreign and domestic, both inside and outside the Party. We thank Marx, Engels, Lenin and Stalin for giving us a weapon. This weapon is not a machine-gun, but Marxism-Leninism.

In his book *"Left-Wing" Communism, an Infantile Disorder* written in 1920, Lenin described the quest of the Russians for revolutionary theory.[2] Only after several decades of hardship and suffering did the Russians find Marxism. Many things in China were the same as, or similar to, those in Russia before the October Revolution. There was the same feudal oppression. There was similar economic and cultural backwardness. Both countries were backward, China even more so. In both countries alike, for the sake of national regeneration progressives braved hard and bitter struggles in their quest for revolutionary truth.

From the time of China's defeat in the Opium War of 1840,[3] Chinese progressives went through untold hardships in their quest for truth from the Western countries. Hung Hsiu-chuan,[4] Kang Yu-wei,[5] Yen Fu[6] and Sun Yat-sen were representative of those who had looked to the West for truth before the Communist Party of China was born. Chinese who then sought progress would read any book containing the new knowledge from the West. The number of students sent to Japan, Britain, the United

States, France and Germany was amazing. At home, the imperial examinations[7] were abolished and modern schools sprang up like bamboo shoots after a spring rain; every effort was made to learn from the West. In my youth, I too engaged in such studies. They represented the culture of Western bourgeois democracy, including the social theories and natural sciences of that period, and they were called "the new learning" in contrast to Chinese feudal culture, which was called "the old learning." For quite a long time, those who had acquired the new learning felt confident that it would save China, and very few of them had any doubts on this score, as the adherents of the old learning had. Only modernization could save China, only learning from foreign countries could modernize China. Among the foreign countries, only the Western capitalist countries were then progressive, as they had successfully built modern bourgeois states. The Japanese had been successful in learning from the West, and the Chinese also wished to learn from the Japanese. The Chinese in those days regarded Russia as backward, and few wanted to learn from her. That was how the Chinese tried to learn from foreign countries in the perild from the 1840s to the beginning of the 20th century.

Imperialist aggression shattered the fond dreams of the Chinese about learning from the West. It was very odd—why were the teachers always committing aggression against their pupil? The Chinese learned a good deal from the West, but they could not make it work and were never able to realize their ideals. Their repeated struggles, including such a country-wide movement as the Revolution of 1911,[8] all ended in failure. Day by day, conditions in the country got worse, and life was made impossible. Doubts arose, increased and deepened. World War I shook the whole globe. The Russians made the October Revolution and created the world's first socialist state. Under the leadership of Lenin and Stalin, the revolutionary energy of the great proletariat and labouring people of Russia, hitherto latent and unseen by foreigners, suddenly erupted like a volcano, and the Chinese and all mankind began to see the Russians in a new light. Then, and only then, did the Chinese enter an entirely new era in their thinking and their life. They found Marxism-Leninism, the universally applicable truth, and the face of China began to change.

It was through the Russians that the Chinese found Marxism. Before the October Revolution, the Chinese were not only ignorant of Lenin and Stalin, they did not even know of Marx and Engels. The salvoes of the October Revolution brought us Marxism-Leninism. The October Revolution helped progressives in China, as throughout the world, to adopt the proletarian world outlook as the instrument for studying a nation's destiny and considering anew their own problems. Follow the path of the Russians—that was their conclusion. In 1919, the May 4th Movement took place in China. In 1921, the Communist Party of China was founded. Sun Yat-sen, in the depths of despair, came across the October Revolution and the Communist Party of China. He welcomed the October Revolution, welcomed Russian help to the Chinese and welcomed co-operation of the Communist Party of China. Then Sun Yat-sen died and Chiang Kai-shek rose to power. Over a long period of twenty-two years, Chiang Kai-shek dragged China into ever more hopeless straits. In this period, during the anti-fascist Second World War in which the Soviet Union was the main force, three big imperialist powers were knocked out, while two others were weakened. In the whole world only one big imperialist power, the United States of America, remained uninjured. But the United States faced a grave domestic crisis. It wanted to enslave the whole world; it supplied arms to help Chiang Kai-shek slaughter several million Chinese. Under the leadership of the Communist Party of China, the Chinese people, after driving out Japanese imperialism, waged the People's War of Liberation for three years and have basically won victory.

Thus Western bourgeois civilization, bourgeois democracy and the plan for a bourgeois republic have all gone bankrupt in the eyes of the Chinese people. Bourgeois democracy has given way to people's democracy under the leadership of the working class and the bourgeois republic to the people's republic. This has made it possible to achieve socialism and communism through the people's republic, to abolish classes and enter a world of Great Harmony. Kang Yu-wei wrote *Ta Tung Shu*, or the *Book of Great Harmony*, but he did not and could not find the way to achieve Great Harmony. There are bourgeois republics in foreign lands, but China cannot have a bourgeois republic because she is a country suffering under imperialist oppression. The only way is through a people's republic led by the working class.

All other ways have been tried and failed. Of the people who hankered after those ways, some have fallen, some have awakened and some are changing their ideas. Events are developing so swiftly that many feel the abruptness of the change and the need to learn anew. This state of mind is understandable and we welcome this worthy desire to learn anew.

The vanguard of the Chinese proletariat learned Marxism-Leninism after the October Revolution and founded the Communist Party of China. It entered at once into political struggles and only now, after a tortuous course of twenty-eight years, has it won basic victory. From our twenty-eight years' experience we have drawn a conclusion similar to the one Sun Yat-sen drew in his testament from his "experience of forty years"; that is, we are deeply convinced that to win victory, "we must arouse the masses of the people and unite in a common struggle with those nations of the world which treat us as equals." Sun Yat-sen had a world outlook different from ours and started from a different class standpoint in studying and tackling problems; yet, in the 1920s he reached a conclusion basically the same as ours on the question of how to struggle against imperialism.

Twenty-four years have passed since Sun Yat-sen's death, and the Chinese revolution, led by the Communist Party of China, has made tremendous advances both in theory and practice and has radically changed the face of China. Up to now the principal and fundamental experience the Chinese people have gained is twofold:

1. Internally, arouse the masses of the people. That is, unite the working class, the peasantry, the urban petty bourgeoisie and the national bourgeoisie, form a domestic united front under the leadership of the working class, and advance from this to the establishment of a state which is a people's democratic dictatorship under the leadership of the working class and based on the alliance of workers and peasants.
2. Externally, unite in a common struggle with those nations of the world which treat us as equals and unite with the peoples of all countries. That is, ally ourselves with the Soviet Union, with the People's Democracies and with the proletariat and the broad masses of the people in all other countries, and form an international united front.

"You are leaning to one side." Exactly. The forty years' experience of Sun Yat-sen and the twenty-eight years' experience of the Communist Party have taught us to lean to one side, and we are firmly convinced that in order to win victory and consolidate it we must lean to one side. In the light of the experiences accumulated in these forty years and these twenty-eight years, all Chinese without exception must lean either to the side of imperialism or to the side of socialism. Sitting on the fence will not do, nor is there a third road. We oppose the Chiang Kai-shek reactionaries who lean to the side of imperialism, and we also oppose the illusions about a third road.

"You are too irritating." We are talking about how to deal with domestic and foreign reactionaries, the imperialists and their running dogs, not about how to deal with anyone else. With regard to such reactionaries, the question of irritating them or not does not arise. Irritated or not irritated, they will remain the same because they are reactionaries. Only if we draw a clear line between reactionaries and revolutionaries, expose the intrigues and plots of the reactionaries, arouse the vigilance and attention of the revolutionary ranks, heighten our will to fight and crush the enemy's arrogance can we isolate the reactionaries, vanquish them or supersede them. We must not show the slightest timidity before a wild beast. We must learn from Wu Sung[9] on the Chingyang Ridge. As Wu Sung saw it, the tiger on Chingyang Ridge was a man-eater, whether irritated or not. Either kill the tiger or be eaten by him—one or the other.

"We want to do business." Quite right, business will be done. We are against no one except the domestic and foreign reactionaries who hinder us from doing business. Everybody should know that it is none other than the imperialists and their running dogs, the Chiang Kai-shek reactionaries, who hinder us from doing business and also from establishing diplomatic relations with foreign countries. When we have beaten the internal and external reactionaries by uniting all domestic and international forces, we shall be able to do business and establish diplomatic relations with all foreign countries on the basis of equality, mutual benefit and mutual respect for territorial integrity and sovereignty.

"Victory is possible even without international help." This is a mistaken idea. In the epoch in which imperialism exists, it is impossible for a genuine people's revolution to win victory in any country without various forms of help from the international revolutionary forces, and even if victory were won, it could not be consolidated. This was the case with the victory and consolidation of the great October Revolution, as Lenin and Stalin told us long ago. This was also the case with the overthrow of the three imperialist powers in World War II and the establishment of the People's Democracies. And this is also the case with the present and the future of People's China. Just imagine! If the Soviet Union had not existed, if there had been no victory in the anti-fascist Second World War, if Japanese imperialism had not been defeated, if the People's Democracies had not come into being, if the oppressed nations of the East were not rising in struggle and if there were no struggle of the masses of the people against their reactionary rulers in the United States, Britain, France, Germany, Italy, Japan and other capitalist countries—if not for all these in combination, the international reactionary forces bearing down upon us would certainly be many times greater than now. In such circumstances, could we have won victory? Obviously not. And even with victory, there could be no consolidation. The Chinese people have had more than enough experience of this kind. This experience was reflected long ago in Sun Yat-sen's deathbed statement on the necessity of uniting with the international revolutionary forces.

"We need help from the British and U.S. governments." This, too, is a naive idea in these times. Would the present rulers of Britain and the United States, who are imperialists, help a people's state? Why do these countries do business with us and, supposing they might be willing to lend us money on terms of mutual benefit in the future, why would they do so? Because their capitalists want to make money and their bankers want to earn interest to extricate themselves from their own crisis—it is not a matter of helping the Chinese people. The Communist Parties and progressive groups in these countries are urging their governments to establish trade and even diplomatic relations with us. This is goodwill, this is help, this cannot be mentioned in the same breath with the conduct of the bourgeoisie in the same countries. Throughout his life, Sun Yat-sen appealed countless times to the capitalist countries for help and got nothing but heartless rebuffs. Only once in his whole life did Sun Yat-sen receive foreign help, and that was Soviet help. Let readers refer to Dr. Sun Yat-sen's testament; his earnest advice was not to look for help from the imperialist countries but to "unite with those nations of the world which treat us as equals." Dr. Sun had experience,; he had suffered, he had been deceived. We should remember his words and not allow ourselves to be deceived again. Internationally, we belong to the side of the anti-imperialist front headed by the Soviet Union, and so we can turn only to this side for genuine and friendly help, not to the side of the imperialist front.

"You are dictatorial." My dear sirs, you are right, that is just what we are. All the experience the Chinese people have accumulated through several decades teaches us to enforce the people's democratic dictatorship, that is, to deprive the reactionaries of the right to speak and let the people alone have that right.

Who are the people? At the present stage in China, they are the working class, the peasantry, the urban petty bourgeoisie and the national bourgeoisie. These classes, led by the working class and the Communist Party, unite to form their own state and elect their own government; they enforce their dictatorship over the running dogs of imperialism—the landlord class and bureaucrat-bourgeoisie, as well as the representatives of those classes, the Kuomintang reactionaries and their accomplices—suppress them, allow them only to behave themselves and not to be unruly in word or deed. If they speak or act in an unruly way, they will be promptly stopped and punished. Democracy is practised within the ranks of the people, who enjoy the rights of freedom of speech, assembly, association and so on. The right to vote belongs only to the people, not to the reactionaries. The combination of these two aspects, democracy for the people and dictatorship over the reactionaries, is the people's democratic dictatorship.

Why must things be done this way? The reason is quite clear to everybody. If things were not done this way, the revolution would fail, the people would suffer, the country would be conquered.

"Don't you want to abolish state power?" Yes, we do, but not right now; we cannot do it yet. Why? Because imperialism still exists, because domestic reaction still exists, because classes still exist in our country. Our present task is to strengthen the people's state apparatus—mainly the people's army, the people's police and the people's courts—in order to consolidate national defence and protect the people's interests. Given this condition, China can develop steadily, under the leadership of the working class and the Communist Party, from an agricultural into an industrial country and from a new-democratic into a socialist and communist society, can abolish classes and realize the Great Harmony. The state apparatus, including the army, the police and the courts, is the instrument by which one class oppresses another. It is an instrument for the oppression of antagonistic classes; it is violence and not "benevolence." "You are not benevolent!" Quite so. We definitely do not apply a policy of benevolence to the reactionaries and towards the reactionary activities of the reactionary classes. Our policty of benevolence is applied only within the ranks of the people, not beyond them to the reactionaries or to the reactionary activities of reactionary classes.

The people's state protects the people. Only when the people have such a state can they educate and remould themselves by democratic methods on a country-wide scale, with everyone taking part, and shake off the influence of domestic and foreign reactionaries (which is still very strong, will survive for a long time and cannot be quickly destroyed), rid themselves of the bad habits and ideas acquired in the old society, not allow themselves to be led astray by the reactionaries, and continue to advance—to advance towards a socialist and communist society.

Here, the method we employ is democratic, the method of persuasion, not of compulsion. When anyone among the people breaks the law, he too should be punished, imprisoned or even sentenced to death; but this is a matter of a few individual cases, and it differs in principle from the dictatorship exercised over the reactionaries as a class.

As for the members of the reactionary classes and individual reactionaries, so long as they do not rebel, sabotage or create trouble after their political power has been overthrown, land and work will be given to them as well in order to allow them to live and remould themselves through labour into new people. If they are not willing to work, the people's state will compel them to work. Propaganda and educational work will be done among them too and will be done, moreover, with as much care and thoroughness as among the captured army officers in the past. This, too, may be called a "policy of benevolence" if you like, but it is imposed by us on the members of the enemy classes and cannot be mentioned in the same breath with the work of self-education which we carry on within the ranks of the revolutionary people.

Such remoulding of members of the reactionary classes can be accomplished only by a state of the people's democratic dictatorship under the leadership of the Communist Party. When it is well done, China's major exploiting classes, the landlord class and the bureaucrat-bourgeoisie (the monopoly capitalist class), will be eliminated for good. There remain the national bourgeoisie; at the present stage, we can already do a good deal of suitable educational work with many of them. When the time comes to realize socialism, that is, to nationalize private enterprise, we shall carry the work of educating and remoulding them a step further. The people have a powerful state apparatus in their hands—there is no need to fear rebellion by the national bourgeoisie.

The serious problem is the education of the peasantry. The peasant economy is scattered, and the socialization of agriculture, judging by the Soviet Union's experience, will require a long time and painstaking work. Without socialization of agriculture, there can be no complete, consolidated socialism. The steps to socialize agriculture must be co-ordinated with the development of a powerful industry having state enterprise as its backbone.[10] The state of the people's democratic dictatorship must systematically solve the problems of industrialization. Since it is not proposed to discuss economic problems in detail in this article, I shall not go into them further.

In 1924 a famous manifesto was adopted at the Kuomintang's First National Congress, which Sun Yat-sen himself led and in which Communists participated. The manifesto stated:

> The so-called democratic system in modern states is usually monopolized by the bourgeoisie and has become simply an instrument for oppressing the common people. On the other hand, the Kuomintang's Principle of Democracy means a democratic system shared by all the common people and not privately owned by the few.

Apart from the question of who leads whom, the Principle of Democracy stated above corresponds as a general political programme to what we call People's Democracy or New Democracy. A state system which is shared only by the common people and which the bourgeoisie is not allowed to own privately—add to this the leadership of the working class, and we have the state system of the people's democratic dictatorship.

Chiang Kai-shek betrayed Sun Yat-sen and used the dictatorship of the bureaucrat-bourgeoisie and the landlord class as an instrument for oppressing the common people of China. This counter-revolutionary dictatorship was enforced for twenty-two years and has only now been overthrown by the common people of China under our leadership.

The foreign reactionaries who accuse us of practising "dictatorship" or "totalitarianism" are the very persons who practise it. They practise the dictatorship or totalitarianism of one class, the bourgeoisie, over the proletariat and the rest of the people. They are the very persons Sun Yat-sen spoke of as the bourgeoisie of modern states who oppress the common people. And it is from these reactionary scoundrels that Chiang Kai-shek learned his counter-revolutionary dictatorship.

Chu Hsi, a philosopher of the Sung Dynasty, wrote many books and made many remarks which are now forgotten, but one remark is still remembered, "Deal with a man as he deals with you."[11] This is just what we do; we deal with the imperialists and their running dogs, the Chiang Kai-shek reactionaries, as they deal with us. That is all there is to it!

Revolutionary dictatorship and counter-revolutionary dictatorship are by nature opposites, but the former was learned from the latter. Such learning is very important. If the revolutionary people do not master this method of ruling over the counter-revolutionary classes, they will not be able to maintain their state power, domestic and foreign reaction will overthrow that power and restore its own rule over China, and disaster will befall the revolutionary people.

The people's democratic dictatorship is based on the alliance of the working class, the peasantry and the urban petty bourgeoisie, and mainly on the alliance of the workers and the peasants, because these two classes comprise 80 to 90 per cent of China's population. These two classes are the main force in overthrowing imperialism and the Kuomintang reactionaries. The transition from New Democracy to socialism also depends mainly upon their alliance.

The people's democratic dictatorship needs the leadership of the working class. For it is only the working class that is most farsighted, most selfless and most thoroughly revolutionary. The entire history of revolution proves that without the leadership of the working class revolution fails and that with the leadership of the working class revolution triumphs. In the epoch of imperialism, in no country can any other class lead any genuine revolution to victory. This is clearly proved by the fact that the many revolutions led by China's petty bourgeoisie and national bourgeoisie all failed.

The national bourgeoisie at the present stage is of great importance. Imperialism, a most ferocious enemy, is still standing alongside us. China's modern industry still forms a very small proportion of the national economy. No reliable statistics are available, but it is estimated, on the basis of certain data, that before the War of Resistance Against Japan the value of output of modern industry constituted only about 10 per cent of the total value of output of the national economy. To counter imperialist oppression and to raise her backward economy to a higher level, China must utilize all the factors of urban and rural capitalism that are beneficial and not harmful to the national economy and the people's livelihood; and we must unite with the national bourgeoisie in common struggle. Our present policy is to regulate capitalism, not to destroy it. But the national bourgeoisie cannot be the leader of the revolution, nor should it have the chief role in state power. The reason it cannot be the leader of the revolution and should not have the chief role in state power is that the social and economic position of the national bourgeoisie determines its weakness; it lacks foresight and sufficient courage and many of its members are afraid of the masses.

Sun Yat-sen advocated "arousing the masses of the people" or "giving assistance to the peasants and workers." But who is to "arouse" them or "give assistance" to them? Sun Yat-sen had the petty bourgeoisie and the national bourgeoisie in mind. As a matter of fact, they cannot do so. Why did forty years of revolution under Sun Yat-sen end in failure? Because in the epoch of imperialism the petty bourgeoisie and the national bourgeoisie cannot lead any genuine revolution to victory.

Our twenty-eight years have been quite different. We have had much valuable experience. A well-disciplined Party armed with the theory of Marxism-Leninism, using the method of self-criticism and linked with the masses of the people; an army under the leadership of such a Party; a united front of all revolutionary classes and all revolutionary groups under the leadership of such a Party—these are the three main weapons with which we have defeated the enemy. They distinguish us from our predecessors. Relying on them, we have won basic victory. We have travelled a tortuous road. We have struggled against opportunist deviations in our Party, both Right and "Left." Whenever we made serious mistakes on these three matters, the revolution suffered setbacks. Taught by mistakes and setbacks, we have become wiser and handle our affairs better. It is hard for any political party or person to avoid mistakes, but we should make as few as possible. Once a mistake is made, we should correct it, and the more quickly and throughly the better.

To sum up our experience and concentrate it into one point, it is: the people's democratic dictatorship under the leadership of the working class (through the Communist Party) and based upon the alliance of workers and peasants. This dictatorship must unite as one with the international revolutionary forces. This is our formula, our principal experience, our main programme.

Twenty-eight years of our Party are a long period, in which we have accomplished only one thing—we have won basic victory in the revolutionary war. This calls for celebration, because it is the people's victory, because it is a victory in a country as large as China. But we still have much work to do; to use the analogy of a journey, our past work is only the first step in a long march of ten thousand *li*. Remnants of the enemy have yet to be wiped out. The serious task of economic construction lies before us. We shall soon put aside some of the things we know well and be compelled to do things we don't know well. This means difficulties. The imperialists reckon that we will not be able to manage our economy; they are standing by and looking on, awaiting our failure.

We must overcome difficulties, we must learn what we do not know. We must learn to do economic work from all who know how, no matter who they are. We must esteem them as teachers, learning from them respectfully and conscientiously. We must not pretend to know when we do not know. We must not put on bureaucratic airs. If we dig into a subject for several months, for a year or two, for three or five years, we shall eventually master it. At first some of the Soviet Communists also were not very good at handling economic matters and the imperialists awaited their failure too. But the Communist Party of the Soviet Union emerged victorious and, under the leadership of Lenin and Stalin, it learned not only how to make the revolution but also how to carry on construction. It has built a great and splendid socialist state. The Communist Party of the Soviet Union is our best teacher and we must learn from it. The situation both at home and abroad is in our favour, we can rely fully on the weapon of the people's democratic dictatorship, unite the people throughout the country, the reactionaries excepted, and advance steadily to our goal.

NOTES

1. Also known as the world of Great Harmony. It refers to a society based on public ownership, free from class exploitation and oppression—a lofty ideal long cherished by the Chinese people. Here the realm of Great Harmony means communist society.
2. See V. I. Lenin, *"Left-Wing" Communism, an Infantile Disorder,* Chapter 2. Lenin said: "For nearly half a century—approximately from the 'forties to the 'nineties—advanced thinkers in Russia, under the oppression of an unparalleled savage and reactionary tsardom, eagerly sought for the correct revolutionary theory and followed each and every 'last word' in Europe and America in this sphere with astonishing diligence and thoroughness. Russia achieved Marxism, the only correct revolutionary theory, veritably through *suffering,* by half a century of unprecedented torment and sacrifice, of unprecedented revolutionary heroism, incredible energy, devoted searching, study, testing in practice, disappointment, verification and comparison with European experience."
3. Faced with the opposition of the Chinese people to her traffic in opium, Britain sent forces in 1840–1842 to invade Kwangtung and other coastal regions of China under the pretext of protecting trade. The troops in Kwangtung, led by Lin Tse-hau fought a war of resistance.
4. Hung Hsiu-chuan (1814–1864), who was born in Kwangtung, was the leader of a peasant revolutionary war in the middle of the 19th century. In 1851 he led a mass uprising in Kwangsi and proclaimed the establishment of the Tsiping Heavenly Kingdom, which held many provinces and fought the Ching Dynasty for fourteen

years. In 1864 this revolutionary war failed and Hung Hsiu-chuan committed suicide by poison.

5. Kang Yu-wei (1858–1927), of Nanhai County, Kwangtung Province. In 1895, after China had been defeated by Japanese imperialism in the previous year, he led thirteen hundred candidates for the third grade in the imperial examinations at Peking in submitting a "ten thousand word memorial" to Emperor Kuang Hsu, asking for "constitutional reform and modernization" and asking that the autocratic monarchy be changed into a constitutional monarchy. In 1898, in an attempt to introduce reforms, the emperor promoted Kang Yu-wei together with Tan Sze-tung, Liang Chi-chao and others to key posts in the government. Later, the Empress Dowager Tzu Hsi, representing the die-hards, again took power and the reform movement failed. Kang Yu-wei and Liang Chi-chao fled abroad and formed the Protect-the-Emperor Party, which became a reactionary political faction in opposition to the bourgeois and petty bourgeois revolutionaries represented by Sun Yat-sen. Among Kang's works were *Forgeries in the Classics of the Confucian Canon, Confucius as a Reformer,* and *Ta Tung Shu* or the *Book of Great Harmony.*
6. Yen Fu (1853–1921), of Foochow, Fukien Province, studied at a naval academy in Britain. After the Sino-Japanese War of 1894, he advocated constitutional monarchy and reforms to modernize China. His translations of T. H. Huxley's *Evolution and Ethics,* Adam Smith's *The Wealth of Nations,* J. S. Mill's *System of Logic,* Montesquieu's *L'Esprit des Lois,* and other works were vehicles for the spread of European bourgeois thought in China.
7. A system of examinations adopted by China's autocratic dynasties. It was a method used by the feudal ruling class for selecting personnel to govern the people and also for enticing the intellectuals. The system, dating from the 7th century, persisted into the early 20th century.
8. The Revolution of 1911 overthrew the autocratic regime of the Ching Dynasty. On October 10 of that year, a section of the New Army, at the urging of the revolutionary societies of the bourgeoisie and petty bourgeoisie, staged an uprising in Wuchang. This was followed by uprisings in other provinces, and very soon the rule of the Ching Dynasty crumbled. On January 1, 1912, the Provisional Government of the Republic of China was set up in Nanking, and Sun Yat-sen was elected Provisional President. The revolution achieved victory through the alliance of the bourgeoisie, peasants, workers and urban petty bourgeoisie. But because the group which led the revolution was compromising in nature, failed to bring real benefits to the peasants and yielded to the pressure of imperialism and the feudal forces, state power fell into the hands of the Northern warlord Yuan Shih-kai, and the revolution failed.
9. A hero in the novel *Shui Hu Chuan (Heroes of the Marshes),* who killed a tiger with his bare hands on the Chingyang Ridge. This is one of the most popular episodes in that famous novel.
10. For the relation between the socialization of agriculture and the industrialization of the country, see *On the Question of Agricultural Co-operation* (Sections 7 and 8), a report made by Comrade Mao Zedong July 31, 1955 at the Conference of the Secretaries of the Provincial, Municipal and Autonomous Region Committees of the Chinese Communist Party. In this report Comrade Mao Zedong, on the basis of Soviet experience and our own country's practice, greatly developed the thesis that socialization of agriculture should proceed in step with socialist industrialization.
11. The quotation is from Chu Hsi's commentary on the *Confucian Doctrine of the Mean,* Chapter 13.

36

ON MARX AND MARXISM

MIKHAIL BAKUNIN

Among Marx's earliest critics were "anarcho-communists," including Mikhail Bakunin (1814–1876). A Russian anarchist (from the Greek *an-archos,* meaning "no rule" or "no government"), Bakunin believed that Marx's version of communism would not lead to "the withering away of the state," as Marxists claim. On the contrary, Bakunin predicted, the supposedly temporary interim state that Marx called "the dictatorship of the proletariat" would prove to be a permanent dictatorship over the proletariat by state officials who would jealously guard their own power and privilege. Bakunin insisted that state power must be smashed once and for all by a proletarian revolution. Only then, he claimed, could people combine and associate as free and equal producers.

Source: Mikhail Bakunin, Selected Writings, *translated by Steven Cox and Olive Stevens (London: Jonathan Cape, 1973), pp. 233, 235–240. Reprinted by permission.*

ON MARX AND MARXISM

Having lived almost exclusively for about thirty years in the midst of German workers, refugees like himself, and with a circle of friends and more or less intelligent disciples belonging by birth or contact to the bourgeois world, Herr Karl Marx naturally came to the point of forming a school, a kind of small-scale communist Church, made up of fervent believers and scattered all over Germany. Although restricted in numerical terms, this Church is expertly organized, and thanks to extensive contacts with working men's associations in all the key points of Germany it is already a force to be reckoned with. Herr Marx naturally enjoys a position close to supreme authority in the Church, and it has to be admitted in all fairness that he is adept at handling his little army of fanatical supporters so as continually to enhance his prestige and his power over the imagination of the German workers. . . .

II. A LETTER TO THE EDITORIAL BOARD OF LA LIBERTÉ

Zurich, October 5th, 1872

Gentlemen,

Having published the verdict of excommunication which the Marxist Hague Congress has just passed against myself, in all fairness you will surely publish my reply. Here it is.

The triumph of Herr Marx and his followers has been complete. Certain of a majority which had been a long time in preparation and which was organized with great skill and care, if without much respect for the principles of Morality, Truth and Justice which are so often to be found in their speeches and so seldom in their actions, the Marxists have shed their masks and, in the typical manner of power-loving men, always in the name of that popular sovereignty which in future will serve as a stepping-stone for all pretenders to control of the masses, they have boldly ordained the enslavement of the people of the International.

If the International were less deeply rooted, if it was based, as they imagine, only on the organization of centres of control, instead of on the real solidarity of the actual interests and aspirations of the proletariat of every country in the civilized world, regardless of any governmental tutelage, the decrees of that dismal Hague Congress, the all too pliant and faithful embodiment of Marxist theory and practice, would have been enough to kill it. They would have brought down both ridicule and odium upon that fine association, in whose foundation I would like to add that Herr Marx played an intelligent, vigorous part.

A State, a government, a universal dictatorship! The dream of a Gregory VII, a Boniface VIII, a Charles V or a Napoleon, recurring under new guises but always with the same pretensions, in the camp of socialist democracy! Is it possible to imagine anything more absurd, but also more loathsome?

To claim that even the most intelligent and best-intentioned group of individuals will be capable of becoming the mind, soul and guiding and unifying will of the revolutionary moment and economic organization of the proletariat of every land is such an outrage against common sense and historical experience that one can only wonder how a man as clever as Herr Marx could have conceived it.

The Popes at least had the excuse of the absolute truth which they said the Holy Ghost had given into their hands, and which they were bound to believe. Herr Marx has no such excuse, and I shall not insult him by thinking that he imagines himself to have scientifically invented something approaching absolute truth. But granted that the absolute does not exist, there can be no infallible dogma for the International and consequently no official political or economic theory, and our congresses should never aspire to the role of ecumenical councils proclaiming compulsory principles for all adherents and believers.

There is only one law binding all the members, individuals, sections and federations of the International, a law which constitutes its one true basis. In all its scope, consequences and applications, it is *the international solidarity of workers in all jobs and all countries in their economic struggle against the exploiters of labour.* It is the real organization of that solidarity through the spontaneous action of the working classes, and the absolutely free federation—all the stronger for being free—of the working masses of all tongues and nations, not their unification by decree and under the aegis of any government, which constitutes the real, living unity of the International.

Who can doubt that it is out of this increasingly widespread organization of the militant solidarity of the proletariat against bourgeois exploitation that the political struggle of the proletariat against the bourgeoisie must rise and grow? The Marxists and ourselves are unanimous on this point. But now comes the question that divides us so deeply from the Marxists.

We think that the policy of the proletariat must necessarily be a revolutionary one, aimed directly and solely at the destruction of States. We do not see how it is possible to talk about international solidarity and yet to intend preserving States—unless in some dream of the universal State, meaning universal slavery, the dream of the great emperors and popes—because by its very nature the State is a breach of that solidarity and therefore a permanent cause of war. Nor can we conceive how it is possible to talk about the liberty of the proletariat or the real deliverance of the masses within and by means of the State. State means dominion, and all dominion involves the subjugation of the masses and consequently their exploitation for the sake of some ruling minority.

We do not accept, even in the process of revolutionary transition, either constituent assemblies, provisional governments or so-called revolutionary dictatorships; because we are convinced that revolution is only sincere, honest and real in the hands of the masses, and that when it is concentrated into those of a few ruling individuals it inevitably and immediately becomes reaction. That is our belief, but this is not the moment to expand on it.

The Marxists profess quite different ideas. They are worshipers of State power, and necessarily also prophets of political and social discipline and champions of order established from the top downwards, always in the name of universal suffrage and the sovereignty of the masses, for whom they save the honour and privilege of obeying leaders, elected masters. The only kind of emancipation the Marxists accept is what they expect to come out of their so-called People's State *(Volksstaat).* They are so unopposed to patriotism that their International flies the flag of Pan-Germanism all too often. Between the policies of Bismarck and Marx there may well be a marked difference, but between the Marxists and ourselves there is a chasm. They are for government, we, for our part, are anarchists.

It is these two main attitudes which today split the International into two camps. On the one side Germany, practically alone; on the other, to a greater or lesser degree, Italy, Spain, the Swiss Jura, a large part of France, Belgium, Holland, and soon the Slav peoples. These two trends clashed at the Hague Congress, and, thanks to the cunning of Herr Marx and the utterly artificial organization of that Congress, the German trend won.

Does this mean that the crucial question was resolved? It was not even properly debated; the majority voted like a well-drilled regiment and crushed all debate beneath its vote. The contradiction therefore looms more menacingly than ever, and Herr Marx himself, despite the intoxication of victory, certainly does not imagine that he can be rid of it so cheap. And even if he had momentarily entertained such a foolish hope, the united protest of the Jura, Spanish, Belgian and Dutch delegations (not counting Italy, which did not even bother to send delegates to such a blatantly rigged Congress), that protest, so moderate in form but all the more forceful and significant in essence, must soon have disabled him.

In itself, that protest is clearly only a feeble

precursor of the storm of opposition which will break in every country truly imbued with the principles and passion of social revolution. And that whole storm will have been raised by the Marxists' fatal preoccupation with making the political question a plank of the International, and a binding principle.

In fact, no rapprochement is now possible between these two trends. Only the praxis of social revolution, great new historical experiments and the logic of events might eventually lead them to a common solution, and, convinced as we are of the value of our own principle, we hope that the Germans themselves—the workers of Germany, not their leaders—will then join us at last to raze those people's prisons which are called States and to pass sentence on politics, which is in fact nothing but the art of subduing and fleecing the masses. . . .

If I try hard, I can understand how despots crowned or uncrowned could have dreamed of world power, but what is to be said when a friend of the proletariat, a revolutionary who claims that he genuinely supports the emancipation of the masses, proceeds to set himself up as controller and supreme arbiter of every revolutionary movement which may break out in every country, and dares to dream of subjecting the proletariat of all those countries to a single approach hatched out of a single brain—his own!

I believe that Herr Marx is a very serious if not very honest revolutionary, and that he really is in favour of the rebellion of the masses, and I wonder how he manages to overlook the fact that the establishment of a universal dictatorship, collective or individual, a dictatorship which would create the post of a kind of chief engineer of world revolution, ruling and controlling the insurrectionary activity of the masses in all countries, as a machine might be controlled—that the establishment of such a dictatorship would in itself suffice to kill revolution and warp and paralyse all popular movements. . . .

. . . The political State in every country, he says, is always the product and faithful reflection of its economic situation; to change the former, one has only to change the latter. This is the whole secret of political evolutions, according to Herr Marx. He pays no heed to other elements in history, such as the effect—obvious though it is—of political, judicial and religious institutions on the economic situation. He says that "hardship produces political slavery—the State," but does not allow for the converse: "Political slavery—the State—reproduces and maintains hardship as a condition of its existence, so that in order to destroy hardship the State must be destroyed." And the strange thing is that the man who forbids his opponents to condemn political slavery, the State, as an *actual* cause of hardship should be instructing his friends and disciples in the German Social Democratic Party to consider the seizure of political power and liberties as the absolutely essential precondition for economic emancipation. . . .

In Herr Marx's People's State, so we are told, there will be no privileged class. Everybody will be equal, not only from the judicial and political but also from the economic standpoint. This is the promise at any rate, although judging by the means of action and the path it is intended to follow, I very much doubt whether it can ever be honoured. So there will be no more class, but a government, and please note, an extremely complicated government which, not content with governing and administering the masses politically, like all the governments of today, will also administer them economically, by taking over the production and *fair* sharing of wealth, agriculture, the establishment and development of factories, the organization and control of trade, and lastly the injection of capital into production by a single banker, the State. All this will require vast knowledge and a lot of heads brimful of brains. It will be the reign of the *scientific mind,* the most aristocratic, despotic, arrogant and contemptuous of all regimes. There will be a new class, a new hierarchy of real or bogus learning, and the world will be divided into a dominant, science-based minority and a vast, ignorant majority. And then let the ignorant masses beware! . . .

One may well ask whether the proletariat would be in the position of a ruling class, and over whom would it rule? This means that yet another proletariat would emerge, which would be subject to the new sovereignty and the new State. For instance, the Marxists, as is well known, are not well disposed towards the peasant rabble, who, being on the lowest cultural level, would doubtless be governed by the urban and factory proletariat; or, if one were to look at this problem from the national point of view, considering Germans and Slavs, then presumably, for the same reason, Slavs would be in a condition of slavery to a triumphant German proletariat, and therefore in the same situation as the lowest class is now to its own bourgeoisie.

If there is a State, then there is inevitably supremacy, and therefore slavery: a State without open or veiled slavery is inconceivable—that is why we are opposed to the State.

What does raising the proletariat to the level of government mean? Surely the whole proletariat is not going to head the administration? There are about forty million Germans. Does it mean that all forty million will be members of the government? Will all the people be rulers, and will there be no one to be ruled? In that case there will be no government and no State, but if there is a State, then there are subjects, that is, slaves.

This dilemma in the Marxist theory can easily be solved. A people's administration, according to them, must mean a people's administration by virtue of a small number of representatives chosen by the people. The universal right of each individual among all the people to elect so-called representatives and members of the government, that is the final word of the Marxists and of the democratic school, and it is a deception which would conceal the despotism of a governing minority, all the more dangerous because it appears as a sham expression of the people's will.

Therefore, whichever way you look at this question, you reach the same sad result: that the vast majority, the great mass of people, would be governed by a privileged minority. But this minority, say the Marxists, will consist of workers. Well, perhaps *former* workers, who would stop being workers the moment they became rulers or representatives, and would then come to regard the whole blue-collared world from government heights, and would not represent the people but themselves and their pretensions in the government of the people. Anyone who does not see this does not know anything about human nature.

But those who would be chosen would be burning with conviction, and would also be trained socialists! The expression "scholarly socialist," or "scientific socialist," which one is always meeting in the writings and speeches of the Lassalists and Marxists, itself proves that this sham people's government would be no other than the completely despotic rule of the masses by a new and very small aristocracy of actual or alleged "scholars." The people are no "scholars," and therefore they are as a whole to be freed from the toils of government, and as a whole they are to make up the herd that is governed. What a splendid freedom!

The Marxists realize the contradiction in this, and, realizing that the governing of educated people is the most difficult, humiliating and despicable thing in the world, and will be a real dictatorship, whatever democratic form it will take, console themselves with the thought that this dictatorship will be temporary and short-lived. They say that its only concern and purpose will be to educate and raise the people, both economically and politically, to the stage at which all administration will soon become unnecessary, and the State, having lost all of its political, that is sovereign, character, will itself turn into a completely free organization of economic interests and communes.

This is the real contradiction. If their State is really going to be a people's government, then why should it abolish itself, and if its abolition is essential for the real emancipation of the people, then how dare they call it a people's government? By the polemic we have used against them, we have made them realize that liberty or anarchy, that is the free organization of the working masses from the bottom up, is the final aim of social development, and that any State, including their people's State, is a yoke, as it gives birth to depotism on the one side and slavery on the other.

They say that this sort of governmental yoke, this dictatorship, is an essential step leading to the attainment of complete freedom for the people; and that anarchy or freedom is the aim, but the State or dictatorship is the means. Therefore in order to emancipate the masses they must first be enslaved.

On this contradiction we must for the time being end our argument. They affirm that only dictatorship, *theirs* of course, can create a popular will. We reply that no dictatorship can have any other aim except to perpetuate itself, and that it is capable of instilling and fostering only slavery in the masses that endure it. Liberty can only be created by liberty, that is by mass rebellion and the free organization of the working masses from the bottom upwards.

37

ANARCHIST COMMUNISM

PETER KROPOTKIN

Like Bakunin, Peter Kropotkin (1842–1921) was born into the Russian nobility, became an anarchist, and was one of Marx's—and Marxism's—most ardent and outspoken critics. As a young man Kropotkin renounced his title of prince, choosing instead to devote his life to bettering the lot of poor peasants. Arrested and sent to Siberia, he escaped and, like many radicals before him—including Marx—made his way to England, where he spent three decades in exile as a tireless defender of the anarchist cause. Much influenced by the writings of Charles Darwin, Kropotkin came to believe that the process of evolution was leading to the transition to a communal and cooperative anarchist society. Returning to Russia after the 1917 revolution, Kropotkin hoped to influence the course of the new society, but he failed to do so and died in despair.

Source: Peter Kropotkin, "Anarchist Communism: Its Basis and Principles," in Revolutionary Pamphlets *(New York: Vanguard Press, 1927), pp. 46–57, 68–75.*

ANARCHIST COMMUNISM: ITS BASIS AND PRINCIPLES

I

Anarchism, the no-government system of socialism, has a double origin. It is an outgrowth of the two great movements of thought in the economic and the political fields which characterize the nineteenth century, and especially its second part. In common with all socialists, the anarchists hold that the private ownership of land, capital, and machinery has had its time; that it is condemned to disappear; and that all requisites for production must, and will, become the common property of society, and be managed in common by the producers of wealth. And in common with the most advanced representatives of political radicalism, they maintain that the ideal of the political organization of society is a condition of things where the functions of government are reduced to a minimum, and the individual recovers his full liberty of initiative and action for satisfying, by means of free groups and federations—freely constituted—all the infinitely varied needs of the human being.

As regards socialism, most of the anarchists arrive at its ultimate conclusion, that is, at a complete negation of the wage-system and at communism. And with reference to political organization, by giving a further development to the above-mentioned part of the radical program, they arrive at the conclusion that the ultimate aim of society is the reduction of the functions of government to *nil*—that is, to a society without government, to an-archy. The anarchists maintain, moreover, that such being the ideal of social and political organization, they must not remit it to future centuries, but that only those changes in our social organization which are in accordance with the above double ideal, and constitute an approach to it, will have a chance of life and be beneficial for the commonwealth.

As to the method followed by the anarchist thinker, it entirely differs from that followed by the utopists. The anarchist thinker does not resort to metaphysical conceptions (like "natural rights," the "duties of the State," and so on) to establish what are, in his opinion, the best conditions for realizing the greatest happiness of humanity. He follows, on the contrary, the course traced by the modern philosophy of evolution. He studies human society as it is now and was in the past; and without either endowing humanity as a whole, or separate individuals, with superior qualities which they do not possess, he merely considers society as an aggregation of organisms trying to find out the best ways of combining the wants of the individual with those of cooperation for the welfare of the species. He studies society and tries to discover its *tendencies*, past and present, its growing needs, intellectual and economic, and in his ideal he merely points out in which direction evolution goes. He distinguishes between the real wants and tendencies of human aggregations and the accidents (want of knowledge, migrations, wars, conquests) which have prevented these tendencies from being satisfied. And he concludes that the two most prominent, although often unconscious, tendencies throughout our history have been: first, a tendency towards integrating labor for the production of all riches in common, so as finally to render it impossible to discriminate the part of the common production due to the separate individual; and second, a tendency towards the fullest freedom of the individual in the prosecution of all aims, beneficial both for himself and for society at large. The ideal of the anarchist is thus a mere summing-up of what he considers to be the next phase of evolution. It is no longer a matter of faith; it is a matter for scientific discussion.

In fact, one of the leading features of this century is the growth of socialism and the rapid spreading of socialist views among the working-classes. How could it be otherwise? We have witnessed an unparalleled sudden increase of our powers of production, resulting in an accumulation of wealth which has outstripped the most sanguine expectations. But owing to our wage system, this increase of wealth—due to the combined efforts of men of science, of managers, and workmen as well—has resulted only in an unprecedented accumulation of wealth in the hands of the owners of capital; while an increase of misery for great numbers, and an insecurity of life for all, have been the lot of the workmen. The unskilled laborers, in continuous search for labor, are falling into an unheard-of destitution. And even the best paid artisans and skilled workmen labor under the permanent menace of being thrown, in their turn, into the same conditions as the unskilled paupers, in consequence of some of the continuous and unavoidable fluctuations of industry and caprices of capital.

The chasm between the modern millionaire who squanders the produce of human labor in a gorgeous and vain luxury, and the pauper reduced to a miserable and insecure existence, is thus growing wider and wider, so as to break the very unity of society—the harmony of its life—and to endanger the progress of its further development.

At the same time, workingmen are less and less inclined to patiently endure this division of society into two classes, as they themselves become more and more conscious of the wealth-producing power of modern industry, of the part played by labor in the production of wealth, and of their own capacities of organization. In proportion as all classes of the community take a more lively part in public affairs, and knowledge spreads among the masses, their longing for equality becomes stronger, and their demands for social reorganization become louder and louder. They can be ignored no more. The worker claims his share in the riches he produces; he claims his share in the management of production; and he claims not only some additional well-being, but also his full rights in the higher enjoyments of science and art. These claims, which formerly were uttered only by the social reformer, begin now to be made by a daily growing minority of those who work in the factory or till the acre. And they so conform to our feelings of justice that they find support in a daily growing minority among the privileged classes themselves. Socialism becomes thus *the* idea of the nineteenth century; and neither coercion nor pseudo-reforms can stop its further growth.

Much hope of improvement was placed, of course, in the extension of political rights to the working classes. But these concessions, unsupported as they were by corresponding changes in economic relations, proved delusions. They did not materially improve the conditions of the great bulk of the workmen. Therefore, the watchword of socialism is: "Economic freedom as the only secure basis for political freedom." And as long as the present wage system, with all its bad consequences, remains unaltered, the socialist watchword will continue to inspire the workmen. Socialism will continue to grow until it has realized its program.

Side by side with this great movement of thought in economic matters, a like movement has been going on with regard to political rights, political organization, and the functions of government. Government has been submitted to the same criticism as capital. While most of the radicals saw in universal suffrage and republican institutions the last word of political wisdom, a further step was made by the few. The very functions of government and the State, as also their relations to the individual, were submitted to a sharper and deeper criticism. Representative government having been tried by experiment on a wide field, its defects became more and more prominent. It became obvious that these defects are not merely accidental but inherent in the system itself. Parliament and its executive proved to be unable to attend to all the numberless affairs of the community and to conciliate the varied and often opposite interests of the separate parts of a State. Election proved unable to find out the men who might represent a nation, and manage, otherwise than in a party spirit, the affairs they are compelled to legislate upon. These defects become so striking that the very principles of the representative system were criticized and their justness doubted.

Again, the dangers of a centralized government became still more conspicuous when the socialists came to the front and asked for a further increase of the powers of government by entrusting it with the management of the immense field covered now by the economic relations between individuals. The question was asked whether a government entrusted with the management of industry and trade would not become a permanent danger for liberty and peace, and whether it even would be able to be a good manager?

The socialists of the earlier part of this century did not fully realize the immense difficulties of the problem. Convinced as they were of the necessity of economic reforms, most of them took no notice of the need of freedom for the individual. And we have had social reformers ready to submit society to any kind of theocracy, or dictatorship in order to obtain reforms in a socialist sense. Therefore we have seen in England and also on the Continent the division of men of advanced opinions into political radicals and socialists—the former looking with distrust on the latter, as they saw in them a danger for the political liberties which have been won by the civilized nations after a long series of struggles. And even now, when the socialists all over Europe have become political parties, and profess the democratic faith, there remains among most impartial men a well-founded fear of the *Volksstaat* or "popular State" being as great a danger to liberty as any form of autocracy if its government be entrusted with the management of all the social organization including the production and distribution of wealth.

Recent evolution, however, has prepared the way for showing the necessity and possibility of a higher form of social organization which may guarantee economic freedom without reducing the individual to the role of a slave to the State. The origins of government have been carefully studied, and all metaphysical conceptions as to its divine or "social contract" derivation having been laid aside, it appears that it is among us of a relatively modern origin, and that its powers have grown precisely in proportion as the division of society into the privileged and unprivileged classes was growing in the course of ages. Representative government has also been reduced to its real value—that of an instrument which has rendered services in the struggle against autocracy, but not an ideal of free political organization. As to the system of philosophy which saw in the State a leader of progress, it was more and more shaken as it became evident that progress is the most effective when it is not checked by State interference. It has thus become obvious that a further advance in social life does not lie in the direction of a further concentration of power and regulative functions in the hands of a governing body, but in the direction of decentralization, both territorial and functional—in a subdivision of public functions with respect both to their sphere of action and to the character of the functions; it is in the abandonment to the initiative of freely constituted groups of all those functions which are now considered as the functions of government.

This current of thought has found its expression not merely in literature, but also to a limited extent in life. The uprise of the Paris Commune, followed by that of the Commune of Cartagena—a movement of which the historical bearing seems to have been quite overlooked—opened a new page of history. If we analyze not only this movement in itself, but also the impression it left in the minds and the tendencies manifested during the communal revolution, we must recognize in it an indication showing that in the future human agglomerations which are more advanced in their social development will try to start an independent life; and that they will endeavor to convert the more backward parts of a nation by example, instead of imposing their opinions by law and force, or submitting themselves to the majority-rule, which always is a mediocrity-rule. At the same time the failure of representative government within the Commune itself proved that self-government and self-administration must be carried further than in a merely territorial sense. To be effective they must also be carried into the various functions of life within the free community. A merely territorial limitation of the sphere of action of government will not do—representative government being as deficient in a city as it is a nation. Life gave thus a further point in favor of the no-government theory, and a new impulse to anarchist thought.

Anarchists recognize the justice of both the just-mentioned tendencies towards economic and political freedom, and see in them two different manifestations of the very same need of equality which constitutes the very essence of all struggles mentioned by history. Therefore, in common with all socialists, the anarchist says to the political reformer: "No substantial reform in the sense of political equality and no limitation of the powers of government can be made as long as society is divided into two hostile camps, and the laborer remains, economically speaking, a slave to his employer." But to the state socialist we say also: "You cannot modify the existing conditions of property without deeply modifying at the same time the political organization. You must limit the powers of government and renounce parliamentary rule. To each new economic phase of life corresponds a new political phase. Absolute monarchy corresponded to the system of serfdom. Representative government corresponds to capital-rule. Both, however, are class-rule. But in a society where the distinction between capitalist and laborer has disappeared, there is no need of such a government; it would be an anachronism, a nuisance. Free workers would require a free organization, and this cannot have any other basis than free agreement and free cooperation, without sacrificing the autonomy of the individual to the all-pervading interference of the State. The no-capitalist system implies the no-government system."

Meaning thus the emancipation of man from the oppressive powers of capitalism and government as well, the system of anarchism becomes a synthesis of the two powerful currents of thought which characterize our century.

In arriving at these conclusions anarchism proves to be in accordance with the conclusions arrived at by the philosophy of evolution. By bringing to light the plasticity of organization, the philosophy of evolution has shown the admirable adaptability of organisms to their conditions of life, and the ensuing development of such faculties as render more complete both the adaptations of the aggregates to their surroundings and those of each of the constituent parts of the aggregate to the needs of free cooperation. It has familiarized us with the circumstance that throughout organic nature the capacities for life in common grow in proportion as the integration of organisms into compound aggregates becomes more and more complete; and it has enforced thus the opinion already expressed by social moralists as to the perfectibility of human nature. It has shown us that, in the long run of the struggle for existence, "the fittest" will prove to be those who combine intellectual knowledge with the knowledge necessary for the production of wealth, and not those who are now the richest because they, or their ancestors, have been momentarily the strongest.

By showing that the "struggle for existence" must be conceived not merely in its restricted sense of a struggle between individuals for the means of subsistence but in its wider sense of adaptation of all individuals of the species to the best conditions for the survival of the species, as well as for the greatest possible sum of life and happiness for each and all, it has permitted us to deduce the laws of moral science from the social needs and habits of mankind. It has shown us the infinitesimal part played by positive law in moral evolution, and the immense part played by the natural growth of altruistic feelings, which develop as soon as the conditions of life favor their growth. It has thus enforced the opinion of social reformers as to the necessity of modifying the conditions of life for improving man, instead of trying to improve human nature by moral teachings while life works in an opposite direction. Finally, by studying human society from the biological point of view, it has come to the conclusions arrived at by anarchists from the study of history and present tendencies as to further progress being in the line of socialization of wealth and integrated labor combined with the fullest possible freedom of the individual.

It has happened in the long run of ages that

everything which permits men to increase their production, or even to continue it, has been appropriated by the few, The land, which derives its value precisely from its being necessary for an ever-increasing population, belongs to the few, who may prevent the community from cultivating it. The coal-pits, which represent the labor of generations, and which also derive their value from the wants of the manufacturers and railroads, from the immense trade carried on and the density of population, belong again to the few, who have even the right of stopping the extractions of coal if they choose to give another use of their capital. The lace-weaving machine, which represents, in its present state of perfection, the work of three generations of Lancashire weavers, belongs also to the few; and if the grandsons of the very same weaver who invented the first lace-weaving machine claim their right to bring one of these machines into motion, they will be told "Hands off! this machine does not belong to you!" The railroads, which mostly would be useless heaps of iron if not for the present dense population, its industry, trade, and traffic, belong again to the few—to a few shareholders, who may not even know where the railway is situated which brings them a yearly income larger than that of a medieval king. And if the children of those people who died by thousands in digging the tunnels should gather and go—a ragged and starving crowd—to ask bread or work from the shareholders, they would be met with bayonets and bullets.

Who is the sophist who will dare to say that such an organization is just? But what is unjust cannot be beneficial to mankind; and *it is not.* In consequence of this monstrous organization, the son of a workman, when he is able to work, finds no acre to till, no machine to set in motion, unless he agrees to sell his labor for a sum inferior to its real value. His father and grandfather have contributed to drain the field, or erect the factory, to the full extent of their capacities—and nobody can do more than that—but he comes into the world more destitute than a savage. If he resorts to agriculture, he will be permitted to cultivate a plot of land, but on the condition that he gives up part of his product to the landlord. If he resorts to industry, he will be permitted to work, but on the condition that out of the thirty shillings he has produced, ten shillings or more will be pocketed by the owner of the machine. We cry out against the feudal barons who did not permit anyone to settle on the land otherwise than on payment of one quarter of the crops to the lord of the manor; but we continue to do as they did—we extend their system. The forms have changed, but the essence has remained the same. And the workman is compelled to accept the feudal conditions which we call "free contract," because nowhere will he find better conditions. Everything has been appropriated by somebody; he *must* accept the bargain, or starve.

Owing to this circumstance our production takes a wrong turn. It takes no care of the needs of the community; its only aim is to increase the profits of the capitalist. And we have, therefore,—the continuous fluctuations of industry, the crisis coming periodically nearly every ten years, and throwing out of employment several hundred thousand men who are brought to complete misery, whose children grow up in the gutter, ready to become inmates of the prison and workhouse. The workmen being unable to purchase with their wages the riches they are producing, industry must search for markets elsewhere, amidst the middle classes of other nations. It must find markets, in the East, in Africa, anywhere; it must increase, by trade, the number of its serfs in Egypt, in India, on the Congo. But everywhere it finds competitors in other nations which rapidly enter into the same line of industrial development. And wars, continuous wars, must be fought for the supremacy in the world-market—wars for the possession of the East, wars for getting possession of the seas, wars for the right of imposing heavy duties on foreign merchandise. The thunder of European guns never ceases; whole generations are slaughtered from time to time; and we spend in armaments the third of the revenue of our States—a revenue raised, the poor know with what difficulties.

And finally, the injustice of our partition of wealth exercises the most deplorable effect on our morality. Our principles of morality say: "Love your neighbour as yourself"; but let a child follow this principle and take off his coat to give it to the shivering pauper, and his mother will tell him that he must never understand moral principles in their direct sense. If he lives according to them, he will go barefoot, without alleviating the misery around him! Morality is good on the lips, not in deeds. Our preachers say, "Who works, prays," and everybody endeavors to make others work for him. They say, "Never lie!" and politics are a big lie. And we accustom ourselves and our children to live under this double-faced morality, which is hypocrisy, and to conciliate our double-facedness by sophistry. Hypocrisy and sophistry become the very basis of our life. But society cannot live under such a morality. It cannot last so: it must, it will, be changed.

The question is thus no more a mere question of bread. It covers the whole field of human activity. But it has at its bottom a question of social economy, and we conclude: The means of production and of satisfaction of all needs of society, having been created by the common efforts of all, must be at the disposal of all. The private appropriation of requisites for production is neither just nor beneficial. All must be placed on the same footing as producers and consumers of wealth. That will be the only way for society to step out of the bad conditions which have been created by centuries of wars and oppression. That will be the only guarantee for further progress in a direction of equality and freedom, which have always been the real, although unspoken goal of humanity. . . .

Representative government has accomplished its historical mission; it has given a mortal blow to court-rule; and by its debates it has awakened public interest in public questions. But to see in it the government of the future socialist society is to commit a gross error. Each economic phase of life implies its own political phase; and it is impossible to touch the very basis of the present economic life—private property—without a corresponding change in the very basis of the political organization. Life already shows in which direction the change will be made. Not in increasing the powers of the State, but in resorting to free organization and free federation in all those branches which are now considered as attributes of the State.

The objections of the above may be easily foreseen. It will be said of course: "But what is to be done with those who do not keep their agreements? What with those who are not inclined to work? What with those who would prefer breaking the written laws of society, or—on the anarchist hypothesis—its unwritten customs? Anarchism may be good for a higher humanity—not for the men of our own times."

First of all, there are two kinds of agreements: there is the free one which is entered upon by free consent, as a free choice between different courses equally open to each of the agreeing parties. And there is the enforced agreement, imposed by one party upon the other, and accepted by the latter from sheer necessity; in fact, it is no agreement at all; it is a mere submission to necessity. Unhappily, the great bulk of what are now described as agreements belong to the latter category. When a workman sells his labor to an employer and knows perfectly well that some part of the value of his produce will be unjustly taken by the employer; when he sells it without even the slightest guarantee of being employed so much as six consecutive months, it is a sad mockery to call that a free contract. Modern economists may call it free, but the father of political economy—Adam Smith—was never guilty of such a misrepresentation. As long as three-quarters of humanity are compelled to enter into agreements of that description, force is of course necessary, both to enforce the supposed agreements and to maintain such a state of things. Force—and a great deal of force—is necessary to prevent the laborers from taking possession of what they consider unjustly appropriated by the few; and force is necessary to continually bring new "uncivilized nations" under the same conditions.

But we do not see the necessity of force for

enforcing agreements freely entered upon. We never heard of a penalty imposed on a man who belonged to the crew of a lifeboat and at a given moment preferred to abandon the association. All that his comrades would do with him, if he were guilty of a gross neglect, would probably be to refuse to have anything further to do with him. Nor did we hear of fines imposed on a contributor to the dictionary for a delay in his work, or of *gendarmes* driving the volunteers of Garibaldi to the battlefield. Free agreements need not be enforced.

As to the so-often repeated objection that no one would labor if he were not compelled to do so by sheer necessity, we heard enough of it before the emancipation of slaves in America, as well as before the emancipation of serfs in Russia. And we have had the opportunity of appreciating it at its just value. So we shall not try to convince those who can be convinced only by accomplished facts. As to those who reason, they ought to know that, if it really was so with some parts of humanity at its lowest stages, or if it is so with some small communities, or separate individuals, brought to sheer despair by ill success in their struggle against unfavorable conditions, it is not so with the bulk of the civilized nations. With us, work is a habit, and idleness an artificial growth. Of course, when to be a manual worker means to be compelled to work all one's life long for ten hours a day, and often more, at producing some part of something—a pin's head, for instance; when it means to be paid wages on which a family can live only on the condition of the strictest limitation of all its needs; when it means to be always under the menace of being thrown tomorrow out of employment—and we know how frequent are the industrial crises, and what misery they imply; when it means, in a very great number of cases, premature death in a paupers' infirmary, if not in the workhouse; when to be a manual worker signifies to wear a life-long stamp of inferiority in the eyes of those very people who live on the work of these "hands"; when it always means the renunciation of all those higher enjoyments that science and art give to man—oh, then there is no wonder that everybody—the manual workers as well—has but one dream: that of rising to a condition where others would work for him.

Overwork is repulsive to human nature—not work. Overwork for supplying the few with luxury—not work for the well-being of all. Work is a physiological necessity, a necessity of spending accumulated bodily energy, a necessity which is health and life itself. If so many branches of useful work are so reluctantly done now, it is merely because they mean overwork, or they are improperly organized. But we know—old Franklin knew it—that four hours of useful work every day would be more than sufficient for supplying everybody with the comfort of a moderately well-to-do middle-class house, if we all gave ourselves to productive work, and if we did not waste our productive powers as we do waste them now.

As to the childish question, repeated for fifty years: "Who would do disagreeable work?" frankly I regret that none of our *savants* has ever been brought to do it, be it for only one day in his life. If there is still work which is really disagreeable in itself, it is only because our scientific men have never cared to consider the means of rendering it less so. They have always known that there were plenty of starving men who would do it for a few cents a day.

As to the third—the chief—objection, which maintains the necessity of a government for punishing those who break the law of society, there is so much to say about it that it hardly can be touched incidentally. The more we study the question, the more we are brought to the conclusion that society itself is responsible for the anti-social deeds perpetrated in its midst, and that no punishment, no prisons, and no hangmen can diminish the numbers of such deeds; nothing short of a reorganization of society itself.

Three quarters of all the acts which are brought before our courts every year have their origin, either directly or indirectly, in the present disorganized state of society with regard to the production and distribution of wealth—not in perversity of human nature. As to the relatively few anti-social deeds which result from anti-social inclinations of separate individuals, it is not by prisons, nor even by resorting to the hangmen, that we can diminish their numbers. By our prisons, we merely multiply them and render them worse. By our detectives, our "price of blood," our executions, and our jails, we spread in society such a terrible flow of basest passions and habits, that he who should realize the effects of these institutions to their full extent would be frightened by what society is doing under the pretext of maintaining morality. We *must* search for other remedies, and the remedies have been indicated long since.

Of course now, when a mother in search of food and shelter for her children must pass by shops filled with the most refined delicacies of refined gluttony; when gorgeous and insolent luxury is displayed side by side with the most execrable misery; when the dog and the horse of a rich man are far better cared for than millions of children whose mothers earn a pitiful salary in the pit or the manufactory; when each "modest" evening dress of a lady represents eight months, or one year, of human labor; when enrichment at somebody else's expense is the avowed aim of the "upper classes," and no distinct boundary can be traced between honest and dishonest means of making money—then force is the only means for maintaining such a state of things. Then an army of policemen, judges, and hangmen becomes a necessary institution.

But if all our children—all children are *our* children—received a sound instruction and education—and we have the means of giving it; if every family lived in a decent home—and they *could* at the present high pitch of our production; if every boy and girl were taught a handicraft at the same time as he or she receives scientific instruction, and *not* to be a manual producer of wealth were considered as a token of inferiority; if men lived in closer contact with one another, and had continually to come into on those public affairs which now are vested in the few; and if, in consequence of a closer contact, we were brought to take as lively an interest in our neighbors' difficulties and pains as we formerly took in those of our kinsfolk—then we should not resort to policemen and judges, to prisons and executions. Anti-social deeds would be nipped in the bud, not punished. The few contests which would arise would be easily settled by arbitrators; and no more force would be necessary to impose their decisions than is required now for enforcing the decisions of the family tribunals of China.

And here we are brought to consider a great question: what would become of morality in a society which recognized no laws and proclaimed the full freedom of the individual. Our answer is plain. Public morality is independent from, and anterior to, law and religion. Until now, the teachings of morality have been associated with religious teachings. But the influence which religious teachings formerly exercised on the mind has faded of late, and the sanction which morality derived from religion has no longer the power it formerly had. Millions and millions grow in our cities who have lost the old faith. Is it a reason for throwing morality overboard, and for treating it with the same sarcasm as primitive cosmogony?

Obviously not. No society is possible without certain principles of morality generally recognized. If everyone grew accustomed to deceiving his fellow-men; if we never could rely on each other's promise and words; if everyone treated his fellow as an enemy, against whom every means of warfare is justifiable—no society could exist. And we see, in fact, that notwithstanding the decay of religious beliefs, the principles of morality remain unshaken. We even see irreligious people trying to raise the current standard of morality. The fact is that moral principles are independent of religious beliefs: they are anterior to them. The primitive Tchuktchis have no religion: they have only superstitions and fear of the hostile forces of nature; and nevertheless we find with them the very same principles of morality which are taught by Christians and Buddhists, Mussulmans and Hebrews. Nay, some of their practices imply a much higher standard of tribal morality than that which appears in our civilized society.

In fact, each new religion takes its moral principles from the only real stock of morality—the moral habits which grow with men as soon as they unite to live together in tribes, cities, or nations. No animal society is possible without resulting in a growth of certain moral habits of mutual support and even self-sacrifice for the common well-being. These habits are a necessary condition for the welfare of the species in its struggle for life—cooperation of individuals being a much more important factor in the struggle for the preservation of the species than the so-much-spoken-of physical struggle between individuals for the means of existence. The "fittest" in the organic world are those who grow accustomed to life in society; and life in society necessarily implies moral habits. As to mankind, it has during its long existence developed in its midst a nucleus of social habits, of moral habits, which cannot disappear as long as human societies exist. And therefore, notwithstanding the influences to the contrary which are now at work in consequence of our present economic relations, the nucleus of our moral habits continues to exist. Law and religion only formulate them and endeavor to enforce them by their sanction.

Whatever the variety of theories of morality, all can be brought under three chief catagories: the morality of religion; the utilitarian morality; and the theory of moral habits resulting from the very needs of life in society. Each religious morality sanctifies its prescriptions by making them originate from revelation; and it tries to impress its teachings on the mind by a promise of reward, or punishment, either in this or in a future life. The utilitarian morality maintains the idea of reward, but it finds it in man himself. It invites men to analyze their pleasures, to classify them, and to give preference to those which are most intense and most durable. We must recognize, however, that, although it has exercised some influence, this system has been judged too artificial by the great mass of human beings. And finally—whatever its varieties—there is the third system of morality which sees in moral actions—in those actions which are most powerful in rendering men best fitted for life in society—a mere necessity of the individual to enjoy the joys of his brethren, to suffer when some of his brethren are suffering; a habit and a second nature, slowly elaborated and perfected by life in society. That is the morality of mankind; and that is also the morality of anarchism.

Such are, in a very brief summary, the leading principles of anarchism. Each of them hurts many a prejudice, and yet each of them results from an analysis of the very tendencies displayed by human society. Each of them is rich in consequences and implies a thorough revision of many a current opinion. And anarchism is not a mere insight into a remote future. Already now, whatever the sphere of action of the individual, he can act, either in accordance with anarchist principles or on an opposite line. And all that may be done in that direction will be done in the direction to which further development goes. All that may be done in the opposite way will be an attempt to force humanity to go where it will *not* go.

38

LOOKING BACKWARD

EDWARD BELLAMY

Like Kropotkin, the American Socialist Edward Bellamy (1850–1898) thought that the process of "evolution" was leading inevitably to a cooperative Socialist society. But, unlike the anarchists, Bellamy believed that the state would continue to have a role under socialism, albeit a very different one. Bellamy put these thoughts into his best-selling novel *Looking Backward*, published in 1888. There Bellamy's late nineteenth-century hero, Julian West, falls into a deep, trancelike sleep, awakening (or so it seems) a century later to discover the socialist "evolution" that had occurred in the interim. His host, Dr. Leete, and the minister, Mr. Barton, lament the evils of the old capitalist system and explain the advantages of the new socialist society.

Source: Edward Bellamy, Looking Backward *(Boston: Ticknor, 1888).*

By way of attempting to give the reader some general impression of the way people lived together in those days, and especially of the relations of the rich and poor to one another, perhaps I cannot do better than to compare society as it then was to a prodigious coach which the masses of humanity were harnessed to and dragged toilsomely along a very hilly and sandy road. The driver was hunger, and permitted no lagging, though the pace was necessarily very slow. Despite the difficulty of drawing the coach at all along so hard a road, the top was covered with passengers who never got down, even at the steepest ascents. These seats on top were very breezy and comfortable. Well up out of the dust, their occupants could enjoy the scenery at their leisure, or critically discuss the merits of the straining team. Naturally such places were in great demand and the competition for them was keen, every one seeking as the first end in life to secure a seat on the coach for himself and to leave it to his child after him. By the rule of the coach a man could leave his seat to whom he wished, but on the other hand there were many accidents by which it might at any time be wholly lost. For all that they were so easy, the seats were very insecure, and at every sudden jolt of the coach persons were slipping out of them and falling to the ground, where they were instantly compelled to take hold of the rope and help to drag the coach on which they had before ridden so pleasantly. It was naturally regarded as a terrible misfortune to lose one's seat, and the apprehension that this might happen to them or their friends was a constant cloud upon the happiness of those who rode.

But did they think only of themselves? you ask. Was not their very luxury rendered intolerable to them by comparison with the lot of their brothers and sisters in the harness, and the knowledge that their own weight added to their toil? Had they no compassion for fellow beings from whom fortune only distinguished them? Oh, yes; commiseration was frequently expressed by those who rode for those who had to pull the coach, especially when the vehicle came to a bad place in the road, as it was constantly doing, or to a particular steep hill. At such times, the desperate straining of the team, their agonized leaping and plunging under the pitiless lashing of hunger, the many who fainted at the rope and were trampled in the mire, made a very distressing spectacle which often called forth highly creditable displays of feeling on the top of the coach. At such times the passengers would call down encouragingly to the toilers of the rope, exhorting them to patience, and holding out hopes of possible compensation in another world for the hardness of their lot, while others contributed to buy salves and liniments for the crippled and injured. It was agreed that it was a great pity that the coach should be so hard to pull, and there was a sense of general relief when the specially bad piece of road was gotten over. This relief was not, indeed, wholly on account of the team, for there was always some danger at these bad places of a general overturn in which all would lose their seats.

It must in truth be admitted that the main effect of the spectacle of the misery of the toilers at the rope was to enhance the passengers' sense of the value of their seats upon the coach, and to cause them to hold on to them more desperately than before. If the passengers could only have felt assured that neither they nor their friends would ever fall from the top, it is probable that, beyond contributing to the funds for liniments and bandages, they would have troubled themselves extremely little about those who dragged the coach.

I am well aware that this will appear to the men and women of the twentieth century as incredible inhumanity, but there are two facts, both very curious, which partly explain it. In the first place, it was firmly and sincerely believed that there was no other way in which Society could get along, except the many pulled at the rope and the few rode, and not only this, but that no very radical improvement even was possible, either in the harness, the coach, the roadway, or the distribution of the toil. It had always been as it was, and it always would be so. It was a pity, but it could not be helped, and philosophy forbade wasting compassion on what was beyond remedy.

The other fact is yet more curious, consisting in a singular hallucination which those on the top of the coach generally shared, that they were not exactly like their brothers and sisters who pulled at the rope, but of finer clay, in some way belonging to a higher order of beings who might justly expect to be drawn. This seems unaccountable, but, as I once rode on this very coach and shared that very hallucination, I ought to be believed. The strangest thing about the hallucination was that those who had but just climbed up from the ground, before they had outgrown the marks of the rope upon their hands, began to fall under its influence. As for those whose parents and grandparents before them had been so fortunate as to keep their seats on the top, the conviction they cherished of the essential difference between their sort of humanity and the common article was absolute. . . .

[PRODUCTION AND DISTRIBUTION]

[T]he warehouse . . . [provided a] remarkable illustration . . . of the prodigiously multiplied efficiency which perfect organization can give to labor. It is like a gigantic mill, into the hopper of which goods are being constantly poured by the train-load and ship-load, to issue at the other end in packages of pounds and ounces, yards and inches, pints and gallons, corresponding to the infinitely complex personal needs of half a million people. Dr. Leete, with the assistance of data furnished by me as to the way goods were sold in my day, figured out some astounding results in the way of the economies effected by the modern system.

As we set out homeward, I said: "After what I have seen today, together with what you have told me, and what I learned under Miss Leete's tutelage at the sample store, I have a tolerably clear idea of your system of distribution, and how it enables you to dispense with a circulating medium. But I should like very much to know something more about your system of production. You have told me in general how your industrial army is levied and organized, but who directs its efforts? What supreme authority determines what shall be done in every department, so that enough of everything is produced and yet no labor wasted? It seems to me that this must be a wonderfully complex and difficult function, requiring very unusual endowments."

"Does it indeed seem so to you?" responded Dr. Leete. "I assure you that it is nothing of the kind, but on the other hand so simple, and depending on principles so obvious and easily applied, that the functionaries at Washington to whom it is trusted require to be nothing more than men of fair abilities to discharge it to the entire satisfaction of the nation. The machine which they direct is indeed a vast one, but so logical in its principles and direct and simple in its workings, that it all but runs itself; and nobody but a fool could derange it, as I think you will agree after a few words of explanation. Since you already have a pretty good idea of the working of the distributive system, let us begin at that end. Even in your day statisticians were able to tell you the number of yards of cotton, velvet, woolen, the number of barrels of flour, potatoes, butter, number of pairs of shoes, hats, and umbrellas annually consumed by the nation. Owing to the fact that production was in private hands, and that there was no way of getting statistics of actual distribution, these figures were not exact, but they were nearly so. Now that every pin which is given out from a national warehouse is recorded, of course the figures of consumption for any week, month, or year, in the possession of the department of distribution at the end of that period, are precise. On these figures, allowing for tendencies to increase or decrease and for any special causes likely to affect demand, the estimates, say for a year ahead, are based. These estimates, with a proper margin for security, having been accepted by the general administration, the responsibility of the distributive department ceases until the goods are delivered to it. I speak of the estimates being furnished for an entire year ahead, but in reality they cover that much time only in case of the great staples for which the demand can be calculated on as steady. In the great majority of smaller industries for the product of which popular taste fluctuates, and novelty is frequently required, production is kept barely ahead of consumption, the distributive department furnishing frequent estimates based on the weekly state of demand.

"Now the entire field of productive and constructive industry is divided into ten great departments, each representing a group of allied industries, each particular industry being in turn represented by a subordinate bureau, which has a complete record of the plant and force under its control, of the present product, and means of increasing it. The estimates of the distributive department, after adoption by the administration, are sent as mandates to the ten great departments, which allot them to the subordinate bureaus representing the particular industries, and these set the men at work. Each bureau is responsible for the task given it, and this responsibility is enforced by departmental oversight and that of the administration; nor does the distributive department accept the product without its own inspection; while even if in the hands of the consumer an article turns out unfit, the system enables the fault to be traced back to the original workman. The production of the commodities for actual public consumption does not, of course, require by any means all the national force of workers. After the necessary contingents have been detailed for the various industries, the amount of labor left for other employment is expended in creating fixed capital, such as buildings, machinery, engineering works, and so forth."

"One point occurs to me," I said, "on which I should think there might be dissatisfaction. Where there is no opportunity for private enterprise, how is there any assurance that the claims of small minorities of the people to have articles produced, for which there is no wide demand, will be respected? An official decree at any moment may deprive them of the means of gratifying some special taste, merely because the majority does not share it."

"That would be tyranny indeed," replied Dr. Leete, "and you may be very sure that it does not happen with us, to whom liberty is as dear as equality or fraternity. As you come to know our system better, you will see that our officials are in fact, and not merely in name, the agents and servants of the people. The administration has no power to stop the production of any commodity for which there continues to be a demand. Suppose the demand for any article declines to such a point that its production becomes very costly. The price has to be raised in proportion, of course, but as long as the consumer cares to pay it, the production goes on. Again, suppose an article not before produced is demanded. If the administration doubts the reality of the demand, a popular petition guaranteeing a certain basis of consumption compels it to produce the desired article. A government, or a majority, which should undertake to tell the people, or a minority, what they were to eat, drink, or wear, as I believe governments in America did in your day, would be regarded as a curious anachronism indeed. Possibly you had reasons for tolerating these infringements of personal independence, but we should not think them endurable. I am glad you raised this point, for it has given me a chance to show you how much more direct and efficient is the control over production exercised by the individual citizen now than it was in your day, when what you called private initiative prevailed, though it should have been called capitalist initiative, for the average private citizen had little enough share in it."

"You speak of raising the price of costly articles," I said, "How can prices be regulated in a country where there is no competition between buyers or sellers?"

"Just as they were with you," replied Dr. Leete. "You think that needs explaining," he added, as I looked incredulous, "but the explanation need not be long; the cost of the labor which produced it was recognized as the legitimate basis of the price of an article in your day, and so it is in ours. In your day, it was the difference in wages that made the difference in the cost of labor; now it is the relative number of hours constituting a day's work in different trades, the maintenance of the worker being equal in all cases. The cost of a man's work in a trade so difficult that in order to attract volunteers the hours have to be fixed at four a day is twice as great as that in a trade where the men work eight hours. The result as to the cost of labor, you see, is just the same as if the man working four hours were paid, under your system, twice the wages the other gets. This calculation applied to the labor employed in the various processes of a manufactured article gives its price relatively to other articles. Besides the cost of production and transportation, the factor of scarcity affects the prices of some commodities. As regards the great staples of life, of which an abundance can always be secured, scarcity is eliminated as a factor. There is always a large surplus kept on hand from which any fluctuations of demand or supply can be corrected, even in most cases of bad crops. The prices of the staples grow less year by year, but rarely, if ever, rise. There are, however, certain classes of articles permanently, and others temporarily, unequal to the demand, as, for example, fresh fish or dairy products in the latter category, and the products of high skill and rare materials in the other. All that can be done here is to equalize the inconvenience of the scarcity. This is done by temporarily raising the price if the scarcity be temporary, or fixing it high if it be permanent. High prices in your day meant restriction of the articles affected to the rich, but nowadays, when the means of all are the same, the effect is only that those to whom the articles seem most desirable are the ones who purchase them. Of course the nation, as any other caterer for the public needs must be, is frequently left with small lots of goods on its hands by changes in taste, unseasonable weather, and various other causes. These it has to dispose of at a sacrifice just as merchants often did in your day, charging up the loss to the expenses of the business. Owing, however, to the vast body of consumers to which such lots can be simultaneously offered, there is rarely any difficulty in getting rid of them at trifling loss. I have given you now some general notion of our system of production, as well as distribution. Do you find it as complex as you expected?"

I admitted that nothing could be much simpler.

"I am sure," said Dr. Leete, "that it is within the truth to say that the head of one of the myriad private businesses of your day, who had to maintain sleepless vigilance against the fluctuations of the market, the machinations of his rivals, and the failure of his debtors, had a far more trying task than the group of men at Washington who nowadays direct the industries of the entire nation. All this merely shows, my dear fellow, how much easier it is to do things the right way than the wrong. It is easier for a general up in a balloon, with perfect survey of the field, to manoeuvre a million men to victory than for a sergeant to manage a platoon in a thicket."

"The general of this army, including the flower of the manhood of the nation, must be the foremost man in the country, really greater even than the President of the United States," I said.

"He is the President of the United States," replied Dr. Leete, "or rather the most important function of the presidency is the headship of the industrial army."

"How is he chosen?" I asked.

"I explained to you before," replied Dr. Leete, "when I was describing the force of the motive of emulation among all grades of the industrial army, that the line of promotion for the meritorious lies through three grades to the officer's grade, and thence up through the lieutenancies to the captaincy or foremanship, and superintendency or colonel's rank. Next, with an intervening grade in some of the larger trades, come the general of the guild, under whose immediate control all the operations of the trade are conducted. This officer is at the head of the national bureau representing his trade, and is responsible for its work to the administration. The general of his guild holds a splendid position, and one which amply satisfies the ambition of most men, but above his rank, which may be compared—to follow the military analogies familiar to you—to that of a general of division or major-general, is that of the chiefs of the ten great departments, or groups of allied trades. The chiefs of these ten grand divisions of the industrial army may be compared to your commanders of army corps, or lieutenant-generals, each having from a dozen to a score of generals of separate guilds reporting to him. Above these ten great officers, who form his council, is the general-in-chief, who is the President of the United States.

"The general-in-chief of the industrial army must have passed through all the grades below him, from the common laborers up. Let us see how he rises. As I have told you, it is simply by the excellence of his record as a worker that one rises through the grades of the privates and becomes a candidate for a lieutenancy. Through the lieutenancies he rises to the colonelcy, or superintendent's position, by appointment from above, strictly limited to the candidates of the best records. The general of the guild appoints to the ranks under him, but he himself is not appointed, but chosen by suffrage."

"By suffrage!" I exclaimed. "Is not that ruinous to the discipline of the guild, by tempting the candidates to intrigue for the support of the workers under them?"

"So it would be, no doubt," replied Dr. Leete, "if the workers had any suffrage to exercise, or anything to say about the choice. But they have nothing. Just here comes in a peculiarity of our system. The general of the guild is chosen from among the superintendents by vote of the honorary members of the guild, that is, of those who have served their time in the guild and received their discharge. As you know, at the age of forty-five we are mustered out of the army of industry, and have the residue of life for the pursuit of our own improvement or recreation. Of course, however, the associations of our active lifetime retain a powerful hold on us. The companionships we formed then remain our companionships till the end of life. We always continue honorary members of our former guilds, and retain the keenest and most jealous interest in their welfare and repute in the hands of the following generation. In the clubs maintained by the honorary members of the several guilds, in which we meet socially, there are no topics of conversation so commonly as those which relate to these matters, and the young aspirants for guild leadership who can pass the criticism of us old fellows are likely to be pretty well equipped. Recognizing this fact, the nation entrusts to the honorary members of each guild the election of its general, and I venture to claim that no previous form of society could have developed a body of electors so ideally adapted to their office, as regards absolute impartiality, knowledge of the special qualifications and record of candidates, solicitude for the best result, and complete absence of self-interest.

"Each of the ten lieutenant-generals or heads of departments is himself elected from among the generals of the guilds grouped as a department, by vote of the honorary members of the guilds thus grouped. Of course there is a tendency on the part of each guild to vote for its own general, but no guild of any group has nearly enough votes to elect a man not supported by most of the others. I assure you that these elections are exceedingly lively."

"The President, I suppose, is selected from among the ten heads of the great departments," I suggested.

"Precisely, but the heads of departments are not eligible to the presidency till they have been a certain number of years out of office. It is rarely that a man passes through all the grades to the headship of a department much before he is forty, and at the end of a five years' term he is usually forty-five. If more, he still serves through his term, and if less, he is nevertheless discharged from the industrial army at its termination. It would not do for him to return to the ranks. The interval before he is a candidate for the presidency is intended to give time for him to recognize fully that he has returned into the general mass of the nation, and is identified with it rather than with the industrial army.

Moreover, it is expected that he will employ this period in studying the general condition of the army, instead of that of the special group of guilds of which he was the head. From among the former heads of departments who may be eligible at the time, the President is elected by vote of all the men of the nation who are not connected with the industrial army."

"The army is not allowed to vote for President?"

"Certainly not. That would be perilous to its discipline, which it is the business of the President to maintain as the representative of the nation at large. His right hand for this purpose is the inspectorate, a highly important department of our system; to the inspectorate come all complaints or information as to defects in goods, insolence or inefficiency of officials, or dereliction of any sort in the public service. The inspectorate, however, does not wait for complaints. Not only is it on the alert to catch and sift every rumor of a fault in the service, but it is its business, by systematic and constant oversight and inspection of every branch of the army, to find out what is going wrong before anybody else does. The President is usually not far from fifty when elected, and serves five years, forming an honorable exception to the rule of retirement at forty-five. At the end of his term of office, a national Congress is called to receive his report and approve or condemn it. If it is approved, Congress usually elects him to represent the nation for five years more in the international council. Congress, I should also say, passes on the reports of the outgoing heads of departments, and a disapproval renders any one of them ineligible for President. But it is rare, indeed, that the nation has occasion for other sentiments than those of gratitude toward its high officers. As to their ability, to have risen from the ranks, by tests so various and severe, to their positions, is proof in itself of extraordinary qualities, while as to faithfulness, our social system leaves them absolutely without any other motive than that of winning the esteem of their fellow citizens. Corruption is impossible in a society where there is neither poverty to be bribed nor wealth to bribe, while as to demagoguery or intrigue for office, the conditions of promotion render them out of the question."

"One point I do not quite understand," I said. "Are the members of the liberal professions eligible to the presidency? and if so, how are they ranked with those who pursue the industries proper?"

"They have no ranking with them," replied Dr. Leete. "The members of the technical professions, such as engineers and architects, have a ranking with the constructive guilds; but the members of the liberal professions, the doctors and teachers, as well as the artists and men of letters who obtain remissions of industrial service, do not belong to the industrial army. On this ground they vote for the President, but are not eligible to his office. One of its main duties being the control and discipline of the industrial army, it is essential that the President should have passed through all its grades to understand his business."

"That is reasonable," I said; "but if the doctors and teachers do not know enough of industry to be President, neither, I should think, can the President know enough of medicine and education to control those departments."

"No more does he," was the reply. "Except in the general way that he is responsible for the enforcement of the laws as to all classes, the President has nothing to do with the faculties of medicine and education, which are controlled by boards of regents of their own, in which the President is ex-officio chairman, and has the casting vote. These regents, who, of course, are responsible to Congress, are chosen by the honorary members of the guilds of education and medicine, the retired teachers and doctors of the country."

"Do you know," I said, "the method of electing officials by votes of the retired members of the guilds is nothing more than the application on a national scale of the plan of government by alumni, which we used to a slight extent occasionally in the management of our higher educational institutions."

"Did you, indeed?" exclaimed Dr. Leete,

with animation. "That is quite new to me, and I fancy will be to most of us, and of much interest as well. There has been great discussion as to the germ of the idea, and we fancied that there was for once something new under the sun. Well! well! In your higher educational institutions! that is interesting indeed. You must tell me more of that."

"Truly, there is very little more to tell than I have told already," I replied. "If we had the germ of your idea, it was but as a germ. . . ." *[Later Julian West attends a church service and hears the following sermon.—Eds.]*

MR. BARTON'S SERMON

"We have had among us, during the past week, a critic from the nineteenth century, a living representative of the epoch of our great-grandparents. It would be strange if a fact so extraordinary had not somewhat strongly affected our imaginations. Perhaps most of us have been stimulated to some effort to realize the society of a century ago, and figure to ourselves what it must have been like to live then. In inviting you now to consider certain reflections upon this subject which have occurred to me, I presume that I shall rather follow than divert the course of your own thoughts. . . .

"Although the idea of the vital unity of the family of mankind, the reality of human brotherhood, was very far from being apprehended by them as the moral axiom it seems to us, yet it is a mistake to suppose that there was no feeling at all corresponding to it. I could read you passages of great beauty from some of their writers which show that the conception was clearly attained by a few, and no doubt vaguely by many more. Moreover, it must not be forgotten that the nineteenth century was in name Christian, and the fact that the entire commercial and industrial frame of society was the embodiment of the anti-Christian spirit must have had some weight, though I admit it was strangely little, with the nominal followers of Jesus Christ.

"When we inquire why it did not have more, why, in general, long after a vast majority of men had agreed as to the crying abuses of the existing social arrangement, they still tolerated it, or contented themselves with talking of petty reforms in it, we come upon an extraordinary fact. It was the sincere belief of even the best of men at that epoch that the only stable elements in human nature, on which a social system could be safely founded were its worst propensities. They had been taught and believed that greed and self-seeking were all that held mankind together, and that all human associations would fall to pieces if anything were done to blunt the edge of these motives or curb their operation. In a word, they believed—even those who longed to believe otherwise—the exact reverse of what seems to us self-evident; they believed, that is, that the anti-social qualities of men, and not their social qualities, were what furnished the cohesive force of society. It seemed reasonable to them that men lived together solely for the purpose of overreaching and oppressing one another, and of being overreached and oppressed, and that while a society that gave full scope to these propensities could stand, there would be little chance for one based on the idea of co-operation for the benefit of all. It seems absurd to expect any one to believe that convictions like these were ever seriously entertained by men; but that they were not only entertained by our great-grandfathers, but were responsible for the long delay in doing away with the ancient order, after a conviction of its intolerable abuses had become general, is as well established as any fact in history can be. Just here you will find the explanation of the profound pessimism of the literature of the last quarter of the nineteenth century, the note of melancholy in its poetry, and the cynicism of its humor.

"Feeling that the condition of the race was unendurable, they had no clear hope of anything better. They believed that the evolution of humanity had resulted in leading it into a *cul de sac*, and that there was no way of getting forward. The frame of men's minds at this time is strikingly illustrated by treatises which have come down to us, and may even now be consulted in our libraries by the curious, in which laborious arguments are pursued to prove that despite the evil plight of men, life was still, by some slight preponderance of considerations, probably better worth living than leaving. Despising themselves, they despised their Creator. There was a general decay of religious belief. Pale and watery gleams, from skies thickly veiled by doubt and dread, alone lighted up the chaos of earth. That men should doubt Him whose breath is in their nostrils, or dread the hands that moulded them, seems to us indeed a pitiable insanity; but we must remember that children who are brave by day have sometimes foolish fears at night. The dawn has come since then. It is very easy to believe in the fatherhood of God in the twentieth century. . . .

"You know the story of that last, greatest, and most bloodless of revolutions. In the time of one generation men laid aside the social traditions and practices of barbarians, and assumed a social order worthy of rational and human beings. Ceasing to be predatory in their habits, they became co-workers, and found in fraternity, at once, the science of wealth and happiness. 'What shall I eat and drink, and wherewithal shall I be clothed?' stated as a problem beginning and ending in self, had been an anxious and an endless one. But when once it was conceived, not from the individual, but the fraternal standpoint, 'What shall we eat and drink, and wherewithal shall we be clothed?'—its difficulties vanished.

"Poverty with servitude had been the result, for the mass of humanity, of attempting to solve the problem of maintenance from the individual standpoint, but no sooner had the nation become the sole capitalist and employer than not alone did plenty replace poverty, but the last vestige of the serfdom of man to man disappeared from earth. Human slavery, so often vainly scotched, at last was killed. The means of subsistence no longer doled out by men to women, by employer to employed, by rich to poor, was distributed from a common stock as among children at the father's table. It was impossible for a man any longer to use his fellowmen as tools for his own profit. His esteem was the only sort of gain he could thenceforth make out of him. There was no more either arrogance or servility in the relations of human beings to one another. For the first time since the creation every man stood up straight before God. The fear of want and the lust of gain became extinct motives when abundance was assured to all and immoderate possessions were made impossible of attainment. There were no more beggars nor almoners. Equity left charity without an occupation. The ten commandments became well-nigh obsolete in a world where there was no temptation to theft, no occasion to lie either for fear or favor, no room for envy where all were equal, and little provocation to violence where men were disarmed of power to injure one another. Humanity's ancient dream of liberty, equality, fraternity, mocked by so many ages, at last was realized.

"As in the old society the generous, the just, the tender-hearted had been placed at a disadvantage by the possession of those qualities, so in the new society the cold-hearted, the greedy, and self-seeking found themselves out of joint with world. Now that the conditions of life for the first time ceased to operate as a forcing process to develop the brutal qualities of human nature, and the premium which had heretofore encouraged selfishness was not only removed, but placed upon unselfishness, it was for the first time possible to see what unperverted human nature really was like. The depraved tendencies, which had previously overgrown and obscured the better to so large an extent, now withered like cellar fungi in the open air, and the nobler qualities showed a sudden luxuriance which turned cynics into panegyrists and for the first time in human history tempted mankind to fall in love with itself. Soon was fully revealed, what the divines and philosophers of the old world never would have believed, that human nature in its essential qualities is good, not bad, that men by their natural intention and structure are generous, not selfish, pitiful, not cruel, sympathetic, not arrogant, godlike in aspiration, instinct with divinest impulses of tenderness and self-sacrifice, images of God indeed, not the travesties upon Him they had seemed. The constant pressure, through numberless generations, of conditions of life which might have perverted angels, had not been able to essentially alter the natural nobility of the stock, and these conditions once removed, like a bent tree, it had sprung back to its normal uprightness. . . .

"But how is it with us who stand on this height which they gazed up to? Already we have well-nigh forgotten, except when it is especially called to our minds by some occasion like the present, that it was not always with men as it is now. It is a strain on our imaginations to conceive the social arrangements of our immediate ancestors. We find them grotesque. The solution of the problem of physical maintenance so as to banish care and crime, so far from seeming to us an ultimate attainment, appears but as a preliminary to anything like real human progress. We have but relieved ourselves of an impertinent and needless harassment which hindered our ancestors from undertaking the real ends of existence. We are merely stripped for the race; no more. We are like a child which has just learned to stand upright and to walk. It is a great event, from the child's point of view, when he first walks. Perhaps he fancies that there can be little beyond that achievement, but a year later he has forgotten that he could not always walk. His horizon did but widen when he rose, and enlarge as he moved. A great event indeed, in one sense, was his first step, but only as a beginning, not as the end. His true career was but then first entered on. The enfranchisement of humanity in the last century, from mental and physical absorption in working and scheming for the mere bodily necessities, may be regarded as a species of second birth of the race, without which its first birth to an existence that was but a burden would forever have remained unjustified, but whereby it is now abundantly vindicated. Since then, humanity has entered on a new phase of spiritual development, an evolution of higher faculties, the very existence of which in human nature our ancestors scarcely suspected. In place of the dreary hopelessness of the nineteenth century, its profound pessimism as to the future of humanity, the animating idea of the present age is an enthusiastic conception of the opportunities of our earthly existence, and the unbounded possibilities of human nature. The betterment of mankind from generation to generation, physically, mentally, morally, is recognized as the one great object supremely worthy of effort and of sacrifice. We believe the race for the first time to have entered on the realization of God's ideal of it, and each generation must now be a step upward.

"Do you ask what we look for when unnumbered generations shall have passed away? I answer, the way stretches far before us, but the end is lost in light. For twofold is the return of man to God 'who is our home,' the return of the individual by the way of death, and the return of the race by the fulfilment of the evolution, when the divine secret hidden in the germ shall be perfectly unfolded. With a tear for the dark past, turn we then to the dazzling future, and, veiling our eyes, press forward. The long and weary winter of the race is ended. Its summer has begun. Humanity has burst the chrysalis. The heavens are before it."

39

WHY WE NEED SOCIALISM IN AMERICA

MICHAEL HARRINGTON

The American socialist Michael Harrington (1928–1989) argued that the United States needed socialism, albeit of a nonauthoritarian and distinctly democratic variety. Once the facts about unemployment, poverty, homelessness, hopelessness, and despair became known, he hoped, Americans would be compassionate enough to turn to socialism as the only just, equitable—and, above all, democratic—alternative to a corporate capitalist society that placed a premium on profit, to the neglect of other, more worthy goals. Only in a democratic socialist society, Harrington believed, could the American dream of equal freedom and opportunity for all, regardless of class or race, really come true.

Source: Michael Harrington, "Why We Need Socialism in America," Dissent *(May–June 1970), pp. 240–242, 280–287. Reprinted by permission.*

America needs socialism. Our technology has produced unprecedented wealth, rotted great cities, threatened the very air and water, and embittered races, generations, and social classes.

Our vision of society, even when most liberal, is too conservative to resolve these contradictions, for they are aspects of a system that has a deep, even principled commitment to the wrong priorities. And while significant reforms—often socialist in inspiration—have modified some of the extreme forms of capitalist injustice, the post-Keynesian welfare state still allows huge corporations to make decisions of fundamental social importance without consulting either those who are affected or those who work for them.

But isn't it an act of leftist nostalgia to indict American society in this way? Today, one is told, the United States is the richest country in the history of mankind, and its remaining problems can be taken care of by pragmatic technicians acting within the framework of the welfare state.

It is precisely this conventional assumption about our present and future that I propose to challenge. I will show that our affluence is so misshapen that it does not even meet the needs of the majority of the people. The most humane of technocrats cannot cope with the basic causes of these antisocial policies, if only because they are located in an entrenched and possessive system of power. Only a democratic mass movement could challenge this vested interest in our current crises. And it is just possible that the "success" of American capitalism will accomplish what its sweatshops failed to do: make socialism politically relevant.

I say these things with a full knowledge of the ways in which the socialist idea has been confused, betrayed, and eviscerated during the past 150 years. Indeed, one of the aims of this essay is to try to face up to these difficulties with candor and to make the idea of socialism more precise. If that attempt is successful, what will emerge at the end of this study will not be the promise of a magical cure-all to bring complete and eternal happiness to all men but a more modest yet still audacious program for making America a good society.

IS REFORM OF THE WELFARE STATE ENOUGH?

There are three basic reasons why the reform of the welfare state will not solve our most urgent problems:

- the class structure of capitalist society vitiates, or subverts, almost every such effort toward social justice;
- private, corporate power cannot tolerate the comprehensive and democratic planning we desperately need;
- and even if these first two obstacles to providing every citizen with a decent house, income, and job were overcome, the system still has an inherent tendency to make affluence self-destructive.

In thus documenting the limits of the welfare state it may seem that I am contemptuous of past reforms or of those liberals who do not share my conviction that there must be fundamental, structural change. Nothing could be further from the truth. The welfare state was an enormous advance over the cruelty and indifference to human suffering that characterized early capitalism. It was achieved through struggle and great sacrifice—sometimes of life itself—on the part of "ordinary" people who, even though they had usually been denied an adequate education, tutored the wealthy in some of the fundamentals of social decency. And to the extent that there is a mass "left wing" in the United States, it is composed largely of precisely those groups—trade unionists, minorities, middle-class idealists—which fought these great battles and are determined to preserve the gains they brought.

Far from being simply a matter of keeping the record straight, this point has profound political implications for the future. It is important that socialists demonstrate the inherent inability of the welfare state, based as it is upon a capitalist economy and social structure, to deal with problems that demand anticapitalist allocations of resources. But that does not mean, as some young leftists in recent times have thought, that the welfare state is to be dismissed as a "fraud" that prevents the people from coming to truly radical conclusions. For if millions of Americans are to become socialists they will do so because, in the struggle to make that welfare state respond to their immediate needs they will have discovered that they must go beyond it. If socialists were arrogantly to dismiss these battles as irrelevant, they would play no role when masses of their fellow citizens turned left.

Socialists, then, must be in the forefront of every fight to defend and extend the welfare state, even as they criticize its inability to solve fundamental problems and even as they propose alternatives to it. In this context, the following analysis of the severe limits capitalism imposes upon the welfare state is designed not to prove that liberals are foolish and deluded, but that their liberal values can only be completely realized on the basis of a socialist program.

The welfare state, for all its value, tends to provide benefits in inverse relationship to human need. And not—the point is crucial—because there is a conspiracy of the affluent, but as a "natural" consequence of the division of society into unequal social classes.

Through vigorous and radical reforms it is possible to offset—though not to remove—this inherent tendency within capitalist society to distribute public benefits according to the inequalities of private wealth. Any movement that attempts to carry out such reforms will be going against the grain of the system itself. This has not kept socialists from participating in every one of these struggles, nor will it in the future. But if the gains are to be permanent, if they are not to be reversed when a period of social innovation is followed by a swing back to capitalist normality, then there must be basic, structural changes. Instead of episodic victories within an antisocial environment, there must be a concerted effort to create a new human environment. . . .

THE VISION OF SOCIALISM

Though the changes I have been talking about go far beyond any proposals by major political movements in neocapitalist society, they are still only transitional measures. They would profoundly improve and humanize the old order but would not yet constitute a new and revolutionary order. So it is now necessary to look beyond scarcity to the ultimate vision of socialism itself.

In envisaging the transcendent potential of social change I am not, I hope, indulging in holiday rhetoric to console those who spend their lives in mundane struggles—nor am I implying that history will one day enter paradise. But in the particulars of this or that conflict, each increment of progress can be better structured if it is related to the vision of a qualitative change in the human condition. If, as I will argue in a moment, the abolition of money and work are basic socialist values, that has some bearing on tomorrow's urgent trade union negotiations and on the next welfare measure in the legislature. It was, for example, a prophetic notion of more dignity for human beings which led the British socialists in 1945 to reject a means test for the new social services they were providing.

There is also a certain danger in carrying out the socialist idea to its ultimate conclusions. It was first pointed out by that great antisocialist, Fyodor Dostoevsky, and it has since gained in relevance. Dostoevsky argued that messianic socialism, the pretence of a total earthly salvation analogous to Christian redemption, would lead to totalitarianism. Man, he said, cannot be so completely refashioned, and those who claim to do so will, in the name of nonviolence and brotherhood, be driven to force and dictatorship. Dostoevsky did not understand his own prejudices when he made this analysis, but the alarm he sounded was quite real.

Now it is not true, as some conservatives think, that the Communist countries are the proof of Dostoevsky's prophecy. For, as I noted earlier, Marx himself had understood as early as in the 1840s that the attempt to base socialism on an economy of scarcity would lead to new forms of exploitation and repression, not to socialism. Even so, Dostoevsky did brilliantly intuit the logic and psychology of totalitarianism, the way in which the promise of total cooperation and consensus can become the excuse for total coercion and terror. With the means of scientific manipulation developed since Dostoevsky's time, advanced societies could, in the name of absolute justice, act out the injustices which he perceived but in a far more efficient technological way than he could have foreseen.

It is therefore important to insist upon the limitations of socialism as a prelude to describing how it seeks to break through some of our present limits. It proposes a solution, not to all human ills, but to those based upon the economic, social, and political conditions of life. In contrast to what Marx thought, it may well be that once man stops dying from famines and depressions and starts to die only from death, there will be a resurgence of the religious spirit, not an end to it. "Under Communism," Sidney Hook once wrote, "man ceases to suffer as an animal and suffers as a human. He therefore moves from the plane of the pitiful to the plane of the tragic."[1]

To grant that socialism is not a final redemption should not, however, paralyze the imagination, for even within these limits there are enormous possibilities. For instance, I think that Stanley Moore overreacted in his legitimate hostility to the demands of some of the youthful New Leftists for "Gemeinschaft Now!" "Is it not enough," Moore wrote, "for the proletarian revolution to abolish the division of labor between wage workers and capitalists? Why does Marx suggest in the *German Ideology* that communism will eliminate *all* division of labor?"[2] For there are present tendencies, and there is a certain future socialist potential, toward redefining work along the lines Marx suggested.

In what follows there will be a "dialectical" tension. On the one hand, I want to avoid that absolutist view of socialism which is so transcendental that it drives its true believers to totalitarianism and an antisocialist society; on the other hand, I want to suggest the truly radical potential for human change that exists today. And with these caveats, I would stress two elements as crucial in my definition of the socialist future. Society should move toward, even if it never reaches, the abolition of work and money.

Can Work Be Abolished? Should It?

Marx's vision of socialism was as radical as Stanley Moore complains it was. I quote extensively, not because it comes from Marx, but because I think it remains an accurate perception of the most desirable possibility of social change.

> The realm of freedom [Marx held] begins first with the fact that work ceases to be determined by need and external expediency; so in the nature of things it will be located beyond the sphere of material production in the proper sense of the word. As the savage must wrestle with nature to satisfy his needs and to maintain and reproduce his life, so must civilized man do the same thing under all social forms and possible modes of production. With his development, man expands the realm of material necessity and his own needs; but at the same time, he expands the productive forces which satisfy them. In this sphere, freedom can only emerge if socialized man [*vergesellschafteter Mensch*], the associated producers [*assozierte Produzenten*] regulate their relation to nature rationally and bring it under communal [*gemeinschaftliche*] control, rather than being ruled by it as by a blind power; and if this is accomplished with the least expenditure of effort and under conditions worthy and adequate to human nature. But this remains always as the realm of necessity. Beyond that there begins the true realm of freedom where the development of man's powers becomes an end in itself, a realm which can only bloom on the basis of the realm of necessity. The shortening of the working day is its fundamental premise.[3]

Essentially Marx is saying that, in the fullness of socialism, all men will work like artists, out of an inner need and satisfaction, and not because they are forced to earn their daily bread. In arguing that even in the planned, socially controlled society, work is still unfree as long as it is compulsory, Marx was anticipating that passionate antisocialist, Friedrich Nietzsche, who wrote, "Phew! To speak as if an increase in the impersonality inside a mechanized plant will make a new society and turn the scandal of slavery into a virtue!"[4]

By now we have become so accustomed to the regime of compulsory (in an economic sense) labor that we have lost even the memory of the precapitalist period when leisure was more common. For, as Marx documented in his brilliant history of the bourgeois struggle to lengthen the working day and week, the limit that Massachusetts law set upon the labor of children in the nineteenth century defined the normal working day for an adult in the seventeenth century.[5] In the Middle Ages the working year was only 150–200 days.[6] Nietzsche's insight reflected, if from a reactionary point of view, an instinctive understanding of working people whose lives had been subjected to the calculation of clocks and the division of labor. A hundred or so years later we have "progressed" to the point where we have forgotten how natural it is not to work.

What Marx understood, however, and Nietzsche did not, was that the application of science and technology make it possible—even necessary—to change the very nature of work. Marx had glimpsed the coming of automation as early as the late 1850s. Just before the passage I have quoted on the realm of freedom, he wrote, "The actual wealth of society and the possibility of a continued expansion of its process of reproduction do not depend upon the duration of surplus labor, but upon its productivity and the more or less fertile conditions of production under which it is performed."[7]

In other words, the evolution of technology would progressively reduce the need for human labor, and this economic trend would make possible the socialist realm of freedom. In his notes for *Das Kapital,* Marx was even more specific about the tendency he summarized in Volume Three of that work. He not only argued that the increasing productivity of machine production would make it possible for society progressively to reduce labor time; he held that it would become a necessity.[8] The output of an automated economy, Marx said, would increase so fast that, if title to consumption were still determined by labor time, society could not possibly use up its own production. Therefore, as a matter of survival, such an economy would have to shorten the working day and increase the consumption of the masses. In order to release these surging forces of production, a new mode of production becomes a practical necessity.

Is it poetic license to say that Marx was talking about automation? Now it is obvious that he did not have advance knowledge of the computers and cybernated equipment that were not invented until long after his death. But it is extraordinary that his analysis of the capitalist dynamic did lead him to anticipate in broad outline what automation would mean. Marx had rightly seen (and Joseph Schumpeter thought it his great accomplishment) that one of the basic laws of motion in capitalist society was for competition to beget monopoly and a consequent tendency to increase investment in machines (in the Marxist vocabulary, for constant capital to grow in relationship to variable capital, thus changing the "organic composition" of capital itself). "In this transformation," Marx said, "it is neither the immediate labor which man himself performs, nor the time during which he works, but the appropriation of his common productivity . . . in a word, the development of the socialized individual, which is the basic source of richness and production."[9]

This reference to the "socialized individual" has a very specific economic meaning. The increasing investment per worker who tends more and more sophisticated machines enables the individual to produce out of all proportion to his own physical powers. Through science and its application to industry, one man can do as much as a hundred, or a thousand men used to do. Moreover—and if this is not an anticipation of automation, what is it?—"men relate more and more to the productive process as watchers and regulators."[10]

The Promise, or Threat, of Automation

Within capitalism this develoment threatens the very existence of the system: success is suicidal. On the one hand, capitalism "uses all the power of science and nature, of social cooperation and social exchange, to make the creation of wealth (relatively) independent of the amount of labor time expended."[11] On the other hand, capitalism proposes to measure, and consume, this output in terms of labor time which sets a limit upon what can be sold; the worker, who through technology produces as if he were a thousand men, is paid as an individual. So the increase in productivity within a class society—where its benefits are necessarily maldistributed—has a tendency to decrease effective demand. An unprecedented accomplishment, Marx concluded, would contain the seeds of crisis.[12]

The basic technological trend Marx predicted has indeed come to pass. Yet the crisis it was supposed to occasion has not. Why?

Marx, it turned out, was wrong to think that capitalism was necessarily helpless to deal with its own abundance. There has been widespread state intervention to correct the "natural" tendency of the system to catastrophe (though, more often than not, these measures were introduced at the behest of the labor and socialist movements and against the determined opposition of a significant section of business). But this does not mean that the neo-Keynesian complacency of the National Commission on Technology, Automation and Economic Progress is justified. Federal fiscal policy, the Commission said in summarizing the prevailing reform attitude, could supply the deficiencies in aggregate demand for any rate of technological innovation.[13] If productivity increase eliminated particular jobs, then government action would create an economic environment in which new work would be forthcoming. In other words, Marx's insight was partially validated and partially annulled. The society would indeed have to spend socially in order to buy back its own incredible output; and by doing so it could contain even a revolutionary technology within the established framework.

But this optimism ignores the evidence presented in this essay: that government spending, precisely because it follows a commercial calculus, has "solved" one crisis by worsening other crises. For if capitalism was more flexible than Marx thought, it still had to design, or stumble into, ameliorative programs that would preserve the structural injustices of the society. It created 1.7 million "jobs" to prosecute the tragedy in Vietnam without hesitation, but it would only fund a handful of social employments; it provided billions in disguised welfare for the housing of the rich and a pittance for the poor; etc. And these perverse appropriations were not miscalculations or the result of ill will, but expressions of the most basic values of the system itself.

This is the key to that paradox presented by the National Commission of the Causes and Prevention of Violence under Dr. Milton Eisenhower: that after the most prosperous decade in the nation's history, it is in imminent danger of building a hate-ridden, strife-torn anti-utopia.

Can All Men Be Creative?

Socialism would be free of precisely those constraints which make it structurally impossible for capitalism to make a truly social use of its productivity. In the immediate future, a democratically socialized society could use this enormous economic power to meet the needs of America and to aid in the industrialization of the world. There is so much work that needs to be done within this country and internationally that the next several generations, at least, must put the "socialized individual" to work meeting basic needs. Yet in the more distant future it is not only possible, but perhaps necessary, for society to enter that Kingdom of Freedom which Marx described. Once the basic needs of all of mankind are provided for, and productivity still grows, men may be forced to live without compulsory work. The sentence decreed in the Garden of Eden will have been served.

I would not suggest that a psychic transition of this character will be easy. It is a familar phenomenon that some people are crushed by retirement, bewildered when the compulsion of work is removed from their lives. At a conference sponsored by DISSENT in 1969, Meyer Schapiro, a brilliant art critic and socialist, placed this kind of crisis in a thoughtful context. The ideal of the artist, of freely chosen and loving work, Schapiro said, is problematic even for the the artists themselves and would be infinitely more difficult to apply in the lives of the masses of people. For every successful painter or sculptor there are many others whose hopes are disappointed. And even those who do succeed often require tremendous sacrifice from their family and friends in order to develop their genius.

I suspect that Schapiro has touched upon one of the fundamental social-psychological issues of the twenty-first century: whether, in an economy of abundance, men can find within themselves and their relations with one another, rather than in external necessity, a reason for living. The problem with this aspect of the ultimate socialist projection arises because Marx's cultural vision was so thoroughly aristocratic. He hoped for nothing less than that every citizen become a Renaissance man. "In a Communist society," he and Engels wrote, "there will be no painters, but only highly developed men who, among other things, paint."[14]

But it was Trotsky, among the Marxists, whose optimism was the most audacious:

> Man will become immeasurably stronger, wiser and subtler; his movements more rhythmic, his voice more musical. The forms of life will become dynamically dramatic. The average human type will rise to the heights of an Aristotle, a Goethe, a Marx. And above this ridge, new peaks will arise.[15]

In part at least, this soaring vision is an expression of that dangerous messianism I described earlier. Yet, if one understands it as the statement of a limit toward which mankind strives but perhaps will never reach, it serves to free the mind from the narrowness of the present. The human body has been changing under capitalism: in the United States, Selective Service exams show that height is on the increase in the twentieth century; and, of course, athletic records, and presumably biological prowess, have been dramatically extended. A higher living standard, with good diet and medical care, certainly can make people more beautiful, as the rich discovered a long time ago. In the realm of intelligence there are no comparative statistics but the qualitative growth in the number of scientists, and educated people generally, must mean that some of man's genetic potential has been saved from the savage fate scarcity and starvation used to visit upon it.

We may well be on the eve of psychic mutations. Our unprecedented, man-made environments produce new kinds of people. The question is not whether this will happen but how it will take place: under commercial priorities (Marcuse's pessimistic vision); under totalitarian control (Orwell's fear); or consciously chosen and shaped by a free political and social movement.

Men Freed of the Curse of Money

The end of compulsory labor is one socialist ultimate; the abolition of money is another.

As many economists have recognized, money is the basis of a system of "rationing by the purse." In a society of maldistributed incomes it is obviously unjust that an elite should enjoy luxuries while a mass are denied necessities. Long before the socialist movement will even be in sight of its final aims, it can ameliorate this outrage by the redistribution of income, for then the rations will at least be more justly shared. But this reform might even be assimilated to an Adam Smithian model of the economy. As Paul Samuelson remarks, Smith would now agree that dollar wealth has to be distributed "in an 'ethically optimal' manner—and kept so by non-distorting, nonmarket intervention" in order to get the most efficient production and "to give people what they really deem is best for them."[16]

Socialists should propose to go well beyond such a change and eventually to challenge the principle of money itself. In a discussion of property which produces unearned income John Strachey argued that, given such a phenomenon, "a moral poison is bound to permeate the society."[17] And as long as access to goods and pleasures is rationed according to the possession of money, there is a pervasive venality, an invitation to miserliness and hostility to one's neighbor. Particularly in the area of necessities no one should be required to choose between needs or to sacrifice them in order to get luxuries—and that is what money makes inevitable.

Socialism should therefore work toward making more and more goods and services free: medicine, housing, transportation, a healthy diet, etc. The standard response of many economists to such a proposition is that cliché of Economics One: nothing is really free. All commodities cost something to produce and if the individual does not pay for them directly, then some one does indirectly. But this is to miss the enormous social gain that would occur if society were to make all the fundamentals of life free. There would, surely, be a collective payment for these goods but the change in moral atmosphere created by such a new mode of distribution would be profound.

The other standard criticism of free goods is the charge that they invite waste. People, one is told, will lavishly misuse their new rights, and a socialist society will therefore be the least efficient in human history. That prediction is partly based on the parochial assumption that man will act in a radically new environment exactly as he did in the old, that the greed and acquisitiveness of several hundred years of capitalism are of the human essence. It is not even necessary to become particularly visionary in responding to this, for the theory and practice of recent years has provided a basis for the socialist hope.

In his famous essay on the economics of socialism, Oskar Lange argued that those goods and services for which demand is relatively inelastic can be made free without running the risk of wastefulness. Salt is a classic example. The amount of it consumed in good times or in bad is relatively invariant. If it were made free it is doubtful that individuals would suddenly and vastly increase their use of it. Similarly with transportation within a city. If that were made free, there would unquestionably be a large increase in the use of transit facilities, since people would be much more likely to visit one another, to go on outings, etc. Yet who can say that such an increase in sociability and recreation is "wasteful"? And who would want to ride a subway simply because it is free?

There is some experience to go on. In California there is a private medical plan run by the Kaiser company. It has succeeded in sharply reducing the cost of care while improving the service. According to the thesis about the inherent greediness of men, the people who subscribe should use their rights more than the citizen who pays a higher cost. In fact, the Kaiser patients go to the doctor less than do the patients of expensive fee-for-service systems. As an article in *Fortune* put it, "Kaiser's experience refutes the widely held belief that if medical services are 'free,' or virtually free, the public will stampede to them."[18]

Socialism, then, is not simply a program for socializing investments and ownership and redistributing wealth, important as all those goals are. It retains the notion of a truly new order of things and it asserts this through the vision of seeking, in the distant but conceivable future, to abolish compulsory work and the rationing system of money as far as is humanly possible. Perhaps I can sum up this vision by retelling a famous socialist parable.

In desert societies—including the American Southwest—water is so precious that it is money. People fight and die and connive over it; governments covet it; marriages are made and broken because of it. If one had talked to a person who had only known that desert and told him that in the city there are public water fountains and that children are even sometimes allowed to turn on the fire hydrants in the summer and to frolic in the water, he would be sure that you were crazy. For he knows, with an existential certitude, that it is human nature to fight over water.

Mankind has lived now for several millennia in the desert. Our minds and emotions are conditioned by that bitter experience; we do not dare to think that things could be otherwise. Yet there are signs that we are, without really having planned it that way, marching out of the desert. There are some who loathe to leave behind the consolation of familiar brutalities; there are others who, in one way or another, would like to impose the law of the desert upon the Promised Land. It may even be possible that mankind cannot bear too much happiness.

It is also possible that we will seize this opportunity and make of the earth a homeland rather than an exile. That is the socialist project. It does not promise or even seek to abolish the human condition. That is impossible. It does propose to end that invidious competition and venality which, because scarcity allowed no other alternatives, we have come to think are inseparable from our humanity.

Under socialism there will be no end to history—but there may be a new history.

NOTES

1. Sidney Hook, *Towards the Understanding of Karl Marx* (New York: John Day & Co., 1933), p. 14.
2. Stanley Moore, "Utopian Themes in Marx and Mao: A Critique for Modern Revisionists, *Dissent,* March–April 1970, p. 170 (reprinted from *Monthly Review,* June 1968).
3. *Das Kapital,* in *MEW,* 25:828.
4. Friedrich Nietzsche, *Morgenröte,* in *Nietzsche's Werke* (Salzburg: Bergland), 2:475.
5. *MEW,* 23:287.
6. Ernest Mandel, *Introduction to Marxist Economic Theory* (New York: Young Socialist Alliance, 1967), p. 13.
7. *MEW,* 25:828.
8. Karl Marx, *Grundrisse der Kritik der Politischen Oeconomie* (Berlin: Dietz Verlag, 1953), p. 592.
9. *Ibid.,* p. 593.
10. *Ibid.,* p. 592.
11. *Ibid.,* p. 593.
12. *Ibid.,* p. 594.
13. National Commission on Technology, Automation and Economic Progress, *Technology and the American Economy: Report, 1966* (Washington, D.C.: GPO), 1:9 ff.
14. *MEW,* 3:378.
15. Trotsky, *Literature and Revolution,* p. 256.
16. Paul Samuelson, *Economics,* 7th ed. (New York: McGraw-Hill, 1967), pp. 610–611.
17. Strachey, *Contemporary Capitalism,* p. 140.
18. Edmund K. Faltermayer, "Better Care at Less Cost Without Miracles," *Fortune,* January 1970, p. 83. See also "NHI [National Health Insurance]: What It Is, What It Isn't," *Federationist,* January 1970.

PART SEVEN
FASCISM

Fascism emerged after World War I as a reaction against the two leading ideologies of the time, liberalism and socialism. Both liberalism and socialism, the fascists complained, divide the members of society against each other—liberals by emphasizing the individual, socialists by stressing the conflict between social classes. In contrast, fascism presents a picture of individuals and classes as merely parts of a larger, all-embracing whole—the society or state—which can be strong only when all the parts unite behind a single party and a supreme leader.

This was the core of the fascist ideology as it developed in Italy under Benito Mussolini (1883–1945) and in Germany under Adolf Hitler (1889–1945). Mussolini's Fascist party took its name from the Italian word *fasciare*, to fasten or bind, and its derivative *fasci*, meaning group. Fascism was the force that could bind Italy together, Mussolini declared. Fascism would lead Italy to a new empire as glorious as the Roman Empire of ancient times. Everything and everyone would have to be dedicated to the service of the state, which was the legal and institutional embodiment of the power, unity, and majesty of the Italian people, or nation. As Mussolini and his followers repeated over and over, "Everything in the state, nothing outside the state, nothing against the state."

As this slogan suggests, fascism in its pure form is a totalitarian ideology. In fact, the Italian Fascists coined the word "totalitarian" to define their antidemocratic aims and to distinguish themselves from liberalism and socialism, which they saw as advocating democracy. Democracy requires equality of some sort, whether it be in the liberals' insistence on equal opportunity for individuals or the socialists' insistence on equal power for all in a classless society. But Mussolini and his followers had no use for either democracy or equality. Democracy is all talk and no action; equality merely restrains the strong in order to protect the weak. The Fascists did appeal to the masses for support, to be sure, but in their view the common people were to exercise power not by thinking or speaking for themselves, but by blindly following their leaders to victory. As another of Mussolini's many slogans put the point, "Believe, obey, fight!"

Hitler and his National Socialists, or Nazis for short, adopted a similar position in Germany in the 1920s and 1930s. With Hitler as supreme leader, the Nazi party was to unify all German-speaking peoples into a single state that would go on to become a great new empire (or Reich). Hence the Nazi slogan. *"Ein volk, ein Reich, ein Führer"*—one people, one empire, one leader.

The chief difference between German Nazism and Italian fascism was the racial element in Nazi theory. For Nazis, the fundamental fact of human life is race. There is no such thing as a single or universal human nature, for human beings belong to different races. Far from being equal, furthermore, each race has its own unique characteristics and its own destiny. One race, the Aryan, is naturally stronger, more intelligent, and more creative than all the others, and the destiny of this "master race" is to subject all other races to its rule.

Aside from this important difference, fascism and Nazism are fundamentally alike. Both grew out of a combination of forces that developed during the nineteenth century—the Counter-Enlightenment, elitism, irrationalism, and nationalism. The Counter-Enlightenment included a number of thinkers, such as Joseph de Maistre, who rejected the key elements of eighteenth-century Enlightenment thought (for a classic exposition of Enlightenment thought, see Immanuel Kant's essay "What Is Enlightenment?" in Part Three; for some of de Maistre's reactions to the Enlightenment, see Part Four). The Counter-Enlightenment thinkers denied that reason by itself can bring about great progress and improvement in human life. Counter-Enlightenment theorists and various elitist theories of the late 1800s were alike, moreover, in denying that the common people can ever become capable of ruling themselves. In this way both contributed to the antidemocratic character of fascism. This was also true of such "irrationalists" as Georges Sorel (1847–1922), who maintained that "myths" and emotions play a greater part than reason in moving the masses to action.

Finally, and perhaps most significantly, fascists are intensely nationalistic. Nationalism is the belief that the world is naturally divided into distinct nations, or peoples, each of which ought to be united in its own political unit, or nation-state. Although nationalistic tendencies have been evident in many parts of the world throughout history, they became especially powerful in the nineteenth century, particularly in Italy and Germany—two countries that were not forged into distinct nation-states until the 1860s and 1870s. The desire to preserve and strengthen this unity seems to have played a large part in the rise of Italian fascism and German Nazism.

Mussolini and Hitler both died in 1945, the former killed by anti-Fascist Italian guerillas, the latter a suicide in his bunker in Berlin. Their defeat in World War II dealt a crushing blow to the Fascists and Nazis, if not a fatal one. For we should not forget that fascism was not confined to Italy and Germany, nor has it altogether disappeared—as the activities of various Fascists and neo-Nazis in Europe, South Africa, and the Americas clearly remind us. Hitler and Mussolini may be dead, but their legacy lingers.

40

CIVILIZATION AND RACE

JOSEPH-ARTHUR DE GOBINEAU

Why do great empires and civilizations rise to power and glory, only to fall into decay? In the nineteenth century a French diplomat named Joseph-Arthur de Gobineau (1816–1882) thought he had found a simple answer to this question: race. In his *Essay on the Inequality of Human Races* (1853–1855), from which the following selection is taken, Gobineau argued that the mingling of races led, and must continue to lead, to the downfall of great civilizations.

Source: Joseph-Arthur de Gobineau, The Inequality of Human Races, *translated by Adrian Collins (New York: Howard Fertig, 1967; reprint of 1915 ed.), pp. 1–2, 25, 150–151, 154–155, 178–179, 205–211.*

. . . The racial question overshadows all other problems of history, it holds the key to them all, and the inequality of the races from whose fusion a people is formed is enough to explain the whole course of its destiny. Every one must have had some inkling of this colossal truth, for every one must have seen how certain agglomerations of men have descended on some country, and utterly transformed its way of life; how they have shown themselves able to strike out a new vein of activity where, before their coming, all had been sunk in torpor. Thus, to take an example, a new era of power was opened for Great Britain by the Anglo-Saxon invasion, thanks to a decree of Providence, which by sending to this island some of the peoples governed by the sword of your Majesty's illustrious ancestors, was to bring two branches of the same nation under the sceptre of a single house—a house that can trace its glorious title to the dim sources of the heroic nation itself.

Recognizing that both strong and weak races exist, I preferred to examine the former, to analyse their qualities, and especially to follow them back to their origins. By this method I convinced myself at last that everything great, noble, and fruitful in the works of man on this earth, in science, art, and civilization, derives from a single starting-point, is the development of a single germ and the result of a single thought; it belongs to one family alone, the different branches of which have reigned in all the civilized countries of the universe. . . .

THE INEQUALITY OF HUMAN RACES

CHAPTER I THE MORTAL DISEASE OF CIVILIZATIONS AND SOCIETIES PROCEEDS FROM GENERAL CAUSES COMMON TO THEM ALL

THE fall of civilizations is the most striking, and, at the same time, the most obscure, of all the phenomena of history. It is a calamity that strikes fear into the soul, and yet has always something so mysterious and so vast in reserve, that the thinker is never weary of looking at it, of studying it, of groping for its secrets. No doubt the birth and growth of peoples offer a very remarkable subject for the observer; the successive development of societies, their gains, their conquests, their triumphs, have something that vividly takes the imagination and holds it captive. But all these events, however great one may think them, seem to be easy of explanation; one accepts them as the mere outcome of the intellectual gifts of man. Once we recognize these gifts, we are not astonished at their results; they explain, by the bare fact of their existence, the great stream of being whose source they are. So, on this score, there need be no difficulty or hesitation. But when we see that after a time of strength and glory all human societies come to their decline and fall—all, I say, not this or that; when we see in what awful silence the earth shows us, scattered on its surface, the wrecks of the civilizations that have preceded our own—not merely the famous civilizations, but also many others, of which we know nothing but the names, and some, that lie as skeletons of stone deep world-old forests, and have not left us even this shadow of a memory; when the mind returns to our modern States, reflects on their extreme youth, and confesses that they are a growth of yesterday, and that some of them are already toppling to their fall: then at last we recognize, not without a certain philosophic shudder, that the words of the prophets on the instability of mortal things apply with the same rigour to civilizations as to peoples, to people as to States, to States as to individuals; and we are forced to affirm that every assemblage of men, however ingenious the network of social relations that protects it, acquires on the very day of its birth, hidden among the elements of its life, the seed of an inevitable death.

But what is this seed, this principle of death? Is it uniform, as its results are, and do all civilizations perish from the same cause?

At first sight we are tempted to answer in the negative; for we have seen the fall of many empires, Assyria, Egypt, Greece, Rome, amid the clash of events that had no likeness one to the other. Yet, if we pierce below the surface, we soon find that this very necessity of coming to an end, that weighs imperiously on all societies without exception, presupposes such a general cause, which, though hidden, cannot be explained away. When we start from this fixed principle of natural death—a principle unaffected by all the cases of violent death,—we see that all civilizations, after they have lasted some time, betray to the observer some little symptoms of uneasiness, which are difficult to define, but not less difficult to deny; these are of a like nature in all times and all places. We may admit one obvious point of difference between the fall of States and that of civilizations, when we see the same kind of culture sometimes persisting in a country under foreign rule and weathering every storm of calamity, at other times being destroyed or changed by the slightest breath of a contrary wind; but we are, in the end, more and more driven to the idea that the principle of death which can be seen at the base of all societies is not only inherent in their life, but also uniform and the same for all.

. . . How and why is a nation's vigour lost? How does it degenerate? These are the questions which we must try to answer. Up to the present, men have been content with finding the word, without unveiling the reality that lies behind. This further step I shall now attempt to take.

The word *degenerate*, when applied to a people, means (as it ought to mean) that the people has no longer the same intrinsic value as it had before, because it has no longer the same blood in its veins, continual adulterations having gradually affected the quality of that blood. In other words, though the nation bears the name given by its founders, the name no longer connotes the same race; in fact, the man of a decadent time, the *degenerate* man properly so called, is a different being, from the racial point of view from the heroes of the great ages. I agree that he still keeps something of their essence; but the more he degenerates the more attenuated does this "something" become. The heterogeneous elements that henceforth prevail in him give him quite a different nationality—a very original one, no doubt, but such originality is not to be envied. He is only a very distant kinsman of those he still calls his ancestors. He, and his civilization with him, will certainly die on the day when the primordial race-unit is so broken up and swamped by the influx of foreign elements, that its effective qualities have no longer a sufficient freedom of action. It will not, of course, absolutely disappear, but it will in practice be so beaten down and enfeebled, that its power will be felt less and less as time goes on. It is at this point that all the results of degeneration will appear, and the process may be considered complete.

CHAPTER XIII THE HUMAN RACES ARE INTELLECTUALLY UNEQUAL; MANKIND IS NOT CAPABLE OF INFINITE PROGRESS

In order to appreciate the intellectual differences between races, we ought first to ascertain the degree of stupidity to which mankind can descend. We know already the highest point that it can reach, namely civilization.

Most scientific observers up to now have been very prone to make out the lowest types as worse than they really are.

Nearly all the early accounts of a savage tribe paint it in hideous colours, far more hideous than the reality. They give it so little power of reason and understanding, that it seems to be on a level with the monkey and below the elephant. It is true that we find the contrary opinion. If a captain is well received in an island, if he meets, as he believes, with a kind and hospitable welcome, and succeeds in making a few natives do a small amount of work with his sailors, then praises are showered on the happy people. They are declared to be fit for anything and capable of everything; and sometimes the enthusiasm bursts all bounds, and swears it has found among them some higher intelligences.

We must appeal from both judgments—harsh and favourable alike. The fact that certain Tahitians have helped to repair a whaler does not make their nation capable of civilization.

Because a man of Tonga-Tabu shows goodwill to strangers, he is not necessarily open to ideas of progress. Similarly, we are not entitled to degrade a native of a hitherto unknown coast to the level of the brute, just because he receives his first visitors with a flight of arrows, or because he is found eating raw lizards and mud pies. Such a banquet does not certainly connote a very high intelligence or very cultivated manners. But even in the most hideous cannibal there is a spark of the divine fire, and to some extent the flame of understanding can always be kindled in him. There are no tribes so low that they do not pass some judgments, true or false, just or unjust, on the things around them; the mere existence of such judgments is enough to show that in every branch of mankind some ray of intelligence is kept alive. It is this that makes the most degraded savages accessible to the teachings of religion and distinguishes them in a special manner, of which they are themselves conscious, from even the most intelligent beasts.

Are however these moral possibilities, which lie at the back of every man's consciousness, capable of infinite extension? Do all men possess in an equal degree an unlimited power of intellectual development? In other words, has every human race the capacity for becoming equal to every other? The question is ultimately concerned with the infinite capacity for improvement possessed by the species as a whole, and with the equality of races. I deny both points.

The idea of an infinite progress is very seductive to many modern philosophers, and they support it by declaring that our civilization has many merits and advantages which our differently trained ancestors did not possess. They bring forward all the phenomena that distinguished our modern societies. I have spoken of these already; but I am glad to be able to go through them again.

We are told that our scientific opinions are truer than they were; that our manners are, as a rule, kindly, and our morals better than those of the Greeks and Romans. Especially with regard to political liberty, they say, have we ideas and feelings, beliefs and tolerances, that prove our superiority. There are even some hopeful theorists who maintain that our institutions should lead us straight to that garden of the Hesperides which was sought so long, and with such ill-success, since the time when the ancient navigators reported that it was not in the Canaries. . . .

A little more serious consideration of history will show what truth there is in these high claims. . . .

CHAPTER XVI RECAPITULATION; THE RESPECTIVE CHARACTERISTICS OF THE THREE GREAT RACES; THE SUPERIORITY OF THE WHITE TYPE, AND, WITHIN THIS TYPE, OF THE ARYAN FAMILY

I HAVE shown the unique place in the organic world occupied by the human species, the profound physical, as well as moral, differences separating it from all other kinds of living creatures. Considering it by itself, I have been able to distinguish, on physiological grounds alone, three great and clearly marked types, the black, the yellow, and the white. However uncertain the aims of physiology may be, however meagre its resources, however defective its methods, it can proceed thus far with absolute certainty.

The negroid variety is the lowest, and stands at the foot of the ladder. The animal character, that appears in the shape of the pelvis, is stamped on the negro from birth, and foreshadows his destiny. His intellect will always move within a very narrow circle. He is not however a mere brute, for behind his low receding brow, in the middle of his skull, we can see signs of a powerful energy, however crude its objects. If his mental faculties are dull or even non-existent, he often has an intensity of desire, and so of will, which may be called terrible. Many of his senses, especially taste and smell, are developed to an extent unknown to the other two races.

The very strength of his sensations is the most striking proof of his inferiority. All food is good in his eyes, nothing disgusts or repels him.

What he desires is to eat, to eat furiously, and to excess; no carrion is too revolting to be swallowed by him. It is the same with odours; his inordinate desires are satisfied with all, however coarse or even horrible. To these qualities may be added an instability and capriciousness of feeling, that cannot be tied down to any single object, and which, so far as he is concerned, do away with all distinctions of good and evil. We might even say that the violence with which he pursues the object that has aroused his senses and inflamed his desires is a guarantee of the desires being soon satisfied and the object forgotten. Finally, he is equally careless of his own life and that of others: he kills willingly, for the sake of killing; and this human machine, in whom it is so easy to arouse emotion, shows, in face of suffering, either a monstrous indifference or a cowardice that seeks a voluntary refuge in death.

The yellow race is the exact opposite of this type. The skull points forward, not backward. The forehead is wide and bony, often high and projecting. The shape of the face is triangular, the nose and chin showing none of the coarse protuberances that mark the negro. There is further a general proneness to obesity, which, though not confined to the yellow type, is found there more frequently than in the others. The yellow man has little physical energy, and is inclined to apathy; he commits none of the strange excesses so common among negroes. His desires are feeble, his will-power rather obstinate than violent; his longing for material pleasures, though constant, is kept within bounds. A rare glutton by nature, he shows far more discrimination in his choice of food. He tends to mediocrity in everything; he understands easily enough anything not too deep or sublime. He has a love of utility and a respect for order, and knows the value of a certain amount of freedom. He is practical, in the narrowest sense of the word. He does not dream or theorize; he invents little, but can appreciate and take over what is useful to him. His whole desire is to live in the easiest and most comfortable way possible. The yellow races are thus clearly superior to the black. Every founder of a civilization would wish the backbone of this society, his middle class, to consist of such men. But no civilized society could be created by them; they could not supply its nerve-force, or set in motion the springs of beauty and action.

We come now to the white peoples. These are gifted with reflective energy, or rather with an energetic intelligence. They have a feeling for utility, but in a sense far wider and higher, more courageous and ideal, than the yellow races; a perseverance that takes account of obstacles and ultimately finds a means of overcoming them; a greater physical power, an extraordinary instinct for order, not merely as a guarantee of peace and tranquillity, but as an indispensable means of self-preservation. At the same time, they have a remarkable, and even extreme, love of liberty, and are openly hostile to the formalism under which the Chinese are glad to vegetate, as well as to the strict despotism which is the only way of governing the negro.

The white races are, further, distinguished by an extraordinary attachment to life. They know better how to use it, and so, as it would seem, set a greater price on it; both in their own persons and those of others, they are more sparing of life. When they are cruel, they are conscious of their cruelty; it is very doubtful whether such a consciousness exists in the negro. At the same time, they have discovered reasons why they should surrender this busy life of theirs, that is so precious to them. The principal motive is honour, which under various names has played an enormous part in the ideas of the race from the beginning. I need hardly add that the word honour, together with all the civilizing influences connoted by it, is unknown to both the yellow and the black man.

On the other hand, the immense superiority of the white peoples in the whole field of the intellect is balanced by an inferiority in the intensity of their sensations. In the world of the senses, the white man is far less gifted than the others, and so is less tempted and less absorbed by considerations of the body, although in physical structure he is far the most vigorous.

Such are the three constituent elements of the human race. I call them secondary types, as I think myself obliged to omit all discussion of the Adamite man. From the combination, by intermarriage, of the varieties of these types come the tertiary groups. The quaternary formations are produced by the union of one of these tertiary types, or of a pure-blooded tribe, with another group taken from one of the two foreign species.

Below these categories others have appeared—and still appear. Some of these are very strongly characterized, and form new and distinct points of departure, coming as they do from races that have been completely fused. Others are incomplete, and ill-ordered, and, one might even say, anti-social, since their elements, being too numerous, too disparate, or too barbarous, have had neither the time nor the opportunity for combining to any fruitful purpose. No limits, except the horror excited by the possibility of infinite intermixture, can be assigned to the number of these hybrid and chequered races that make up the whole of mankind.

It would be unjust to assert that every mixture is bad and harmful. If the three great types had remained strictly separate, the supremacy would no doubt have always been in the hands of the finest of the white races, and the yellow and black varieties would have crawled for ever at the feet of the lowest of the whites. Such a state is so far ideal, since it has never been beheld in history; and we can imagine it only by recognizing the undisputed superiority of those groups of the white races which have remained the purest.

It would not have been all gain. The superiority of the white race would have been clearly shown, but it would have been bought at the price of certain advantages which have followed the mixture of blood. Although these are far from counter-balancing the defects they have brought in their train, yet they are sometimes to be commended. Artistic genius, which is equally foreign to each of the three great types, arose only after the intermarriage of white and black. Again, in the Malayan variety, a human family was produced from the yellow and black races that had more intelligence than either of its ancestors. Finally, from the union of white and yellow, certain intermediary peoples have sprung, who are superior to the purely Finnish tribes as well as to the negroes.

I do not deny that these are good results. The world of art and great literature that comes from the mixture of blood, the improvement and ennoblement of inferior races—all these are wonders for which we must needs be thankful. The small have been raised. Unfortunately, the great have been lowered by the same process; and this is an evil that nothing can balance or repair. Since I am putting together the advantages of racial mixtures, I will also add that to them is due the refinement of manners and beliefs, and especially the tempering of passion and desire. But these are merely transitory benefits, and if I recognize that the mulatto, who may become a lawyer, a doctor, or a business man, is worth more than his negro grandfather, who was absolutely savage, and fit for nothing, I must also confess that the Brahmans of primitive India, the heroes of the Iliad and the Shahnameh, the warriors of Scandinavia—the glorious shades of noble races that have disappeared—give us a higher and more brilliant idea of humanity, and were more active, intelligent, and trusty instruments of civilization and grandeur than the peoples, hybrid a hundred times over, of the present day. And the blood even of these was no longer pure.

However it has come about, the human races, as we find them in history, are complex; and one of the chief consequences has been to throw into disorder most of the primitive characteristics of each type. The good as well as the bad qualities are seen to diminish in intensity with repeated intermixture of blood; but they also scatter and separate off from each other, and are often mutually opposed. The white race originally possessed the monopoly of beauty, intelligence, and strength. By its union with other varieties, hybrids were created, which were beautiful without strength, strong without intelligence, or, if intelligent, both weak and ugly. Further, when the quantity of white blood was increased to an indefinite amount of successive infusions, and not by a single admixture, it no longer carried with it its natural advantages, and often merely increased the confusion already existing in the racial elements. Its strength, in fact, seemed to be its only remaining quality, and even its strength served only to promote disorder. The apparent anomaly is easily explained. Each stage of a perfect mixture produces a new type from diverse elements, and develops special faculties. As soon as further elements are added, the vast difficulty of harmonizing the whole creates a state of anarchy. The more this increases, the more do even the best and richest of the new contributions diminish in value, and by their mere presence add fuel to an evil which they cannot abate. If mixtures of blood are, to a certain extent, beneficial to the mass of mankind, if they raise and ennoble it, this is merely at the expense of mankind itself, which is stunted, abased, enervated, and humiliated in the persons of its noblest sons. Even if we admit that it is better to turn a myriad of degraded beings into mediocre men than to preserve the race of princes whose blood is adulterated and impoverished by being made to suffer this dishonourable change, yet there is still the unfortunate fact that the change does not stop here; for when the mediocre men are once created at the expense of the greater, they combine with other mediocrities, and from such unions, which grow ever more and more degraded, is born a confusion which, like that of Babel, ends in utter impotence, and leads societies down to the abyss of nothingness whence no power on earth can rescue them.

Such is the lesson of history. It shows us that all civilizations derive from the white race, that none can exist without its help, and that a society is great and brilliant only so far as it preserves the blood of the noble group that created it, provided that this group itself belongs to the most illustrious branch of our species.

Of the multitude of peoples which live or have lived on the earth, ten alone have risen to the position of complete societies. The remainder have gravitated round these more or less independently, like planets round their suns. If there is any element of life in these ten civilizations that is not due to the impulse of the white races, any seed of death that does not come from the inferior stocks that mingled with them, then the whole theory on which this book rests is false. On the other hand, if the facts are as I say, then we have an irrefragable proof of the nobility of our own species. Only the actual details can set the final seal of truth on my system, and they alone can show with sufficient exactness the full implications of my main thesis, that peoples degenerate only in consequence of the various admixtures of blood which they undergo; that their degeneration corresponds exactly to the quantity and quality of the new blood, and that the rudest possible shock to the vitality of a civilization is given when the ruling elements in a society and those developed by racial change have become so numerous that they are clearly moving away from the homogeneity necessary to their life, and it therefore becomes impossible for them to be brought into harmony and so acquire the common instincts and interests, the common logic of existence, which is the sole justification for any social bond whatever. There is no greater curse than such disorder, for however bad it may have made the present state of things, it promises still worse for the future.

41

THE DOCTRINE OF FASCISM

BENITO MUSSOLINI

As founder and leader of the Fascist party of Italy, Benito Mussolini (1883–1945) brought together the various elements that make fascism a distinctive ideology. As a young man Mussolini considered himself a Marxian socialist, but World War I convinced him that nations, not social classes, are the primary forces in history and politics. After seizing control of the Italian government in 1922, Mussolini set out to convert Italy into a modern industrial and military power in order to create a new Italian empire. The following article, published under Mussolini's name but written by philosophers sympathetic to fascism, appeared in the *Enciclopedia Italiana* in 1932.

Source: The Social and Political Doctrines of Contemporary Europe, *edited by Michael Oakeshott (Cambridge: Cambridge University Press, 1939), pp. 164–179.*

FUNDAMENTAL IDEAS

1. Like every sound political conception, Fascism is both practice and thought; action in which a doctrine is immanent, and a doctrine which, arising out of a given system of historical forces, remains embedded in them and works there from within. Hence it has a form correlative to the contingencies of place and time, but it has also a content of thought which raises it to a formula of truth in the higher level of the history of thought. In the world one does not act spiritually as a human will dominating other wills without a conception of the transient and particular reality under which it is necessary to act, and of the permanent and universal reality in which the first has its being and its life. In order to know men it is necessary to know man; and in order to know man it is necessary to know reality and its laws. There is no concept of the State which is not fundamentally a concept of life: philosophy or intuition, a system of ideas which develops logically or is gathered up into a vision or into a faith, but which is always, at least virtually, an organic conception of the world.

2. Thus Fascism could not be understood in many of its practical manifestations as a party organization, as a system of education, as a discipline, if it were not always looked at in the light of its whole way of conceiving life, a spiritualized way. The world seen through Fascism is not this material world which appears on the surface, in which man is an individual separated from all others and standing by himself, and in which he is governed by a natural law that makes him instinctively live a life of selfish and momentary pleasure. The man of Fascism is an individual who is nation and fatherland, which is a moral law, binding together individuals and the generations into a tradition and a mission, suppressing the instinct for a life enclosed within the brief round of pleasure in order to restore within duty a higher life free from the limits of time and space: a life in which the individual, through the denial of himself, through the sacrifice of his own private interests, through death itself, realizes that completely spiritual existence in which his value as a man lies.

3. Therefore it is a spiritualized conception, itself the result of the general reaction of modern times against the flabby materialistic positivism of the nineteenth century. Anti-positivistic, but positive: not sceptical, nor agnostic, nor pessimistic, nor passively optimistic, as are, in general, the doctrines (all negative) that put the centre of life outside man, who with his free will can and must create his own world. Fascism desires an active man, one engaged in activity with all his energies: it desires a man virilely conscious of the difficulties that exist in action and ready to face them. It conceives of life as a struggle, considering that it behooves man to conquer for himself that life truly worthy of him, creating first of all in himself the instrument (physical, moral, intellectual) in order to construct it. Thus for the single individual, thus for the nation, thus for humanity. Hence the high value of culture in all its forms (art, religion, science), and the enormous importance of education. Hence also the essential value of work, with which man conquers nature and creates the human world (economic, political, moral, intellectual).

4. This positive conception of life is clearly an ethical conception. It covers the whole of reality, not merely the human activity which controls it. No action can be divorced from moral judgement; there is nothing in the world which can be deprived of the value which belongs to everything in its relation to moral ends. Life, therefore, as conceived by the Fascist, is serious, austere, religious: the whole of it is poised in a world supported by the moral and responsible forces of the spirit. The Fascist disdains the "comfortable" life.

5. Fascism is a religious conception in which man is seen in his immanent relationship with a superior law and with an objective Will that transcends the particular individual and raises him to conscious membership of a spiritual

society. Whoever has seen in the religious politics of the Fascist regime nothing but mere opportunism has not understood that Fascism besides being a system of government is also, and above all, a system of thought.

6. Fascism is an historical conception, in which man is what he is only in so far as he works with the spiritual process in which he finds himself, in the family or social group, in the nation and in the history in which all nations collaborate. From this follows the great value of tradition, in memories, in language, in customs, in the standards of social life. Outside history man is nothing. Consequently Fascism is opposed to all the individualistic abstractions of a materialistic nature like those of the eighteenth century; and it is opposed to all Jacobin utopias and innovations. It does not consider that "happiness" is possible upon earth, as it appeared to be in the desire of the economic literature of the eighteenth century, and hence it rejects all teleological theories according to which mankind would reach a definitive stabilized condition at a certain period in history. This implies putting oneself outside history and life, which is a continual change and coming to be. Politically, Fascism wishes to be a realistic doctrine; practically, it aspires to solve only the problems which arise historically of themselves and that of themselves find or suggest their own solution. To act among men, as to act in the natural world, it is necessary to enter into the process of reality and to master the already operating forces.

7. Against individualism, the Fascist conception is for the State; and it is for the individual in so far as he coincides with the State, which is the conscience and universal will of man in his historical existence. It is opposed to classical Liberalism, which arose from the necessity of reacting against absolutism, and which brought its historical purpose to an end when the State was transformed into the conscience and will of the people. Liberalism denied the State in the interests of the particular individual; Fascism reaffirms the State as the true reality of the individual. And if liberty is to be the attribute of the real man, and not of that abstract puppet envisaged by individualistic Liberalism, Fascism is for liberty. And for the only liberty which can be a real thing, the liberty of the State and of the individual within the State. Therefore, for the Fascist, everything is in the State, and nothing human or spiritual exists, much less has value, outside the State. In this sense Fascism is totalitarian, and the Fascist State, the synthesis and unity of all values, interprets, develops and gives strength to the whole life of the people.

8. Outside the State there can be neither individuals nor groups (political parties, associations, syndicates, classes). Therefore Fascism is opposed to Socialism, which confines the movement of history within the class struggle and ignores the unity of classes established in one economic and moral reality in the State; and analogously it is opposed to class syndicalism. Fascism recognizes the real exigencies for which the socialist and syndicalist movement arose, but while recognizing them wishes to bring them under the control of the State and give them a purpose within the corporative system of interests reconciled within the unity of the State.

9. Individuals form classes according to the similarity of their interests, they form syndicates according to differentiated economic activities within these interests; but they form first, and above all, the State, which is not to be thought of numerically as the sum-total of individuals forming the majority of a nation. And consequently Fascism is opposed to Democracy, which equates the nation to the majority, lowering it to the level of that majority; nevertheless it is the purest form of democracy if the nation is conceived, as it should be, qualitatively and not quantitatively, as the most powerful idea (most powerful because most moral, most coherent, most true) which acts within the nation as the conscience and the will of a few, even of One, which ideal tends to become active within the conscience and the will of all—that is to say, of all those who rightly constitute a nation by reason of nature, history or race, and

have set out upon the same line of development and spiritual formation as one conscience and one sole will. Not a race,[1] nor a geographically determined region, but as a community historically perpetuating itself, a multitude unified by a single idea, which is the will to existence and to power: consciousness of itself, personality.

10. This higher personality is truly the nation in so far as it is the State. It is not the nation that generates the State, as according to the old naturalistic concept which served as the basis of the political theories of the national States of the nineteenth century. Rather the nation is created by the State, which gives to the people, conscious of its own moral unity, a will and therefore an effective existence. The right of a nation to independence derives not from a literary and ideal consciousness of its own being, still less from a more or less unconscious and inert acceptance of a *de facto* situation, but from an active consciousness, from a political will in action and ready to demonstrate its own rights: that is to say, from a state already coming into being. The State, in fact, as the universal ethical will, is the creator of right.

11. The nation as the State is an ethical reality which exists and lives in so far as it develops. To arrest its development is to kill it. Therefore the State is not only the authority which governs and gives the form of laws and the value of spiritual life to the wills of individuals, but it is also a power that makes its will felt abroad, making it known and respected, in other words, demonstrating the fact of its universality in all the necessary directions of its development. It is consequently organization and expansion, at least virtually. Thus it can be likened to the human will which knows no limits to its development and realizes itself in testing its own limitlessness.

12. The Fascist State, the highest and most powerful form of personality, is a force, but a spiritual force, which takes over all the forms of the moral and intellectual life of man. It cannot therefore confine itself simply to the functions of order and supervision as Liberalism desired. It is not simply a mechanism which limits the sphere of the supposed liberties of the individual. It is the form, the inner standard and the discipline of the whole person; it saturates the will as well as the intelligence. Its principle, the central inspiration of the human personality living in the civil community, pierces into the depths and makes its home in the heart of the man of action as well as of the thinker, of the artist as well as of the scientist: it is the soul of the soul.

13. Fascism, in short, is not only the giver of laws and the founder of institutions, but the educator and promoter of spiritual life. It wants to remake, not the forms of human life, but its content, man, character, faith. And to this end it requires discipline and authority that can enter into the spirits of men and there govern unopposed. Its sign, therefore, is the Lictors' rods, the symbol of unity, of strength and justice.

POLITICAL AND SOCIAL DOCTRINE

1. When in the now distant March of 1919 I summoned to Milan, through the columns of the *Popolo d'Italia*, my surviving supporters who had followed me since the constitution of the Fasces of Revolutionary Action, founded in January 1915, there was no specific doctrinal plan in my mind. I had known and lived through only one doctrine, that of the Socialism of 1903–4 up to the winter of 1914, almost ten years. My experience in this had been that of a follower and of a leader, but not that of a theoretician. My doctrine, even in that period, had been a doctrine of action. An unequivocal Socialism, universally accepted, did not exist after 1905, when the Revisionist Movement began in Germany under Bernstein and there was formed in opposition to that, in the see-saw of tendencies, an extreme revolutionary movement, which in Italy never emerged from the condition of mere words, whilst in Russian Socialism it was the prelude to Bolshevism. Reform, Revolution, Centralization—even the

echoes of the terminology are now spent; whilst in the great river of Fascism are to be found the streams which had their source in Sorel, Peguy, in the Lagardelle of the *Mouvement Socialiste* and the groups of Italian Syndicalists, who between 1904 and 1914 brought a note of novelty into Italian Socialism. . . .

In 1919, at the end of the War, Socialism as a doctrine was already dead: it existed only as hatred, it had still only one possibility, especially in Italy, that of revenge against those who had wished for the War and who should be made to expiate it. The *Popolo d'Italia* expressed it in its sub-title—"The Newspaper of Combatants and Producers." The word "producers" was already the expression of a tendency. Fascism was not given out to the wet nurse of a doctrine elaborated beforehand round a table: it was born of the need for action; it was not a party, but in its first two years it was a movement against all parties. The name which I gave to the organization defined its characteristics. Nevertheless, whoever rereads, in the now crumpled pages of the time, the account of the constituent assembly of the *Fasci italiani di Combattimento* will not find a doctrine, but a series of suggestions, of anticipations, of admonitions, which when freed from the inevitable vein of contingency, were destined later, after a few years, to develop into a series of doctrinal attitudes which made of Fascism a self-sufficient political doctrine able to face all others, both past and present. "If the bourgeoisie," I said at that time, "thinks to find in us a lightning-conductor, it is mistaken. We must go forward in opposition to Labour. . . . We want to accustom the working classes to being under a leader, to convince them also that it is not easy to direct an industry or a commercial undertaking successfully. . . . We shall fight against technical and spiritual retrogression. . . . The successors of the present regime still being undecided, we must not be unwilling to fight for it. We must hasten; when the present regime is superseded, we must be the ones to take its place. The right of succession belongs to us because we pushed the country into the War and we lead it to victory. The present method of political representation cannot be sufficient for us, we wish for a direct representation of individual interests. . . . It might be said against this programme that it is a return to the corporations. It doesn't matter! . . . I should like, nevertheless, the Assembly to accept the claims of national syndicalism from the point of view of economics. . . ."

Is it not surprising that from the first day in the Piazza San Sepolcro there should resound the word "Corporation" which was destined in the course of the revolution to signify one of the legislative and social creations at the base of the regime?

2. The years preceding the March on Rome were years during which the necessity of action did not tolerate enquiries or complete elaborations of doctrine. Battles were being fought in the cities and villages. There were discussions, but—and this is more sacred and important—there were deaths. People knew how to die. The doctrine—beautiful, well-formed, divided into chapters and paragraphs and surrounded by a commentary—might be missing; but there was present something more decisive to supplant it—Faith. Nevertheless, he who recalls the past with the aid of books, articles, votes in Parliament, the major and the minor speeches, he who knows how to investigate and weigh evidence, will find that the foundations of the doctrine were laid while the battle was raging. It was precisely in these years that Fascist thought armed itself, refined itself, moving towards one organization of its own. The problems of the individual and the State; the problems of authority and liberty; political and social problems and those more specifically national; the struggle against liberal, democratic, socialist, Masonic, demagogic doctrines was carried on at the same time as the "punitive expeditions." But since the "system" was lacking, adversaries ingenuously denied that Fascism had any power to make a doctrine of its own, while the doctrine rose up, even though tumultuously, at first under the aspect of a violent and dogmatic negation, as happens to all ideas that break new

ground, then under the positive aspect of a constructive policy which, during the years 1926, 1927, 1928, was realized in the laws and institutions of the regime.

Fascism is to-day clearly defined not only as a regime but as a doctrine. And I mean by this that Fascism to-day, self-critical as well as critical of other movements, has an unequivocal point of view of its own, a criterion, and hence an aim, in face of all the material and intellectual problems which oppress the people of the world.

3. Above all, Fascism, in so far as it considers and observes the future and the development of humanity quite apart from the political considerations of the moment, believes neither in the possibility nor in the utility of perpetual peace. It thus repudiates the doctrine of Pacifism—born of a renunciation of the struggle and an act of cowardice in the face of sacrifice. War alone brings up to their highest tension all human energies and puts the stamp of nobility upon the peoples who have the courage to meet it. All other trials are substitutes, which never really put a man in front of himself in the alternative of life and death. A doctrine, therefore, which begins with a prejudice in favour of peace is foreign to Fascism; as are foreign to the spirit of Fascism, even though acceptable by reason of the utility which they might have in given political situations, all internationalistic and socialistic systems which, as history proves, can be blown to the winds when emotional, idealistic and practical movements storm the hearts of peoples. Fascism carries over this anti-pacifist spirit even into the lives of individuals. The proud motto of the *Squadrista*, "Me ne frego" ["I don't give a damn"], written on the bandages of a wound is an act of philosophy which is not only stoical, it is the epitome of a doctrine that is not only political: it is education for combat, the acceptance of the risks which it brings; it is a new way of life for Italy. Thus the Fascist accepts and loves life, he knows nothing of suicide and despises it; he looks on life as duty, ascent, conquest: life which must be noble and full: lived for oneself, but above all for those others near and far away, present and future.

4. The "demographic" policy of the regime follows from these premises. Even the Fascist does in fact love his neighbour, but this "neighbour" is not for him a vague and ill-defined concept; love for one's neighbour does not exclude necessary educational severities, and still less differentiations and distances. Fascism rejects universal concord, and, since it lives in the community of civilized peoples, it keeps them vigilantly and suspiciously before its eyes, it follows their states of mind and the changes in their interests and it does not let itself be deceived by temporary and fallacious appearances.

5. Such a conception of life makes Fascism the precise negation of that doctrine which formed the basis of the so-called Scientific or Marxian Socialism: the doctrine of historical Materialism, according to which the history of human civilizations can be explained only as the struggle of interest between the different social groups and as arising out of change in the means and instruments of production. That economic improvements—discoveries of raw materials, new methods of work, scientific inventions—should have an importance of their own, no one denies, but that they should suffice to explain human history to the exclusion of all other factors is absurd: Fascism believes, now and always, in holiness and in heroism, that is in acts in which no economic motive—remote or immediate—plays a part. With this negation of historical materialism, according to which men would be only by-products of history, who appear and disappear on the surface of the waves while in the depths the real directive forces are at work, there is also denied the immutable and irreparable "class struggle" which is the natural product of this economic conception of history, and above all it is denied that the class struggle can be the primary agent of social changes. Socialism, being thus wounded in these two primary tenets of its doctrine, nothing of it is left save the sentimental aspiration—old as humanity—towards a social order in which the sufferings and the pains of the humblest folk could be alleviated. But here Fascism rejects the concept of an economic "happiness" which would be

realized socialistically and almost automatically at a given moment of economic evolution by assuring to all a maximum prosperity. Fascism denies the possibility of the materialistic conception of "happiness" and leaves it to the economists of the first half of the eighteenth century; it denies, that is, the equation of prosperity with happiness, which would transform men into animals with one sole preoccupation: that of being well-fed and fat, degraded in consequence to a merely physical existence.

6. After Socialism, Fascism attacks the whole complex of democratic ideologies and rejects them both in their theoretical premises and in their applications or practical manifestations. Fascism denies that the majority, through the mere fact of being a majority, can rule human societies; it denies that this majority can govern by means of a periodical consultation; it affirms the irremediable, fruitful and beneficent inequality of men, who cannot be levelled by such a mechanical and extrinsic fact as universal suffrage. By democratic regimes we mean those in which from time to time the people is given the illusion of being sovereign, while true effective sovereignty lies in other, perhaps irresponsible and secret, forces. Democracy is a regime without a king, but with very many kings, perhaps more exclusive, tyrannical and violent than one king even though a tyrant. This explains why Fascism, although before 1922 for reasons of expediency it made a gesture of republicanism, renounced it before the March on Rome, convinced that the question of the political forms of a State is not pre-eminent to-day, and that studying past and present monarchies, past and present Republics it becomes clear that monarchy and republic are not to be judged *sub specie aeternitatis* [from the perspective of eternity], but represent forms in which the political evolution, the history, the tradition, the psychology of a given country are manifested. Now Fascism overcomes the antithesis between monarchy and republic which retarded the movements of democracy, burdening the former with every defect and defending the latter as the regime of perfection. Now it has been seen that there are inherently reactionary and absolutistic republics, and monarchies that welcome the most daring political and social innovations.

7. "Reason, Science," said Renan (who was inspired before Fascism existed) in one of his philosophical Meditations, "are products of humanity, but to expect reason directly from the people and through the people is a chimera. It is not necessary for the existence of reason that everybody should know it. In any case, if such an initiation should be made, it would not be made by means of base democracy, which apparently must lead to the extinction of every difficult culture, and every higher discipline. The principle that society exists only for the prosperity and the liberty of the individuals who compose it does not seem to conform with the plans of nature, plans in which the species alone is taken into consideration and the individual seems to be sacrificed. It is strongly to be feared lest the last word of democracy thus understood (I hasten to say that it can also be understood in other ways) would be a social state in which a degenerate mass would have no other care than to enjoy the ignoble pleasures of vulgar men."

Thus far Renan. Fascism rejects in democracy the absurd conventional lie of political equalitarianism clothed in the dress of collective irresponsibility and the myth of happiness and indefinite progress. But if democracy can be understood in other ways, that is, if democracy means not to relegate the people to the periphery of the State, then Fascism could be defined as an "organized, centralized, authoritarian democracy."

8. In face of Liberal doctrines, Fascism takes up an attitude of absolute opposition both in the field of politics and in that of economics. It is not necessary to exaggerate—merely for the purpose of present controversies—the importance of Liberalism in the past century, and to make of that which was one of the numerous doctrines sketched in that century a religion of humanity for all times, present and future. . . . The "Liberal" century, after having accumulated an infinity of Gordian knots, tried to untie

them by the hecatomb of the World War. Never before has any religion imposed such a cruel sacrifice. Were the gods of Liberalism thirsty for blood? Now Liberalism is about to close the doors of its deserted temples because the peoples feel that its agnosticism in economics, its indifferentism in politics and in morals, would lead, as they have led, the States to certain ruin. In this way one can understand why all the political experiences of the contemporary world are anti-Liberal, and it is supremely ridiculous to wish on that account to class them outside of history; as if history were a hunting ground reserved to Liberalism and its professors, as if Liberalism were the definitive and no longer surpassable message of civilization.

9. But the Fascist repudiations of Socialism, Democracy, Liberalism must not make one think that Fascism wishes to make the world return to what it was before 1789, the year which has been indicated as the year of the beginning of the liberal-democratic age. One does not go backwards. The Fascist doctrine has not chosen De Maistre as its prophet. Monarchical absolutism is a thing of the past and so also is every theocracy. So also feudal privileges and division into impenetrable and isolated castes have had their day. The theory of Fascist authority has nothing to do with the police State. A party that governs a nation in a totalitarian way is a new fact in history. References and comparisons are not possible. Fascism takes over from the ruins of Liberal Socialistic democratic doctrines those elements which still have a living value. It preserves those that can be called the established facts of history, it rejects all the rest, that is to say the idea of a doctrine which holds good for all times and all peoples. If it is admitted that the nineteenth century has been the century of Socialism, Liberalism and Democracy, it does not follow that the twentieth must also be the century of Liberalism, Socialism and Democracy. Political doctrines pass; peoples remain. It is to be expected that this century may be that of authority, a century of the "Right," a Fascist century. If the nineteenth was the century of the individual (Liberalism means individualism) it may be expected that this one may be the century of "collectivism" and therefore the century of the State. That a new doctrine should use the still vital elements of other doctrines is perfectly logical. No doctrine is born quite new, shining, never before seen. No doctrine can boast of an absolute "originality." It is bound, even if only historically, to other doctrines that have been, and to develop into other doctrines that will be. Thus the scientific socialism of Marx is bound to the Utopian Socialism of the Fouriers, the Owens and the Saint-Simons; thus the Liberalism of the nineteenth century is connected with the whole "Enlightenment" of the eighteenth century. Thus the doctrines of democracy are bound to the *Encyclopédie*. Every doctrine tends to direct the activity of men towards a determined objective; but the activity of man reacts upon the doctrine, transforms it, adapts it to new necessities or transcends it. The doctrine itself, therefore, must be, not words, but an act of life. Hence, the pragmatic veins in Fascism, its will to power, its will to be, its attitude in the face of the fact of "violence" and of its own courage.

10. The keystone of Fascist doctrine is the conception of the State, of its essence, of its tasks, of its ends. For Fascism the State is an absolute before which individuals and groups are relative. Individuals and groups are "thinkable" in so far as they are within the State. The Liberal State does not direct the interplay and the material and spiritual development of the groups, but limits itself to registering the results; the Fascist State has a consciousness of its own, a will of its own, on this account it is called an "ethical" State. In 1929, at the first quinquennial assembly of the regime, I said: "For Fascism, the State is not the night-watchman who is concerned only with the personal security of the citizens; nor is it an organization for purely material ends, such as that of guaranteeing a certain degree of prosperity and a relatively peaceful social order, to achieve which a council of administration would be sufficient, nor is it a creation of mere politics with no contact with the material and complex reality of the

lives of individuals and the life of peoples. The State, as conceived by Fascism and as it acts, is a spiritual and moral fact because it makes concrete the political, juridical, economic organization of the nation and such an organization is, in its origin and in its development, a manifestation of the spirit. The State is the guarantor of internal and external security, but it is also the guardian and the transmitter of the spirit of the people as it has been elaborated through the centuries in language, custom, faith. The State is not only present, it is also past, and above all future. It is the State which, transcending the brief limit of individual lives, represents the immanent conscience of the nation. The forms in which States express themselves change, but the necessity of the State remains. It is the State which educates citizens for civic virtue, makes them conscious of their mission, calls them to unity; harmonizes their interests in justice; hands on the achievements of thought in the sciences, the arts, in law, in human solidarity; it carries men from the elementary life of the tribe to the highest human expression of power which is Empire; it entrusts to the ages the names of those who died for its integrity or in obedience to its laws; it puts forward as an example and recommends to the generations that are to come the leaders who increased its territory and the men of genius who gave it glory. When the sense of the State declines and the disintegrating and centrifugal tendencies of individuals and groups prevail, national societies move to their decline."

11. From 1929 up to the present day these doctrinal positions have been strengthened by the whole economico-political evolution of the world. It is the State alone that grows in size, in power. It is the State alone that can solve the dramatic contradictions of capitalism. What is called the crisis cannot be overcome except by the State, within the State. . . . But when one says liberalism, one says the individual; when one says Fascism, one says the State. But the Fascist State is unique; it is an original creation. It is not reactionary, but revolutionary in that it anticipates the solutions of certain universal problems. These problems are no longer seen in the same light: in the sphere of politics they are removed from party rivalries, from the supreme power of parliament, from the irresponsibility of assemblies; in the sphere of economics they are removed from the sphere of the syndicates' activities—activities that were ever widening their scope and increasing their power both on the workers' side and on the employers'—removed from their struggles and their designs; in the moral sphere they are divorced from ideas of the need for order, discipline and obedience, and lifted into the plane of the moral commandments of the fatherland. Fascism desires the State to be strong, organic and at the same time founded on a wide popular basis. The Fascist State has also claimed for itself the field of economics and, through the corporative, social and educational institutions which it has created, the meaning of the State reaches out to and includes the farthest off-shoots; and within the State, framed in their respective organizations, there revolve all the political, economic and spiritual forces of the nation. A State founded on millions of individuals who recognize it, feel it, are ready to serve it, is not the tyrannical State of the medieval lord. It has nothing in common with the absolutist States that existed either before or after 1789. In the Fascist State the individual is not suppressed, but rather multiplied, just as in a regiment a soldier is not weakened but multiplied by the number of his comrades. The Fascist State organizes the nation, but it leaves sufficient scope to individuals; it has limited useless or harmful liberties and has preserved those that are essential. It cannot be the individual who decides in this matter, but only the State.

12. The Fascist State does not remain indifferent to the fact of religion in general and to that particular positive religion which is Italian Catholicism. The State has no theology, but it has an ethic. In the Fascist State religion is looked upon as one of the deepest manifestations of the spirit; it is, therefore, not only respected, but defended and protected. The Fascist State does not create a "God" of its own, as

Robespierre once, at the height of the Convention's foolishness, wished to do; nor does it vainly seek, like Bolshevism, to expel religion from the minds of men; Fascism respects the God of the ascetics, of the saints, of the heroes, and also God as seen and prayed to by the simple and primitive heart of the people.

13. The Fascist State is a will to power and to government. In it the tradition of Rome is an idea that has force. In the doctrine of Fascism Empire is not only a territorial, military or mercantile expression, but spiritual or moral. One can think of an empire, that is to say a nation that directly or indirectly leads other nations, without needing to conquer a single square kilometre of territory. For Fascism the tendency to Empire, that is to say, to the expansion of nations, is a manifestation of vitality; its opposite, staying at home, is a sign of decadence: peoples who rise or re-rise are imperialist, peoples who die are renunciatory. Fascism is the doctrine that is most fitted to represent the aims, the states of mind, of a people, like the Italian people, rising again after many centuries of abandonment or slavery to foreigners. But Empire calls for discipline, co-ordination of forces, duty and sacrifice; this explains many aspects of the practical working of the regime and the direction of many of the forces of the State and the necessary severity shown to those who would wish to oppose this spontaneous and destined impulse of the Italy of the twentieth century, to oppose it in the name of the superseded ideologies of the nineteenth, repudiated wherever great experiments of political and social transformation have been courageously attempted: especially where, as now, peoples thirst for authority, for leadership, for order. If every age has its own doctrine, it is apparent from a thousand signs that the doctrine of the present age is Facism. That it is a doctrine of life is shown by the fact that it has resuscitated a faith. That this faith has conquered minds is proved by the fact that Fascism has had its dead and its martyrs.

Fascism henceforward has in the world the universality of all those doctrines which, by fulfilling themselves, have significance in the history of the human spirit.

NOTE

1. "Race; it is an emotion, not a reality; ninety-five per cent of it is emotion." Mussolini.

42

NATION AND RACE

ADOLF HITLER

Adolf Hitler (1889–1945) was neither an original nor a consistent thinker, but his blend of fascism and racism proved to be one of the most potent ideological forces in history. The following selections are from Hitler's autobiography, *Mein Kampf*, which he wrote in 1924 while imprisoned for leading an attempt to overthrow the government of the German province of Bavaria. The selections reveal Hitler's racial ideas and anti-Semitism, his hatred of socialism and liberalism, and other ideas he and the Nazis pursued once they gained power in Germany in 1933.

Source: excerpts from Mein Kampf *by Adolf Hitler, translated by Ralph Manheim (New York: Houghton Mifflin, 1943), pp. 40–45, 284–329, 378–385.*

More than any theoretical literature, my daily reading of the Social Democratic press enabled me to study the inner nature of these thought-processes.

For what a difference between the glittering phrases about freedom, beauty, and dignity in the theoretical literature, the delusive welter of words seemingly expressing the most profound and laborious wisdom, the loathsome humanitarian morality—all this written with the incredible gall that comes with prophetic certainty—and the brutal daily press, shunning no villainy, employing every means of slander, lying with a virtuosity that would bend iron beams, all in the name of this gospel of a new humanity. The one is addressed to the simpletons of the middle, not to mention the upper, educated, "classes," the other to the masses.

For me immersion in the literature and press of this doctrine and organization meant finding my way back to my own people.

What had seemed to me an unbridgable gulf became the source of a greater love than ever before.

Only a fool can behold the work of this villainous poisoner and still condemn the victim. The more independent I made myself in the next few years, the clearer grew my perspective, hence my insight into the inner causes of the Social Democratic successes. I now understood the significance of the brutal demand that I read only Red papers, attend only Red meetings, read only Red books, etc. With plastic clarity I saw before my eyes the inevitable result of this doctrine of intolerance.

The psyche of the great masses is not receptive to anything that is half-hearted and weak.

Like the woman, whose psychic state is determined less by grounds of abstract reason than by an indefinable emotional longing for a force which will complement her nature, and who, consequently, would rather bow to a strong man than dominate a weakling, likewise the masses love a commander more than a petitioner and feel inwardly more satisfied by a doctrine, tolerating no other beside itself, than by the granting of liberalistic freedom with which, as a rule, they can do little, and are prone to feel that they have been abandoned. They are equally unaware of their shameless spiritual terrorization and the hideous abuse of their human freedom, for they absolutely fail to suspect the inner insanity of the whole doctrine. All they see is the ruthless force and brutality of its calculated manifestations, to which they always submit in the end.

If Social Democracy is opposed by a doctrine of greater truth, but equal brutality of methods, the latter will conquer, though this may require the bitterest struggle.

Before two years had passed, the theory as well as the technical methods of Social Democracy were clear to me.

I understood the infamous spiritual terror which this movement exerts, particularly on the bourgeoisie, which is neither morally nor mentally equal to such attacks; at a given sign it unleashes a veritable barrage of lies and slanders against whatever adversary seems most dangerous, until the nerves of the attacked persons break down and, just to have peace again, they sacrifice the hated individual.

However, the fools obtain no peace.

The game begins again and is repeated over and over until fear of the mad dog results in suggestive paralysis.

Since the Social Democrats best know the value of force from their own experience, they most violently attack those in whose nature they detect any of this substance which is so rare. Conversely, they praise every weakling on the opposing side, sometimes cautiously, sometimes loudly, depending on the real or supposed quality of his intelligence.

They fear an impotent, spineless genius less than a forceful nature of moderate intelligence.

But with the greatest enthusiasm they commend weaklings in both mind and force.

They know how to create the illusion that this is the only way of preserving the peace, and at the same time, stealthily but steadily, they conquer one position after another, sometimes by silent blackmail, sometimes by actual theft, at moments when the general attention is directed toward other matters, and either does not want to be disturbed or considers the matter too small to raise a stir about, thus again irritating the vicious antagonist.

This is a tactic based on precise calculation of all human weaknesses, and its result will lead to success with almost mathematical certainty unless the opposing side learns to combat poison gas with poison gas.

It is our duty to inform all weaklings that this is a question of to be or not to be.

I achieved an equal understanding of the importance of physical terror toward the individual and the masses.

Here, too, the psychological effect can be calculated with precision.

Terror at the place of employment, in the factory, in the meeting hall, and on the occasion of mass demonstrations will always be successful unless opposed by equal terror.

In this case, to be sure, the party will cry bloody murder; though it has long despised all state authority, it will set up a howling cry for that same authority and in most cases will actually attain its goal amid the general confusion: it will find some idiot of a higher official who, in the imbecilic hope of propitiating the feared adversary for later eventualities, will help this world plague to break its opponent.

The impression made by such a success on the minds of the great masses of supporters as well as opponents can only be measured by those who know the soul of a people, not from books, but from life. For while in the ranks of their supporters the victory achieved seems a triumph of the justice of their own cause, the defeated adversary in most cases despairs of the successes of any further resistance.

. . .

There are some truths which are so obvious that for this very reason they are not seen or at least not recognized by ordinary people. They sometimes pass by such truisms as though blind and are most astonished when someone suddenly discovers what everyone really ought to know. Columbus's eggs lie around by the hundreds of thousands, but Columbuses are met with less frequently.

Thus men without exception wander about in the garden of Nature; they imagine that they know practically everything and yet with few exceptions pass blindly by one of the most patent principles of Nature's rule: the inner segregation of the species of all living beings on this earth.

Even the most superficial observation shows that Nature's restricted form of propagation and increase is an almost rigid basic law of all the innumerable forms of expression of her vital urge. Every animal mates only with a member of the same species. The titmouse seeks the titmouse, the finch the finch, the stork the stork, the field mouse the field mouse, the dormouse the dormouse, the wolf the she-wolf, etc.

Only unusual circumstances can change this, primarily the compulsion of captivity or any other cause that makes it impossible to mate within the same species. But then Nature begins to resist this with all possible means, and her most visible protest consists either in refusing further capacity for propagation to bastards or in limiting the fertility of later offspring; in most cases, however, she takes away the power of resistance to disease or hostile attacks.

This is only too natural.

Any crossing of two beings not at exactly the same level produces a medium between the level of the two parents. This means: the offspring will probably stand higher than the racially lower parent, but not as high as the higher one. Consequently, it will later succumb in the struggle against the higher level. Such mating is contrary to the will of Nature for a higher breeding of all life. The precondition for this does not lie in associating superior and inferior, but in the total victory of the former. The stronger must dominate and not blend with the weaker, thus sacrificing his own greatness. Only the born weakling can view this as cruel, but he after all is only a weak and limited man; for if this law did not prevail, any conceivable higher development of organic living beings would be unthinkable.

The consequence of this racial purity, universally valid in Nature, is not only the sharp outward delimitation of the various races, but their uniform character in themselves. The fox is always a fox, the goose a goose, the tiger a tiger, etc., and the difference can lie at most in the varying measure of force, strength, intelligence, dexterity, endurance, etc., of the individual specimens. But you will never find a fox who in his inner attitude might, for example, show humanitarian tendencies toward geese, as similarly there is no cat with a friendly inclination toward mice.

Therefore, here, too, the struggle among themselves arises less from inner aversion than from hunger and love. In both cases, Nature looks on calmly, with satisfaction, in fact. In the struggle for daily bread all those who are weak and sickly or less determined succumb, while the struggle of the males for the female grants the right or opportunity to propagate only to the healthiest. And struggle is always a means for improving a species' health and power of resistance and, therefore, a cause of its higher development.

If the process were different, all further and higher development would cease and the opposite would occur. For, since the inferior always predominates numerically over the best, if both had the same possibility of preserving life and propagating, the inferior would multiply so much more rapidly that in the end the best would inevitably be driven into the background, unless a correction of this state of affairs were undertaken. Nature does just this by subjecting the weaker part to such severe living conditions that by them alone the number is limited, and by not permitting the remainder to increase promiscuously, but making a new and ruthless choice according to strength and health.

No more than Nature desires the mating of weaker with stronger individuals, even less does she desire the blending of a higher with a lower race, since, if she did, her whole work of higher breeding, over perhaps hundreds of thousands of years, might be ruined with one blow.

Historical experience offers countless proofs of this. It shows with terrifying clarity that in every mingling of Aryan blood with that of lower peoples the result was the end of the cultured people. North America, whose population consists in by far the largest part of Germanic elements who mixed but little with the lower colored peoples, shows a different humanity and culture from Central and South America, where the predominantly Latin immigrants often mixed with the aborigines on a large scale. By this one example, we can clearly and distinctly recognize the effect of racial mixture. The Germanic inhabitant of the American continent, who has remained racially pure and unmixed, rose to be master of the continent; he will remain the master as long as he does not fall a victim to defilement of the blood.

The result of all racial crossing is therefore in brief always the following:

a. Lowering of the level of the higher race;
b. Physical and intellectual regression and hence the beginning of a slowly but surely progressing sickness.

To bring about such a development is, then, nothing else but to sin against the will of the eternal creator.

And as a sin this act is rewarded.

When man attempts to rebel against the iron logic of Nature, he comes into struggle with the principles to which he himself owes his existence as a man. And this attack must lead to his own doom.

Here, of course, we encounter the objection of the modern pacifist, as truly Jewish in its effrontery as it is stupid! "Man's rôle is to overcome Nature!"

Millions thoughtlessly parrot this Jewish nonsense and end up by really imagining that they themselves represent a kind of conqueror of Nature; though in this they dispose of no other weapon than an idea, and at that such a miserable one, that if it were true no world at all would be conceivable.

But quite aside from the fact that man has never yet conquered Nature in anything, but at most has caught hold of and tried to lift one or another corner of her immense gigantic veil of eternal riddles and secrets, that in reality he invents nothing but only discovers everything, that he does not dominate Nature, but has only risen on the basis of his knowledge of various laws and secrets of Nature to be lord over those other living creatures who lack this knowledge—quite aside from all this, an idea cannot overcome the preconditions for the development of being of humanity, since the idea itself depends only on man. Without human beings there is no human idea in this world, therefore, the idea as such is always conditioned by the presence of human beings and hence of all the laws which created the precondition for their existence.

And not only that! Certain ideas are even tied up with certain men. This applies most of all to those ideas whose content originates, not in an exact scientific truth, but in the world of emotion, or, as it is so beautifully and clearly expressed today, reflects an "inner experience." All these ideas, which have nothing to do with cold logic as such, but represent only pure expressions of feeling, ethical conceptions, etc., are chained to the existence of men, to whose intellectual imagination and creative power they owe their existence. Precisely in this case the preservation of these definite races and men is the precondition for the existence of these ideas. Anyone, for example, who really desired the victory of the pacifistic idea in this world with all his heart would have to fight with all the means at his disposal for the conquest of the world by the Germans; for, if the opposite should occur, the last pacifist would die out with the last German, since the rest of the world has never fallen so deeply as our own people, unfortunately, has for this nonsense so contrary to Nature and reason. Then, if we were serious, whether we liked it or not, we would have to wage wars in order to arrive at pacifism. This and nothing else was what Wilson, the American world savior, intended, or so at least our German visionaries believed—and thereby his purpose was fulfilled.

In actual fact the pacifistic-humane idea is perfectly all right perhaps when the highest type of man has previously conquered and subjected the world to an extent that makes him the sole ruler of this earth. Then this idea lacks the power of producing evil effects in exact proportion as its practical application becomes rare and finally impossible. Therefore, first struggle and then we shall see what can be done. Otherwise mankind has passed the high point of its development and the end is not the domination of any ethical idea but barbarism and consequently chaos. At this point someone or other may laugh, but this planet once moved through the ether for millions of years without human beings and it can do so again some day if men forget that they owe their higher existence, not to the ideas of a few crazy ideologists, but to the knowledge and ruthless application of Nature's stern and rigid laws.

Everything we admire on this earth today—science and art, technology and inventions—is only the creative product of a few peoples and originally perhaps of *one* race. On them depends the existence of this whole culture. If they perish, the beauty of this earth will sink into the grave with them.

However much the soil, for example, can influence men, the result of the influence will always be different depending on the races in question. The low fertility of a living space may spur the one race to the highest achievements; in others it will only be the cause of bitterest poverty and final undernourishment with all its consequences. The inner nature of peoples is always determining for the manner in which outward influences will be effective. What leads the one to starvation trains the other to hard work.

All great cultures of the past perished only because the originally creative race died out from blood poisoning.

The ultimate cause of such a decline was their forgetting that all culture depends on men and not conversely; hence that to preserve a certain culture the man who creates it must be preserved. This preservation is bound up with the rigid law of necessity and the right to victory of the best and stronger in this world.

Those who want to live, let them fight, and those who do not want to fight in this world of eternal struggle do not deserve to live.

Even if this were hard—that is how it is! Assuredly, however, by far the harder fate is that which strikes the man who thinks he can overcome Nature, but in the last analysis only mocks her. Distress, misfortune, and diseases are her answer.

The man who misjudges and disregards the racial laws actually forfeits the happiness that seems destined to be his. He thwarts the triumphal march of the best race and hence also the precondition for all human progress, and remains, in consequence, burdened with all the sensibility of man, in the animal realm of helpless misery.

It is idle to argue which race or races were the original representative of human culture and hence the real founders of all that we sum up under the word "humanity." It is simpler to raise this question with regard to the present, and here an easy, clear answer results. All the human culture, all the results of art, science, and technology that we see before us today, are almost exclusively the creative product of the Aryan. This very fact admits of the not unfounded inference that he alone was the founder of all higher humanity, therefore representing the prototype of all that we understand by the word "man." He is the Prometheus of mankind from whose bright forehead the divine spark of genius has sprung at all times, forever kindling anew that fire of knowledge which illumined the night of silent mysteries and thus caused man to climb the path to mastery over the other beings of this earth. Exclude him—and perhaps after a few thousand years darkness will again descend on the earth, human culture will pass, and the world turn to a desert.

If we were to divide mankind into three groups, the founders of culture, the bearers of culture, the destroyers of culture, only the Aryan could be considered as the representative of the first group. From him originate the foundations and walls of all human creation, and only the outward form and color are determined by the changing traits of character of the various peoples. He provides the mightiest building stones and plans for all human progress and only the execution corresponds to the nature of the varying men and races. In a few decades, for example, the entire east of Asia will possess a culture whose ultimate foundation will be Hellenic spirit and Germanic technology, just as much as in Europe. Only the *outward* form—in part at least—will bear the features of Asiatic character. It is not true, as some people think, that Japan adds European technology to its culture; no, European science and technology are trimmed with Japanese characteristics. The foundation of actual life is no longer the special Japanese culture, although it determines the color of life—because outwardly, in consequence of its inner difference, it is more conspicuous to the European—but the gigantic scientific-technical achievements of Europe and America; that is, of Aryan peoples. Only on the basis of these achievements can the Orient follow general human progress. They furnish the basis of the struggle for daily bread, create weapons and implements for it, and only the outward form is gradually adapted to Japanese character.

If beginning today all further Aryan influence on Japan should stop, assuming that Europe and America should perish, Japan's present rise in science and technology might continue for a short time; but even in a few years the well would dry up, the Japanese special character would gain, but the present culture would freeze and sink back into the slumber from which it was awakened seven decades ago by the wave of Aryan culture. Therefore, just as the present Japanese development owes its life to Aryan origin, long ago in the gray past foreign influence and foreign spirit awakened the Japanese culture of that time. The best proof of this is furnished by the fact of its subsequent sclerosis and total petrifaction. This can occur in a people only when the original creative racial nucleus has been lost, or if the external influence which furnished the impetus and the material for the first development in the cultural field was later lacking. But if it is established that a people receives the most essential basic materials of its culture from foreign races, that it assimilates and adapts them, and that then, if further external influence is lacking, it rigidifies again and again, such a race may be designated as "*culture-bearing,*" but never as "*culture-creating.*" An examination of the various peoples from this standpoint points to the fact that practically none of them were originally *culture-founding*, but almost always *culture-bearing*.

Approximately the following picture of their development always results:

Aryan races—often absurdly small numerically—subject foreign peoples, and then, stimulated by the special living conditions of the new territory (fertility, climatic conditions, etc.) and assisted by the multitude of lower-type beings standing at their disposal as helpers, develop the intellectual and organizational capacities dormant within them. Often in a few millenniums or even centuries they create cultures which originally bear all the inner characteristics of their nature, adapted to the above-indicated special qualities of the soil and subjected beings. In the end, however, the conquerors transgress against the principle of blood purity, to which they had first adhered; they begin to mix with the subjugated inhabitants and thus end their own existence; for the fall of man in paradise has always been followed by his expulsion. . . .

We see this most distinctly in connection with the race which has been and is the bearer of human cultural development—the Aryans. As soon as Fate leads them toward special conditions, their latent abilities begin to develop in a more and more rapid sequence and to mold themselves into tangible forms. The cultures which they found in such cases are nearly always decisively determined by the existing soil, the given climate, and—the subjected people. This last item, to be sure, is almost the most decisive. The more primitive the technical foundations for a cultural activity, the more necessary is the presence of human helpers who, organizationally assembled and employed, must replace the force of the machine. Without this possibility of using lower human beings, the Aryan would never have been able to take his first steps toward his future culture; just as without the help of various suitable beasts which he knew how to tame, he would not have arrived at a technology which is now gradually permitting him to do without these beasts. The saying, "The Moor has worked off his debt, the Moor can go," unfortunately has only too deep a meaning. For thousands of years the horse had to serve man and help him lay the foundations of a development which now, in consequence of the motor car, is making the horse superfluous. In a few years his activity will have ceased, but without his previous collaboration man might have had a hard time getting where he is today.

Thus, for the formation of higher cultures the existence of lower human types was one of the most essential preconditions, since they alone were able to compensate for the lack of technical aids without which a higher development is not conceivable. It is certain that the first culture of humanity was based less on the tamed animal than on the use of lower human beings.

Only after the enslavement of subjected races did the same fate strike beasts, and not the other way around, as some people would like to think. For first the conquered warrior drew the plow—and only after him the horse. Only pacifistic fools can regard this as a sign of human depravity, failing to realize that this development had to take place in order to reach the point where today these sky-pilots could force their drivel on the world.

The progress of humanity is like climbing an endless ladder; it is impossible to climb higher without first taking the lower steps. Thus, the Aryan had to take the road to which reality directed him and not the one that would appeal to the imagination of a modern pacifist. The road of reality is hard and difficult, but in the end it leads where our friend would like to bring humanity by dreaming, but unfortunately removes more than bringing it closer.

Hence it is no accident that the first cultures arose in places where the Aryan, in his encounters with lower peoples, subjugated them and bent them to his will. They then became the first technical instrument in the service of a developing culture.

Thus, the road which the Aryan had to take was clearly marked out. As a conqueror he subjected the lower beings and regulated their practical activity under his command, according to his will and for his aims. But in directing them to a useful, though arduous activity, he not only spared the life of those he subjected; perhaps he gave them a fate that was better than their previous so-called "freedom." As long as he ruthlessly upheld the master attitude, not only did he really remain master, but also the preserver and increaser of culture. For culture was based exclusively on his abilities and hence on his actual survival. As soon as the subjected people began to raise themselves up and probably approached the conqueror in language, the sharp dividing wall between master and servant fell. The Aryan gave up the purity of his blood and, therefore, lost his sojourn in the paradise which he had made for himself. He became submerged in the racial mixture, and gradually, more and more, lost his cultural capacity, until at last, not only mentally but also physically, he began to resemble the subjected aborigines more than his own ancestors. For a time he could live on the existing cultural benefits, but then petrifaction set in and he fell a prey to oblivion.

Thus cultures and empires collapsed to make place for new formations.

Blood mixture and the resultant drop in the racial level is the sole cause of the dying out of old cultures; for men do not perish as a result of lost wars, but by the loss of that force of resistance which is contained only in pure blood.

All who are not of good race in this world are chaff.

And all occurrences in world history are only the expression of the races' instinct of self-preservation, in the good or bad sense. . . .

. . . The Aryan is not greatest in his mental qualities as such, but in the extent of his willingness to put all his abilities in the service of the community. In him the instinct of self-preservation has reached the noblest form, since he willingly subordinates his own ego to the life of the community and, if the hour demands, even sacrifices it.

Not in his intellectual gifts lies the source of the Aryan's capacity for creating and building culture. If he had just this alone, he could only act destructively, in no case could he organize; for the innermost essence of all organization requires that the individual renounce putting forward his personal opinion and interests and sacrifice both in favor of a larger group. Only by way of this general community does he again recover his share. Now, for example, he no longer works directly for himself, but with his activity articulates himself with the community, not only for his own advantage, but for the advantage of all. The most wonderful elucidation of this attitude is provided by his word "work," by which he does not mean an activity for maintaining life in itself, but exclusively a creative effort that does not conflict with the interests of the community. Otherwise he designates human activity, in so far as it serves the instinct of self-preservation without consideration for his fellow men, as theft, usury, robbery, burglary, etc.

This state of mind, which subordinates the interests of the ego to the conservation of the community, is really the first premise for every truly human culture. From it alone can arise all the great works of mankind, which bring the founder little reward, but the richest blessings to posterity. Yes, from it alone can we understand how so many are able to bear up faithfully under a scanty life which imposes on them nothing but poverty and frugality, but gives the community the foundations of its existence. Every worker, every peasant, every inventor, official, etc., who works without ever being able to achieve any happiness or prosperity for himself, is a representative of this lofty idea, even if the deeper meaning of his activity remains hidden in him.

What applies to work as the foundation of human sustenance and all human progress is true to an even greater degree for the defense of man and his culture. In giving one's own life for the existence of the community lies the crown of all sense of sacrifice. It is this alone that prevents what human hands have built from being overthrown by human hands or destroyed by Nature.

Our own German language possesses a word which magnificently designates this kind of activity: *Pflichterfüllung* (fulfillment of duty); it means not to be self-sufficient but to serve the community.

The basic attitude from which such activity arises, we call—to distinguish it from egoism and selfishness—idealism. By this we understand only the individual's capacity to make sacrifices for the community, for his fellow men.

How necessary it is to keep realizing that idealism does not represent a superfluous expression of emotion, but that in truth it has been, is, and will be, the premise for what we designate as human culture, yes, that it alone created the concept of "man"! It is to this inner attitude that the Aryan owes his position in this world, and to it the world owes man; for it alone formed from pure spirit the creative force which, by a unique pairing of the brutal fist and the intellectual genius, created the monuments of human culture.

Without his idealistic attitude all, even the most dazzling faculties of the intellect, would remain mere intellect as such—outward appearance without inner value, and never creative force.

But, since true idealism is nothing but the subordination of the interests and life of the individual to the community, and this in turn is the precondition for the creation of organizational forms of all kinds, it corresponds in its innermost depths to the ultimate will of Nature. It alone leads men to voluntary recognition of the privilege of force and strength, and thus makes them into a dust particle of that order which shapes and forms the whole universe. . . .

The mightiest counterpart to the Aryan is represented by the Jew. In hardly any people in the world is the instinct of self-preservation developed more strongly than in the so-called "chosen." Of this, the mere fact of the survival of this race may be considered the best proof. Where is the people which in the last two thousand years has been exposed to so slight changes of inner disposition, character, etc., as the Jewish people? What people, finally, has gone through greater upheavals than this one—and nevertheless issued from the mightiest catastrophes of mankind unchanged? What an infinitely tough will to live and preserve the species speaks from these facts!

The mental qualities of the Jew have been schooled in the course of many centuries. Today he passes as "smart," and this in a certain sense he has been at all times. But his intelligence is not the result of his own development, but of visual instruction through foreigners. For the human mind cannot climb to the top without steps; for every step upward he needs the foundation of the past, and this in the comprehensive sense in which it can be revealed only in general culture. All thinking is based only in small part on man's own knowledge, and mostly on the experience of the time that has preceded. The general cultural level provides the individual man, without his noticing it as a rule, with such a profusion of preliminary knowledge that, thus armed, he can more easily take further steps of his own. The boy of today, for example, grows up among a truly vast number of technical acquisitions of the last centuries, so that he takes for granted and no longer pays attention to much that a hundred years ago was a riddle to even the greatest minds, although for following and understanding our progress in the field in question it is of decisive importance to him. If a very genius from the twenties of the past century should suddenly leave his grave today, it would be harder for him even intellectually to find his way in the present era than for an average boy of fifteen today. For he would lack all the infinite preliminary education which our present contemporary unconsciously, so to speak, assimilates while growing up amidst the manifestations of our present general civilization.

Since the Jew—for reasons which will at once become apparent—was never in possession of a culture of his own, the foundations of his intellectual work were always provided by others. His intellect at all times developed through the cultural world surrounding him.

The reverse process never took place.

For if the Jewish people's instinct of self-preservation is not smaller but larger than that of other peoples, if his intellectual faculties can easily arouse the impression that they are equal to the intellectual gifts of other races, he lacks completely the most essential requirement for a cultured people, the idealistic attitude.

In the Jewish people the will to self-sacrifice does not go beyond the individual's naked instinct of self-preservation. Their apparently great sense of solidarity is based on the very primitive herd instinct that is seen in many other living creatures in this world. It is a noteworthy fact that the herd instinct leads to mutual support only as long as a common danger makes this seem useful or inevitable. The same pack of wolves which has just fallen on its prey together disintegrates when hunger abates into its individual beasts. The same is true of horses which try to defend themselves against an assailant in a body, but scatter again as soon as the danger is past.

It is similar with the Jew. His sense of sacrifice is only apparent. It exists as long as the existence of the individual makes it absolutely necessary. However, as soon as the common enemy is conquered, the danger threatening all averted and the booty hidden, the apparent harmony of the Jews among themselves ceases, again making way for their old causal tendencies. The Jew is only united when a common danger forces him to be or a common booty entices him; if these two grounds are lacking, the qualities of the crassest egoism come into their own, and in the twinkling of an eye the united people turns into a horde of rats, fighting bloodily among themselves.

If the Jews were alone in this world, they would stifle in filth and offal; they would try to get ahead of one another in hate-filled struggle and exterminate one another, in so far as the absolute absence of all sense of self-sacrifice, expressing itself in their cowardice, did not turn battle into comedy here too.

So it is absolutely wrong to infer any ideal sense of sacrifice in the Jews from the fact that they stand together in struggle, or, better expressed, in the plundering of their fellow men.

Here again the Jew is led by nothing but the naked egoism of the individual.

That is why the Jewish state—which should be the living organism for preserving and increasing a race—is completely unlimited as to territory. For a state formation to have a definite spatial setting always presupposes an idealistic attitude on the part of the state-race, and especially a correct interpretation of the concept of work. In the exact measure in which this attitude is lacking, any attempt at forming, even of preserving, a spatially delimited state fails. And thus the basis on which alone culture can arise is lacking.

Hence the Jewish people, despite all apparent intellectual qualities, is without any true culture, and especially without any culture of its own. For what sham culture the Jew today possesses is the property of other peoples, and for the most part it is ruined in his hands.

In judging the Jewish people's attitude on the question of human culture, the most essential characteristic we must always bear in mind is that there has never been a Jewish art and accordingly there is none today either; that above all the two queens of all the arts, architecture and music, owe nothing original to the Jews. What they do accomplish in the field of art is either patchwork or intellectual theft. Thus, the Jew lacks those qualities which distinguish the races that are creative and hence culturally blessed.

To what an extent the Jew takes over foreign culture, imitating or rather ruining it, can be seen from the fact that he is mostly found in the art which seems to require least original invention, the art of acting. But even here, in reality, he is only a "juggler," or rather an ape; for even here he lacks the last touch that is required for real greatness; even here he is not the creative genius, but a superficial imitator, and all the twists and tricks that he uses are powerless to conceal the inner lifelessness of his creative gift. Here the Jewish press most lovingly helps him along by raising such a roar of hosannahs about even the most mediocre bungler, just so long as he is a Jew, that the rest of the world actually ends up by thinking that they have an artist before them, while in truth it is only a pitiful comedian.

No, the Jew possesses no culture-creating force of any sort, since the idealism, without which there is no true higher development of man, is not present in him and never was present. Hence his intellect will never have a constructive effect, but will be destructive, and in very rare cases perhaps will at most be stimulating, but then as the prototype of the "force which always wants evil and nevertheless creates good." Not through him does any progress of mankind occur, but in spite of him.

Since the Jew never possessed a state with definite territorial limits and therefore never called a culture his own, the conception arose that this was a people which should be reckoned among the ranks of the *nomads*. This is a fallacy as great as it is dangerous. The nomad does possess a definitely limited living space, only he does not cultivate it like a sedentary peasant, but lives from the yield of his herds with which he wanders about in his territory. The outward reason for this is to be found in the small fertility of a soil which simply does not permit of settlement. The deeper cause, however, lies in the disparity between the technical culture of an age or people and the natural poverty of a living space. There are territories in which even the Aryan is enabled only by his technology, developed in the course of more than a thousand years, to live in regular settlements, to master broad stretches of soil and obtain from it the requirements of life. If he did not possess this technology, either he would have to avoid these territories or likewise have to struggle along as a nomad in perpetual wandering, provided that his thousand-year-old education and habit of settled residence did not make this seem simply unbearable to him. We must bear in mind that in the time when the American continent was being opened up, numerous Aryans fought for their livelihood as trappers, hunters, etc., and often in larger troops with wife and children, always on the move, so that their existence was completely like that of the nomads. But as soon as their increasing number and better implements permitted them to clear the wild soil and make a stand against the natives, more and more settlements sprang up in the land.

Probably the Aryan was also first a nomad, settling in the course of time, but for that very reason he was never a Jew! No, the Jew is no nomad; for the nomad had also a definite attitude toward the concept of work which could serve as a basis for his later development in so far as the necessary intellectual premises were present. In him the basic idealistic view is present, even if in infinite dilution, hence in his whole being he may seem strange to the Aryan peoples, but not unattractive. In the Jew, however, this attitude is not at all present; for that reason he was never a nomad, but only and always a *parasite* in the body of other peoples. That he sometimes left his previous living space has nothing to do with his own purpose, but results from the fact that from time to time he was thrown out by the host nations he had misused. His spreading is a typical phenomenon for all parasites; he always seeks a new feeding ground for his race.

This, however, has nothing to do with nomadism, for the reason that a Jew never thinks of leaving a territory that he has occupied, but remains where he is, and he sits so fast that even by force it is very hard to drive him out. His extension to ever-new countries occurs only in the moment in which certain conditions for his existence are there present, without which—unlike the nomad—he would not change his residence. He is and remains the typical parasite, a sponger who like a noxious bacillus keeps spreading as soon as a favorable medium invites him. And the effect of his existence is also like that of spongers: wherever he appears, the host people dies out after a shorter or longer period.

Thus, the Jew of all times has lived in the states of other peoples, and there formed his own state, which, to be sure, habitually sailed under the disguise of "religious community" as long as outward circumstances made a complete revelation of his nature seem inadvisable. But as soon as he felt strong enough to do without the protective cloak, he always dropped the veil and suddenly became what so many of the others previously did not want to believe and see: the Jew.

The Jew's life as a parasite in the body of other nations and states explains a characteristic which once caused Schopenhauer, as has already been mentioned, to call him the "great master in lying." Existence impels the Jew to lie, and to lie perpetually, just as it compels the inhabitants of the northern countries to wear warm clothing.

His life within other peoples can only endure for any length of time if he succeeds in arousing the opinion that he is not a people but a "religious community," though of a special sort.

And this is the first great lie.

In order to carry on his existence as a parasite on other peoples, he is forced to deny his inner nature. The more intelligent the individual Jew is, the more he will succeed in this deception. Indeed, things can go so far that large parts of the host people will end by seriously believing that the Jew is really a Frenchman or an Englishman, a German or an Italian, though of a special religious faith. Especially state authorities, which always seem animated by the historical fraction of wisdom, most easily fall a victim to this infinite deception. Independent thinking sometimes seems to these circles a true sin against holy advancement, so that we may not be surprised if even today a Bavarian state ministry, for example, still has not the faintest idea that the Jews are members of a *people* and not of a "*religion*" though a glance at the Jew's own newspapers should indicate this even to the most modest mind. The *Jewish Echo* is not yet an official organ, of course, and consequently is unauthoritative as far as the intelligence of one of these government potentates is concerned.

The Jew has always been a people with definite racial characteristics and never a religion; only in order to get ahead he early sought for a means which could distract unpleasant attention from his person. And what would have been more expedient and at the same time more innocent than the "embezzled" concept of a religious community? For here, too, everything is borrowed or rather stolen. Due to his own original special nature, the Jew cannot possess a religious institution, if for no other reason because he lacks idealism in any form, and hence belief in a hereafter is absolutely foreign to him. And a religion in the Aryan sense cannot be imagined which lacks the conviction of survival after death in some form. Indeed, the Talmud is not a book to prepare a man for the hereafter, but only for a practical and profitable life in this world.

The Jewish religious doctrine consists primarily in prescriptions for keeping the blood of Jewry pure and for regulating the relation of Jews among themselves, but even more with the rest of the world; in other words, with non-Jews. But even here it is by no means ethical problems that are involved, but extremely modest economic ones. Concerning the moral value of Jewish religious instruction, there are today and have been at all times rather exhaustive studies (not by Jews; the drivel of the Jews themselves on the subject is, of course, adapted to its purpose) which make this kind of religion seem positively monstrous according to Aryan conceptions. The best characterization is provided by the product of this religious education, the Jew himself. His life is only of this world, and his spirit is inwardly as alien to true Christianity as his nature two thousand years previous was to the great founder of the new doctrine. Of course, the latter made no secret of his attitude toward the Jewish people, and when necessary he even took to the whip to drive from the temple of the Lord this adversary of all humanity, who then as always saw in religion nothing but an instrument for his business existence. In return, Christ was nailed to the cross, while our present-day party Christians debase themselves to begging for Jewish votes at elections and later try to arrange political swindles with atheistic Jewish parties—and this against their own nation.

On this first and greatest lie, that the Jews are not a race but a religion, more and more lies are based in necessary consequence. Among them is the lie with regard to the language of the Jew. For him it is not a means for expressing his thoughts, but a means for concealing them. When he speaks French, he thinks Jewish, and while he turns out German verses, in his life he only expresses the nature of his nationality. As long as the Jew has not become the master of the other peoples, he must speak their languages whether he likes it or not, but as soon as they became his slaves, they would all have to learn a universal language (Esperanto, for instance!), so that by this additional means the Jews could more easily dominate them!

To what an extent the whole existence of this people is based on a continuous lie is shown incomparably by the *Protocols of the Wise Men of Zion*, so infinitely hated by the Jews. They are based on a forgery, the *Frankfurter Zeitung* moans and screams once every week: the best proof that they are authentic. What many Jews may do unconsciously is here consciously exposed. And that is what matters. It is completely indifferent from what Jewish brain these disclosures originate; the important thing is that with positively terrifying certainty they reveal the nature and activity of the Jewish people and expose their inner contexts as well as their ultimate final aims. The best criticism applied to them, however, is reality. Anyone who examines the historical development of the last hundred years from the standpoint of this book will at once understand the screaming of the Jewish press. For once this book has become the common property of a people, the Jewish menace may be considered as broken. . . .

With satanic joy in his face, the black-haired Jewish youth lurks in wait for the unsuspecting girl whom he defiles with his blood, thus stealing her from her people. With every means he tries to destroy the racial foundations of the people he has set out to subjugate. Just as he himself systematically ruins women and girls, he does not shrink back from pulling down the blood barriers for others, even on a large scale. It was and it is Jews who bring the Negroes into the Rhineland, always with the same secret thought and clear aim of ruining the hated white race by the necessarily resulting bastardization, throwing it down from its cultural and political height, and himself rising to be its master.

For a racially pure people which is conscious of its blood can never be enslaved by the Jew. In this world he will forever be master over bastards and bastards alone.

And so he tries systematically to lower the racial level by a continuous poisoning of individuals.

And in politics he begins to replace the idea of democracy by the dictatorship of the proletariat.

In the organized mass of Marxism he has found the weapon which lets him dispense with democracy and in its stead allows him to subjugate and govern the peoples with a dictatorial and brutal fist.

He works systematically for revolutionization in a twofold sense: economic and political.

Around peoples who offer too violent a resistance to attack from within he weaves a net of enemies, thanks to his international influence, incites them to war, and finally, if necessary, plants the flag of revolution on the very battlefields.

In economics he undermines the states until the social enterprises which have become unprofitable are taken from the state and subjected to his financial control.

In the political field he refuses the state the means for its self-preservation, destroys the foundations of all national self-maintenance and defense, destroys faith in the leadership, scoffs at its history and past, and drags everything that is truly great into the gutter.

Culturally he contaminates art, literature, the theater, makes a mockery of natural feeling, overthrows all concepts of beauty and sublimity, of the noble and the good, and instead drags men down into the sphere of his own base nature.

Religion is ridiculed, ethics and morality represented as outmoded, until the last props of a nation in its struggle for existence in this world have fallen.

Now begins the great last revolution. In gaining political power the Jew casts off the few cloaks that he still wears. The democratic people's Jew becomes the blood-Jew and tyrant over peoples. In a few years he tries to exterminate the national intelligentsia and by robbing the peoples of their natural intellectual leadership makes them ripe for the slave's lot of permanent subjugation.

The most frightful example of this kind is offered by Russia, where he killed or starved about thirty million people with positively fanatical savagery, in part amid inhuman tortures, in order to give a gang of Jewish journalists and stock exchange bandits domination over a great people.

The end is not only the end of the freedom of the peoples oppressed by the Jew, but also the end of this parasite upon the nations. After the death of his victim, the vampire sooner or later dies too. . . .

In the first volume I have dealt with the word "folkish," in so far as I was forced to establish that this term seems inadequately defined to permit the formation of a solid fighting community. All sorts of people, with a yawning gulf between everything essential in their opinions, are running around today under the blanket term "folkish." Therefore, before I proceed to the tasks and aims of the National Socialist German Workers' Party, I should like to give a clarification of the concept "folkish," as well as its relation to the party movement.

The concept "folkish" seems as vaguely defined, open to as many interpretations and as unlimited in practical application as, for instance, the word "religious," and it is very hard to conceive of anything absolutely precise under this designation, either in the sense of intellectual comprehension or of practical effects. The designation "religious" only becomes tangibly conceivable in the moment when it becomes connected with a definitely outlined form of its practice. It is a very lovely statement and usually apt, to describe a man's nature as "profoundly religious." Perhaps there are a few people who feel satisfied by such a very general description, to whom it can even convey a definite, more or less sharp, picture of that soul-state. But, since the great masses consist neither of philosophers nor of saints, such a very general religious idea will as a rule mean to the individual only the liberation of his individual thought and action, without, however, leading to that efficacy which arises from religious inner longing in the moment when, from the purely metaphysical infinite world of ideas, a clearly delimited faith forms. Assuredly, this is not the end in itself, but only a means to the end; yet it is the indispensably necessary means which alone makes possible the achievement of the end. This end, however, is not only ideal, but in the last analysis also eminently practical. And in general we must clearly acknowledge the fact that the highest ideals always correspond to a deep vital necessity, just as the nobility of the most exalted beauty lies in the last analysis only in what is logically most expedient.

By helping to raise man above the level of bestial vegetation, faith contributes in reality to the securing and safeguarding of his existence. Take away from present-day mankind its education-based, religious-dogmatic principles—or, practically speaking, ethical-moral principles—by abolishing this religious education, but without replacing it by an equivalent, and the result will be a grave shock to the foundations of their existence. We may therefore state that not only does man live in order to serve higher ideals, but that, conversely, these higher ideals also provide the premise for his existence. Thus the circle closes.

Of course, even the general designation "religious" includes various basic ideas or convictions, for example, the indestructibility of the soul, the eternity of its existence, the existence of a higher being, etc. But all these ideas, regardless how convincing they may be for the individual, are submitted to the critical examination of this individual and hence to a fluctuating affirmation or negation until emotional divination or knowledge assumes the binding force of apodictic faith. This, above all, is the fighting factor which makes a breach and opens the way for the recognition of basic religious views.

Without clearly delimited faith, religiosity with its unclarity and multiplicity of form would not only be worthless for human life, but would probably contribute to general disintegration.

The situation with the term "folkish" is similar to that with the term "religious." In it, too, there lie various basic realizations. Though of eminent importance, they are, however, so unclearly defined in form that they rise above the value of a more or less acceptable opinion only if they are fitted into the framework of a political party as basic elements. *For the realization of philosophical ideals and of the demands derived from them no more occurs through men's pure feeling or inner will in themselves than the achievement of freedom through the general longing for it. No, only when the ideal urge for independence gets a fighting organization in the form of military instruments of power can the pressing desire of a people be transformed into glorious reality.*

Every philosophy of life, even if it is a thousand times correct and of highest benefit to humanity, will remain without significance for the practical shaping of a people's life, as long as its principles have not become the banner of a fighting movement which for its part in turn will be a party as long as its activity has not found completion in the victory of its ideas and its party dogmas have not become the new state principles of a people's community.

But if a spiritual conception of a general nature is to serve as a foundation for a future development, the first presupposition is to obtain unconditional clarity with regard to the nature, essence, and scope of this conception, since only on such a basis can a movement be formed which by the inner homogeneity of its convictions can develop the necessary force for struggle. From general ideas a political program must be stamped, from a general philosophy of life a definite political faith. The latter, since its goal must be practically attainable, will not only have to serve the idea in itself, but will also have to take into consideration the means of struggle which are available and must be used for the achievement of this idea. The abstractly correct spiritual conception, which the theoretician has to proclaim, must be coupled with the practical knowledge of the politician. And so an eternal ideal, serving as the guiding star of mankind, must unfortunately resign itself to taking the weaknesses of this mankind into consideration, if it wants to avoid shipwreck at the very outset on the shoals of general human inadequacy. To draw from the realm of the eternally true and ideal that which is humanly possible for small mortals, and make it take form, the search after truth must be coupled with knowledge of the people's psyche.

This transformation of a general, philosophical, ideal conception of the highest truth into a definitely delimited, tightly organized political community of faith and struggle, unified in spirit and will, is the most significant achievement, since on its happy solution alone the possibility of the victory of an idea depends. From the army of often millions of men, who as individuals more or less clearly and definitely sense these truths, and in part perhaps comprehend them, *one* man must step forward who with apodictic force will form granite principles from the wavering idea-world of the broad masses and take up the struggle for their sole correctness, until from the shifting waves of a free thought-world there will arise a brazen cliff of solid unity in faith and will.

The general right for such an activity is based on necessity, the personal right on success. . . .

If from the word "folkish" we try to peel out the innermost kernel of meaning, we arrive at the following:

Our present political world view, current in Germany, is based in general on the idea that creative, culture-creating force must indeed be attributed to the state, but that it has nothing to do with racial considerations, but is rather a product of economic necessities, or, at best, the natural result of a political urge for power. This underlying view, if logically developed, leads not only to a mistaken conception of basic racial forces, but also to an underestimation of the individual. For a denial of the difference between the various races with regard to their general culture-creating forces must necessarily extend this greatest of all errors to the judgment of the individual. The assumption of the equality of the races then becomes a basis for a similar way of viewing peoples and finally individual men. And hence international Marxism itself is only the transference, by the Jew, Karl Marx, of a philosophical attitude and conception, which had actually long been in existence, into the form of a definite political creed. Without the subsoil of such generally existing poisoning, the amazing success of this doctrine would never have been possible. Actually Karl Marx was only the *one* among millions who, with the sure eye of the prophet, recognized in the morass of a slowly decomposing world the most essential poisons, extracted them, and, like a wizard, prepared them into a concentrated solution for the swifter annihilation of the independent existence of free nations of this earth. And all this in the service of his race.

His Marxist doctrine is a brief spiritual extract of the philosophy of life that is generally current today. And for this reason alone any struggle of our so-called bourgeois world against it is impossible, absurd in fact, since this bourgeois world is also essentially infected by these poisons, and worships a view of life which in general is distinguished from the Marxists only by degrees and personalities. The bourgeois world is Marxist, but believes in the possibility of the rule of certain groups of men (bourgeoisie), while Marxism itself systematically plans to hand the world over to the Jews.

In opposition to this, the folkish philosophy finds the importance of mankind in its basic racial elements. In the state it sees on principle only a means to an end and construes its end as the preservation of the racial existence of man. Thus, it by no means believes in an equality of the races, but along with their difference it recognizes their higher or lesser value and feels itself obligated, through this knowledge, to promote the victory of the better and stronger, and demand the subordination of the inferior and weaker in accordance with the eternal will that dominates this universe. Thus, in principle, it serves the basic aristocratic idea of Nature and believes in the validity of this law down to the last individual. It sees not only the different value of the races, but also the different value of individuals. From the mass it extracts the importance of the individual personality, and thus, in contrast to disorganizing Marxism, it has an organizing effect. It believes in the necessity of an idealization of humanity, in which alone it sees the premise for the existence of humanity. But it cannot grant the right to existence even to an ethical idea if this idea represents a danger for the racial life of the bearers of a higher ethics; for in a bastardized and niggerized world all the concepts of the humanly beautiful and sublime, as well as all ideas of an idealized future of our humanity, would be lost forever.

Human culture and civilization on this continent are inseparably bound up with the presence of the Aryan. If he dies out or declines, the dark veils of an age without culture will again descend on this globe.

The undermining of the existence of human culture by the destruction of its bearer seems in the eyes of a folkish philosophy the most execrable crime. Anyone who dares to lay hands on the highest image of the Lord commits sacrilege against the benevolent creator of this miracle and contributes to the expulsion from paradise.

And so the folkish philosophy of life corresponds to the innermost will of Nature, since it restores that free play of forces which must lead to a continuous mutual higher breeding, until at last the best of humanity, having achieved possession of this earth, will have a free path for activity in domains which will lie partly above it and partly outside it.

We all sense that in the distant future humanity must be faced by problems which only a highest race, become master people and supported by the means and possibilities of an entire globe, will be equipped to overcome. . . .

It is self-evident that so general a statement of the meaningful content of a folkish philosophy can be interpreted in thousands of ways. And actually we find hardly a one of our newer political formations which does not base itself in one way or another on this world view. And, by its very existence in the face of the many others, it shows the difference of its conceptions. And so the Marxist world view, led by a unified top organization, is opposed by hodge-podge of views which even as ideas are not very impressive in face of the solid, hostile front. Victories are not gained by such feeble weapons! Not until the international world view—politically led by organized Marxism—is confronted by a folkish world view, organized and led with equal unity, will success, supposing the fighting energy to be equal on both sides, fall to the side of eternal truth.

A philosophy can only be organizationally comprehended on the basis of a definite formulation of that philosophy, and what dogmas represent for religious faith, party principles are for a political party in the making.

Hence an instrument must be created for the folkish world view which enables it to fight, just as the Marxist party organization creates a free path for internationalism.

This is the goal pursued by the National Socialist German Workers' Party.

That such a party formulation of the folkish concept is the precondition for the victory of the folkish philosophy of life is proved most sharply by a fact which is admitted indirectly at least by the enemies of such a party tie. Those very people who never weary of emphasizing that the folkish philosophy is not the "hereditary estate" of an individual, but that it slumbers or "lives" in the hearts of God knows how many millions, thus demonstrate the fact that the general existence of such ideas was absolutely unable to prevent the victory of the hostile world view, classically represented by a political party. If this were not so, the German people by this time would have been bound to achieve a gigantic victory and not be standing at the edge of an abyss. What gave the international world view success was its representation by a political party organized into storm troops; what caused the defeat of the opposite world view was its lack up to now of a unified body to represent it. Not by unlimited freedom to interpret a general view, but only in the limited and hence integrating form of a political organization can a world view fight and conquer.

Therefore, I saw my own task especially in extracting those nuclear ideas from the extensive and unshaped substance of a general world view and remolding them into more or less dogmatic forms which in their clear delimitation are adapted for holding solidly together those men who swear allegiance to them. In other words: *From the basic ideas of a general folkish world conception the National Socialist German Workers' Party takes over the essential fundamental traits, and from them, with due consideration of practical reality, the times, and the available human material as well as its weaknesses, forms a political creed which, in turn, by the strict organizational integration of large human masses thus made possible, creates the precondition for the victorious struggle of this world view.*

PART EIGHT
LIBERATION IDEOLOGIES

Several contemporary ideologies include the word "liberation" in their name. One thinks immediately, for example, of "women's liberation" as well as "black liberation," "gay liberation," "liberation theology," and, more recently still, "animal liberation." In one sense, of course, these are vastly different ideologies in that each addresses different groups—women, black people, gays, and so on. But these groups need not be opposed or antithetical in their aims. Indeed, one liberation movement's membership may, and often does, overlap with another's. For that matter, there would be no contradiction in a gay, black woman, liberation theologian dedicating herself to the defense of animal rights. But by and large we can view these various liberation ideologies as separate members of an extended ideological family.

This family shares several common characteristics. First, each liberation ideology addresses itself to a particular group, sex, race, class, species, and so on. Second, this group is in some sense oppressed by another (blacks oppressed by whites, women by men, gays by "straights," animals by humans). Third, the ideology aims to liberate the oppressed group from its oppressors, not only by removing external obstacles (for example, laws that discriminate against black people), but by exposing, criticizing, and overcoming *internal* barriers—or in the poet William Blake's phrase, the "mind-forged manacles"—to their self-emancipation. These internal obstacles might include, for example, self-loathing, low self-esteem, feelings of inferiority, incompetence and stupidity, and so on. A fourth feature common to all liberation ideologies is their attempt to "raise the consciousness" of the oppressed, thereby enabling them to free themselves from their own internalized fetters. (This feature, as we shall note in a moment, does not apply in the case of animal liberation.) Fifth and finally, liberation ideologies are also addressed to the oppressors, who, as Hegel and Rousseau both noted, are enslaved by their own sense of superiority. "The one who thinks himself the master of others," Rousseau wrote, "is as much a slave as they."

The ideology of "black liberation" is addressed to black people, particularly those whose feelings of inferiority have been intensified by their having accepted uncritically the dominant "white" standards of talent, intelligence, beauty, "normal" behavior, musical tastes, and so on. Black liberationists have raised the consciousness of blacks, affirming the integrity and legitimacy of African-American culture, proclaiming that "black is beautiful," and encouraging black history's recovery and remembrance of black people's contributions to Western history and culture. In these and many other ways the ideology of black liberation helps people of color to discover, criticize, and break their own mind-forged manacles. But it also leads white people to examine their own deep-seated attitudes and prejudices as a prelude to overcoming them.

Much the same is true of the ideology of women's liberation. That ideology is, of course, addressed to women of all races, on the assumption that women of every color and creed and class face problems that are unique to them as women. In addition to overt discrimination—legal and economic barriers, sexual harassment in the workplace and elsewhere—women face the covert or hidden obstacles of "sexist" attitudes and beliefs. Such attitudes and beliefs include, for example, views about what is and is not "women's work," about women as "sex objects" who enjoy pain and humiliation, and many others as well. The women's liberation movement has helped to raise women's consciousness by exposing and criticizing sexist attitudes in the classroom, the workplace, the family—and in women's own minds as well. Many women, that is, have accepted sexist stereotypes about women's limitations and shortcomings. By exposing and criticizing these false beliefs, the women's liberation movement helps women to break down these internalized barriers. But the ideology of women's liberation is also addressed to men, encouraging them to examine their own hidden or half-conscious sexist stereotypes and attitudes toward women. Thus women's liberation attempts to liberate both women and men from the mutually stifling confines of sexual prejudice.

The ideology of gay liberation is of relatively recent vintage. Homosexual men and women face numerous obstacles, particularly if their sexual preference is publicly known. Many gay men and women prefer to keep their homosexuality a secret, fearing that they will lose their jobs, housing, health insurance coverage, and other benefits that heterosexuals or "straights" take for granted. In addition to such overt discrimination, many gays experience the more subtle oppression that comes from internalizing "straight" or "homophobic" beliefs about and attitudes toward sexual "deviants" or "perverts." Such people sometimes suffer from feelings of guilt, worthlessness, and self-loathing. Some contemplate suicide; others engage in other kinds of self-destructive actions and practices. The ideology of the gay liberation movement attempts to counter this by exposing and criticizing homophobic beliefs and attitudes, by instilling a sense of "gay pride," and by encouraging gays to "come out of the closet" and openly proclaim their sexual preference. This ideology is also addressed to "straights," inviting them to examine and overcome their own homophobic beliefs and attitudes.

The primary audience of liberation theology is poor people, particularly peasants in Latin America and elsewhere, who face not only overt oppression from landlords and army death squads, but who have internalized the "culture of silence." The latter refers to deep-seated beliefs about one's own powerlessness and helplessness—the belief that one's views and voice will not and cannot make any difference in one's condition. One is, in short, doomed or "fated" to suffer in silence, to accept one's unhappy lot in life as the will of God or other forces beyond one's control. Liberation theology attempts to expose and criticize these attitudes in order to help poor peasants overcome them. It does so by offering a radical interpretation of the gospels that views Jesus as a liberator and a champion of the poor and downtrodden. Rightly understood, His teachings can help the poor to find their voices and to liberate themselves from the forces that oppress them. In addition to being addressed to the poor and oppressed, liberation theology also speaks to their affluent oppressors, inviting them to exercise their "option for the poor" by taking an active part in the peasants' struggles against poverty and oppression.

The ideology of animal liberation is likewise intended to liberate an oppressed group, in this case nonhuman animals, from their human oppressors. Many, perhaps most, humans harbor "speciesist" views about the innate inferiority of animals and the superiority of human beings. We humans therefore feel free to kill and eat them, wear their fur, and perform painful experiments on them. It is precisely this prejudice that the animal liberation movement aims to expose and overcome. One qualification is of course necessary in the case of animal liberation. Since one cannot reason with or raise the consciousness of nonhuman animals, the addressee must therefore be their oppressors, namely, humans who participate in, or benefit from, the suffering and deaths of animals. The ideology of animal liberation aims, in other words, to raise the consciousness of humans, thereby helping them to change their speciesist attitudes and actions.

43

LETTER FROM BIRMINGHAM JAIL

MARTIN LUTHER KING, JR.

Although American liberals in the 1960s favored granting civil rights to African-Americans, many advocated a gradualist strategy to achieve this goal and criticized the confrontational tactics—including the use of civil disobedience, sit-ins, and protest marches—favored by some black leaders. One of these leaders was the Reverend Dr. Martin Luther King, Jr., who wrote the following essay while confined to a cell in the Birmingham, Alabama, jail for leading a march against segregation. The immediate provocation for the letter was a statement by several white clergymen, who complained that the demonstrations he led were "unwise," "untimely," and "extreme." To this, King responded that black people had already waited too long and too patiently to be "given" rights that were already theirs. The time for waiting was over, he said, and the time had come to act, albeit nonviolently.

LETTER FROM BIRMINGHAM JAIL[1]

April 16, 1963

MY DEAR FELLOW CLERGYMEN:

While confined here in the Birmingham city jail, I came across your recent statement calling my present activities "unwise and untimely." Seldom do I pause to answer criticism of my work and ides. If I sought to answer all criticisms that cross my desk, my secretaries would have little time for anything other than such correspondence in the course of the day, and I would have no time for constructive work. But since I feel that you are men of genuine good will and that your criticisms are sincerely set forth, I want to try to answer your statement in what I hope will be patient and reasonable terms.

I think I should indicate why I am here in Birmingham, since you have been influenced by the view which argues against "outsiders coming in." I have the honor of serving as president of the Southern Christian Leadership Conference, an organization operating in every southern state, with headquarters in Atlanta, Georgia. We have some eighty-five affiliated organizations across the south, and one of them is the Alabama Christian Movement for Human Rights. Frequently we share staff, educational and financial resources with our affiliates. Several months ago the affiliate here in Birmingham asked us to be on call to engage in a nonviolent direct-action program if such were deemed necessary. We readily consented, and when the hour came we lived up to our promise. So I, along with several members of my staff, am here because I was invited here. I am here because I have basic organizational ties here.

Beyond this, I am in Birmingham because injustice is here. Just as the prophets of the eighth century B.C. left their villages and carried their "thus saith the Lord" far beyond the boundaries of their home towns, and just as the Apostle Paul left his village of Tarsus and carried the gospel of Jesus Christ to the far corners of the Greco-Roman world, so am I compelled to carry the gospel of freedom beyond my own home town. Like Paul, I must constantly respond to the Macedonian call for aid.

Moreover, I am cognizant of the interrelatedness of all communities and states. I cannot sit idly by in Atlanta and not be concerned about what happens in Birmingham. Injustice anywhere is a threat to justice everywhere. We are caught in an inescapable network of mutuality, tied in a single garment of destiny. Whatever affects one directly, affects all indirectly. Never again can we afford to live with the narrow, provincial "outside agitator" idea. Anyone who lives inside the United States can never be considered an outsider anywhere within its bounds.

You deplore the demonstrations taking place in Birmingham. But your statement, I am sorry to say, fails to express a similar concern for the conditions that brought about the demonstrations. I am sure that none of you would want to rest content with the superficial kind of social analysis that deals merely with effects and does not grapple with underlying causes. It is unfortunate that demonstrations are taking place in Birmingham at this time, but I would say in even more emphatic terms that it is even more unfortunate that the city's white power structure left the Negro community with no alternative.

In any nonviolent campaign there are four basic steps: collection of the facts to determine whether injustices exist; negotiation; self-purification; and direct action. We have gone through all these steps in Birmingham. There can be no gainsaying the fact that racial injustice engulfs this community. Birmingham is probably the most thoroughly segregated city in the United States. Its ugly record of brutality is widely known. Negroes have experienced grossly unjust treatment in the courts. There have been more unsolved bombings of Negro homes and churches in Birmingham than in any other city in the nation. These are the hard, brutal facts of the case. On the basis of these conditions, Negro leaders sought to negotiate with the city fathers. But the latter consistently refused to engage in good-faith negotiation.

Then, last September, came the opportunity to talk with leaders of Birmingham's economic community. In the course of the negotiations, certain promises were made by the merchants—for example, to remove the stores' humiliating racial signs. On the basis of these promises, the Reverend Fred Shuttlesworth and the leaders of the Alabama Christian Movement for Human Rights agreed to a moratorium on all demonstrations. As the weeks and months went by, we realized that we were the victims of a broken promise. A few signs, briefly removed, returned; the others remained.

As in so many past experiences, our hopes had been blasted, and the shadow of deep disappointment settled upon us. We had no alternative except to prepare for direct action, whereby we would present our very bodies as a means of laying our case before the conscience of the local and the national community. Mindful of the difficulties involved, we decided to undertake a process of self-purification. We began a series of workshops on nonviolence, and we repeatedly asked ourselves: "Are you able to accept blows without retaliating?" "Are you able to endure the ordeal of jail?" We decided to schedule our direct-action program for the Easter season, realizing that except for Christmas, this is the main shopping period of the year. Knowing that a strong economic-withdrawal program would be the by-product of direct action, we felt that this would be the best time to bring pressure to bear on the merchants for the needed change.

Then it occurred to us that Birmingham's mayoral election was coming up in March, and we speedily decided to postpone action until after election day. When we discovered that the Commissioner of Public Safety, Eugene "Bull" Connor, had piled up enough votes to be in the run-off, we decided again to postpone action until the day after the run-off so that the demonstrations could not be used to cloud the issues. Like many others, we waited to see Mr. Connor defeated, and to this end we endured postponement after postponement. Having aided in this community need, we felt that our direct-action program could be delayed no longer.

You may well ask: "Why direct action? Why sit-ins, marches and so forth? Isn't negotiation a better path?" You are quite right in calling for negotiation. Indeed, this is the very purpose of direct action. Nonviolent direct action seeks to create such a crisis and foster such a tension that a community which has constantly refused to negotiate is forced to confront the issue. It seeks so to dramatize the issue that it can no longer be ignored. My citing the creation of tension as part of the work of the nonviolent-resister may sound rather shocking. But I must confess that I am not afraid of the word "tension." I have earnestly opposed violent tension, but there is a type of constructive, nonviolent tension which is necessary for growth. Just as Socrates felt that it was necessary to create a tension in the mind so that individuals could rise from the bondage of myths and half-truths to the unfettered realm of creative analysis and objective appraisal, so must we see the need for nonviolent gadflies to create the kind of tension in society that will help men rise from the dark depths of prejudice and racism to the majestic heights of understanding and brotherhood.

The purpose of our direct-action program is to create a situation so crisis-packed that it will inevitably open the door to negotiation. I therefore concur with you in your call for negotiation. Too long has our beloved Southland been bogged down in a tragic effort to live in monologue rather than dialogue.

One of the basic points in your statement is that the action that I and my associates have taken in Birmingham is untimely. Some have asked: "Why didn't you give the new city administration time to act?" The only answer that I can give to this query is that the new Birmingham administration must be prodded about as much as the outgoing one, before it will act. We are sadly mistaken if we feel that the election of Albert Boutwell as mayor will bring the millennium to Birmingham. While Mr. Boutwell is a much more gentle person than Mr. Connor, they are both segregationists, dedicated to maintenance of the status quo. I have hope that Mr. Boutwell will be reasonable enough to see the futility of massive resistance to desegregation. But he will not see this without pressure from devotees of civil rights. My friends, I must say to you that we have not made a single gain in civil rights without determined legal and nonviolent pressure. Lamentably, it is an historical fact that privileged groups seldom give up their privileges voluntarily. Individuals may see the moral light and voluntarily give up their unjust posture; but, as Reinhold Niebuhr has reminded us, groups tend to be more immoral than individuals.

We know through painful experience that freedom is never voluntarily given by the oppressor; it must be demanded by the oppressed. Frankly, I have yet to engage in a direct-action campaign that was "well timed" in the view of those who have not suffered unduly from the disease of segregation. For years now I have heard the word "Wait!" It rings in the ear of every Negro with piercing familiarity. This "Wait" has almost always meant "Never." We must come to see, with one of our distinguished jurists, that "justice too long delayed is justice denied."

We have waited for more than 340 years for our constitutional and God-given rights. The nations of Asia and Africa are moving with jetlike speed toward gaining political independence, but we still creep at horse-and-buggy pace toward gaining a cup of coffee at a lunch counter. Perhaps it is easy for those who have never felt the stinging darts of segregation to say, "Wait." But when you have seen vicious mobs lynch your mothers and fathers at will and drown your sisters and brothers at whim; when you have seen hate-filled policemen curse, kick and even kill your black brothers and sisters; when you see the vast majority of your twenty million Negro brothers smothering in an airtight cage of poverty in the midst of an affluent society; when you suddenly find your tongue twisted and your speech stammering as you seek to explain to your six-year-old daughter why she can't go to the public amusement park that has just been advertised on television, and see tears welling up in her eyes when she is told that Funtown is closed to colored children, and see ominous clouds of inferiority beginning to form in her little mental sky, and see her beginning to distort her personality by developing an unconscious bitterness toward white people; when you have to concoct an answer for a five-year-old son who is asking: "Daddy, why do white people treat colored people so mean?"; when you take a cross-country drive and find it necessary to sleep night after night in the uncomfortable corners of your automobile because no motel will accept you; when you are humiliated day in and day out by nagging signs reading "white" and "colored"; when your first name becomes "nigger," your middle name becomes "boy" (however old you are) and your last name becomes "John," and your wife and mother are never given the respected title "Mrs."; when you are harried by day and haunted by night by the fact that you are a Negro, living constantly at tiptoe stance, never quite knowing what to expect next, and are plagued with inner fears and outer resentments; when you are forever fighting a degenerating sense of "nobodiness"—then you will understand why we find it difficult to wait. There comes a time when the cup of endurance runs over, and men are no longer willing to be plunged into the abyss of despair. I hope, sirs, you can understand our legitimate and unavoidable impatience.

You express a great deal of anxiety over our willingness to break laws. This is certainly a legitimate concern. Since we so diligently urge people to obey the Supreme Court's decision of 1954 outlawing segregation in the public schools, at first glance it may seem rather paradoxical for us consciously to break laws. One may well ask: "How can you advocate breaking some laws and obeying others?" The answer lies in the fact that there are two types of laws: just and unjust. I would be the first to advocate obeying just laws. One has not only a legal but a moral responsibility to obey just laws. Conversely, one has a moral responsibility to disobey unjust laws. I would agree with St. Augustine that "an unjust law is no law at all."

Now, what is the difference between the two? How does one determine whether a law is just or unjust? A just law is a man-made code the squares with the moral law or the law of God. An unjust law is a code that is out of harmony with the moral law. To put it in the terms of St. Thomas Aquinas: An unjust law is a human law that is not rooted in eternal law and natural law. Any law that uplifts human personality is just. Any law that degrades human personality is unjust. All segregation statutes are unjust because segregation distorts the soul and damages the personality. It gives the segregator a false sense of superiority and the segregated a false sense of inferiority. Segregation, to use the terminology of the Jewish philosopher Martin Buber, substitutes an "I-it" relationship for an "I-thou" relationship and ends up relegating persons to the status of things. Hence segregation is not only politically, economically and sociologically unsound, it is morally wrong and sinful. Paul Tillich has said that sin is separation. Is not segregation an existential expression of man's tragic separation, his awful estrangement, his terrible sinfulness? Thus it is that I can urge men to obey the 1954 decision of the Supreme Court, for it is morally right; and I can urge them to disobey segregation ordinances, for they are morally wrong.

Let us consider a more concrete example of just and unjust laws. An unjust law is a code that a numerical or power majority group compels a minority group to obey but does not make binding on itself. This is *difference* made legal. By the same token, a just law is a code that a majority compels a minority to follow and that it is willing to follow itself. This is *sameness* made legal.

Let me give another explanation. A law is unjust if it is inflicted on a minority that, as a result of being denied the right to vote, had no part in enacting or devising the law. Who can say that the legislature of Alabama which set up that state's segregation laws was democratically elected? Throughout Alabama all sorts of devious methods are used to prevent Negroes from becoming registered voters, and there are some counties in which, even though Negroes constitute a majority of the population, not a single Negro is registered. Can any law enacted under such circumstances be considered democratically structured?

Sometimes a law is just on its face and unjust in its application. For instance, I have been arrested on a charge of parading without a permit. Now, there is nothing wrong in having an ordinance which requires a permit for a parade. But such an ordinance becomes unjust when it is used to maintain segregation and to deny citizens the First-Amendment privilege of peaceful assembly and protest.

I hope you are able to see the distinction I am trying to point out. In no sense do I advocate evading or defying the law, as would the rabid segregationist. That would lead to anarchy. One who breaks an unjust law must do so openly, lovingly, and with a willingness to accept the penalty. I submit that an individual who breaks a law that conscience tells him is unjust, and who willingly accepts the penalty of imprisonment in order to arouse the conscience of the community over its injustice, is in reality expressing the highest respect for law.

Of course, there is nothing new about this kind of civil disobedience. It was evidenced sublimely in the refusal of Shadrach, Meshach and Abednego to obey the laws of Nebuchadnezzar, on the ground that a higher moral law was at stake. It was practiced superbly by the early Christians, who were willing to face hungry lions and the excruciating pain of chopping blocks rather than submit to certain unjust laws of the Roman Empire. To a degree, academic freedom is a reality today because Socrates practiced civil disobedience. In our own nation, the

Boston Tea Party represented a massive act of civil disobedience.

We should never forget that everything Adolf Hitler did in Germany was "legal" and everything the Hungarian freedom fighters did in Hungary was "illegal." It was "illegal" to aid and comfort a Jew in Hitler's Germany. Even so, I am sure that, had I lived in Germany at the time, I would have aided and comforted my Jewish brothers. If today I lived in a Communist country where certain principles dear to the Christian faith are suppressed, I would openly advocate disobeying that country's antireligious laws.

I must make two honest confessions to you, my Christian and Jewish brothers. First, I must confess that over the past few years I have been gravely disappointed with the white moderate. I have almost reached the regrettable conclusion that the Negro's great stumbling block in his stride toward freedom is not the White Citizen's Counciler or the Ku Klux Klanner, but the white moderate, who is more devoted to "order" than to justice; who prefers a negative peace which is the absence of tension to a positive peace which is the presence of justice; who constantly says: "I agree with you in the goal you seek, but I cannot agree with your methods of direct action"; who paternalistically believes he can set the timetable for another man's freedom; who lives by a mythical concept of time and who constantly advises the Negro to wait for a "more convenient season." Shallow understanding from people of good will is more frustrating than absolute misunderstanding from people of ill will. Lukewarm acceptance is much more bewildering than outright rejection.

I had hoped that the white moderate would understand that law and order exist for the purpose of establishing justice and that when they fail in this purpose they become the dangerously structured dams that block the flow of social progress. I had hoped that the white moderate would understand that the present tension in the South is a necessary phase of the transition from an obnoxious negative peace, in which the Negro passively accepted his unjust plight, to a substantive and positive peace, in which all men will respect the dignity and worth of human personality. Actually, we who engage in nonviolent direct action are not the creators of tension. We merely bring to the surface the hidden tension that is already alive. We bring it out in the open, where it can be seen and dealt with. Like a boil that can never be cured so long as it is covered up but must be opened with all its ugliness to the natural medicines of air and light, injustice must be exposed, with all the tension its exposure creates, to the light of human conscience and the air of national opinion before it can be cured.

In your statement you assert that our actions, even though peaceful, must be condemned because they precipitate violence. But is this a logical assertion? Isn't this like condemning a robbed man because his possession of money precipitated the evil act of robbery? Isn't this like condemning Socrates because his unswerving commitment to truth and his philosophical inquiries precipitated the act by the misguided populace in which they made him drink hemlock? Isn't this like condemning Jesus because his unique God-consciousness and never-ceasing devotion to God's will precipitated the evil act of crucifixion? We must come to see that, as the federal courts have consistently affirmed, it is wrong to urge an individual to cease his efforts to gain his basic constitutional rights because the quest may precipitate violence. Society must protect the robbed and punish the robber.

I had also hoped that the white moderate would reject the myth concerning time in relation to the struggle for freedom. I have just received a letter from a white brother in Texas. He writes: "All Christians know that the colored people will receive equal rights eventually, but it is possible that you are in too great a religious hurry. It has taken Christianity almost two thousand years to accomplish what it has. The teachings of Christ take time to come to earth." Such an attitude stems from a tragic misconception of time, from the strangely irrational notion that there is something in the very flow of time that will inevitably cure all ills. Actually, time itself is neutral; it can be used either destructively or constructively. More and more I feel that the people of ill will have used time much more effectively than have the people of good will. We will have to repent in this generation not merely for the hateful words and actions of the bad people but for the appalling silence of the good people. Human progress never rolls in on wheels of inevitability; it comes through the tireless efforts of men willing to be co-workers with God, and without this hard work, time itself becomes an ally of the forces of social stagnation. We must use time creatively, in the knowledge that the time is always ripe to do right. Now is the time to make real the promise of democracy and transform our pending national elegy into a creative psalm of brotherhood. Now is the time to lift our national policy from the quicksand of racial injustice to the solid rock of human dignity.

You speak of our activity in Birmingham as extreme. At first I was rather disappointed that fellow clergymen would see my nonviolent efforts as those of an extremist. I began thinking about the fact that I stand in the middle of two opposing forces in the Negro community. One is a force of complacency, made up in part of Negroes who, as a result of long years of oppression, are so drained of self-respect and a sense of "somebodiness" that they have adjusted to segregation; and in part of a few middle-class Negroes who, because of a degree of academic and economic security and because in some ways they profit by segregation, have become insensitive to the problems of the masses. The other force is one of bitterness and hatred, and it comes perilously close to advocating violence. It is expressed in the various black nationalist groups that are springing up across the nation, the largest and best-known being Elijah Muhammad's Muslim movement. Nourished by the Negro's frustration over the continued existence of racial discrimination, this movement is made up of people who have lost faith in America, who have absolutely repudiated Christianity, and who have concluded that the white man is an incorrigible "devil."

I have tried to stand between these two forces, saying that we need emulate neither the "do-nothingism" of the complacent nor the hatred and despair of the black nationalist. For there is the more excellent way of love and nonviolent protest. I am grateful to God that, through the influence of the Negro church, the way of nonviolence became an integral part of our struggle.

If this philosophy had not emerged, by now many streets of the South would, I am convinced, be flowing with blood. And I am further convinced that if our white brothers dismiss as "rabble-rousers" and "outside agitators" those of us who employ nonviolent direct action, and if they refuse to support our nonviolent efforts, millions of Negroes will, out of frustration and despair, seek solace and security in black-nationalist ideologies—a development that would inevitably lead to a frightening racial nightmare.

Oppressed people cannot remain oppressed forever. The yearning for freedom eventually manifests itself, and that is what has happened to the American Negro. Something within has reminded him of his birthright of freedom, and something without has reminded him that it can be gained. Consciously or unconsciously, he has been caught up by the *Zeitgeist*, and with his black brothers of Africa and his brown and yellow brothers of Asia, South America and the Caribbean, the United States Negro is moving with a sense of great urgency toward the promised land of racial justice. If one recognizes this vital urge that has engulfed the Negro community, one should readily understand why public demonstrations are taking place. The Negro has many pent-up resentments and latent frustrations, and he must release them. So let him march; let him make prayer pilgrimages to the city hall; let him go on freedom rides—and try to understand why he must do so. If his repressed emotions are not released in nonviolent ways, they will seek expression through violence; this is not a threat but a fact of history. So I have not said to my people: "Get rid of your discontent." Rather, I have tried to say that this normal and healthy discontent can be channeled into the creative outlet of nonviolent direct action. And now this approach is being termed extremist.

But though I was initially disappointed at being categorized as an extremist, as I continued to think about the matter I gradually gained a measure of satisfaction from the label. Was not Jesus an extremist for love: "Love your enemies, bless them that curse you, do good to them that hate you, and pray for them which despitefully use you, and persecute you." Was not Amos an extremist for justice: "Let justice roll down like waters and righteousness like an ever-flowing stream." Was not Paul an extremist for the Christian gospel: "I bear in my body the marks of the Lord Jesus." Was not Martin Luther an extremist: "Here I stand; I cannot do otherwise, so help me God." And John Bunyan: "I will stay in jail to the end of my days before I make a butchery of my conscience." And Abraham Lincoln: "This nation cannot survive half slave and half free." And Thomas Jefferson: "We hold these truths to be self-evident, that all men are created equal . . ." So the question is not whether we will be extremists, but what kind of extremists we will be. Will we be extremists for hate or for love? Will we be extremists for the preservation of injustice or for the extension of justice? In that dramatic scene on Calvary's hill three men were crucified. We must never forget that all three were crucified for the same crime—the crime of extremism. Two were extremists for immorality, and thus fell below their environment. The other, Jesus Christ, was an extremist for love, truth and goodness, and thereby rose above his environment. Perhaps the South, the nation and the world are in dire need of creative extremists.

I had hoped that the white moderate would see this need. Perhaps I was too optimistic; perhaps I expected too much. I suppose I should have realized that few members of the oppressor race can understand the deep groans and passionate yearnings of the oppressed race, and still fewer have the vision to see that injustice must be rooted out by strong, persistent and determined action. I am thankful, however, that some of our white brothers in the South have grasped the meaning of this social revolution and committed themselves to it. They are still all too few in quantity, but they are big in quality. Some . . . have written about our struggle in eloquent and prophetic terms. Others have marched with us down nameless streets of the South. They have languished in filthy, roach-infested jails, suffering the abuse and brutality of policemen who view them as "dirty nigger-lovers." Unlike so many of their moderate brothers and sisters, they have recognized the urgency of the moment and sensed the need for powerful "action" antidotes to combat the disease of segregation.

Let me take note of my other major disappointment. I have been so greatly disappointed with the white church and its leadership. Of course, there are some notable exceptions. I am not unmindful of the fact that each of you has taken some significant stands on this issue. I commend you, Reverend Stallings, for your Christian stand on this past Sunday, in welcoming Negroes to your worship service on a nonsegregated basis. I commend the Catholic leaders of this state for integrating Spring Hill College several years ago.

But despite these notable exceptions, I must honestly reiterate that I have been disappointed with the church. I do not say this as one of those negative critics who can always find something wrong with the church. I say this as a minister of the gospel, who loves the church; who was nurtured in its bosom; who has been sustained by its spiritual blessings and who will remain true to it as long as the cord of life shall lengthen.

When I was suddenly catapulted into the leadership of the bus protest in Montgomery, Alabama, a few years ago, I felt we would be supported by the white church. I felt that the white ministers, priests and rabbis of the South would be among our strongest allies. Instead, some have been outright opponents, refusing to understand the freedom movement and misrepresenting its leaders; all too many others have been more cautious than courageous and have remained silent behind the anesthetizing security of stained-glass windows.

In spite of my shattered dreams, I came to Birmingham with the hope that the white religious leadership of this community would see the justice of our cause and, with deep moral concern, would serve as the channel through which our just grievances could reach the power structure. I had hoped that each of you would understand. But again I have been disappointed.

I have heard numerous southern religious leaders admonish their worshipers to comply with a desegregation decision because it is the law, but I have longed to hear white ministers declare: "Follow this decree because integration is morally right and because the Negro is your brother." In the midst of blatant injustices inflicted upon the Negro, I have watched white churchmen stand on the sideline and mouth pious irrelevancies and sanctimonious trivialities. In the midst of a mighty struggle to rid our nation of racial and economic injustice, I have heard many ministers say: "Those are social issues, with which the gospel has no real concern." And I have watched many churches commit themselves to a completely otherworldly religion which makes a strange, un-Biblical distinction between body and soul, between the sacred and the secular.

I have traveled the length and breadth of Alabama, Mississippi, and all the other southern states. On sweltering summer days and crisp autumn mornings I have looked at the South's beautiful churches with their lofty spires pointing heavenward. I have beheld the impressive outlines of her massive religious-education buildings. Over and over I have found myself asking: "What kind of people worship here? Who is their God? Where were their voices when the lips of Governor Barnett dripped with words of interposition and nullification? Where were they when Governor Wallace gave a clarion call for defiance and hatred? Where were their voices of support when bruised and weary Negro men and women decided to rise from the dark dungeons of complacency to the bright hills of creative protest?"

Yes, these questions are still in my mind. In deep disappointment I have wept over the laxity of the church. But be assured that my tears have been tears of love. There can be no deep disappointment where there is not deep love. Yes, I love the church. How could I do otherwise? I am in the rather unique position of being the son, the grandson and the great-grandson of preachers. Yes, I see the church as the body of Christ. But, oh! How we have blemished and scarred that body through social neglect and through fear of being nonconformists.

There was a time when the church was very powerful—in the time when the early Christians rejoiced at being deemed worthy to suffer for what they believed. In those days the church was not merely a thermometer that recorded the ideas and principles of popular opinion; it was a thermostat that transformed the mores of society. Whenever the early Christians entered a town, the people in power became disturbed and immediately sought to convict the Christians for being "disturbers of the peace" and "outside agitators." But the Christians pressed on, in the conviction that they were "a colony of heaven," called to obey God rather than man. Small in number, they were big in commitment. They were too God-intoxicated to be "astronomically intimidated." By their effort and example they brought an end to such ancient evils as infanticide and gladiatorial contests.

Things are different now. So often the contemporary church is a weak, ineffectual voice with an uncertain sound. So often it is an archdefender of the status quo. Far from being disturbed by the presence of the church, the power structure of the average community is consoled by the church's silent—and often even vocal—sanction of things as they are.

But the judgment of God is upon the church as never before. If today's church does not recapture the sacrificial spirit of the early church, it will lose its authenticity, forfeit the loyalty of millions, and be dismissed as an irrelevant social club with no meaning for the twentieth century. Every day I meet young people whose disappointment with the church has turned into outright disgust.

Perhaps I have once again been too optimistic. Is organized religion too inextricably bound to the status quo to save our nation and the world? Perhaps I must turn my faith to the inner spiritual church, the church within the church, as the true *ekklesia* [congregation] and the hope of the world. But again I am thankful to God that some noble souls from the ranks of organized religion have broken loose from the paralyzing chains of conformity and joined us as active partners in the struggle for freedom. They have left their secure congregations and walked the streets of Albany, Georgia, with us. They have gone down the highways of the South on tortuous rides for freedom. Yes, they have gone to jail with us. Some have been dismissed from their churches, have lost the support of their bishops and fellow ministers. But they have acted in the faith that right defeated is stronger than evil triumphant. Their witness has been the spiritual salt that has preserved the true meaning of the gospel in these troubled times. They have carved a tunnel of hope through the dark mountain of disappointment.

I hope the church as a whole will meet the challenge of this decisive hour. But even if the church does not come to the aid of justice, I have no despair about the future. I have no fear about the outcome of our struggle in Birmingham, even if our motives are at present misunderstood. We will reach the goal of freedom in Birmingham and all over the nation, because the goal of America is freedom. Abused and scorned though we may be, our destiny is tied up with America's destiny. Before the pilgrims landed at Plymouth, we were here. Before the pen of Jefferson etched the majestic words of the Declaration of Independence across the pages of history, we were here. For more than two centuries our forebears labored in this country without wages; they made cotton king; they built the homes of their masters while suffering gross injustice and shameful humiliation—and yet out of a bottomless vitality they continued to thrive and develop. If the inexpressible cruelties of slavery could not stop us, the opposition we now face will surely fail. We will win our freedom because the sacred heritage of our nation and the eternal will of God are embodied in our echoing demands.

Before closing I feel impelled to mention one other point in your statement that has troubled me profoundly. You warmly commended the Birmingham police force for keeping "order" and "preventing violence." I doubt that you would have so warmly commended the police force if you had seen its dogs sinking their teeth into unarmed, nonviolent Negroes. I doubt that you would so quickly commend the policemen if you were to observe their ugly and inhumane treatment of Negroes here in the city jail; if you were to watch them push and curse old Negro women and young Negro girls; if you were to see them slap and kick old Negro men and young boys; if you were to observe them, as they did on two occasions, refuse to give us food because we wanted to sing our grace together. I cannot join you in your praise of the Birmingham police department.

It is true that the police have exercised a degree of discipline in handling the demonstrators. In this sense they have conducted themselves rather "nonviolently" in public. But for what purpose? To preserve the evil system of segregation. Over the past few years I have consistently preached that nonviolence demands that the means we use must be as pure as the ends we seek. I have tried to make clear that it is wrong to use immoral means to attain moral ends. But now I must affirm that it is just as wrong, or perhaps even more so, to use moral means to preserve immoral ends. Perhaps Mr. Connor and his policemen have been rather nonviolent in public, as was Chief Pritchett in Albany, Georgia, but they have used the moral means of nonviolence to maintain the immoral end of racial injustice. As T. S. Eliot has said:

"The last temptation is the greatest treason: To do the right deed for the wrong reason."

I wish you had commended the Negro sit-inners and demonstrators of Birmingham for their sublime courage, their willingness to suffer and their amazing discipline in the midst of great provocation. One day the South will recognize its real heroes. They will be the James Merediths, with the noble sense of purpose that enables them to face jeering and hostile mobs, and with the agonizing loneliness that characterizes the life of the pioneer. They will be old, oppressed, battered Negro women, symbolized in a seventy-two-year-old woman in Montgomery, Alabama, who rose up with a sense of dignity and with her people decided not to ride segregated buses, and who responded with ungrammatical profundity to one who inquired about her weariness: "My feets is tired, but my soul is at rest." They will be the young high school and college students, the young ministers of the gospel and a host of their elders, courageously and nonviolently sitting in at lunch counters and willingly going to jail for conscience' sake. One day the South will know that when these disinherited children of God sat down at lunch counters, they were in reality standing up for what is best in the American dream and for the most sacred values in our Judaeo-Christian heritage, thereby bringing our nation back to those great wells of democracy which were dug deep by the founding fathers in their formulation of the Constitution and the Declaration of Independence.

Never before have I written so long a letter. I'm afraid it is much too long to take your precious time. I can assure you that it would have been much shorter if I had been writing from a comfortable desk, but what else can one do when he is alone in a narrow jail cell, other than write long letters, think long thoughts and pray long prayers?

If I have said anything in this letter that overstates the truth and indicates an unreasonable impatience, I beg you to forgive me. If I have said anything that understates the truth and indicates my having a patience that allows me to settle for anything less than brotherhood, I beg God to forgive me.

I hope this letter finds you strong in the faith. I also hope that circumstances will soon make it possible for me to meet each of you, not as an integrationist or a civil-rights leader but as a fellow clergyman and a Christian brother. Let us all hope that the dark clouds of racial prejudice will soon pass away and the deep fog of misunderstanding will be lifted from our fear-drenched communities, and in some not too distant tomorrow the radiant stars of love and brotherhood will shine over our great nation with all their scintillating beauty.

Yours for the cause of Peace and Brotherhood,
MARTIN LUTHER KING, JR.

NOTES

1. AUTHOR'S NOTE: This response to a published statement by eight fellow clergymen from Alabama (Bishop C. C. J. Carpenter, Bishop Joseph A. Durick, Rabbi Hilton L. Grafman, Bishop Paul Hardin, Bishop Holan B. Harmon, the Reverend George M. Murray, the Reverend Edward V. Ramage and the Reverend Earl Stallings) was composed under somewhat constricting circumstances. Begun on the margins of the newspaper in which the statement appeared while I was in jail, the letter was continued on scraps of writing paper supplied by a friendly Negro trusty, and concluded on a pad my attorneys were eventually permitted to leave me. Although the text remains in substance unaltered, I have indulged in the author's prerogative of polishing it for publication.

44

BLACK POWER

STOKELEY CARMICHAEL AND CHARLES V. HAMILTON

After he coined the phrase, "black power," Stokely Carmichael became one of the most controversial figures in the civil rights movement of the 1960s. He and Charles Hamilton, a political scientist, spelled out the implications of this idea in their book, *Black Power: The Politics of Liberation in America* (1967), from which the following excerpt is taken. Carmichael (1941–) was Chairman of the Student Nonviolent Coordinating Committee in 1966, then Prime Minister of the Black Panthers from 1967 to 1969, when he moved to Guinea. Hamilton (1929–) now holds the position of Wallace S. Sayre Professor of Government at Columbia University.

Source: Stokeley Carmichael and Charles V. Hamilton, Black Power: The Politics of Liberation in America *(New York: Random House, 1967), pp. 37–39, 44–55.*

BLACK POWER: ITS NEED AND SUBSTANCE

. . .

Black people must redefine themselves, and only *they* can do that. Throughout this country, vast segments of the black communities are beginning to recognize the need to assert their own definitions, to reclaim their history, their culture; to create their own sense of community and togetherness. There is a growing resentment of the word "Negro," for example, because this term is the invention of our oppressor; it is *his* image of us that he describes. Many blacks are now calling themselves African-Americans, Afro-Americans or black people because that is *our* image of ourselves. When we begin to define our own image, the stereotypes—that is, lies—that our oppressor has developed will begin in the white community and end there. The black community will have a positive image of itself that *it* has created. This means we will no longer call ourselves lazy, apathetic, dumb, good-timers, shiftless, etc. Those are words used by white America to define us. If we accept these adjectives, as some of us have in the past, then we see ourselves only in a negative way, precisely the way white America wants us to see ourselves. Our incentive is broken and our will to fight is surrendered. From now on we shall view ourselves as African-Americans and as black people who are in fact energetic, determined, intelligent, beautiful and peace-loving.

There is a terminology and ethos peculiar to the black community of which black people are beginning to be no longer ashamed. Black communities are the only large segments of this society where people refer to each other as brother—soul-brother, soul-sister. Some people may look upon this as *ersatz*, as make-believe, but it is not that. It is real. It is a growing sense of community. It is a growing realization that black Americans have a common bond not only among themselves, but with their African brothers. In *Black Man's Burden*, John O. Killens described his trip to ten African countries as follows:

> Everywhere I went people called me brother. . . . "Welcome, American brother." It was a good feeling for me, to be in Africa. To walk in a land for the first time in your entire life knowing within yourself that your color would not be held against you. No black man ever knows this in America [p. 160].

More and more black Americans are developing this feeling. They are becoming aware that they have a history which pre-dates their forced introduction to this country. African-American history means a long history beginning on the continent of Africa, a history not taught in the standard textbooks of this country. It is absolutely essential that black people know this history, that they know their roots, that they develop an awareness of their cultural heritage. Too long have they been kept in submission by being told that they had no culture, no manifest heritage, before they landed on the slave auction blocks in this country. If black people are to know themselves as a vibrant, valiant people, they must know their roots. And they will soon learn that the Hollywood image of man-eating cannibals waiting for, and waiting on, the Great White Hunter is a lie.

With redefinition will come a clearer notion of the role black Americans can play in this world. This role will emerge clearly out of the unique, common experiences of Afro-Asians. Killens concludes:

> I believe furthermore that the American Negro can be the bridge between the West and Africa-Asia. We black Americans can serve as a bridge to mutual understanding. The one thing we black Americans have in common with the other colored peoples of the world is that we have all felt the cruel and ruthless heel of white supremacy. We have all been "niggerized" on one level or another. And all of us are determined to "de-niggerize" the earth. To rid the world of "niggers" is the Black Man's Burden, human reconstruction is the grand objective [p. 176].

Only when black people fully develop this sense of community, of themselves, can they begin to deal effectively with the problems of racism in *this* country. This is what we mean by a new consciousness; this is the vital first step. . . .

The adoption of the concept of Black Power is one of the most legitimate and healthy developments in American politics and race relations in our time. The concept of Black Power speaks to all the needs mentioned in this chapter. It is a call for black people in this country to unite, to recognize their heritage, to build a sense of community. It is a call for black people to begin to define their own goals, to lead their own organizations and to support those organizations. It is a call to reject the racist institutions and values of this society.

The concept of Black Power rests on a fundamental premise: *Before a group can enter the open society, it must first close ranks.* By this we mean that group solidarity is necessary before a group can operate effectively from a bargaining position of strength in a pluralistic society. Traditionally, each new ethnic group in this society has found the route to social and political viability through the organization of its own institutions with which to represent its needs within the larger society. Studies in voting behavior specifically, and political behavior generally, have made it clear that politically the American pot has not melted. Italians vote for Rubino over O'Brien; Irish for Murphy over Goldberg, etc. This phenomenon may seem distasteful to some, but it has been and remains today a central fact of the American political system. . . .

The point is obvious: black people must lead and run their own organizations. Only black people can convey the revolutionary idea—and it is a revolutionary idea—that black people are able to do things themselves. Only they can help create in the community an aroused and continuing black consciousness that will provide the basis for political strength. In the past, white allies have often furthered white supremacy without the whites involved realizing it, or even wanting to do so. Black people must come together and do things for themselves. They must achieve self-identity and self-determination in order to have their daily needs met.

Black Power means, for example, that in Lowndes County, Alabama, a black sheriff can end police brutality. A black tax assessor and tax collector and county board of revenue can lay, collect, and channel tax monies for the building of better roads and schools serving black people. In such areas as Lowndes, where black people have a majority, they will attempt to use power to exercise control. This is what they seek: control. When black people lack a majority, Black Power means proper representation and sharing of control. It means the creation of power bases, of strength, from which black people can press to change local or nation-wide patterns of oppression—instead of from weakness.

It does not mean *merely* putting black faces into office. Black visibility is not Black Power. Most of the black politicians around the country today are not examples of Black Power. The power must be that of a community, and emanate from there. The black politicians must start from there. The black politicians must stop being representatives of "downtown" machines, whatever the cost might be in terms of lost patronage and holiday handouts.

Black Power recognizes—it must recognize—the ethnic basis of American politics as well as the power-oriented nature of American politics. Black Power therefore calls for black people to consolidate behind their own, so that they can bargain from a position of strength. But while we endorse the *procedure* of group solidarity and identity for the purpose of attaining certain goals in the body politic, this does not mean that black people should strive for the same kind of rewards (i.e., end results) obtained by the white society. The ultimate values and goals are not domination or exploitation of other groups, but rather an effective share in the total power of the society.

Nevertheless, some observers have labeled those who advocate Black Power as racists; they have said that the call for self-identification and self-determination is "racism in reverse" or "black supremacy." This is a deliberate and absurd lie. There is no analogy—by any stretch of definition or imagination—between the advocates of Black Power and white racists. Racism is not merely exclusion on the basis of race but exclusion for the purpose of subjugating or maintaining subjugation. The goal of the racists is to keep black people on the bottom, arbitrarily and dictatorially, as they have done in this country for over three hundred years. The goal of black self-determination and black self-identity—Black Power—is full participation in the decision-making processes affecting the lives of black people, and recognition of the virtues in themselves as black people. The black people of this country have not lynched whites, bombed their churches, murdered their children and manipulated laws and institutions to maintain oppression. White racists have. Congressional laws, one after the other, have not been necessary to stop black people from oppressing others and denying others the full enjoyment of their rights. White racists have made such laws necessary. The goal of Black Power is positive and functional to a free and viable society. No white racist can make this claim. . . .

It is a commentary on the fundamentally racist nature of this society that the concept of group strength for black people must be articulated—not to mention defended. No other group would submit to being led by others. Italians do not run the Anti-Defamation League of B'nai B'rith. Irish do not chair Christopher Columbus Societies. Yet when black people call for black-run and all-black organizations, they are immediately classed in a category with the Ku Klux Klan. This is interesting and ironic, but by no means surprising: the society does not expect black people to be able to take care of their business, and there are many who prefer it precisely that way.

In the end, we cannot and shall not offer any guarantees that Black Power, if achieved, would be non-racist. No one can predict human behavior. Social change always has unanticipated consequences. If black racism is what the larger society fears, we cannot help them. We can only state what we hope will be the result, given the fact that the present situation is unacceptable and that we have no real alternative but to work for Black Power. The final truth is that the white society is not entitled to reassurances, even if it were possible to offer them.

We have outlined the meaning and goals of Black Power; we have also discussed one major thing which it is not. There are others of greater importance. The advocates of Black Power reject the old slogans and meaningless rhetoric of previous years in the civil rights struggle. The language of yesterday is indeed irrelevant: progress, non-violence, integration, fear of "white backlash," coalition. Let us look at the rhetoric and see why these terms must be set aside or redefined.

One of the tragedies of the struggle against racism is that up to this point there has been no national organization which could speak to the growing militancy of young black people in the urban ghettos and the black-belt South. There has been only a "civil rights" movement, whose tone of voice was adapted to an audience of middle class whites. It served as a sort of buffer zone between that audience and angry young blacks. It claimed to speak for the needs of a community, but it did not speak in the tone of that community. None of its so-called leaders could go into a rioting community and be listened to. In a sense, the blame must be shared—along with the mass media—by those leaders for what happened in Watts, Harlem, Chicago, Cleveland and other places. Each time the black people in those cities saw Dr. Martin Luther King get slapped they became angry. When they saw little black girls bombed to death *in a church* and civil rights workers ambushed and murdered, they were angrier, and when nothing happened, they were steaming mad. We had nothing to offer that they could see, except to go out and be beaten again. We helped to build their frustration.

We had only the old language of love and suffering. And in most places—that is, from the liberals and middle class—we got back the old language of patience and progress. The civil rights leaders were saying to the country: "Look, you guys are supposed to be nice guys, and we are only going to do what we are supposed to do. Why do you beat us up? Why don't you give us what we ask? Why don't you straighten yourselves out?" For the masses of black people, this language resulted in virtually nothing. In fact, their objective day-to-day condition worsened. The unemployment rate among black people increased while that among whites declined. Housing conditions in the black communities deteriorated. Schools in the black ghettos continued to plod along on outmoded techniques, inadequate curricula, and with all too many tired and indifferent teachers. Meanwhile, the President picked up the refrain of "We Shall Overcome" while the Congress passed civil rights law after civil rights law, only to have them effectively nullified by deliberately weak enforcement. "Progress is being made," we were told.

Such language, along with admonitions to remain nonviolent and fear the white backlash, convinced some that the course was the *only* course to follow. It misled some into believing that a black minority could bow its head and get whipped into a meaningful position of power. The very notion is absurd. The white society devised the language, adopted the rules and had the black community narcotized into believing that that language and those rules were, in fact, relevant. The black community was told time and again how *other* immigrants finally won *acceptance:* that is, by following the Protestant Ethic of Work and Achievement. They worked hard; therefore, they achieved. We were not told that it was by building Irish Power, Italian Power, Polish Power or Jewish Power that these groups got themselves together and operated from positions of strength. We were not told that "the American dream" wasn't designed for black people. That while today, to whites, the dream may *seem* to include black people, it cannot do so by the very nature of this nation's political and economic system, which imposes institutional racism on the black masses if not upon every individual black. A notable comment on that "dream" was made by Dr. Percy Julian, the black scientist and director of the Julian Research Institute in Chicago, a man for whom the dream seems to have come true. While not subscribing to "black power" as he understood it, Dr. Julian clearly understood the basis for it: "The false concept of basic Negro inferiority is one of the curses that still lingers. It is a problem created by the white man. Our children just no longer are going to accept the patience we were taught by our generation. We were taught a pretty little lie—excel and the whole world lies open before you. I *obeyed the injunction and found it to be wishful thinking.*" (Authors' italics.)[1]

A key phrase in our buffer-zone days was non-violence. For years it has been thought that black people would not literally fight for their lives. Why this has been so is not entirely clear; neither the larger society nor black people are noted for passivity. The notion apparently stems from the years of marches and demonstrations and sit-ins where black people did not strike back and the violence always came from white mobs. There are many who still sincerely believe in that approach. From our viewpoint, rampaging white mobs and white night-riders must be made to understand that their days of free head-whipping are over. Black people should and must fight back. Nothing more quickly repels someone bent on destroying you than the unequivocal message: "O.K., fool, make your move, and run the same risk I run—of dying."

When the concept of Black Power is set forth, many people immediately conjure up notions of violence. The country's reaction to the Deacons for Defense and Justice, which originated in Louisiana, is instructive. Here is a group which realized that the "law" and law enforcement agencies would not protect people, so they had to do it themselves. If a nation fails to protect its citizens, then that nation cannot condemn those who take up the task themselves. The Deacons and all other blacks who resort to self-defense represent a simple answer to a simple question: what man would not defend his family and home from attack?

But this frightened some white people, because they knew that black people would now fight back. They knew that this was precisely what *they* would have long since done if *they* were subjected to the injustices and oppression heaped on blacks. Those of us who advocate Black Power are quite clear in our own minds that a "non-violent" approach to civil rights is an approach black people cannot afford and a luxury white people do not deserve. It is crystal clear to us—and it must become so with the white society—*that there can be no social order without social justice.* White people must be made to understand that they must stop messing with black people, or the blacks *will* fight back!

Next, we must deal with the term "integration." According to its advocates, social justice will be accomplished by "integrating the Negro into the mainstream institutions of the society from which he has been traditionally excluded." This concept is based on the assumption that there is nothing of value in the black community and that little of value could be created among black people. The thing to do is siphon off the "acceptable" black people into the surrounding middle-class white community.

The goals of integrationists are middle-class goals, articulated primarily by a small group of Negroes with middle-class aspirations or status. Their kind of integration has meant that a few blacks "make it," leaving the black community, sapping it of leadership potential and know-how. As we noted in Chapter I, those token Negroes—absorbed into a white mass—are of no value to the remaining black masses. They become meaningless show-pieces for a conscience-soothed white society. Such people will state that they would prefer to be treated "only as individuals, not as Negroes"; that they "are not and should not be preoccupied with race." This is a totally unrealistic position. In the first place, black people have not suffered as individuals but as members of a group; therefore, their liberation lies in group action. This is why SNCC—and the concept of Black Power—affirms that helping *individual* black people to solve their problems on an *individual* basis does little to alleviate the mass of black people. Secondly, while color blindness *may* be a sound goal ultimately, we must realize that race is an overwhelming fact of life in this historical period. There is no black man in this country who can live "simply as a man." His blackness is an ever-present fact of this racist society, whether he recognizes it or not. It is unlikely that this or the next generation will witness the time when race will no longer be relevant in the conduct of public affairs and in public policy decision-making. To realize this and to attempt to deal with it does not make one a racist or overly preoccupied with race; it puts one in the forefront of a significant *struggle.* If there is no intense struggle today, there will be no meaningful results tomorrow.

"Integration" as a goal today speaks to the problem of blackness not only in an unrealistic way but also in a despicable way. It is based on complete acceptance of the fact that in order to have a decent house or education, black people must move into a white neighborhood or send their children to a white school. This reinforces, among both black and white, the idea that "white" is automatically superior and "black" is by definition inferior. For this reason, "integration" is a subterfuge for the maintenance of white supremacy. It allows the nation to focus on a handful of Southern black children who get into white schools at a great price, and to ignore the ninety-four percent who are left in unimproved all-black schools. Such situations will not change until black people become equal in a way that means something, and integration ceases to be a one-way street. Then integration does not mean draining skills and energies from the black ghetto into white neighborhoods. To sprinkle black children among white pupils in outlying schools is at best a stop-gap measure. The goal is not to take black children out of the black community and expose them to white middle-class values; the goal is to build and strengthen the black community.

"Integration" also means that black people must give up their identity, deny their heritage. We recall the conclusion of Killian and Grigg: "At the present time, integration as a solution to the race problem demands that the Negro foreswear his identity as a Negro." The fact is that integration, as traditionally articulated, would abolish the black community. The fact is that what must be abolished is not the black community, but the dependent colonial status that has been inflicted upon it.

The racial and cultural personality of the black community must be preserved and that community must win its freedom while preserving its cultural integrity. Integrity includes a pride—in the sense of self-acceptance, not chauvinism—in being black, in the historical attainments and contributions of black people. No person can be healthy, complete and mature if he must deny a part of himself; this is what "integration" has required thus far. This is the essential difference between integration as it is currently practiced and the concept of Black Power. . . .

NOTE

1. *The New York Times* (April 30, 1967), p. 30.

45

A VINDICATION OF THE RIGHTS OF WOMAN

MARY WOLLSTONECRAFT

Mary Wollstonecraft (1759–1797) wrote *A Vindication of the Rights of Woman* (1792) as a response to Thomas Paine's *Rights of Man* (1791). Although he claimed that "the rights of man" are natural and universal, Wollstonecraft noted, Paine overlooked the rights of the other half of the human race, namely, women. Setting about to rectify this oversight, she constructed the first systematic defense of women's rights against male domination.

Source: Mary Wollstonecraft, A Vindication of the Rights of Woman *(Philadelphia: Matthew Carey, 1794), pp. 87–109.*

OBSERVATIONS ON THE STATE OF DEGRADATION TO WHICH WOMAN IS REDUCED BY VARIOUS CAUSES

That woman is naturally weak, or degraded by a concurrence of circumstances, is, I think, clear. But this position I shall simply contrast with a conclusion, which I have frequently heard fall from sensible men in favour of an aristocracy: that the mass of mankind cannot be anything, or the obsequious slaves, who patiently allow themselves to be driven forward, would feel their own consequence, and spurn their chains. Men, they further observe, submit everywhere to oppression, when they have only to lift up their heads to throw off the yoke; yet, instead of asserting their birthright, they quietly lick the dust, and say, "Let us eat and drink, for to-morrow we die." Women, I argue from analogy, are degraded by the same propensity to enjoy the present moment, and at last despise the freedom which they have not sufficient virtue to struggle to attain. But I must be more explicit.

With respect to the culture of the heart, it is unanimously allowed that sex is out of the question; but the line of subordination in the mental powers is never to be passed over. Only "absolute in loveliness," the portion of rationality granted to woman is, indeed, very scanty; for denying her genius and judgment, it is scarcely possible to divine what remains to characterise intellect.

The stamen of immortality, if I may be allowed the phrase, is the perfectibility of human reason; for, were man created perfect, or did a flood of knowledge break in upon him, when he arrived at maturity, that precluded error, I should doubt whether his existence would be continued after the dissolution of the body. But, in the present state of things, every difficulty in morals that escapes from human discussion, and equally baffles the investigation of profound thinking, and the lightning glance of genius, is an argument on which I build my belief of the immortality of the soul. Reason is, consequentially, the simple power of improvement; or, more properly speaking, of discerning truth. Every individual is in this respect a world in itself. More or less may be conspicuous in one being than another; but the nature of reason must be the same in all, if it be an emanation of divinity, the tie that connects the creature with the Creator; for, can that soul be stamped with the heavenly image, that is not perfected by the exercise of its own reason? Yet outwardly ornamented with elaborate care, and so adorned to delight man, "that with honour he may love," the soul of woman is not allowed to have this distinction, and man, ever placed between her and reason, she is always represented as only created to see through a gross medium, and to take things on trust. But dismissing these fanciful theories, and considering woman as a whole, let it be what it will, instead of a part of man, the inquiry is whether she have reason or not. If she have, which, for a moment, I will take for granted, she was not created merely to be the solace of man, and the sexual should not destroy the human character.

Into this error men have, probably, been led by viewing education in a false light; not considering it as the first step to form a being advancing gradually towards perfection; but only as a preparation for life. On this sensual error, for I must call it so, has the false system of female manners been reared, which robs the whole sex of its dignity, and classes the brown and fair with the smiling flowers that only adorn the land. This has ever been the language of men, and the fear of departing from a supposed sexual character, has made even women of superior sense adopt the same sentiments. Thus understanding, strictly speaking, has been denied to woman; and instinct, sublimated into wit and cunning, for the purposes of life, has been substituted in its stead.

The power of generalising ideas, of drawing comprehensive conclusions from individual observations, is the only acquirement, for an immortal being, that really deserves the name of knowledge. Merely to observe, without endeavouring to account for anything, may (in a very incomplete manner) serve as the common sense of life; but where is the store laid up that is to clothe the soul when it leaves the body?

This power has not only been denied to women; but writers have insisted that it is inconsistent, with a few exceptions, with their sexual character. Let men prove this, and I shall grant that woman only exists for man. I must, however, previously remark, that the power of generalising ideas, to any great extent, is not very common amongst men or women. But this exercise is the true cultivation of the understanding; and everything conspires to render the cultivation of the understanding more difficult in the female than the male world.

I am naturally led by this assertion to the main subject of the present chapter, and shall now attempt to point out some of the causes that degrade the sex, and prevent women from generalising their observations.

I shall not go back to the remote annals of antiquity to trace the history of woman; it is sufficient to allow that she has always been either a slave or a despot, and to remark that each of these situations equally retards the progress of reason. The grand source of female folly and vice has ever appeared to me to arise from narrowness of mind; and the very constitution of civil governments has put almost insuperable obstacles in the way to prevent the cultivation of the female understanding; yet virtue can be built on no other foundation. The same obstacles are thrown in the way of the rich, and the same consequences ensue.

Necessity has been proverbially termed the mother of invention; the aphorism may be extended to virtue. It is an acquirement, and an acquirement to which pleasure must be sacrificed; and who sacrifices pleasure when it is within the grasp, whose mind has not been opened and strengthened by adversity, or the pursuit of knowledge goaded on by necessity? Happy is it when people have the cares of life to struggle with, for these struggles prevent their becoming a prey to enervating vices, merely from idleness. But if from their birth men and women be placed in a torrid zone, with the meridian sun of pleasure darting directly upon them, how can they sufficiently brace their minds to discharge the duties of life, or even to relish the affections that carry them out of themselves?

Pleasure is the business of woman's life, according to the present modification of society; and while it continues to be so, little can be expected from such weak beings. Inheriting in a lineal descent from the first fair defect in nature—the sovereignty of beauty—they have, to maintain their power, resigned the natural rights which the exercise of reason might have procured them, and chosen rather to be short-lived queens than labour to obtain the sober pleasures that arise from equality. Exalted by their inferiority (this sounds like a contradiction), they constantly demand homage as women, though experience should teach them that the men who pride themselves upon paying this arbitrary insolent respect to the sex, with the most scrupulous exactness, are most inclined to tyrannise over, and despise the very weakness they cherish. . . .

Ah! why do women—I write with affectionate solicitude—condescend to receive a degree of attention and respect from strangers different from that reciprocation of civility which the dictates of humanity and the politeness of civilisation authorise between man and man? And why do they not discover, when "in the noon of beauty's power," that they are treated like queens only to be deluded by hollow respect, till they are led to resign, or not assume, their natural prerogatives? Confined, then, in cages like the feathered race, they have nothing to do but to plume themselves, and stalk with mock majesty from perch to perch. It is true they are provided with food and raiment, for which they neither toil nor spin; but health, liberty, and virtue are given in exchange. But where, amongst mankind, has been found sufficient strength of mind to enable a being to resign these adventitious prerogatives—one who, rising with the calm dignity of reason above opinion, dared to be proud of the privileges inherent in man? And it is vain to expect it whilst hereditary power chokes the affections, and nips reason in the bud.

The passions of men have thus placed women on thrones, and till mankind become more reasonable, it is to be feared the women will avail themselves of the power which they attain with the least exertion, and which is the most indisputable. They will smile—yes, they will smile, though told that:

In beauty's empire is no mean,
And woman, either slave or queen,
Is quickly scorned when not adored.

But the adoration comes first, and the scorn is not anticipated.

Louis XIV, in particular, spread factitious manners, and caught, in a specious way, the whole nation in his toils; for, establishing an artful chain of despotism, he made it the interest of the people at large individually to respect his station, and support his power. And women, whom he flattered by a puerile attention to the whole sex, obtained in his reign that prince-like distinction so fatal to reason and virtue.

A king is always a king, and a woman always a woman. His authority and her sex ever stand between them and rational converse. With a lover, I grant, she should be so, and her sensibility will naturally lead her to endeavour to excite emotion, not to gratify her vanity, but her heart. This I do not allow to be coquetry; it is the artless impulse of nature. I only exclaim against the sexual desire of conquest when the heart is out of the question.

This desire is not confined to women. "I have endeavoured," says Lord Chesterfield, "to gain the hearts of twenty women, whose persons I would not have given a fig for." The libertine who, in a gust of passion, takes advantage of unsuspecting tenderness, is a saint when compared with this cold-hearted rascal—for I like to use significant words. Yet only taught to please, women are always on the watch to please, and with true heroic ardour endeavour to gain hearts merely to resign or spurn them when the victory is decided and conspicuous.

I must descend to the minutiæ of the subject.

I lament that women are systematically degraded by receiving the trivial attentions which men think it manly to pay to the sex, when in fact, they are insultingly supporting their own superiority. It is not condescension to bow to an inferior. So ludicrous, in fact, do these ceremonies appear to me that I scarcely am able to govern my muscles when I see a man start with eager and serious solicitude to lift a handkerchief or shut a door, when the *lady* could have done it herself, had she only moved a pace or two.

A wild wish has just flown from my heart to my head, and I will not stifle it, though it may excite a horse-laugh. I do earnestly wish to see the distinction of sex confounded in society, unless where love animates the behaviour. For this distinction is, I am firmly persuaded, the foundation of the weakness of character ascribed to woman; is the cause why the understanding is neglected, whilst accomplishments are acquired with sedulous care; and the same cause accounts for their preferring the graceful before the heroic virtues.

Mankind, including every description, wish to be loved and respected by *something*, and the common herd will always take the nearest road to the completion of their wishes. The respect paid to wealth and beauty is the most certain and unequivocal, and, of course, will always attract the vulgar eye of common minds. Abilities and virtues are absolutely necessary to raise men from the middle rank of life into notice, and the natural consequence is notorious—the middle rank contains most virtue and abilities. Men have thus, in one station at least, an opportunity of exerting themselves with dignity, and of rising by the exertions which really improve a rational creature; but the whole female sex are, till their character is formed, in the same condition as the rich, for they are born—I now speak of a state of civilisation—with certain sexual privileges; and whilst they are gratuitously granted them, few will ever think of works of supererogation to obtain the esteem of a small number of superior people.

When do we hear of women who, starting out of obscurity, boldly claim respect on account of their great abilities or daring virtues? Where are they to be found? "To be observed, to be attended to, to be taken notice of with sympathy, complacency, and approbation, are all the advantages which they seek." True! my male readers will probably exclaim; but let them, before they draw any conclusion, recollect that this was not written originally as descriptive of women, but of the rich. In Dr. [Adam] Smith's *Theory of Moral Sentiments* I have found a general character of people of rank and fortune, that, in my opinion, might with the greatest propriety be applied to the female sex. I refer the sagacious reader to the whole comparison, but must be allowed to quote a passage to enforce an argument that I mean to insist on, as the one most conclusive against a sexual character. For if, excepting warriors, no great men of any denomination have ever appeared amongst the nobility, may it not be fairly inferred that their local situation swallowed up the man, and produced a character similar to that of women, who are *localised*—if I may be allowed the word—by the rank they are placed in by *courtesy?* Women, commonly called ladies, are not to be contradicted in company, are not allowed to exert any manual strength; and from them the negative virtues only are expected, when any virtues are expected—patience, docility, good humour, and flexibility—virtues incompatible with any vigorous exertion of intellect. Besides, by living more with each other, and being seldom absolutely alone, they are more under the influence of sentiments than passions. Solitude and reflection are necessary to give to wishes the force of passions, and to enable the imagination to enlarge the object, and make it the most desirable. The same may be said of the rich; they do not sufficiently deal in general ideas, collected by impassioned thinking or calm investigation, to acquire that strength of character on which great resolves are built. . . .

In the middle rank of life, to continue the comparison, men, in their youth, are prepared for professions, and marriage is not considered as the grand feature in their lives; whilst women, on the contrary, have no other scheme to sharpen their faculties. It is not business, extensive plans, or any of the excursive flights of ambition, that engross their attention; no, their thoughts are not employed in rearing such noble structures. To rise in the world, and have the liberty of running from pleasure to pleasure, they must marry advantageously, and to this object their time is sacrificed, and their persons often legally prostituted. A man when he enters any profession has his eye steadily fixed on some future advantage (and the mind gains great strength by having all its efforts directed to one point), and, full of his business, pleasure is considered as mere relaxation; whilst women seek for pleasure as the main purpose of existence. In fact, from the education, which they receive from society, the love of pleasure may be said to govern them all; but does this prove that there is a sex in souls? It would be just as rational to declare that the courtiers in France, when a destructive system of despotism had formed their character, were not men, because liberty, virtue, and humanity, were sacrificed to pleasure and vanity. Fatal passions, which have ever domineered over the *whole* race!

The same love of pleasure, fostered by the whole tendency of their education, gives a trifling turn to the conduct of women in most circumstances; for instance, they are ever anxious about secondary things; and on the watch for adventures instead of being occupied by duties.

A man, when he undertakes a journey, has, in general, the end in view; a woman thinks more of the incidental occurrences, the strange things that may possibly occur on the road; the impression that she may make on her fellow-travellers; and, above all, she is anxiously intent on the care of the finery that she carries with her, which is more than ever a part of herself, when going to figure on a new scene; when, to use an apt French turn of expression, she is going to produce a sensation. Can dignity of mind exist with such trivial cares?

In short, women, in general, as well as the rich of both sexes have acquired all the follies and vices of civilisation, and missed the useful fruit. It is not necessary for me always to premise that I speak of the condition of the whole sex, leaving exceptions out of the question. Their senses are inflamed, and their understandings neglected, consequently they become the prey of their senses, delicately termed sensibility, and are blown about by every momentary gust of feeling. Civilised women are, therefore, so weakened by false refinement, that, respecting morals, their condition is much below what it would be were they left in a state nearer to nature. Ever restless and anxious, their over-exercised sensibility not only renders them uncomfortable themselves, but troublesome, to use a soft phrase, to others. All their thoughts turn on things calculated to excite emotion and feeling, when they should reason, their conduct is unstable, and their opinions are wavering—not the wavering produced by deliberation or progressive views, but by contradictory emotions. By fits and starts they are warm in many pursuits; yet this warmth, never concentrated into perseverance, soon exhausts itself; exhaled by its own heat, or meeting with some other fleeting passion, to which reason has never given any specific gravity, neutrality ensues. Miserable, indeed, must be that being whose cultivation of mind has only tended to inflame its passions! A distinction should be made between inflaming and strengthening them. The passions thus pampered, whilst the judgment is left unformed, what can be expected to ensue? Undoubtedly, a mixture of madness and folly!

This observation should not be confined to the *fair* sex; however, at present, I only mean to apply it to them.

Novels, music, poetry, and gallantry, all tend to make women the creatures of sensation, and their character is thus formed in the mould of folly during the time they are acquiring accomplishments, the only improvement they are excited, by their station in society, to acquire. This overstretched sensibility naturally relaxes the other powers of the mind, and prevents intellect from attaining that sovereignty which it ought to attain to render a rational creature useful to others, and content with its own station; for the exercise of the understanding, as life advances, is the only method pointed out by nature to calm the passions.

Satiety has a very different effect, and I have often been forcibly struck by an emphatical description of damnation; when the spirit is represented as continually hovering with abortive eagerness round the defiled body, unable to enjoy anything without the organs of sense. Yet, to their senses, are women made slaves, because it is by their sensibility that they obtain present power.

And will moralists pretend to assert that this is the condition in which one-half of the human race should be encouraged to remain with listless inactivity and stupid acquiescence? Kind instructors! what were we created for? To remain, it may be said, innocent; they mean in a state of childhood. We might as well never have been born, unless it were necessary that we should be created to enable man to acquire the noble privilege of reason, the power of discerning good from evil, whilst we lie down in the dust from whence we were taken, never to rise again.

It would be an endless task to trace the variety of meannesses, cares, and sorrows, into which women are plunged by the prevailing opinions, that they were created rather to feel than reason, and that all the power they obtain must be obtained by their charms and weakness:

Fine by defect, and amiably weak!

And, made by this amiable weakness entirely dependent, excepting what they gain by illicit sway, on man, not only for protection, but advice, is it surprising, that, neglecting the duties that reason alone points out, and shrinking from trials calculated to strengthen their minds, they only exert themselves to give their defects a graceful covering, which may serve to heighten their charms in the eye of the voluptuary, though it sink them below the scale of moral excellence.

Fragile in every sense of the word, they are obliged to look up to man for every comfort. In the most trifling danger they cling to their support, with parasitical tenacity, piteously demanding succour; and their *natural* protector extends his arm, or lifts up his voice, to guard the lovely trembler—from what? Perhaps the frown of an old cow, or the jump of a mouse; a rat would be a serious danger. In the name of reason, and even common sense, what can save such beings from contempt; even though they be soft and fair.

These fears, when not affected, may produce some pretty attitudes; but they show a degree of imbecility which degrades a rational creature in a way women are not aware of—for love and esteem are very distinct things.

I am fully persuaded that we should hear of none of these infantine airs, if girls were allowed to take sufficient exercise, and not confined in close rooms till their muscles are relaxed, and their powers of digestion destroyed. To carry the remark still further, if fear in girls, instead of being cherished, perhaps, created, were treated in the same manner as cowardice in boys, we should quickly see women with more dignified aspects. It is true, they could not then with equal propriety be termed the sweet flowers that smile in the walk of man; but they would be more respectable members of society, and discharge the important duties of life by the light of their own reason. "Educate women like men," says Rousseau, "and the more they resemble our sex the less power they have over us." This is the very point I aim at. I do not wish them to have power over men; but over themselves. . . .

And what is sensibility? "Quickness of sensation, quickness of perception, delicacy." This is it defined by Dr. [Samuel] Johnson; and the definition gives me no other idea than of the most exquisitely polished instinct. I discern not a trace of the image of God in either sensation or matter. Refined seventy times seven they are still material; intellect dwells not there; nor will fire ever make lead gold!

I come round to my old argument: if woman be allowed to have an immortal soul, she must have, as the employment of life, an understanding to improve. And when, to render the present state more complete, though everything proves it to be but a fraction of a mighty sum, she is incited by present gratification to forget her grand destination, nature is counteracted, or she was born only to procreate and rot. Or, granting brutes of every description a soul, though not a reasonable one, the exercise of instinct and sensibility may be the step which they are to take, in this life, towards the attainment of reason in the next; so that through all eternity they will lag behind man, who, why we cannot tell, had the power given him of attaining reason in his first mode of existence.

When I treat of the peculiar duties of women, as I should treat of the peculiar duties of a citizen or father, it will be found that I do not mean to insinuate that they should be taken out of their families, speaking of the majority. "He that hath wife and children," says Lord [Francis] Bacon, "hath given hostages to fortune; for they are impediments to great enterprises, either of virtue or mischief. Certainly the best works, and of greatest merit for the public, have proceeded from the unmarried or childless men." I say the same of women. But the welfare of society is not built on extraordinary exertions; and were it more reasonably organised, there would be still less need of great abilities, or heroic virtues.

In the regulation of a family, in the education of children, understanding, in an unsophisticated sense, is particularly required—strength both of body and mind; yet the men who, by their writings, have most earnestly laboured to domesticate women, have endeavoured, by arguments dictated by a gross appetite, which satiety had rendered fastidious, to weaken their bodies and cramp their minds. But, if even by these sinister methods they really *persuaded* women, by working on their feelings, to stay at home, and fulfil the duties of a mother and mistress of a family, I should cautiously oppose opinions that led women to right conduct, by prevailing on them to make the discharge of such important duties the main business of life, through reason were insulted. Yet, and I appeal to experience, if by neglecting the understanding they be as much, nay, more detached from these domestic employments, than they could be the most serious intellectual pursuit, though it may be observed, that the mass of mankind will never vigorously pursue an intellectual object, I may be allowed to infer that reason is absolutely necessary to enable a woman to perform any duty properly, and I must again repeat, that sensibility is not reason.

The comparison with the rich still occurs to me; for, when men neglect the duties of humanity, women will follow their example; a common stream hurries them both along with thoughtless celerity. Riches and honours prevent a man from enlarging his understanding, and enervate all his powers by reversing the order of nature, which has ever made true pleasure the reward of labour. Pleasure—enervating pleasure—is, likewise, within women's reach without earning it. But, till hereditary possessions are spread abroad, how can we expect men to be proud of virtue? And, till they are, women will govern them by the most direct means, neglecting their dull domestic duties to catch the pleasure that sits lightly on the wing of time.

46

OPPRESSION

MARILYN FRYE

Oppression takes many forms, including those subtle forms that are half-hidden in our language and habits of thought. So argues the feminist author and activist Marilyn Frye (1941–), who teaches philosophy at Michigan State University. Frye is the author of *The Politics of Reality*, from which the following essay below is taken, and other essays in feminism and philosophy.

OPPRESSION

It is a fundamental claim of feminism that women are oppressed. The word "oppression" is a strong word. It repels and attracts. It is dangerous and dangerously fashionable and endangered. It is much misused, and sometimes not innocently.

The statement that women are oppressed is frequently met with the claim that men are oppressed too. We hear that oppressing is oppressive to those who oppress as well as to those they oppress. Some men cite as evidence of their oppression their much-advertised inability to cry. It is tough, we are told, to be masculine. When the stresses and frustrations of being a man are cited as evidence that oppressors are oppressed by their oppressing, the word "oppression" is being stretched to meaningless; it is treated as though its scope includes any and all human experience of limitation of suffering no matter the cause, degree or consequence. Once such usage has been put over on us, then if ever we deny that any person or group is oppressed, we seem to imply that we think they never suffer and have no feelings. We are accused of insensitivity; even of bigotry. For women, such accusation is particularly intimidating, since sensitivity is one of the few virtues that has been assigned to us. If we are found insensitive, we may fear we have no redeeming traits at all and perhaps are not real women. Thus are we silenced before we begin: the name of our situation drained of meaning and our guilt mechanisms tripped.

But this is nonsense. Human beings can be miserable without being oppressed, and it is perfectly consistent to deny that a person or group is oppressed without denying that they have feelings or that they suffer.

We need to think clearly about oppression, and there is much that mitigates against this. I do not want to undertake to prove that women are oppressed (or that men are not), but I want to make clear what is being said when we say it. We need this word, this concept, and we need it to be sharp and sure.

I

The root of the word "oppression" is the element "press." *The press of the crowd; pressed into military service; to press a pair of pants; printing press; press the button.* Presses are used to mold things or flatten them or reduce them in bulk, sometimes to reduce them by squeezing out the gases or liquids in them. Something pressed is something caught between or among forces and barriers which are so related to each other that jointly they restrain, restrict or prevent the thing's motion or mobility. Mold. Immobilize. Reduce.

The mundane experience of the oppressed provides another clue. One of the most characteristic and ubiquitous features of the world as experienced by oppressed people is the double bind—situations in which options are reduced to a very few and all of them expose one to penalty, censure or deprivation. For example, it is often a requirement upon oppressed people that we smile and be cheerful. If we comply, we signal our docility and our acquiescence in our situation. We need not, then, be taken note of. We acquiesce in being made invisible, in our occupying no space. We participate in our own erasure. On the other hand, anything but the sunniest countenance exposes us to being perceived as mean, bitter, angry or dangerous. This means, at the least, that we may be found "difficult" or unpleasant to work with, which is enough to cost one one's livelihood; at worst, being seen as mean, bitter, angry or dangerous has been known to result in rape, arrest, beating and murder. One can only choose to risk one's preferred form and rate of annihilation.

Another example: It is common in the United States that women, especially younger women, are in a bind where neither sexual activity nor sexual inactivity is all right. If she is heterosexually active, a woman is open to censure and punishment for being loose, unprincipled or a whore. The "punishment" comes in the form of criticism, snide and embarrassing remarks, being treated as an easy lay by men, scorn from her more restrained female friends. She may have to lie and hide her behavior from her parents. She must juggle the risks of unwanted pregnancy and dangerous contraceptives. On the other hand, if she refrains from heterosexual activity, she is fairly constantly harassed by men who try to persuade her into it and pressure her to "relax" and "let her hair down"; she is threatened with labels like "frigid," "uptight," "man-hater," "bitch" and "cocktease." The same parents who would be disapproving of her sexual activity may be worried by her inactivity because it suggests she is not or will not be popular, or is not sexually normal. She may be charged with lesbianism. If a woman is raped, then if she has been heterosexually active she is subject to the presumption that she liked it (since her activity is presumed to show that she likes sex), and if she has not been heterosexually active, she is subject to the presumption that she liked it (since she is supposedly "repressed and frustrated"). Both heterosexual activity and heterosexual nonactivity are likely to be taken as proof that you wanted to be raped, and hence, of course, weren't *really* raped at all. You can't win. You are caught in a bind, caught between systematically related pressures.

Women are caught like this, too, by networks of forces and barriers that expose one to penalty, loss or contempt whether one works outside the home or not, is on welfare or not, bears children or not, raises children or not, marries or not, stays married or not, is heterosexual, lesbian, both or neither. Economic necessity; confinement to racial and/or sexual job ghettos; sexual harassment; sex discrimination; pressures of competing expectations and judgments about *women, wives* and *mothers* (in the society at large, in racial and ethnic subcultures and in one's own mind); dependence (full or partial) on husbands, parents or the state; commitment to political ideas; loyalties to racial or ethnic or other "minority" groups; the demands of self-respect and responsibilities to others. Each of these factors exists in complex tension with every other, penalizing or prohibiting all of the apparently available options. And nipping at one's heels, always, is the endless pack of little things. If one dresses one way, one is subject to the assumption that one is advertising one's sexual availability; if one dresses another way, one appears to "not care about oneself" or to be "unfeminine." If one uses "strong language," one invites categorization as a whore or slut; if one does not, one invites categorization as a "lady" —one too delicately constituted to cope with robust speech or the realities to which it presumably refers.

The experience of oppressed people is that the living of one's life is confined and shaped by forces and barriers which are not accidental or occasional and hence avoidable, but are systematically related to each other in such a way as to catch one between and among them and restrict or penalize motion in any direction. It is the experience of being caged in: all avenues, in every direction, are blocked or booby trapped.

Cages. Consider a birdcage. If you look very closely at just one wire in the cage, you cannot see the other wires. If your conception of what is before you is determined by this myopic focus, you could look at that one wire, up and down the length of it, and be unable to see why a bird would not just fly around the wire any time it wanted to go somewhere. Furthermore, even if, one day at a time, you myopically inspected each wire, you still could not see why a bird would have trouble going past the wires to get anywhere. There is no physical property of any one wire, *nothing* that the closest scrutiny could discover, that will reveal how a bird could be inhibited or harmed by it except in the most accidental way. It is only when you step back, stop looking at the wires one by one, microscopically, and take a macroscopic view of the whole cage, that you can see why the bird does not go anywhere; and then you will see it in a moment. It will require no great subtlety of mental powers. It is perfectly *obvious* that the bird is surrounded by a network of systematically related barriers, no one of which would be the least hindrance to its flight, but which, by their relations to each other, are as confining as the solid walls of a dungeon.

It is now possible to grasp one of the reasons why oppression can be hard to see and recognize: one can study the elements of an oppressive structure with great care and some good will without seeing the structure as a whole, and hence without seeing or being able to understand that one is looking at a cage and that there are people there who are caged, whose motion and mobility are restricted, whose lives are shaped and reduced.

The arresting of vision at a microscopic level yields such common confusion as that about the male door-opening ritual. This ritual, which is remarkably widespread across classes and races, puzzles many people, some of whom do and some of whom do not find it offensive. Look at the scene of the two people approaching a door. The male steps slightly ahead and opens the door. The male holds the door open while the female glides through. Then the male goes through. The door closes after them. "Now how," one innocently asks, "can those crazy women's libbers say that is oppressive? The guy *removed* a barrier to the lady's smooth and unruffled progress." But each repetition of this ritual has a place in a pattern, in fact in several patterns. One has to shift the level of one's perception in order to see the whole picture.

The door-opening pretends to be a helpful service, but the helpfulness is false. This can be seen by noting that it will be done whether or not it makes any practical sense. Infirm men and men burdened with packages will open doors for able-bodied women who are free of physical burdens. Men will impose themselves awkwardly and jostle everyone in order to get to the door first. The act is not determined by convenience or grace. Furthermore, these very numerous acts of unneeded or even noisome "help" occur in counterpoint to a pattern of men not being helpful in many practical ways in which women might welcome help. What *women* experience is a world in which gallant princes charming commonly make a fuss about being helpful and providing small services when help and services are of little or no use, but in which there are rarely ingenious and adroit princes at hand when substantial assistance is really wanted either in mundane affairs or in situations of threat, assault or terror. There is no help with the (his) laundry; no help typing a report at 4:00 a.m.; no help in mediating disputes among relatives or children. There is nothing but advice that women should stay indoors after dark, be chaperoned by a man, or when it comes down to it, "lie back and enjoy it."

The gallant gestures have no practical meaning. Their meaning is symbolic. The door-opening and similar services provided are services which really are needed by people who are for one reason or another incapacitated—unwell, burdened with parcels, etc. So the message is that women are incapable. The detachment of the acts from the concrete realities of what women need and do not need is a vehicle for the message that women's actual needs and interests are unimportant or irrelevant. Finally, these gestures imitate the behavior of servants toward masters and thus mock women, who are in most respects the servants and caretakers of men. The message of the false helpfulness of male gallantry is female dependence, the invisibility or insignificance of women, and contempt for women.

One cannot see the meanings of these rituals if one's focus is riveted upon the individual event in all its particularity, including the particularity of the individual man's present conscious intentions and motives and the individual woman's conscious perception of the event in the moment. It seems sometimes that people take a deliberately myopic view and fill their eyes with things seen microscopically in order not to see macroscopically. At any rate, whether it is deliberate or not, people can and do fail to see the oppression of women because they fail to see macroscopically and hence fail to see the various elements of the situation as systematically related in larger schemes.

As the cageness of the birdcage is a macroscopic phenomenon, the oppressiveness of the situations in which women live our various and different lives is a macroscopic phenomenon. Neither can be *seen* from a microscopic perspective. But when you look macroscopically you can see it—a network of forces and barriers which are systematically related and which conspire to the immobilization, reduction and molding of women and the lives we live.

II

The image of the cage helps convey one aspect of the systematic nature of oppression. Another is the selection of occupants of the cages, and analysis of this aspect also helps account for the invisibility of the oppression of women.

It is as a woman (or as a Chicana/o or as a Black or Asian or lesbian) that one is entrapped.

> *"Why can't I go to the park; you let Jimmy go!"*
> *"Because it's not safe for girls."*
> *"I want to be a secretary, not a seamstress; I don't want to learn to make dresses."*
> *"There's no work for negroes in that line; learn a skill where you can earn your living."*

When you question why you are being blocked, why this barrier is in your path, the answer has not to do with individual talent or merit, handicap or failure; it has to do with your membership in some category understood as a "natural" or "physical" category. The "inhabitant" of the "cage" is not an individual but a group, all those of a certain category. If an individual is oppressed, it is in virtue of being a member of a group or category of people that is systematically reduced, molded, immobilized. Thus, to recognize a person as oppressed, one has to see that individual *as* belonging to a group of a certain sort.

There are many things which can encourage or inhibit perception of someone's membership in the sort of group or category in question here. In particular, it seems reasonable to suppose that if one of the devices of restriction and definition of the group is that of is that of physical confinement or segregation, the confinement and separation would encourage recognition of the group as a group. This in turn would encourage the macroscopic focus which enables one to recognize oppression and encourages the individuals' identification and solidarity with other individuals of the group or category. But physical confinement and segregation of the group as a group is not common to all oppressive structures, and when an oppressed group is geographically and demographically dispersed the perception of it as a group is inhibited. There may be little or nothing in the situation of the individuals encouraging the macroscopic focus which would reveal the unity of the structure bearing down on all members of that group.

A great many people, female and male and of every race and class, simply do not believe that *woman* is a category of oppressed people, and I think that this is in part because they have been fooled by the dispersal and assimilation of women throughout and into the systems of the class and race which organize men. Our simply being dispersed makes it difficult for women to have knowledge of each other and hence difficult to recognize the shape of our common cage. The dispersal and assimilation of women throughout economic classes and races also divides us against each other practically and economically and thus attaches *interest* to the inability to see: for some, jealousy of their benefits, and for some, resentment of the others' advantages.

To get past this, it helps to notice that in fact women of races and classes *are* together in a ghetto of sorts. There is a women's place, a sector, which is inhabited by women of all classes and races, and it is not defined by geographical boundaries but by function. The function is the service of men and men's interests as men define them, which includes the bearing and rearing of children. The details of the service and the working conditions vary by race and class, for men of different races and classes have different interests, perceive their interests differently, and express their needs and demands in different rhetorics, dialects and languages. But there are also some constants.

Whether in lower, middle or upper-class home or work situations, women's service always includes personal service (the work of maids, butlers, cooks, personal secretaries), sexual service (including provision for his genital sexual needs and bearing his children, but also including "being nice," "being attractive for him," etc.), and ego service (encouragement, support, praise, attention). Women's service work also is characterized everywhere by the fatal combination of responsibility and powerlessness: we are held responsible and we hold ourselves responsible for good outcomes for men and children in almost every respect though we have in almost no case power adequate to that project. The details of the subjective experience of this servitude are local. They vary with economic class and race and ethnic tradition as well as the personalities of the men in question. So also are the details of the forces which coerce our tolerance of this servitude particular to the different situations in which different women live and work.

All this is not to say that women do not have, assert and manage sometimes to satisfy our own interests, nor to deny that in some cases and in some respects women's independent interests do overlap with men's. But at every race/class level and even across race/class lines men do not serve women as women serve men. "Women's sphere" may be understood as the "service sector," taking the latter expression much more widely and deeply than is usual in discussions of the economy.

III

It seems to be the human condition that in one degree or another we all suffer frustration and limitation, all encounter unwelcome barriers, and all are damaged and hurt in various ways. Since we are a social species, almost all of our behavior and activities are structured by more than individual inclination and the conditions of the planet and its atmosphere. No human is free of social structures, nor (perhaps) would happiness consist in such freedom. Structure consists of boundaries, limits and barriers; in a structured whole, some motions and changes are possible, and others are not. If one is looking for an excuse to dilute the word "oppression," one can use the fact of social structure as an excuse and say that everyone is oppressed. But if one would rather get clear about what oppression is and is not, one needs to sort out the sufferings, harms and limitations and figure out which are elements of oppression and which are not.

From what I have already said here, it is clear that if one wants to determine whether a particular suffering, harm or limitation is part of someone's being oppressed, one has to look at it *in context* in order to tell whether it is an element in an oppressive structure: one has to see if it is part of an enclosing structure of forces and barrier which tends to the immobilization and reduction of a group or category of people. One has to look at how the barrier or force fits with others and to whose benefit or detriment it works. As soon as one looks at examples, it becomes obvious that not everything which frustrates or limits a person is oppressive, and not every harm or damage is due to or contributes to oppression.

If a rich white playboy who lives off income from his investments in South African diamond mines should break a leg in a skiing accident at Aspen and wait in pain in a blizzard for hours before he is rescued, we may assume that in that period he suffers. But the suffering comes to an end; his leg is repaired by the best surgeon money can buy and he is soon recuperating in a lavish suite, sipping Chivas Regal. Nothing in this picture suggests a structure of barriers and forces. He is a member of several oppressor groups and does not suddenly become oppressed because he is injured and in pain. Even if the accident was caused by someone's malicious negligence, and hence someone can be blamed for it and morally faulted, that person still has not been an agent of oppression.

Consider also the restriction of having to drive one's vehicle on a certain side of the road.

There is no doubt that this restriction is almost unbearably frustrating at times, when one's lane is not moving and the other lane is clear. There are surely times, even, when abiding by this regulation would have harmful consequences. But the restriction is obviously wholesome for most of us most of the time. The restraint is imposed for our benefit, and does benefit us; its operation tends to encourage our *continued* motion, not to immobilize us. The limits imposed by traffic regulations are limits most of us would cheerfully impose on ourselves given that we knew others would follow them too. They are part of a structure which shapes our behavior, not to our reduction and immobilization, but rather to the protection of our continued ability to move and act as we will.

Another example: The boundaries of a racial ghetto in an American city serve to some extent to keep white people from going in, as well as to keep ghetto dwellers from going out. A particular white citizen may be frustrated or feel deprived because s/he cannot stroll around there and enjoy the "exotic" aura of a "foreign" culture, or shop for bargains in the ghetto swap shops. In fact, the existence of the ghetto, of racial segregation, does deprive the white person of knowledge and harm her/his character by nurturing unwarranted feeling of superiority. But this does not make the white person in this situation a member of an oppressed race or a person oppressed because of her/his race. One must look at the barrier. It limits the activities and the access of those on both sides of it (though to different degrees). But it is a product of the intention, planning and action of whites for the benefit of whites, to secure and maintain privileges that are available to whites generally, as members of the dominant and privileged group. Though the existence of the barrier has some bad consequences for whites, the barrier does not exist in a systematic relationship with other barriers and forces forming a structure oppressive to whites; quite the contrary. It is part of a structure which oppresses the ghetto dwellers and thereby (and by white intention) protects and furthers white interests as dominant white culture understands them. This barrier is not oppressive to whites, even though it is a barrier to whites.

Barriers have different meanings to those on opposite sides of them, even though they are barriers to both. The physical walls of a prison no more dissolve to let an outsider in than to let an insider out, but for the insider they are confining and limiting while to the outsider they may mean protection from what s/he takes to be threats posed by insiders—freedom from harm or anxiety. A set of social and economic barriers and forces separating two groups may be felt, even painfully, by members of both groups and yet may mean confinement to one and liberty and enlargement of opportunity to the other.

The service sector of the wives/mommas/assistants/girls is almost exclusively a woman-only sector; its boundaries not only enclose women but to a very great extent keep men out. Some men sometimes encounter this barrier and experience it as a restriction on this movement, their activities, their control of their choices of "lifestyle." Thinking they might like the simple nurturant life (which they may imagine to be quite free of stress, alienation and hard work), and feeling deprived since it seems closed to them, they thereupon announce the discovery that they are oppressed, too, by "sex roles." But that barrier is erected and maintained by men, for the benefit of men. It consists of cultural and economic forces and pressures in a cultural and economy controlled by men in which, at every economic level and in all racial and ethnic subcultures, economy, tradition—and even ideologies of liberation—work to keep at least local culture and economy in male control.

The boundary that sets apart women's sphere is maintained and promoted by men generally for the benefit of men generally, and men do benefit from its existence, even the man who bumps into it and complains of the inconvenience. That barrier is protecting his classification and status as a male, as superior, as having a right to sexual access to a female or females. It protects a kind of citizenship which is superior to that of females of his class and race, his access to a wider range of better paying and higher status work, and his right to prefer unemployment to the degradation of doing lower status or "women's" work.

If a person's life or activity is affected by some force or barrier that person encounters, one may not conclude that the person is oppressed simply because the person encounters that barrier or force; nor simply because the encounter is unpleasant, frustrating or painful to that person at that time; nor simply because the existence of the barrier or force, or the processes which maintain or apply it, serve to deprive that person of something of value. One must look at the barrier or force and answer certain questions about it. Who constructs and maintains it? Whose interests are served by its existence? Is it part of a structure which tends to confine, reduce and immobilize some group? Is the individual a member of the confined group? Various forces, barriers and limitations a person may encounter or live with may be part of an oppressive structure or not, and if they are, that person may be on either the oppressed or the oppressor side of it. One cannot tell which by how loudly or how little the person complains.

IV

Many of the restrictions and limitations we live with are more or less internalized and self-monitored, and are part of our adaptations to the requirements and expectations imposed by the needs and tastes and tyrannies of others. I have in mind such things as women's cramped postures and attenuated strides and men's restraint of emotional self-expression (except for anger). Who gets what out of the practice of those disciplines, and who imposes what penalties for improper relaxations of them? What are the rewards of this self-discipline?

Can men cry? Yes, in the company of women. If a man cannot cry, it is in the company of men that he cannot cry. It is men, not women, who require this restraint; and men not only require it, they reward it. The man who maintains a steely or tough or laid-back demeanor (all are forms which suggest invulnerability) marks himself as a member of the male community and is esteemed by other men. Consequently, the maintenance of that demeanor contributes to the man's self-esteem. It is felt as good, and he can feel good about himself. The way this restriction fits into the structures of men's lives is as one of the socially required behaviors which, if carried off, contribute to their acceptance and respect by significant others and to their own self-esteem. It is to their benefit to practice this discipline.

Consider, by comparison, the discipline of women's cramped physical postures and attenuated stride. This discipline can be relaxed in the company of women; it generally is at its most strenuous in the company of men. Like men's emotional restraint, women's physical restraint is required by men. But unlike the case of men's emotional restraint, women's physical restraint is not rewarded. What do we get for it? Respect and esteem and acceptance? No. They mock us and parody our mincing steps. We look silly, incompetent, weak and generally contemptible. Our exercise of this discipline tends to low esteem and low self-esteem. It does not benefit us. It fits in a network of behaviors through which we constantly announce to others our membership in a lower caste and our unwillingness and/or inability to defend our bodily or moral integrity. It is degrading and part of a pattern of degradation.

Acceptable behavior for both groups, men and women, involves a required restraint that seems in itself silly and perhaps damaging. But the social effect is drastically different. The woman's restraint is part of a structure oppressive to women; the man's restraint is part of a structure oppressive to women.

V

One is marked for application of oppressive pressures by one's membership in some group or category. Much of one's suffering and frustration befalls one partly or largely because one is a member of that category. In the case at hand, it is the category, *woman*. Being a woman is a major factor in my not having a better job than I do; being a woman selects me as a likely victim of sexual assault or harassment; it is my being a woman that reduces the power of my anger to a proof of my insanity. If a woman has little or no economic or political power, or achieves little of what she wants to achieve, a major causal factor in this is that she is a woman. For any woman of any race or economic class, being a woman is significantly attached to whatever disadvantages and deprivations she suffers, be they great or small.

None of this is the case with respect to a person's being a man. Simply being a man is not what stands between him and a better job; whatever assaults and harassments he is subject to, being male is not what selects him for victimization; being male is not a factor which would make his anger impotent—quite the opposite. If a man has little or no material or political power, or achieves little of what he wants to achieve, his being male is no part of the explanation. Being male is something he has going *for* him, even if race or class or age or disability is going against him.

Women are oppressed, *as women.* Members of certain racial and/or economic groups and classes, both the males and the females, are oppressed *as* members of those races and/or classes. But men are not oppressed *as men.*

. . . and isn't it strange that any of us should have been confused and mystified about such a simple thing?

47

GAY LIBERATION

RICHARD MOHR

One of the aims of the Gay Liberation movement, as philosopher Richard Mohr observes, is to enable "gay" or homosexual men and women to be happy, healthy, contributing members of a society that recognizes and accepts differences in sexual preference among its members. To do this requires "raising the consciousness" not only of gay people, but of their heterosexual or "straight" neighbors and co-workers as well. Only by confronting their own "homophobia"—that is, their fear of homosexuals and homosexuality—can people criticize and overcome its stunting and stifling effects.

Source: Richard Mohr, Gays/Justice. *New York: Columbia University Press, 1988), pp. 21–45. Reprinted by permission.*

BUT AREN'T GAYS WILLFULLY THE WAY THEY ARE?

It is generally conceded that if sexual orientation is something over which an individual—for whatever reason—has virtually no control, then discrimination against gays is deplorable, as it is against racial and ethnic classes, because it holds people accountable without regard for anything they themselves have done. And to hold a person accountable for that over which the person has no control is a central form of prejudice.

Attempts to answer the question whether or not sexual orientation is something that is reasonably thought to be within one's own control usually appeal simply to various claims of the biological or "mental" sciences. But the ensuing debate over genes, hormones, twins, early childhood development, and the like—though now pointing in lopsided preponderance toward the conclusion that homosexuality is either genetically determined or a permanent result of early childhood familial configurations—need not be firmly or finally settled beyond doubt in order to answer the morally and socially relevant questions over responsibility, choice, and necessity. One need only look at the social record to answer the question. All that is needed to answer the question is to look at the actual experience of gays in current society and it becomes fairly clear that sexual orientation is not likely a matter of choice. For coming to have a homosexual identity simply does not have the same sort of structure that decision-making has.

On the one hand, the "choice" of the gender of a sexual partner does not seem to express a trivial desire which might as easily be fulfilled by a simple substitution of the desired object: picking the gender of a sex partner is decidedly dissimilar to picking a flavor of ice cream. If an ice-cream parlor is out of one's flavor, one simply picks another. And if people were persecuted, threatened with jail terms, shattered careers, loss of family and housing, exposed to fatal disease and the like for eating, say, rocky road ice cream, no one would ever eat it; everyone would pick another easily available flavor. But gay sex seems not to be like that. If sexual orientation were an easy choice, Kinsey's statistics on the incidence of homosexuality in America, issued as they were when gay sex was everywhere a felony, would not have been shocking —they would simply have been preposterous, utterly unbelievable, virtually self-refuting.

On the other hand, even if establishing a sexual orientation is not like making a relatively trivial choice, perhaps it is like making the central and serious life-choices by which individuals try to establish themselves as being of some type. Again, if one examines gay experience, this seems not to be the case. For one never sees anyone setting out to become a homosexual, in the way one does see people setting out to become doctors, lawyers, and bricklayers. One does not find gays-to-be picking some end—"At some point in the future, I want to become a homosexual"—and then set about planning and acquiring the ways and means to that end, in the way one does see people deciding that they want to become lawyers, and then sees them plan what courses to take and what sort of temperaments, habits, and skills to develop in order to become lawyers.

The gay experience is quite different. Typically, gay persons-to-be simply find themselves having homosexual encounters and yet at least initially resisting quite strongly the identification of being a homosexual. Such a person even very likely resists having such encounters, but ends up having them anyway. Only with time, luck, and great personal effort does the person gradually come, if she does, to accept her orientation, to view it as a given material condition of life, coming as materials do with certain capacities and limitations. The person then begins to act in accordance with her orientation and its capacities, seeing its actualization as a requisite for an integrated personality and as a central component of personal well-being. As a result, the experience of coming out *to oneself* has for gays the basic structure of a discovery, not the structure of a choice. Far from signaling immorality, the coming out process affords one of the few remaining opportunities in ever more bureaucratic, mechanistic, and socialistic societies to manifest courage.

Nevertheless, two groups of self-identified homosexuals hold that sexual orientation *is* a matter of choice and, indeed, is better for being so. One group is lesbians who claim that having same-sex relations is chiefly politically motivated, and that pulling out of heterosexual relations and beginning homosexual ones is the politically correct thing to do, given the horrors of heterosexuality. However, as far as actual sexual behavior goes, this claim simply overlooks the psychobiological truth (seemingly obvious, but in any case proven by Masters and Johnson) that one's sexual arousals are not subject to the blandishments of one's will. Sexual arousal is something that comes over one independently of the will; indeed, willing sexual arousal defeats it. In sexual acts, one does not choose the gender (or genders) which can excite one. One may choose to identify oneself with a sexual orientation, but if one has successful sex acts in accordance with that orientation, it is because one is preconfigured or primed to respond to sexual cues of one sort rather than another.

Other gays who hold that sexual orientation is a matter of choice do so because they believe that the categories of sexuality themselves are not cast up from nature but are products of social construction, in much the way stereotypes are social constructions, so that sexual categories manifest themselves differently in different historical eras. If this belief is true, nature cannot compel one to be, say, a homosexual, for while nature has always been around, homosexuality did not (in this view) exist *as a social category* before the last century. One must therefore choose to fall into one category or another after the categories are socially created. Constructivists accuse biological or social determinists of merely being apologists and excuse-makers trying to fend off moral censure through metaphysics and of actually belittling gays by making sexual orientation a process as determinate, mechanical, and hapless as the earth circling the sun in 365.25 days or water freezing at 32 degrees.

As a normative theory, constructionism is objectionable in two ways. First, it takes a Stalinistic view of the social and hard sciences in that it calls for drawing their findings into line with a predetermined social ideology. It requires, for instance, dismissing the experience of gay people *discovering* that they are gay as a grand scale self-deception despite the honesty, clarity, and perspicuity with which their stories are told.

Second, to be free does not require that a person be a blank slate capable of creating and then reconstructing every possible component of the self. Rather, to be free is to be able to make something of oneself. One does not hear the social constructivists claiming that blacks cannot be free if it is the case that their race is not chosen. In the social dimensions of sexuality, one acts freely by taking responsibility for it. In taking responsibility for their sexuality—even though it may not be of their choosing—and doing something about it and society's response to it, gays are justifiably proud of themselves and make something of themselves.

That gays do take responsibility for sexuality and come out—virtually always in isolation and even into conditions of pervasive and imminent oppression—is a sign of the indomitability of the *individual* human spirit and a justification for viewing the individual as the proper locus of value in society.

HOW WOULD SOCIETY AT LARGE BE CHANGED IF HOMOSEXUAL ACTS WERE DECRIMINALIZED AND GAYS SOCIALLY TOLERATED OR EVEN ACCEPTED?

Recommendations to change social policy with regard to gays are invariably met with claims that to do so would invite the destruction of civilization itself: after all, isn't that what did Rome in? Actually Rome's decay paralleled not the flourishing of homosexuality but its repression under the later Christianized emperors. Predictions of American civilization's imminent demise have been as premature as they have been frequent. Civilization has shown itself rather resilient here, in large part because of the country's traditional commitments to a respect for privacy, to individual liberties, and especially to people minding their own business. These all give society an open texture and the flexibility to try out things to see what works. And because of this, one need not now speculate about what changes reforms of gay social policy might bring to society at large. For many reforms have already been tried out here and there, and nothing weird has resulted from them.

Half the states have decriminalized homosexual acts. Can you guess which of the following states still have sodomy laws: Wisconsin, Minnesota; New Mexico, Arizona; Vermont, New Hampshire; Nebraska, Kansas. One from each pair does and one does not. And yet one would be hard pressed to point out any substantial difference between the members of each pair. (If you're interested: the second of each pair has such laws.) Empirical studies have shown that there is no increase in other crimes in states that have decriminalized gay sex. Decriminalization is not a primrose path to hell.

Neither has the passage of legislation barring discrimination against gays ushered in the end of civilization. Some fifty counties and municipalities, including Los Angeles, Boston, and New York, have passed such statutes and among the states and colonies, Wisconsin and the District of Columbia have model protective codes. Again, no more brimstone has fallen in these places than elsewhere. Staunchly antigay cities like Miami and Houston have not been spared the AIDS crisis.

Berkeley, California, has even passed domestic partner legislation giving gay couples the same rights to city benefits as married couples and yet Berkeley has not become more weird than it already was.

Seemingly hysterical predictions that the American family would collapse if such reforms were passed have proven false, just as the same dire predictions that the availability of divorce would lessen the ideal and desirability of marriage proved completely unfounded. Indeed if current discrimination, which drives gays into hiding and into anonymous relations, was lifted, far from seeing gays raze American families, one would see gays forming them. Virtually all gays express a desire to have a permanent lover. Many would like to raise or foster children—perhaps from among those alarming number of gay kids who have been beaten up and thrown out of their "families" for being gay. A surprising number of gays—especially lesbians—do have children, either from former heterosexual lives or through artificial insemination. Indeed it is not fanciful to suppose that technology will eventually do for the relation between procreation and sexual orientation what it has done for the relation between strength and gender. In general, when afforded the opportunity, gays have shown an amazing tendency to nest.

Society currently makes gay coupling very difficult: a life of hiding is a tense and pressured existence not easily shared with another. And society seems to find gay love even more threatening than gay sex. The latter society might excuse as an aberrant compulsion but the former is surely a matter of choice that shows a commitment and indicates that the homosexual does not view her or his condition as some sort of permanent flaw. In turn, this choice shows that more usual couplings are not a matter of destiny but of personal responsibility. And *that* society finds scary: the so-called basic unit of society—the family—turns out not to be a unique immutable atom, but can adopt different parts, be adapted to different needs, and even improved. Gays might even have a thing or two to teach others about divisions of labor, the relation of sensuality to intimacy, and the stages of development in love relations.

If discrimination ceased, the energies that the typical gay person wastes worrying in the closet would be released for use in personal flourishing. From this release would be generated the many spinoff benefits that accrue to society at large when its individual members thrive—goodwill, charity, and civic spirit.

Finally, and perhaps paradoxically, in extending to gays the rights and benefits it has reserved for its dominant culture and extended selectively to others, America would confirm its deeply held, nearly religious vision of itself as a morally progressing nation, a nation itself advancing and serving as a beacon for others—especially with regard to human rights. The words with which our national pledge ends—"with liberty and justice for all"—are not a description of the present but a call for the future. Ours is a nation given to a prophetic political rhetoric which acknowledges that morality is not arbitrary and that justice is not merely the expression of the current collective will. It is this vision that led, even in the absence of much articulate moral argument, the black civil rights movement to its successes. Those congressmen who opposed that movement and its centerpiece, the 1964 Civil Rights Act, on obscurantist grounds, but who lived long enough and were noble enough, came in time to express their heartfelt regret and shame at what they had done. It is to be hoped and someday to be expected that those who now grasp at anything to oppose the extension of that which is best about America to gays will one day feel the same.

48

LIBERATION THEOLOGY

GUSTAVO GUTIERREZ

An increasingly influential movement within Christianity, especially the Roman Catholic Church, the "theology of liberation" views Jesus Christ as the champion and liberator of poor and oppressed people. Christ's teachings, as interpreted by liberation theologians such as Father Gustavo Gutierrez (1927–) of Peru, are aimed as much at social justice in this world as salvation in the next. Far from being "normal" or "natural" features of human life, poverty and oppression are the products of sin—of greed and lust for power—among the affluent. Liberation theology aims at raising the consciousness not only of the poor, but also of affluent people, who are asked to confront and overcome their own sin by exercising the "option for the poor."

Source: Gustavo Gutierrez, A Theology of Liberation, *2nd ed., translated by Sister Caridad Inda and John Eagleson (Maryknoll, NY: Orbis Books, 1988), chap. 2. Reprinted by permission.*

LIBERATION AND DEVELOPMENT

The world today is experiencing a profound and rapid sociocultural transformation. But the changes do not occur at a uniform pace, and the discrepancies in the change process have differentiated the various countries and regions of our planet.

Contemporary man has become clearly aware of this unequal process of transformation, of its economic causes, and of the basic relationships which combine to determine conditions and approaches. He examines his own circumstances and compares them to those of others; since he lives in a world where communication is fast and efficient, the conditions in which others live are no longer distant and unknown. But man goes beyond the limited expectations which such a comparison might create. He sees the process of transformation as a quest to satisfy the most fundamental human aspirations—liberty, dignity, the possibility of personal fulfillment for all. Or at least he would like the process to be moving toward these goals. He feels that the satisfaction of these aspiratons should be the purpose of all organization and social activity. He knows also that all his plans are possible, able to be at least partially implemented.

Finally, history demonstrates that the achievements of humanity are cumulative; their effects and the collective experience of the generations open new perspectives and allow for even greater achievements in the generations yet to come.

The phenomenon of the awareness of differences among countries characterizes our era, due to the bourgeoning of communications media; it is particularly acute in those countries less favored by the evolution of the world economy—the poor countries where the vast majority of people live. The inhabitants of these countries are aware of the unacceptable living conditions of most of their countrymen. They confirm the explanation that these inequalities are caused by a type of relationship which often has been imposed upon them. For these reasons, the efforts for social change in these areas are characterized both by a great urgency and by conflicts stemming from differences of expectations, degrees of pressure, and existing systems of relationships and power. It is well to clarify, on the one hand, that the current (and very recent) level of expectations of the poor countries goes far beyond a mere imitation of the rich countries and is of necessity somewhat indistinct and imprecise. On the other hand, both the internal heterogeneity and the presence of external determinants in these societies contribute to defining different needs in different groups. All of this causes a dynamics of action which is inevitably conflictual.

The poor countries are not interested in modeling themselves after the rich countries, among other reasons because they are increasingly more convinced that the status of the latter is the fruit of injustice and coercion. It is true that the poor countries are attempting to overcome material insufficiency and misery, but it is in order to achieve a more human society.

THE CONCEPT OF DEVELOPMENT

The term *development* seems tentatively to have synthesized the aspirations of people today for more human living conditions. The term itself is not new, but its current usage in the social sciences is new, for it responds to a different set of issues which has emerged only recently. Indeed, the old wealth-poverty antinomy no longer expresses all the problems and contemporary aspirations of mankind. . . .

Approaches

The concept of development has no clear definition; there are a variety of ways to regard it. Rather than reviewing them all at length, we will recall briefly the general areas involved.

Development can be regarded as purely economic, and in that sense it would be synonymous with *economic growth*.

The degree of development of a country could be measured, for example, by comparing its gross national product or its per capita income with those of a country regarded as highly developed. It is also possible to refine this gauge and make it more complex, but the presuppositions would still be the same: development consists above all in increased wealth, or, at most, a higher level of well-being.

Historically, this is the meaning which appears first. What led to this point of view was perhaps the consideration of the process in England, the first country to develop and, understandably enough, the first to be studied by economists. This viewpoint was later reinforced by the mirage which the well-being of the rich nations produced.

Those who champion this view today, at least explicitly, are few in number. Currently its value lies in serving as a yardstick to measure more integral notions. However, this focus continues to exist in a more or less subtle form in the capitalistic view of development.

The deficiencies of the above-mentioned view have led to another more important and more frequently held one. According to it, development is a *total social process*, which includes economic, social, political, and cultural aspects. This notion stresses the interdependence of the different factors. Advances in one area imply advances in all of them and, conversely, the stagnation of one retards the growth of the rest.

A consideration of development as a total process leads one to consider also all the external and internal factors which affect the economic evolution of a nation as well as to evaluate the distribution of goods and services and the system of relationships among the agents of its economic life. This has been carefully worked out by social scientists concerned with so-called Third World countries. They have reached the conclusion that the dynamics of world economics leads simultaneously to the creation of greater wealth for the few and greater poverty for the many.

From all this flows a strategy of development which, taking into account the different factors, will allow a country to advance both totally and harmoniously and to avoid dangerous setbacks.

To view development as a total social process necessarily implies for some an ethical dimension, which presupposes a concern for human values. The step toward an elaboration of a *humanistic perspective* of development is thus taken unconsciously, and it prolongs the former point of view without contradicting it.

François Perroux worked consistently along these lines. Development for him means "the combination of mental and social changes of a people which enable them to increase, cumulatively and permanently, their total real production." Going even further, he says "Development is achieved fully in the measure that, by reciprocity of services, it prepares the way for reciprocity of consciousness."[1]

It would be a mistake to think that this point of view, which is concerned with human values, is the exclusive preserve of scholars of a Christian inspiration. Converging viewpoints are found in Marxist-inspired positions.

This humanistic approach attempts to place the notion of development in a wider context: a historical vision in which mankind assumes control of its own destiny. But this leads precisely to a change of perspective which—after certain additions and corrections—we would prefer to call liberation. We shall attempt to clarify this below.

THE PROCESS OF LIBERATION

From the Critique of Developmentalism to Social Revolution

The term *development* has synthesized the aspirations of poor peoples during the last few decades. Recently, however, it has become the object of severe criticism due both to the deficiencies of the development policies proposed to the poor countries to lead them out of their underdevelopment and also to the lack of concrete achievements of the interested governments. This is the reason why *developmentalism (desarrollismo)*, a term derived from *develop-*

ment (desarrollo), is now used in a pejorative sense, especially in Latin America.

Much has been said in recent times about development. Poor countries competed for the help of the rich countries. There were even attempts to create a certain development mystique. Support for development was intense in Latin America in the '50s, producing high expectations. But since the supporters of development did not attack the roots of the evil, they failed and caused instead confusion and frustration.

One of the most important reasons for this turn of events is that development—approached from an economic and modernizing point of view—has been frequently promoted by international organizations closely linked to groups and governments which control the world economy. The changes encouraged were to be achieved within the formal structure of the existing institutions without challenging them. Great care was exercised, therefore, not to attack the interests of large international economic powers nor those of their natural allies, the ruling domestic interest groups. Furthermore, the so-called changes were often nothing more than new and underhanded ways of increasing the power of strong economic groups.

Developmentalism thus came to be synonymous with *reformism* and modernization, that is to say, synonymous with timid measures, really ineffective in the long run and counterproductive to achieving a real transformation. The poor countries are becoming ever more clearly aware that their underdevelopment is only the by-product of the development of other countries, because of the kind of relationship which exists between the rich and the poor countries. Moreover, they are realizing that their own development will come about only with a struggle to break the domination of the rich countries.

This perception sees the conflict implicit in the process. Development must attack the root causes of the problems and among them the deepest is economic, social, political and cultural dependence of some countries upon others—an expression of the domination of some social classes over others. Attempts to bring about changes within the existing order have proven futile. This analysis of the situation is at the level of scientific rationality. Only a radical break from the status quo, that is, a profound transformation of the private property system, access to power of the exploited class, and a social revolution that would break this dependence would allow for the change to a new society, a socialist society—or at least allow that such a society might be possible.

In this light, to speak about the process of *liberation* begins to appear more appropriate and richer in human content. Liberation in fact expresses the inescapable moment of radical change which is foreign to the ordinary use of the term *development*. Only in the context of such a process can a policy of development be effectively implemented, have any real meaning, and avoid misleading formulations.

Man, the Master of his Own Destiny

To characterize the situation of the poor countries as dominated and oppressed leads one to speak of economic, social, and political liberation. But we are dealing here with a much more integral and profound understanding of human existence and its historical future.

A broad and deep aspiration for liberation inflames the history of mankind in our day, liberation from all that limits or keeps man from self-fulfillment, liberation from all impediments to the exercise of his freedom. Proof of this is the awareness of new and subtle forms of oppression in the heart of advanced industrial societies, which often offer themselves as models to the underdeveloped countries. In them subversion does not appear as a protest against poverty, but rather against wealth. The context in the rich countries, however, is quite different from that of the poor countries: we must beware of all kinds of imitations as well as new forms of imperialism—revolutionary this time—of the rich countries, which consider themselves central to the history of mankind. Such mimicry would only lead the revolutionary groups of the Third World to a new deception regarding their own reality. They would be led to fight against windmills.

But, having acknowledged this danger, it is important to remember also that the poor countries would err in not following these events closely since their future depends at least partially upon what happens on the domestic scene in the dominant countries. Their own efforts at liberation cannot be indifferent to that proclaimed by growing minorities in rich nations. There are, moreover, valuable lessons to be learned by the revolutionaries of the countries on the periphery, who could in turn use them as corrective measures in the difficult task of building a new society.

What is at stake in the South as well as in the North, in the West as well as the East, on the periphery and in the center is the possibility of enjoying a truly human existence, a free life, a dynamic liberty which is related to history as a conquest. We have today an ever-clearer vision of this dynamism and this conquest, but their roots stretch into the past.

The fifteenth and sixteenth centuries are important milestones in man's understanding of himself. His relationship with nature changed substantially with the emergence of experimental science and the techniques of manipulation derived from it. Relying on these achievements, man abandoned his former image of the world and himself. . . . Because of science man took a step forward and began to regard himself in a different way. This process indicates why the best philosophical tradition is not merely an armchair product; it is rather the reflective and thematic awareness of man's experience of his relationships with nature and with other men. And these relationships are interpreted and at the same time modified by advances in technological and scientific knowledge.

Descartes is one of the great names of the new physics which altered man's relationship to nature. He laid the cornerstone of a philosophical reflection which stressed the primacy of thought and of "clear and distinct ideas," and so highlighted the creative aspects of human subjectivity. Kant's "Copernican Revolution" strengthened and systematized this point of view. For him our concept ought not to conform to the objects, but rather "the objects, or, in which is the same thing, that experience, which alone as given objects they are *cognized*, must conform to my conceptions." The reason is that "we only cognize in things *a priori* that which we ourselves place in them." Kant was aware that this leads to a "new method" of thought, to a knowledge which is critical of its foundations and thus abandons its naiveté and enters an adult stage.

Hegel followed this approach, introducing with vitality and urgency the theme of history. To a great extent his philosophy is a reflection on the French Revolution. This historical event had vast repercussions, for it proclaimed the right of every man to participate in the direction of the society to which he belongs. For Hegel man is aware of himself "only by being acknowledged or 'recognized' " by another consciousness. But this being recognized by another presupposes an initial conflict, "a life-and-death struggle," because it is "solely by risking life that freedom is obtained."[2]

Through the lord-bondsman dialectic (resulting from this original confrontation), the historical process will then appear as the genesis of consciousness and therefore of the gradual liberation of man. Through the dialectical process man constructs himself and attains a real awareness of his own being; he liberates himself in the acquisition of genuine freedom which through work transforms the world and educates man. For Hegel "world history is the progression of the awareness of freedom." Moreover, the driving force of history is the difficult conquest of freedom, hardly perceptible in its initial stages. It is the passage from awareness of freedom to real freedom. "It is Freedom in itself that comprises within itself the infinite necessity of bringing itself to consciousness and thereby, since knowledge about itself is its very nature, to reality." Thus man gradually takes hold of the reins of his own destiny. He looks ahead and turns towards a society in which he will be free of all alienation and servitude. This focus will initiate a new dimension in philosophy: social criticism.

Marx deepened and renewed this line of thought in his unique way . . . The new attitude was expressed clearly in the famous *Theses on Feuerbach*, in which Marx presented concisely but penetratingly the essential elements of his approach. In them, especially in the First Thesis, Marx situated himself equidistant between the old materialism and idealism; more precisely, he presented his position as the dialectical transcendence of both. Of the first he retained the affirmation of the objectivity of the external world; of the second he kept man's transforming capacity. For Marx, to know was something indissolubly linked to the transformation of the world through work. Basing his thought on these first intuitions, he went on to construct a scientific understanding of historical reality. He analyzed capitalistic society, in which were found concrete instances of the exploitation of man by his fellows and of one social class by another. Pointing the way towards an era in history when man can live humanly, Marx created categories which allowed for the elaboration of a science of history.

The door was opened for science to help man take one more step on the road to critical thinking. It made him more aware of the socio-economic determinants of his ideological creations and therefore freer and more lucid in relation to them. But at the same time these new insights enabled man to have greater control and rational grasp of his historical initiatives. (This interpretation is valid unless of course one holds a dogmatic and mechanistic interpretation of history.) These initiatives ought to assure the change from the capitalistic mode of production to the socialistic mode, that is to say, to one oriented towards a society in which man can begin to live freely and humanly. He will have controlled nature, created the conditions for a socialized production of wealth, done away with private acquisition of excessive wealth, and established socialism.

But modern man's aspirations include not only liberation from *exterior* pressures which prevent his fulfillment as a member of a certain social class, country, or society. He seeks likewise an *interior* liberation, in an individual and intimate dimension; he seeks liberation not only on a social plane but also on a psychological. He seeks an interior freedom understood however not as an ideological evasion from social confrontation or as the internalization of a situation of dependency. Rather it must be in relation to the real world of the human psyche as understood since Freud.

A new frontier was in effect opened up when Freud highlighted the unconscious determinants of human behavior, with repression as the central element of man's psychic make-up. Repression is the result of the conflict between instinctive drives and the cultural and ethical demands of the social environment. For Freud, unconscious motivations exercise a tyrannical power and can produce aberrant behavior. This behavior is controllable only if the subject becomes aware of these motivations through an accurate rending of the new language of meanings created by the unconscious. Since Hegel we have seen *conflict* used as a germinal explanatory category and *awareness* as a step in the conquest of freedom. In Freud however they appear in a psychological process which ought also to lead to a fuller liberation of man.

The scope of liberation on the collective and historical level does not always and satisfactorily include psychological liberation. Psychological liberation includes dimensions which do not exist in or are not sufficiently integrated with collective, historical liberation. We are not speaking here, however, of facilely separating them or putting them in opposition to another. "It seems to me," writes David Cooper, "that a cardinal failure of all past revolutions has been the dissociation of liberation on the mass social level, i.e., liberation of whole classes in economic and political terms, and liberation on the level of the individual and the concrete groups in which he is directly engaged. If we are to talk of revolution today our talk will be meaningless unless we effect some union between the macro-social and micro-social, and between 'inner reality' and 'outer reality.' "[3] Moreover, alienation and exploitation as well as the very struggle for liberation from them have ramifications on the personal and psychological planes which it would be dangerous to overlook in the process of constructing a new society and a new man. These personal aspects—considered not as excessively privatized, but rather as encompassing all human dimensions—are also under consideration in the contemporary debate concerning greater participation of all in political activity. This is so even in a socialist society.

In this area, Marcuse's attempt, under the influence of Hegel and Marx, to use the psychoanalytical categories for social criticism is important. Basing his observations on a work which Freud himself did not hold in high regard, *Civilization and its Discontents*, Marcuse analyzes the *over-repressive* character of the affluent society and envisions the possibility of a non-repressive society, a possibility skeptically denied by Freud. Marcuse's analyses of advanced industrial society, capitalistic or socialistic, lead him to denounce the emergence of a one-dimensional and oppressive society. In order to achieve this non-repressive society, however, it will be necessary to challenge the values espoused by the society which denies man the possibility of living freely. Marcuse labels this the Great Refusal: "the specter of a revolution which subordinates the development of the productive forces and higher standards of living to the requirements of creating solidarity for the human species, for abolishing poverty and misery beyond all national frontiers and spheres of interest, for the attainment of peace."[4]

We are not suggesting, of course, that we should endorse without question every aspect of this development of ideas. There are ambiguities, critical observations to be made, and points to be clarified. Many ideas must be reconsidered in the light of a history that advances inexorably, simultaneously confirming and rejecting previous assertions. Ideas must be reconsidered too in light of praxis, which is the proving ground of all theory, and in light of socio-cultural realities very different from those from which the ideas emerged. But all this should not lead us to an attitude of distrustful reserve toward these ideas; rather it should suggest that the task to be undertaken is formidable. And the task is all the more urgent because these reflections are attempts to express a deeply-rooted sentiment in today's masses: the aspiration to liberation. This aspiration is still confusedly perceived, but there is an ever greater awareness of it. Furthermore, for many people in various ways this aspiration—in Vietnam or Brazil, New York or Prague—has become a norm for their behavior and a sufficient reason to lead lives of dedication. Their commitment is the backbone which validates and gives historical viability to the development of the ideas outlined above.

To conceive of history as a process of the liberation of man is to consider freedom as a historical conquest; it is to understand that the step from an abstract to a real freedom is not taken without a struggle against all the forces that oppress man, a struggle full of pitfalls, detours, and temptations to run away. The goal is not only better living conditions, a radical change of structures, a social revolution; it is much more: the continuous creation, never ending, of a new way to be a man, a *permanent cultural revolution.*

In other words, what is at stake above all is a dynamic and historical conception of man, oriented definitively and creatively toward his future, acting in the present for the sake of tomorrow. Teilhard de Chardin has remarked that man has taken hold of the reins of evolution. History, contrary to essentialist and static thinking, is not the development of potentialities preexistent in man; it is rather the conquest of new, qualitatively different ways of being a man in order to achieve an ever more total and complete fulfillment of the individual in solidarity with all mankind.

The Concept of Liberation Theologically Considered

Although we will consider liberation from a theological perspective more extensively later, it is important at this time to attempt an initial treatment in the light of what we have just discussed.

The term *development* is relatively new in the texts of the ecclesiastical magisterium. Except for a brief reference by Pius XII, the subject is broached for the first time by John XXIII in the encyclical letter *Mater et Magistra*. *Pacem in terris* gives the term special attention. *Gaudium et spes* dedicates a whole section to it, though the treatment is not original. All these documents stress the urgency of eliminating the existing injustices and the need for an economic development geared to the service of man. Finally, *Populorum progressio* discusses development as its central theme. Here the language and ideas are clearer; the adjective *integral* is added to development, putting things in a different context and opening new perspectives.

These new viewpoints were already hinted at in the sketchy discussion of Vatican Council II on dependence and liberation. *Gaudium et spes* points out that "nations on the road to progress . . . continually fall behind while often their *dependence* on wealthier nations deepens more rapidly, even in the economic sphere" (no. 9). Later it acknowledges that "although nearly all peoples have gained their independence, it is still far from true that they are free from excessive inequalities and from every form of *undue dependence*" (no. 85).

These assertions should lead to a discernment of the need to be free from the dependence, to be liberated from it. The same *Gaudium et spes* on two occasions touches on liberation and laments the fact that it is seen exclusively as the fruit of human effort: "Many look forward to a genuine and total *emancipation* of humanity wrought solely by human effort. They are convinced that the future rule of man over the earth will satisfy every desire of his heart" (no. 10). Or it is concerned that liberation be reduced to a purely economic and social level: "Among the forms of modern atheism is that which anticipates the *liberation* of man especially through his economic and social emancipation" (no. 20).[5] These assertions presuppose, negatively speaking, that liberation must be placed in a wider context; they criticize a narrow vision. They allow, therefore, for the possibility of a "genuine and total" liberation.

Unfortunately, this wider perspective is not elaborated. We find some indications, however, in the texts in which *Gaudium et spes* speaks of the birth of a "new humanism, one in which man is defined first of all by his responsibility toward his brothers and toward history" (no. 55). There is a need for men who are makers of history, "men who are truly new and artisans of a new humanity" (no. 30), men moved by the desire to build a really new society. Indeed, the conciliar document asserts that beneath economic and political demands "lies a deeper and more widespread longing. Persons and societies thirst for a full and free life worthy of man—one in which they can subject to their own welfare all that the modern world can offer them so abundantly" (no. 9).

All this is but a beginning. It is an oft-noted fact that *Gaudium et spes* in general offers a rather irenic description of the human situation; it touches up the uneven spots, smoothes the rough edges, avoids the more conflictual aspects, and stays away from the sharper confrontations among social classes and countries.

The encyclical *Populorum progressio* goes a step further. In a somewhat isolated text it speaks clearly of "building a world where every man, no matter what his race, religion or nationality, can live a fully human life, freed from servitude imposed on him by other men or by natural forces over which he has not sufficient control" (no. 47). It is unfortunate, however, that this idea was not expanded in the encyclical. From this point of view, *Populorum progressio* is a transitional document. Although it energetically denounces the "international imperialism of money," "situations whose injustice cries to heaven," and the growing gap between rich and poor countries, ultimately it addresses itself to the great ones of this world urging them to carry out the necessary changes. The outright use of the language of liberation, instead of its mere suggestion, would have given a more decided and direct thrust in favor of the oppressed, encouraging them to break with their present situation and take control of their own destiny.

The theme of liberation appears more completely discussed in the message from eighteen bishops of the Third World, published as a specific response to the call made by *Populorum progressio*. It is also treated frequently—almost to the point of being a synthesis of its message—in the conclusions of the Second General Conference of Latin American Bishops held in Medellín, Colombia, in 1968, which have more doctrinal authority than the eighteen bishops' message. In both these documents the focus has changed. The situation is not judged from the point of view of the countries at the center, but rather of those on the periphery, providing insiders' experience of their anguish and aspirations.

The product of a profound historical movement, this aspiration to liberation is beginning to be accepted by the Christian community as a sign of the times, as a call to commitment and interpretation. The Biblical message, which presents the work of Christ as a liberation, provides the framework for this interpretation. Theology seems to have avoided for a long time reflecting on the conflictual character of human history, the confrontations among men, social classes, and countries. St. Paul continuously reminds us, however, of the paschal core of Christian existence and of all of human life: the passage from the old man to the new, from sin to grace, from slavery to freedom.

"For freedom Christ has set us free" (Gal. 5:1), St. Paul tells us. He refers here to liberation from sin insofar as it represents a selfish turning in upon oneself. To sin is to refuse to love one's neighbors and, therefore, the Lord himself. Sin—a breach of friendship with God and others—is according to the Bible the ultimate cause of poverty, injustice, and the oppression in which men live. In describing sin as the ultimate cause we do not in any way negate the structural reasons and the objective determinants leading to these situations. It does, however, emphasize the fact that things do not happen by chance and that behind an unjust structure there is a personal or collective will responsible—a willingness to reject God and neighbor. It suggests, likewise, that a social transformation, no matter how radical it may be, does not automatically achieve the suppression of all evils.

But St. Paul asserts not only that Christ liberated us; he also tells us that he did it in order that we might be free. Free for what? Free to love. "In the language of the Bible," writes Bonhoeffer, "freedom is not something man has for himself but something he has for others. . . . It is not a possession, a presence, an object, . . . but a relationship and nothing else. In truth, freedom is a relationship between two persons. Being free means 'being free for the other,' because the other has bound me to him. Only in relationship with the other am I free."[6] The freedom to which we are called presupposes the going out of oneself, the breaking down of our selfishness and of all the structures that support our selfishness; the foundation of this freedom is openness to others. The fullness of liberation—a free gift from Christ—is communion with God and with other men.

CONCLUSION

Summarizing what has been said above, we can distinguish three reciprocally interpenetrating levels of meaning of the term *liberation*, or in other words, three approaches to the process of liberation.

In the first place, *liberation* expresses the aspirations of oppressed peoples and social classes, emphasizing the conflictual aspect of the economic, social, and political process which puts them at odds with wealthy nations and oppressive classes. In contrast, the word *development*, and above all the policies characterized as developmentalist [*desarrollista*], appear somewhat aseptic, giving a false picture of a tragic and conflictual reality. The issue of development does in fact find its true place in the more universal, profound, and radical perspective of liberation. It is only within this framework that *development* finds its true meaning and possibilities of accomplishing something worthwhile.

At a deeper level, *liberation* can be applied to an understanding of history. Man is seen as assuming conscious responsibility for his own destiny. This understanding provides a dynamic context and broadens the horizons of the desired social changes. In this perspective the unfolding of all of man's dimensions is demanded—a man who makes himself throughout his life and throughout history. The gradual conquest of true freedom leads to the creation of a new man and a qualitatively different society. This vision provides, therefore, a better understanding of what in fact is at stake in our times.

Finally, the world *development* to a certain extent limits and obscures the theological problems implied in the process designated by this term. On the contrary the word *liberation* allows for another approach leading to the Biblical sources which inspire the presence and action of man in history. In the Bible, Christ is presented as the one who brings us liberation. Christ the Savior liberates man from sin, which is the ultimate root of all disruption of friendship and of all injustice and oppression. Christ makes man truly free, that is to say, he enables man to live in communion with him; and this is the basis for all human brotherhood.

This is not a matter of three parallel or chronologically successive processes, however. There are three levels of meaning of a single, complex process, which finds its deepest sense and its full realization in the saving work of Christ. These levels of meaning, therefore, are interdependent. A comprehensive view of the matter presupposes that all three aspects can be considered together. In this way two pitfalls will be avoided: first, *idealist* or *spiritualist* approaches, which are nothing but ways of evading a harsh and demanding reality, and second, shallow analyses and programs of short-term effect initiated under the pretext of meeting immediate needs.

NOTES

1. "La notion de développement," in *L'économie de XXe siècle,* 2nd ed., enl., (Paris: Presses Universitaires de France, 1964), pp. 155 and 171.
2. *The Phenomenology of Mind,* trans. J. B. Baillie (New York: The Humanities Press, Inc., 1964), pp. 229, 232–233.
3. "Introduction" in the anthology (Stokely Carmichael, John Gerassi, Paul Sweezy, Herbert Marcuse, Lucien Goldmann et al.) *To Free a Generation: The Dialectics of Liberation,* ed. David Cooper (London: Collier Books, 1968), pp. 9–10.
4. *An Essay on Liberation* (Boston: Beacon Press, 1969), pp. ix–x.
5. In the texts quoted here the italics are ours.
6. *Creation and Fall, Temptation* (New York: The Macmillan Company, 1966), p. 37.

49

ALL ANIMALS ARE EQUAL

PETER SINGER

Just as oppressed people suffer from discriminatory beliefs and attitudes—women from sexism, people of color from racism, gays from homophobia—so too, says the Australian philosopher Peter Singer (1946–), do animals suffer from "speciesism." Speciesism is the belief that one particular animal species—the human species—is innately superior to all others. This supposed superiority leads humans to engage in the morally unjustifiable oppression, exploitation, and slaughter of other species. According to Singer, the aim of the animal liberation movement is to expose, criticize, and overcome these widely shared speciesist attitudes.

Source: Peter Singer, "All Animals Are Equal," Philosophic Exchange, *1 (Summer 1974). Reprinted by permission of Peter Singer.*

In recent years a number of oppressed groups have campaigned vigorously for equality. The classic instance is the Black Liberation movement, which demands an end to the prejudice and discrimination that has made blacks second-class citizens. The immediate appeal of the black liberation movement and its initial, if limited, success made it a model for other oppressed groups to follow. We became familiar with liberation movements for Spanish-Americans, gay people, and a variety of other minorities. When a majority group—women—began their campaign, some thought we had come to the end of the road. Discrimination on the basis of sex, it has been said, is the last universally accepted form of discrimination, practiced without secrecy or pretense even in those liberal circles that have long prided themselves on their freedom from prejudice against racial minorities.

One should always be wary of talking of "the last remaining form of discrimination." If we have learnt anything from liberation movements, we should have learnt how difficult it is to be aware of latent prejudice in our attitudes to particular groups until this prejudice is forcefully pointed out.

A liberation movement demands an expansion of our moral horizons and an extension or reinterpretation of the basic moral principle of equality. Practices that were previously regarded as natural and inevitable come to be seen as the result of an unjustifiable prejudice. Who can say with confidence that all his or her attitudes and practices are beyond criticism? If we wish to avoid being numbered amongst the oppressors, we must be prepared to re-think even our most fundamental attitudes. We need to consider them from the point of view of those most disadvantaged by our attitudes, and the practices that follow from these attitudes. If we can make this unaccustomed mental switch we may discover a pattern in our attitudes and practices that consistently operates so as to benefit one group—usually the one to which we ourselves belong—at the expense of another. In this way we may come to see that there is a case for a new liberation movement. My aim is to advocate that we make this mental switch in respect of our attitudes and practices towards a very large group of beings: members of species other than our own—or, as we popularly though misleadingly call them, animals. In other words, I am urging that we extend to other species the basic principle of equality that most of us recognize should be extended to all members of our own species.

All this may sound a little far-fetched, more like a parody of other liberation movements than a serious objective. In fact, in the past the idea of "The Rights of Animals" really has been used to parody the case for women's rights. When Mary Wollstonecraft, a forerunner of later feminists, published here *Vindication of the Rights of Women* in 1792, her ideas were widely regarded as absurd, and they were satirized in an anonymous publication entitled *A Vindication of the Rights of Brutes.* The author of this satire (actually Thomas Taylor, a distinguished Cambridge philosopher) tried to refute Wollstonecraft's reasonings by showing that they could be carried one stage further. If sound when applied to women, why should the arguments not be applied to dogs, cats, and horses? They seemed to hold equally well for these "brutes"; yet to hold that brutes had rights was manifestly absurd; therefore the reasoning by which this conclusion had been reached must be unsound, and if unsound when applied to brutes, it must also be unsound when applied to women, since the very same arguments had been used in each case.

One way in which we might reply to this argument is by saying that the case for equality between men and women cannot validly be extended to nonhuman animals. Women have a right to vote, for instance, because they are just as capable of making rational decisions as men are; dogs, on the other hand, are incapable of understanding the significance of voting, so they cannot have the right to vote. There are many other obvious ways in which men and women resemble each other closely, while humans and other animals differ greatly. So, it might be said, men and women are similar beings, and should have equal rights, while humans and nonhumans are different and should not have equal rights.

The thought behind this reply to Taylor's analogy is correct up to a point, but it does not go far enough. There *are* important differences between humans and other animals, and these differences must give rise to *some* differences in the rights that each have. Recognizing this obvious fact, however, is no barrier to the case for extending the basic principle of equality to nonhuman animals. The differences that exist between men and women are equally undeniable, and the supporters of Women's Liberation are aware that these differences may give rise to different rights. Many feminists hold that women have the right to an abortion on request. It does not follow that since these same people are campaigning for equality between men and women they must support the right of men to have abortions too. Since a man cannot have an abortion, it is meaningless to talk of his right to have one. Since a pig can't vote, it is meaningless to talk of its right to vote. There is no reason why either Women's Liberation or Animal Liberation should get involved in such nonsense. The extension of the basic principle of equality from one group to another does not imply that we must treat both groups in exactly the same way, or grant exactly the same rights to both groups. Whether we should do so will depend on the nature of the members of the two groups. The basic principle of equality, I shall argue, is equality of consideration; and equal consideration for different beings may lead to different treatment and different rights.

So there is a different way of replying to Taylor's attempt to parody Wollstonecraft's arguments, a way which does not deny the differences between humans and nonhumans, but goes more deeply into the question of equality, and concludes by finding nothing absurd in the idea that the basic principle of equality applies to so-called "brutes." I believe that we reach this conclusion if we examine the basis on which our opposition to discrimination on grounds of race or sex ultimately rests. We will then see that we would be on shaky ground if we were to demand equality for blacks, women, and other grounds of oppressed humans while denying equal consideration to nonhumans.

When we say that all human beings, whatever their race, creed or sex, are equal, what is it that we are asserting? Those who wish to defend a hierarchical, inegalitarian society have often pointed out that by whatever test we choose, it simply is not true that all humans are equal. Like it or not, we must face the fact that humans come in different shapes and sizes; they come with differing moral capacities, differing intellectual abilities, differing amounts of benevolent feeling and sensitivity to the needs of others, differing abilities to communicate effectively, and differing capacities to experience pleasure and pain. In short, if the demand for equality were based on the actual equality of all human beings, we would have to stop demanding, equality. It would be an unjustifiable demand.

Still, one might cling to the view that the demand for equality among human beings is based on the actual equality of the different races and sexes. Although humans differ as individuals in various ways, there are no differences between the races and sexes *as such*. From the mere fact that a person is black, or a women, we cannot infer anything else about that person. This, it may be said, is what is wrong with racism and sexism. The white racist claims that whites are superior to blacks, but this is false—although there are differences between individuals, some blacks are superior to some whites in all of the capacities and abilities that could conceivably be relevant. The opponent of sexism would say the same: a person's sex is no guide to his or her abilities, and this is why it is unjustifiable to discriminate on the basis of sex.

This is a possible line of objection to racial and sexual discrimination. It is not, however, the way that someone really concerned about equality would choose, because taking this line could, in some circumstances, force one to accept a most inegalitarian society. The fact that humans differ as individuals, rather than as races or sexes, is a valid reply to someone who defends a hierarchical society like, say, South Africa, in which all whites are superior in status to all blacks. The existence of individual variations that cut across the lines of race or sex, however, provides us with no defence at all against a more sophisticated opponent of equality, one who proposes that, say, the interests of those with I.Q. ratings above 100 be preferred to the interests of those with I.Q.s below 100. Would a hierarchical society of this sort really be so much better than one based on race or sex? I think not. But if we tie the moral principle of equality to the factual equality of the different races or sexes, taken as a whole, our opposition to racism and sexism does not provide us with any basis for objecting to this kind of inegalitarianism.

There is a second important reason why we ought not to base our opposition to racism and sexism on any kind of factual equality, even the limited kind which asserts that variations in capacities and abilities are spread evenly between the different races and sexes: we can have no absolute guarantee that these abilities and capacities really are distributed evenly, without regard to race or sex, among human beings. So far as actual abilities are concerned, there do seem to be certain measurable differences between both races and sexes. These differences do not, of course, appear in each case, but only when averages are taken. More important still, we do not yet know how much of these differences is really due to the different genetic endowments of the various races and sexes, and how much is due to environmental differences that are the result of past and continuing discrimination. Perhaps all of the important differences will eventually prove to be environmental rather than genetic. Anyone opposed to racism and sexism will certainly hope that this will be so, for it will make the task of ending discrimination a lot easier; nevertheless it would be dangerous to rest the case against racism and sexism on the belief that all significant differences are environmental in origin. The opponent of, say, racism who takes this line will be unable to avoid conceding that if differences in ability did after all prove to have some genetic connection with race, racism would in some way be defensible.

It would be folly for the opponent of racism to stake his whole case on a dogmatic commitment to one particular outcome of a difficult scientific issue which is still a long way from being settled. While attempts to prove that differences in certain selected abilities between races and sexes are primarily genetic in origin have certainly not been conclusive, the same must be said of attempts to prove that these differences are largely the result of environment. At this stage of the investigation we cannot be certain which view is correct, however much we may hope it is the latter.

Fortunately, there is no need to pin the case for equality to one particular outcome of this scientific investigation. The appropriate response to those who claim to have found evidence of genetically-based differences in ability between the races or sexes is not to stick to the belief that the genetic explanation must be wrong, whatever evidence to the contrary may turn up: instead we should make it quite clear that the claim to equality does not depend on intelligence, moral capacity, physical strength, or similar matters of fact. Equality is a moral ideal, not a simple assertion of fact. There is no logically compelling reason for assuming that a factual difference in ability between two people justifies any difference in the amount of consideration we give to satisfying their needs and interests. The principle of the equality of human beings is not a description of an alleged actual equality among humans: it is a prescription of how we should treat humans.

Jeremy Bentham incorporated the essential basis of moral equality into his utilitarian system of ethics in the formula: "Each to count for one and none for more than one." In other words, the interests of every being affected by an action are to be taken into account and given the same weight as the like interests of any other being. A later utilitarian, Henry Sidgwick, put the point in this way: "The good of any one individual is of no more importance, from the point of view (if I may say so) of the Universe, than the good of any other."[1] More recently, the leading figures in contemporary moral philosophy have shown a great deal of agreement in specifying as a fundamental presupposition of their moral theories some similar requirement which operates so as to give everyone's interests equal consideration—although they cannot agree on how this requirement is best formulated.[2]

It is an implication of this principle of equality that our concern for others ought not to depend on what they are like, or what abilities they possess—although precisely what this concern requires us to do may vary according to the characteristics of those affected by what we do. It is on this basis that the case against racism and the case against sexism must both ultimately rest; and it is in accordance with this principle that speciesism is also to be condemned. If possessing a higher degree of intelligence does not entitle one human to use another for his own ends, how can it entitle humans to exploit nonhumans?

Many philosophers have proposed the principle of equal consideration of interests, in some form or other, as a basic moral principle; but, as we shall see in more detail shortly, not many of them have recognised that this principle applies to members of other species as well as to our own. Bentham was one of the few who did realize this. In a forward-looking passage, written at a time when black slaves in the British dominions were still being treated much as we now treat nonhuman animals, Bentham wrote:

> The day *may* come when the rest of the animal creation may acquire those rights which never could have been witholden from them but by the hand of tyranny. The French have already discovered that the blackness of the skin is no reason why a human being should be abandoned without redress to the caprice of a tormentor. It may one day come to be recognized that the number of the legs, the villosity of the skin, or the termination of the *os sacrum*, are reasons equally insufficient for abandoning a sensitive being to the same fate. What else is it that should trace the insuperable line? Is it the faculty of reason, or perhaps the faculty of discourse? But a full-grown horse or dog is beyond comparison a more rational, as well as a more conversable animal, than an infant of a day, or a week, or even a month, old. But suppose they were otherwise, what would it avail? The question is not, Can they reason? nor Can they *talk*? but, *Can they suffer*?[3]

In this passage Bentham points to the capacity for suffering as the vital characteristic that gives a being the right to equal consideration. The capacity for suffering—or more strictly, for suffering and/or enjoyment or happiness—is not just another characteristic like the capacity for language, or for higher mathematics. Bentham is not saying that those who try to mark "the insuperable line" that determines whether the interests of a being should be considered happen to have selected the wrong characteristic. The capacity for suffering and enjoying things is a pre-requisite for having interests at all, a condition that must be satisfied before we can speak of interests in any meaningful way. It would be nonsense to say that it was not in the interests of a stone to be kicked along the road by a schoolboy. A stone does not have interests because it cannot suffer. Nothing that we can do to it could possibly make any difference to its welfare. A mouse, on the other hand, does have an interest in not being tormented, because it will suffer if it is.

If a being suffers, there can be no moral justification for refusing to take that suffering into consideration. No matter what the nature of the being, the principle of equality requires that its suffering be counted equally with the like suffering—in so far as rough comparisons can be made—of any other being. If a being is not capable of suffering, or of experiencing enjoyment or happiness, there is nothing to be taken into account. This is why the limit of sentience (using the term as a convenient, if not strictly accurate, shorthand for the capacity to suffer or experience enjoyment or happiness) is the only defensible boundary of concern for the interests of others. To mark this boundary by some characteristic like intelligence or rationality would be to mark it in an arbitrary way. Why not choose some other characteristic, like skin color?

The racist violates the principle of equality by giving greater weight to the interests of members of his own race, when there is a clash between their interests and the interests of those of another race. Similarly the speciesist allows the interests of his own species to override the greater interests of members of other species.[4] The pattern is the same in each case. Most human beings are speciesists. I shall now very briefly describe some of the practices that show this.

For the great majority of human beings, especially in urban, industrialized societies, the most direct form of contact with members of other species is at meal-times: we eat them. In doing so we treat them purely as means to our ends. We regard their life and well-being as subordinate to our taste for a particular kind of dish. I say "taste" deliberately; this is purely a matter of pleasing our palate. There can be no defence of eating flesh in terms of satisfying nutritional needs, since it has been established beyond doubt that we could satisfy our need for protein and other essential nutrients far more efficiently with a diet that replaced animal flesh by soy beans, or products derived from soy beans, and other high-protein vegetable products.[5]

It is not merely the act of killing that indicates what we are ready to do to other species in order to gratify our tastes. The suffering we inflict on the animals while they are alive is perhaps an even clearer indication of our speciesism than the fact that we are prepared to kill them.[6] In order to have meat on the table at a price that people can afford, our society tolerates methods of meat production that confine sentient animals in cramped, unsuitable conditions for the entire durations of their lives. Animals are treated like machines that convert fodder into flesh, and any innovation that results in a higher "conversion ratio" is liable to be adopted. As one authority on the subject has said, "cruelty is acknowledged only when profitability ceases."[7] . . .

Since, as I have said, none of these practices cater for anything more than our pleasures of taste, our practice of rearing and killing other animals in order to eat them is a clear instance of the sacrifice of the most important interests of other beings in order to satisfy trivial interests of our own. To avoid speciesism we must stop this practice, and each of us has a moral obligation to cease supporting the practice. Our custom is all the support that the meat-industry needs. The decision to cease giving it that support may be difficult, but it is no more difficult than it would have been for a white Southerner to go against the traditions of his society and free his slaves: if we do not change our dietary habits, how can we censure those slaveholders who would not change their own way of living?

The same form of discrimination may be observed in the widespread practice of experimenting on other species in order to see if certain substances are safe for human beings, or to test some psychological theory about the effect of severe punishment on learning, or to try out various new compounds just in case something turns up. . . .

In the past, argument about vivisection has often missed this point, because it has been put in absolutist terms: Would the abolitionist be prepared to let thousands die if they could be saved by experimenting on a single animal? The way to reply to this purely hypothetical question is to pose another: Would the experimenter be prepared to perform his experiment on an orphaned human infant, if that were the only way to save many lives? (I say "orphan" to avoid the complication of parental feelings, although in doing so I am being overfair to the experimenter, since the nonhuman subjects of experiments are not orphans.) If the experimenter is not prepared to use an orphaned human infant, then his readiness to use nonhumans is simple discrimination, since adult apes, cats, mice and other mammals are more aware of what is happening to them, more self-directing and, so far as we can tell, at least as sensitive to pain, as any human infant. There seems to be no relevant characteristic that human infants possess that adult mammals do not have to the same or a higher degree. (Someone might try to argue that what makes it wrong to experiment on a human infant is that the infant will, in time and if left alone, develop into more than the nonhuman, but one would then, to be consistent, have to oppose abortion, since the fetus has the same potential as the infant—indeed, even contraception and abstinence might be wrong on this ground, since the egg and sperm, considered jointly, also have the same potential. In any case, this argument still gives us no reason for selecting a nonhuman, rather than a human with severe and irreversible brain damage, as the subject for our experiments.)

The experimenter, then, shows a bias in favor of his own species whenever he carries out an experiment on a nonhuman for a purpose that he would not think justified him in using a human being at an equal or lower level of sentience, awareness, ability to be self-directing, etc. No one familiar with the kind of results yielded by most experiments on animals can have the slightest doubt that if this bias were eliminated the number of experiments performed would be a minute fraction of the number performed today.

Experimenting on animals, and eating their flesh, are perhaps the two major forms of speciesism in our society. By comparison, the third and last form of speciesism is so minor as to be insignificant, but it is perhaps of some special interest to those for whom this article was written. I am referring to speciesism in contemporary philosophy.

Philosophy ought to question the basic assumptions of the age. Thinking through, critically and carefully, what most people take for granted is, I believe, the chief task of philosophy, and it is this task that makes philosophy a worthwhile activity. Regrettably, philosophy does not always live up to its historic role. Philosophers are human beings and they are subject to all the preconceptions of the society to which they belong. Sometimes they succeed in breaking free of the prevailing ideology: more often they become its most sophisticated defenders. So, in this case, philosophy as practiced in the universities today does not challenge anyone's preconceptions about our relations with other species. By their writings, those philosophers who tackle problems that touch upon the issue reveal that they make the same unquestioned assumptions as most other humans, and what they say tends to confirm the reader in his or her comfortable speciesist habits.

I could illustrate this claim by referring to the writings of philosophers in various fields—for instance, the attempts that have been made by those interested in rights to draw the boundary of the sphere of rights so that it runs parallel to the biological boundaries of the species *homo sapiens*, including infants and even mental defectives, but excluding those other beings of equal or greater capacity who are so useful to us at mealtimes and in our laboratories. I think it would be a more appropriate conclusion to this article, however, if I concentrated on the problem with which we have been centrally concerned, the problem of equality.

It is significant that the problem of equality, in moral and political philosophy, is invariably formulated in terms of human equality. The effects of this is that the question of the equality of other animals does not confront the philosopher, or student, as an issue itself—and this is already an indication of the failure of philosophy to challenge accepted beliefs. Still, philosophers have found it difficult to discuss the issue of human equality without raising, in a paragraph or two, the question of the status of other animals. The reason for this, which should be apparent from what I have said already, is that if humans are to be regarded as equal to one another, we need some sense of "equal" that does not require any actual, descriptive equality of capacities, talents or other qualities. If equality is to be related to any actual characteristics of humans, these characteristics must be some lowest common denominator, pitched so low that no human lacks them—but then the philosopher comes up against the catch that any such set of characteristics which covers *all* humans will not be possessed *only by humans*. In other words, it turns out that in the only sense in which we can truly say, as an assertion of fact, that all humans are equal, at least some members of other species are also equal—equal, that is, to each other and to humans. If, on the other hand, we regard the statement "All humans are equal" in some non-factual way, perhaps as a prescription, then, as I have already argued, it is even more difficult to exclude non-humans from the sphere of equality.

This result is not what the egalitarian philosopher originally intended to assert. Instead of accepting the radical outcome to which their own reasonings naturally point, however, most philosophers try to reconcile their beliefs in human equality and animal inequality by arguments that can only be described as devious.

As a first example, I take William Frankena's well-known article "The Concept of Social Justice." Frankena opposes the idea of basing justice on merit, because he sees that this could lead to highly inegalitarian results. Instead he proposes the principle that

> . . . all men are to be treated as equals, not because they are equal, in any respect, but simply because they are human. They are human because they have emotions and desires, and are able to think, and hence are capable of enjoying a good life in a sense in which other animals are not.[8]

But what is this capacity to enjoy the good life which all humans have, but no other animals? Other animals have emotions and desires, and appear to be capable of enjoying a good life. We may doubt that they can think—although the behavior of some apes, dolphins and even dogs suggests that some of them can—but what is the relevance of thinking? Frankena goes on to admit that by "the good life" he means "not so much the morally good life as the happy or satisfactory life," so thought would appear to be unnecessary for enjoying the good life; in fact to emphasise the need for thought would make difficulties for the egalitarian since only some people are capable of leading intellectually satisfying lives, or morally good lives. This makes it difficult to see what Frankena's principle of equality has to do with simply being *human*. Surely every sentient being is capable of leading a life that is happier or less miserable than some alternative life, and hence has a claim to be taken into account. In this respect the distinction between humans and nonhumans is not a sharp division, but rather a continuum along which we move gradually, and with overlaps between the species, from simple capacities for enjoyment and satisfaction, or pain and suffering, to more complex ones.

Faced with a situation in which they see a need for some basis for the moral gulf that is commonly thought to separate humans and animals but can find no concrete difference that will do the job without undermining the equality of humans, philosophers tend to waffle. They resort to high-sounding phrases like "the intrinsic dignity of the human individual";[9] They talk of the "intrinsic worth of all men" as if men (humans?) had some worth that other beings did not.[10] or they say that humans, and only humans, are "ends in themselves," while "everything other than a person can only have value for a person."[11]

This idea of a distinctive human dignity and worth has a long history; it can be traced back directly to the Renaissance humanists, for instance, to Pico della Mirandola's *Oration on the Dignity of Man*. Pico and other humanists based their estimate of human dignity on the idea that man possessed the central, pivotal position in the "Great Chain of Being" that led from the lowliest forms of matter to God himself; this view of the universe, in turn, goes back to both classical and Judeo-Christian doctrines. Contemporary philosophers have cast off these metaphysical and religious shackles and freely invoke the dignity of mankind without needing to justify the idea at all. Why should we not attribute "intrinsic dignity" or "intrinsic worth" to ourselves? Fellow humans are unlikely to reject the accolades we so generously bestow on them, and those to whom we deny the honor are unable to object. Indeed, when one thinks only of humans, it can be very liberal, very progressive, to talk of the dignity of all human beings. In so doing, we implicitly condemn slavery, racism, and other violations of human rights. We admit that we ourselves are in some fundamental sense on a par with the poorest, most ignorant members of our own species. It is only when we think of humans as no more than a small sub-group of all the beings that inhabit our planet that we may realize that in elevating our own species we are at the same time lowering the relative status of all other species.

The truth is that the appeal to the intrinsic dignity of human beings appears to solve the egalitarian's problems only as long as it goes unchallenged. Once we ask *why* it should be that all humans—including infants, mental defectives, psychopaths, Hitler, Stalin and the rest—have some kind of dignity or worth that no elephant, pig, or chimpanzee can ever achieve, we see that this question is as difficult to answer as our original request for some relevant fact that justifies the inequality of humans and other animals. In fact, these two questions are really one: talk of intrinsic dignity or moral worth only takes the problem back one step, because any satisfactory defence of the claim that all and only humans have intrinsic dignity would need to refer to some relevant capacities or characteristics that all and only humans possess. Philosophers frequently introduce ideas of dignity, respect and worth at the point at which other reasons appear to be lacking, but this is hardly good enough. Fine phrases are the last resource of those who have run out of arguments.

In case there are those who still think it may be possible to find some relevant characteristic that distinguishes all humans from all members of other species, I shall refer again, before I conclude, to the existence of some humans who quite clearly are below the level of awareness, self-consciousness, intelligence, and sentience, of many non-humans. I am thinking of humans with severe and irreparable brain damage, and also of infant humans. To avoid the complication of the relevance of a being's potential, however, I shall henceforth concentrate on permanently retarded humans.

Philosophers who set out to find a characteristic that will distinguish humans from other animals rarely take the course of abandoning these groups of humans by lumping them in and with the other animals. It is easy to see why they do not. To take this line without re-thinking our attitudes to other animals would entail that we have the right to perform painful experiments on retarded humans for trivial reasons; similarly it would follow that we had the right to rear and kill these humans for food. To most philosophers these consequences are as unacceptable as the view that we should stop treating nonhumans in this way.

Of course, when discussing the problem of equality it is possible to ignore the problem of mental defectives, or brush it aside as if somehow insignificant.[12] This is the easiest way out. What else remains? My final example of speciesism in contemporary philosophy has been selected to show what happens when a writer is prepared to face the question of human equality and animal inequality without ignoring the existence of mental defectives, and without resorting to obscurantist mumbo-jumbo. Stanley Benn's clear and honest article "Egalitarianism and Equal Consideration of Interests"[13] fits this description.

Benn, after noting the usual "evident human inequalities" argues, correctly I think, for equality of consideration as the only possible basis for egalitarianism. Yet Benn, like other writers, is thinking only of "equal consideration of human interests." Benn is quite open in his defence of this restriction of equal consideration:

> . . . not to possess human shape is a disqualifying condition. However faithful or intelligent a dog may be, it would be a monstrous sentimentality to attribute to him interests that could be weighed in an equal balance with those of human beings . . . if, for instance, one had to decide

between feeding a hungry baby or a hungry dog, anyone who chose the dog would generally be reckoned morally defective, unable to recognize a fundamental inequality of claims.

This is what distinguishes our attitude to animals from our attitude to imbeciles. It would be odd to say that we ought to respect equally the dignity or personality of the imbecile and of the rational man . . . but there is nothing odd about saying that we should respect their interests equally, that is, that we should give to the interests of each the same serious consideration as claims to considerations necessary for some standard of well-being that we can recognize and endorse.

Benn's statement of the basis of the consideration we should have for imbeciles seems to me correct, but why should there be any fundamental inequality of claims between a dog and a human imbecile? Benn sees that if equal consideration depended on rationality, no reason could be given against using imbeciles for research purposes, as we now use dogs and guinea pigs. This will not do: "But of course we do distinguish imbeciles from animals in this regard," he says. That the common distinction is justifiable is something Benn does not question; his problem is how it is to be justified. The answer he gives is this:

. . . we respect the interests of men and give them priority over dogs not *insofar* as they are rational, but because rationality is the human norm. We say it is *unfair* to exploit the deficiencies of the imbecile who falls short of the norm, just as it would be unfair, and not just ordinarily dishonest, to steal from a blind man. If we do not think in this way about dogs, it is because we do not see the irrationality of the dog as a deficiency or a handicap, but as normal for the species. The characteristics, therefore, that distinguish the normal man from the normal dog make it intelligible for us to talk of other men having interests and capacities, and therefore claims, of precisely the same kind as we make on our own behalf. But although these characteristics may provide the point of the distinction between men and other species, they are not in fact the qualifying conditions for membership, or the distinguishing criteria of the class of morally considerable persons; and this is precisely because a man does not become a member of a different species, with its own standards of normality, by reason of not possessing these characteristics.

The final sentence of this passage gives the argument away. An imbecile, Benn concedes, may have no characteristics superior to those of a dog; nevertheless this does not make the imbecile a member of "a different species" as the dog is. *Therefore* it would be "unfair" to use the imbecile for medical research as we use the dog. But why? That the imbecile is not rational is just the way things have worked out, and the same is true of the dog—neither is any more responsible for their mental level. If it is unfair to take advantage of an isolated defect, why is it fair to take advantage of a more general limitation? I find it hard to see anything in this argument except a defence of preferring the interests of members of our own species because they are members of our own species. To those who think there might be more to it, I suggest the following mental exercise. Assume that it has been proven that there is a difference in the average, or normal, intelligence quotient for two different races, say whites and blacks. Then substitute the term "white" for every occurrence of "men" and "black" for every occurrence of "dog" in the passage quoted; and substitute "high I.Q." for "rationality" and when Benn talks of "imbeciles" replace this term by "dumb whites"—that is, whites who fall well below the normal white I.Q. score. Finally, change "species" to "race." Now re-read the passage. It has become a defence of a rigid, no-exceptions division between whites and blacks, based on I.Q. scores, *not withstanding an admitted overlap* between whites and blacks in this respect. The revised passage is, of course, outrageous, and this is not only because we have made fictitious assumptions in our substitutions. The point is that in the original passage Benn was defending a rigid division in the amount of consideration due to members of different species, despite admitted cases of overlap. If the original did not, at first reading strike us as being as outrageous as the revised version does, this is largely because although we are not racists ourselves, most of us are speciesists. Like the other articles, Benn's stands as a warning of the ease with which the best minds can fall victim to a prevailing ideology.

NOTES

1. *The Methods of Ethics* (7th Ed.), p. 382.
2. For example, R. M. Hare, *Freedom and Reason* (Oxford, 1963) and J. Rawls, *A Theory of Justice* (Harvard, 1972); for a brief account of the essential agreement on this issue between these and other positions, see R. M. Hare, "Rules of War and Moral Reasoning." *Philosophy and Public Affairs,* vol. 1. no. 2 (1972).
3. *Introduction to the Principles of Morals and Legislation,* ch. XVII.
4. I owe the term "speciesism" to Richard Ryder.
5. In order to produce 1 lb. of protein in the form of beef or veal, we must feed 21 lbs. of protein to the animal. Other forms of livestock are slightly less inefficient, but the average ratio in the U.S. is still 1:8. It has been estimated that the amount of protein lost to humans in this way is equivalent to 90% of the annual world protein deficit. For a brief account, see Frances Moore Lappé, *Diet for a Small Planet* (Friends of The Earth/Ballantine, New York 1971), pp. 4–11.
6. Although one might think that killing a being is obviously the ultimate wrong one can do it, I think that the infliction of suffering is a clearer indication of speciesism because it might be argued that at least part of what is wrong with killing a human is that most humans are conscious of their existence over time, and have desires and purposes that extend into the future—see, for instance, M. Tooley, "Abortion and Infanticide," *Philosophy and Public Affairs,* vol. 2, no. 1 (1972). Of course, if one took this view one would have to hold—as Tooley does—that killing a human infant or mental defective is not in itself wrong, and is less serious than killing certain higher mammals that probably do have a sense of their own existence over time.
7. Ruth Harrison, *Animal Machines* (Stuart, London, 1964).
8. In R. Brandt (ed.) *Social Justice* (Prentice-Hall, Englewood Cliffs, 1962), p. 19.
9. Frankena, *op. cit.,* p. 23.
10. H. A. Bedau, "Egalitarianism and the Idea of Equality" in *Nomos IX: Equality.* cd. J. R. Pennock and J. W. Chapman, New York, 1967.
11. G. Vlastos, "Justice and Equality" in Brandt, *Social Justice,* p. 48.
12. For example, Bernard Williams, "The Idea of Equality," in *Philosophy, Politics and Society* (second series), ed. P. Laslett and W. Runciman (Blackwell, Oxford, 1962), p. 118; J. Rawls, *A Theory of Justice,* pp. 509–510.
13. *Nomos IX: Equality;* the passages quoted are on p. 62ff.

PART NINE

"GREEN" POLITICS: ECOLOGY AS IDEOLOGY

Few can doubt that the world of the late twentieth century is beset by an ecological crisis of unprecedented proportions. The killing of forests and lakes by acid rain; the depletion of the earth's protective ozone layer; the pollution of our air and water; radioactive fallout from nuclear power plants; the destruction of tropical rain forests; the death of birds, fish, and mammals from oil spills; the rapid extinction of hundreds of species—these and many other events are all part of that interconnected series of crises that is often spoken of as a single "environmental" crisis. This crisis can be traced, in large part, to the rise and rapid proliferation of particular technologies, such as the internal combustion engine and the nuclear reactor. But the environmental crisis can also be traced to *ideologies*—that is, to widely shared and still prevalent ideas and beliefs about our relation to nature and to other species.

The ecology or "green" movement is a relatively recent arrival on the political scene. And, like other political movements, it has its own ideology—or, as many Greens prefer to say, an "ethic." This ideology or ethic—which is, as yet, not fully formed—is critical of other mainstream ideologies, right and left alike. Liberalism, Marxism, and modern conservatism are alike, the Greens say, in picturing human beings as "masters" or "conquerors" of nature, which in turn is viewed as being without intrinsic value or worth. An alternative "green" ideology invites us to see ourselves as members of a species that exists in, and because of, nature. Nature nurtures us and our fellow species. We are all part of a wonderfully intricate and complex web of life. To the degree that we are greedy and selfish, to the extent that we are ignorant and heedless of our proper place in nature, we endanger this delicate web. Yet this is precisely what we humans have done. And, unless we change our ways—and our basic beliefs—very soon, we and our children and grandchildren will pay a heavy price.

Quite obviously, then, the "green" movement and its ideology raise deep and difficult questions about what it means to be a human being and how humans are related to nature, to other species, and to future generations. Difficult as these questions are, however, we will have to ask and attempt to answer them aright if our species and others are to survive and flourish. But where might the answers be found? Some Greens say that the answers are to be found in the life sciences, such as biology, ethology, and ecology. Others say that the answers are to be found in philosophy or religion—in the meditations of Dr. Albert Schweitzer and Mahatma Gandhi, for example—or perhaps in the ideas and practices of supposedly "primitive" peoples such as our own Native American forebears. Still others claim that we must invent an entirely new religion or perhaps a "planetary ethic" with a respect for the earth and all life at its core. But whatever the source, say the Greens, the answers cannot be found in older ideologies, for they do not even pose the questions in the first place. Hence the need for an alternative ideology or ethic.

Although it is too early to say precisely what a "green" ideology would look like, several fundamental features are already quite clear. The first and most important of these is that all things are connected. Every species, including our own, lives in interdependent relations with every other species, and with the environment that sustains us all. From this a second feature follows: All life, and the environment that sustains it, is intrinsically valuable and therefore deserving of recognition, respect, and protection. A third feature is the recognition that all human actions, however small or seemingly insignificant, have consequences for the biosphere. A fourth feature of an emerging "green" ideology is its emphasis on individual or personal, as well as political or collective, responsibility. The slogan, "Think globally and act locally," succinctly summarizes this view. From this follows a fifth feature—a "green" conception of democracy as a decentralized, "grass-roots" form of self-rule that maximizes the opportunity for individual participation and personal responsibility at the local level.

Most Greens would probably agree that these five features form the core of their environmental ethic or ideology. But, despite a fairly widespread agreement about fundamental principles and ends, Greens are apt to disagree about the means for achieving those ends. Some say that the "green" movement should act as an interest group within the present political system; others say that the system is in need of a fundamental transformation. Some Greens favor low-key, subtle strategies for educating and informing the public; others opt for highly visible campaigns of protest and acts of civil disobedience; and more radical environmentalists favor acts of "eco-terrorism" or "monkey-wrenching" to stop polluters, developers, dumpers of toxic wastes, and others from despoiling the environment.

But whatever their differences regarding strategy, most Greens are in broad agreement regarding ends. Theirs is a voice that we shall hear more often, and more loudly, as this century ends and another begins.

50

THE LAND ETHIC

ALDO LEOPOLD

One of the fathers of the modern environmental movement, the ecologist Aldo Leopold (1886–1948), brought a broad scientific training to his inquiries into our attitudes toward nature and its myriad creatures. His *A Sand County Almanac* (1949) combines observations on wildlife and human life and the way in which the two are irrevocably intertwined. If humans and other species are to survive and flourish, he believed, we will have to develop a more acute awareness of our interdependence with other species and the habitat that sustains us all.

THE LAND ETHIC

When god-like Odysseus returned from the wars in Troy, he hanged all on one rope a dozen slave-girls of his household whom he suspected of misbehavior during his absence.

This hanging involved no question of propriety. The girls were property. The disposal of property was then, as now, a matter of expediency, not of right and wrong.

Concepts of right and wrong were not lacking from Odysseus's Greece: witness the fidelity of his wife through the long years before at last his black-prowed galleys clove the wine-dark seas for home. The ethical structure of that day covered wives, but had not yet been extended to human chattels. During the three thousand years which have since elapsed, ethical criteria have been extended to many fields of conduct, with corresponding shrinkages in those judged by expediency only.

THE ETHICAL SEQUENCE

This extension of ethics, so far studied only by philosophers, is actually a process in ecological evolution. Its sequences may be described in ecological as well as in philosophical terms. An ethic, ecologically, is a limitation on freedom of action in the struggle for existence. An ethic, philosophically, is a differentiation of social from anti-social conduct. These are two definitions of one thing. The thing has its origin in the tendency of interdependent individuals or groups to evolve modes of co-operation. The ecologist calls these symbioses. Politics and economics are advanced symbioses in which the original free-for-all competition has been replaced, in part, by co-operative mechanisms with an ethical content.

The complexity of co-operative mechanisms has increased with population density, and with the efficiency of tools. It was simpler, for example, to define the anti-social uses of sticks and stones in the days of the mastodons than of bullets and billboards in the age of motors.

The first ethics dealt with the relation between individuals; the Mosaic Decalogue is an example. Later accretions dealt with the relation between the individual and society. The Golden Rule tries to integrate the individual to society; democracy to integrate social organization to the individual.

There is as yet no ethic dealing with man's relation to land and to the animals and plants which grow upon it. Land, like Odysseus' slave-girls, is still property. The land-relation is still strictly economic, entailing privileges but not obligations.

The extension of ethics to this third element in human environment is, if I read the evidence correctly, an evolutionary possibility and an ecological necessity. It is the third step in a sequence. The first two have already been taken. Individual thinkers since the days of Ezekiel and Isaiah have asserted that the despoliation of land is not only inexpedient but wrong. Society, however, has not yet affirmed their belief. I regard the present conservation movement as the embryo of such an affirmation.

An ethic may be regarded as a mode of guidance for meeting ecological situations so new or intricate, or involving such deferred reactions, that the path of social expediency is not discernible to the average individual. Animal instincts are modes of guidance for the individual in meeting such situations. Ethics are possibly a kind of community instinct in-the-making.

THE COMMUNITY CONCEPT

All ethics so far evolved rest upon a single premise: that the individual is a member of a community of interdependent parts. His instincts prompt him to compete for his place in that community, but his ethics prompt him also to co-operate (perhaps in order that there may be a place to compete for).

The land ethic simply enlarges the boundaries of the community to include soils, waters, plants, and animals, or collectively, the land.

This sounds simple: do we not already sing our love for and obligation to the land of the free and the home of the brave? Yes, but just what and whom do we love? Certainly not the soil, which we are sending helter-skelter downriver.

Certainly not the waters, which we assume have no function except to turn turbines, float barges, and carry off sewage. Certainly not the plants, of which we exterminate whole communities without batting an eye. Certainly not the animals, of which we have already extirpated many of the largest and most beautiful species. A land ethic of course cannot prevent the alteration, management, and use of these "resources," but it does affirm their right to continued existence, and, at least in spots, their continued existence in a natural state.

In short, a land ethic changes the role of *Homo sapiens* from conqueror of the land-community to plain member and citizen of it. It implies respect for his fellow-members, and also respect for the community as such.

In human history, we have learned (I hope) that the conqueror role is eventually self-defeating. Why? Because it is implicit in such a role that the conqueror knows, *ex cathedra*, just what makes the community clock tick, and just what and who is valuable, and what and who is worthless, in community life. It always turns out that he knows neither, and this is why his conquests eventually defeat themselves.

In the biotic community, a parallel situation exists. Abraham knew exactly what the land was for: it was to drip milk and honey into Abraham's mouth. At the present moment, the assurance with which we regard this assumption is inverse to the degree of our education.

The ordinary citizen today assumes that science knows what makes the community clock tick; the scientist is equally sure that he does not. He knows that the biotic mechanism is so complex that its workings may never be fully understood.

That man is, in fact, only a member of a biotic team is shown by an ecological interpretation of history. Many historical events, hitherto explained solely in terms of human enterprise, were actually biotic interactions between people and land. The characteristics of the land determined the facts quite as potently as the characteristics of the men who lived on it.

Consider, for example, the settlement of the Mississippi valley. In the years following the Revolution, three groups were contending for its control: the native Indian, the French and English traders, and the American settlers. Historians wonder what would have happened if the English at Detroit had thrown a little more weight into the Indian side of those tipsy scales which decided the outcome of the colonial migration into the cane-lands of Kentucky. It is time now to ponder the fact that the cane-lands, when subjected to the particular mixture of forces represented by the cow, plow, fire, and axe of the pioneer, became bluegrass. What if the plant succession inherent in this dark and bloody ground had, under the impact of these forces, given us some worthless sedge, shrub, or weed? Would Boone and Kenton have held out? Would there have been any overflow into Ohio, Indiana, Illinois, and Missouri? Any Louisiana Purchase? Any transcontinental union of new states? Any Civil War?

Kentucky was one sentence in the drama of history. We are commonly told what the human actors in this drama tried to do, but we are seldom told that their success, or the lack of it, hung in large degree on the reaction of particular soils to the impact of the particular forces exerted by their occupancy. In the case of Kentucky, we do not even know where the bluegrass came from—whether it is a native species, or a stowaway from Europe.

Contrast the cane-lands with what hindsight tells us about the Southwest, where the pioneers were equally brave, resourceful, and persevering. The impact of occupancy here brought no bluegrass, or other plant fitted to withstand the bumps and buffetings of hard use. This region, when grazed by livestock, reverted through a series of more and more worthless grasses, shrubs, and weeds to a condition of unstable equilibrium. Each recession of plant types bred erosion; each increment to erosion bred a further recession of plants. The result today is a progressive and mutual deterioration, not only of plants and soils, but of the animal community subsisting thereon. The early settlers did not expect this: on the ciénegas of New Mexico some even cut ditches to hasten it. So subtle has been its progress that few residents of the region are aware of it. It is quite invisible to the tourist who finds this wrecked landscape colorful and charming (as indeed it is, but it bears scant resemblance to what it was in 1848).

This same landscape was "developed" once before, but with quite different results. The Pueblo Indians settled the Southwest in pre-Columbian times, but they happened *not* to be equipped with range livestock. Their civilization expired, but not because their land expired.

In India, regions devoid of any sod-forming grass have been settled, apparently without wrecking the land, by the simple expedient of carrying the grass to the cow, rather than vice versa. (Was this the result of some deep wisdom, or was it just good luck? I do not know.)

In short, the plant succession steered the course of history; the pioneer simply demonstrated, for good or ill, what successions inhered in the land. Is history taught in this spirit? It will be, once the concept of land as a community really penetrates our intellectual life.

THE ECOLOGICAL CONSCIENCE

Conservation is a state of harmony between men and land. Despite nearly a century of propaganda, conservation still proceeds at a snail's pace; progress still consists largely of letterhead pieties and convention oratory. On the back forty we still slip two steps backward for each forward stride.

The usual answer to this dilemma is "more conservation education." No one will debate this, but is it certain that only the *volume* of education needs stepping up? Is something lacking in the *content* as well?

It is difficult to give a fair summary of its content in brief form, but, as I understand it, the content is substantially this: obey the law, vote right, join some organizations, and practice what conservation is profitable on your own land; the government will do the rest.

Is not this formula too easy to accomplish anything worthwhile? It defines no right or wrong, assigns no obligation, calls for no sacrifice, implies no change in the current philosophy of values. In respect to land-use, it urges only enlightened self-interest. Just how far will such education take us? An example will perhaps yield a partial answer.

By 1930 it had become clear to all except the ecologically blind that southwestern Wisconsin's topsoil was slipping seaward. In 1933 the farmers were told that if they would adopt certain remedial practices for five years, the public would donate CCC labor to install them, plus the necessary machinery and materials. The offer was widely accepted, but the practices were widely forgotten when the five-year contract period was up. The farmers continued only those practices that yielded an immediate and visible economic gain for themselves.

This led to the idea that maybe farmers would learn more quickly if they themselves wrote the rules. Accordingly the Wisconsin Legislature in 1937 passed the Soil Conservation District Law. This said to farmers, in effect: *We, the public, will furnish you free technical service and loan you specialized machinery, if you will write your own rules for land-use. Each county may write its own rules, and these will have the force of law.* Nearly all the counties promptly organized to accept the proffered help, but after a decade of operation, *no county has yet written a single rule.* There has been visible progress in such practices as strip-cropping, pasture renovation, and soil liming, but none in fencing woodlots against grazing, and none in excluding plow and cow from steep slopes. The farmers, in short, have selected those remedial practices which were profitable anyhow, and ignored those which were profitable to the community, but not clearly profitable to themselves.

When one asks why no rules have been written, one is told that the community is not yet ready to support them; education must precede rules. But the education actually in progress makes no mention of obligations to land over and above those dictated by self-interest. The net result is that we have more education but less soil, fewer healthy woods, and as many floods as in 1937.

The puzzling aspect of such situations is that the existence of obligations over and above self-interest is taken for granted in such rural community enterprises as the betterment of roads, schools, churches, and baseball teams. Their existence is not taken for granted, nor as yet seriously discussed, in bettering the behavior of the water that falls on the land, or in the preserving of the beauty or diversity of the farm landscape. Land-use ethics are still governed wholly by economic self-interest, just as social ethics were a century ago.

To sum up: we asked the farmer to do what he conveniently could to save his soil, and he has done just that, and only that. The farmer who clears the woods off a 75 per cent slope, turns his cows into the clearing, and dumps its rainfall, rocks, and soil into the community creek, is still (if otherwise decent) a respected member of society. If he puts lime on his fields and plants his crops on contour, he is still entitled to all the privileges and emoluments of his Soil Conservation District. The District is a beautiful piece of social machinery, but it is coughing along on two cylinders because we have been too timid, and too anxious for quick success, to tell the farmer the true magnitude of his obligations. Obligations have no meaning without conscience, and the problem we face is the extension of the social conscience from people to land.

No important change in ethics was ever accomplished without an internal change in our intellectual emphasis, loyalties, affections, and convictions. The proof that conservation has not yet touched these foundations of conduct lies in the fact that philosophy and religion have not yet heard of it. In our attempt to make conservation easy, we have made it trivial.

SUBSTITUTES FOR A LAND ETHIC

When the logic of history hungers for bread and we hand out a stone, we are at pains to explain how much the stone resembles bread. I now describe some of the stones which serve in lieu of a land ethic.

One basic weakness in a conservation system based wholly on economic motives is that most members of the land community have no economic value. Wildflowers and songbirds are examples. Of the 22,000 higher plants and animals native to Wisconsin, it is doubtful whether more than 5 per cent can be sold, fed, eaten, or otherwise put to economic use. Yet these creatures are members of the biotic community, and if (as I believe) its stability depends on its integrity, they are entitled to continuance.

When one of these non-economic categories is threatened, and if we happen to love it, we invent subterfuges to give it economic importance. At the beginning of the century songbirds were supposed to be disappearing. Ornithologists jumped to the rescue with some distinctly shaky evidence to the effect that insects would eat us up if birds failed to control them. The evidence had to be economic in order to be valid.

It is painful to read these circumlocutions today. We have no land ethic yet, but we have at least drawn nearer the point of admitting that birds should continue as a matter of biotic right, regardless of the presence or absence of economic advantage to us.

A parallel situation exists in respect of predatory mammals, raptorial birds, and fish-eating birds. Time was when biologists somewhat overworked the evidence that these creatures preserve the health of game by killing weaklings, or that they control rodents for the farmer, or that they prey only on "worthless" species. Here again, the evidence had to be economic in order to be valid. It is only in recent years that we hear the more honest argument that predators are members of the community, and that no special interest has the right to exterminate them for the sake of a benefit, real or fancied, to itself. Unfortunately this enlightened view is still in the talk stage. In the field the extermination of predators goes merrily on: witness the impending erasure of the timber wolf by fiat of Congress, the Conservation Bureaus, and many state legislatures.

Some species of trees have been "read out of the party" by economics-minded foresters because they grow too slowly, or have too low a sale value to pay as timber crops: white cedar, tamarack, cypress, beech, and hemlock are examples. In Europe, where forestry is ecologically more advanced, the non-commercial tree species are recognized as members of the native forest community, to be preserved as such, within reason. Moreover, some (like beech) have been found to have a valuable function in building up soil fertility. The interdependence of the forest and its constituent tree species, ground flora, and fauna is taken for granted.

Lack of economic value is sometimes a character not only of species or groups, but of entire biotic communities: marshes, bogs, dunes, and "deserts" are examples. Our formula in such cases is to relegate their conservation to government as refuges, monuments, or parks. The difficulty is that these communities are usually interspersed with more valuable private lands; the government cannot possibly own or control such scattered parcels. The net effect is that we have relegated some of them to ultimate extinction over large areas. If the private owner were ecologically minded, he would be proud to be the custodian of a reasonable proportion of such areas, which add diversity and beauty to his farm and to his community.

In some instances, the assumed lack of profit in these "waste" areas has proved to be wrong, but only after most of them had been done away with. The present scramble to reflood muskrat marshes is a case in point.

There is a clear tendency in American conservation to relegate to government all necessary jobs that private landowners fail to perform. Government ownership, operation, subsidy, or regulation is now widely prevalent in forestry, range management, soil and watershed management, park and wilderness conservation, fisheries management, and migratory bird management, with more to come. Most of this growth in governmental conservation is proper and logical, some of it is inevitable. That I imply no disapproval of it is implicit in the fact that I have spent most of my life working for it. Nevertheless the question arises: What is the ultimate magnitude of the enterprise? Will the tax base carry its eventual ramifications? At what point will governmental conservation, like the mastodon, become handicapped by its own dimensions? The answer, if there is any, seems to be in a land ethic, or some other force which assigns more obligation to the private landowner.

Industrial landowners and users, especially lumbermen and stockmen, are inclined to wail long and loudly about the extension of government ownership and regulation to land, but (with notable exceptions) they show little disposition to develop the only visible alternative: the voluntary practice of conservation on their own lands.

When the private landowner is asked to perform some unprofitable act for the good of the community, he today assents only with outstretched palm. If the act costs him cash this is fair and proper, but when it costs only forethought, open-mindedness, or time, the issue is at least debatable. The overwhelming growth of land-use subsides in recent years must be ascribed, in large part, to the government's own agencies for conservation education: the land bureaus, the agricultural colleges, and the extension services. As far as I can detect, no ethical obligation toward land is taught in these institutions.

To sum up: a system of conservation based solely on economic self-interest is hopelessly lopsided. It tends to ignore, and thus eventually to eliminate, many elements in the land community that lack commercial value, but that are (as far as we know) essential to its healthy functioning. It assumes, falsely, I think, that the economic parts of the biotic clock will function without the uneconomic parts. It tends to relegate to government many functions eventually too large, too complex, or too widely dispersed to be performed by government.

An ethical obligation on the part of the private owner is the only visible remedy for these situations.

THE LAND PYRAMID

An ethic to supplement and guide the economic relation to land presupposes the existence of some mental image of land as a biotic mechanism. We can be ethical only in relation to something we can see, feel, understand, love, or otherwise have faith in.

The image commonly employed in conservation education is "the balance of nature." For reasons too lengthy to detail here, this figure of speech fails to describe accurately what little we know about the land mechanism. A much truer image is the one employed in ecology: the biotic pyramid. I shall first sketch the pyramid as a symbol of land, and later develop some of its implications in terms of land-use.

Plants absorb energy from the sun. This energy flows through a circuit called the biota, which may be represented by a pyramid consisting of layers. The bottom layer is the soil. A plant layer rests on the soil, an insect layer on the plants, a bird and rodent layer on the insects, and so on up through various animal groups to the apex layer, which consists of the larger carnivores.

The species of a layer are alike not in where they came from, or in what they look like, but rather in what they eat. Each successive layer depends on those below it for food and often for other services, and each in turn furnishes food and services to those above. Proceeding upward, each successive layer decreases in numerical abundance. Thus, for every carnivore there are hundreds of his prey, thousands of their prey, millions of insects, uncountable plants. The pyramidal form of the system reflects this numerical progression from apex to base. Man shares an intermediate layer with the bears, raccoons, and squirrels which eat both meat and vegetables.

The lines of dependency for food and other services are called food chains. Thus soil-oak-deer-Indian is a chain that has now been largely converted to soil-corn-cow-farmer. Each species, including ourselves, is a link in many chains. The deer eats a hundred plants other than oak, and the cow a hundred plants other than corn. Both, then, are links in a hundred chains. The pyramid is a tangle of chains so complex as to seem disorderly, yet the stability of the system proves it to be a highly organized structure. Its functioning depends on the co-operation and competition of its diverse parts.

In the beginning, the pyramid of life was low and squat, the food chains short and simple. Evolution has added layer after layer, link after link. Man is one of thousands of accretions to the height and complexity of the pyramid. Science has given us many doubts, but it has given us at least one certainty: the trend of evolution is to elaborate and diversify the biota.

Land, then, is not merely soil; it is a fountain of energy flowing through a circuit of soils, plants, and animals. Food chains are the living channels which conduct energy upward; death and decay return it to the soil. The circuit is not closed; some energy is dissipated in decay, some is added by absorption from the air, some is stored in soils, peats, and long-lived forests; but it is a sustained circuit, like a slowly augmented revolving fund of life. There is always a net loss by downhill wash, but this is normally small and offset by the decay of rocks. It is deposited in the ocean and, in the course of geological time, raised to form new lands and new pyramids.

The velocity and character of the upward flow of energy depend on the complex structure of the plant and animal community, much as the upward flow of sap in a tree depends on its complex cellular organization. Without this complexity, normal circulation would presumably not occur. Structure means the characteristic numbers, as well as the characteristic kinds and functions, of the component species. This interdependence between the complex structure of the land and its smooth functioning as an energy unit is one of its basic attributes.

When a change occurs in one part of the circuit, many other parts must adjust themselves to it. Change does not necessarily obstruct or divert the flow of energy; evolution is a long series of self-induced changes, the net result of which has been to elaborate the flow mechanism and to lengthen the circuit. Evolutionary changes, however, are usually slow and local. Man's invention of tools has enabled him to make changes of unprecedented violence, rapidity, and scope.

One change is in the composition of floras and faunas. The larger predators are lopped off the apex of the pyramid; food chains, for the first time in history, become shorter rather than longer. Domesticated species from other lands are substituted for wild ones, and wild ones are moved to new habitats. In this world-wide pooling of faunas and floras, some species get out of bounds as pests and diseases; others are extinguished. Such effects are seldom intended or foreseen; they represent unpredicted and often untraceable readjustments in the structure. Agricultural science is largely a race between the emergence of new pests and the emergence of new techniques for their control.

Another change touches the flow of energy through plants and animals and its return to the soil. Fertility is the ability of soil to receive, store, and release energy. Agriculture, by overdrafts on the soil, or by too radical a substitution of domestic for native species in the superstructure, may derange the channels of flow or deplete storage. Soils depleted of their storage, or of the organic matter which anchors it, wash away faster than they form. This is erosion.

Waters, like soil, are part of the energy circuit. Industry, by polluting waters or obstructing them with dams, may exclude the plants and animals necessary to keep energy in circulation.

Transportation brings another basic change: the plants or animals grown in one region are now consumed and returned to the soil in another. Transportation taps the energy stored in rocks, and in the air, and uses it elsewhere; thus we fertilize the garden with nitrogen gleaned by the guano birds from the fishes of seas on the other side of the Equator. Thus the formerly localized and self-contained circuits are pooled on a world-wide scale.

The process of altering the pyramid for human occupation releases stored energy, and this often gives rise, during the pioneering period, to a deceptive exuberance of plant and animal life, both wild and tame. These releases of biotic capital tend to becloud or postpone the penalties of violence. . . .

This thumbnail sketch of land as an energy circuit conveys three basic ideas:

1. That land is not merely soil.
2. That the native plants and animals kept the energy circuit open; others may or may not.
3. That man-made changes are of a different order than evolutionary changes, and have effects more comprehensive than is intended or foreseen.

These ideas, collectively, raise two basic issues: Can the land adjust itself to the new order? Can the desired alterations be accomplished with less violence?

Biotas seem to differ in their capacity to sustain violent conversion. Western Europe, for example, carries a far different pyramid than Caesar found there. Some large animals are lost; swampy forests have become meadows or plowland; many new plants and animals are introduced, some of which escape as pests; the remaining natives are greatly changed in distribution and abundance. Yet the soil is still there and, with the help of imported nutrients, still fertile; the waters flow normally; the new structure seems to function and to persist. There is no visible stoppage or derangement of the circuit.

Western Europe, then, has a resistant biota. Its inner processes are tough, elastic, resistant to strain. No matter how violent the alterations, the pyramid, so far, has developed some new *modus vivendi* which preserves its habitability for man, and for most of the other natives.

Japan seems to present another instance of radical conversion without disorganization.

Most other civilized regions, and some as yet barely touched by civilization, display various stages of disorganization, varying from initial symptoms to advanced wastage. In Asia Minor and North Africa diagnosis is confused by climatic changes, which may have been either the cause or the effect of advanced wastage. In the United States the degree of disorganization varies locally; it is worst in the Southwest, the Ozarks, and parts of the South, and least in New England and the Northwest. Better land-uses may still arrest it in the less advanced regions.

In parts of Mexico, South America, South Africa, and Australia a violent and accelerating wastage is in progress, but I cannot assess the prospects.

This almost world-wide display of disorganization in the land seems to be similar to disease in an animal, except that it never culminates in complete disorganization or death. The land recovers, but at some reduced level of complexity, and with a reduced carrying capacity for people, plants, and animals. Many biotas currently regarded as "lands of opportunity" are in fact already subsisting on exploitative agriculture, i.e., they have already exceeded their sustained carrying capacity. Most of South America is overpopulated in this sense.

In arid regions we attempt to offset the process of wastage by reclamation, but it is only too evident that the prospective longevity of reclamation projects is often short. In our own West, the best of them may not last a century.

The combined evidence of history and ecology seem to support one general deduction: the less violent the man-made changes, the greater the probability of successful readjustment in the pyramid. Violence, in turn, varies with human population density; a dense population requires a more violent conversion. In this respect, North America has a better chance for permanence than Europe, if she can contrive to limit her density.

This deduction runs counter to our current philosophy, which assumes that because a small increase in density enriched human life, an indefinite increase will enrich it indefinitely. Ecology knows of no density relationship that holds for indefinitely wide limits. All gains from density are subject to a law of diminishing returns.

Whatever may be the equation for men and land, it is improbable that we as yet know all its terms. Recent discoveries in mineral and vitamin nutrition reveal unsuspected dependencies in the up-circuit: incredibly minute quantities of certain substances determine the value of soils to plants, of plants to animals. What of the down-circuit? What of the vanishing species, the preservation of which we now regard as an esthetic luxury? They helped build the soil; in what unsuspected ways may they be essential to its maintenance? Professor Weaver proposes that we use prairie flowers to reflocculate the wasting soils of the dust bowl; who knows for what purpose cranes and condors, otters and grizzlies may some day be used?

LAND HEALTH AND THE A-B CLEAVAGE

A land ethic, then, reflects the existence of an ecological conscience, and this in turn reflects a conviction of individual responsibility for the health of the land. Health is the capacity of the land for self-renewal. Conservation is our effort to understand and preserve this capacity.

Conservationists are notorious for their dissensions. Superficially these seem to add up to mere confusion, but a more careful scrutiny reveals a single plane of cleavage common to many specialized fields. In each field one group (A) regards the land as soil, and its function as commodity-production; another group (B) regards the land as a biota, and its function as something broader. How much broader is admittedly in a state of doubt and confusion.

In my own field, forestry, Group A is quite content to grow trees like cabbages, with cellulose as the basic forest commodity. It feels no inhibition against violence; its ideology is agronomic. Group B, on the other hand, sees forestry as fundamentally different from agronomy because it employs natural species, and manages a natural environment rather than creating an artificial one. Group B prefers natural reproduction on principle. It worries on biotic as well as economic grounds about the loss of species like chestnut, and the threatened loss of the white pines. It worries about a whole series of secondary forest functions: wildlife, recreation, watersheds, wilderness areas. To my mind, Group B feels the stirrings of an ecological conscience.

In the wildlife field, a parallel cleavage exists. For Group A the basic commodities are sport and meat; the yardsticks of production are ciphers of take in pheasants and trout. Artificial propagation is acceptable as a permanent as well as a temporary recourse—if its unit costs permit. Group B, on the other hand, worries about a whole series of biotic side-issues. What is the cost in predators of producing a game crop? Should we have further recourse to exotics? How can management restore the shrinking species, like prairie grouse, already hopeless as shootable game? How can management restore the threatened rarities, like trumpeter swan and whooping crane? Can management principles be extended to wildflowers? Here again it is clear to me that we have the same A-B cleavage as in forestry.

In the larger field of agriculture I am less competent to speak, but there seem to be somewhat parallel cleavages. Scientific agriculture was actively developing before ecology was born; hence a slower penetration of ecological concepts might be expected. Moreover the farmer, by the very nature of his techniques, must modify the biota more radically than the forester or the wildlife manager. Nevertheless, there are many discontents in agriculture which seem to add up to a new vision of "biotic farming."

Perhaps the most important of these is the new evidence that poundage or tonnage is no measure of the food-value of farm crops; the products of fertile soil may be qualitatively as well as quantitatively superior. We can bolster poundage from depleted soils by pouring on imported fertility, but we are not necessarily bolstering food-value. The possible ultimate ramifications of this idea are so immense that I must leave their exposition to abler pens.

The discontent that labels itself "organic farming," while bearing some of the earmarks of a cult, is nevertheless biotic in its direction, particularly in its insistence on the importance of soil flora and fauna.

The ecological fundamentals of agriculture are just as poorly known to the public as in other fields of land-use. For example, few educated people realize that the marvelous advances in technique made during recent decades are improvements in the pump, rather than the well. Acre for acre, they have barely sufficed to offset the sinking level of fertility.

In all of these cleavages, we see repeated the same basic paradoxes: man the conqueror *versus* man the biotic citizen; science the sharpener of his sword *versus* science the searchlight on his universe; land the slave and servant *versus* land the collective organism. Robinson's injunction to Tristram may well be applied, at this juncture, to *Homo sapiens* as a species in geological time:

Whether you will or not
You are a King, Tristram, for you are one
Of the time-tested few that leave the
world,
When they are gone, not the same place it
was.
Mark what you leave.

THE OUTLOOK

It is inconceivable to me that an ethical relation to land can exist without love, respect, and admiration for land, and a high regard for its value. By value, I of course mean something far broader than mere economic value; I mean value in the philosophical sense.

Perhaps the most serious obstacle impeding the evolution of a land ethic is the fact that our educational and economic system is headed away from, rather than toward, an intense consciousness of land. Your true modern is separated from the land by many middlemen, and by innumerable physical gadgets. He has no vital relation to it; to him it is the space between cities on which crops grow. Turn him loose for a day on the land, and if the spot does not happen to be a golf links or a "scenic" area, he is bored stiff. If crops could be raised by hydroponics instead of farming, it would suit him very well. Synthetic substitutes for wood, leather, wool, and other natural land products suit him better than the originals. In short land is something he has "outgrown."

Almost equally serious as an obstacle to a land ethic is the attitude of the farmer for whom the land is still and adversary, or a taskmaster that keeps him in slavery. Theoretically, the mechanization of farming ought to cut the farmer's chains, but whether it really does is debatable.

One of the requisites for an ecological comprehension of land is an understanding of ecology, and this is by no means co-extensive with "education"; in fact, much higher education seems deliberately to avoid ecological concepts. An understanding of ecology does not necessarily originate in courses bearing ecological labels; it is quite as likely to be labeled geography, botany, agronomy, history, or economics. This is as it should be, but whatever the label, ecological training is scarce.

The case for a land ethic would appear hopeless but for the minority which is in obvious revolt against these "modern" trends.

The "key-log" which must be moved to release the evolutionary process for an ethic is simply this: quit thinking about decent land-use as solely an economic problem. Examine each question in terms of what is ethically and esthetically right, as well as what is economically expedient. A thing is right when it tends to preserve the integrity, stability, and beauty of the biotic community. It is wrong when it tends otherwise.

It of course goes without saying that economic feasibility limits the tether of what can or cannot be done for land. It always has and it always will. The fallacy the economic determinists have tied around our collective neck, and which we now need to cast off, is the belief that economics determines *all* land-use. This is simply not true. An innumerable host of actions and attitudes, comprising perhaps the bulk of all land relations, is determined by the land-users' tastes and predilections, rather than by his purse. The bulk of all land relations hinges on investments of time, forethought, skill, and faith rather than on investments of cash. As a land-user thinketh, so is he.

I have purposely presented the land ethic as a product of social evolution because nothing so important as an ethic is ever "written." Only the most superficial student of history supposes that Moses "wrote" the Decalogue; it evolved in the minds of a thinking community, and Moses wrote a tentative summary of it for a "seminar." I say tentative because evolution never stops.

The evolution of a land ethic is an intellectual as well as emotional process. Conservation is paved with good intentions which prove to be futile, or even dangerous, because they are devoid of critical understanding either of the land, or of economic land-use. I think it is a truism that as the ethical frontier advances from the individual to the community, its intellectual content increases.

The mechanism of operation is the same for any ethic: social approbation for right actions; social disapproval for wrong actions.

By and large, our present problem is one of attitudes and implements. We are remodeling the Alhambra with a steam-shovel, and we are proud of our yardage. We shall hardly relinquish the shovel, which after all has many good points, but we are in need of gentler and more objective criteria for its successful use.

WILDERNESS

Wilderness is the raw material out of which man has hammered the artifact called civilization.

Wilderness was never a homogeneous raw material. It was very diverse, and the resulting artifacts are very diversive. These differences in the end-product are known as cultures. The rich diversity of the world's cultures reflects a corresponding diversity in the wilds that gave them birth.

For the first time in the history of the human species, two changes are now impending. One is the exhaustion of wilderness in the more habitable portions of the globe. The other is the world-wide hybridization of cultures through modern transport and industrialization. Neither can be prevented, and perhaps should not be, but the question arises whether, by some slight amelioration of the impending changes, certain values can be preserved that would otherwise be lost.

To the laborer in the sweat of his labor, the raw stuff on his anvil is an adversary to be conquered. So was wilderness an adversary to the pioneer.

But to the laborer in repose, able for the moment to cast a philosophical eye on his world, that same raw stuff is something to be loved and cherished, because it gives definition and meaning to his life. This is a plea for the preservation of some tag-ends of wilderness, as museum pieces, for the edification of those who may one day wish to see, feel, or study the origins of their cultural inheritance.

THE REMNANTS

Many of the diverse wildernesses out of which we have hammered America are already gone; hence in any practical program the unit areas to be preserved must vary greatly in size and in degree of wildness.

No living man will see again the long-grass prairie, where a sea of prairie flowers lapped at the stirrups of the pioneer. We shall do well to find a forty here and there on which the prairie plants can be kept alive as species. There were a hundred such plants, many of exceptional beauty. Most of them are quite unknown to those who have inherited their domain.

But the short-grass prairie, where Cabeza de Vaca saw the horizon under the bellies of the buffalo, is still extant in a few spots of 10,000-acre size, albeit severely chewed up by sheep, cattle, and dry-farmers. If the forty-niners are worth commemorating on the walls of state capitols, is not the scene of their mighty hegira worth commemorating in several national prairie reservations?

No living man will see again the virgin pineries of the Lake States, or the flatwoods of the coastal plain, or the giant hardwoods; of these, samples of a few acres each will have to suffice. But there are still several blocks of maple-hemlock of thousand-acre size; there are similar blocks of Appalachian hardwoods, of southern hardwood swamp, of cypress swamp, and of Adirondack spruce. Few of these tag-ends are secure from prospective cuttings, and fewer still from prospective tourist roads.

One of the fastest-shrinking categories of wilderness is coastlines. Cottages and tourist roads have all but annihilated wild coasts on both oceans, and Lake Superior is now losing the last large remnant of wild shoreline on the Great Lakes. No single kind of wilderness is more intimately interwoven with history, and none nearer the point of complete disappearance.

In all of North America east of the Rockies, there is only one large area formally reserved as a wilderness: the Quetico-Superior International Park in Minnesota and Ontario. This magnificent block of canoe-country, a mosaic of lakes and rivers, lies mostly in Canada, and can be about as large as Canada chooses to make it, but its integrity is threatened by two recent developments: the growth of fishing resorts served by pontoon-equipped airplanes, and a jurisdictional dispute whether the Minnesota end of the area shall be all National Forest, or partly State Forest. The whole region is in danger of power impoundments, and this regrettable cleavage among proponents of wilderness may end in giving power the whip-hand.

In the Rocky Mountain states, a score of areas in the National Forests, varying in size from a hundred thousand to half a million acres, are withdrawn as wilderness, and closed to roads, hotels, and other inimical uses. In the National Parks the same principle is recognized, but no specific boundaries are delimited. Collectively, these federal areas are the backbone of the wilderness program, but they are not so secure as the paper record might lead one to believe. Local pressures for new tourist roads knock off a chip here and a slab there. There is perennial pressure for extension of roads for forest-fire control, and these, by slow degrees, become public highways. Idle CCC camps presented a widespread temptation to build new and often needless roads. Lumber shortages during the war gave the impetus of military necessity to many road extensions, legitimate and otherwise. At the present moment, ski-tows and ski-hotels are being promoted in many mountain areas, often without regard to their prior designation as wilderness.

One of the most insidious invasions of wilderness is via predator control. It works thus: wolves and lions are cleaned out of a wilderness area in the interest of big-game management. The big-game herds (usually deer or elk) then increase to the point of overbrowsing the range. Hunters must then be encouraged to harvest the surplus, but modern hunters refuse to operate far from a car; hence a road must be built to provide access to the surplus game. Again and again, wilderness areas have been split by this process, but it still continues.

The Rocky Mountain system of wilderness areas covers a wide gamut of forest types, from the juniper breaks of the Southwest to the "illimitable woods where rolls the Oregon." It is lacking, however, in desert areas, probably because of that under-aged brand of esthetics which limits the definitions of "scenery" to lakes and pine trees.

In Canada and Alaska there are still large expanses of virgin country

> Where nameless men by nameless rivers wander
> and in strange valleys die strange deaths alone.

A representative series of these areas can, and should, be kept. Many are of negligible or negative value for economic use. It will be contended, of course, that no deliberate planning to this end is necessary; that adequate areas will survive anyhow. All recent history belies so comforting an assumption. Even if wild spots do survive, what of their fauna? The woodland caribou, the several races of mountain sheep, the pure form of woods buffalo, the barren ground grizzly, the freshwater seals, and the whales are even now threatened. Of what use are wild areas destitute of their distinctive faunas? There are now organizations and development groups actively embarked on the industrialization of the Arctic wastes, and plans even larger are actively being pressed. The wilderness of the Far North as yet has no formal protection and though still extensive, is beginning to dwindle.

To what extent Canada and Alaska will be able to see and grasp their opportunities is anybody's guess. Pioneers usually scoff at any effort to perpetuate pioneering.

WILDERNESS FOR RECREATION

Physical combat for the means of subsistence was, for unnumbered centuries, an economic fact. When it disappeared as such, a sound instinct led us to preserve it in the form of athletic sports and games.

Physical combat between men and beasts was, in like manner, an economic fact, now preserved as hunting and fishing for sport.

Public wilderness areas are, first of all, a means of perpetuating, in sport form, the more virile and primitive skills in pioneering travel and subsistence.

Some of these skills are of generalized distribution; the details have been adapted to the American scene, but the skill is world-wide. Hunting, fishing, and foot travel by pack are examples.

Two of them, however, are as American as a hickory tree; they have been copied elsewhere, but they were developed to their full perfection only on this continent. One of these is canoe travel, and the other is travel by pack-train. Both are shrinking rapidly. Your Hudson Bay Indian now has a put-put, and your mountaineer a Ford. If I had to make a living by canoe or packhorse, I should likely do likewise, for both are grueling labor. But we who seek wilderness travel for sport are foiled when we are forced to compete with mechanized substitutes. It is bootless to execute a portage to the tune of motor launches, or to turn out your bellmare in the pasture of a summer hotel. It is better to stay home.

Wilderness areas are first of all a series of sanctuaries for the primitive arts of wilderness travel, especially canoeing and packing.

I suppose some will wish to debate whether it is important to keep these primitive arts alive. I shall not debate it. Either you know it in your bones, or you are very, very old.

European hunting and fishing are largely devoid of the thing that wilderness areas might be the means of preserving in this country. Europeans do not camp, cook, or do their own work in the woods if they can avoid doing so. Work chores are delegated to beaters and servants, and a hunt carries the atmosphere of a picnic, rather than of pioneering. The test of skill is confined largely to the actual taking of game or fish.

There are those who decry wilderness sports as "undemocratic" because the recreational carrying capacity of a wilderness is small, as compared with a golf links or a tourist camp. The basic error in such argument is that it applies the philosophy of mass-production to what is intended to counteract mass-production. The value of recreation is not a matter of ciphers. Recreation is valuable in proportion to the intensity of its experiences, and to the degree to which it *differs from* and *contrasts with* workaday life. By these criteria, mechanized outings are at best a milk-and-water affair.

Mechanized recreation already has seized nine-tenths of the woods and mountains; a decent respect for minorities should dedicate the other tenth to wilderness.

WILDERNESS FOR SCIENCE

The most important characteristic of an organism is that capacity for internal self-renewal known as health.

There are two organisms whose processes of self-renewal have been subjected to human interference and control. One of these is man himself (medicine and public health). The other is land (agriculture and conservation).

The effort to control the health of land has not been very successful. It is now generally understood that when soil loses fertility, or washes away faster than it forms, and when water systems exhibit abnormal floods and shortages, the land is sick.

Other derangements are known as facts, but are not yet thought of as symptoms of land sickness. The disappearance of plants and animal species without visible cause, despite efforts to protect them, and the irruption of others as pests despite efforts to control them, must, in the absence of simpler explanations, be regarded as symptoms of sickness in the land organism. Both are occurring too frequently to be dismissed as normal evolutionary events.

The status of thought on these ailments of the land is reflected in the fact that our treatments for them are still prevailingly local. Thus when a soil loses fertility we pour on fertilizer, or at best alter its tame flora and fauna, without considering the fact that its wild flora and fauna, which built the soil to begin with, may likewise be important to its maintenance. It was recently discovered, for example, that good tobacco crops depend, for some unknown reason, on the preconditioning of the soil by wild ragweed. It does not occur to us that such unexpected chains of dependency may have wide prevalence in nature.

When prairie dogs, ground squirrels, or mice increase to pest levels we poison them, but we do not look beyond the animal to find the cause of the irruption. We assume that animal troubles must have animal causes. The latest scientific evidence points to derangements of the *plant* community as the real seat of rodent irruptions, but few explorations of this clue are being made.

Many forest plantations are producing one-log or two-log trees on soil which originally grew three-log and four-log trees. Why? Thinking foresters know that the cause probably lies not in the tree, but in the micro-flora of the soil, and that it may take more years to restore the soil flora than it took to destroy it.

Many conservation treatments are obviously superficial. Flood-control dams have no relation to the cause of floods. Check dams and terraces do not touch the cause of erosion. Refuges and hatcheries to maintain the supply of game and fish do not explain why the supply fails to maintain itself.

In general, the trend of the evidence indicates that in land, just as in the human body, the symptoms may lie in one organ and the cause in another. The practices we now call conservation are, to a large extent, local alleviations of biotic pain. They are necessary, but they must not be confused with cures. The art of land doctoring is being practiced with vigor, but the science of land health is yet to be born.

A science of land health needs, first of all, a

base datum of normality, a picture of how healthy land maintains itself as an organism.

We have two available norms. One is found where land physiology remains largely normal despite centuries of human occupation. I know of only one such place: northeastern Europe. It is not likely that we shall fail to study it.

The other and most perfect norm is wilderness. Paleontology offers abundant evidence that wilderness maintained itself for immensely long periods; that its component species were rarely lost, neither did they get out of hand; that weather and water built soil as fast or faster than it was carried away. Wilderness, then, assumes unexpected importance as a laboratory for the study of land-health.

One cannot study the physiology of Montana in the Amazon; each biotic province needs its own wilderness for comparative studies of used and unused land. It is of course too late to salvage more than a lopsided system of wilderness study areas, and most of these remnants are far too small to retain their normality in all respects. Even the National Parks, which run up to a million acres each in size, have not been large enough to retain their natural predators, or to exclude animal diseases carried by livestock. Thus the Yellowstone has lost its wolves and cougars, with the result that elk are ruining the flora, particularly on the winter range. At the same time the grizzly bear and the mountain sheep are shrinking, the latter by reason of disease.

While even the largest wilderness areas become partially deranged, it required only a few wild acres for J. E. Weaver to discover why the prairie flora is more drouth-resistant than the agronomic flora which has supplanted it. Weaver found that the prairie species practice "team work" underground by distributing their root-systems to cover all levels, whereas the species comprising the agronomic rotation overdraw one level and neglect another, thus building up cumulative deficits. An important agronomic principle emerged from Weaver's researches.

Again, it required only a few wild acres for Togrediak to discover why pines on old fields never achieve the size or wind-firmness of pines on uncleared forest soils. In the latter case, the roots follow old root channels, and thus strike deeper.

In many cases we literally do not know how good a performance to expect of healthy land unless we have a wild area for comparison with sick ones. Thus most of the early travelers in the Southwest describe the mountain rivers as originally clear, but a doubt remains, for they may, by accident, have seen them at favorable seasons. Erosion engineers had no base datum until it was discovered that exactly similar rivers in the Sierra Madre of Chihuahua, never grazed or used for fear of Indians, show at their worst a milky hue, not too cloudy for a trout fly. Moss grows to the water's edge on their banks. Most of the corresponding rivers in Arizona and New Mexico are ribbons of boulders, mossless, soilless, and all but treeless. The preservation and study of the Sierra Madre wilderness by an international experiment station, as a norm for the cure of sick land on both sides of the border, would be a good-neighbor enterprise well worthy of consideration.

In short all available wild areas, large or small, are likely to have value as norms for land science. Recreation is not their only, or even their principal, utility.

WILDERNESS FOR WILDLIFE

The National Parks do not suffice as a means of perpetuating the larger carnivores; witness the precarious status of the grizzly bear, and the fact that the park system is already wolfless. Neither do they suffice for mountain sheep; most sheep herds are shrinking.

The reasons for this are clear in some cases and obscure in others. The parks are certainly too small for such a far-ranging species as the wolf. Many animal species, for reasons unknown, do not seem to thrive as detached islands of population.

The most feasible way to enlarge the area available for wilderness fauna is for the wilder parts of the National Forests, which usually surround the Parks, to function as parks in respect to threatened species. That they have not so functioned is tragically illustrated in the case of the grizzly bear.

In 1909, when I first saw the West, there were grizzlies in every major mountain mass, but you could travel for months without meeting a conservation officer. Today there is some kind of conservation officer "behind every bush," yet as wildlife bureaus grow, our most magnificent mammal retreats steadily toward the Canadian border. Of the 6000 grizzlies officially reported as remaining in areas owned by the United States, 5000 are in Alaska. Only five states have any at all. There seems to be a tacit assumption that if grizzlies survive in Canada and Alaska, that is good enough. It is not good enough for me. The Alaskan bears are a distinct species. Relegating grizzlies to Alaska is about like relegating happiness to heaven; one may never get there.

Saving the grizzly requires a series of large areas from which roads and livestock are excluded, or in which livestock damage is compensated. Buying out scattered livestock ranches is the only way to create such areas, but despite large authority to buy and exchange lands, the conservation bureaus have accomplished virtually nothing toward this end. The Forest Service has established a grizzly range in Montana, but I know of a mountain range in Utah in which the Forest Service actually promoted a sheep industry, despite the fact that it harbored the sole remnant of grizzlies in that state.

Permanent grizzly ranges and permanent wilderness areas are of course two names for one problem. Enthusiasm about either requires a long view of conservation, and a historical perspective. Only those able to see the pageant of evolution can be expected to value its theater, the wilderness, or its outstanding achievement, the grizzly. But if education really educates, there will, in time, be more and more citizens who understand that relics of the old West add meaning and value to the new. Youth yet unborn will pole up the Missouri with Lewis and Clark, or climb the Sierras with James Capen Adams, and each generation in turn will ask: Where is the big white bear? It will be a sorry answer to say he went under while conservationists weren't looking.

DEFENDERS OF WILDERNESS

Wilderness is a resource which can shrink but not grow. Invasions can be arrested or modified in a manner to keep an area usable either for recreation, or for science, or for wildlife, but the creation of new wilderness in the full sense of the word is impossible.

It follows, then, that any wilderness program is a rearguard action, through which retreats are reduced to a minimum. The Wilderness Society was organized in 1935 "for the one purpose of saving the wilderness remnants in America." The Sierra Club is doing yeoman work toward the same end.

It does not suffice, however, to have a few such societies, nor can one be content that Congress has enacted a bill aimed at wilderness preservation. Unless there be wilderness-minded men scattered through all the conservation bureaus, the societies may never learn of new invasions until the time for action has passed. Furthermore, a militant minority of wilderness-minded citizens must be on watch throughout the nation and vigilantly available for action.

In Europe, where wilderness has now retreated to the Carpathians and Siberia, every thinking conservationist bemoans its loss. Even in Britain, which has less room for land-luxuries than almost any other civilized country, there is a vigorous if belated movement for saving a few small spots of semi-wild land.

Ability to see the cultural value of wilderness boils down, in the last analysis, to a question of intellectual humility. The shallow-minded modern who has lost his rootage in the land assumes that he has already discovered what is important; it is such who prate of empires, political or economic, that will last a thousand years. It is only the scholar who appreciates that all history consists of successive excursions from a single starting-point, to which man returns again and again to organize yet another search for a durable scale of values. It is only the scholar who understands why the raw wilderness gives definition and meaning to the human enterprise.

CONSERVATION ESTHETIC

Barring love and war, few enterprises are undertaken with such abandon, or by such diverse individuals, or with so paradoxical a mixture of appetite and altruism, as that group of avocations known as outdoor recreation. It is, by common consent, a good thing for people to get back to nature. But wherein lies the goodness, and what can be done to encourage its pursuit? On these questions there is confusion of counsel, and only the most uncritical minds are free from doubt.

Recreation became a problem with a name in the days of the elder Roosevelt, when the railroads which had banished the countryside from the city began to carry city-dwellers, *en masse,* to the countryside. It began to be noticed that the greater the exodus, the smaller the per-capita ration of peace, solitude, wildlife, and scenery, and the longer the migration to reach them.

The automobile has spread this once mild and local predicament to the outermost limits of good roads—it has made scarce in the hinterlands something once abundant on the back forty. But that something must nevertheless be found. Like ions shot from the sun, the week-enders radiate from every town, generating heat and friction as they go. A tourist industry purveys bed and board to bait more ions, faster, further. Advertisements on rock and rill confide to all and sundry the whereabouts of new retreats, landscapes, hunting-grounds, and fishing-lakes just beyond those recently overrun. Bureaus build roads into new hinterlands, then buy more hinterlands to absorb the exodus accelerated by the roads. A gadget industry pads the bumps against nature-in-the-raw; woodcraft becomes the art of using gadgets. And now, to cap the pyramid of banalities, the trailer. To him who seeks in the woods and mountains only those things obtainable from travel or golf, the present situation is tolerable. But to him who seeks something more, recreation has become a self-destructive process of seeking but never quite finding, a major frustration of mechanized society.

The retreat of the wilderness under the barrage of motorized tourists is no local thing; Hudson Bay, Alaska, Mexico, South Africa are giving way, and South America and Siberia are next. Drums along the Mohawk are now honks along the rivers of the world. *Homo sapiens* putters no more under his own vine and fig tree; he has poured into his gas tank the stored motivity of countless creatures aspiring through the ages to wiggle their way to pastures new. Ant-like he swarms the continents.

This is Outdoor Recreation, Latest Model.

Who now is the recreationist, and what does he seek? A few samples will remind us.

Take a look, first, at any duck marsh. A cordon of parked cars surrounds it. Crouched on each point of its reedy margin is some pillar of society, automatic ready, trigger finger itching to break, if need be, every law of commonwealth or commonweal to kill a duck. That he is already overfed in no way dampens his avidity for gathering his meat from God.

Wandering in the near-by woods is another pillar, hunting rare ferns or new warblers. Because his kind of hunting seldom calls for theft or pillage, he disdains the killer. Yet, like as not, in his youth he was one.

At some near-by resort is still another nature-lover—the kind who writes bad verse on birchbark. Everywhere is the unspecialized motorist whose recreation is mileage, who has run the gamut of the National Parks in one summer, and now is headed for Mexico City and points south.

Lastly, there is the professional, striving through countless conservation organizations to give the nature-seeking public what it wants, or to make it want what he has to give.

Why, it may be asked, should such a diversity of folk be bracketed in a single category? Because each, in his own way, is a hunter. And why does each call himself a conservationist? Because the wild things he hunts for have eluded his grasp, and he hopes by some necromancy of laws, appropriations, regional plans, reorganization of departments, or other form of mass-wishing to make them stay put.

Recreation is commonly spoken of as an economic resource. Senate committees tell us, in reverent ciphers, how many millions the public spends in its pursuit. It has indeed an economic aspect—a cottage on a fishing-lake, or even a duck-point on a marsh, may cost as much as the entire adjacent farm.

It has also an ethical aspect. In the scramble for unspoiled places, codes and decalogues evolve. We hear of "outdoor manners." We indoctrinate youth. We print definitions of "What is a sportsman?" and hang a copy on the wall of whosoever will pay a dollar for the propagation of the faith.

It is clear, though, that these economic and ethical manifestations are results, not causes, of the motive force. We seek contacts with nature because we derive pleasure from them. As in opera, economic machinery is employed to create and maintain facilities. As in opera, professionals make a living out of creating and maintaining them, but it would be false to say of either that the basic motive, the *raison d'être*, is economic. The duck-hunter in his blind and the operatic singer on the stage, despite the disparity of their accoutrements, are doing the same thing. Each is reviving, in play, a drama formerly inherent in daily life. Both are, in the last analysis, esthetic exercises.

Public policies for outdoor recreation are controversial. Equally conscientious citizens hold opposite views on what it is and what should be done to conserve its resource-base. Thus the Wilderness Society seeks to exclude roads from the hinterlands, and the Chamber of Commerce to extend them, both in the name of recreation. The game-farmer kills hawks and the bird-lover protects them in the name of shotgun and field-glass hunting respectively. Such factions commonly label each other with short and ugly names, when, in fact, each is considering a different component of the recreational process. These components *differ widely in their characteristics or properties.* A given policy may be true for one but false for another.

It seems timely, therefore, to segregate the components, and to examine the distinctive characteristics or properties of each.

We begin with the simplest and most obvious: the physical objects that the outdoorsman may seek, find, capture, and carry away. In this category are wild crops such as game and fish, and the symbols or tokens of achievement such as heads, hides, photographs, and specimens.

All these things rest upon the idea of *trophy*. The pleasure they give is, or should be, in the seeking as well as in the getting. The trophy, whether it be a bird's egg, a mass of trout, a basket of mushrooms, the photograph of a bear, the pressed specimen of a wild flower, or a note tucked into the cairn on a mountain peak, is a *certificate*. It attests that its owner has been somewhere and done something—that he has exercised skill, persistence, or discrimination in the age-old feat of overcoming, outwitting, or reducing-to-possession. These connotations which attach to the trophy usually far exceed its physical value.

But trophies differ in their reactions to mass-pursuit. The yield of game and fish can, by means of propagation or management, be increased so as to give each hunter more, or to give more hunters the same amount. During the past decade a profession of wildlife management has sprung into existence. A score of universities teach its techniques, conduct research for bigger and better wild animal crops. However, when carried too far, this stepping-up of yields is subject to a law of diminishing returns. Very intensive management of game or fish lowers the unit value of the trophy by artificializing it.

Consider, for example, a trout raised in a hatchery and newly liberated in an over-fished stream. The stream is no longer capable of natural trout production. Pollution has fouled its waters, or deforestation and trampling have warmed or silted them. No one would claim that this trout has the same value as a wholly wild one caught out of some unmanaged stream in the high Rockies. Its esthetic connotations are inferior, even though its capture may require skill. (Its liver, one authority says, is also so degenerated by hatchery feeding as to forebode an early death.) Yet several over-fished states now depend almost entirely on such man-made trout.

All intergrades of artificiality exist, but as mass-use increases it tends to push the whole gamut of conservation techniques toward the artificial end, and the whole scale of trophy-values downward.

To safeguard this expensive, artificial, and more or less helpless trout, the Conservation Commission feels impelled to kill all herons and terns visiting the hatchery where it was raised, and all mergansers and otters inhabiting the stream in which it is released. The fisherman perhaps feels no loss in this sacrifice of one kind of wild life for another, but the ornithologist is ready to bite off ten-penny nails. Artificialized management has, in effect, bought fishing at the expense of another and perhaps higher recreation; it has paid dividends to one citizen out of capital stock belonging to all. The same kind of biological wildcatting prevails in game management. In Europe, where wild-crop statistics are available for long periods, we even know the "rate of exchange" of game for predators. Thus, in Saxony one hawk is killed for each seven game birds bagged, and one predator of some kind for each three head of small game.

Damage to plant life usually follows artificialized management of animals—for example, damage to forests by deer. One may see this in north Germany, in northeast Pennsylvania, the Kaibab, and in dozens of other less publicized regions. In each case over-abundant deer, when deprived of their natural enemies, have made it impossible for deer food plants to survive or reproduce. Beech, maple, and yew in Europe, ground hemlock and white cedar in the eastern states, mountain mahogany and cliff-rose in the West, are deer foods threatened by artificialized deer. The composition of the flora, from wild flowers to forest trees, is gradually impoverished, and the deer in turn are dwarfed by malnutrition. There are no stags in the woods today like those whose antlers decorate the walls of feudal castles.

On the English heaths, reproduction of trees is inhibited by rabbits over-protected in the process of cropping partridges and pheasants. On scores of tropical islands both flora and fauna have been destroyed by goats introduced for meat and sport. It would be hard to calculate the mutual injuries by and between mammals deprived of their natural predators, and ranges stripped of their natural food plants. Agricultural crops caught between these upper and nether millstones of ecological mismanagement are saved only at the cost of endless indemnities and barbed wire.

We generalize, then, by saying that mass-use tends to dilute the quality of organic trophies like game and fish, and to induce damage to other resources such as non-game animals, natural vegetation, and farm crops.

The same dilution and damage is not apparent in the yield of "indirect" trophies, such as photographs. Broadly speaking, a piece of scenery snapped by a dozen tourist cameras daily is not physically impaired thereby, nor does it suffer if photographed a hundred times. The camera industry is one of the few innocuous parasites on wild nature.

We have, then, a basic difference in reaction to mass-use as between two categories of physical objects pursued as trophies.

Let us now consider another component of recreation, which is more subtle and complex: the feeling of isolation in nature. That this is acquiring a scarcity-value that is very high to some persons is attested by the wilderness controversy. Wilderness areas are by official definition roadless, with roads built only to their edges. They are thus advertised as unique, as indeed they are. But before long trails are congested, there is pressure for access from the air; or an unexpected fire necessitates splitting an area in two with a road to haul fire-fighters. Or the congestion induced by publicity may whip up the price of guides and packers, whereupon somebody discovers that the wilderness policy is undemocratic. Or the local Chamber of Commerce, at first quiescent at the novelty of a hinterland officially labeled as "wild," tastes its first blood of tourist money. It then wants more, wilderness or no wilderness. The jeep and the airplane, creatures of the ever mounting pressure from humanity, thus eliminate the opportunity for isolation in nature.

In short, the very scarcity of wild places, reacting with the *mores* of advertising and promotion, tends to defeat any deliberate effort to prevent their growing still more scarce.

It is clear without further discussion that mass-use involves a direct dilution of the opportunity for solitude; that when we speak of roads, campgrounds, trails, and toilets as "development" of recreational resources, we speak falsely in respect to this component. Such accommodations for the crowd are not developing (in the sense of adding or creating) anything. On the contrary, they are merely water poured into the already-thin soup.

We now contrast with the isolation-component that very distinct if simple one which we may label "fresh-air" and "change of scene." Mass-use neither destroys nor dilutes this value. The thousandth tourist who clicks the gate of the National Park breathes approximately the same air, and experiences the same contrast with Monday-at-the-office, as does the first. One might even believe that the gregarious assault on the outdoors enhances the contrast. We may say, then, that the fresh-air and change-of-scene component is like the photographic trophy—it withstands mass-use without damage.

We come now to another component: the perception of the natural processes by which the land and the living things upon it have achieved their characteristic forms (evolution) and by which they maintain their existence (ecology). That thing called "nature study," despite the shiver it brings to the spines of the elect, constitutes the first embryonic groping of the mass-mind toward perception.

The outstanding characteristic of perception is that it entails no consumption and no dilution of any resource. The swoop of a hawk, for example, is perceived by one as the drama of evolution. To another it is only a threat to the full frying-pan. The drama may excite a hundred successive witnesses, the threat only one—for he responds with a shotgun.

To promote perception is the only truly creative part of recreational engineering.

This fact is important, and its potential power for bettering "the good life" only dimly understood. When Daniel Boone first entered into the forests and prairies of "the dark and bloody ground," he reduced to his possession the pure essence of "outdoor America." He didn't call it that, but what he found is the thing we now seek, and we here deal with things not names.

Recreation, however, is not the outdoors, but our reaction to it. Daniel Boone's reaction depended not only on the quality of what he saw, but on the quality of the mental eye with which he saw it. Ecological science has wrought a change in the mental eye. It has disclosed origins and functions for what to Boone were only facts. It has disclosed mechanisms for what to Boone were only attributes. We have no yardstick to measure this change, but we may safely say that, as compared with the competent ecologist of the present day, Boone saw only the surface of things. the incredible intricacies of the plant and animal community—the intrinsic beauty of the organism called America, then in the full bloom of her maidenhood—were as invisible and incomprehensible to Daniel Boone as they are today to Babbitt. The only true development in American recreational resources is the development of the perceptive faculty in Americans. All of the other acts we grace by the name are, at best, attempts to retard or mask the process of dilution.

Let no man jump to the conclusion that Babbitt must take his Ph.D in ecology before he can "see" his country. On the contrary, the Ph.D may become as callous as an undertaker to the mysteries at which he officiates. Like all real treasures of the mind, perception can be split into infinitely small fractions without losing its quality. The weeds in a city lot convey the same lesson as the redwoods; the farmer may see in his cow-pasture what may not be vouchsafed to the scientist adventuring in the South Seas.

Perception, in short, cannot be purchased with either learned degrees or dollars; it grows at home as well as abroad, and he who has a little may use it to as good advantage as he who has much. As a search for perception, the recreational stampede is footless and unnecessary.

There is, lastly, a fifth component: the sense of husbandry. It is unknown to the outdoorsman who works for conservation with his vote rather than with his hands. It is realized only when some art of management is applied to land by some person of perception. That is to say, its enjoyment is reserved for landholders too poor to buy their sport, and land administrators with a sharp eye and an ecological mind. The tourist who buys access to his scenery misses it altogether; so also the sportsman who hires the state, or some underling, to be his gamekeeper. The Government, which essays to substitute public for private operation of recreational lands, is unwittingly giving away to its field officers a large share of what it seeks to offer its citizens. We foresters and game managers might logically pay for, instead of being paid for, our job as husbandmen of wild crops.

That a sense of husbandry exercised in the production of crops may be quite as important as the crops themselves is realized to some extent in agriculture, but not in conservation. American sportsmen hold in small esteem the intensive game-cropping of the Scottish moors and the German forests, and in some respects rightly. But they overlook entirely the sense of husbandry developed by the European landholder in the process of cropping. We have no such thing as yet. It is important. When we conclude that we must bait the farmer with subsidies to induce him to raise a forest, or with gate receipts to induce him to raise game, we are merely admitting that the pleasures of husbandry-in-the-wild are as yet unknown both to the farmer and to ourselves.

Scientists have an epigram: ontogeny repeats phylogeny. What they mean is that the development of each individual repeats the evolutionary history of the race. This is true of mental as well as physical things. The trophy-hunter is the caveman reborn. Trophy-hunting is the prerogative of youth, racial or individual, and nothing to apologize for.

The disquieting thing in the modern picture is the trophy-hunter who never grows up, in whom the capacity for isolation, perception, and husbandry is undeveloped, or perhaps lost. He is the motorized ant who swarms the continents before learning to see his own back yard, who consumes but never creates outdoor satisfactions. For him the recreational engineer dilutes the wilderness and artificializes its trophies in the fond belief that he is rendering a public service.

The trophy-recreationist has peculiarities that contribute in subtle ways to his own undoing. To enjoy he must possess, invade, appropriate. Hence the wilderness that he cannot personally see has no value to him. Hence the universal assumption that an unused hinterland is rendering no service to society. To those devoid of imagination, a blank place on the map is a useless waste; to others, the most valuable part. (Is my share in Alaska worthless to me because I shall never go there? Do I need a road to show me the arctic prairies, the goose pastures of the Yukon, the Kodiak bear, the sheep meadows behind McKinley?)

It would appear, in short, that the rudimentary grades of outdoor recreation consume their resource-base; the higher grades, at least to a degree, create their own satisfactions with little or no attrition of land or life. It is the expansion of transport without a corresponding growth of perception that threatens us with qualitative bankruptcy of the recreational process. Recreational development is a job not of building roads into lovely country, but of building receptivity into the still unlovely human mind.

51

EARTH FIRST!

DAVE FOREMAN

A radical environmentalist, Dave Foreman argues that present-day ecological crises are too severe to justify half-hearted or piecemeal measures to solve them. Wilderness has ultimate value, over and above any value that humans may place on it. In keeping with this view, Foreman's version of radical environmentalism—sometimes called "deep ecology"—advocates all measures necessary to ensure the integrity and survival of animals, plants, and the ecosystems that sustain them. Like the characters in Edward Abbey's novel, *The Monkey Wrench Gang* (1975), Foreman and other members of Earth First! favor, and have been accused of practicing, pro-environmental sabotage or "monkey-wrenching" to stop strip-miners, loggers, dam-builders, and other "developers" from further despoiling North American wilderness.

Source: Dave Foreman, "Earth First!" The Progressive *(October 1981), pp. 39–42. Reprinted by permission from* The Progressive, *409 East Main Street, Madison, WI 53703.*

The early conservation movement in the United States was a child—and no bastard child—of the Establishment. The founders of the Sierra Club, the Audubon Society, the Wilderness Society, and the wildlife conservation groups were, as a rule, wealthy pillars of American society. They were an elite band—sportsmen of the Teddy Roosevelt variety, naturalists like John Burroughs, outdoorsmen in the mold of John Muir, pioneer foresters and ecologists on the order of Aldo Leopold, and wealthy social visionaries like Robert Marshall. No anarchistic Luddites these.

When such groups as the Sierra Club grew into the politically effective force that blocked Echo Park Dam in 1956 and got the Wilderness Act passed in 1964, their members were likely to be physicians, mathematicians, and nuclear physicists. To be sure, in the 1950s and 1960s a few oddball refugees from the American mainstream joined the conservation outfits. But it was not until Earth Day in 1970 that the environmental movement received its first influx of real anti-establishment radicals as anti-war protesters found a new cause—the environment. Suddenly, in environmental meetings beards appeared alongside crewcuts—and the rhetoric quickened.

The militancy was short-lived. Along with dozens of other products of the 1960s who went to work for conservation groups in the early 1970s, I discovered that a suit and tie gained access to regional foresters and members of Congress. We learned to moderate our opinions along with our dress. We heard that extremists were ignored in the councils of government, that the way to get a Senator to put his arm around your shoulders and drop a wilderness bill in the hopper was to consider the conflicts—mining, timber, grazing—and pare back the offending acreage. Of course we were good patriotic Americans. Of course we were concerned with the production of red meat, timber, and minerals. We tried to demonstrate that preserving wilderness did not conflict all that much with the gross national product and that clean air actually helped the economy. We argued that we could have our booming industry and still sink oil wells in pristine areas.

Our moderate stance appeared to pay off when the first avowed conservationist since Teddy Roosevelt took the helm at the White House in 1977. Suddenly our colleagues—self-professed conservationists—occupied important and decisive positions in the Carter Administration. Editorials proclaimed that environmentalism had been enshrined in the Establishment, that conservation was here to stay. A new environmental ethic was at hand: Environmental Quality and Continued Economic Progress.

But although we had access—indeed, influence—in high places, something seemed amiss. When the chips were down, conservation still lost out to industry. But these were our *friends* turning us down. We tried to understand the problems they faced in the real political world. We gave them the benefit of the doubt. We failed to sue when we should have. . . .

I wondered about all this on a gray day in January 1979, as I sat in my private office in the headquarters of the Wilderness Society, only three blocks from the White House in Washington, D.C. I had just returned from a news conference at the South Agriculture Building, where the Forest Service had announced a disappointing decision on RARE II—the second Roadless Area Review and Evaluation (a twenty-month exercise by the Forest Service to determine which National Forest lands should be protected in their natural condition).

As I loosened my tie, propped my cowboy boots up on my desk, and popped the top to another Stroh's, I thought about RARE II and why it had gone so wrong. Jimmy Carter, supposedly a great friend of wilderness, was President. Dr. M. Rupert Cutler, a former assistant executive director of the Wilderness Society, was assistant secretary of agriculture over the Forest Service and had conceived the RARE II program. But we had lost to the timber, mining, and cattle interests on every point. Of sixty million acres still roadless and undeveloped in the 220 million acres of National Forests, the Department of Agriculture was recommending only fifteen million for wilderness protection from road building and timber cutting.

Moreover, damn it, we—the conservationists—had been moderate. The antienvironmental side had been extreme, radical, emotional. Their arguments had been easily shot full of holes. We had been factual, rational. We had provided more—and better—serious public comment. But we had lost. And now we were worried that some local wilderness group might go off the reservation and sue the Forest Service over the clearly inadequate environmental impact statement for RARE II. We didn't want a suit—because we knew we could win and were afraid of the political consequences of such a victory. We might make some powerful Senators and Representatives angry. So those of us in Washington were plotting on how to keep the grass roots in line. But, vaguely, something seemed wrong to me.

After RARE II, I left my position as issues coordinator for the Wilderness Society in Washington to return to New Mexico and my old job as the Society's Southwest representative. I was particularly concerned with the overgrazing on the 180 million acres of public lands in the West managed by the Department of Interior's Bureau of Land Management (BLM). For years, these lands—rich in wildlife, scenic, recreational, and wilderness values—had been the private preserve of stockgrowers in the West. BLM had done little to manage national lands or to control the serious overgrazing that was sending millions of tons of topsoil down the Colorado, Rio Grande, and other rivers; wiping out wildlife habitat, and generally beating the land to hell.

Prodded by a Natural Resources Defense Council suit, BLM began to try to get a handle on the overgrazing problem through a series of environmental impact statements. These confirmed that most BLM lands were seriously overgrazed and recommended cuts in animal numbers. But after the expected outcry from the few thousands ranchers leasing BLM land and their political cronies in Congress and state capitals, BLM backtracked so quickly that a fair number of knees must have been dislocated. Why were BLM and the Department of Interior so gutless?

While that question gnawed at my innards, I was growing increasingly disturbed about the trends in the conservation organizations themselves. When I had originally gone to work for the Wilderness Society in 1973, the way to get a job with a conservation group was to prove yourself first as a volunteer. It helped to have the right academic background, but experience as a capable grass-roots conservation activist was more important.

We realized that we would not receive the salary we could earn in government or private industry but we didn't expect it. We were working for nonprofit groups funded by the contributions of concerned people. Give us enough to keep food on the table, pay rent, buy a six-pack—we didn't want to get rich. But a change occurred after the mid-1970s. Now young people seeking to work for conservation groups were career-oriented, they had relevant degrees (science, law—not history or English), they saw jobs in environmental organizations in the same light as jobs in government or industry. One was a stepping stone to another, more powerful position later on. They were less part of a cause and more part of a profession.

A gulf began to grow between staff and volunteers. We also began to squabble over salaries. We were no longer content to be paid subsistence, and the figures in our salaries chalked up our status in the movement. Perrier and brie replaced Bud and beans.

Within the Wilderness Society, Celia Hunter, prominent Alaskan conservationist and outfitter, World War II pilot, and feminist, had been executive director while I was in Washington. Celia instituted staff discussions, democratic decision-making, more equitable salaries, and emphasis on results instead of flash. But the governing council of the Society, controlled by retired Federal bureaucrats, was not sympathetic; the council preferred a hierarchy dominated by a strong male figure (there was a definite undercurrent of sexism in the struggle).

The council found this strong male figure in Bill Turnage, an eager young businessman who had made his mark by marketing Ansel Adams. Turnage took over as executive director late in 1978, and within two years he had replaced virtually all those on the staff under Celia with professional organization people. The clique running things on the governing council also moved to bring millionaires with a vague environmental interest onto the council. We were, it seemed to some of us, becoming indistinguishable from those we were ostensibly fighting.

I resigned my position in June 1980.

But what of the rest of the movement? Were there any radicals anywhere? Anyone to take the hard stands? Sadly, no. The national groups—Sierra Club, Friends of the Earth, Audubon Society, Wilderness Society, and the rest—took almost identical middle-of-the-road positions on most issues. And then those half-a-loaf demands were readily compromised further. The top conservation staffs of these groups fretted about keeping local conservationists (and some of their field staffs) in line, keeping them from becoming extreme or unreasonable, keeping them from blowing moderate national strategy on a variety of issues.

For years I was a strong advocate of this approach. We could, I believed, gain more wilderness by a moderate tack, we would stir up less opposition by keeping a low profile. We could inculcate conservation in the Establishment by using rational, economic arguments. The last thing we needed was somebody running amok. We needed to present a solid front. We all had to be on the same bandwagon. Even Friends of the Earth, which had started out to be the radical among us back in the heady Earth Day era, had gravitated to the center and, as a rule, was a comfortable member of the informal coalition of environmental organizations.

A major crack in my personal moderation appeared early in 1979, when I returned from Washington to the small ranching community of Glenwood, New Mexico. I had lived there earlier for six years and, although a known conservationist, was fairly well accepted. Shortly after my return, *The New York Times* published an article on RARE II, with the Gila National Forest around Glenwood as chief exhibit. To my amazement, the article included a quote from a rancher, whom I considered to be a friend, threatening *my* life because of wilderness lockups! A couple of days later I was accosted on the street by four men, one of whom ran the town cafe at which I had eaten many a fried steak. They threatened my life because of RARE II.

I was not afraid, but I was irritated—and surprised. I had been a leading moderate among New Mexico conservationists. I had successfully convinced them to propose fewer RARE II areas on the Gila National Forest as wilderness. What had backfired? I thought again about the different approaches to RARE II: the moderate, subdued one advanced by the major conservation groups: the howling, impassioned, extreme stand set forth by off-road-vehicle zealots, many ranchers, local boosters, loggers, and miners. They looked like fools. We looked like statesmen. Who won? They did.

The last straw fell last Fourth of July in Moab, Utah. There the local county commission sent a flag-flying bulldozer into an area the Bureau of Land Management had identified as a possible study area for wilderness review. The bulldozer incursion was to be an opening salvo for the so-called Sagebrush Rebellion, a move by chambers of commerce, ranchers, and right-wing fanatics in the West to claim all Federal public lands for the states and eventual transfer to private hands. The Rebellion was clearly an extremist effort, lacking the support of even many conservative members of Congress in the West. But BLM was afraid to stop the county commission.

"What have we really accomplished?" I thought. "Are we any better off as far as saving the Earth now than we were ten years ago?" I ticked off the real problems: world population growth, destruction of tropical forests, expanding slaughter of African wildlife, oil pollution of the ocean acid rain, carbon dioxide buildup in the atmosphere, spreading deserts on every continent, destruction of native peoples and the imposition of one world culture (European), plans to carve up Antarctica, deep seabed mining, nuclear proliferation, recombinant DNA research, toxic wastes. It was staggering. And I feared we had done nothing to reverse the tide. Indeed, it had accelerated.

And then: Ronald Reagan. James "Rape 'n' Ruin" Watt is Secretary of the Interior. The Forest Service is Louisiana-Pacific's. Interior is Exxon's. The Environmental Protection Agency is Dow's. Already, the Reagan Administration and the Republican Senate talk of gutting the gutless Alaska Lands Bill. The Clean Air Act, up for renewal, faces a Government more interested in corporate black ink than human lungs. The lands of the Bureau of Land Management appear to our Interior Department obscenely naked without the garb of oil wells. Meanwhile, the Agriculture Department will direct the Forest Service in ridding the National Forests of those disgustingly decadent and diseased old-growth trees. The cowboys have the grazing lands and God help the hiker, coyote, or blade of grass that gets in their way.

Maybe—some of us began to feel, even before Reagan's election—it was time for a new joker in the deck: a militant, uncompromising group unafraid to say what needed to be said or to back it up with stronger actions than the established organizations were willing to take. This idea had been kicking around for a couple of years; finally last year several of us (including, among others, Susan Morgan, formerly educational director for the Wilderness Society; Howie Wolke, former Wyoming representative for Friends of the Earth; Bart Koehler, former Wyoming representative for the Wilderness Society, and myself) decided that the time for talk was past. We formed a new national group, EARTH FIRST! We set out to be radical in style, positions, philosophy, and organization in order to be effective and to avoid the pitfalls of co-option and moderation which we had already experienced.

What, we asked ourselves as we sat around a campfire in the Wyoming mountains, were the advantages, the reasons for environmental radicalism?

- To state honestly the views held by many conservationists.
- To demonstrate that the Sierra Club and its allies were raging moderates, believers in the system, and to refute the Reagan/Watt contention that they were "extremist environmentalists."
- To balance such anti-environmental radicals as the Grand County commission and provide a broader spectrum of viewpoints.
- To return some vigor, joy, and enthusiasm to the allegedly tired environmental movement.
- To keep the established groups honest. By stating a pure, non-compromise proEarth position, we felt EARTH FIRST! could help keep the other groups from straying too far from their philosophical base.
- To give an outlet to many hard-line conservationists who were no longer active because of disenchantment with compromise politics and the co-option of environmental organizations.
- To provide a productive fringe since it seems that ideas, creativity, and energy spring up on the fringe and later spread into the middle.
- To inspire others to carry out activities straight from the pages of *The Monkey Wrench Gang* even though EARTH FIRST!, we agreed, would itself be ostensibly law-abiding.
- To question the system: to help develop a new world view, a biocentric paradigm, an Earth philosophy. To fight, with uncompromising passion, for Mother Earth.

The name—EARTH FIRST!—was chosen deliberately because it succinctly summed up the one thing on which we could all agree. That in *any* decision, consideration for the health of the Earth must come first, or, as Aldo Leopold said, "A thing is right when it tends to preserve the integrity, stability, and beauty of the biotic community. It is wrong when it tends otherwise."

In a true Earth-radical group, concern for

wilderness preservation must be the keystone. The idea of wilderness, after all, is the most radical in human thought—more radical than Paine, than Marx, than Mao, Wilderness says: Human beings are not dominant. Earth is not for *Homo sapiens* alone, human life is but one life form on the planet and has no right to take exclusive possession. Yes, wilderness for its own sake, without any need to justify it for human benefit. Wilderness for wilderness. For grizzlies and whales and titmice and rattlesnakes and stink bugs. And . . . wilderness for human beings. Because it is the laboratory of three million years of human evolution—and because it is home.

It is not enough to protect our few remaining bits of wilderness. The only hope for Earth (and humanity for that matter) is to withdraw huge areas as inviolate natural sanctuaries from the depredations of modern industry and technology. Keep Cleveland, Los Angeles. Contain them. Try to make them habitable. But identify areas—big areas—that can be restored to a semblance of natural conditions, reintroduce the griz and wolf and prairie grasses, and declare them off limits to modern civilization.

In the United States pick an area for each of our major ecosystems and recreate the American wilderness—not in little pieces of a thousand acres but in chunks of a million or ten million. Move out the people and cars. Reclaim the roads and plowed land. It is not enough any longer to say no more dams on our wild rivers. We must begin tearing down some dams already built—beginning with Glen Canyon, Hetch Hetchy, Tellico, and New Melones—and freeing shackled rivers.

This emphasis on wilderness is not to ignore other environmental issues or to abandon the people who suffer because of them. In the United States blacks and Chicanos of the inner cities are the ones most affected by air and water pollution, the ones most trapped by the unnatural confines of urbanity. So we decided that not only should ecomilitants be concerned with these human environmental problems: we should also make common ground with other progressive elements of society whenever possible.

Obviously, for a group more committed to Gila monsters and mountain lions than to people, there will not be a total alliance with the other social movements. But there are issues where Earth radicals can cooperate with feminist, Indian rights, anti-nuke, peace, civil rights, and civil liberties groups. The inherent conservatism of the conservation community has made it wary of snuggling too close to these questionable (in their minds) leftist organizations. We hoped that the way might be paved for better cooperation from the entire conservation movement.

We believed that new tactics were needed—something more than commenting on dreary environmental impact statements and writing letters to members of Congress. Politics in the streets. Civil disobedience. Media stunts. Holding the villains up to ridicule. Using music to charge the cause.

Action is the key. Action is more important than philosophical hair-splitting or endless refining of dogma (for which radicals are so well known). Let our actions set the finer points of our philosophy. And let us recognize that diversity is not only the spice of life, it is also the strength. All that would be required to join us, we decided. was a belief in Earth first. Apart from that, EARTH FIRST! would be big enough to contain street poets and cowboy bar bouncers, agnostics and pagans, vegetarians and raw steak eaters, pacifists and those who think that turning the other cheek is a good way to get a sore face.

Radicals frequently verge toward a righteous seriousness. But we felt that if we couldn't laugh at ourselves we would be merely another bunch of dangerous fanatics who should be locked up (like the oil companies). Not only does humor preserve individual and group sanity, it retards hubris, a major cause of environmental rape, and it is also an effective weapon. Additionally, fire, passion, courage, and emotionalism are called for. We have been too reasonable, too calm, too understanding. It's time to get angry, to cry, to let rage flow at what the human cancer is doing to Mother Earth, to be uncompromising. For EARTH FIRST! it is all or nothing. Win or lose. No truce or cease fire. No surrender. No partitioning of the territory.

Ever since the Earth goddesses of ancient Greece were supplanted by the macho Olympians, repression of women and Earth has gone hand in hand with imperial organization. EARTH FIRST! decided to be nonorganizational: no officers, no bylaws or constitution, no incorporation, no tax status; just a collection of women and men committed to the Earth. At the turn of the century William Graham Sumner wrote a famous essay entitled "The Conquest of the United States by Spain." His thesis was that Spain had ultimately won the Spanish American War because the United States took on the imperialism and totalitarianism of Spain as a result. We felt that if we took on the organization of the industrial state, we would soon accept their anthropocentric paradigm (much as Audubon and the Sierra Club already had).

In keeping with that view, EARTH FIRST! took the shape of a circle, a group of thirteen women and men around the country who more or less direct the movement, and a collection of regional contacts. We also have local affiliates (so far in Alaska, Montana, Wyoming, Colorado, Arizona, New Mexico, Utah, Arkansas, Maine, and Virginia). We publish a newsletter eight times a year and are developing position papers on a range of issues from automobiles to overgrazing. We also send out press releases. Membership is free, although we do encourage members to kick in ten bucks or more, if they can afford it, to help with expenses. We have not sought any grants or funding with strings attached, nor do we plan to have paid staff (although we hope to have field organizers receiving expenses in the tradition of the Wobblies).

And, when we are inspired, we *act.*

Massive, powerful, like some creation of Darth Vader's, Glen Canyon Dam squats in the canyon of the Colorado River on the Arizona-Utah border and backs the cold dead waters of Lake Powell some 180 miles upstream, drowning the most awesome and magical canyon on Earth. More than any other single entity, Glen Canyon Dam is the symbol of the destruction of wilderness, of the technological rape of the West. The finest fantasy of eco-warriors in the West is the destruction of the dam and the liberation of the Colorado. So it was only proper that on March 21, 1981—on the Spring Equinox, the traditional time of rebirth—EARTH FIRST! held its first national gathering at Glen Canyon Dam.

On that morning, seventy-five members of EARTH FIRST! lined the walkway of the Colorado River Bridge 700 feet above the once free river and watched five compatriots busy at work with an awkward black bundle on the massive dam just upstream. Those on the bridge carried placards reading "Damn Watt, Not Rivers." "Free the Colorado," and "Let It Flow." The four men and one woman on the dam attached ropes to a grill on the dam, shouted out "EARTH FIRST!" and let 300 feet of black plastic unfurl down the side of the dam, creating the impression of a growing crack. Those on the bridge returned the cheer.

A few minutes later, Edward Abbey, author of *The Monkey Wrench Gang,* a novel of environmental sabotage in the Southwest, told the protesters of the "green and living wilderness" that was Glen Canyon only nineteen years ago:

"And they took it away from us. The politicians of Arizona, Utah, New Mexico, and Colorado, in cahoots with the land developers, city developers, industrial developers of the Southwest, stole this treasure from us in order to pursue and promote their crackpot ideology of growth, profit and power—growth for the sake of power, power for the sake of growth."

Speaking toward the future, Abbey offered this advice: "Oppose. Oppose the destruction of our homeland by these alien forces from Houston, Tokyo, Manhattan, Washington, D.C., and the Pentagon. And if opposition is not enough, we must resist. And if resistance is not enough, then subvert."

Abbey then launched a nationwide petition campaign demanding the dismantling of Glen

Canyon Dam. Hardly had he finished speaking when Park Service police and Coconino County sheriff's deputies arrived on the scene. While they questioned the organizers of the illegal assembly and tried to disperse it, outlaw country singer Johnny Sagebrush led the demonstrators in song for another twenty minutes.

The Glen Canyon Dam caper brought EARTH FIRST! an unexpected degree of media attention. Membership in our group has spiraled to more than a thousand with members from Maine to Hawaii. Even the Government is interested—according to reliable reports, the FBI dusted the entire Glen Canyon Dam crack for fingerprints!

Last Fourth of July more than 200 EARTH FIRST!ers gathered in Moab, Utah, for the first Sagebrush Patriot Rally to express support for Federal public land and to send a message to anti-Earth fanatics that there are Americans who are patriotic about *their* wilderness.

When a few of us kicked off EARTH FIRST! we sensed a growing environmental radicalism in the country but we did not expect the response we have received. Maybe EARTH FIRST! isin the right place at the right time. Tom Turner, editor of Friends of the Earth's *Not Man Apart*, recently wrote to us to say:

"Russ Train once said, 'Thank God for Dave Brower—he makes it so easy for the rest of us to appear reasonable.' Youze guys are about to make Dave Brower look reasonable, and more power to you!"

The cynical may smirk. "But what can you really accomplish? How can you fight Exxon, Coors, David Rockefeller, Japan, and the other great corporate giants of the Earth? How, indeed, can you fight the dominant dogmas of Western Civilization?"

Perhaps it *is* a hopeless quest. But is that relevant? Is that important? No, what is important is that one who loves Earth can do no less. Maybe a species will be saved or a forest will go uncut or a dam will be torn down. Maybe not. A monkey wrench thrown into the gears of the machine may not stop it. But it might delay it. Make it cost more. And it feels good to put it there.

52

WHAT IS SOCIAL ECOLOGY?

MURRAY BOOKCHIN

Anarchist Murray Bookchin (1921–   ) is one of the most prominent representatives of the school of thought known as "social ecology." In common with Dave Foreman and other advocates of "deep ecology," Bookchin and social ecologists trace the roots of contemporary environmental crises to the ideas and ideologies that have dominated the Western world, especially in the last few centuries. In contrast with the deep ecologists, however, Bookchin outlines an ecological view that emphasizes the value of human community and finds room for modern technology of an appropriate scale.

Source: Murray Bookchin, The Modern Crisis *(Philadelphia: New Society Publisher, 1986). Copyright © Murray Bookchin, New Society Publishers, Philadelphia, PA, and Santa Cruz, CA. (800) 333–9093.*

We are clearly beleaguered by an ecological crisis of monumental proportions—a crisis that visibly stems from the ruthless exploitation and pollution of the planet. We rightly attribute the social sources of this crisis to a competitive marketplace spirit that reduces the entire world of life, including humanity, to merchandisable objects, to mere commodities with price tags that are to be sold for profit and economic expansion. The ideology of this spirit is expressed in the notorious marketplace maxim: "Grow or die!"—a maxim that identifies limitless growth with "progress" and the "mastery of nature" with "civilization." The results of this tide of exploitation and pollution have been grim enough to yield serious forecasts of complete planetary breakdown, a degree of devastation of soil, forests, waterways, and atmosphere that has no precedent in the history of our species.

In this respect, our market-oriented society is unique in contrast with other societies in that it places no limits on growth and egotism. The antisocial principles that "rugged individualism" is the primary motive for social improvement and competition the engine for social progress stand sharply at odds with all past eras that valued selflessness as the authentic trait of human nobility and cooperation as the authentic evidence of social virtue, however much these prized attributes were honored in the breach. Our marketplace society has, in effect, made the worst features of earlier times into its more honored values and exhibited a degree of brutality in the global wars of this century that makes the cruelties of history seem mild by comparison.

In our discussions of modern ecological and social crises, we tend to ignore a more underlying mentality of domination that humans have used for centuries to justify the domination of each other and, by extension, of nature. I refer to an image of the natural world that sees nature itself as "blind," "mute," "cruel," "competitive," and "stingy," a seemingly demonic "realm of necessity" that opposes "man's" striving for freedom and self-realization. Here, "man" seems to confront a hostile "otherness" against which he must oppose his own powers of toil and guile. History is thus presented to us as a Promethean drama in which "man" heroically defies and willfully asserts himself against a brutally hostile and unyielding natural world. Progress is seen as the extrication of humanity from the muck of a mindless, unthinking, and brutish domain or what Jean-Paul Sartre so contemptuously called the "slime of history," into the presumably clear light of reason and civilization.

This image of a demonic and hostile nature goes back to the Greek world and even earlier, to the Gilgamesh Epic of Sumerian society. But it reached its high point during the past two centuries, particularly in the Victorian Age, and persists in our thinking today. Ironically, the idea of a "blind," " mute," "cruel," "competitive," and "stingy" nature forms the basis for the very social sciences and humanities that profess to provide us with a civilized alternative to nature's "brutishness" and "law of claw and fang." Even as these disciplines stress the "unbridgeable gulf" between nature and society in the classical tradition of a dualism between the physical and the mental, economics literally defines itself as the study of "scarce resources" (read: "stingy nature") and "unlimited needs," essentially rearing itself on the interconnection between nature and humanity. By the same token, sociology sees itself as the analysis of "man's" ascent from "animality." Psychology, in turn, particularly in its Freudian form, is focused on the control of humanity's unruly "internal nature" through rationality and the imperatives imposed on it by "civilization"—with the hidden agenda of sublimating human powers in the project of controlling "external nature."

Many class theories of social development, particularly Marxian socialism, have been rooted in the belief that the "domination of man by man" emerges from the need to "dominate nature," presumably with the result that once nature is subjugated, humanity will be cleansed of the "slime of history" and enter into a new era of freedom. However warped these self-definitions of our major social and humanistic disciplines may be, they are still embedded in nature and humanity's relationships with the natural world, even as they try to bifurcate the two and impart a unique autonomy to cultural development and social evolution.

Taken as a whole, however, it is difficult to convey the enormous amount of mischief this image of nature has done to our ways of thinking, not to speak of the ideological rationale it has provided for human domination. More so than any single notion in the history of religion and philosophy, the image of a "blind," "mute,"' "cruel," "competitive," and "stingy" nature has opened a wide, often unbridgeable chasm between the social world and the natural world, and in its more exotic ramifications, between mind and body, subject and object, reason and physicality, technology and "raw materials," indeed, the whole gamut of dualisms that have fragmented not only the world of nature and society but the human psyche and its biological matrix.

From Plato's view of the body as a mere burden encasing an ethereal soul, to René Descartes' harsh split between the God-given rational and the purely mechanistic physical, we are the heirs of a historic dualism: between, firstly, a misconceived nature as the opponent of every human endeavor, whose "domination" must be lifted from the shoulders of humanity (even if human beings themselves are reduced to mere instruments of production to be ruthlessly exploited with a view toward their eventual liberation), and, secondly, a domineering humanity whose goal is to subjugate the natural world, including human nature itself. Nature, in effect, emerges as an affliction that must be removed by the technology and methods of domination that excuse human domination in the name of "human freedom."

This all-encompassing image of an intractable nature that must be tamed by a rational humanity has given us a domineering form of reason, science, and technology—a fragmentation of humanity into hierarchies, classes, state institutions, gender, and ethnic divisions. It has fostered nationalistic hatreds, imperialistic adventures, and a global philosophy of rule that identifies order with dominance and submission. In slowly corroding every familial, economic, aesthetic, ideological, and cultural tie that provided a sense of place and meaning for the individual in a vital human community, this antinaturalistic mentality has filled the awesome vacuum created by an utterly nihilistic and antisocial development with massive urban entities that are neither cities nor villages, with ubiquitous bureaucracies that impersonally manipulate the lives of faceless masses of atomized human beings, with giant corporate enterprises that spill beyond the boundaries of the world's richest nations to conglomerate on a global scale and determine the material life of the most remote hamlets on the planet, and finally, with highly centralized State institutions and military forces of unbridled power that threaten not only the freedom of the individual but the survival of the species.

The split that clerics and philosophers projected centuries ago in their visions of a soulless nature and a denatured soul has been realized in the form of a disastrous fragmentation of humanity and nature, indeed, in our time, of the human psyche itself. A direct line or logic of events flows almost unrelentingly from a warped image of the natural world to the warped contours of the social world, threatening to bury society in a "slime of history" that is not of nature's making but of man's—specifically, the early hierarchies from which economic classes emerged; the systems of domination, initially of woman by man, that have yielded highly rationalized systems of exploitation; and the vast armies of warriors, priests, monarchs, and bureaucrats who emerged from the simple status groups of tribal society to become the institutionalized tyrants of a market society.

That this authentic jungle of "claw and fang" we call the "free market" is an extension of human competition into nature—an ideological, self-serving fiction that parades under such labels as social Darwinism and sociobiology—hardly requires emphasis any longer. Lions are turned into "Kings of the Beasts" only by human kings, be they imperial monarchs or corporate ones; ants belong to the "lowly" in nature only by virtue of ideologies spawned in temples, palaces, manors, and, in our own time, by subservient apologists of the powers that be. The reality, as we shall see, is different, but a nature conceived as "hierarchical," not to speak of the other "brutish" and very bourgeois traits imputed to it, merely reflects a human condition in which dominance and submission are ends in themselves, which has brought the very existence of our biosphere into question.

Far from being the mere "object" of culture (technology, science, and reason), nature is always with us: as the parody of our self-image, as the cornerstone of the very disciplines which deny it a place in our social and self-formation, even in the protracted infancy of our young which renders the mind open to cultural development and creates those extended parental and sibling ties from which an organized society emerged.

And nature is always with us as the conscience of the transgressions we have visited on the planet—and the terrifying revenge that awaits us for our violation of the ecological balance.

What distinguishes social ecology is that it negates the harsh image we have traditionally created of the natural world and its evolution. And it does so not by dissolving the social into the natural, like sociobiology, or by imparting mystical properties to nature that place it beyond the reach of human comprehension and rational insight. Indeed, as we shall see, social ecology places the human mind, like humanity itself, within a natural context and explores it in terms of its own natural history, so that the sharp cleavages between thought and nature, subject and object, mind and body, and the social and natural are overcome, and the traditional dualisms of western culture are transcended by an evolutionary interpretation of consciousness with its rich wealth of gradations over the course of natural history.

Social ecology "radicalizes" nature, or more precisely, our understanding of natural phenomena, by questioning the prevailing marketplace image of nature from an ecological standpoint: nature as a constellation of communities that are neither "blind" nor "mute," "cruel" nor "competitive," "stingy" nor "necessitarian" but, freed of all anthropocentric moral trappings, a *participatory* realm of interactive life-forms whose most outstanding attributes are fecundity, creativity, and directiveness, marked by complementarity that renders the natural world the *grounding* for an ethics of freedom rather than domination.

Seen from an ecological standpoint, life-forms are related in an ecosystem not by the "rivalries" and "competitive" attributes imputed to them by Darwinian orthodoxy, but by the mutualistic attributes emphasized by a growing number of contemporary ecologists—an image pioneered by Peter Kropotkin. Indeed, social ecology challenges the very premises of "fitness" that enter into the Darwinian drama of evolutionary development with its fixation on "survival" rather than differentiation and fecundity. As William Trager has emphasized in his insightful work on symbiosis:

> The conflict in nature between different kinds of organisms has been popularly expressed in phrases like the "struggle for existence" and the "survival of the fittest." Yet few people realized that mutual cooperation between organisms—symbiosis—is just as important, and that the "fittest" may be the one that helps another to survive.

It is tempting to go beyond this pithy and highly illuminating judgement to explore an ecological notion of natural evolution based on the development of *ecosystems,* not merely individual species. This is a concept of evolution as the dialectical development of ever-variegated, complex, and increasingly fecund *contexts* of plant-animal communities as distinguished from the traditional notion of biological evolution based on the atomistic development of single life-forms, a characteristically entrepreneurial concept of the isolated "individual," be it animal, plant, or bourgeois—a creature which fends for itself and either "survives" or "perishes" in a marketplace "jungle." As ecosystems become more complex and open a greater variety of evolutionary pathways, due to their own richness of diversity and increasingly flexible forms of organic life, it is not only the environment that "chooses" what "species" are "fit" to survive but species themselves, in mutualistic complexes as well as singly, that introduce a dim element of "choice"—by no means "intersubjective" or "willful" in the *human* meaning of these terms.

Concomitantly, these ensembles of species alter the environment of which they are part and exercise an increasingly *active* role in their own evolution. Life, in this *ecological* conception of evolution, ceases to be the passive *tabula rasa* on which eternal forces which we loosely call "the environment" inscribe the destiny of "*a* species," an atomistic term that is meaningless outside the context of an ecosystem within which a life-form is truly definable with respect to other species.

Life is active, interactive, procreative, relational, and contextual. It is not a passive lump of "stuff," a form of metabolic "matter" that awaits the action of "forces" external to it and is mechanically "shaped" by them. Ever striving and always producing new life-forms, there is a sense in which life is self-directive in its own evolutionary development, not passively reactive to an inorganic or organic world that impinges upon it from outside and "determines" its destiny in isolation from the ecosystems which it constitutes and of which it is a part.

And this much is clear in social ecology: our studies of "food webs" (a not quite satisfactory term for describing the interactivity that occurs in an ecosystem or, more properly, an ecological *community*) demonstrate that the complexity of biotic interrelationships, their diversity and intricacy, is a crucial factor in assessing an ecosystem's stability. In contrast to biotically complex temperate zones, relatively simple desert and arctic ecosystems are very fragile and break down easily with the loss or numerical decline of only a few species. The thrust of biotic evolution over great eras of organic evolution has been toward the increasing diversification of species and their interlocking into highly complex, basically mutualistic relationships, without which the widespread colonization of the planet by life would have been impossible.

Unity in diversity (a concept deeply rooted in the western philosophical tradition) is not only the determinant of an ecosystem's stability; it is the source of an ecosystem's fecundity, of its innovativeness, of its evolutionary potential to create newer, still more complex life-forms and biotic interrelationships, even in the most inhospitable areas of the planet. Ecologists have not sufficiently stressed the fact that a multiplicity of life-forms and organic interrelationships in a biotic community opens new evolutionary pathways of development, a greater variety of evolutionary interactions, variations, and degrees of flexibility in the capacity to evolve, and is hence crucial not only in the community's stability but also in its innovativeness in the natural history of life.

The ecological principle of unity in diversity grades into a richly mediated social principle, hence my use of the term *social* ecology. Society, in turn, attains its "truth," its self-actualization, in the form of richly articulated, mutualistic networks of people based on community, roundedness of personality, diversity of stimuli and activities, an increasing wealth of experience, and a variety of tasks. Is this grading of ecosystem diversity into social diversity, based on humanly scaled, decentralized communities, merely analogic reasoning?

My answer would be that it is not a superficial analogy but a deep-seated continuity between nature and society that social ecology recovers from traditional nature philosophy without its archaic dross of cosmic hierarchies, static absolutes, and cycles. In the case of social ecology, it is not in the *particulars* of differentiation that plant-animal communities are ecologically united with human communities; rather, it is the *logic* of differentiation that makes it possible to relate the mediations of nature and society into a continuum.

What makes unity in diversity in nature more than a suggestive ecological metaphor for unity in diversity in society is the underlying fact of wholeness. By wholeness I do not mean any finality of closure in a development, any "totality" that leads to a terminal "reconciliation" of all "Being" in a complete identity of subject and object or a reality in which no further development is possible or meaningful. Rather, I mean varying degrees of the actualization of potentialities, the organic unfolding of the wealth of particularities that are latent in the as-yet-undeveloped potentiality. This potentiality can be a newly planted seed, a newly born infant, a newly formed community, a newly emerging society—yet, given their radically different specificity, they are all united by a processual reality, a shared "metabolism" of development, a unified catalysis of growth as distinguished from mere "change" that provides us with the most insightful way of *understanding* them we can possibly achieve. Wholeness is literally the unity that finally gives order to the particularity of each of these phenomena; it is what has emerged from the process, what integrates the particularities into a unified form, what renders the unity an operable reality and a "being" in the literal sense of the term—an order as the actualized *unity* of its diversity from the flowing and emergent process that yields its self-realization, the fixing of its directiveness into a clearly contoured form, and the creation in a dim sense of a "self" that is identifiable with respect to the "others" with which it interacts. Wholeness is the *relative* completion of a phenomenon's potentiality, the fulfillment of latent possibility as such, all its concrete manifestations aside, to become more than the realm of mere possibility and attain the "truth" or fulfilled reality of possibility. To think this way—in terms of potentiality, process, mediation, and wholeness—is to reach into the most underlying nature of things, just as to know the biography of a human being and the history of a society is to know them in their authentic reality and depth.

The natural world is no less encompassed by this processual dialectic and developmental ecology than the social, although in ways that do not involve will, degrees of choice, values, ethical goals, and the like. Life itself, as distinguished from the nonliving, however, emerges from the inorganic latent with all the potentialities and particularities it has immanently produced from the logic of its own nascent forms of self-organization. Obviously, so does society as distinguished from biology, humanity as distinguished from animality, and individuality as distinguished from humanity in the generic sense of the word. But these distinctions are not absolutes. They are the unique and closely interrelated phases of a shared continuum, of a process that is united precisely by its own differentiations just as the phases through which an embryo develops are both distinct from and incorporated into its complete gestation and its organic specificity.

This continuum is not simply a philosophical construct. It is an earthy anthropological fact which lives with us daily as surely as it explains the emergence of humanity out of mere animality. Individual socialization is the highly nuanced "biography" of that development in everyday life and in everyone as surely as the anthropological socialization of our species is part of its history. I refer to the biological basis of all human socialization: the protracted infancy of the human child that renders its cultural development possible, in contrast to the rapid growth of nonhuman animals, a rate of growth that quickly forecloses their ability to form a culture and develop sibling affinities of a lasting nature; the instinctual maternal drives that extend feelings of care, sharing, intimate consociation, and finally love and a sense of responsibility for one's own kin into the institutional forms we call "society"; and the sexual division of labor, age-ranking, and kin-relationships which, however culturally conditioned and even mythic in some cases, formed and still inform so much of social institutionalization today. These formative elements of society rest on biological facts and, placed in the contextual analysis I have argued for, require ecological analysis.

In emphasizing the nature-society continuum with all its gradations and "mediations," I do not wish to leave the impression that the known ways and forms in which society emerged from nature and still embodies the natural world in a shared process of cumulative growth follow a logic that is "inexorable" or "preordained" by a telos that mystically guides the unfolding by a supranatural and suprasocial process. Potentiality is not necessity; the logic of a process is not a form of inexorable "law"; the truth of a development is what is *implicit* in any unfolding and defined by the extent to which it achieves stability, variety, fecundity, and enlarges the "realm of freedom," however dimly freedom is conceived.

No specific "stage" of a process necessarily yields a still later one or is "presupposed" by it—but certain obvious conditions, however varied, blurred, or even idiosyncratic, form the determining ground for still other conditions that can be expected to emerge. Freedom and, ultimately, a degree of subjectivity that make choice and will possible along rational lines may be desiderata that the natural world renders possible and in a "self"-directive way plays an active role in achieving. But in no sense are these desiderata predetermined certainties that must unfold, nor is any such unfolding spared the very real possibility that it will become entirely regressive or remain unfulfilled and incomplete. That the *potentiality* for freedom and consciousness exists in nature and society; that nature and society are not merely "passive" in a development toward freedom and consciousness, a passivity that would make the very notion of potentiality mystical just as the notion of "necessity" would make it meaningless by definition; that natural and social history bear existential witness to the potentiality and processes that form subjectivity and bring consciousness more visibly on the horizon in the very natural history of mind—all constitute no guarantee that these latent desiderata are certainties or lend themselves to systematic elucidation and teleological explanations in any traditional philosophical sense.

Our survey of organic and social experience may stir us to interpret a development we know to have occurred as reason to presuppose that potentiality, wholeness, and *graded* evolution are realities after all, no less real than our own existence and personal histories, but presuppositions they remain. Indeed, no outlook in philosophy can ever exist that is free of presuppositions, any more than speculation can exist that is free of some stimulus by the objective world. The only truth about "first philosophy," from Greek times onward, is that what is "first" in any philosophical outlook are the presuppositions it adopts, the background of unformulated experience from which these presuppositions emerge, and the intuition of a coherence that must be validated by reality as well as speculative reason.

One of the most provocative of the graded continuities between nature and society is the nonhierarchical relationships that exist in an ecosystem, and the extent to which they provide a grounding for a nonhierarchical society. It is meaningless to speak of hierarchy in an ecosystem and in the succession of ecosystems which, in contrast to a monadic species-oriented development, form the true story of natural evolution. There is no "king of the beasts" and no "lowly serf"—presumably, the lion and the ant—in ecosystem relationships. Such terms, including words like "cruel nature," "fallen nature," "domineering nature," and even "mutualistic nature" (I prefer to use the word "complementary" here) are projections of our own social relationships into the natural world. Ants are as important as lions and eagles in ecosystems; indeed, their recycling of organic materials gives them a considerable "eminence" in the maintenance of the stability and integrity of an area.

As to accounts of "dominance-submission" relationships between individuals such as "alpha" and "beta" males, utterly asymmetrical relationships tend to be grouped under words like "hierarchy" that are more analogic, often more metaphoric, than real. It becomes absurd, I think, to say that the "dominance" of a "queen bee," who in no way knows that she is a "queen" and whose sole function in a beehive is reproductive, is in any way equatable with an "alpha" male baboon, whose "status" tends to suffer grave diminution when the baboon troop moves from the plains to the forest. By the same token, it is absurd to equate "patriarchal harems" among red deer with "matriarchal" elephant herds, which simply expel bulls when they reach puberty and in no sense "dominate" them. One could go through a whole range of asymmetrical relationships to show that, even among our closest primate relatives, which include the utterly "pacific" orangutans as well as the seemingly "aggressive" chimpanzees, words like "dominance" and "submission" mean very different relationships depending upon the species one singles out and the circumstances under which they live.

I cannot emphasize too strongly that hierarchy in society is an *institutional* phenomenon, not a biological one. It is a product of organized, carefully crafted power relationships. . . .

What renders social ecology so important in comparing ecosystems to societies is that it decisively challenges the very function of hierarchy as a way of *ordering* reality, of dealing with differentiation and variation—with "otherness" as such. Social ecology ruptures the association of order with hierarchy. It poses the question of whether we can experience the "other," not hierarchically on a "scale of one to ten" with a continual emphasis on "inferior" and "superior," but ecologically, as variety that enhances the unity of phenomena, enriches wholeness, and more closely resembles a food-web than a pyramid. That hierarchy exists today as an even more fundamental problem than social classes, that domination exists today as an even more fundamental problem than economic exploitation, can be attested to by every conscious feminist, who can justly claim that long before man began to exploit man through the formation of social classes, he began to dominate woman in patriarchal and hierarchical relationships.

We would do well to remember that the abolition of classes, exploitation, and even the State is no guarantee whatever that people will cease to be ranked hierarchically and dominated according to age, gender, race, physical qualities, and often quite frivolous and irrational categories, unless liberation focuses as much on hierarchy and domination as it does on classes and exploitation. This is the point where socialism, in my view, must extend itself into a broader libertarian tradition that reaches back into the tribal or band-type communities ancestral to what we so smugly call "civilization," a tradition, indeed an abiding human impulse, that has surged to the surface of society in every revolutionary period, only to be brutally contained by those purely societal forms called "hierarchies."

Social ecology raises all of these issues in a fundamentally new light, and establishes entirely new ways of resolving them. I have tried to show that nature is always present in the human condition, and in the very ideological constructions that deny its presence in societal relationships. The notion of dominating nature literally *defines* all our social disciplines, including socialism and psychoanalysis. It is the apologia *par excellence* for the domination of human by human. Until that apologia is removed from our sensibilities in the rearing of the young, the first step in socialization as such, and replaced by an ecological sensibility that sees "otherness" in terms of complementarity rather than rivalry, we will never achieve human emancipation . . . .

The ideas I have advanced so far take their point of departure from a radically different image of nature than the prevailing western one, in which philosophical dualism, economics, sociology, psychology, and even socialism have their roots. As a social ecologist, I see nature as essentially creative, directive, mutualistic, fecund, and marked by complementarity, not "mute," "blind," "cruel," "stingy," or "necessitarian." This shift in focus from a marketplace to an ecological image of nature obliges me to challenge the time-honored notion that the domination of human by human is necessary in order to "dominate nature." In emphasizing how meaningless this rationale for hierarchy and domination is, I conclude—with considerable historical justification, which our own era amply illuminates with its deployment of technology primarily for purposes of social control—that the idea of dominating nature stems from human domination, initially in hierarchical forms as feminists so clearly understand, and later in class and statist forms.

Accordingly, my ecological image of nature leads me to drastically redefine my conception of economics, sociology, psychology, and even socialism, which, ironically, advance a shared dualistic gospel of a radical separation of society from nature even as they rest on a militant imperative to "subdue" nature, be it as "scarce resources," the realm of "animality," "internal nature," or "external nature." Hence, I have tried to re-vision history not only as an account of power over human beings that by far outweighs any attempt to gain power over things, but also as power ramified into centralized states and urban environments, a technology, science, and rationality of social control, and a message of "liberation" that conceals the most awesome features of domination, notably, the traditional socialist orthodoxies of the last century.

At the juncture where nature is conceived either as a ruthless, competitive marketplace or a creative, fecund biotic community, two radically divergent pathways of thought and sensibility emerge, following contrasting directions and conceptions of the human future. One ends in a totalitarian and antinaturalistic terminus for society: centralized, statist, technocratic, corporate, and sweepingly repressive. The other ends in a libertarian and ecological beginning for society: decentralized, stateless, artistic, collective, and sweepingly emancipatory. These are not tendentious words. It is by no means certain that western humanity, currently swept up in a counterrevolution of authoritarian values and adaptive impulses, would regard a libertarian vision as less pejorative than a totalitarian one. Whether or not my own words seem tendentious, the full logic of my view should be seen: the view we hold of the natural world profoundly shapes the image we develop of the social worlds, even as we assert the "supremacy" and "autonomy" of culture over nature.

In what sense does social ecology view nature as a grounding for an ethics of freedom? If the story of natural evolution is not understandable in Locke's atomistic account of a particular species' evolution, if that story is basically an account of ecosystem evolution toward ever more complex and flexible evolutionary pathways, then natural history itself cannot be seen simply as "necessitarian," "governed" by "inexorable laws" and imperatives. Every organism is in some sense "willful," insofar as it seeks to preserve itself, to maintain its identity, to resist a kind of biological entropy that threatens its integrity and complexity. However dimly, every organism transforms the essential attributes of self-maintenance that earn it the status of a distinct form of life into a capacity to choose alternatives that favor its survival and well-being—not merely to react to stimuli as a purely physico-chemical ensemble.

This dim, germinal freedom is heightened by the growing wealth of ecological complexity that confronts evolving life in synchronicity with evolving ecosystems. The elaboration of possibilities that comes with the elaboration of diversity and the growing multitude of alternatives confronting species development opens newer and more fecund pathways for organic development. Life is not passive in the face of these possibilities for its evolution. It drives toward them actively in a shared process of mutual stimulation between organisms and their environment (including the living and non-living environment they create) as surely as it also actively creates and colonizes the niches that cradle a vast diversity of life-forms in our richly elaborated biosphere . . .

Here, in this ecological concept of natural evolution, lies a hidden message of freedom based on the "inwardness of life," to use Hans Jonas's excellent expression, and the ever greater diversification produced by natural evolution. Ecology is united with society in new terms that reveal moral tension in natural history, just as Marx's simplistic image of the "savage" who "wrestles with nature" reveals a moral tension in social history.

We must beware of being prejudiced by our own fear of prejudice. Organismic philosophies can surely yield totalitarian, hierarchical, and eco-fascistic results. We have good reason to be concerned over so-called nature philosophies that gives us the notion of *Blut and Boden* and "dialectical materialism," which provide the ideological justification for the horrors of Nazism and Stalinism. We have good reason to be concerned over a mysticism that yields social quietism at best and the aggressive activism of reborn Christianity and certain Asian gurus at worst. We have even better reason to be concerned over the eco-fascism of Garrett Hardin's "lifeboat ethic" with its emphasis on scarce resources and the so-called tragedy of the commons, an ethic which services genocidal theories of imperialism and a global disregard for human misery. So, too, sociobiology, which roots all the savage features of "civilization" in our genetic constitution. Social ecology offers the coordinates for an entirely different pathway in exploring our relationship to the natural world—one that accepts neither genetic and scientistic theories of "natural necessity" at one extreme, nor a romantic and mystical zealotry that reduces the rich variety of reality and evolution to a cosmic "oneness" and energetics at the other extreme. For in both cases, it is not only our vision of the world and the unity of nature and society that suffers, but the "natural history" of freedom and the basis for an objective ethics of liberation as well.

We cannot avoid the use of conventional reason, present-day modes of science, and modern technology. They, too, have their place in the future of humanity and humanity's metabolism with the natural world. But we can establish new *contexts* in which these modes of rationality, science, and technology have their proper place—an *ecological* context that does not deny other, more qualitative modes of knowing and producing which are participatory and emancipatory. We can also foster a new sensibility toward otherness that, *in a nonhierarchical society*, is based on complementarity rather than rivalry, and new communities that, scaled to human dimensions, are tailored to the ecosystem in which they are located and open a new, decentralized, self-managed public realm for new forms of selfhood as well as directly democratic forms of social management.

53

WHAT HAS POSTERITY EVER DONE FOR ME?

ROBERT HEILBRONER

"Why should I do anything for posterity?" goes the old saying. "After all, what has posterity ever done for me?" This attitude, according to economist Robert Heilbroner (1919–), is dangerous to the health, the well-being—even the very existence—of future generations. If future people are to exist and flourish, Heilbroner argues, we shall have to widen our circle of concern to include people who will inhabit the earth long after we are all dead.

Will mankind survive? Who knows? The question I want to put is more searching: Who cares? It is clear that most of us today do not care—or at least do not care enough. How many of us would be willing to give up some minor convenience—say, the use of aerosols—in the hope that this might extend the life of man on earth by a hundred years? Suppose we also knew with a high degree of certainty that humankind could not survive a thousand years unless we gave up our wasteful diet of meat, abandoned all pleasure driving, cut back on every use of energy that was not essential to the maintenance of a bare minimum. Would we care enough for posterity to pay the price of its survival?

I doubt it. A thousand years is unimaginably distant. Even a century far exceeds our powers of empathetic imagination. By the year 2075, I shall probably have been dead for three quarters of a century. My children will also likely be dead, and my grandchildren, if I have any, will be in their dotage. What does it matter to me, then, what life will be like in 2075, much less 3075? Why should I lift a finger to affect events that will have no more meaning for me seventy-five years after my death than those that happened seventy-five years before I was born?

There is no rational answer to that terrible question. No argument based on reason will lead me to care for posterity or to lift a finger in its behalf. Indeed, by every rational consideration, precisely the opposite answer is thrust upon us with irresistible force. As a Distinguished Professor of political economy at the University of London has written in the current winter issue of *Business and Society Review:*

> Suppose that, as a result of using up all the world's resources, human life did come to an end. So what? What is so desirable about an indefinite continuation of the human species, religious convictions apart? It may well be that nearly everybody who is already here on earth would be reluctant to die, and that everybody has an instinctive fear of death. But one must not confuse this with the notion that, in any meaningful sense, generations who are yet unborn can be said to be better off if they are born than if they are not.

Thus speaks the voice of rationality. It is echoed in the book *The Economic Growth Controversy* by a Distinguished Younger Economist from the Massachusetts Institute of Technology:

> . . . Geological time [has been] made comprehensible to our finite human minds by the statement that the 4.5 billion years of the earth's history [are] equivalent to once around the world in an SST. . . . Man got on eight miles before the end, and industrial man got on six feet before the end. . . . Today we are having a debate about the extent to which man ought to maximize the length of time that he is on the airplane.
>
> According to what the scientists now think, the sun is gradually expanding and 12 billion years from now the earth will be swallowed up by the sun. This means that our airplane has time to go round three more times. Do we want man to be on it for all three times around the world? Are we interested in man being on for another eight miles? Are we interested in man being on for another six feet? Or are we only interested in man for a fraction of a millimeter—our lifetimes?
>
> That led me to think: Do I care what happens a thousand years from now? . . . Do I care when man gets off the airplane? I think I basically [have come] to the conclusion that I don't care whether man is on the airplane for another eight feet, or if man is on the airplane another three times around the world.

Is it an outrageous position? I must confess it outrages me. But this is not because the economists' arguments are "wrong"—indeed, within their rational framework they are indisputably right. It is because their position reveals the limitations—worse, the suicidal dangers—of what we call "rational argument" when we confront questions that can only be decided by an appeal to an entirely different faculty from that of cool reason. More than that, I suspect that if there is cause to fear for man's survival it is because the calculus of logic and reason will be applied to problems where they have as little validity, even as little bearing, as the calculus of feeling or sentiment applied to the solution of a problem in Euclidean geometry.

If reason cannot give us a compelling argument to care for posterity—and to care desperately and totally—what can? For an answer, I turn to another distinguished economist whose fame originated in his profound examination of moral conduct. In 1759, Adam Smith published "The Theory of Moral Sentiments," in which he posed a question very much like ours, but to which he gave an answer very different from that of his latter-day descendants.

Suppose, asked Smith, that "a man of humanity" in Europe were to learn of a fearful earthquake in China—an earthquake that swallowed up its millions of inhabitants. How would that man react? He would, Smith mused, "make many melancholy reflections upon the precariousness of human life, and the vanity of all the labors of man, which could thus be annihilated in a moment. He would, too, perhaps, if he was a man of speculation, enter into many reasonings concerning the effects which this disaster might produce upon the commerce of Europe, and the trade and business of the world in general." Yet, when this fine philosophizing was over, would our "man of humanity" care much about the catastrophe in distant China? He would not. As Smith tells us, he would "pursue his business or his pleasure, take his repose or his diversion, with the same ease and tranquillity as if nothing had happened."

But now suppose, Smith says, that our man were told he was to lose his little finger on the morrow. A very different reaction would attend the contemplation of this "frivolous disaster." Our man of humanity would be reduced to a tormented state, tossing all night with fear and dread—whereas "provided he never saw them, he will snore with the most profound security over the ruin of a hundred millions of his brethren."

Next, Smith puts the critical question: Since the hurt to his finger bulks so large and the catastrophe in China so small, does this mean that a man of humanity, given the choice, would prefer the extinction of a hundred million Chinese in order to save his little finger? Smith is unequivocal in his answer. "Human nature startles at the thought," he cries, "and the world in its greatest depravity and corruption never produced such a villain as would be capable of entertaining it."

But what stays our hand? Since we are all such creatures of self-interest (and is not Smith the very patron saint of the motive of self-interest?), what moves us to give precedence to the rights of humanity over those of our own immediate well-being? The answer, says Smith, is the presence within us all of a "man within the beast," an inner creature of conscience whose insistent voice brooks no disobedience: "It is the love of what is honorable and noble, of the grandeur and dignity, and superiority of our own characters."

It does not matter whether Smith's eighteenth-century view of human nature in general or morality in particular appeals to the modern temper. What matters is that he has put the question that tests us to the quick. For it is one thing to appraise matters of life and death by the principles of rational self-interest and quite another *to take responsibility for our choice*. I cannot imagine the Distinguished Professor from the University of London personally consigning humanity to oblivion with the same equanimity with which he writes off its demise. I am certain that if the Distinguished Younger Economist from M.I.T. were made responsible for determining the precise length of stay of humanity on the SST, he would agonize over the problem and end up by exacting every last possible inch for mankind's journey.

Of course, there are moral dilemmas to be faced even if one takes one's stand on the "survivalist" principle. Mankind cannot expect to continue on earth indefinitely if we do not curb population growth, thereby consigning billions or tens of billions to the oblivion of nonbirth. Yet, in this case, we sacrifice some portion of life-to-come in order that life itself may be preserved. This essential commitment to life's continuance gives us the moral authority to take measures, perhaps very harsh measures, whose justification cannot be found in the precepts of rationality, but must be sought in the unbearable anguish we feel if we imagine ourselves as the executioners of mankind.

This anguish may well be those "religious convictions," to use the phrase our London economist so casually tosses away. Perhaps to our secular cast of mind, the anguish can be easily accepted as the furious power of the biogenetic force we see expressed in every living organism. Whatever its source, when we ask if mankind "should" survive, it is only here that we can find a rationale that gives us the affirmation we seek.

This is not to say we will discover a religious affirmation naturally welling up within us as we careen toward Armageddon. We know very little about how to convince men by recourse to reason and nothing about how to convert them to religion. A hundred faiths contend for believers today, a few perhaps capable of generating that sense of caring for human salvation on earth. But, in truth, we do not know if "religion" will win out. An appreciation of the magnitude of the sacrifices required to perpetuate life may well tempt us to opt for "rationality"—to enjoy life while it is still to be enjoyed on relatively easy terms, to write mankind a shorter ticket on the SST so that some of us may enjoy the next millimeter of the trip in first-class seats.

Yet I am hopeful that in the end a survivalist ethic will come to the fore—not from the reading of a few books or the passing twinge of a pious lecture, but from an experience that will bring home to us, as Adam Smith brought home to his "man of humanity," the personal responsibility that defies all the homicidal promptings of reasonable calculation. Moreover, I believe that the coming generations, in their encounters with famine, war, and the threatened life-carrying capacity of the globe, may be given just such an experience. It is a glimpse into the void of a universe without man. I must rest my ultimate faith on the discovery by these future generations, as the ax of the executioner passes into their hands, of the transcendent importance of posterity for them.

PART TEN

THE FUTURE OF IDEOLOGY

"Anyone wishing to lead a quiet life," wrote the Russian revolutionary Leon Trotsky, "has done badly to be born in the twentieth century." Ours has been a century of wars and revolution, of concentration camps and gulags, of genocide and hydrogen bombs. The ferocity of these conflicts was increased in part by new developments in technology, and particularly in the creation of newer and ever more murderous weapons of war. But political ideologies have also inspired and intensified these conflicts. The Russian Revolution of 1917, the rise of Mussolini and Hitler, the systematic murder of millions of people—all these, and many more, are traceable to political ideologies of one kind or another. Clearly our century has been an age of ideology.

As the twentieth century comes to an end, however, some people are asking whether the age of ideology might be ending too. After all, they say, communism has crumbled in Eastern Europe and faces serious challenges in the Soviet Union and China. Democracies are replacing dictatorships. Everywhere people are demanding the right to shape their own destinies as they see fit. In short, ideology no longer seems to divide the world as it once did. An awareness of common hopes—the hope for peace, for prosperity, for a world fit for habitation by our children and grandchildren—is replacing the fear and hostility exacerbated by ideological differences. Even so, we continue to fear that the awesome weapons of war might be unleashed, as President Kennedy once said, through madness or miscalculation. We share another fear as well: that even if the planet escapes nuclear destruction, it may nevertheless be destroyed more slowly but no less surely by a series of interconnected environmental catastrophes. Therefore, some say, we can no longer afford (if ever we could) the luxury of ideological differences and disagreements. This makes it possible to believe that we can now put aside our differences and work together for the good of all.

As advanced by Daniel Bell and others, this "end of ideology" thesis offers an appealing vision of present possibilities and future prospects. But is it true? Can ideology "end"? Our own view is that this is highly unlikely, if only because—as we noted in the "Introduction"—ideologies perform four important functions for those who subscribe to them. First, they help to *explain* political phenomena that would otherwise remain puzzling or mysterious. Second, they supply standards for *evaluat-*

ing political situations and developments. Third, ideologies provide their adherents with a means of *orienting* themselves in the complicated and changing political world. And fourth, ideologies provide a *program* of political action. It is unlikely that reasonably intelligent citizens could make their way in the world without an ideology to perform these four important—and probably indispensable—functions.

Although ideology per se is unlikely to end, it can be profoundly transformed. And that, we believe, is precisely what is happening as the twentieth century nears its end. Some ideologies, such as the Marxist-Leninist version of socialism, appear to be dying, whereas others—such as the newer ecological or "green" ideology—are emerging and gaining in influence and importance. Meanwhile, an older ideology—liberalism—is experiencing a revival. Indeed, Francis Fukuyama contends that liberalism—understood as the defense of individual rights and private property against state encroachment—has defeated its ideological rivals and emerged as *the* dominant ideology of our time. The older history of ideological conflict has come to an end, with a single ideology triumphant.

Inasmuch as predictions about "the end of ideology" (Bell) and the "end of history" (Hegel, Marx, and Fukuyama) have been made before and have always failed to be borne out by events, we remain skeptical. We suspect that history—to turn Hegel's own phrase against him—is too "cunning" for humans, however clever, to predict its future course with any accuracy.

All ideologies are born of crises of one kind or another. If there is one crisis that looms large on the near horizon of history, that is surely the ecological crisis. Far from being a single crisis, this is in fact a series of interconnected problems requiring immediate attention. These range from the technical—How, for example, shall we dispose of toxic wastes?—to the philosophical—What is our place in and relation to nature? What duties or obligations, if any, do human beings have toward animals, or toward rivers, mountains, and forests? What are our obligations toward future generations?

If older ideologies, including liberalism, cannot answer these questions in any satisfactory way, then it appears likely that an alternative ideology will emerge to challenge and perchance replace it. That is the expectation, at any rate, being voiced by many modern Greens in Europe and elsewhere.

What the coming century holds for us and our children, no one knows. But we can be reasonably certain that ideologies and ideological differences, far from disappearing, will continue to transform the political terrain of the twenty-first century.

54

THE END OF IDEOLOGY—REVISITED

DANIEL BELL

Daniel Bell (1919–), a sociologist, is a former socialist who has been linked since the late 1960s with neoconservatism (see selection 28). In 1960 his book, *The End of Ideology: On the Exhaustion of Political Ideas in the Fifties*, provoked a controversy among scholars. In 1988 Bell "revisited" this controversy, and took a look ahead, in the essay from which the following selection is taken.

Source: Daniel Bell, "The End of Ideology Revisited—Part II," Government and Opposition, *Volume 23, No. 3 (Summer 1988), pp. 325–331. Reprinted by permission.*

In respect to political consequences, the "End of Ideology" . . . has some resonance today because we are in a new cycle of disillusionment in the communist world. There were the Moscow Trials and the Nazi-Soviet pact in the late 1930s; the Khrushchev revelations and the Hungarian uprising in 1956; the Prague spring of 1968 and the smashing by the Brezhnev regime of Dubček's effort to propose a "socialism with a human face." There is one startling difference in the present situation. The previous disillusionments were moral, intellectual and political. The admitted failures this time are primarily *economic*.

Whatever the previous disenchantments, the overriding argument for the superiority of socialism was that the anarchy of the market is replaced by conscious social organization. As Engels wrote, in *Socialism: Utopian and Scientific:* "The laws of society come under man's control, and men, for the first time, can make their own history." The justification for Stalin's forced industrialization and brutal collectivism in agriculture was that the Soviet Union could make the leap from a backward nation to a modern state only through the mechanisms of central planning and the primacy of heavy industry as the basis for later differentiation of production and the expansion of consumption. After the Second World War, with the emergence of the "Third World," the Soviet model was touted as the only workable model for "under-developed countries," whose economic expansion was being held back by "unequal exchange" and "dependency" on the capitalist societies.

But what Deng Xiaoping and Mikhail Gorbachev have conceded is that central planning has become cumbersome and inflexible, and that the economies of both countries have begun to stagnate. At the same time, the extraordinary economic successes of Japan, South Korea, the smaller East Asian countries, as well as Brazil, within a shorter period of time than in the Soviet Union, have provided a very different mixed market/state economic model for Third-World countries.

In China and the Soviet Union, the new policies seek to provide material incentives geared to output, the introduction of market mechanisms, a large leeway for enterprise managers to make their own production and pricing decisions, and a degree of competition to weed out the inefficient firms even at the cost of bankruptcies and unemployment. What, then, is the economic meaning of "socialism"? In the 1920s, the American journalist Lincoln Steffens returned from the Soviet Union and fashioned a phrase that for decades became the banner for all progressive-minded persons: "I have seen the future and it works." As a character in the satirical novel *Mother Russia* by Robert Littell (1978) remarks about Soviet life: "I have seen the future, and it needs work."

On the political level, the situation in Eastern Europe presents a mirthless paradox that completes the ideological re-inversion of Marxism. On his road to discovering the materialist foundations of society Marx had sought to show that Hegel's views of political life were "illusions" derived from a false relation between ideology and reality. In his *Critique of Hegel's Philosophy of Right* and *On the Jewish Question*, Marx argued that Hegel had inverted the relation of state to civil society by postulating a false autonomy to the former. And Engels, picking up that theme, in his monograph on *Feuerbach and the Outcome of German Classical Philosophy* (1888) wrote: "The State presents itself to us as the first ideological power over mankind," for though it was created by "society" to safeguard the general interest, it "makes itself independent in regard to society; and indeed, the more so, the more it becomes the organ of a particular class, the more it directly enforces the supremacy of that class."

This statement could be—it is—an adequate formulation of the relation of state to society in Poland, i.e., of the regime to the working class; and, in the Soviet Union, of the *nomenklatura*, the "new class" of privilege, to the remainder of the society.

The ideology *of* Marxism is the belief in the inevitable polarization in advanced Western society between capitalist and worker and the victory of the proletariat as the necessary outcome of the cunning of reason. This is the "philosophy of history" that replaced the Augustinian *parousia* as the faith system which prophesied the "leap from the kingdom of necessity into the kingdom of freedom."[1] Does anyone still believe in those illusions?

But a different intellectual and theoretical issue is at stake. The fundamental theorem of Marxian sociology is that, *au fond*, all social structure is class structure, and is the relevant unit of politics, even for the analysis of culture. What is striking in almost all societies, particularly in the West, is not only the rapid shrinking of the industrial working class but the break-up of the economic class as the fundamental axis of social division. Every society (with the exception of Japan) is a "plural society" with large admixtures of minorities. And apart from the multiple identities of gender, age, religion, education and occupation, ethnic identities seem to become more and more salient as group attachment and conflicts between groups on ethnic, linguistic, religious, communal and similar lines seem to be sources today of cultural/political identifications. Yet in the *Communist Manifesto*, Marx had written:

> National differences and antagonisms between people are already tending to disappear more and more, owing to the development of the bourgeosie, the growth of free trade and a world market, and the increasing uniformity of industrial processes and of the corresponding conditions of life. The rule of the proletariat will efface these differences and antagonisms even more.

Apart from the fact that there is less cooperation and solidarity within the international working class today than at any time in the past hundred years, what is striking is the rise of national tensions in almost every part of the world, as much in the Communist world as anywhere else. How, on Marxist grounds, can one explain the rivalry between the Soviet Union and China; the smouldering war between China and Vietnam; the occupation of Cambodia by Vietnamese puppets; the armed wall between Albania and Yugoslavia; and the threatened break-up of Yugoslavia itself, as ancient antagonisms between Serb and Croat, Serb and Albanian, etc. become visible? What is one to say of the large minority enclaves of Hungarian national groups in Romania, of the Baltic peoples within the Soviet Union, of the Muslim nationalities in Central Asia whose demographic growth rates threaten to overwhelm the balance of nationalities within the Soviet Union?

As one approaches the twenty-first century, the problems of colour, of tribalism, of ethnic differences—in south-east Asia, the Middle East, the fratricidal hatred in the Muslim world—all bespeak an agenda of issues which contemporary sociology, least of all Marxism, is ill-prepared to understand. One sees, particularly in Marxism, how much our sociological categories were framed within the context of Western society, and how the themes of Enlightenment, rationality, industrialization, consciousness, class, development, the idea of "historic nations" and social evolution, became our prisms of understanding. And how irrelevant Marx, and even Weber and Durkheim, may be.

TWO IDEOLOGICAL MODES

In our time, we have seen two contrasting ideological modes which have dominated the politics of the past two hundred years. One is the mode which mobilizes what William James once called "the will to believe," the "passional and volitional" tendencies that drive men to go beyond logic in order to satisfy emotional needs. The break-down of religious attachments, the turn to this-worldly concerns, the spur of modernity, all gave impetus to the ascent up the faith-ladders of secular utopias. The desiccation of the old ideologies, however, has now been followed by a "revolt against modernity," by the return of the repressed, the surging impulses of religious fundamentalisms which invoke both traditional symbols as well as accommodations to the wealth of the world or, as in Islam, a martyrdom in the next one. The fusion of passion and ideology of blood and race, that we saw first in the "reactionary modernism" of the National Socialist regime, now reappears in the new spasms of rage throughout the world, as in the Iran of the Ayatollah Khomeni, and we see, again, the same blood-chilling slogans and practices that result when such atavisms and technology are fused in the new "triumphs of the will."

The second mode is the ideology in power, the totalitarian regimes that compel conformity by emphasizing, through posters and slogans, the "little red book," or the "cult of personality," the hammered repetitions of the quotations from the founders or the obligatory visit to the tomb of Lenin ("Lenin lives"), the participatory obedience to the system. This is ideology as ritualized code and ritualized communication, the ideological caul which envelops people and makes the rest of the world opaque. As Václav Havel, the Czech playwright and one of the inspirers of the great document of dissent, Charter 77, writes of the deceits of belief: the facade of ideology "offers human beings the illusion of an identity . . . and of morality while making it easier for them to *part* with them," to be stripped of an individual identity within the casing of the system.[2]

Yet such ideology, because it is used for an uneasy legitimacy, breaks down as well. One reason is that, at first recourse, the easiest mode of conformity is terror. Yet terror, as in the rampant executions in Stalin's day, or the diffuse hysteria of the Red Guards, has its limits. People seek for a normalization in their lives, even if it is the normalization of the dull conformity of a grey everyday life, and overt terror cannot be resorted to again, once its legitimacy has been destroyed, as in the instance of the 1956 revelations of Stalin's paranoia.

There is also a fact, which ideological discourse (left and right) tends to obscure, that few movements are monolithic or can sustain such uniformity for long. There are, first, the structural rigidites that breed pressure for change: the increasing inability to operate a large, complex modern society from a narrow base of power, either for economic management or political direction, so that widening the arena of decision-making, and providing for some decentralization and individual initiatives, become necessary if a society is not to sag or stagnate. Whether such needs can be translated into institutional change is, of course, the crucial question.

More intangible may be the psychological elements that play a role in the transformation of such societies. It may be the humiliation that a Khrushchev felt at being forced to play the clown at Stalin's whim, as well as the recognition of the structural problems that led to his reform efforts. Or the humiliations of a Deng Xiaoping, forced to be a pig farmer during the Cultural Revolution, may have been a motivating element in his revision of Mao Zedong's thought. Nor should one underestimate the elements of idealism that often linger in the minds and hearts of old communists, even those in power, which led a Nagy and the communist intellectuals in Hungary or a Dubček in Czechoslovakia a dozen years later to seek for a socialism with a human face.

Beyond all these may be the most powerful solvent of all—the inescapable and immutable need of men for a moral justification for their acts, moral justifications which in the end encounter the test of rival beliefs and of some transcendental standards. Perhaps the most malevolent and self-defeating theorem in Marxist thought is the moral relativism that undergirds the theory of historical materialism. As Engels wrote in *Anti-Dühring:*

> We . . . reject every presumptuous attempt to impose upon us any dogmatic morality whatever as eternal, final, immutable ethical laws under the pretext that also the moral world has its permanent principles which stand above history and national differences. We maintain, on the contrary, that all past theories of morality are the product, in the last instance, of the contemporary economic conditions of society. And just as society hitherto has moved in class antagonisms, so has morality always been a class morality . . . .[3]

In the name of a higher morality, the Bolsheviks lied and cheated and executed hundreds of thousands of persons. In denouncing bourgeois democracy as a sham, the Communists worked with the Nazis to destroy the Weimar Republic in the 1930s. Painfully, painfully, socialists learned during the Second World War and after that democracy and legal rights are an inviolable condition for a decent society and that liberty, necessarily, has to be prior even to socialism.

As for culture and religion, it may be that, in their origins, they derive from the material conditions of their times, but once created they take on lives of their own, with the power to continue, if they can reach the well-springs of moral beliefs that are renewed over time. The continuity of culture is the rebuttal to any historicism, and the recurrent impulse to seek truth is the insistent beat that erodes the stones of total power. No political system can exist outside the context of moral justifications. But a moral order, if it is to exist without coercion or deceit, has to transcend the parochialisms of interests and tame the appetites of passions. And that is the defeat of ideology.

But all this now is only one chain of ideological thought, in that larger domain of what Nietzsche called *ketten-denken*, the fetters of the chain-thinkers. Today in the widening gyre of passional discourse, the links entangle and ideology has come to designate almost any creed held with the will to believe, held with dogmatism or stridency—the ideologies of Black Power, the New Right, Feminism, et al. The historicity of the term has lost its context and only the pejorative and invidious penumbra, but no conceptual clarity, remains. Ideology has become an irretrievably fallen word. And so is sin.

NOTES

1. The phrase occurs in Engels's *Anti-Dühring* (1877) where Engels, citing the huge advances in wealth in the Western capitalist societies, remarks that the possibilities of socialism are now *here.* (Italics in the original.)
2. Václav Havel, et al., *The Power of the Powerless,* London, Hutchinson, 1985.
3. Friedrich Engels, *Anti-Dühring,* Chicago, C. H. Kerr & Co., 1935; original publication in German, 1877, pp. 93–94.

55

THE END OF HISTORY?

FRANCIS FUKUYAMA

What is the significance of the apparent collapse of Marxism-Leninism? In this controversial essay, Francis Fukuyama, a former deputy director of the U.S. State Department's policy planning staff, suggests that it marks the end, or fulfillment, of history itself.

Source: Francis Fukuyama, "The End of History?" The National Interest *(Summer 1989), pp. 3–5, 8–15, 18. Reprinted by permission of International Creative Management.*

In watching the flow of events over the past decade or so, it is hard to avoid the feeling that something very fundamental has happened in world history. The past year has seen a flood of articles commemorating the end of the Cold War, and the fact that "peace" seems to be breaking out in many regions of the world. Most of these analyses lack any larger conceptual framework for distinguishing between what is essential and what is contingent or accidental in world history, and are predictably superficial. If Mr. Gorbachev were ousted from the Kremlin or a new Ayatollah proclaimed the millennium from a desolate Middle Eastern capital, these same commentators would scramble to announce the rebirth of a new era of conflict.

And yet, all of these people sense dimly that there is some larger process at work, a process that gives coherence and order to the daily headlines. The twentieth century saw the developed world descend into a paroxysm of ideological violence, as liberalism contended first with the remnants of absolutism, then bolshevism and fascism, and finally an updated Marxism that threatened to lead to the ultimate apocalypse of nuclear war. But the century that began full of self-confidence in the ultimate triumph of Western liberal democracy seems at its close to be returning full circle to where it started: not to an "end of ideology" or a convergence between capitalism and socialism, as earlier predicted, but to an unabashed victory of economic and political liberalism.

The triumph of the West, of the Western *idea*, is evident first of all in the total exhaustion of viable systematic alternatives to Western liberalism. In the past decade, there have been unmistakable changes in the intellectual climate of the world's two largest communist countries, and the beginnings of significant reform movements in both. But this phenomenon extends beyond high politics and it can be seen also in the ineluctable spread of consumerist Western culture in such diverse contexts as the peasants' markets and color television sets now omnipresent throughout China, the cooperative restaurants and clothing stores opened in the past year in Moscow, the Beethoven piped into Japanese department stores, and the rock music enjoyed alike in Prague, Rangoon, and Tehran.

What we may be witnessing is not just the end of the Cold War, or the passing of a particular period of postwar history, but the end of history as such: that is, the end point of mankind's ideological evolution and the universalization of Western liberal democracy as the final form of human government. This is not to say that there will no longer be events to fill the pages of *Foreign Affairs*'s yearly summaries of international relations, for the victory of liberalism has occurred primarily in the realm of ideas or consciousness and is as yet incomplete in the real or material world. But there are powerful reasons for believing that it is the ideal that will govern the material world *in the long run.* To understand how this is so, we must first consider some theoretical issues concerning the nature of historical change.

The notion of the end of history is not an original one. Its best known propagator was Karl Marx, who believed that the direction of historical development was a purposeful one determined by the interplay of material forces, and would come to an end only with the achievement of a communist utopia that would finally resolve all prior contradictions. But the concept of history as a dialectical process with a beginning, a middle, and an end was borrowed by Marx from his great German predecessor, Georg Wilhelm Friedrich Hegel.

For better or worse, much of Hegel's historicism has become part of our contemporary intellectual baggage. The notion that mankind has progressed through a series of primitive stages of consciousness on his path to the present, and that these stages corresponded to concrete forms of social organization, such as tribal, slave-owning, theocratic, and finally democratic-egalitarian societies, has become inseparable from the modern understanding of man. Hegel was the first philosopher to speak the language of modern social science, insofar as man for him was the product of his concrete historical and social environment and not, as earlier natural right theorists would have it, a collection of more or less fixed "natural" attributes. The mastery and transformation of man's natural environment through the application of science and technology was originally not a Marxist concept, but a Hegelian one. Unlike later historicists whose historical relativism degenerated into relativism *tout court*, however, Hegel believed that history culminated in an absolute moment—a moment in which a final, rational form of society and state became victorious.

It is Hegel's misfortune to be known now primarily as Marx's precursor, and it is our misfortune that few of us are familiar with Hegel's work from direct study, but only as it has been filtered through the distorting lens of Marxism. In France, however, there has been an effort to save Hegel from his Marxist interpreters and to resurrect him as the philosopher who most correctly speaks to our time. Among those modern French interpreters of Hegel, the greatest was certainly Alexandre Kojève, a brilliant Russian emigre who taught a highly influential series of seminars in Paris in the 1930s at the *Ecole Practique des Hautes Etudes.* While largely unknown in the United States, Kojève had a major impact on the intellectual life of the continent. Among his students ranged such future luminaries as Jean-Paul Sartre on the Left and Raymond Aron on the Right; postwar existentialism borrowed many of its basic categories from Hegel via Kojève.

Kojève sought to resurrect the Hegel of the *Phenomenology of Mind*, the Hegel who proclaimed history to be at an end in 1806. For as early as this Hegel saw in Napoleon's defeat of the Prussian monarchy at the Battle of Jena the victory of the ideals of the French Revolution, and the imminent universalization of the state incorporating the principles of liberty and equality. Kojève, far from rejecting Hegel in light of the turbulent events of the next century and a half, insisted that the latter had been essentially correct. The Battle of Jena marked the end of history because it was at that point that the *vanguard* of humanity (a term quite familiar to Marxists) actualized the principles of the French Revolution. While there was considerable work to be done after 1806—abolishing slavery and the slave trade, extending the franchise to workers, women, blacks, and other racial minorities, etc.—the basic *principles* of the liberal democratic state could not be improved upon. The two world wars in this century and their attendant revolutions and upheavals simply had the effect of extending those principles spatially, such that the various provinces of human civilization were brought up to the level of its most advanced outposts, and of forcing those societies in Europe and North America at the vanguard of civilization to implement their liberalism more fully.

The state that emerges at the end of history is liberal insofar as it recognizes and protects through a system of law man's universal right to freedom, and democratic insofar as it exists only with the consent of the governed. For Kojève, this so-called "universal homogenous state" found real-life embodiment in the countries of postwar Western Europe—precisely those flabby, prosperous, self-satisfied, inward-looking, weak-willed states whose grandest project was nothing more heroic than the creation of the Common Market. But this was only to be expected. For human history and the conflict that characterized it was based on the existence of "contradictions": primitive man's quest for mutual recognition, the dialectic of the master and slave, the transformation and mastery of nature, the struggle for the universal recognition of rights, and the dichotomy between proletarian and capitalist. But in the universal homogenous state, all prior contradictions are resolved and all human needs are satisfied. There is no struggle or conflict over "large" issues, and consequently no need for generals or statesmen; what remains is primarily economic activity. And indeed, Kojève's life was consistent with his teaching. Believing that there was no more work for philosophers as well, since Hegel (correctly understood) had already achieved absolute knowledge, Kojève left teaching after the war and spent the remainder of his life working as a bureaucrat in the European Economic Community, until his death in 1968.

To his contemporaries at mid-century, Kojève's proclamation of the end of history must have seemed like the typical eccentric solipsism of a French intellectual, coming as it did on the heels of World War II and at the very height of the Cold War. To comprehend how Kojève could have been so audacious as to assert that history has ended, we must first of all understand the meaning of Hegelian idealism. . . .

Have we in fact reached the end of history? Are there, in other words, any fundamental "contradictions" in human life that cannot be resolved in the context of modern liberalism, that would be resolvable by an alternative political-economic structure? If we accept the idealist premises laid out above, we must seek an answer to this question in the realm of ideology and consciousness. Our task is not to answer exhaustively the challenges to liberalism promoted by every crackpot messiah around the world, but only those that are embodied in important social or political forces and movements, and which are therefore part of world history. For our purposes, it matters very little what strange thoughts occur to people in Albania or Burkina Faso, for we are interested in what one could in some sense call the common ideological heritage of mankind.

In the past century, there have been two major challenges to liberalism, those of fascism and of communism. The former saw the political weakness, materialism, anomie, and lack of community of the West as fundamental contradictions in liberal societies that could only be resolved by a strong state that forged a new "people" on the basis of national exclusiveness. Fascism was destroyed as a living ideology by World War II. This was a defeat, of course, on a very material level, but it amounted to a defeat of the idea as well. What destroyed fascism as an idea was not universal moral revulsion against it, since plenty of people were willing to endorse the idea as long as it seemed the wave of the future, but its lack of success. After the war, it seemed to most people that German fascism as well as its other European and Asian variants were bound to self-destruct. There was no material reason why new fascist movements could not have sprung up again after the war in other locales, but for the fact that expansionist ultranationalism, with its promise of unending conflict leading to disastrous military defeat, had completely lost its appeal. The ruins of the Reich chancellory as well as the atomic bombs dropped on Hiroshima and Nagasaki killed this ideology on the level of consciousness as well as materially, and all of the proto-fascist movements spawned by the German and Japanese examples like the Peronist movement in Argentina or Subhas Chandra Bose's Indian National Army withered after the war.

The ideological challenge mounted by the other great alternative to liberalism, communism, was far more serious. Marx, speaking Hegel's language, asserted that liberal society contained a fundamental contradiction that could not be resolved within its context, that between capital and labor, and this contradiction has constituted the chief accusation against liberalism ever since. But surely, the class issue has actually been successfully resolved in the West. As Kojève (among others) noted, the egalitarianism of modern America represents the essential achievement of the classless society envisioned by Marx. This is not to say that there are not rich people and poor people in the United States, or that the gap between them has not grown in recent years. But the root causes of economic inequality do not have to do with the underlying legal and social structure of our society, which remains fundamentally egalitarian and moderately redistributionist, so much as with the cultural and social characteristics of the groups that make it up, which are in turn the historical legacy of premodern conditions. Thus black poverty in the United States is not the inherent product of liberalism, but is rather the "legacy of slavery and racism" which persisted long after the formal abolition of slavery.

As a result of the receding of the class issue, the appeal of communism in the developed

Western world, it is safe to say, is lower today than any time since the end of the First World War. This can be measured in any number of ways: in the declining membership and electoral pull of the major European communist parties, and their overtly revisionist programs; in the corresponding electoral success of conservative parties from Britain and Germany to the United States and Japan, which are unabashedly pro-market and antistatist; and in an intellectual climate whose most "advanced" members no longer believe that bourgeois society is something that ultimately needs to be overcome. This is not to say that the opinions of progressive intellectuals in Western countries are not deeply pathological in any number of ways. But those who believe that the future must inevitably be socialist tend to be very old, or very marginal to the real political discourse of their societies.

One may argue that the socialist alternative was never terribly plausible for the North Atlantic world, and was sustained for the last several decades primarily by its success outside of this region. But its precisely in the non-European world that one is most struck by the occurrence of major ideological transformations. Surely the most remarkable changes have occurred in Asia. Due to the strength and adaptability of the indigenous cultures there, Asia became a battleground for a variety of imported Western ideologies early in this century. Liberalism in Asia was a very weak reed in the period after World War I; it is easy today to forget how gloomy Asia's political future looked as recently as ten or fifteen years ago. It is easy to forget as well how momentous the outcome of Asian ideological struggles seemed for world political development as a whole.

The first Asian alternative to liberalism to be decisively defeated was the fascist one represented by Imperial Japan. Japanese fascism (like its German version) was defeated by the force of American arms in the Pacific war, and liberal democracy was imposed on Japan by a victorious United States. Western capitalism and political liberalism when transplanted to Japan were adapted and transformed by the Japanese in such a way as to be scarcely recognizable. Many Americans are now aware that Japanese industrial organization is very different from that prevailing in the United States or Europe, and it is questionable what relationship the factional maneuvering that takes place with the governing Liberal Democratic Party bears to democracy. Nonetheless, the very fact that the essential elements of economic and political liberalism have been so successfully grafted onto uniquely Japanese traditions and institutions guarantees their survival in the long run. More important is the contribution that Japan has made in turn to world history by following in the footsteps of the United States to create a truly universal consumer culture that has become both a symbol and an underpinning of the universal homogenous state. V.S. Naipaul travelling in Khomeini's Iran shortly after the revolution noted the omnipresent signs advertising the products of Sony, Hitachi, and JVC, whose appeal remained virtually irresistible and gave the lie to the regime's pretensions of restoring a state based on the rule of the *Shariah*. Desire for access to the consumer culture, created in large measure by Japan, has played a crucial role in fostering the spread of economic liberalism throughout Asia, and hence in promoting political liberalism as well.

The economic success of the other newly industrializing countries (NICs) in Asia following on the example of Japan is by now a familiar story. What is important from a Hegelian standpoint is that political liberalism has been following economic liberalism, more slowly than many had hoped but with seeming inevitability. Here again we see the victory of the idea of the universal homogenous state. South Korea had developed into a modern, urbanized society with an increasingly large and well-educated middle class that could not possibly be isolated from the larger democratic trends around them. Under these circumstances it seemed intolerable to a large part of this population that it should be ruled by an anachronistic military regime while Japan, only a decade or so ahead in economic terms, had parliamentary institutions for over forty years. Even the former socialist regime in Burma, which for so many decades existed in dismal isolation from the larger trends dominating Asia, was buffeted in the past year by pressures to liberalize both its economy and political system. It is said that unhappiness with strongman Ne Win began when a senior Burmese officer went to Singapore for medical treatment and broke down crying when he saw how far socialist Burma had been left behind by its ASEAN neighbors.

But the power of the liberal idea would seem much less impressive if it had not infected the largest and oldest culture in Asia, China. The simple existence of communist China created an alternative pole of ideological attraction, and as such constituted a threat to liberalism. But the past fifteen years have seen an almost total discrediting of Marxism-Leninism as an economic system. Beginning with the famous third plenum of the Tenth Central Committee in 1978, the Chinese Communist party set about decollectivizing agriculture for the 800 million Chinese who still lived in the countryside. The role of the state in agriculture was reduced to that of a tax collector, while production of consumer goods was sharply increased in order to give peasants a taste of the universal homogenous state and thereby an incentive to work. The reform doubled Chinese grain output in only five years, and in the process created for Deng Xiaoping a solid political base from which he was able to extend the reform to other parts of the economy. Economic statistics do not begin to describe the dynamism, initiative, and openness evident in China since the reform began.

China could not now be described in any way as a liberal democracy. At present, no more than 20 percent of its economy has been marketized, and most importantly it continues to be ruled by a self-appointed Communist party which has given no hint of wanting to devolve power. Deng has made none of Gorbachev's promises regarding democratization of the political system and there is no Chinese equivalent of *glasnost*. The Chinese leadership has in fact been much more circumspect in criticizing Mao and Maoism than Gorbachev with respect to Brezhnev and Stalin, and the regime continues to pay lip service to Marxism-Leninism as its ideological underpinning. But anyone familiar with the outlook and behavior of the new technocratic elite now governing China knows that Marxism and ideological principle have become virtually irrelevant as guides to policy, and that bourgeois consumerism has a real meaning in that country for the first time since the revolution. The various slowdowns in the pace of reform, the campaigns against "spiritual pollution" and crackdowns on political dissent are more properly seen as tactical adjustments made in the process of managing what is an extraordinarily difficult political transition. By ducking the question of political reform while putting the economy on a new footing, Deng has managed to avoid the breakdown of authority that has accompanied Gorbachev's *perestroika*. Yet the pull of the liberal idea continues to be very strong as economic power devolves and the economy becomes more open to the outside world. There are currently over 20,000 Chinese students studying in the U.S. and other Western countries, almost all of them the children of the Chinese elite. It is hard to believe that when they return home to run the country they will be content for China to be the only country in Asia unaffected by the larger democratizing trend. The student demonstrations in Beijing that broke out first in December 1986 and recurred recently on the occasion of Hu Yao-bang's death were only the beginning of what will inevitably be mounting pressure for change in the political system as well.

What is important about China from the standpoint of world history is not the present state of the reform or even its future prospects. The central issue is the fact that the People's Republic of China can no longer act as a beacon for illiberal forces around the world, whether they be guerrillas in some Asian jungle or middle class students in Paris. Maoism, rather than being the pattern for Asia's future, became an anachronism, and it was the mainland Chinese who in fact were decisively influenced by the prosperity and dynamism of their overseas co-ethnics—the ironic ultimate victory of Taiwan.

Important as these changes in China have been, however, it is developments in the Soviet Union—the original "homeland of the world proletariat"—that have put the final nail in the coffin of the Marxist-Leninist alternative to liberal democracy. It should be clear that in terms of formal institutions, not much has changed in the four years since Gorbachev has come to power: free markets and the cooperative movement represent only a small part of the Soviet economy, which remains centrally planned; the political system is still dominated by the Communist party, which has only begun to democratize internally and to share power with other groups; the regime continues to assert that it is seeking only to modernize socialism and that its ideological basis remains Marxism-Leninism; and, finally, Gorbachev faces a potentially powerful conservative opposition that could undo many of the changes that have taken place to date. Moreover, it is hard to be too sanguine about the chances for success of Gorbachev's proposed reforms, either in the sphere of economics or politics. But my purpose here is not to analyze events in the short-term, or to make predictions for policy purposes, but to look at underlying trends in the sphere of ideology and consciousness. And in that respect, it is clear that an astounding transformation has occurred.

Emigres from the Soviet Union have been reporting for at least the last generation now that virtually nobody in that country truly believed in Marxism-Leninism any longer, and that this was nowhere more true than in the Soviet elite, which continued to mouth Marxist slogans out of sheer cynicism. The corruption and decadence of the late Brezhnev-era Soviet state seemed to matter little, however, for as long as the state itself refused to throw into question any of the fundamental principles underlying Soviet society, the system was capable of functioning adequately out of sheer inertia and could even muster some dynamism in the realm of foreign and defense policy. Marxism-Leninism was like a magical incantation which, however absurd and devoid of meaning, was the only common basis on which the elite could agree to rule Soviet society.

What has happened in the four years since Gorbachev's coming to power is a revolutionary assault on the most fundamental institutions and principles of Stalinism, and their replacement by other principles which do not amount to liberalism *per se* but whose only connecting thread is liberalism. This is most evident in the economic sphere, where the reform economists around Gorbachev have become steadily more radical in their support for free markets, to the point where some like Nikolai Shmelev do not mind being compared in public to Milton Friedman. There is a virtual consensus among the currently dominant school of Soviet economists now that central planning and the common system of allocation are the root cause of economic inefficiency, and that if the Soviet system is ever to heal itself, it must permit free and decentralized decision-making with respect to investment, labor, and prices. After a couple of initial years of ideological confusion, these principles have finally been incorporated into policy with the promulgation of new laws on enterprise autonomy, cooperatives, and finally in 1988 on lease arrangements and family farming. There are, of course, a number of fatal flaws in the current implementation of the reform, most notably the absence of a thoroughgoing price reform. But the problem is no longer a *conceptual* one: Gorbachev and his lieutenants seem to understand the economic logic of marketization well enough, but like the leaders of a Third World country facing the IMF, are afraid of the social consequences of ending consumer subsidies and other forms of dependence on the state sector.

In the political sphere, the proposed changes to the Soviet constitution, legal system, and party rules amount to much less than the establishment of a liberal state. Gorbachev has spoken of democratization primarily in the sphere of internal party affairs, and has shown little intention of ending the Communist party's monopoly of power; indeed, the political reform seeks to legitimize and therefore strengthen the CPSU's rule. Nonetheless, the general principles underlying many of the reforms—that the "people" should be truly responsible for their own affairs, that higher political bodies should be answerable to lower ones, and not vice versa, that the rule of law should prevail over arbitrary police actions, with separation of powers and an independent judiciary, that there should be legal protection for property rights, the need for open discussion of public issues and the right of public dissent, the empowering of the Soviets as a forum in which the whole Soviet people can participate, and of a political culture that is more tolerant and pluralistic—come from a source fundamentally alien to the USSR's Marxist-Leninist tradition, even if they are incompletely articulated and poorly implemented in practice.

Gorbachev's repeated assertions that he is doing no more than trying to restore the original meaning of Leninism are themselves a kind of Orwellian doublespeak. Gorbachev and his allies have consistently maintained that intraparty democracy was somehow the essence of Leninism, and that the various liberal practices of open debate, secret ballot elections, and rule of law were all part of the Leninist heritage, corrupted only later by Stalin. While almost anyone would look good compared to Stalin, drawing so sharp a line between Lenin and his successor is questionable. The essence of Lenin's democratic centralism was centralism, not democracy; that is, the absolutely rigid, monolithic, and disciplined dictatorship of a hierarchically organized vanguard Communist party, speaking in the name of the *demos*. All of Lenin's vicious polemics against Karl Kautsky, Rosa Luxemburg, and various other Menshevik and Social Democratic rivals, not to mention his contempt for "bourgeois legality" and freedoms, centered around his profound conviction that a revolution could not be successfully made by a democratically run organization.

Gorbachev's claim that he is seeking to return to the true Lenin is perfectly easy to understand: having fostered a thorough denunciation of Stalinism and Brezhnevism as the root of the USSR's present predicament, he needs some point in Soviet history on which to anchor the legitimacy of the CPSU's continued rule. But Gorbachev's tactical requirements should not blind us to the fact that the democratizing and decentralizing principles which he has enunciated in both the economic and political spheres are highly subversive of some of the most fundamental precepts of both Marxism and Leninism. Indeed, if the bulk of the present economic reform proposals were put into effect, it is hard to know how the Soviet economy would be more socialist than those of other Western countries with large public sectors.

The Soviet Union could in no way be described as a liberal or democratic country now, nor do I think that it is terribly likely that *perestroika* will succeed such that the label will be thinkable any time in the near future. But at the end of history it is not necessary that all societies become successful liberal societies, merely that they end their ideological pretensions of representing different and higher forms of human society. And in this respect I believe that something very important has happened in the Soviet Union in the past few years: the criticisms of the Soviet system sanctioned by Gorbachev have been so thorough and devastating that there is very little chance of going back to either Stalinism or Brezhnevism in any simple way. Gorbachev has finally permitted people to say what they had privately understood for many years, namely, that the magical incantations of Marxism-Leninism were nonsense, that Soviet socialism was not superior to the West in any respect but was in fact a monumental failure. The conservative opposition in the USSR, consisting both of simply workers afraid of unemployment and inflation and of party officials fearful of losing their jobs and privileges, is outspoken and may be strong enough to force Gorbachev's ouster in the next few years. But what both groups desire is tradition, order, and authority; they manifest no deep commitment to Marxism-Leninism, except insofar as they have invested much of their own lives in it. For authority to be restored in the Soviet Union after Gorbachev's demolition work, it must be on the basis of some new and vigorous ideology which has not yet appeared on the horizon.

If we admit for the moment that the fascist and communist challenges to liberalism are dead, are there any other ideological competitors left? Or put another way, are there contradictions in liberal society beyond that of class that are not resolvable? Two possibilities suggest themselves, those of religion and nationalism.

The rise of religious fundamentalism in recent years within the Christian, Jewish, and Muslim traditions has been widely noted. One is inclined to say that the revival of religion in some way attests to a broad unhappiness with the impersonality and spiritual vacuity of liberal consumerist societies. Yet while the emptiness at the core of liberalism is most certainly a defect in the ideology—indeed, a flaw that one does not need the perspective of religion to recognize—it is not at all clear that it is remediable through politics. Modern liberalism itself was historically a consequence of the weakness of religiously-based societies which, failing to agree on the nature of the good life, could not provide even the minimal preconditions of peace and stability. In the contemporary world only Islam has offered a theocratic state as a political alternative to both liberalism and communism. But the doctrine has little appeal for non-Muslims, and it is hard to believe that the movement will take on any universal significance. Other less organized religious impulses have been successfully satisfied within the sphere of personal life that is permitted in liberal societies.

The other major "contradiction" potentially unresolvable by liberalism is the one posed by nationalism and other forms of racial and ethnic consciousness. It is certainly true that a very large degree of conflict since the Battle of Jena has had its roots in nationalism. Two cataclysmic world wars in this century have been spawned by the nationalism of the developed world in various guises, and if those passions have been muted to a certain extent in postwar Europe, they are still extremely powerful in the Third World. Nationalism has been a threat to liberalism historically in Germany, and continues to be one in isolated parts of "post-historical" Europe like Northern Ireland.

But it is not clear that nationalism represents an irreconcilable contradiction in the heart of liberalism. In the first place, nationalism is not one single phenomenon but several, ranging from mild cultural nostalgia to the highly organized and elaborately articulated doctrine of National Socialism. Only systematic nationalisms of the latter sort can qualify as a formal ideology on the level of liberalism or communism. The vast majority of the world's nationalist movements do not have a political program beyond the negative desire of independence *from* some other group or people, and do not offer anything like a comprehensive agenda for socio-economic organization. As such, they are compatible with doctrines and ideologies that do offer such agendas. While they may constitute a source of conflict for liberal societies, this conflict does not arise from liberalism itself so much as from the fact that the liberalism in question is incomplete. Certainly a great deal of the world's ethnic and nationalist tension can be explained in terms of peoples who are forced to live in unrepresentative political systems that they have not chosen.

While it is impossible to rule out the sudden appearance of new ideologies or previously unrecognized contradictions in liberal societies, then, the present world seems to confirm that the fundamental principles of socio-political organization have not advanced terribly far since 1806. Many of the wars and revolutions fought since that time have been undertaken in the name of ideologies which claimed to be more advanced than liberalism, but whose pretensions were ultimately unmasked by history. In the meantime, they have helped to spread the universal homogenous state to the point where it could have a significant effect on the overall character of international relations. . . .

The passing of Marxism-Leninism first from

China and then from the Soviet Union will mean its death as a living ideology of world historical significance. For while there may be some isolated true believers left in places like Managua, Pyongyang, or Cambridge, Massachusetts, the fact that there is not a single large state in which it is a going concern undermines completely its pretensions to being in the vanguard of human history. And the death of this ideology means the growing "Common Marketization" of international relations, and the diminution of the likelihood of large-scale conflict between states.

This does not by any means imply the end of international conflict *per se*. For the world at that point would be divided between a part that was historical and a part that was post-historical. Conflict between states still in history, and between those states and those at the end of history, would still be possible. There would still be a high and perhaps rising level of ethnic and nationalist violence, since those are impulses incompletely played out, even in parts of the post-historical world. Palestinians and Kurds, Sikhs and Tamils, Irish Catholics and Walloons, Armenians and Azeris, will continue to have their unresolved grievances. This implies that terrorism and wars of national liberation will continue to be an important item on the international agenda. But large-scale conflict must involve large states still caught in the grip of history, and they are what appear to be passing from the scene.

The end of history will be a very sad time. The struggle for recognition, the willingness to risk one's life for a purely abstract goal, the worldwide ideological struggle that called forth daring, courage, imagination, and idealism, will be replaced by economic calculation, the endless solving of technical problems, environmental concerns, and the satisfaction of sophisticated consumer demands. In the post-historical period there will be neither art nor philosophy, just the perpetual caretaking of the museum of human history. I can feel in myself, and see in others around me, a powerful nostalgia for the time when history existed. Such nostalgia, in fact, will continue to fuel competition and conflict even in the post-historical world for some time to come. Even though I recognize its inevitability, I have the most ambivalent feelings for the civilization that has been created in Europe since 1945, with its north Atlantic and Asian offshoots. Perhaps this very prospect of centuries of boredom at the end of history will serve to get history started once again.

56

WORD AND FLESH

WENDELL BERRY

Our final selection is by Wendell Berry (1934–), a novelist, essayist, and farmer from Port Royal, Kentucky. In contrast to many of the other writers whose work appears in this volume, Berry warns against the dangers of relying on large abstractions and grand theories. Instead, he suggests that the answers to many of our problems, especially environmental problems, lie in a greater concern for the local and particular—such as the neighborhood and community—rather than the global and abstract.

Toward the end of *As You Like It*, Orlando says: "I can live no longer by thinking." He is ready to marry Rosalind. It is time for incarnation. Having thought too much, he is at one of the limits of human experience, or of human sanity. If his love does put on flesh, we know he must sooner or later arrive at the opposite limit, at which he will say, "I can live no longer without thinking." Thought—even consciousness—seems to live between these limits: the abstract and the particular, the word and the flesh.

All public movements of thought quickly produce a language that works as a code, useless to the extent that it is abstract. It is readily evident, for example, that you can't conduct a relationship with another person in terms of the rhetoric of the civil rights movement or the women's movement—as useful as those rhetorics may initially have been to personal relationships.

The same is true of the environment movement. The favorite adjective of this movement now seems to be "planetary." This word is used, properly enough, to refer to the interdependence of places, and to the recognition, which is desirable and growing, that no place on the earth can be completely healthy until all places are.

But the word "planetary" also refers to an abstract anxiety or an abstract passion that is desperate and useless exactly to the extent that it is abstract. How, after all, can anybody—any particular body—do anything to heal a planet? The suggestion that anybody could do so is preposterous. The heroes of abstraction keep galloping in on their white horses to save the planet—and they keep falling off in front of the grandstand.

What we need, obviously, is a more intelligent—which is to say, a more accurate—description of the problem. The description of a problem as planetary arouses a motivation for which, of necessity, there is no employment. The adjective "planetary" describes a problem in such a way that it cannot be solved. In fact, though we now have serious problems nearly everywhere on the planet, we have no problem that can accurately be described as planetary. And, short of the total annihilation of the human race, there is no planetary solution.

There are also no national, state, or county problems, and no national, state, or county solutions. That will-o'-the-wisp, the large-scale solution to the large-scale problem, which is so dear to governments, universities, and corporations, serves mostly to distract people from the small, private problems that they may, in fact, have the power to solve.

The problems, if we describe them accurately, are all private and small. Or they are so initially.

The problems are our lives. In the "developed" countries, at least, the large problems occur because all of us are living either partly wrong or almost entirely wrong. It was not just the greed of corporate shareholders and the hubris of corporate executives that put the fate of Prince William Sound into one ship; it was also our demand that energy be cheap and plentiful.

The economies of our communities and households are wrong. The answers to the human problems of ecology are to be found in economy. And the answers to the problems of economy are to be found in culture and in character. To fail to see this is to go on dividing the world falsely between guilty producers and innocent consumers.

The planetary versions—the heroic versions—of our problems have attracted great intelligence. But these problems, as they are caused and suffered in our lives, our households, and our communities, have attracted very little intelligence.

There are some notable exceptions. A few people have learned to do a few things better. But it is discouraging to reflect that, though we have been talking about most of our problems for decades, we are still mainly *talking* about them. The civil rights movement has not given us better communities. The women's movement has not given us better marriages or better households. The environment movement has not changed our parasitic relationship to nature.

We have failed to produce new examples of

good home and community economies, and we have nearly completed the destruction of the examples we once had. Without examples, we are left with theory and the bureaucracy and meddling that come with theory. We change our principles, our thoughts, and our words, but these are changes made in the air. Our lives go on unchanged.

For the most part, the subcultures, the countercultures, the dissenters, and the opponents continue mindlessly—or perhaps just helplessly—to follow the pattern of the dominant society in its extravagance, its wastefulness, its dependencies, and its addictions. The old problem remains: How do you get intelligence *out* of an institution or an organization?

My small community in Kentucky has lived and dwindled for at least a century under the influence of four kinds of organizations: governments, corporations, schools, and churches—all of which are distant (either actually or in interest), centralized, and consequently abstract in their concerns.

Governments and corporations (except for employees) have no presence in our community at all, which is perhaps fortunate for us, but we nevertheless feel the indifference or the contempt of governments and corporations for communities such as ours.

We have had no school of our own for nearly thirty years. The school system takes our young people, prepares them for "the world of tomorrow"—which it does not expect to take place in any rural area—and gives back "expert" (that is, extremely generalized) ideas.

The church is present in the town. We have two churches. But both have been used by their denominations, for almost a century, to provide training and income for student ministers, who do not stay long enough even to become disillusioned.

For a long time, then, the minds that have most influenced our town have not been *of* the town and so have not tried even to perceive, much less to honor, the good possibilities that are there. They have not wondered on what terms a good and conserving life might be lived there. In this my community is not unique but is like almost every other neighborhood in our country and in the "developed" world.

The question that *must* be addressed, therefore, is not how to care for the planet, but how to care for each of the planet's millions of human and natural neighborhoods, each of its millions of small pieces and parcels of land, each one of which is in some precious way different from all the others. Our understandable wish to preserve the planet must somehow be reduced to the scale of our competence—that is, to the wish to preserve all of its humble households and neighborhoods.

What can accomplish this reduction? I will say again, without overweening hope but with certainty nonetheless, that only love can do it. Only love can bring intelligence out of the institutions and organizations, where it aggrandizes itself, into the presence of the work that must be done.

Love is never abstract. It does not adhere to the universe or the planet or the nation or the institution or the profession, but to the singular sparrows of the street, the lilies of the field, "the least of these my brethren." Love is not, by its own desire, heroic. It is heroic only when compelled to be. It exists by its willingness to be anonymous, humble, and unrewarded.

The older love becomes, the more clearly it understands its involvement in partiality, imperfection, suffering, and mortality. Even so, it longs for incarnation. It can live no longer by thinking.

And yet to put on flesh and do the flesh's work, it must think.

In his essay on Kipling, George Orwell wrote: "All left-wing parties in the highly industrialized countries are at bottom a sham, because they make it their business to fight against something which they do not really wish to destroy. They have internationalist aims, and at the same time they struggle to keep up a standard of life with which those aims are incompatible. We all live by robbing Asiatic coolies, and those of us who are 'enlightened' all maintain that those coolies ought to be set free; but our standard of living, and hence our 'enlightenment,' demands that the robbery shall continue."

This statement of Orwell's is clearly applicable to our situation now; all we need to do is change a few nouns. The religion and the environmentalism of the highly industrialized countries are at bottom a sham, because they make it their business to fight against something they do not really wish to destroy. We all live by robbing nature, but our standard of living demands that the robbery shall continue.

We must achieve the character and acquire the skills to live much poorer than we do. We must waste less. We must do more for ourselves and each other. It is either that or continue merely to think and talk about changes that we are inviting catastrophe to make.

The great obstacle is simply this: the conviction that we cannot change because we are dependent on what is wrong. But that is the addict's excuse, and we know that it will not do.

How dependent, in fact, are we? How dependent are our neighborhoods and communities? How might our dependences be reduced? To answer these questions will require better thoughts and better deeds than we have been capable of so far.

We must have the sense and the courage, for example, to see that the ability to transport food for hundreds or thousands of miles does not necessarily mean that we are well off. It means that the food supply is more vulnerable and more costly than a local food supply would be. It means that consumers do not control or influence the healthfulness of their food supply and that they are at the mercy of the people who have the control and influence. It means that, in eating, people are using large quantities of petroleum that other people in another time are almost certain to need.

Our most serious problem, perhaps, is that we have become a nation of fantasists. We believe, apparently, in the infinite availability of finite resources. We persist in land-use methods that reduce the potentially infinite power of soil fertility to a finite quantity, which we then proceed to waste as if it were an infinite quantity. We have an economy that depends not on the quality and quantity of necessary goods and services but on the moods of a few stockbrokers. We believe that democratic freedom can be preserved by people ignorant of the history of democracy and indifferent to the responsibilities of freedom.

Our leaders have been for many years as oblivious to the realities and dangers of their time as were George III and Lord North. They believe that the difference between war and peace is still the overriding political difference—when, in fact, the difference has diminished to the point of insignificance. How would you describe the difference between modern war and modern industry—between, say, bombing and strip mining, or between chemical warfare and chemical manufacturing? The difference seems to be only that in war the victimization of humans is directly intentional and in industry it is "accepted" as a "trade-off."

Were the catastrophes of Love Canal, Bhopal, Chernobyl, and the *Exxon Valdez* episodes of war or of peace? They were, in fact, peacetime acts of aggression, intentional to the extent that the risks were known and ignored.

We are involved unremittingly in a war not against "foreign enemies," but against the world, against our freedom, and indeed against our existence. Our so-called industrial accidents should be looked upon as revenges of Nature. We forget that Nature is necessarily party to all our enterprises and that she imposes conditions of her own.

Now she is plainly saying to us: "If you put the fates of whole communities or cities or regions or ecosystems at risk in single ships or factories or power plants, then I will furnish the drunk or the fool or the imbecile who will make the necessary small mistake."